Management

A Global Perspective

McGRAW-HILL SERIES IN MANAGEMENT

Consulting Editors
Fred Luthans
Keith Davis

Schlesinger, Eccles, and Gabarro: *Managing Behavior in Organizations: Text, Cases and Readings*
Schroeder: *Operations Management: Decision Making in the Operations Function*
Steers and Porter: *Motivation and Work Behavior*
Steiner: *Industry, Society, and Change: A Casebook*
Steiner and Steiner: *Business, Government, and Society: A Managerial Perspective, Text and Cases*
Steinhoff and Burgess: *Small Business Management Fundamentals*
Sutermeister: *People and Productivity*
Walker: *Human Resource Strategy*
Weihrich: *Management Excellence: Productivity through MBO*
Weihrich and Koontz: *Management: A Global Perspective*
Werther and Davis: *Human Resources and Personnel Management*
Wofford, Gerloff, and Cummins: *Organizational Communications: The Keystone to Managerial Effectiveness*
Yoffie: *International Trade and Competition*

Also Available from McGraw-Hill

SCHAUM'S OUTLINE SERIES IN ACCOUNTING, BUSINESS, & ECONOMICS

Most outlines include basic theory, definitions, and hundreds of solved problems and supplementary problems with answers.

Titles on the Current List Include:

Accounting I, 3d edition
Accounting II, 3d edition
Advanced Accounting
Advanced Business Law
Bookkeeping & Accounting, 2d edition
Business Law
Business Mathematics
Business Statistics, 2d edition
Contemporary Mathematics of Finance
Cost Accounting I, 2d edition
Cost Accounting II
Development Economics
Financial Accounting
Intermediate Accounting I, 2d edition
Intermediate Accounting II
International Economics, 3d edition

Introduction to Mathematical Economics, 2d edition
Investments
Macroeconomic Theory, 2d edition
Managerial Accounting
Managerial Economics
Managerial Finance
Mathematical Methods for Business & Economics
Mathematics of Finance
Microeconomic Theory, 3d edition
Money and Banking
Operations Management
Personal Finance
Principles of Economics
Statistics and Econometrics

Available at your College Bookstore. A complete listing of Schaum titles may be obtained by writing to: Schaum Division
McGraw-Hill, Inc.
Princeton Road, S-1
Hightstown, NJ 08520

Management

A Global Perspective
Tenth Edition

Heinz Weihrich
Professor of International Management
University of San Francisco

Harold Koontz
Late Professor of Management
University of California, Los Angeles

McGraw-Hill, Inc.
New York   St. Louis   San Francisco   Auckland
Bogotá   Caracas   Lisbon   London   Madrid
Mexico   Milan   Montreal   New Dehli   Paris
San Juan   Singapore   Sydney   Tokyo   Toronto

to Ursula and Mary

MANAGEMENT: A Global Perspective

Copyright © 1993 by McGraw-Hill, Inc. All rights reserved. Previously published under the titles of: *Management,* copyright © 1988, 1984, 1980, 1976 by McGraw-Hill, Inc., all rights reserved; and *Principles of Management: An Analysis of Managerial Functions,* copyright © 1972, 1968, 1964, 1959, 1955 by McGraw-Hill, Inc., all rights reserved. Copyright renewed 1983 by Harold D. Koontz. Printed in the United States of America. Except as permitted under the United States Copyright Act of 1976, no part of this publication may be reproduced or distributed in any form or by any means, or stored in a data base or retrieval system, without the prior written permission of the publisher.

2 3 4 5 6 7 8 9 0 DOC DOC 9 0 9 8 7 6 5 4 3

ISBN 0-07-069170-3

This book was set in Bookman by Ruttle, Shaw & Wetherill, Inc.
The editors were Lynn Richardson and Dan Alpert;
the designer was Robin Hoffmann;
the production supervisor was Leroy A. Young.
R. R. Donnelley & Sons Company was printer and binder.

Library of Congress Cataloging-in-Publication Data

Koontz, Harold, (date).
    Management: a global perspective / Heinz Weihrich, Harold Koontz.
    — 10th ed.
        p.   cm. — (McGraw-Hill series in management)
    The authors' names appear in reverse order on the t.p. of the 9th ed.
    Includes bibliographical references and indexes.
    ISBN 0-07-069170-3
    1. Management.   2. Industrial management.   I. Weihrich, Heinz.
    II. Title.   III. Series.
    HD31.K6   1993
    658—dc20   92–14916

INTERNATIONAL EDITION

Copyright © 1993

Exclusive rights by McGraw-Hill, Inc. for manufacture and export. This book cannot be re-exported from the country to which it is consigned by McGraw-Hill. The International Edition is not available in North America.

When ordering this title, use ISBN 0-07-112892-1

Management

A Global Perspective
Tenth Edition

Heinz Weihrich
Professor of International Management
University of San Francisco

Harold Koontz
Late Professor of Management
University of California, Los Angeles

McGraw-Hill, Inc.
New York   St. Louis   San Francisco   Auckland
Bogotá   Caracas   Lisbon   London   Madrid
Mexico   Milan   Montreal   New Dehli   Paris
San Juan   Singapore   Sydney   Tokyo   Toronto

to Ursula and Mary

MANAGEMENT: A Global Perspective

Copyright © 1993 by McGraw-Hill, Inc. All rights reserved. Previously published under the titles of: *Management,* copyright © 1988, 1984, 1980, 1976 by McGraw-Hill, Inc., all rights reserved; and *Principles of Management: An Analysis of Managerial Functions,* copyright © 1972, 1968, 1964, 1959, 1955 by McGraw-Hill, Inc., all rights reserved. Copyright renewed 1983 by Harold D. Koontz. Printed in the United States of America. Except as permitted under the United States Copyright Act of 1976, no part of this publication may be reproduced or distributed in any form or by any means, or stored in a data base or retrieval system, without the prior written permission of the publisher.

2 3 4 5 6 7 8 9 0 DOC DOC 9 0 9 8 7 6 5 4 3

ISBN 0-07-069170-3

This book was set in Bookman by Ruttle, Shaw & Wetherill, Inc.
The editors were Lynn Richardson and Dan Alpert;
the designer was Robin Hoffmann;
the production supervisor was Leroy A. Young.
R. R. Donnelley & Sons Company was printer and binder.

Library of Congress Cataloging-in-Publication Data

Koontz, Harold, (date).
    Management: a global perspective / Heinz Weihrich, Harold Koontz.
    — 10th ed.
        p.   cm. — (McGraw-Hill series in management)
    The authors' names appear in reverse order on the t.p. of the 9th ed.
    Includes bibliographical references and indexes.
    ISBN 0-07-069170-3
    1. Management.   2. Industrial management.   I. Weihrich, Heinz.
II. Title.   III. Series.
HD31.K6   1993
658—dc20   92–14916

INTERNATIONAL EDITION

Copyright © 1993

Exclusive rights by McGraw-Hill, Inc. for manufacture and export. This book cannot be re-exported from the country to which it is consigned by McGraw-Hill. The International Edition is not available in North America.

When ordering this title, use ISBN 0-07-112892-1

About the Authors

Heinz Weihrich is Professor of International Management at the University of San Francisco. He received his doctorate from the University of California at Los Angeles (UCLA) and was a visiting scholar at the University of California at Berkeley. His fields of work are in management, international management, and behavioral science. He has taught at Arizona State University, at the University of California at Los Angeles, and in Europe.

Dr. Weihrich has published more than fifty books, including various editions and translations, and is now the sole author of *Essentials of Management,* 5th edition. Another of his books, *Management Excellence: Productivity through MBO,* discussing a goal-driven management system, has been translated into Spanish, Italian, German, Greek, Korean, and Japanese. More than a hundred of his articles have been published in several languages in journals such as *Human Resource Planning, Journal of Systems Management, Management International Review, Long Range Planning,* and *Academy of Management Executive.*

In addition to pursuing his academic interests, Dr. Weihrich is active in management consulting as well as executive and organizational development in the United States, Europe, Africa, and Asia. His consulting and business experiences include work with companies such as Eastman Kodak, Volkswagen, and Hughes Aircraft. He is also an active member of Toastmasters International. He was elected as a Fellow of the International Academy of Management, the highest honor conferred by the international management movement, and is listed in *International Businessmen's Who's Who, Men of Achievement, Dictionary of International Biography, Who's Who in the West, Who's Who in America,* and *Who's Who in the World.*

The late **Harold Koontz** was active as a business and government executive, university professor, company board chairman and director, management consultant, worldwide lecturer to top-management groups, and author of many books and articles. From 1950 he was Professor of Management and from 1962 Mead Johnson Professor of Management at the University of California at Los Angeles; from 1978 to 1982 he was World Chancellor at the International Academy of Management. He was the author or coauthor of nineteen books and ninety journal articles, and his *Principles of Management* (now in its tenth edition as *Management: A Global Perspective*) has been translated into sixteen languages. His *Board of Directors and Effective Management* was given the Academy of Management Book Award in 1968.

After taking his doctorate at Yale, Professor Koontz served as Assistant to the Trustees of the New Haven Railroad, Chief of the Traffic Branch of the War Production Board, Assistant to the Vice President of the Association of American Railroads, Assistant to the President of Trans World Airlines, and Director of Sales for Convair. He acted as management consultant for, among others, Hughes Tool Company, Hughes Aircraft Company, Purex Corporation, KLM Royal Dutch Airlines, Metropolitan Life Insurance Company, Occidental Petroleum Corporation, and General Telephone Company. Professor Koontz's honors include election as a Fellow of the American and the International Academies of Management and a term of service as President of the American Academy of Management. He received the Mead Johnson Award in 1962 and the Society for Advancement of Management Taylor Key Award in 1974 and is listed in *Who's Who in America, Who's Who in Finance and Industry,* and *Who's Who in the World.* Harold Koontz passed away in 1984.

Contents
in Brief

Contents

Part 3.   **Organizing**   **241**

Chapter 9.   The Nature of Organizing and Entrepreneuring   **243**

Chapter 10.   Organizational Structure: Departmentation   **265**

Chapter 11.   Line/Staff Authority and Decentralization   291

Chapter 19.   Communication   536

Summary of Major Principles, or Guides, for Leading   564

Chapter 23.   Overall Control and toward the Future through Preventive Control   660

Preface

This book prepares men and women for the exciting, challenging, and rewarding career of managing in an international environment as we move toward the twenty-first century. As the title indicates, this up-to-date tenth edition recognizes and responds to the global nature of managing.

Prior editions of the book have been published in sixteen languages. The global perspectives will appeal to those who realize that in the new world order, walls are crumbling and new alliances among companies and peoples are being formed. Beyond the discussion of managerial issues in the United States, about equal attention is given to topics in the New Europe and in the Pacific Rim countries. By acquiring a global outlook and applying the book's principles, concepts, and theories in their daily work, readers can surely become more effective as managers.

Who Will Benefit from This Book?

All persons who work in organizations will benefit from learning about managing. They include students in colleges and universities, aspiring managers, those who already have managerial skills and want to become more effective, and other professionals who want to improve their understanding of the organization in which they work. This book is for people in all kinds of organizations, not just business firms; it is relevant to nonbusiness organizations as well, such as government, health care, educational institutions, and other not-for-profit enterprises.

Managerial functions are essentially the same for first-level supervisors, middle managers, and top executives. To be sure, there are considerable variations in environment, scope of authority, and types of problems in the positions. Yet all managers undertake the same basic functions to obtain results by establishing an environment for effective and efficient performance of individuals working together in groups.

Organization of the Book

As in previous editions, managerial knowledge is classified according to the functions of planning, organizing, staffing, leading, and controlling. A systems model, shown on the inside cover and used in part openings throughout the book, integrates these functions into a system and also links an enterprise with its environment. The suggested open-systems view is even more important now than in the past, as the external environment has become more challenging through internationalization.

Part 1 covers the basis of global management theory and practice and also introduces the systems model that serves as the framework of the book. To set forth the new perspective of this edition, Part 1 includes chapters on management and its relations to the external environment, social responsibility, and ethics. Moreover, to emphasize the book's international orientation, Part 1 now also includes a chapter on global and comparative management. Parts 2 through 6 discuss the managerial functions of planning, organizing, staffing, leading, and controlling. A summary of relevant principles, or guides, for each function (highlighted on gray pages) follows the last chapter in the respective parts.

The global perspective of managing is emphasized in each part closing (highlighted on colored paper), which deals exclusively with important international issues. Specifically, the closings for Parts 2 through 6 focus on managerial practices in Japan and the People's Republic of China, which are compared with practices in the United States. Moreover, all six part closings have an International Focus section that gives special attention to important issues, such as the New Europe and how managers can prepare for the next decade, or the importance of quality service in Europe, the United States, and Japan. The car industry best illustrates the internationalization of businesses. For example, the Ford Escort (Europe) is assembled in the United Kingdom and Germany, yet the parts for this car are produced in at least fifteen countries. To explain the global competitiveness of automobile companies, Part Closings 1 through 5 have a global car industry case, and the Part 6 Closing has two such cases.

Revision Work for This Edition

This tenth edition is the result of the most comprehensive revision work since the book was first published by the late professors Harold Koontz and Cyril O'Donnell. While material that was well received over the years has been retained, much new information has been added. For example, this edition builds on the strong characteristics of the ninth edition—such as breadth, depth, and the use of examples and cases—identified in the textbook survey published in the *Academy of Management Review;** at the same time, many modern ideas, techniques, and features have been added, especially those providing a global perspective of managing.

Two major influences guided the revision work for this edition. The first is the valuable feedback from teachers, scholars, and students who used past editions

---

* Allen C. Bluedorn, "Resources for the Introductory Management Course," *Academy of Management Review* (July 1986), pp. 684–691.

of this book at various levels of academic and practical management education in a wide variety of universities and operating enterprises. The second major influence is the great volume of research, new ideas, and advanced techniques, especially those being applied to management from the behavioral, social, and physical sciences. The emphasis is on managerial practice based on sound theory.

Although not all changes can be mentioned here, certain revision work should be pointed out. All chapters have been updated. The number of chapters has been reduced to twenty-three from the twenty-five in the ninth edition. For example, the ninth-edition chapters "The Nature and Purpose of Staffing" and "Selection: Matching the Person with the Job" are now combined in Chapter 13. Similarly, the chapters "Managing and the Human Factor" and "Motivation" are merged in this edition (Chapter 16). While some material has been condensed, other topics have been expanded. Certain topics have also been reorganized. "Committees and Group Decision Making," for example, is now in Part 5, "Leading." The topic "Creativity and Innovation" has been moved from the chapter on managing and the human factor to Chapter 8, "Decision Making."

New topics.   These are some of the new topics in this edition:

- What General Electric learned in France (Chapter 4)
- Korean managerial practices (Chapter 4)
- Michael Porter's Competitive Advantage of Nations (Chapter 4)
- The New Europe: preparing for the next decade (Part 1 Closing)
- The car market in the New Europe (Part 1 Closing)
- A case on the globalization of Federal Express (Chapter 8)
- Planning, organizing, staffing, leading, and controlling practices in Japan and the People's Republic of China (closings for Parts 2 through 6)
- Planning for the New Europe (Part 2 Closing)
- A global car industry case on Daimler-Benz and how the company needs to prepare for the twenty-first century (Part 2 Closing)
- The new international executive team at Apple Computer (Chapter 9)
- Organization structures for the global environment (Chapter 10)
- An international case on Siemens, the sleeping giant (Chapter 10)
- A case on the restructuring of Korea's Daewoo (Chapter 12)
- Organizing for quality service in Europe, the United States, and Japan (Part 3 Closing)
- A global car industry case showing how the Lexus, a Japanese car, was developed (Part 3 Closing)
- A comparison of workweek differences in various countries (Chapter 13)
- The global orientation of Procter & Gamble (Chapter 13)
- A comparison of CEOs in various countries (Chapter 14)
- An example of management development at China Resources (Chapter 15)
- The German/European model for training and development (Part 4 Closing)
- Comparisons of leadership approaches at Honda, Chrysler, and Daimler-Benz (Part 4 Closing)
- A Perspective on disillusioned middle managers (Chapter 16)
- The impact of the human factor in managing at Olivetti in Italy (Chapter 16)

- Worker participation in the New Europe (Chapter 18)
- A Perspective on how communications differ in various countries (Chapter 19)
- A case on the Challenger Space Shuttle accident, which shook the nation (Chapter 19)
- Description of the managerial function of leading as carried out in different cultures (Part 5 Closing)
- A case on controlling the decentralized Unilever Company (Chapter 20)
- Telecommunications battles in Europe (Chapter 21)
- Maquiladora companies in Mexico (Chapter 22)
- Quality circles in Japan (Chapter 22)
- A case on General Electric "enlightening" Hungary (Chapter 22)
- Implications of the European Community 1992 (EC 1992) program for managers in the New Europe (Part 6 Closing)
- The importance of quality and continuous improvement for gaining the competitive edge (Part 6 Closing)
- A global car industry case showing the competitive challenges for carmakers (Part 6 Closing)

Other important or expanded topics.   Here are some other important or expanded topics in this edition:

- The most admired companies in America (Chapter 1)
- The importance of the role of women in managing (discussed throughout the book, see, for example, the Chapter 17 Perspective on Marisa Bellisario, a very effective CEO in Europe)
- McKinsey's 7-S framework, which was the conceptual framework for the book *In Search of Excellence,* by Peters and Waterman (Chapter 2)
- A model for ethical decision making (Chapter 3)
- Code of ethics for government service (Chapter 3)
- Porter's generic competitive strategies (Chapter 7)
- Decision support systems (Chapter 8)
- Entrepreneuring and intrapreneuring (Chapter 9)
- Organization culture (Chapter 12)
- Strategic career management (Chapter 14)
- The role of microcomputers, telecommuting, and computer networks (Chapter 21)
- Productivity of knowledge workers for gaining a competitive advantage (Chapter 22)
- Computer-aided design (CAD), computer-aided manufacturing (CAM), and manufacturing automation protocol (MAP) (Chapter 22)

Additional features.   Other features of this book are as follows:

- Many examples are given from companies such as Compaq, Eastman Kodak, General Electric, General Motors, IBM, Lufthansa, McDonald's, 3M Company (Post-it Notes), and Volkswagen.

- Each chapter ends with two cases, many of which are international. Many cases are based on the consulting experience of the authors. Sometimes company names are disguised, to protect confidentiality, but some cases reveal the names of firms (such as People Express, Honda, McDonald's, the University of California, and IBM) and even the name of a country (South Africa).
- Throughout the book, many real-life situations illustrate managerial concepts and theories.
- Boxed inserts called "Perspectives" or "International Perspectives" provide additional insights.
- Each chapter has two recommendations for "Exercises/Action Steps" that get students involved in investigating management practices.
- Frequent references to nonbusiness organizations are made.
- New terms have been added to the already comprehensive glossary.

Learning Assistance

The integrative systems model on the inside cover gives an overview of the content and organization of the book. The model is discussed in detail in Chapter 1. Parts 2 through 6 are each introduced with the model, together with a list of chapters included in the respective part.

Each chapter begins with a notable quote and learning objectives and concludes with a summary, a list of key ideas and concepts for review, discussion questions, and two activities called "Exercises/Action Steps" that are designed to prompt readers' involvement in learning about management. There are also two cases for each chapter.

Following the last chapter in Parts 2 through 6—those dealing with the five managerial functions of planning, organizing, staffing, leading, and controlling—is a summary of major principles, or guides, for the respective function. Each of the six parts has a part closing that focuses on various global aspects of management. (In addition, important international aspects of managing are marked with globe or flag ornaments throughout the text.)

Supplemental Materials

The text is accompanied by a full ancillary program with items designed to complement both the instructor's teaching efforts and the students' learning process. These materials include a Student Study Guide and a comprehensive Instructor's Manual, both by John Halff; Overhead Transparency Acetates; a Test Bank, authored by Heinz Weihrich; and a video program. For information and costs on any supplementary materials, please contact your local McGraw-Hill representative.

Acknowledgments

The late Dr. Harold Koontz is sorely missed by those who knew him. At a memorial session at an Academy of Management meeting, Professor Ronald Greenwood stated that "Howdy" Koontz was many years ahead of his time. Indeed, his inspiration and guidance popularized the classification of management knowledge according to the managerial functions, a framework now used around the world. He will long be remembered for his contributions to management and for his many books, especially the first edition of this book (with Cyril O'Donnell), originally published as *Principles of Management* in 1955 and continuously updated ever since.

Professor Koontz and I are indebted to so many persons that a complete acknowledgment would be encyclopedic. Many scholars, writers, and managers are acknowledged through references in the text. Many managers with whom we have served in business, government, education, and other enterprises have contributed by word and example. Thousands of managers in all kinds of enterprises in various countries have honored us over the years by allowing us to test our ideas in executive training classes and lectures. In particular, many Eastman Kodak managers around the world have generously shared their international experience. Similarly, the managers in an executive program in Switzerland and those at China Resources in Hong Kong provided opportunities to learn about their culture and their managerial practices. To the executives of these and many other companies with whom we have been privileged to work as directors, consultants, or teachers, we are grateful for the opportunity to gain the clinical practice of managing.

Many colleagues, scholars, managers, and students have contributed their ideas and suggestions to this book. My good friend Professor Keith Davis, at Arizona State University, was particularly generous with his time. One of my mentors at UCLA, Professor George S. Steiner, has done much to stimulate my interest in the development of the TOWS Matrix for strategic planning. Professors Peter F. Drucker, George S. Odiorne, and Gene Seyna, to whom my book *Management Excellence: Productivity through MBO* has been dedicated, have sharpened my thinking about goal-driven management systems and managerial productivity. John Halff, the author of the *Study Guide* and the *Instructor's Resource Manual,* has diligently read the text and made very important recommendations over the years.

In previous editions, special appreciation was expressed to those who contributed in many important ways. While they are not named here, their contributions have been important for this edition as well.

We are very indebted to our academic colleagues who contributed, at various stages, to the development of this edition. They include Professors Theodore Andersen, University of California–Los Angeles; Richard D. Babcock, University of San Francisco; Allen Bluedorn, University of Missouri–Columbia; James Buckenmyer, Southeast Missouri State University; Donna E. Bush, Middle Tennessee State University; Marjorie Chan, California State University–Stanislaus; James G. Coe, Taylor University; Thomas P. Cullen, Cornell University; James Daly, Long Island University–Southampton; Diana Dean, Linfield College; Santa Deb, University of San Francisco; Claudia Harris, University of Scranton; Stuart Klein, Cleveland State University; John J. Kustura, Saint Louis University–Parks College; Agia H. Meleka, California State University–Northridge; Marta Mooney, Fordham University; James R. Necessary, Ball State University; Gary R. Oddou, San Jose State University; Larry A. Pace, University of Tennessee–Knoxville; Andrew J. Papageorge, California State University–Stanislaus; Jill Russell, Camden County

College; Susanne Schmalz, University of Southwestern Louisiana; Sat P. Sharma, Morris Brown College; Peter Stonebreaker, Northeastern Illinois University; John N. Yanouzas, University of Connecticut; A. L. Zimmerman, University of Notre Dame; and Asghar Zomorrodian, University of Southern California.

We wish to thank the many people at McGraw-Hill who were involved in publishing this edition: Seibert G. Adams; Laura Givner; Frederick Perkins and Javier Neyra B., whose contributions helped make the book, in its previous editions, a best-seller in the Spanish-speaking world; Lynn Richardson; Alan Sachs; June Smith; and Laura Warner, who skillfully managed this and previous editions from manuscript to bound book.

Finally, my wife Ursula helped greatly with her patience and understanding when yet another deadline for the book had to be met. To her and Mary Koontz this book is dedicated.

Heinz Weihrich

Management

A Global Perspective

PART

The Basis of Global Management Theory and Practice

Leadership complements management; it doesn't replace it.[1]

Management: Science, Theory, and Practice

Chapter Objectives

After completing this chapter, you should be able to:

1. Define and describe the nature and purpose of management.
2. Understand that management, as used in this book, applies to all kinds of organizations and to managers at all organizational levels.
3. Recognize that the aim of all managers is to create a "surplus."
4. Identify excellent and admired companies and their characteristics.
5. Understand the concepts of productivity, effectiveness, and efficiency.
6. Explain that management as practiced is an art in which the underlying theory and science are applied in light of situations.
7. Demonstrate that concepts, theories, principles, and techniques furnish the basic elements of operational science.
8. Realize that managing requires a systems approach and that practice must always take into account situations and contingencies.
9. Define the managerial functions of planning, organizing, staffing, leading, and controlling.
10. Understand how this book is organized.

One of the most important human activities is managing. Ever since people began forming groups to accomplish aims they could not achieve as individuals, managing has been essential to ensure the coordination of individual efforts. As society has come to rely increasingly on group effort, and as many organized groups have become large, the task of managers has been rising in importance. The purpose of this book is to promote excellence among all persons in organizations, especially among managers, aspiring managers, and other professionals.*

DEFINITION OF MANAGEMENT: ITS NATURE AND PURPOSE

Management is *the process of designing and maintaining an environment in which individuals, working together in groups, efficiently accomplish selected aims.* This basic definition needs to be expanded:

1. As managers, people carry out the managerial functions of planning, organizing, staffing, leading, and controlling.
2. Management applies to any kind of organization.
3. It applies to managers at all organizational levels.
4. The aim of all managers is the same: to create a surplus.
5. Managing is concerned with productivity; this implies effectiveness and efficiency.

The Functions of Management

Many scholars and managers have found that the analysis of management is facilitated by a useful and clear organization of knowledge. In studying management, therefore, it is helpful to break it down into five managerial functions—planning, organizing, staffing, leading, and controlling—around which can be or-

---

* At times the term "nonmanagers" is used in reference to persons who have no subordinates. Thus, nonmanagers include professionals who may have a high status in organizations.

ganized the knowledge that underlies those functions. Thus, the concepts, principles, theory, and techniques of management are grouped into these five functions.

This framework has been used and tested for many years. Although there are different ways of organizing managerial knowledge, most textbook authors today have adopted this or a similar framework even after experimenting at times with alternative ways of structuring knowledge.

Although the emphasis in this book is on managers' tasks that pertain to designing an internal environment for performance within an organization, it must never be overlooked that managers must operate in the external environment of an enterprise as well.[2] Clearly, managers cannot perform their tasks well unless they have an understanding of, and are responsive to, the many elements of the external environment—economic, technological, social, political, and ethical factors that affect their areas of operations. Moreover, many organizations operate now in different countries. Therefore, this book takes a global perspective of managing.

Management as an Essential for Any Organization

Managers are charged with the responsibility of taking actions that will make it possible for individuals to make their best contributions to group objectives. Management thus applies to small and large organizations, to profit and not-for-profit enterprises, to manufacturing as well as service industries. The term "enterprise" refers to businesses, government agencies, hospitals, universities, and other organizations, since almost everything said in this book refers to business as well as nonbusiness organizations. Effective managing is the concern of the corporation president, the hospital administrator, the government first-line supervisor, the Boy Scout leader, the bishop in the church, the baseball manager, and the university president.

Managerial Functions at Different Organizational Levels and Women in Management

In this book, no basic distinction is made between managers, executives, administrators, and supervisors. To be sure, a given situation may differ considerably among various levels in an organization or various types of enterprises. Similarly, the scope of authority held may vary and the types of problems dealt with may be considerably different. Furthermore, the person in a managerial role may be directing people in the sales, engineering, or finance department. But the fact remains that, as managers, all obtain results by establishing an environment for effective group endeavor.

All managers carry out managerial functions, but the time spent for each function may differ. Figure 1-1 shows an approximation of the relative time spent for each function, although top-level managers in modern corporations probably spend more time leading than the researchers found. Top-level managers spend more time on planning and organizing than do lower-level managers. Leading, on the other hand, takes a great deal of time for first-line supervisors. Time spent on controlling varies only slightly for managers at various levels.

FIGURE 1-1

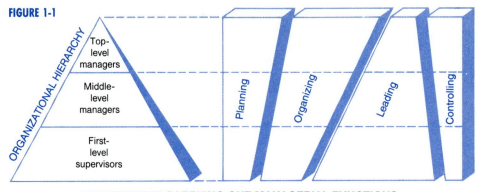

TIME SPENT IN CARRYING OUT MANAGERIAL FUNCTIONS.

Partly based on and adapted from Thomas A. Mahoney, Thomas H. Jerdee, and Stephen J. Carroll, "The Job(s) of Management," *Industrial Relations* (February 1965), pp. 97–110.

Managerial skills and the organizational hierarchy.   Robert L. Katz identified three kinds of skills for administrators.[3] To these may be added a fourth—the ability to design solutions.

1. **Technical skill** is knowledge of and proficiency in activities involving methods, processes, and procedures. Thus, it involves working with tools and specific techniques. For example, mechanics work with tools, and their supervisors should have the ability to teach them how to use these tools. Similarly, accountants apply specific techniques in doing their job.
2. **Human skill** is the ability to work with people; it is cooperative effort; it is teamwork; it is the creation of an environment in which people feel secure and free to express their opinions.
3. **Conceptual skill** is the ability to see the "big picture," to recognize significant elements in a situation, and to understand the relationships among the elements.
4. **Design skill** is the ability to solve problems in ways that will benefit the enterprise. To be effective, particularly at upper organizational levels, managers must be able to do more than see a problem. They must have, in addition, the skill of a good design engineer in working out a practical solution to a problem. If managers merely see the problem and become "problem watchers," they will fail. Managers must also have that valuable skill of being able to design a workable solution to the problem in the light of the realities they face.

The relative importance of these skills may differ at various levels in the organization hierarchy. As shown in Figure 1-2, technical skills are of greatest importance at the supervisory level. Human skills are also helpful in the frequent interactions with subordinates. Conceptual skills, on the other hand, are usually not critical for lower-level supervisors. At the middle-management level, the need for technical skills decreases; human skills are still essential; the conceptual skills gain in importance. At the top management level, conceptual and design abilities and human skills are especially valuable, but there is relatively little need for technical abilities. It is assumed, especially in large companies, that chief executives can utilize the technical abilities of their subordinates. In smaller firms, however, technical experience may still be quite important.

Women in the organizational hierarchy.   In the last decade or so, women have made significant progress in obtaining responsible positions in organizations. Among the reasons for this development are laws governing fair employment practices, changing societal attitudes toward women in the workplace, and the desire of companies to project a favorable image by placing qualified women in managerial positions.

In 1965, readers of the *Harvard Business Review* were surveyed to determine their attitudes toward women in business organizations.[4] About half of the men and women (and there was not much difference between them) responding felt that women seldom expected to achieve or even desired positions of authority.

Twenty years later, in 1985, the results showed that the attitudes toward women in business had changed significantly. Only 9 percent of the men and 4 percent of the women in the survey thought that women do not aspire to top positions. Moreover, it was found that men increasingly saw women as competent, equal colleagues. However, over 50 percent of those answering in the survey thought that women would never be completely accepted in business. This may indeed be discouraging to those women who aspire to top management positions. Yet, 20 years ago, few people would have expected the progress toward equality that has been made since 1965.

Some evidence suggests that women do have difficulties making it to the top. For example, there are no women on the way to the chief executive officer's job

FIGURE 1-2

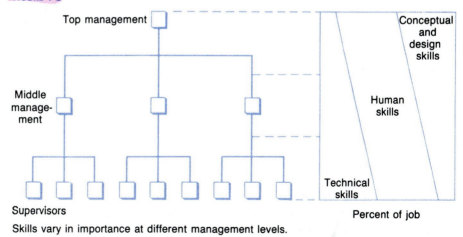

Skills vary in importance at different management levels.

SKILLS AND MANAGEMENT LEVELS.

in the *Fortune* 500 corporations. Discrimination has been given as one reason, according to a *Fortune* article.[5] On the other hand, Marisa Bellisario, who will be discussed in greater detail in Chapter 4, is one of the most successful executives in Italy, with the press calling her "Lady Computer" and the "manager in jeans" (she occasionally wears jeans at work). In fact, companies such as IBM, AT&T, and GTE Corporation have unsuccessfully tried to recruit her.

Another success story involves the internationally oriented Ellen Hancock, a high-ranking top executive at IBM. She heads the company's striving telecommunications business. Educated as a mathematician, she started as a programmer in 1966 and achieved a top position in the 1980s. With computer networking booming, especially in Europe, she decided to relocate her headquarters in London, where she began directing IBM's operation in Europe in 1991. Her international outlook is shown by her statement that "having a line of business headquartered in Europe will give us a different perspective on all our markets."[6]

The Goals of Managers and Organizations

Nonbusiness executives sometimes say that the aim of business managers is simple—to make a profit. But profit is really only a measure of a surplus of sales dollars (or any other currency) over expense dollars. For many business firms, an important goal is the long-term increase in the value of their common stock. In a very real sense, in all kinds of organizations, whether business or nonbusiness, the logical and publicly desirable aim of all managers should be a *surplus*. Thus, managers must establish an environment in which people can accomplish group goals with the least amount of time, money, materials, and personal dissatisfaction or in which they can achieve as much as possible of a desired goal with available resources. In a nonbusiness enterprise such as a police department, as well as in units of a business (such as an accounting department) that are not responsible for total business profits, managers still have goals and should strive to accomplish them with the minimum of resources or to accomplish as much as possible with available resources.

Which are the excellent companies?   In a society such as that in the United States, profitability is an important measure of company excellence. At times, however, other criteria are also used that frequently coincide with financial performance. In their book *In Search of Excellence,* Thomas Peters and Robert Waterman identified 43 companies that they regarded as excellent.[7] In choosing some of the firms, they considered factors such as growth of assets and equity, average return on total capital, and similar measures. They also asked industry experts about the innovativeness of the companies.

The authors identified eight characteristics of excellent enterprises. Specifically, these firms:

- Were oriented toward action
- Learned about the needs of their customers

- Promoted managerial autonomy and entrepreneurship
- Achieved productivity by paying close attention to the needs of their people
- Were driven by a company philosophy often based on the values of their leaders
- Focused on the business they knew best
- Had a simple organization stucture with a lean staff
- Were centralized as well as decentralized, depending on appropriateness

Two years after *In Search of Excellence* was published, *Business Week* took a second look at the companies that Peters and Waterman had considered excellent.[8] The magazine's survey revealed that at least 14 of the 43 companies did not measure up very well to several of the eight characteristics of excellence. Nine companies showed a great decline in earnings. While Peters and Waterman have been criticized in several respects (their methods of collecting and interpreting the data, for example, such as extensive use of anecdotes and quotations from leaders in the field rather than more scientific research sources),[9] the performance review of the firms indicated that success may be only transitory and that it demands continuing hard work to adapt to the changes in the environment.

The late Professor George Odiorne, widely recognized for his contributions to management by objectives, researched the performance of stock prices of the so-called excellent companies.[10] A few companies did very well indeed; but about an equal number did very poorly. Odiorne's analysis was based on this question: If you had invested $1000 in stocks of the companies, how well would you have done? Three companies—Wal-Mart, Amoco, and Intel—performed very well. On the other hand, Avon, Allen Bradley, and Data General did very poorly. In short, if people had invested in all companies considered excellent, the return on their investment would have been mixed at best.

One could take a position that factors other than stock prices should be used as criteria for excellence. Still, the characteristics of excellence identified by Peters and Waterman can have a downside:

1. A *bias for action* can also mean an argument against long-range, strategic planning.
2. *Staying close to the customer* could also mean producing anything the customer wants, even at great cost and without regard to whether or not it fits into the product line.
3. Promoting *autonomy and entrepreneurship* can also mean pursuing new ideas without considering their suitability for a long-term strategy.
4. *Hands-on, value-driven managing* can also result in top managers becoming so involved in the details of the operation that they lose sight of the overall objectives of the firm.
5. *Sticking to the knitting* could be used as an excuse for not searching for meaningful acquisition or mergers.
6. Using *a simple form and a lean staff* could also be an argument against meaningful staff work such as that done by strategic planners. Doing *and* thinking (by staff) are important.

The danger of these prescriptions is that they could result in myopic managing, that is, management with insufficient foresight. A well-known economist making his point for short-term solutions to economic problems said that in the long term we are all dead. Peters and Waterman seem to take this position with respect to managing. Yet we know that many Japanese companies have been successful precisely because they considered the long-term implications of their decisions.

Certainly, Peters and Waterman have done a great service by encouraging companies to have a second look at their managerial approaches. On the other hand, unquestioned pursuit of these authors' management prescriptions can lead to the misapplication of their suggestions. The effective manager is a situational manager who evaluates each approach in light of the circumstances and selects the one that most effectively and efficiently achieves individual and organizational goals.

The most admired companies in America.[11]   *Fortune* magazine questioned more than 8000 senior executives, outside directors, and financial analysts about the reputation of *Fortune* 500 companies on eight criteria: the quality of management; the quality of products or services; innovativeness; the value of long-term investment; financial soundness; competence to attract, develop, and keep good people; corporate responsibility toward the community as well as the environment; and the way corporate assets are used.

The most admired among the 307 companies identified in 1992 was Merck (pharmaceuticals), followed by Rubbermaid (rubber and plastic items), Wal-Mart Stores (retailing), Liz Claiborne (apparel), and Levi Strauss Associates (also apparel). These companies were followed by sixth-ranked Johnson & Johnson (pharmaceuticals), Coca-Cola (beverages), and 3M (scientific and photo equipment). PepsiCo (beverages) and Procter & Gamble (soaps and cosmetics) were equally ranked in ninth place.

As in the 1991 ranking, notably absent in the top ten were IBM and other computer companies. Procter & Gamble dropped from third place in 1991 to ninth in 1992. Levi Strauss, on the other hand, improved its 1991 ranking (from twentieth to fifth) and became the first private company in the top ten.

Customers come first: An important aspect of excellence.   Customers are the reason why businesses exist. Yet this point often tends to be forgotten, although there is ample evidence that staying close to customers can pay off handsomely. Here are some examples:

- After a disappointing 1984 model year, the Cadillac division of General Motors tried another approach in designing the new De Ville model. The company invited customers to tell them what they wanted. Furthermore, they let them test-drive the cars and asked for their opinions and suggestions. The result: a 36 percent increase in sales of the Fleetwood and De Ville models in the last quarter of 1988.

- But customer service goes beyond reaching the ultimate consumer. At Domino's Pizza, emphasis is also placed on the service the headquarters provides for its chain stores. Similarly, firms that supply pizza ingredients are evaluated on their service orientation. Bonuses are given for good service and quality.
- Satisfied customers account for the success of Lands' End, a mail-order house. Customers' trust goes so far that the customers think the company would not sell them anything the people at Lands' End would not buy or wear. A big part of the profits is used for capital expenditures to serve customers even better.

Successes are not magical. In fact, the reasons behind them are deceptively simple—for example, imagining oneself as a customer. But this orientation must be taught to all employees, who have to be monitored so that the company's philosophy is put into practice. Bureaucracy should be kept at a minimum so that customers do have access to communicate their satisfaction as well as dissatisfaction to upper-level managers. Service does not end with a sale but continues to make customers come back.

Productivity, Effectiveness, and Efficiency

Another way to view the aim of all managers is to say that they must be productive. After World War II the United States was the world leader in productivity. But in the late 1960s the deceleration of productivity growth began. Today the urgent need for productivity improvement is recognized by government, private industry, and universities. Often one looks to Japan to find answers to our productivity problem (a subject to be considered later, in Chapter 4), but one tends to overlook the importance of effectively performing the basic managerial and nonmanagerial activities.

Definition of productivity.   Successful companies create a surplus through productive operations. Although there is not complete agreement on the true meaning of **productivity,** let us define it as *the output-input ratio within a time period with due consideration for quality.* It can be expressed as follows:

$$\text{Productivity} = \frac{\text{outputs}}{\text{inputs}} \quad \text{(within a time period, quality considered)}$$

The formula indicates that productivity can be improved (1) by increasing outputs with the same inputs, (2) by decreasing inputs but maintaining the same outputs, or (3) by increasing outputs and decreasing inputs to change the ratio favorably. Companies use several kinds of inputs, such as labor, materials, and capital. Total-factor productivity combines various inputs to arrive at a composite input.[12] In the past, productivity improvement programs were mostly aimed at the worker level.[13] Yet, as Peter F. Drucker, one of the most prolific writers in management, observed, "The greatest opportunity for increasing productivity is surely to be found in knowledge work itself, and especially in management."[14]

Definitions of effectiveness and efficiency.   Productivity implies effectiveness and efficiency in individual and organizational performance. **Effectiveness** is the achievement of objectives. **Efficiency** is the achievement of the ends with the least amount of resources. Managers cannot know whether they are productive unless they first know their goals and those of the organization, a topic that will be discussed in Chapter 6.

MANAGING: SCIENCE OR ART?

Managing, like all other practices—whether medicine, music composition, engineering, accountancy, or even baseball—is an art. It is know-how. It is doing things in the light of the realities of a situation. Yet managers can work better by using the organized knowledge about management. It is this knowledge that constitutes a science. Thus, managing as practice is an *art;* the organized knowledge underlying the practice may be referred to as a *science*. In this context science and art are not mutually exclusive; they are complementary.

As science improves, so should art, as has happened in the physical and biological sciences. To be sure, the science underlying managing is fairly crude and inexact. This is true because the many variables with which managers deal are extremely complex. Nevertheless, such management knowledge can certainly improve managerial practice. Physicians without the advantage of science would be little more than witch doctors. Executives who attempt to manage without management science must trust to luck, intuition, or what they did in the past.

In managing, as in any other field, unless practitioners are to learn by trial and error (and it has been said that managers' errors are their subordinates' trials), there is no place they can turn to for meaningful guidance other than the accumulated knowledge underlying their practice.

THE ELEMENTS OF SCIENCE

Science is organized knowledge. The essential feature of any science is the application of the scientific method to the development of knowledge. Thus, a science comprises clear concepts, theory, and other accumulated knowledge developed from hypotheses (assumptions that something is true), experimentation, and analysis.

The Scientific Approach

The scientific approach, schematically shown in Figure 1-3, first requires clear **concepts**—*mental images of anything formed by generalization from particulars.* These words and terms should be exact, relevant to the things being analyzed, and informative to the scientist and practitioner alike. From this base, the **scientific method** involves the determination of facts through observation. After classifying and analyzing these facts, scientists look for causal relationships. When these

FIGURE 1-3

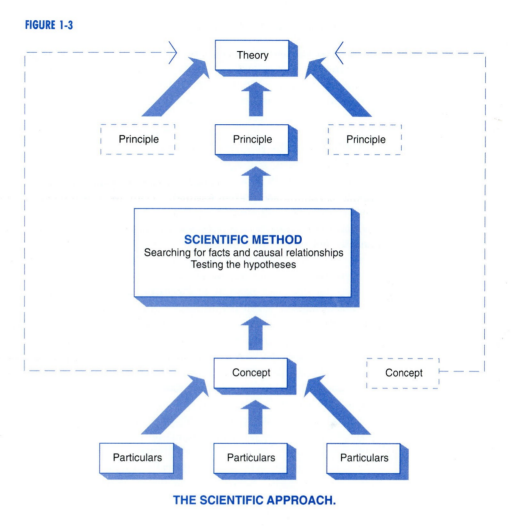

THE SCIENTIFIC APPROACH.

generalizations or hypotheses are tested for accuracy and appear to be true, that is, to reflect or explain reality, they are called "principles." They have value in predicting what will happen in similar circumstances. Principles are not always unquestionably or invariably true, but they are considered valid enough to be used for prediction.

Theory is a systematic grouping of interdependent concepts and principles that gives a framework to, or ties together, a significant area of knowledge. Scattered data, such as the notations left on a blackboard after a group of engineers has been discussing a problem, are not information unless the observer has knowledge of the theory that will explain relationships. Theory is, as Homans has said, "in its lowest form a classification, a set of pigeon holes, a filing cabinet in which fact can accumulate. Nothing is more lost than a loose fact."[15]

The Role of Management Theory[16]

In the field of management, then, the role of theory is to provide a means of classifying significant and pertinent management knowledge. In the area of designing an effective organization structure, for example, there are a number of principles that are interrelated and that have a predictive value for managers. Some principles give guidelines for delegating authority; these include the principle of delegating by results expected, the principle of equality of authority and responsibility, and the principle of unity of command.

Principles in management are fundamental truths (or what are thought to be truths at a given time), explaining relationships between two or more sets of variables, usually an independent variable and a dependent variable. Principles may be *descriptive* or *predictive,* but not prescriptive. That is, they describe how one variable relates to another—what will happen when these variables interact. They do not prescribe what people should do. For example, in physics, if gravity is the only force acting on a falling body, the body will fall at an increasing speed; this principle does not say whether anyone should jump off the roof of a high building. Or take the example of **Parkinson's Law:** *Work tends to expand to fill the time available.* Even if Parkinson's somewhat frivolous principle is correct (as it probably is), it does not mean that a manager should lengthen the time available for people to do a job. As another example, in management the **principle of unity of command** states that *the more often an individual reports to a single superior, the more likely it is that the individual will feel a sense of loyalty and obligation and the less likely it is that there will be confusion about instruction.* The principle merely predicts. It in no sense implies that individuals should never report to more than one person. Rather, it implies that if they do so, their managers must be aware of the possible dangers and should take these risks into account in balancing the advantages and disadvantages of multiple command.

Like engineers who apply physical principles to the design of an instrument, managers who apply theory to managing must usually blend principles with realities. An engineer is often faced with the necessity of combining considerations of weight, size, conductivity, and other factors in designing an instrument. Likewise, a manager may find that the advantages of giving a controller authority to prescribe accounting procedures throughout an organization outweigh the possible costs of multiple authority. But if they know theory, these managers will know that such costs as conflicting instructions and confusion may exist, and they will take steps (such as making the controller's special authority clear to everyone involved) to minimize disadvantages.

Management Techniques

Techniques are essentially ways of doing things, methods of accomplishing a given result. In all fields of practice they are important. They certainly are in managing, even though few really important managerial techniques have been invented. Among them are budgeting, cost accounting, network planning and control techniques like the Program Evaluation and Review Technique (PERT) or the Critical Path Method (CPM), rate-of-return-on-investment control, and various devices of organizational development, all of which will be discussed in later chapters. Techniques normally reflect theory and are a means of helping managers undertake activities most effectively.

A **management fad** can be defined as a managerial interest or practice followed for a period of time with exaggerated zeal or craze. But fads come and go— some slowly, others quickly; some survive and others fall by the wayside. These managerial fads can be found in all managerial functions. *Business Week* identified some that are out and some that are currently in vogue.[17] Let us look at some of those that are "in" in the various managerial functions.

Fads in planning?   One of the fashionable buzzwords is **strategic alliance,** which essentially means that companies cooperate, as in forming a joint venture. These alliances even cut across national boundaries: American Telephone and Telegraph joins forces with Olivetti in Italy (this alliance was not successful and broke up in 1989); General Motors builds cars with the Japanese car manufacturer Toyota.[18]

Fads in organizing?   **Corporate culture** is also "in." It pertains to the values and beliefs shared by employees and the general patterns of their behavior.

Fads in staffing?   Organizations have to be staffed by people who are not only competent but also healthy. This requires **wellness** or **fitness** programs and the management of **stress.** Over 90 percent of the 500 largest companies in the United States have a wellness program or are assisting employees in managing stress or improving their health.[19] **Paying for performance** is also currently fashionable.[20] This simply means measuring the contributions of individuals and rewarding them accordingly. Another term you may hear at times is **demassing,** which is a euphemism for laying off employees or demoting managers.

Fads in leading?   Then there is the **intrapreneur,** a person who acts like an entrepreneur but does so within the organizational environment. Gifford Pinchot, who coined the term, describes intrapreneurs as "those who take hands-on responsibility for creating innovation of any kind within an organization. The intrapreneur may be the creator or inventor but he or she is always the dreamer who figures out how to turn an idea into a profitable reality."[21]

Fads in controlling?   People admire success. Managers, rightly or wrongly, look to Japan to solve their productivity or quality problems. Thus, **quality circles,** widely used in Japan, are seen as a way of improving quality and making U.S. products more competitive.

Fads can become techniques, and they may contribute to the functioning of the organization. (Indeed, some of them will be discussed later in this book.) However, if they are considered short-term solutions to deep-seated problems, or if they are considered quick fixes, then their value may be questioned. On the other hand, if they are integrated into a comprehensive system of management with a real commitment to managerial excellence, then they will be useful techniques.

THE SYSTEMS APPROACH TO OPERATIONAL MANAGEMENT

An organized enterprise does not, of course, exist in a vacuum. Rather, it is dependent on its external environment; it is a part of larger systems such as the industry to which it belongs, the economic system, and society. Thus, the enterprise receives inputs, transforms them, and exports the outputs to the environment, as shown by the very basic model in Figure 1-4. However, this simple model needs to be expanded and developed into a model of operational management that indicates how the various inputs are transformed through the managerial functions of planning, organizing, staffing, leading, and controlling. Clearly, any business or other organization must be described by an open-system model that includes interactions between the enterprise and its external environment.

Inputs and Claimants*

The inputs from the external environment (see Figure 1-5) may include people, capital, and managerial skills, as well as technical knowledge and skills. In addition, various groups of people make demands on the enterprise.[22] For example, employees want higher pay, more benefits, and job security. On the other hand, consumers demand safe and reliable products at reasonable prices. Suppliers want assurance that their products will be bought. Stockholders want not only a high return on their investment but also security for their money. Federal, state, and local governments depend on taxes paid by the enterprise, and they also expect the enterprise to comply with their laws. Similarly, the community demands that enterprises be "good citizens," providing the maximum number of jobs with a minimum of pollution. Other claimants to the enterprise may include financial institutions and labor unions; even competitors have a legitimate claim for fair play. It is clear that many of these claims are incongruent, and it is the manager's job to integrate the legitimate objectives of the claimants. This may need to be done through compromises, trade-offs, and denials of the manager's own ego.

* Claimants may also be called *stakeholders*.

FIGURE 1-4

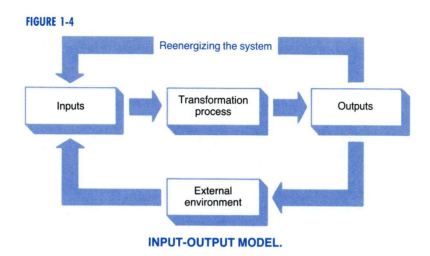

INPUT-OUTPUT MODEL.

The Managerial Transformation Process

It is the task of managers to transform the inputs, in an effective and efficient manner, into outputs. Of course, the transformation process can be viewed from different perspectives. Thus, one can focus on such diverse enterprise functions as finance, production, personnel, and marketing. Writers on management look on the transformation process in terms of their particular approaches to management. Specifically, writers belonging to the human behavior school focus on interpersonal relationships, social systems theorists analyze the transformation by concentrating on social interactions, and those advocating decision theory see the transformation as sets of decisions. However, the most comprehensive and useful approach for discussing the job of managers is to use the managerial functions of planning, organizing, staffing, leading, and controlling as a framework for organizing managerial knowledge; therefore, this is the approach used as the framework of this book (see Figure 1-5).

The Communication System

Communication is essential to all phases of the managerial process for two reasons. First, it integrates the managerial functions. For example, the objectives set in planning are communicated so that the appropriate organization structure can be devised. Communication is essential in the selection, appraisal, and training of managers to fill the roles in this structure. Similarly, effective leadership and the creation of an environment conducive to motivation depend on communication. Moreover, it is through communication that one determines whether events and performance conform to plans. Thus, it is communication that makes managing possible.

FIGURE 1-5

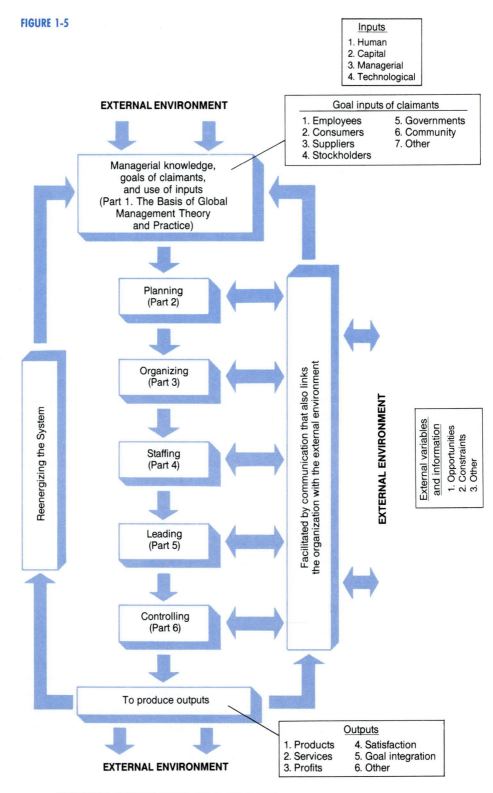

SYSTEMS APPROACH TO MANAGEMENT

The second purpose of the communication system is to link the enterprise with its external environment, where many of the claimants are. For example, one should never forget that customers, who are the reason for the existence of virtually all businesses, are outside a company. It is through the communication system that the needs of customers are identified; this knowledge enables the firm to provide products and services at a profit. Similarly, it is through an effective communication system that the organization becomes aware of competition and other potential threats and constraining factors.

External Variables

Effective managers will regularly scan the external environment. While it is true that managers may have little or no power to change the external environment, they have no alternative but to respond to it. The forces acting in the external environment are discussed in various chapters, especially in Chapters 3, 4, and 7.

Outputs

It is the task of managers to secure and utilize inputs to the enterprise, to transform them through the managerial functions—with due consideration for external variables—into outputs.

Although the kinds of outputs will vary with the enterprise, they usually include many of the following: products, services, profits, satisfaction, and integration of the goals of various claimants to the enterprise. Most of these outputs require no elaboration, and only the last two will be discussed.

The organization must indeed provide many "satisfactions" if it hopes to retain and elicit contributions from its members. It must contribute to the satisfaction not only of basic material needs (for example, employees' needs to earn money for food and shelter or to have job security) but also of needs for affiliation, acceptance, esteem, and perhaps even self-actualization so that one can use his or her potential at the workplace.

Another output is goal integration. As noted above, the different claimants to the enterprise have very divergent—and often directly opposing—objectives. It is the task of managers to resolve conflicts and integrate these aims.

Reenergizing the System

Finally, it is important to notice that in the systems model of operational management some of the outputs become inputs again. Thus, the satisfaction and new knowledge or skills of employees become important human inputs. Similarly, profits, the surplus of income over costs, are reinvested in cash and capital goods, such as machinery, equipment, buildings, and inventory. You will see shortly that the model shown in Figure 1-5 will serve as a framework in this book for organizing managerial knowledge. But let us first look closer at the managerial functions.

THE FUNCTIONS OF MANAGERS[23]

The functions of managers provide a useful structure for organizing management knowledge (see the central part of Figure 1-5). There have been no new ideas, research findings, or techniques that cannot readily be placed in the classifications of planning, organizing, staffing, leading, and controlling.

Planning

Planning involves selecting missions and objectives and the actions to achieve them; it requires decision making, that is, choosing future courses of action from among alternatives. As Chapter 5 will show, there are various types of plans, ranging from overall purposes and objectives to the most detailed actions to be taken, such as ordering a special stainless steel bolt for an instrument or hiring and training workers for an assembly line. No real plan exists until a decision—a commitment of human or material resources or reputation—has been made. Before a decision is made, all that exists is a planning study, an analysis, or a proposal; there is no real plan. The various aspects of planning are discussed in Part 2 of this book.

Organizing[24]

People working together in groups to achieve some goal must have roles to play, much like the parts actors fill in a drama, whether these roles are ones they develop themselves, are accidental or haphazard, or are defined and structured by someone who wants to make sure that people contribute in a specific way to group effort. The concept of a "role" implies that what people do has a definite purpose or objective; they know how their job objective fits into group effort, and they have the necessary authority, tools, and information to accomplish the task.

This can be seen in as simple a group effort as setting up camp on a fishing expedition. Everyone could do anything he or she wanted to do, but activity would almost certainly be more effective and certain tasks would be less likely to be left undone if one or two persons were given the job of gathering firewood, others the assignment of getting water, others the task of starting a fire, others the job of cooking, and so on.

Organizing, then, is that part of managing that involves establishing an intentional structure of roles for people to fill in an organization.[25] It is intentional in the sense of making sure that all the tasks necessary to accomplish goals are assigned and, it is hoped, assigned to people who can do them best.

The purpose of an organization structure is to help in creating an environment for human performance. It is, then, a management tool and not an end in and of itself. Although the structure must define the tasks to be done, the roles so established must also be designed in the light of the abilities and motivations of the people available.

Designing an effective organization structure is not an easy managerial task.

Many problems are encountered in making structures fit situations, including both defining the kinds of jobs that must be done and finding the people to do them. These problems and the essential theory, principles, and techniques of handling them are the subjects of Part 3 of this book.

Staffing

Staffing involves filling, and keeping filled, the positions in the organization structure. This is done by identifying work-force requirements; inventorying the people available; and recruiting, selecting, placing, promoting, appraising, planning the careers of, compensating, and training or otherwise developing both candidates and current jobholders so that tasks are accomplished effectively and efficiently. This subject is dealt with in Part 4 of this book.

Leading

Leading is influencing people so that they will contribute to organization and group goals; it has to do predominantly with the interpersonal aspect of managing. All managers would agree that their most important problems arise from people— their desires and attitudes, their behavior as individuals and in groups—and that effective managers also need to be effective leaders. Since leadership implies followership and people tend to follow those who offer a means of satisfying their own needs, wishes, and desires, it is understandable that leading involves motivation, leadership styles and approaches, and communication. The essentials of these subjects are dealt with in Part 5 of this book.

Controlling

Controlling is measuring and correcting individual and organizational performance to ensure that events conform to plans. It involves measuring performance against goals and plans, showing where deviations from standards exist, and helping to correct them. In short, controlling facilitates the accomplishment of plans. Although planning must precede controlling, plans are not self-achieving. Plans guide managers in the use of resources to accomplish specific goals; then activities are checked to determine whether they conform to the plans.

Control activities generally relate to the measurement of achievement. Some means of controlling, like the budget for expenses, inspection records, and the record of labor-hours lost, are generally familiar. Each measures, and each shows whether plans are working out. If deviations persist, correction is indicated. But what is corrected? Activities, through persons. Nothing can be done about reducing scrap, for example, or buying according to specifications, or handling sales returns unless one knows who is responsible for these functions. Compelling events to conform to plans means locating the persons who are responsible for results that differ from planned action and then taking the necessary steps to improve performance. Thus, outcomes are controlled by controlling what people do. This subject is treated in Part 6.

Coordination, the Essence of Managership

Some authorities consider coordination to be a separate function of the manager. It seems more accurate, however, to regard it as the essence of managership, for achieving harmony among individual efforts toward the accomplishment of group goals. Each of the managerial functions is an exercise contributing to coordination.

Even in the case of a church or a fraternal organization, individuals often interpret similar interests in different ways, and their efforts toward mutual goals do not automatically mesh with the efforts of others. It thus becomes the central task of the manager to reconcile differences in approach, timing, effort, or interest and to harmonize individual goals to contribute to organization goals.

THE SYSTEMS MODEL OF MANAGEMENT AND THE ORGANIZATION OF THIS BOOK

The model of the systems approach to management is also the foundation for organizing managerial knowledge. Note that in Figure 1-5 the numbers shown in the model correspond to the parts of this book. Part 1 covers the basis of global management and the interactions between the organization and its environment. This part cuts across all managerial functions.

As the model in the figure shows, Part 1 deals with basic managerial knowledge such as theory, science, and practice. It also discusses the evolution of management and the various approaches to management. Since organizations are open systems, they interact with the external environment: the domestic and international.

Figure 1-5 also shows that Part 2 deals with the various aspects of **planning** (Chapters 5 to 8). Part 3 is concerned with **organizing** (Chapters 9 to 12), while Part 4 deals with **staffing** (Chapters 13 to 15), Part 5 with **leading** (Chapters 16 to 19), and Part 6 with **controlling** (Chapters 20 to 23). The last chapter also suggests future challenges for managers.

This book has a **global perspective** of management.[26] Increasingly, organizations operate in the global market. Therefore, comparative and international management aspects are discussed not only in Chapter 4 but also throughout the book. Most important, at the end of each of the six parts, significant global managerial aspects are introduced. Specifically, each part has an "International Focus" section. For example, Part 1 focuses on the New Europe, Part 3 on organizing for quality service in Europe, the United States, and Japan. In addition, Parts 2 to 6 discuss the managerial practices of planning, organizing, staffing, leading, and controlling in Japan, the United States, and the People's Republic of China. Each of the part closings also has at least one case dealing with the global car industry. Each case can be analyzed by itself. But a better understanding of the global car industry is gained by reading all the "Global Car Industry Cases."

The model shown in Figure 1-5 is repeated at the beginning of Parts 2 to 6, but with the appropriate part highlighted. This feature of an integrative model shows the relationships of the topics in this book.

SUMMARY

Management is the process of designing and maintaining an environment for the purpose of efficiently accomplishing selected aims. Managers carry out the functions of planning, organizing, staffing, leading, and controlling. Managing is an essential activity at all organizational levels; however, the managerial skills required vary with organizational levels. Although women have made progress in obtaining responsible positions, they still have a long way to go. The goal of all managers is to create a surplus and to be productive, that is, to achieve a favorable output-input ratio within a specific time period with due consideration for quality. Productivity implies effectiveness (achieving objectives) and efficiency (using the least amount of resources).

Managing as practice is an art; organized knowledge about management is a science. The development of management theory involves the development of concepts, principles, and techniques.

The organization is an open system that operates within and interacts with the environment. The systems approach to management includes inputs from the external environment and from claimants, the transformation process, the communication system, external factors, outputs, and a way to reenergize the system. The transformation process consists of the managerial functions, which also provide the framework for organizing knowledge in this book. Throughout the book, but especially in Chapter 4 and in the part closings, international aspects of managing are emphasized.

KEY IDEAS AND CONCEPTS FOR REVIEW

Management
Managerial functions
Managerial skills in the organizational
  hierarchy
Women in the organizational hierarchy
The goal of all managers
Characteristics of excellent companies
Productivity
Effectiveness
Efficiency
Concepts
Scientific method
Principles

Theory
Parkinson's Law
Techniques
Systems approach to operational
  management
Planning
Organizing
Staffing
Leading
Controlling
Coordination
Organization of this book

FOR DISCUSSION

1. Management has been defined as "getting things done through people." Comment on this definition.
2. How would you define "management"? Does your definition differ from the one offered in this book? Explain.

3. What are the managerial functions?
4. How do the required managerial skills differ in the organizational hierarchy?
5. In what fundamental way are the basic goals of all managers at all levels and in all kinds of enterprises the same?
6. What are some of the characteristics of excellent companies (according to Peters and Waterman)? Do the companies you know have these characteristics?
7. What are the differences between productivity, effectiveness, and efficiency?
8. Is managing a science or an art? Could the same explanation apply to engineering or accounting?
9. Look up the terms "science," "theory," and "principle" in a dictionary and determine how they are used. Compare these definitions with the usage of these terms as applied to management in this book. What advantages are there in attempting to identify science, theory, and principles in a book on management?
10. Why do management analysis and practice require a systems approach? Do managers operate in an open or a closed system? Explain.

EXERCISES/ACTION STEPS

1. Interview two local business managers, and ask them how they learned about managing. Ask what kinds of books they might have read on management (e.g., textbooks or popular books such as *In Search of Excellence* by Thomas J. Peters and Robert H. Waterman, Jr., *The One Minute Manager* by Kenneth H. Blanchard, *Theory Z* by William Ouchi, *The Art of Japanese Management* by Richard Tanner Pascale and Anthony G. Athos, and *Reinventing the Corporation: Transforming Your Job and Your Company for the New Information Society* by John Naisbitt and Patricia Aburdene). Probe to what extent these books have helped them to manage. You may also find it interesting to buy one of the best-selling books on management (most are available in paperback) and mention them in the class discussion.
2. Interview two public administrators, and ask them how their job differs from that of business managers. How do they know how well their department, agency, or organization is performing, since profit is probably not one of the criteria for measuring effectiveness and efficiency?

CASES

CASE 1-1
PEOPLE EXPRESS[27]

Donald Burr, the founder and chairperson of People Express, has been hailed in his attempt to build a more humane organization. But his leadership style was changing as the organization grew. Managers at People Express had a distinct managerial style: hard-driving, but giving employees a great deal of freedom. All employees are expected to carry out a great variety of tasks. Thus, pilots help out in handling the baggage. Even top executives rotate from job to job to learn the major aspects of the business. Full-time employees must buy stock in the company, although they receive a large discount.

After the company expanded and experienced its first losses, its emphasis on participative management changed. With the acquisition of Frontier Airlines, Inc., People Express became the fifth largest airline in the country—only 5 years after its formation in 1980. With its growth, however, the firm changed its character from a family-style organization to a more traditional one. Critics maintain that within the company it is even risky to ask unpopular questions. One of the original managing directors, Lori Dubose, who was one of the architects of lifetime employment at People Express, was unexpectedly fired. She thinks now that asking Burr challenging questions was risky and probably was a mistake. Another director, Harold Parety, who did not like being told that he had to be at work from 6 a.m. to 9 p.m. regardless of the workload, quit and formed his own airline (Presidential Airways, Inc.), applying many of People Express's managerial practices.

1. What are some of the consequences to the company of Burr's way of firing an officer?
2. Should a company be managed the same way regardless of its size or its profitability?

INTERNATIONAL CASE 1-2
McDONALD'S: SERVING FAST FOOD AROUND THE WORLD[28]

Ray Kroc opened the first McDonald's restaurant in 1955. He offered a limited menu of high-quality, moderately priced food served fast in spotless surroundings. McDonald's QSC&V (quality, service, cleanliness, and value) was a hit. The chain expanded into every state in the nation. By 1983 it had over 6000 restaurants in the United States.

In 1967 McDonald's opened its first restaurant outside the United States, in Canada. By 1985 international sales represented about one-fifth of McDonald's total revenues. Yet fast food has barely touched many cultures. While 90 percent of the Japanese in Tokyo have eaten a McDonald's hamburger, few outside the cities know what a hamburger is. In Europe, McDonald's maintains a very small percentage of restaurant sales but commands a large share of the fast-food market. It took the company 14 years of planning before it opened a restaurant in Moscow. But the planning paid off. People stand in line up to 2 hours for a hamburger. After waiting for such a long time, they have to pay $14.40 (at the official rate) for a Big Mac and french fries. Despite the high prices, McDonald's restaurant in Moscow attracts more visitors—on the average, 27,000 daily—than Lenin's mausoleum (about 9000 people), which used to be *the* place to see.

The taste for fast food, American-style, is growing more rapidly in countries abroad than at home.

McDonald's international sales have been increasing by a large percentage every year. Every day more than 18 million people in over 40 countries eat at McDonald's.

Its traditional menu has been surprisingly successful. People with diverse dining habits have adopted burgers and fries wholeheartedly. Before McDonald's introduced the Japanese to french fries, potatoes were used in Japan only to make starch. The Germans thought hamburgers were people from the city of Hamburg. Now, McDonald's also serves chicken, sausage, and salads. One of the latest items, a very different product, is pizza. This new venture is risky and can be either a very profitable addition or a costly experiment.

The fast, family-oriented service, the cleanliness, and the value accounted for much of McDonald's success. McDonald's was one of the first restaurants in Europe to welcome families with children. Not only are children welcomed, but in many restaurants they are also entertained with crayons and paper, a playland, or maybe even Ronald McDonald, who can speak twenty languages.

McDonald's golden arches promise the same basic menu and QSC&V in every restaurant. Its products, handling and cooking procedures, and kitchen layouts are standardized and strictly controlled. McDonald's revoked the first French franchises because the franchisees failed to meet its standards for fast service and cleanliness, even though their restaurants were highly profitable. This may have delayed its expansion in France.

The restaurants are run by local managers and crews. Owners and managers must attend the Hamburger University near Chicago to learn how to operate a McDonald's restaurant and maintain QSC&V. The main campus library and modern electronic classrooms (which include simultaneous translation systems) are the envy of many universities. When McDonald's opened in Moscow, a one-page advertisement resulted in 30,000 inquiries about the jobs; 4000 people were interviewed, and some 300 were hired. The pay is about 50 percent higher than the average Soviet salary.

McDonald's ensures consistent products by controlling every stage of distribution. Regional distribution centers purchase products and distribute them to individual restaurants. The centers will buy from local suppliers if the suppliers can meet detailed specifications. McDonald's has had to make some concessions to available products. For example, it is difficult to introduce the Idaho potato in Europe.

McDonald's uses essentially the same competitive strategy in every country: Be first in a market, and establish your brand as rapidly as possible by advertising very heavily. New restaurants are opened with a bang. So many people attended the opening of one Tokyo restaurant that the police closed the street to vehicles. The strategy has helped McDonald's develop a strong share in the fast-food market, even though its U.S. competitors and new local competitors quickly enter the market.

The advertising campaigns are based on local themes and reflect the different environments. In Japan, where burgers are a snack, McDonald's competes against confectioneries and new "fast sushi" restaurants. Many of the charitable causes McDonald's supports abroad have been recommended by the local restaurants.

McDonald's has been willing to relinquish the most control to its Far Eastern operations, where many restaurants are joint ventures with local entrepreneurs, owning 50 percent or more of the restaurant.

European and South American restaurants are generally company-operated or franchised (although there are many affiliates—joint ventures—in France). Like the U.S. franchises, restaurants abroad are allowed to experiment with their menus. In Japan, hamburgers are smaller because they are considered a snack. The Quarter Pounder didn't make much sense to people on a metric system, so it is called a Double Burger. Some of the German restaurants serve beer; some French restaurants serve wine. Some Far Eastern restaurants offer oriental noodles. But these new items must not disrupt existing operations.

Despite success, McDonald's faces tough competitors such as Burger King, Wendy's, Kentucky Fried Chicken, and now also Pizza Hut. And fast food in reheatable containers is now also sold in supermarkets, delicatessens and convenience stores, and even gas stations. McDonald's has done very well, with a great percentage of profits coming now from international operations. But can this success continue?

1. What opportunities and threats did McDonald's face? How did it handle them? What alternatives could it have chosen?
2. Before McDonald's entered the European market, few people believed that fast food could be successful in Europe. Why do you think McDonald's succeeded? What strategies did it follow? How did these differ from its strategies in Asia?
3. What is McDonald's basic philosophy? How does it enforce this philosophy and adapt to different environments?
4. Should McDonald's expand its menu? If you say no, then why not? If you say yes, what kinds of products should it add?
5. Why was McDonald's successful in Moscow?

REFERENCES

1. John P. Kotter, "What Leaders Really Do," *Harvard Business Review* (May–June 1990), p. 103.
2. William H. Peace, "I Thought I Knew What Good Management Was," *Harvard Business Review* (March–April 1986), pp. 59–65.

3. Robert L. Katz, "Skills of an Effective Administrator," *Harvard Business Review* (January–February 1955), pp. 33–42; and Robert L. Katz, "Retrospective Commentary," *Harvard Business Review* (September–October 1974), pp. 101–102.

4. Charlotte Decker Sutton and Kris K. Moore, "Executive Women—20 Years Later," *Harvard Business Review* (September–October 1985), pp. 42–66.

5. Susan Fraker, "Why Women Aren't Getting to the Top, *Fortune* (Apr. 16, 1984), pp. 40–45. In certain firms, such as Federal Express and Hewlett-Packard, and in some industries, such as banking and retailing, chances for promotion to upper-level management are better for women. See Irene Pave, "A Woman's Place Is at GE, Federal Express, P&G . . . ," *Business Week* (June 23, 1986), pp. 75–76. But some women are also leaving the work force, as discussed by Alex Taylor III, "Why Women Managers Are Bailing Out," *Fortune* (Aug. 18, 1986), pp. 16–23; Jaclyn Fierman, "Why Women Still Don't Hit the Top," *Fortune* (July 30, 1990), pp. 40–62.

6. "IBM Goes to Europe," *Fortune* (Jan. 14, 1991), p. 107.

7. Thomas J. Peters and Robert H. Waterman, Jr., *In Search of Excellence* (New York: Harper & Row, Publishers, 1982).

8. "Who's Excellent Now?" *Business Week* (Nov. 5, 1984), pp. 76–88; see also Michael A. Hitt and R. Duane Ireland, "Peters and Waterman Revisited: The Unending Quest for Excellence," *Academy of Management Executive* (May 1987), pp. 91–98.

9. Daniel T. Carroll, "A Disappointing Search for Excellence," *Harvard Business Review* (November–December 1983), pp. 78–88. See also Terence R. Mitchell, "In Search of Excellence versus the 100 Best Companies to Work for in America: A Question of Perspectives and Values," *The Academy of Management Review* (April 1985), pp. 350–355.

10. George Odiorne, *The George Odiorne Letter* (Sept. 22, 1989), pp. 1–3.

11. Kate Ballen, "America's Most Admired Corporations," *Fortune* (Feb. 10, 1992), pp. 40–46.

12. Frank R. Lichtenberg, "What Makes Plant Productivity Grow?" *The Wall Street Journal* (Dec. 24, 1987).

13. Heinz Weihrich, *Management Excellence—Productivity through MBO* (New York: McGraw-Hill Book Company, 1985).

14. Peter F. Drucker, *Management: Tasks, Responsibilities, Practices* (New York: Harper & Row, 1973), p. 69. See also Tim R. V. Davis, "Information Technology and White-Collar Productivity," *Academy of Management Executive* (February 1991), pp. 55–67.

15. G. C. Homans, *The Human Group* (New York: Harcourt, Brace & World, 1958), p. 5.

16. See also Michael T. Matteson and John M. Ivancevich (eds.), *Management Classics,* 3d ed. (Plano, Tex.: Business Publications, 1986).

17. John A. Byrne, "Business Fads: What's In—and Out," *Business Week* (Jan. 20, 1986), pp. 52–61. Peter F. Drucker, probably the most prolific writer on management, notes that the fads change about every 2 1/2 years. The next fad may be in accounting to measure productivity. See "Advice from the Dr. Spock of Business," *Business Week* (Sept. 28, 1987), pp. 61–65.

18. Howard V. Perlmutter and David A. Heenan, "Cooperate to Compete Globally," *Harvard Business Review* (March–April 1986), pp. 136–152; John Rossant, "Can Italy Catch Up?" *Business Week* (June 11, 1990), pp. 34–36.

19. Emily T. Smith, Jody Brott, Alice Cuneo, and Jo Ellen Davis, "Stress: The Test Americans Are Failing," *Business Week* (Apr. 18, 1988), pp. 74–76.

20. Jacob M. Schlesinger, "GM's New Compensation Plan Reflects General Trend Tying Pay to Performance," *The Wall Street Journal* (Jan. 26, 1988).

21. Gifford Pinchot III, *Intrapreneuring* (New York: Harper & Row, Publishers, 1985), p. ix. For a review of books on entrepreneurship, see David E. Gumpert, "Stalking the Entrepreneur," *Harvard Business Review* (May–June 1986), pp. 32–36.

22. See also Grant T. Savage, Timothy W. Nix, Carlton J. Whitehead, and John D. Blair, "Strategies for Assessing and Managing Organizational Stakeholders," *Academy of Management Executive* (May 1991), pp. 61–75.

23. See also Rosabeth Moss Kanter, "The New Managerial Work," *Harvard Business Review* (November–December 1989), pp. 85–92.

24. See also James L. Gibson, John M. Ivancevich, and James H. Donnelly, Jr. (eds.), *Organizations Close-Up—A Book of Readings,* 6th ed. (Plano, Tex.: Business Publications, 1988).

25. For a classic discussion of organizing, see Chester I. Barnard, *The Functions of the Executive* (Cambridge, Mass.: Harvard University Press, 1938).

26. See also *Global Competition—The New Reality*, The Report of the President's Commission on Industrial Competitiveness, vol. I (January 1985).

27. The case is based on a variety of sources, including "Up, Up and Away?—Expansion Is Threatening the 'Humane' Culture at People Express," *Business Week* (Nov. 25, 1985), pp. 80–94; James R. Norman, "People Is Plunging, but Burr Is Staying Cool," *Business Week* (July 7, 1986), pp. 31–32. Note that in 1986, Texas Air Corporation acquired People Express. See James R. Norman, "Nice Going, Frank, but Will It Fly?" *Business Week* (Sept. 29, 1986), pp. 34–35.

28. The case is based on a variety of sources, including interviews and a visit to Hamburger University, as well as the following: Richard Gibson, "McDonald's Sees Nothing to Beef About," *The Wall Street Journal* (Apr. 1, 1988); Frederick H. Katayama, "Japan's Big Mac," *Fortune* (Sept. 15, 1986), pp. 114–120; Stephen Kindel, "Where's the Growth?" *Forbes* (Apr. 23, 1984), p. 80; Kenneth Labich, "America's International Winners," *Fortune* (Apr. 14, 1986), pp. 34–46; Paul Hofheinz, "McDonald's Beats Lenin 3 to 1," *Fortune* (Dec. 17, 1990), p. 11; Donald Henkoff, "Big Mac Attacks with Pizza," *Fortune* (Feb. 26, 1990), pp. 87–89; Jeffrey M. Hertzfeld, "Joint Ventures: Saving the Soviets from Perestroika," *Harvard Business Review* (January–February 1991), pp. 80–91.

History is a record of human progress, a record of the struggle of the advancement of the human mind, of the human spirit, toward some known or unknown objective.

Jawaharlal Nehru

The Evolution of Management Thought and the Patterns of Management Analysis

Chapter Objectives

After studying this chapter, you should be able to:

1. Discuss the "scientific management" thinking of Frederick Taylor and his major followers.
2. Give special attention to the ideas of Henri Fayol and his pioneering theory that managing is a universal activity to be identified and analyzed.
3. Understand the emergence of the behavioral sciences, especially the "social man" concepts of Mayo and his colleagues and the "social system" theory of Chester Barnard.
4. Recognize some recent contributions to management thought.
5. Explain the nature of the "management theory jungle."
6. Describe the various approaches to management, their contributions as well as their limitations.
7. Show how the operational approach to management theory and science has a basic core of its own and also draws from the other approaches.

Despite the inexactness and relative crudity of management theory and science, the development of thought on management dates back to the days when people first attempted to accomplish goals by working together in groups. Although modern operational-management theory dates primarily from the early twentieth century, there was serious thinking and theorizing about managing many years before.

While this chapter can do little more than sketch some of the high spots in the emergence of management thought,[1] it is worthwhile for persons interested in management to know something of the background of the evolution of management thought. Even limited knowledge can help one appreciate the many insights, ideas, and scientific underpinnings that preceded the upsurge in management writing during recent years. Familiarity with the history of management thought may help you avoid rediscovering previously known ideas.

You will see that the many different contributions of writers and practitioners have resulted in different approaches to management, and these make up a "management theory jungle." Later in this chapter you will learn about the different patterns of management analysis and what can be done to untangle the jungle. But let us first focus on the emergence of management thought, summarized in Table 2-1. While it would be too complex and voluminous to include in such a table all the persons who have made significant contributions in the evolution of management thought, major contributors are noted.

FREDERICK TAYLOR AND SCIENTIFIC MANAGEMENT[2]

Frederick Winslow Taylor gave up going to college and started out as an apprentice patternmaker and machinist in 1875, joined the Midvale Steel Company in Philadelphia as a machinist in 1878, and rose to the position of chief engineer after earning a degree in engineering through evening study. He invented high-speed steel-cutting tools and spent most of his life as a consulting engineer. Taylor is generally acknowledged as "the father of scientific management." Probably no other person has had a greater impact on the early development of management. His experience as an apprentice, a common laborer, a foreman, a master mechanic, and then the chief engineer of a steel company gave Taylor ample opportunity to

FREDERICK W. TAYLOR
1856–1912

Historical Pictures Service, Chicago

know firsthand the problems and attitudes of workers and to see the great possibilities for improving the quality of management.

Taylor's patents for high-speed steel-cutting tools and other inventions, as well as his early engineering consulting work, made him so well off that he retired from working for payment in 1901, at the age of 45, and spent the remaining 14 years of his life as an unpaid consultant and lecturer to promote his ideas on scientific management.

Taylor's Major Concern

Taylor's major concern throughout most of his life was to increase efficiency in production, not only to lower costs and raise profits but also to make possible increased pay for workers through their higher productivity. As a young man working in machine shops, he was impressed with the degree of "soldiering" on the job, of making work, and of producing less rather than more, due primarily to the workers' fear that they might work themselves out of a job if they produced more. He saw "soldiering" as a system. From his own experience, he knew that much higher productivity was possible without unreasonable effort by the workers.

Taylor decided that the problem of productivity was a matter of ignorance on the part of both management and labor. Part of this ignorance arose from the fact that neither managers nor workers knew what constituted a "fair day's work" and a "fair day's pay." Moreover, he believed that both managers and workers were concerned too much with how they should divide the surplus that arose from productivity—the split in thinking between pay and profits—and not enough with increasing the surplus so that *both* owners and laborers could get more compensation. In brief, Taylor saw productivity as the answer to both higher wages and higher profits. He believed that the application of scientific methods, instead of custom and rule of thumb, could yield productivity without the expenditure of more human energy or effort.

TABLE 2-1 THE EMERGENCE OF MANAGEMENT THOUGHT	
Name and year of major work	**Major contribution to management**
Scientific management	
Frederick W. Taylor *Shop Management* (1903) *Principles of Scientific Management* (1911) *Testimony before the Special House Committee* (1912)	Acknowledged as "the father of scientific management." His primary concern was to increase productivity through greater efficiency in production and increased pay for workers, through the application of the scientific method. His principles emphasized using science, creating group harmony and cooperation, achieving maximum output, and developing workers.
Henry L. Gantt (1901)	Called for scientific selection of workers and "harmonious cooperation" between labor and management. Developed the Gantt chart (Chapter 21). Stressed the need for training.
Frank and Lillian Gilbreth (1900)	Frank is known primarily for his time and motion studies. Lillian, an industrial psychologist, focused on the human aspects of work and the understanding of workers' personalities and needs.
Modern operational-management theory	
Henri Fayol *Administration Industrielle et Générale* (1916)	Referred to as "the father of modern management theory." Divided industrial activities into six groups: technical, commercial, financial, security, accounting, and managerial. Recognized the need for teaching management. Formulated fourteen principles of management, such as authority and responsibility, unity of command, scalar chain, and esprit de corps.
Behavioral sciences	
Hugo Münsterberg (1912)	Application of psychology to industry and management.
Walter Dill Scott (1911)	Application of psychology to advertising, marketing, and personnel.
Max Weber (translations 1946, 1947)	Theory of bureaucracy.
Vilfredo Pareto (books 1896–1917)	Referred to as "the father of the social systems approach" to organization and management.
Elton Mayo and F. J. Roethlisberger (1933)	Famous studies at the Hawthorne plant of the Western Electric Company. Influence of social attitudes and relationships of work groups on performance.

Taylor's Principles

Taylor's famous work entitled *Principles of Scientific Management* was published in 1911. But one of the best expositions of his philosophy of management is found in his testimony before a committee of the House of Representatives; he was forced to defend his ideas before a group of congressmen, most of whom were hostile because they believed, along with labor leaders, that Taylor's ideas would lead to overworking and displacing workers.[3]

Name and year of major work	Major contribution to management
	Systems theory
Chester Barnard *The Functions of the Executive* (1938)	The task of managers is to maintain a system of cooperative effort in a formal organization. He suggested a comprehensive social systems approach to managing.
	Emergence of modern management thought and recent contributors to management

Many authors are discussed in the book. Major contributors include Chris Argyris, Robert R. Blake, C. West Churchman, Ernest Dale, Keith Davis, Mary Parker Follett, Frederick Herzberg, G. C. Homans, Harold Koontz, Rensis Likert, Douglas McGregor, Abraham H. Maslow, Lyman W. Porter, Herbert Simon, George A. Steiner, Lyndall Urwick, Norbert Wiener, and Joan Woodward.

Peter F. Drucker (1974)	Very prolific writer on many general management topics.
W. Edwards Deming (after World War II)	Introduced quality control in Japan.
Laurence Peter (1969)	Observed that eventually people get promoted to a level where they are incompetent.
William Ouchi (1981)	Discussed selected Japanese managerial practices adapted in the U.S. environment.
Thomas Peters and Robert Waterman (1982)	Identified characteristics of companies they considered excellent.

Source: Some information in this table is based on Claude S. George, Jr., *The History of Management Thought* (Englewood Cliffs, N.J.: Prentice-Hall, 1972).

The fundamental principles that Taylor saw underlying the scientific approach to management are summarized in the Perspective below. You will notice that these basic precepts of Taylor's are not far from the fundamental beliefs of the modern manager. It is true that some of the techniques Taylor and his colleagues and followers developed in order to put his philosophy and principles into practice had certain mechanistic aspects. To determine what a fair day's work was and to help in finding the one best way of doing any *given* job, the careful study of time and motion was widely applied. Likewise, various pay plans based on

Perspective

Taylor's Principles

1. Replacing rules of thumb with science (organized knowledge).
2. Obtaining harmony in group action, rather than discord.
3. Achieving cooperation of human beings, rather than chaotic individualism.
4. Working for maximum output, rather than restricted output.
5. Developing all workers to the fullest extent possible for their own and their company's highest prosperity.

output were used in an attempt to increase the "surplus" (as Taylor referred to "productivity"), to make sure that workers who produced were paid according to their productivity, and to give workers an incentive for performance. As can be seen, techniques such as these were necessary to make Taylor's philosophy work, based as it was on improving productivity, on giving people their best opportunity to be productive, and on rewarding workers for individual productivity. It is likewise true that these techniques could be used, as they often were by many factory owners throughout the world, to increase labor productivity without providing ample reward, adequate training, or managerial help. But this was certainly not what Frederick Taylor had in mind.

On the contrary, throughout Taylor's written work, even though it does seem to be unduly preoccupied with productivity at the shop level, runs a strongly humanistic theme. He believed that workers should be carefully selected and trained and that they should be given the work they were able to do best. He had perhaps an idealist's notion that the interests of workers, managers, and owners could and should be harmonized. Moreover, Taylor emphasized the importance of careful advance planning by managers and the responsibility of managers to design work systems so that workers would be helped to do their best. But as he spoke of management, he never overlooked the fact that "the relations between employers and men [and women]* form without question the most important part of this art."⁴

FOLLOWERS OF TAYLOR

Among the immediate disciples of Taylor were such outstanding pioneers as Henry L. Gantt and Frank and Lillian Gilbreth, to mention only a few.

Henry L. Gantt

Gantt—like Taylor, a mechanical engineer—joined Taylor at the Midvale Steel Company in 1887. He stayed with Taylor in his various assignments until 1901, when he formed his own consulting engineering firm. Although he strongly espoused Taylor's ideas and did much consulting work on the scientific selection of workers and the development of incentive bonus systems, he was far more cautious than Taylor in selling and implementing his scientific-management methods. Like Taylor, he emphasized the need for developing a mutuality of interests between management and labor, a "harmonious cooperation." In doing this, he stressed the importance of teaching, of developing an understanding of systems on the part of both labor and management, and of appreciating that "in all problems of management the human element is the most important one."

---

* Added by the authors of this book.

HENRY L. GANTT
1861–1919

Historical Pictures Service, Chicago

Gantt is perhaps best known for his development of graphic methods of describing plans and making possible better managerial control. He emphasized the importance of time, as well as cost, in planning and controlling work. This led eventually to the famous Gantt chart, which, as we shall see in Chapter 21, is in wide use today and was the forerunner of such modern techniques as the Program Evaluation and Review Technique (PERT). The Gantt chart is regarded by some social historians as the most important social invention of the twentieth century.

Frank and Lillian Gilbreth

The ideas of Taylor were also strongly supported and developed by the famous husband-and-wife team of Frank and Lillian Gilbreth. Frank Gilbreth gave up going to the university to become a bricklayer at the age of 17 in 1885; he rose to the position of chief superintendent of a building contracting firm 10 years later and became a building contractor on his own shortly thereafter. During this period, and quite independently of Taylor's work, he became interested in wasted motions in work; by reducing the number of bricklaying motions from 18 to 5, he made possible the doubling of a bricklayer's productivity with no greater expenditure of effort. His contracting-firm work soon gave way largely to consulting on the improvement of human productivity. After meeting Taylor in 1907, he combined his ideas with Taylor's to put scientific management into effect.

In undertaking his work, Frank Gilbreth was greatly aided and supported by his wife, Lillian. She was one of the earliest industrial psychologists and received her doctor's degree in this field in 1915, 9 years after her marriage and during the period when she was involved in having and raising her celebrated dozen children (later made famous by the book and movie *Cheaper by the Dozen*). After her husband's untimely death in 1924, she carried on his consulting business and was widely acclaimed as the "first lady of management" throughout her long life, which ended in 1972 when she was 93.

FRANK B. GILBRETH
1868–1924
LILLIAN M. GILBRETH
1878–1972

The Bettmann Archive, Inc.

Lillian Gilbreth's interest in the human aspects of work and her husband's interest in efficiency—the search for the one best way of doing a given task—led to a rare combination of talents.[5] It is therefore not surprising that Frank Gilbreth long emphasized that in applying scientific-management principles, we must look at workers first and understand their personalities and needs. It is interesting, too, that the Gilbreths came to the conclusion that it is not the monotony of work that causes so much worker dissatisfaction but, rather, management's lack of interest in workers.

There were, of course, many other management pioneers who built some of their thinking and practice on the ideas and findings of Frederick Taylor. But the discussion of the three mentioned here will give you some idea of Taylor's influence and the nature of the thinking developed by his disciples.

FAYOL: THE FATHER OF MODERN OPERATIONAL-MANAGEMENT THEORY[6]

Perhaps the real father of modern management theory is the French industrialist Henri Fayol. Although there is little evidence that management scholars, either in England or in the United States, paid much heed to Fayol's work or knew much about it until the 1920s or even years later, his acute observations on the principles of general management first appeared in 1916 in French, under the title *Administration Industrielle et Générale*. This monograph, reprinted in French several times, was not translated into English until 1929; even then it was printed by the International Institute of Management at Geneva, and only a few copies were made available for sale outside Great Britain. No English translation was published in the United States until 1949, although the work of Fayol was brought to the attention of American management scholars in 1923 by Sarah Greer's translation of one of Fayol's papers, later incorporated in a collection of papers by Gulick and Urwick.[7] In this same collection, the more general aspects of Fayol's work were referred to in a paper by the British management consultant and scholar Lyndall Urwick.[8]

Industrial Activities

Fayol found that activities of an industrial undertaking could be divided into six groups, as shown in Figure 2-1: (1) technical (production), (2) commercial (buying, selling, and exchanging), (3) financial (search for, and optimum use of, capital), (4) security (protection of property and persons), (5) accounting (including statistics), and (6) managerial (planning, organization, command, coordination, and control). Pointing out that these activities exist in businesses of every size, Fayol observed that the first five were well known, and consequently he devoted most of his book to an analysis of the sixth.

General Principles of Management

Noting that principles of management are flexible, not absolute, and must be usable regardless of changing and special conditions, Fayol listed fourteen, based on his experience. They are summarized in the Perspective.

In concluding his discussion of these principles, Fayol observed that he had made no attempt to be exhaustive but had tried only to describe those he had had the most occasion to use, since some kinds of principles appeared to be indispensable in every undertaking.

FIGURE 2-1

FAYOL'S ACTIVITIES IN INDUSTRIAL UNDERTAKING.

HENRI FAYOL
1841–1925

Ronald T. Greenwood

All on handout

1. *Division of work.* This is the specialization that economists consider necessary for efficiency in the use of labor. Fayol applies the principle to all kinds of work, managerial as well as technical.
2. *Authority and responsibility.* Here Fayol finds authority and responsibility to be related, with the latter arising from the former. He sees authority as a combination of official factors, deriving from the manager's position, and personal factors, "compounded of intelligence, experience, moral worth, past service, etc."
3. *Discipline.* Seeing discipline as "respect for agreements which are directed at achieving obedience, application, energy, and the outward marks of respect," Fayol declares that discipline requires good superiors at all levels.
4. *Unity of command.* This means that employees should receive orders from one superior only.
5. *Unity of direction.* According to this principle, each group of activities with the same objective must have one head and one plan. As distinguished from the fourth principle, it relates to the organization of the "body corporate" rather than to personnel. (Fayol did not in any sense mean that all decisions should be made at the top.)
6. *Subordination of individual to general interest.* This is self-explanatory; when the two are found to differ, management must reconcile them.
7. *Remuneration.* Remuneration and methods of payment should be fair and afford the maximum possible satisfaction to employees and employer.
8. *Centralization.* Without using the term "centralization of authority," Fayol refers to the extent to which authority is concentrated or dispersed. Individual circumstances will determine the degree that will "give the best overall yield."

9. *Scalar chain*. Fayol thinks of this as a "chain of superiors" from the highest to the lowest ranks, which, while not to be departed from needlessly, should be short-circuited when to follow it scrupulously would be detrimental.
10. *Order*. Breaking this into "material" and "social" order, Fayol follows the simple adage of "a place for everything [everyone], and everything [everyone] in its [his or her] place." This is essentially a principle of organization in the arrangement of things and people.
11. *Equity*. Loyalty and devotion should be elicited from personnel by a combination of kindliness and justice on the part of managers when dealing with subordinates.
12. *Stability of tenure*. Finding unnecessary turnover to be both the cause and the effect of bad management, Fayol points out its dangers and costs.
13. *Initiative*. Initiative is conceived of as the thinking out and execution of a plan. Since it is one of the "keenest satisfactions for an intelligent man to experience," Fayol exhorts managers to "sacrifice personal vanity" in order to permit subordinates to exercise it.
14. *Esprit de corps*. This is the principle that "in union there is strength," as well as an extension of the principle of unity of command, emphasizing the need for teamwork and the importance of communication in obtaining it.

Elements of Management

Fayol regarded the elements of management as its functions—planning, organizing, commanding, coordinating, and controlling.[9] A large part of his treatise is given over to an examination of these functions, and his observations are, on the whole, still valid after more than seven decades of study by and experience of others in the field. Throughout Fayol's treatise there exists an understanding of the general applicability of principles. Again and again, he points out that these principles apply not only to business but also to political, religious, philanthropic, military, and other undertakings. Since all enterprises require managing, it follows that the formulation of a theory of management is necessary for effective teaching of the subject.

THE EMERGENCE OF THE BEHAVIORAL SCIENCES[10]

During practically the same period that Taylor, Fayol, and others were concentrating on scientific management and the manager's tasks, many scholars and practitioners were thinking about, experimenting with, and writing on industrial psychology and social theory, both of which, in many instances, were stimulated by the scientific-management movement. We can get the flavor of these developments in the behavioral sciences by looking briefly at the emergence of industrial psychology, the growth of personnel management, the development of a sociological approach to human relations and management, and Chester Barnard's social systems approach.

The Emergence of Industrial Psychology

Acknowledged to be "the father of industrial psychology," Hugo Münsterberg was trained as a psychologist and received his Ph.D. at the University of Leipzig in 1885. He also was trained as a medical doctor and received the M.D. degree at the University of Heidelberg in 1887. At the age of 29, in 1892, Münsterberg went to Harvard at the invitation of psychologist William James to take charge of the psychological laboratory and to act as professor of experimental psychology. In 1910 his interest turned to the application of psychology to industry, where he saw the importance of applying behavioral science to the new scientific-management movement. In his landmark book entitled *Psychology and Industrial Efficiency*, first published in 1912,[11] Münsterberg made it clear that his objectives were to discover (1) how to find people whose mental qualities best fit them for the work they are to do, (2) under what psychological conditions the greatest and most satisfactory output can be obtained from the work of every person, and (3) how a business can influence workers in such a way as to obtain the best possible results from them. Like Taylor, he was interested in the mutuality of interests between managers and workers. He stressed that his approach was even more strongly aimed at workers and that through it he hoped to reduce their working time, increase their wages, and raise their "level of life."

Münsterberg's work was supplemented by the pioneering thinking of Lillian Gilbreth, who attempted in her *Psychology of Management*,[12] published in 1914, to apply early psychological concepts to the practice of scientific management.

Brown Brothers

HUGO MÜNSTERBERG
1863–1916

Another important early behavioral scientist who applied psychology to management was Walter Dill Scott. He received his doctorate in psychology in 1900, wrote many books on the application of psychological concepts to advertising and marketing and on the development of such personnel-management practices as effective selection, and later became president of Northwestern University.[13]

Development of the Sociological Approach to Management

In part preceding and in large part concurrent with the development of scientific management by Taylor and administrative management by Fayol, a considerable amount of thinking and research was being devoted to observing people as products of group behavior. This is sometimes called the "social man" approach to management. Generally regarded as "fathers of organization theory," or the "social systems approach to management," were three outstanding scholars who wrote books and essays at the close of the nineteenth century and during the early years of the twentieth century.

One of these was the German intellectual Max Weber, whose empirical analyses of church, government, the military, and business led him to the belief that hierarchy, authority, and bureaucracy (including clear rules, definition of tasks, and discipline) lie at the foundation of all social organizations. Another contributor to this management approach was the French scholar Emile Durkheim; his doctoral dissertation, published in 1893,[14] and subsequent writings emphasized the idea that groups, by establishing their values and norms, control human conduct in any social organization.

The third was the French-Italian Vilfredo Pareto, who, in a series of lectures and books between 1896 and 1917, earned the right to be called "the father of the social systems approach" to organization and management.[15] Pareto viewed society as an intricate cluster of interdependent units, or elements—that is, as a social system with many subsystems. Among his many ideas was the tendency of social systems to seek equilibrium upon being disturbed by outside or inside influence. His thesis was that social attitudes, or sentiments, function to cause the system to seek an equilibrium when disturbed by these forces. He saw also that it was the task of the elite (the "ruling class") in any society to provide the leadership to maintain the social system.

The Hawthorne Studies

Although these few words inadequately describe the views of the social man or social system pioneers (and space does not permit even the mention of many others), there is no question that they did have considerable influence on Elton Mayo, F. J. Roethlisberger, and others who undertook the famous experiments at the Hawthorne plant of the Western Electric Company between 1927 and 1932.[16] Earlier, from 1924 to 1927, the National Research Council made a study in collaboration with Western Electric to determine the effect of illumination and other conditions on workers and their productivity. Finding that productivity improved when illumination was either increased or decreased for a test group, the researchers were about to declare the whole experiment a failure; however, Elton Mayo, of Harvard, saw in it something unusual and, with Roethlisberger and others, continued the research.

What Mayo and his colleagues found, partly on the basis of the earlier thinking of Pareto, was to have a dramatic effect on management thought. Changing illumination for the test group, modifying rest periods, shortening workdays, and varying incentive pay systems did not seem to explain changes in productivity. Mayo and his researchers then came to the conclusion that other factors were responsible. They found, in general, that the improvement in productivity was due to such social factors as morale, satisfactory interrelationships between members of a work group (a "sense of belonging"), and effective management—a kind of managing that would understand human behavior, especially group behavior, and serve it through such interpersonal skills as motivating, counseling, leading, and communicating. This phenomenon, arising basically from people being "noticed," has been known as the **Hawthorne effect.**

What the Hawthorne studies dramatized was that humans are social—that business operations are a matter not merely of machinery and methods but also of gearing these with the social system to develop a complete sociotechnical system. These experiments led to increased emphasis on the behavioral sciences as applied to management and to the recognition that managers operate in a social system. It should not be inferred from this that prior to the Hawthorne experiments successful managers did not recognize the importance of the human factor, or that management theorists overlooked it. As the brief discussions earlier in this chapter clearly indicate, this is simply not true. But what the work of Mayo and his associates did underscore was the need for a greater and deeper understanding of the social and behavioral aspects of management.

ELTON MAYO
1880–1949

Baker Library, Harvard University
Graduate School of Business Administration

CHESTER I. BARNARD
1886–1961

New Jersey Bell

Chester Barnard and Social Systems Theory

One of the most influential books published in the entire field of management is the classic treatise entitled *The Functions of the Executive*, written by Chester I. Barnard in 1938.[17] A lifelong executive himself and president of the New Jersey Bell Telephone Company from 1927 to 1948, Barnard was a first-rate scholar and intellectual who was greatly influenced by Pareto, Mayo, and other faculty members at Harvard, where he occasionally lectured. His analysis of the manager is truly a social systems approach, since in order to comprehend and analyze the functions of executives, Barnard looked for their major tasks in the system where they operate.

In determining that the tasks of executives (by which he meant all kinds of managers) are to maintain a system of cooperative effort in a formal organization, Barnard addressed himself first to the reasons for, and the nature of, cooperative systems. The book is a social systems approach, concentrating on major elements of the managerial job, containing extraordinary insights on decision making and leadership, and bearing the authority of an intellectual with exceptional executive experience.

RECENT CONTRIBUTORS TO MANAGEMENT THOUGHT

Among the several contributors to management thought are public administrators, business managers, and behavioral scientists, whose important works are discussed throughout this book. We will mention only a few here.

Peter F. Drucker, one of the most prolific writers on general management, has written on a variety of management topics. W. Edwards Deming, an American, has done much to improve the quality of Japanese products, as discussed in Part 6 ("Controlling"). The late Laurence Peter suggested that eventually people get promoted to a level where they are incompetent and no further promotion is possible. Unfortunately, this may result in organizations with incompetent people.[18] William Ouchi, who wrote the best-selling book *Theory Z*, shows how selected management practices may be adapted in the United States.[19] Finally, Thomas Peters and Robert Waterman, as well as Peters and Nancy Austin, discuss characteristics of excellent companies.[20] Most of these works are discussed in greater detail in other parts of this book.

PATTERNS OF MANAGEMENT ANALYSIS: A MANAGEMENT THEORY JUNGLE?[21]

Although academic writers and theorists contributed notably little to the study of management until the early 1950s, previous writings having come largely from practitioners, the past three to four decades have seen a veritable deluge of writing from the academic halls.[22] The variety of approaches to management analysis, the amount of research, and the number of differing views have resulted in much confusion as to what management is, what management theory and science is, and how managerial events should be analyzed. As a matter of fact, Koontz some years ago called this situation "the management theory jungle."[23] Since that time, the vegetation in this jungle has changed somewhat—new approaches have developed, and older approaches have taken on some new meanings with some new words attached—but the developments of management science and theory still have the characteristics of a jungle.

The various approaches to management analysis are summarized in Figure 2-2, where they are grouped into the following categories: (1) the empirical, or case, approach, (2) the interpersonal behavior approach, (3) the group behavior approach, (4) the cooperative social systems approach, (5) the sociotechnical systems approach, (6) the decision theory approach, (7) the systems approach, (8) the mathematical, or "management science," approach, (9) the contingency, or situational, approach, (10) Mintzberg's managerial roles approach, (11) McKinsey's 7-S approach, and (12) the operational approach.

The characteristics, contributions, and limitations are shown in Figure 2-2. The focus here is on the two recent approaches to management—the managerial roles approach and McKinsey's 7-S framework—and the operational approach, which integrates the various perspectives on management.

The Managerial Roles Approach

One of the newer approaches to management theory is the managerial roles approach, popularized by Professor Henry Mintzberg of McGill University.[24] Essentially, his approach is to observe what managers actually do and from such observations come to conclusions as to what managerial activities (or roles) are. Although many researchers have studied the actual work of managers—from chief executives to line supervisors—Mintzberg has given this approach higher visibility.

After systematically studying the activities of five chief executives in a variety of organizations, Mintzberg came to the conclusion that executives do not perform the classical managerial functions—planning, organizing, coordinating, and controlling. Instead, they engage in a variety of other activities.

From his research and the research of others who have studied what managers actually do, Mintzberg has come to the conclusion that managers really fill a series of ten roles as shown in the Perspective.

Perspective

The Ten Managerial Roles Identified by Mintzberg

Interpersonal roles
1. The figurehead role (performing ceremonial and social duties as the organization's representative)
2. The leader role
3. The liaison role (particularly with outsiders)

Informational roles
1. The recipient role (receiving information about the operation of an enterprise)
2. The disseminator role (passing information to subordinates)
3. The spokesperson role (transmitting information to those outside the organization

Decision roles
1. The entrepreneurial role
2. The disturbance-handler role
3. The resource-allocator role
4. The negotiator role (dealing with various persons and groups of persons)

Mintzberg refers to the usual way of classifying managerial functions as "folklore," although most modern management textbooks use this framework. As you will see in the discussion of the operational-management approach, operational theorists have used such managerial functions as planning, organizing, staffing, leading, and controlling as the means of classifying the growing body of managerial knowledge. While the functions are believed to be real, they are not intended to describe all the activities of managers.

Mintzberg's approach has also been criticized. In the first place, the sample of five executives used in his research is far too small to support so sweeping a conclusion. In the second place, in analyzing the actual activities of managers—from chief executives to supervisors—any researcher must realize that all managers do some work that is not purely managerial; one would expect even presidents of large companies to spend some of their time in public and stockholder relations, in fund-raising, and perhaps in dealer relations, marketing, and so on.

In the third place, many of the activities Mintzberg found are, in fact, evidences of planning, organizing, staffing, leading, and controlling. For example,

FIGURE 2-2 **APPROACHES TO MANAGEMENT**

CHARACTERISTICS/ CONTRIBUTIONS	LIMITATIONS	ILLUSTRATION
EMPIRICAL, OR CASE, APPROACH		
Studies experience through cases. Identifies successes and failures.	Situations are all different. No attempt to identify principles. Limited value for developing management theory.	
INTERPERSONAL BEHAVIOR APPROACH		
Focus on interpersonal behavior, human relations, leadership, and motivation. Based on individual psychology.	Ignores planning, organizing, and controlling. Psychological training is not enough to become an effective manager.	FOCUS OF STUDY
GROUP BEHAVIOR APPROACH		
Emphasis on behavior of people in groups. Based on sociology and social psychology. Primarily study of group behavior patterns. The study of large groups is often called "organization behavior."	Often not integrated with management concepts, principles, theory, and techniques. Need for closer integration with organization structure design, staffing, planning, and controlling.	Study of a group / Study of groups interacting with each other
COOPERATIVE SOCIAL SYSTEMS APPROACH		
Concerned with both interpersonal and group behavioral aspects leading to a system of cooperation. Expanded concept includes any cooperative group with a clear purpose.	Too broad a field for the study of management. At the same time, it overlooks many managerial concepts, principles, and techniques.	Organization structure / Common goal
SOCIOTECHNICAL SYSTEMS APPROACH		
Technical system has great effect on social system (personal attitudes, group behavior). Focus on production, office operations, and other areas with close relationships between the technical system and people.	Emphasis only on blue-collar and lower-level office work. Ignores much of other managerial knowledge.	Technical system / Machines / Office operation / Social system / Personal attitudes / Group behavior
DECISION THEORY APPROACH		
Focus on the making of decisions, persons or groups making decisions, and the decision-making process. Some theorists use decision making as a springboard to study all enterprise activities. The boundaries of study are no longer clearly defined.	There is more to managing than making decisions. The focus is at the same time too narrow and too wide.	Process of decision making / Individual decision making / Entire area of business activity / Values of decision makers / DECISION THEORY / Nature of organization structure / Information for decision / Group decision making

CHARACTERISTICS/ CONTRIBUTIONS	LIMITATIONS	ILLUSTRATION

SYSTEMS APPROACH

Systems concepts have broad applicability. Systems have boundaries, but they also interact with the external environment; i.e., organizations are open systems. Recognizes importance of studying interrelatedness of planning, organizing, and controlling in an organization as well as the many subsystems.	Analyses of the interrelatedness of systems and subsystems as well as the interactions of organizations with their external environment. Can hardly be considered a new approach to management.	Open to external environment

MATHEMATICAL OR "MANAGEMENT SCIENCE" APPROACH

Managing is seen as mathematical processes, concepts, symbols, and models. Looks at management as a purely logical process, expressed in mathematical symbols and relationships.	Preoccupation with mathematical models. Many aspects in managing cannot be modeled. Mathematics is a useful tool, but hardly a school or an approach to management.	$E = F (x_i, y_i)$ Yes No

CONTINGENCY OR SITUATIONAL APPROACH

Managerial practice depends on circumstances (i.e, a contingency or a situation). Contingency theory recognizes the influence of given solutions on organizational behavior patterns.	Managers have long realized that there is *no* one best way to do things. Difficulty in determining all relevant contingency factors and showing their relationships. Can be very complex.	Cause → Effect Depends on Contingency Situation

MANAGERIAL ROLES APPROACH

Original study consisted of observations of five chief executives. On the basis of this study, ten managerial roles were identified and grouped into (1) interpersonal, (2) informational, and (3) decision roles.	Original sample was very small. Some activities are not managerial. Activities are evidence of planning, organizing, staffing, leading, and controlling. But some important managerial activities were left out (e.g., appraising managers).	ROLES OF MANAGERS Three interpersonal roles Four decision roles Three informational roles

MCKINSEY'S 7-S FRAMEWORK

The seven S's are (1) strategy, (2) structure, (3) systems, (4) style, (5) staff, (6) shared values, (7) skills.	Although this experienced consulting firm now uses a framework similar to the one found useful by Koontz et al. since 1955 (see Table 2-2) and confirms its practicality, the terms used are not precise and topics are not discussed in depth.	Systems Structure Style Strategy Staff Skills Shared values

OPERATIONAL APPROACH

Draws together concepts, principles, techniques, and knowledge from other fields and managerial approaches. The attempt is to develop science and theory with practical application. Distinguishes between managerial and non-managerial knowledge. Develops classification system built around the managerial functions of plannng, organizing, staffing, leading, and controlling.	Does not, as some authors do, identify "representing" or "coordination" as a separate function. Coordination, for example, is the essence of managership and is the purpose of managing.	Draws knowledge from approaches above. OPERATIONAL APPROACH Integrates the approaches with science and theory that is practical.

what is resource allocation but planning? The entrepreneurial role is certainly an element of planning. And the interpersonal roles are mainly instances of leading. In addition, the informational roles can be fitted into a number of the functional areas.

Nevertheless, looking at what managers really do can have considerable value. In analyzing activities, an effective manager might wish to ascertain how activities and techniques fall into the various fields of knowledge reflected by the basic functions of managers. However, the roles Mintzberg identified appear to be incomplete. Where does one find such unquestionably important managerial activities as structuring an organization, selecting and appraising managers, and determining major strategies? Omissions such as these make one wonder whether the executives in his sample were really effective managers. They certainly raise a serious question as to whether the managerial roles approach, at least as put forth here, is an adequate one on which to base a practical, operational theory of management.

McKinsey's 7-S Approach

The second of the recent approaches—the 7-S framework for management analysis—was developed by the respected consulting firm of McKinsey & Company. This approach has gained in popularity, partly because it became the basis for the research behind two best-selling books, *The Art of Japanese Management*[25] and *In Search of Excellence*.[26] The seven S's are strategy, structure, systems, style, staff, shared values, and skills, as summarized in Table 2-2. However, the author of one of the above-mentioned books admitted that in the attempt to make the key aspects of the model begin with an "s" (to serve as a memory hook), the meaning of some of the terms had to be stretched. For example, in traditional management literature the term "skills" is generally applied to personal skills (for example, technical, human, conceptual), while in the 7-S framework "skills" means the capabilities of the organization as a whole. Organizational capabilities and the lack of such capabilities are generally referred to in management literature as the strengths and weaknesses of the firm.

The outstanding feature of the 7-S model is that it has been tested extensively by McKinsey consultants in their studies of many companies. At the same time, this framework has been used by respected business schools, such as Harvard and Stanford. Thus, theory and practice seem to support each other in the study of management. Perhaps the most surprising fact about the 7-S framework is that it supports, and is similar to, the framework of the managerial functions (planning, organizing, staffing, leading, and controlling) used in this book and in previous editions of this book. Table 2-2 shows the relationship of the seven S's to the organization of this textbook edition.

By using the term "shared values," also sometimes called "superordinate goals," 7-S theorists emphasize that goal statements are very important in determining the destiny of the enterprise, as emphasized in Chapter 6 in this book; they also point out that values must be shared by organization members. Therefore, special attention is given to personal and organizational values in Chapter 12, where we discuss organizational effectiveness.

TABLE 2-2 COMPARISON OF 7-S FRAMEWORK AND THE OPERATIONAL-MANAGEMENT APPROACH	
McKinsey's 7-S framework **for management analysis**	**Textbook reference**
Strategy: Systematic action and allocation of resources to achieve company aims	Strategies, Policies, and Planning Premises (Chap. 7)

Structure: Organization structure and authority/responsibility relationships	Part 3: Organizing, especially:
	   Organizational Structure:
	   Departmentation (Chap. 10)
	   Line/Staff Authority and
	   Decentralization (Chap. 11)

Systems: Procedures and processes such as information systems, manufacturing processes, budgeting and control processes	Part 6: Controlling, especially:
	   The System and Process of
	   Controlling (Chap. 20)
	   Control Techniques and
	   Information Technology (Chap. 21)
	   Productivity and Operations
	   Management (Chap. 22)

Style: The way management behaves and collectively spends its time to achieve organizational goals	Part 5: Leading (Chaps. 16–19)
Staff: The people in the enterprise and their socialization into the organizational culture	Part 4: Staffing (Chaps. 13–15)

Shared values (superordinate goals): The values shared by the members of an organization	Various parts of the book, especially:
	   Effective Organizing and
	   Organizational Culture (Chap. 12)
	   Leadership (Chap. 17)

Skills: Distinctive capabilities of an enterprise	Strategies, Policies, and Planning Premises (Chap. 7)

Source: R. T. Pascale and A. G. Athos, *The Art of Japanese Management* (New York: Warner Books, 1981); R. H. Waterman, Jr., "The Seven Elements of Strategic Fit," in A. A. Thomson, Jr., A. J. Strickland III, and W. E. Fulmer (eds.), *Reading in Strategic Management* (Plano, Tex.: Business Publications, 1984), pp. 333–339.

Identifying key aspects of the management system and showing the interrelatedness of the variables is a positive contribution to management theory. A simple, easy-to-remember framework, such as that suggested by McKinsey, is certainly an effort to be welcomed by practitioners and academicians. Although the terminology it employs is, at times, not quite clear and may have somewhat increased the semantic jungle, the positive contributions of this framework must be recognized.

The Operational, or Management Process, Approach

The operational approach to management theory and science draws together the pertinent knowledge of management by relating it to the managerial job—what managers do. Like other operational sciences, it tries to integrate the concepts, principles, and techniques that underlie the task of managing.

The operational approach recognizes that there is a central core of knowledge about managing that is pertinent only to the field of management. Such matters

FIGURE 2-3

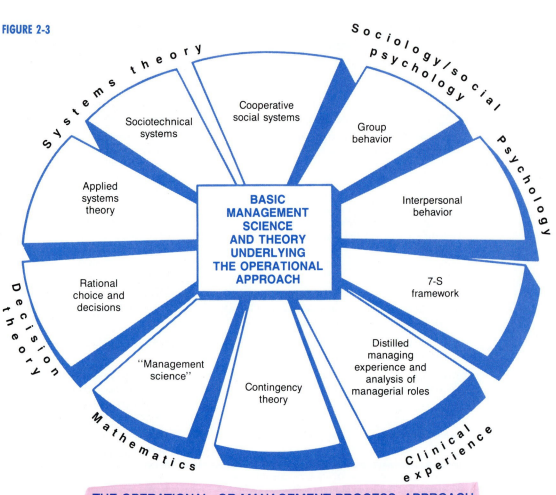

THE OPERATIONAL, OR MANAGEMENT PROCESS, APPROACH.

Management theory and science as a system draw on other areas of organized knowledge. The figure shows how operational-management theory and science, here enclosed in the circle, have a core of basic science and theory and draw from other fields of knowledge pertinent to understanding management. Basic management is thus, in part, an eclectic science and theory.

as line and staff, departmentation, managerial appraisal, and various managerial control techniques involve concepts and theories found only in situations involving managers. In addition, this approach draws on and absorbs knowledge from other fields, including systems theory, decision theory, theories of motivation and leadership, individual and group behavior, social systems, and cooperation and communications, as well as the application of mathematical analyses and concepts.

The nature of the operational approach can be seen in Figure 2-3. As this diagram shows, the operational management school recognizes the existence of a central core of science and theory peculiar to managing and also draws important contributions from various other schools and approaches. As the circle shows, the operational theorist is interested not in all the important knowledge in these various fields but only in that which is deemed most useful and relevant to managing.

Those who subscribe to the operational approach do so with the hope of developing science and theory that have practical application to managing and yet are not so broad as to apply to everything that might have any relationship to the managerial task. They recognize that managing is a difficult task with an immense number of variables affecting it. They realize that any field as complex as managing, which deals with the production and marketing of anything from bread to money, with religion, and with government services, can never be isolated from the physical, biological, or social environment. But they also recognize that some partitioning of knowledge is necessary and that some boundaries must be set if meaningful progress is to be made there or in any other field.

Because the functions of managers are emphasized in the operational approach, it is often called the "management process" school. The great French industrialist and management pioneer Henri Fayol first attempted to organize management knowledge around managerial functions. This approach has been found useful to, and understandable by, practicing managers. It also furnishes a means of distinguishing between managerial knowledge and the special knowledge and expertise of such nonmanagerial fields as marketing and production. In addition, it is a way of integrating into management useful and pertinent knowledge from all schools and approaches.

Although the operationalists generally believe that the fundamentals of management are universal, theorists of this school would readily admit that the problems managers face and the situations in which they operate vary among managerial levels in an enterprise and among different enterprises and that the application of concepts, theories, and techniques will naturally vary. But, as indicated in Chapter 1, this diversity is characteristic of the difference between theory and practice in any field.

SUMMARY

Many writers and practitioners have contributed to the development of management thought. Frederick Taylor's concern was productivity improvement through the application of the scientific method. Henry Gantt developed the Gantt chart. He focused on the selection of workers and cooperation between labor and management. Frank Gilbreth is known for his time and motion studies, while Lillian Gilbreth focused on the human aspects of work.

Henri Fayol, "the father of modern management theory," formulated fourteen principles of management. Hugo Münsterberg applied psychology to industry and management, while Walter Dill Scott applied it to advertising, marketing, and personnel management. Max Weber is known for his theory of bureaucracy. Vilfredo Pareto is considered "the father of the social systems approach." Elton Mayo and F. J. Roethlisberger became famous through their studies of the impact of the social attitudes and relationships of work groups on performance. Chester Barnard suggested a comprehensive social systems approach to managing.

There are many theories about management, and each contributes something to our knowledge of what managers do. The characteristics and contributions as well as the limitations of the various approaches to management were summarized in Figure 2-2, and the managerial roles approach and the 7-S approach were discussed in greater detail. The operational, or management process, approach draws from various "schools" and systematically integrates them.

KEY IDEAS AND CONCEPTS FOR REVIEW

Contributions to scientific management
  (Taylor, Gantt, Frank and Lillian
  Gilbreth)
Fayol's operational-management theory
Contributions to the behavioral sciences
  (Münsterberg, Scott, Weber, Pareto,
  Mayo, and Roethlisberger)
Barnard's social systems theory

Recent contributors (Drucker, Deming,
  Peter, Ouchi, Peters and Waterman)
Management theory jungle
Managerial roles approach
McKinsey's 7-S approach
Operational, or management process,
  approach

FOR DISCUSSION

1. Why has Frederick Taylor been called "the father of scientific management" and Henri Fayol "the father of modern management theory"?
2. What were the contributions of the followers of Taylor, such as Henry Gantt and Frank and Lillian Gilbreth?
3. Taylor, Fayol, and other management pioneers have been accused of seeking and recommending a one best way to do things in managing. To what extent, if at all, is this accusation correct?
4. How, and to what extent, has the development of behavioral thought contributed to management theory?
5. Chester Barnard has been referred to as the originator of the social systems approach to management. Why might he be so regarded?
6. What is meant by the term "management theory jungle"?
7. Identify the various approaches to management analysis. Discuss their characteristics and contributions as well as their limitations.
8. Do the various approaches to the analysis of management represent a management theory jungle, or do they represent simply an intellectual division of labor?
9. As you read the following chapters of this book, watch for signs of convergence of the various approaches to management theory and science. Is it reasonable to refer to the various approaches as the management theory jungle?

EXERCISES/ACTION STEPS

1. Take any four books or articles on management that you like, and ascertain what approach to management each author takes and the extent of the semantic differences among them.
2. Divide the class into groups. Each group should take a management approach, except the operational one, and identify its major elements and its contributions, as well as its limitations. Each group should select a spokesperson to present the findings of the group.

CASES

CASE 2-1
FRED DENNY

"The trouble with management as a field of study and practice," Fred Denny, a space physicist, said to his laboratory head, Claude Greenwood, "is that it has no scientific base. I feel I know what I am doing when I design a guidance system for a missile because I have the space, propulsion, and other sciences available to tell me what to do. But, when you ask me if I am doing a good job as a supervisor of my engineering and technical team, there is nothing, no science of management, to guide me. In my reading of the books on management, I get the idea that managers must operate on a closed-system basis, that the best things managers can do are to be friendly, consult with their subordinates on every little thing, and develop strict rules and procedures so that no subordinate can make a mistake.

"As I think about it, Claude, I cannot see much science in management. And I wonder what good management books, articles, and management development courses are ever going to do any of us. Do we have to wait for centuries when a science of management, as an exact science like physics, is developed?"

Claude Greenwood, having been exposed to a number of management development seminars that had emphasized the usefulness and importance of management knowledge, was taken aback by Fred's outburst. But he was impressed that what his subordinate had said did make a lot of sense. He was, however, at a loss as to how to respond to Fred.

1. If you were Claude Greenwood, how would you respond to Fred Denny's statement?
2. What would you suggest be done to make management more scientific?

CASE 2-2
PATTERNS OF MANAGEMENT AT IBM[27]

Thomas J. Watson, Jr.'s father, an admired industrialist in the 1920s and 1930s, moved IBM into the punch card business. Watson, Jr., moved IBM into the computer field and provided the vision leading to its phenomenal growth against competition from giant companies such as General Electric, RCA, Honeywell, and Remington Rand.

After World War II, IBM grew quickly because of the demand for accounting equipment using punch cards. But it was in the mid-1950s that computers, with their recognized calculating power, became the buzzword of the time.

What made IBM so successful was not technical innovation but marketing and service. In the early days of computers, competitors were equal or better in providing hardware. But many competitors fell short when it came to installing and servicing the equipment.

The early computers were built around electronic tubes. A limiting factor was the need to find people to run them. To satisfy this need, IBM turned to universities for help. A new profession was born: programmers and systems engineers. Around 1958, working against the resistance of IBM engineers, Watson insisted that the electronic tubes be replaced by transistors.

Watson attributes his success to selecting good people, integrating them into teams, providing financial incentives, being concerned about the people, and having open communication channels to them. The selection of people was based not on personal liking but on competence. Another IBM policy was to provide job security—a policy that dates back to the Great Depression. Employees, not just managers, were handsomely paid. Starting in 1955, the company offered stock options that made many of them rich.

Watson, Sr., built an organization culture that is similar to Japanese practices. Sales personnel had to wear white shirts with starched collars. There was also a company song. But Watson, Jr., relaxed the rules. Still, the older and the younger Watsons were perfectionists, paying attention to details. The implicit principles were to value the individual, make customers satisfied, and go out of one's way to do the right thing.

To instill these values, one has to manage by example. Training is also required. Yet until the 1950s, management training was rather primitive, compared with that at General Electric. In 1966, however, it was ruled that people, in order to manage, had to attend a management school. The early programs were based on Harvard's case approach.

Another step in creating a certain corporate culture was to establish an open-door policy. After employees had discussed their concerns with their managers, they could go to individuals at higher levels. In fact, Watson spent about a fifth of his time talking with people who "walked through the open door." This policy, of course, results in open communication and counters the problem of top-management isolation so often found in companies.

Still another factor that contributed to the rather unique corporate culture was the elimination of piecework. This reduced the distinction between white- and blue-collar workers. Also, starting in the late 1950s, all the employees were paid salaries. In addition, employees began to receive medical coverage and other benefits. The company also provided for matching grants for contributions to schools and charities. These changes, too, helped to reduce the distinction between managers and nonmanagers.

IBM has been very successful. But in late 1989, IBM announced that because of changing market situations, it plans to restructure and cut 10,000 jobs. In 1991, John Akers, IBM's CEO, announced additional restructuring of the organization.

1. What factors made IBM successful?
2. Are past managerial practices still effective today? Why or why not?
3. Do you think that the changing market conditions will change IBM's internal management practices?

REFERENCES

1. For one of the most comprehensive histories of management thought, see Daniel A. Wren, *The Evolution of Management Thought* (New York: The Ronald Press Company, 1972; 2d ed., New York: John Wiley & Sons, 1979). See also Claude S. George, Jr., *The History of Management Thought* (Englewood Cliffs, N.J.: Prentice-Hall, 1968).
2. See also Michael T. Matteson and John M. Ivancevich (eds.), *Management Classics*, 3d ed. (Plano, Tex.: Business Publications, 1986); and Charles D. Wrege and Ronald G. Greenwood, *Frederick W. Taylor, The Father of Scientific Management: Myth and Reality* (Homewood, Ill.: Business One Irwin, 1991).
3. Taylor's principal works, *Shop Management* (originally published in 1903), *Principles of Scientific Management* (published in 1911), and *Testimony before the Special House Committee* (given in 1912), are combined in one book entitled *Scientific Management* (New York: Harper & Brothers, 1947). For a review of classic books on management, see Allen C. Bluedorn (ed.), "Special Review Section on the Classics of Management," *Academy of Management Review* (April 1986), pp. 442–464.
4. *Shop Management*, p. 25. For a more recent discussion of Taylor's contributions, see Edwin A. Locke, "The Ideas of Frederick W. Taylor: An Evaluation," *Academy of Management Review* (January 1982), pp. 14–24.
5. Although the Gilbreths were known for their search for the "best way," it should be noted that they really were interested in the "best way" to do something under a given set of realities, not in every possible situation.
6. Henri Fayol, *General and Industrial Management* (New York: Pitman Publishing Corporation, 1949).

7. L. Gulick and L. Urwick (eds.), *Papers on the Science of Administration* (New York: Institute of Public Administration, 1937). Fayol's paper was translated by Greer as "The Administrative Theory of the State."

8. "The Function of Administration," in Gulick and Urwick, *Papers* (1937); see also Ernest R. Archer, "Toward a Revival of the Principles of Management," *Industrial Management* (January–February 1990), pp. 19–22, and L. Urwick, *The Golden Book of Management* (London: N. Neame, 1956).

9. Gulick and Urwick, *Papers* (1937), chap. 5.

10. See also Melville Dalton, *Men Who Manage* (New York: Wiley, 1959).

11. Published in German in 1912 and in English in 1913 (Boston: Houghton Mifflin Company).

12. (New York: Sturgis and Walton Company.) This book was also Dr. Gilbreth's Ph.D. dissertation.

13. Among his books were *Influencing Men in Business* (New York: The Ronald Press Company, 1911), *Increasing Human Efficiency* (New York: The Macmillan Company, 1911), and (with R. C. Clothier) *Personnel Management: Principles, Practices and Point of View* (New York: McGraw-Hill Book Company, 1923).

14. *De la Division du Travail Social* (The Division of Labor) (Paris: F. Alcan, 1893).

15. The most famous of his books was *Trattato di Sociologia Generale*, published in Florence in 1916, with a second edition in 1923; it may be found in English translation as *The Mind and Society: A Treatise on General Sociology* (New York: Harcourt, Brace and Company, 1935; also New York: Dover Publications, 1963).

16. For a full description of these experiments, see Elton Mayo, *The Human Problems of an Industrial Civilization* (New York: The Macmillan Company, 1933), chaps. 3–5; and F. J. Roethlisberger and W. J. Dickson, *Management and the Worker* (Cambridge, Mass.: Harvard University Press, 1939).

17. (Cambridge, Mass.: Harvard University Press, 1938).

18. Laurence J. Peter and Raymond Hall, *The Peter Principle* (New York: Bantam Books, 1969).

19. William G. Ouchi, *Theory Z: How American Business Can Meet the Japanese Challenge* (Reading, Mass.: Addison-Wesley Publishing Company, 1981).

20. Thomas J. Peters and Robert H. Waterman, Jr., *In Search of Excellence* (New York: Harper & Row, Publishers, 1982); and Thomas J. Peters and Nancy Austin, *A Passion for Excellence* (New York: Random House, 1985).

21. See also Harold Koontz, Cyril O'Donnell, and Heinz Weihrich (eds.), *Management—A Book of Readings*, 5th ed. (New York: McGraw-Hill Book Company, 1980).

22. See Ronald G. Greenwood, "Charting the Management Theory Jungle," in Richard M. Hodgetts (ed.), *Readings and Study Guide for Management* (Orlando, Fla.: Academic Press, 1985), pp. 36–38.

23. See Harold Koontz, "The Management Theory Jungle," *Journal of the Academy of Management* (December 1961), pp. 174–188. See also Harold Koontz, "Making Sense of Management Theory," *Harvard Business Review* (July–August 1962), pp. 24ff., and "The Management Theory Jungle Revisited," *Academy of Management Review* (April 1980), pp. 175–187. Much of this material has been drawn from these articles.

24. Especially in his article "The Manager's Job: Folklore and Fact," *Harvard Business Review* (July–August 1975), pp. 49–61, and his book *The Nature of Managerial Work* (New York: Harper & Row, Publishers, 1973).

25. Richard Tanner Pascale and Anthony G. Athos, *The Art of Japanese Management* (New York: Warner Books, 1981).

26. Peters and Waterman, *In Search of Excellence* (1982).

27. The case is based on a variety of sources, including "The Greatest Capitalist in History," *Fortune* (Aug. 31, 1987), pp. 24–35; Paul B. Carroll, "Big Blues, Hurt by a Pricing War: IBM Plans Write-off and Cut of 10,000 Jobs," *The Wall Street Journal* (Dec. 6, 1989); and Carol J. Loomis, "Can John Akers Save IBM?" *Fortune* (July 15, 1991), pp. 40–56.

Chapter 3

No human institution can long exist without some consensus on what is right and what is wrong.[1]

Gerald F. Cavanagh

Management and Society: The External Environment, Social Responsibility, and Ethics

Chapter Objectives

After studying this chapter, you should be able to:

1. Describe the nature of the pluralistic society.
2. Discuss the economic, technological, social, political, and legal environments in which managers operate.
3. Explain the social responsibility of managers and the arguments for and against the social involvement of business.
4. Understand the nature and importance of ethics in managing and ways to institutionalize and raise ethical standards.
5. Recognize differing ethical standards in various societies.

Much of this book deals with the interaction of managers and their subordinates with the environment inside the enterprise, but in most instances the effective manager must also deal with the outside environment. Every time managers plan, they take into account the needs and desires of members of society outside the organization, as well as the needs for material and human resources, technology, and other requirements in the external environment. They do likewise to some degree with almost every other kind of managerial activity.

All managers, whether they operate in a business, a government agency, a church, a charitable foundation, or a university, must, in varying degrees, take into account the elements and forces of their external environment. While they may be able to do little or nothing to change these forces, they have no alternative but to respond to them. They must identify, evaluate, and react to the forces outside the enterprise that may affect its operations. The impact of the external environment on the organization is illustrated in Figure 3-1. The constraining influences of external factors on the enterprise are even more crucial in international management (a fact to be discussed in Chapter 4).

This chapter deals with the impact of the external environment on the organization and the relationships between business and the society in which it operates. First, the focus is on various factors in the domestic environment. Then the discussion expands to the topics of social responsibility and ethical behavior. Let us begin by appreciating what it means to manage in a pluralistic environment.

OPERATING IN A PLURALISTIC SOCIETY

Managers in the United States operate in a **pluralistic society,** in which many organized groups represent various interests. Each group has an impact on other groups, but no one group exerts an inordinate amount of power. Many groups exert some power over business. As explained in Chapter 1, there are many claimants on the organization, and they have divergent goals. It is the task of the manager to integrate their aims.

Working within a pluralistic society has several implications for business.[2]

FIGURE 3-1

THE ORGANIZATION AND ITS EXTERNAL ENVIRONMENT.

First, business power is kept in balance by various groups, such as environmental groups. Second, business interests can be expressed by joining groups such as the Chamber of Commerce. Third, business participates in projects with other responsible groups for the purpose of bettering society; an example is working toward the renewal of inner cities. Fourth, in a pluralistic society there can be conflict or agreement among groups. Finally, in such a society one group is quite aware of what other groups are doing.

THE EXTERNAL ENVIRONMENT: ECONOMIC

It is sometimes thought that the economic environment is of concern only to businesses whose socially approved mission is the production and distribution of goods and services that people want and can pay for. But it is also of the greatest importance to other types of organized enterprises. A government agency takes resources, usually from taxpayers, and provides services desired by the public. A church takes contributions from members and serves their religious and social needs. A university takes resource inputs from taxpayers, students, and contributors of various kinds and transforms these into educational and research services.

Capital

Almost every kind of organization needs capital—machinery, buildings, inventories of goods, office equipment, tools of all kinds, and cash. Some of this may be produced by the organization itself, as when a business builds its own machinery or a church group prepares a church supper. Cash resources may also be generated within an organization to buy capital items outside, as when business profits are used to purchase equipment or when a university collects parking fees to pay for the building of parking structures. But organized enterprises are usually dependent for capital requirements on various suppliers, whose job it is to produce the many materials and other items of capital that an organization requires for its operation.

This means that all kinds of operations are dependent on the availability and prices of needed capital items. Societies vary considerably in this availability. Railroad facilities may be in short supply in Brazil but in plentiful supply in the United States and countries of Western Europe. Capital, in terms of fertilizers and advanced farm machines, may be scarce in rural Russia, and therefore farm productivity may be hampered, but such capital may be plentiful in rural America.

Labor

Another important input from the economic environment is the availability, quality, and price of labor. In some societies, untrained common labor may be plentiful, while highly trained labor may be in short supply. Engineers may be scarce at one time and plentiful at another, as has occurred in the ups and downs of the defense and space operations of the United States.

The price of labor is also an important economic factor for an enterprise, although automation mitigates high labor costs. The relatively high wages in the United States and many European countries often create cost problems for producers in these countries. Many items can be produced at a lower cost in countries such as Mexico, Korea, and Taiwan. It is not surprising that many products requiring high labor input are often made outside the United States.

Price Levels

The input side of an enterprise is clearly affected by price-level changes. If prices go up fairly rapidly, as happened in most parts of the world in the 1970s and early 1980s, the turbulence created in the economic environment on both the input and output sides can be severe. Inflation not only upsets businesses but also has highly disturbing influences on every kind of organization through its effects on the costs of labor, materials, and other items.

Government Fiscal and Tax Policies

Another important input to the enterprise is the nature of government fiscal and tax policies. Although these are, strictly speaking, aspects of the political environment, their economic impact on all enterprises is tremendous. Government control of the availability of credit through fiscal policy has considerable impact not only on business but also on most nonbusiness operations. Similarly, government tax policy affects every segment of our society. The way taxes are levied is also important, not only to business but to people generally. For example, if taxes on business profits are too high, the incentive to go into business or stay in it tends to drop, and investors will look elsewhere to invest their capital. If taxes are levied on sales, prices will rise and people will tend to buy less. If heavy taxes are placed on real estate, people may find it too expensive to own a house and may go to cheaper and less comfortable living quarters.

Customers

One of the most important factors for the success of an enterprise is customers. Without them, a business cannot exist. But to capture customers, a business must try to find out what people want and will buy. Nonbusiness enterprises have "customers" also. Universities and colleges have students and alumni to satisfy. Similarly, police, fire, and government health departments must serve the public.

To be sure, the expectations and demands of the various publics served by organized enterprises are influenced by noneconomic as well as economic factors in the environment. The principal ones are people's attitudes, desires, and expectations, many of which arise from cultural patterns in the social environment. Still, economic factors play a major role. People want as much as possible for their money, whether it goes to businesses, government, or charitable organizations.

Another factor in the market is the appearance of substitute products. For example, publishers of magazines saw their market eroded when advertisers shifted to television. Also, people like different products. Some want a powerboat, others want a sailboat, and still others do not want a boat at all. The needs of industrial buyers change as their products change, as new processes are developed, and as different equipment and materials come on the market. In the long run, any enterprise (at least in free economies) has to serve the different and changing needs of customers. To do otherwise is a sure road to enterprise failure.

THE EXTERNAL ENVIRONMENT: TECHNOLOGICAL

One of the most pervasive factors in the environment is technology. It is science that provides knowledge, and it is technology that uses it. The term **technology** refers to the sum total of the knowledge we have of ways to do things. It includes inventions, it includes techniques, and it includes the vast store of organized knowledge about everything from aerodynamics to zoology. But its main influence is on ways of doing things, on how we design, produce, distribute, and sell goods as well as services.

The Impact of Technology: Benefits and Problems

The impact of technology is seen in new products, new machines, new tools, new materials, and new services.[3] A few of the *benefits* of technology are greater productivity, higher living standards, more leisure time, and a greater variety of products. Consider, for example, the great variety of cars available: subcompacts, compacts, intermediates, full-sized automobiles, and sports and specialty cars. Consider also the many body styles, the various colors, and the many options in engines (sizes), transmissions (manual, automatic), and brakes (mechanical, power).

In addition, one may select tinted glass, power windows, power steering, automatic speed control, air-conditioning, special mirrors, a vinyl roof, a sunroof, and various interior and exterior trims.

But the benefits of technology must be weighed against the *problems* associated with technological developments, such as traffic jams, polluted air and water, energy shortages, and the loss of privacy through the application of computer technology. What is needed is a balanced approach that takes advantage of technology and at the same time minimizes some of the undesirable side effects.

Categories of Technological Change

In a general way, we know that the impact of technology has been wide and pervasive, so much so that we refer to various developments as "revolutions," such as the industrial revolution of the eighteenth century or the computer revolution of the latter half of the twentieth century. But we do not always appreciate the precise developments that make up these revolutions. To better comprehend the wide scope of technological change, consider the following categories and examples:

1. Increased ability to master time and distance for the movement of freight and passengers: railroads, automobiles and trucks, airplanes, space vehicles (to some extent)
2. Increased ability to generate, store, transport, and distribute energy: electricity, nuclear power, the laser
3. Increased ability to design new materials and change the properties of others so that they better serve needs: steel alloys, synthetic fibers, plastics, and new drugs
4. Mechanization or automation of physical processes: the large number of laborsaving devices, from Hargreaves's spinning jenny in 1770 to the largely automatic subway systems in San Francisco and Washington
5. Mechanization or automation of certain mental processes: the computer, which greatly expands our ability to store, manipulate, select, and supply data
6. Extension of the human ability to sense things: radar, the electron microscope, night-vision instruments
7. Increased understanding of individual and group behavior and how to deal with it: psychological bases of motivation, group behavior patterns, improved managerial techniques
8. Increased understanding of diseases and their treatment: inoculations for polio, kidney transplants, antibiotic treatment of infections

THE EXTERNAL ENVIRONMENT: SOCIAL

In any classification of environment elements having an impact on a manager, it is extremely difficult to separate the social, political, and ethical environments. Conceptually, however, it is possible. The *social* environment is made up of the attitudes, desires, expectations, degrees of intelligence and education, beliefs, and customs of people in a given group or society. The *political* and *legal* environment is primarily that complex of laws, regulations, and government agencies and their actions which affects all kinds of enterprises, often to varying degrees. The concept of *social responsibility* requires organizations to consider the impact of their actions on society. The *ethical* environment—which could well be included as an element in the social environment—includes sets of generally accepted and practiced standards of personal conduct. These standards may or may not be codified by law, but for any group to which they are meant to apply, they sometimes have virtually the force of law.

The Complexity of Environmental Forces

The interweaving of these environmental elements makes their study and comprehension exceptionally difficult. To forecast them so that a manager can anticipate and prepare for changes is even more difficult.[4] Social desires, expectations, and pressures give rise to laws and standards of ethics. Social forces, including ethics, normally arise before laws are passed, since the legislative process is notably reactive in the sense that it acts when a crisis is at hand but seldom before. Furthermore, existing laws and regulations, which are so numerous and complex that even the best-trained lawyers cannot know all of them (though they would probably know where to find them), often are brought to our attention in surprising and unusual ways.

Social Attitudes, Beliefs, and Values

Managers of various enterprises have been criticized for not being responsive to the social attitudes, beliefs, and values of particular individuals, groups, or societies. But attitudes and values differ among workers and employers, rich and poor people, college students and alumni, accountants and engineers, Californians and New Yorkers. This variety makes it difficult for managers to design an environment conducive to performance and satisfaction. It is even more difficult to respond to these forces when they are outside the enterprise. Yet managers have no choice but to take them into account in their decision making.

Over the centuries of American social development, a number of social beliefs have evolved that are of significance to the manager. Among the most important of these are the following:

1. The belief that there are opportunities for people who are willing and able to work to take advantage of them
2. A faith in business and a respect for business owners and leaders
3. A belief in competition and competitiveness in all aspects of life, particularly in business
4. A respect for the individual, regardless of race, religion, or creed
5. A respect for authority arising from ownership of property, expert knowledge, and elected or appointed political position

6. A belief in, and respect for, education
7. A faith in logical processes, science, and technology
8. A belief in the importance of change and experimentation to find better ways of doing things

It is true that these and other major beliefs have tended to erode as the country has become more populous and as social problems have forced more government involvement in everyone's life. It is also true, as usually happens in all cultures, that when people's standard of living improves, their expectations for a better life tend to increase even faster. Nonetheless, the long-held American beliefs are still strong, supported as they are by the American work ethic developed by early settlers and immigrants, by a long tradition of individual rights and freedoms, and by our remarkable Constitution.

Perspective

Where Have All the Yuppies Gone?

The 1980s were marked by greed. For example, arbitrageur Ivan Boesky advocated greed, and his illegal greedy behavior landed him in jail. Now, in the early 1990s, America's mood seems to be changing. Whether the President sets the mood or simply reflects it may be argued on either side. President George Bush reflects values that are markedly different from those of previous administrations in this statement: "From now on, any definition of a successful life must include serving others."[5] The notion of "helping those in need," so popular during the Kennedy years, seems to be gaining favor. Conspicuous consumption by the young urban professionals, the yuppies, popular in the early 1980s, is losing appeal. The "me" concern is being overshadowed by the "we" concern. Historian Arthur Schlesinger, Jr., looks optimistically at the 1990s, with young men and women showing more of the idealism of the sixties.

Although there may be core values in a society, different times bring different concerns to the forefront. Societal values are often reflected in corporate concerns. Increasingly, companies are providing services such as child-care facilities, in addition to opportunities for job sharing and flexible working hours.

THE EXTERNAL ENVIRONMENT: POLITICAL AND LEGAL

As was pointed out earlier, the political and legal environment of managers is closely intertwined with the social environment. Laws are ordinarily passed as the result of social pressures and problems. But what is bothersome is that once passed, laws often stay on the books after the socially perceived need for them has disappeared.

The Political Environment

Political environments—the attitudes and actions of political and government leaders and legislators—do change with the ebb and flow of social demands and beliefs. World War II patriotic fervor, affecting virtually every segment of American society and even world society, may be contrasted with the effect on government and other organizations of disillusionment over the unpopular Vietnam conflict. Many legislators who strongly supported involvement in Vietnam did a complete turnabout when people became disenchanted. In many communities, strong sentiments about air and water pollution control subsided when plants that were unable to meet new standards had to be shut down.

Government affects virtually every enterprise and every aspect of life. With respect to business, it acts in two main roles: it promotes and constrains business. For example, it promotes business by stimulating economic expansion and development, by providing assistance through the Small Business Administration, by subsidizing selected industries, by giving tax advantages in certain situations, by supporting research and development, and even by protecting some businesses through special tariffs. Finally, government is also the biggest customer, purchasing goods and services.

The Legal Environment

The other role of government is to constrain and regulate business. Every manager is encircled by a web of laws, regulations, and court decisions—not only on the national level but also on the state and local levels. Some are designed to protect workers, consumers, and communities. Others are designed to make contracts enforceable and to protect property rights. Many are designed to regulate the behavior of managers and their subordinates in business and other enterprises. There is relatively little that a manager can do in any organization that is not in some way concerned with, and often specifically controlled by, a law or regulation.

Many of our laws and regulations are necessary, even though many become obsolete. But they do present a complex environment for all managers. Managers are expected to know the legal restrictions and requirements applicable to their actions. Thus, it is understandable that managers in all kinds of organizations, especially in business and government, usually have a legal expert close at hand as they make their decisions.

In many areas laws are too slow to develop. For example, if one of the many businesses that contributed to the pollution of Lake Erie had gone to the great expense of eliminating the dumping of wastes into the lake, the costs would have put it at the mercy of competitors who did not go to this expense. If the governing body of a single municipality that was polluting the lake had gone to a similar expense, it would probably have had to answer to the taxpayers. Likewise, if one automobile manufacturer had produced a nonpolluting car 40 years ago and had offered it at a price a few hundred dollars higher than the prices of its competitors' models, there can hardly be a question that this company would have been at a competitive disadvantage. It took strong legislation to approach the solution of pollution problems.[6]

Thus, perceptive managers not only must respond to social pressures but also need to foresee and deal with political pressures, as well as laws that might be passed.[7] As can be readily understood, this is not an easy matter.

Business leaders are perceived to wield a great deal of power. Yet over the years, their power has decreased. Institutions such as government, labor unions, and universities have gained power. But with power comes responsibility and accountability. When companies, barely controlled by Toshiba, shipped strategic U.S. products to former Eastern bloc countries in violation of the ban, top executives of Toshiba resigned in recognition that leadership entails not privileges but responsibilities.

THE SOCIAL RESPONSIBILITY OF MANAGERS

In the early 1900s the mission of business firms was exclusively economic. Today, partly owing to the interdependencies of the many groups in our society, the social involvement of business has increased. There is indeed a question as to what the social responsibility of business really is. Moreover, the question of social responsibility, originally associated with businesses, is now being posed with increasing frequency in regard to governments, universities, nonprofit foundations, charitable organizations, and even churches. Thus, we talk about the social responsibility and social responsiveness of all organizations, although the focus of this discussion is on business. Society, awakened and vocal with respect to the urgency of social problems, is asking managers, particularly those at the top, what they are doing to discharge their social responsibilities and why they are not doing more.

Social Responsibility and Social Responsiveness

The concept of **social responsibility** is not new. Although the idea was already considered in the early part of the twentieth century, the modern discussion of social responsibility got a major impetus with the book *Social Responsibilities of the Businessman* by Howard R. Bowen, who suggested that businesses should consider the social implications of their decisions.[9] As might be expected, there is no complete agreement on the definition. In a survey of 439 executives, 68 percent of responding managers agreed with this definition: "Corporate social responsibility is seriously considering the impact of the company's actions on society."[10]

A concept that is newer, but still very similar to social responsibility, is **social responsiveness,** which in simple terms means "the ability of a corporation to relate its operations and policies to the social environment in ways that are mutually beneficial to the company and to society."[11] Both definitions focus on corporations, but these concepts should be expanded (1) to include enterprises other than businesses and (2) to encompass relationships within an enterprise. The main difference between social responsibility and social responsiveness is that the latter implies actions and the "how" of enterprise responses. In this discussion, the terms will be used interchangeably.[12]

Arguments for and against Business Involvement in Social Actions

Although there are arguments for business involvement in social activities, there are also arguments against it, as shown in Table 3-1.

Today many businesses are involved in social actions. A decision as to whether companies should extend their social involvement requires a careful examination of the arguments for and against such actions. Certainly, society's expectations are changing, and the trend seems to be toward greater social responsiveness. In fact, most respondents in a study of *Harvard Business Review* readers consider social responsibility a legitimate and achievable aim for business.[13] Still, the mission of the organization must be taken into account.

The Mission of the Enterprise

Various kinds of organized enterprises have different missions entrusted to them by society.[14] The mission of business is the production and distribution of goods and services. The mission of a police department is the protection of people's safety and welfare. The mission of a state highway department is the design and construction of highways. The mission of a university is teaching and research. And so on.

We should not hold business managers, for example, responsible for solving all social problems. There can hardly be any sense in making it the job of business to furnish public school education or the many other things, like police and fire protection, that the government provides. But business, like any other type of organized enterprise, must interact with, and live in, its environment.

Whether managers achieve their missions and how they do so are matters of great social importance. A society expects and deserves the accomplishment of the missions of approved enterprises. Thus, managers must take into account elements in their surroundings that are important to their success and important to others who may be affected by the actions they take. In other words, managers respond to their environment and become active participants in the community to improve the quality of life. This is what they must do, since the survival of their enterprise depends on successful interaction with all environmental elements, as emphasized in the discussion of organizations as open systems.

Reaction or Proaction?

But to live within an environment and be responsive to it does not mean that managers should merely react in the face of stress. Since no enterprise can be

TABLE 3-1   ARGUMENTS FOR AND AGAINST SOCIAL INVOLVEMENT OF BUSINESS

Arguments for social involvement of business

1. Public needs have changed, leading to changed expectations. Business, it is suggested, received its charter from society and consequently has to respond to the needs of society.

2. The creation of a better social environment benefits both society and business. Society gains through better neighborhoods and employment opportunities; business benefits from a better community, since the community is the source of its work force and the consumer of its products and services.

3. Social involvement discourages additional government regulation and intervention. The result is greater freedom and more flexibility in decision making for business.

4. Business has a great deal of power that, it is reasoned, should be accompanied by an equal amount of responsibility.

5. Modern society is an interdependent system, and the internal activities of the enterprise have an impact on the external environment.

6. Social involvement may be in the interest of stockholders.

7. Problems can become profits. Items that may once have been considered waste (for example, empty soft-drink cans) can be profitably used again.

8. Social involvement creates a favorable public image. Thus, a firm may attract customers, employees, and investors.

9. Business should try to solve the problems that other institutions have not been able to solve. After all, business has a history of coming up with novel ideas.

10. Business has the resources. Specifically, business should use its talented managers and specialists, as well as its capital resources, to solve some of society's problems.

11. It is better to prevent social problems through business involvement than to cure them. It may be easier to help the hard-core unemployed than to cope with social unrest.

Arguments against social involvement of business

1. The primary task of business is to maximize profit by focusing strictly on economic activities. Social involvement could reduce economic efficiency.

2. In the final analysis, society must pay for the social involvement of business through higher prices. Social involvement would create excessive costs for business, which cannot commit its resources to social action.

3. Social involvement can create a weakened international balance of payments situation. The cost of social programs, the reasoning goes, would have to be added to the price of the product. Thus, American companies selling in international markets would be at a disadvantage when competing with companies in other countries that do not have these social costs to bear.

4. Business has enough power, and additional social involvement would further increase its power and influence.

5. Businesspeople lack the social skills to deal with the problems of society. Their training and experience is with economic matters, and their skills may not be pertinent to social problems.

6. There is a lack of accountability of business to society. Unless accountability can be established, business should not get involved.

7. There is not complete support for involvement in social actions. Consequently, disagreements among groups with different viewpoints will cause friction.

Source: Based on William C. Frederick, Keith Davis, and James E. Post, *Business and Society,* 6th ed. (New York: McGraw-Hill Book Company, 1988), chap. 2.

expected to react very quickly to unforeseen developments, an enterprise must practice ways of anticipating developments through forecasts. An alert company, for example, does not wait until its product is obsolete and sales have fallen off before coming out with a new or improved product. A government agency should not wait until its regulations are obsolete and discredited before looking for another way to achieve its objectives. No enterprise should wait for problems to develop before preparing to face them. *Proaction* is an essential part of the planning process.

The Role of the Government

There are many instances in which social changes can be implemented only by the enactment of legislation. However, many managers in business and elsewhere have found it to their advantage to do something about pressing social problems. For example, many businesses have profited by filtering smokestack pollutants and selling or utilizing these recovered wastes. Some companies have made a profit by building low-cost apartment buildings in ghetto areas. The Internal Revenue Service has increased tax collection efficiency and effectiveness by simplifying or eliminating certain burdensome reports and forms. In other words, contributing to the solution of social problems does not always involve net expense. But society may need the bludgeoning force of legislation to get improvements under way.

The Influence of Values and Performance Criteria on Behavior

Even if individual managers have full freedom to act in accordance with the currently conceived social responsibilities, they may not do so because of standards applied in evaluating their performance. Managers, like everyone else, want their performance positively appraised—they seek approval. Therefore, if their success is measured in terms of profit, living within a budget, tax collection as a percentage of income, the volume of blood contributed to a blood bank, or the number of communicants in a church, managers will tend to strive to achieve excellence in these regards. If success is measured in terms of pollution control, the number of convicts returned successfully to society, the dollar support for employees seeking university degrees, the ratio of "disadvantaged" to total number of employees, achievements in raising the productivity of subordinates, or combinations of these and similar goals, then managers will strive to achieve them.

In other words, managers will respond to socially approved values and will give priority to those held in highest esteem. If we want to make sure that organizations respond to social forces, we must clarify social values and then reward managers for their success in responding to them, recognizing, of course, that different organizations have a variety of missions.

The Social Audit

The discussion of social responsibility raises the question of how social performance should be evaluated. This led to the concept of the "social audit," which was first proposed in the 1950s by Howard R. Bowen.[15] But it is only more recently that corporations have seriously concerned themselves with this idea.[16] The **social**

audit has been defined as "a commitment to systematic assessment of and reporting on some meaningful, definable domain of the company's activities that have social impact."[17]

One may distinguish between two types of audits. One is *required* by the government and involves, for example, pollution control, product performance requirements, and equal employment standards. The other kind of social audit concerns a great variety of *voluntary* social programs.[18]

One survey of the *Fortune* 500 firms indicated that 456 companies (91.2 percent) have made social responsibility disclosures in their annual reports.[19] Although these disclosures may not be equated with a social audit, the large number of firms making such disclosures shows that there is a general concern among major corporations about their social responsibility.

It is rather difficult to determine what areas the social audit should encompass. Often the items include pollution and the hiring, training, and promotion of minorities, but there are many other areas. For example, General Electric developed a matrix that facilitates the analysis of the expectations of customers, investors, employees, communities, and other claimants in the following areas: product and technical performance, economic performance, employment performance, environment and natural resources, community welfare and development, and government-business relations, as well as international trade and development.

Another difficulty is determining the amount of money an enterprise spends in selected areas. But cost alone is an inadequate measure. It does not necessarily indicate the results of social involvement. Other problems are the collection of the data and their presentation in a way that accurately reflects the social involvement of an enterprise. There is no doubt that many difficulties are associated with a social audit, but there is evidence that many companies and other organizations in the United States honestly attempt to address themselves to this challenge.

ETHICS IN MANAGING

All persons, whether in business, government, a university, or any other enterprise, are concerned with ethics. In *Webster's Ninth New Collegiate Dictionary,* **ethics** is defined as "the discipline dealing with what is good and bad and with moral duty and obligation." Thus, **personal ethics** has been referred to as "the rules by which an individual lives his or her personal life," and **accounting ethics** pertains to "the code that guides the professional conduct of accountants."[20] **Business ethics** is concerned with truth and justice and has a variety of aspects such as the expectations of society, fair competition, advertising, public relations, social responsibilities, consumer autonomy, and corporate behavior in the home country as well as abroad.[21]

Ethical Theories and a Model for Political Behavior Decisions

In organizations, managers compete for information, influence, and resources. The potential for conflicts in selecting the ends as well as the means to the ends is easy to understand, and the question of what criteria should guide ethical behavior becomes acute.

Three basic types of moral theories in the field of normative ethics have been developed. First, the **utilitarian theory** suggests that plans and actions should be evaluated by their consequences. The underlying idea is that plans or actions should produce the greatest good for the greatest number of people. Second, the **theory based on rights** holds that all people have basic rights. Examples are the rights to freedom of conscience, free speech, and due process. A number of those rights can be found in the Bill of Rights in the Constitution of the United States. Third, the **theory of justice** demands that decision makers be guided by fairness and equity, as well as impartiality.[22]

Gerald Cavanagh, Dennis Moberg, and Manuel Velasquez point out the strengths and weaknesses of each theory and integrate them into a decision tree, shown in Figure 3-2, that can guide managers in making ethical decisions.[23] The theories are best illustrated by the following example:

Sam and Bob are highly motivated research scientists who work in the new-product development lab at General Rubber. Sam is by far the most technically competent scientist in the lab, and he has been responsible for several patents that have netted the company nearly $6 million in the past decade. He is quiet, serious, and socially reserved. In contrast, Bob is outgoing and demonstrative. While Bob lacks the technical track record Sam has, his work has been solid though unimaginative. Rumor has it that Bob will be moved into an administrative position in the lab in the next few years.

According to the lab policy, a $300,000 fund is available every year for the best new-product development idea proposed by a lab scientist in the form of a competitive bid. Accordingly, Sam and Bob both prepare proposals. Each proposal is carefully constructed to detail the benefits to the company and to society if the proposal is accepted, and it is the consensus of other scientists from blind reviews that both proposals are equally meritorious. Both proposals require the entire $300,000 to realize any significant results. Moreover, the proposed line of research in each requires significant mastery of the technical issues involved and minimal need to supervise the work of others.

After submitting his proposal, Sam takes no further action aside from periodically inquiring about the outcome of the bidding process. In contrast, Bob begins to wage what might be termed an open campaign in support of his proposal. After freely admitting his intentions to Sam and others, Bob seizes every opportunity he can to point out the relative advantages of his proposal to individuals who might have some influence over the decision. So effective is this open campaign that considerable informal pressure is placed on those authorized to make the decision on behalf of Bob's proposal. Bob's proposal is funded and Sam's is not.

An ethical analysis of Bob's action in this case could begin by using the decision tree shown in Figure 3-2. The first question in the sequence requires a utilitarian analysis. Clearly, Bob's interests are better served than Sam's. However, the nature of the two proposals seems to require one of the two to be disappointed. Moreover, the outcome in terms of broader interests (i.e., company, society) appears not to be suboptimal, since both proposals were judged

FIGURE 3-2

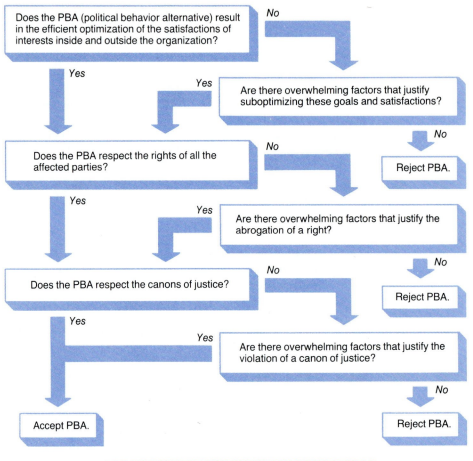

**A DECISION TREE FOR INCORPORATING ETHICS
INTO POLITICAL BEHAVIOR DECISIONS.**

equivalent in the blind reviews. Consequently, it is appropriate to answer the first question affirmatively.

The second question inquires into the rights respected by Bob's behavior. Here again, the evidence seems persuasive that no one's rights were violated. Sam did not have (did not create) the same opportunity to point out the advantages of his proposal to those at whom Bob directed his lobbying campaign, but Bob's open campaign involved no deceit, and Sam's inaction may be taken as implied consent.

It is in light of the third question that Bob's actions are most suspect. Justice would have best been served in this case if there had been a clear situation-relevant difference between the two proposals. The blind reviews found them equivalent, so some other basis for differentiating between the proposals presumably had to be found. Bob's efforts served to create irrelevant differences between them. If anything, Sam's superior technical track record would have been a more relevant factor than Bob's initiative and social skills in determining who should be favored to perform a technical task. Bob's actions in this regard were therefore unjust. Interestingly, had the proposals required supervision of others or the ability to persuade others, Bob's approach would have been justified.[24]

Managers are facing many situations that require ethical judgments, and often there are no easy answers. The model shown in Figure 3-2 provides a conceptual framework that helps managers analyze and evaluate their decisions, as illustrated by the case.[25]

Institutionalizing Ethics

Managers, especially top managers, do have a responsibility to create an organizational environment that fosters ethical decision making by institutionalizing ethics. This means applying and integrating ethical concepts with daily actions. Theodore Purcell and James Weber suggest that this can be accomplished in three ways: (1) by establishing an appropriate company policy or a code of ethics, (2) by using a formally appointed ethics committee, and (3) by teaching ethics in management development programs.[26] The most common way to institutionalize ethics is to establish a code of ethics; much less common is the use of ethics board committees. Management development programs dealing with ethical issues are very seldom used, although companies such as Allied Chemical, International Business Machines, and General Electric have instituted such programs.

Code of Ethics and Its Implementation through a Formal Committee

A **code** is a statement of policies, principles, or rules that guides behavior. Certainly, codes of ethics do not apply only to business enterprises; they should guide the behavior of persons in all organizations and in everyday life.

Perspective

Code of Ethics for Government Service

The federal government has established the following.[27] Any person in government service should:

1. Put loyalty to the highest moral principles and to country above loyalty to persons, party, or Government department.
2. Uphold the Constitution, laws, and regulations of the United States and of all governments therein and never be a party to their evasion.
3. Give a full day's labor for a full day's pay; giving earnest effort and best thought to the performance of duties.

4. Seek to find and employ more efficient and economical ways of getting tasks accomplished.

5. Never discriminate unfairly by the dispensing of special favors or privileges to anyone, whether for remuneration or not; and never accept, for himself or herself or for family members, favors or benefits under circumstances which might be construed by reasonable persons as influencing the performance of governmental duties.

6. Make no private promises of any kind binding upon the duties of office, since a Government employee has no private word which can be binding on public duty.

7. Engage in no business with the Government, either directly or indirectly, which is inconsistent with the conscientious performance of governmental duties.

8. Never use any information gained confidentially in the performance of governmental duties as a means of making private profit.

9. Expose corruption wherever discovered.

10. Uphold these principles, ever conscious that public office is a public trust.

Simply stating a code of ethics is not enough, and the appointment of an ethics committee, consisting of internal and external directors, is considered essential for institutionalizing ethical behavior.[28] The functions of such a committee may include (1) holding regular meetings to discuss ethical issues, (2) dealing with "gray areas," (3) communicating the code to all members of the organization, (4) checking for possible violations of the code, (5) enforcing the code, (6) rewarding compliance and punishing violations, (7) reviewing and updating the code, and (8) reporting activities of the committee to the board of directors.

Factors That Raise Ethical Standards

In the study cited earlier, the two factors that raise ethical standards the most, according to the respondents, are (1) public disclosure and publicity and (2) the increased concern of a well-informed public. These factors are followed by government regulations and by education to increase the professionalism of business managers.[29]

For ethical codes to be effective, provisions must be made for their enforcement. Unethical managers should be held responsible for their actions. This means that privileges and benefits should be withdrawn and sanctions should be applied. Although the enforcement of ethical codes may not be easy, the mere existence of such codes can increase ethical behavior by clarifying expectations. On the other hand, one should not expect ethical codes to solve all problems. In fact, they can create a false sense of security. Effective code enforcement requires consistent ethical behavior and support from top management.

Another factor that could raise ethical standards is the teaching of ethics and values in business and other schools and universities. The Harvard Business School has come under severe criticism by its own president, Derek Bok, for the lack of teaching of human values.[30] With the help of business executives, the school hired Dean John McArthur and faculty members trained to teach ethics to give a new direction to the school. While financial aspects received less attention in the revised curriculum, more emphasis was placed on people skills and ethical behavior. Since Harvard has one of the largest numbers of B-school graduates who often hold top managerial positions, a somewhat greater awareness of the ethical dimension in managing may be expected.

The need for improvement of ethical behavior has become evident by way of some widely publicized cases. Saul Gellerman examined three in greater detail: the Manville Corporation, which apparently hid the real danger of asbestos; Continental Illinois Bank, in which some managers misinterpreted the overall interest of the enterprise; and E. F. Hutton and Company, which pleaded guilty to mail and wire fraud.[31]

In light of his analysis, Gellerman made several suggestions, such as the following:

1. Provide clear guidelines for ethical behavior.
2. Teach ethical guidelines and their importance.[32]
3. In gray areas where there are questions about the ethics of an action, refrain from it.
4. Set up controls (for example, establish an auditing agency reporting to outside directors) that check on illegal or unethical deeds.
5. Conduct frequent and unpredictable audits.
6. Punish trespassers in a meaningful way, and make it public so that it may deter others.
7. Emphasize regularly that loyalty to the company does not excuse improper behavior or actions.

Differing Ethical Standards of Various Societies

Any person in business, government, a university, or some other organization is aware that ethical, as well as legal, standards do differ, particularly among nations and societies.[33] This has long been true. For example, many nations with privately owned companies permit corporations to make contributions to political parties, campaigns, and candidates. (The United States does not.) In some countries, payments to government officials and other persons with political influence to ensure the favorable handling of a business transaction are regarded not as unethical bribes but as proper payments for services rendered. In many cases, payments made to ensure the landing of a contract are even looked upon as a normal and acceptable way of doing business. Consider the Quaker Oats Company, which was faced with a situation in which foreign officials threatened to close the operation if the demand for "payouts" was not met. Or what should a company do when the plant manager's safety will be in question if payoffs are not made?[34]

The question facing responsible American business managers is: What ethical standards should they follow? There is no question of what to do in the United States, and American executives have had to refuse the suggestion of putting money in a "paper bag." In a country where such practices are expected and common, American executives are faced with a difficult problem. With the passage of laws by the U.S. Congress and the adoption of regulations by the Securities and Exchange Commission, not only must American firms report anything that could be called a payoff, but anything else that can be construed as a bribe is now unlawful. Thus, we have attempted to export our standards for doing business to other countries, which can improve ethical standards abroad.

SUMMARY

Managers operate in a complex environment. They are affected by—and to some extent influence—the environment. In the United States, managers operate in a pluralistic society in which many organized groups represent various interests.

In their decision making, managers must consider the external economic environment: capital, labor, price levels, government fiscal and tax policies, and the needs of customers. Technology provides many benefits but also some problems. To understand the scope of technology, one may consider its numerous categories. There is also a complex of social factors. Thus, a manager should understand the social beliefs prevailing in a country. We focused on American beliefs that developed over a period of time. Government affects every enterprise. The political environment changes with the social demands and beliefs. Thus, every organization is affected by laws, regulations, and court decisions.

Corporate social responsibility requires that organizations consider seriously the impact of their actions on society. Similarly, social responsiveness is relating corporate operations and policies to the social environment in ways that are beneficial to the company and society. Determining the appropriate relationships between various organizations and society is not an easy task, and one can make arguments for and against business involvement. Nevertheless, many corporations and other organizations are making serious efforts to establish an environment that is beneficial to individuals, business, and society.

Ethics deals with what is good and bad and with moral duty and obligation. There are three moral theories in normative ethics: the utilitarian theory, the theory based on rights, and the theory of justice. Some authors have suggested that businesses institutionalize ethics and develop a code of ethics. There are also other factors that raise ethical standards. Managers have to make difficult choices when the standards differ in various societies.

KEY IDEAS AND CONCEPTS FOR REVIEW

Pluralistic society
External economic factors
Benefits and problems resulting from
  technology
Categories of technological change
The impact of social attitudes, beliefs,
  and values on decision making
Political environment
Legal environment
Corporate social responsibility
Social responsiveness
Arguments for and against social
  involvement of business

Mission of the enterprise
Role of the government
Values, performance criteria, and
  behavior
Social audit
Ethics
Utilitarian theory of ethics
Ethical theory based on rights
Ethical theory of justice
Institutionalizing ethics
Code of ethics for government service
Factors raising ethical standards

FOR DISCUSSION

1. Why is the environment external to an enterprise so important to all managers? Can any manager avoid being influenced by the external environment?
2. Identify the elements of the external environment that are likely to be the most important to each of the following: a company president, a sales manager, a production manager, a controller, and a personnel manager.
3. What effects do the external social, political, and legal environments have on an enterprise? How do managers respond to these influences?
4. What are the major social responsibilities of business managers? Of government managers? Have these responsibilities changed over the years? How?
5. Briefly explain the major moral theories in the field of normative ethics. How do they relate to the decision tree for incorporating ethics into political behavior decisions?
6. If you were the chief executive officer of a large corporation, how would you "institutionalize" ethics in the organization?
7. List and discuss the benefits and limitations of some codes of ethics.
8. What ethical codes would you recommend for your university, your class, and your family? How should these codes be enforced?

EXERCISES/ACTION STEPS

1. The class should select and read an article published in a recent issue of *The Wall Street Journal, Business Week,* or *Fortune* that involves some ethical issues. Divide the class into groups, and analyze the situation using the decision tree shown in this chapter. Each group, through its spokesperson, should present its analysis.
2. Interview one business manager and one administrator in the local government, and ask how they perceive their social responsibilities. Do these responsibilities relate primarily to the environment external to the organization, or do they also include internal aspects?

CASES

CASE 3-1
BISHOPS' PASTORAL[35]

In 1984 the Catholic bishops issued statements about Catholic social teaching and the U.S economy. The first draft was debated and criticized as being too negative about the free-market economy in the United States. A second draft was then issued that softened the tone, but the message was the same. Some of the key points are the following:

• Economic decisions must be made with due consideration as to whether they help all people.
• Government, corporations, and individuals must help to reduce the inequities created by the free-market system.
• More resources should be allocated for helping the poor and the jobless instead of for military uses.

The purpose of the document is to influence governmental and individual decisions in a way that would bring about a more humane society. The poor, the letter suggests, have not adequately shared the economic resources, and the government has a role to play to bring this about.

These are some of the recommendations in the draft:

• Pursue fiscal and monetary policies that result in full employment.
• Support job-creating programs.
• Remove employment barriers for women and minorities through affirmative action and job training.
• Reform the welfare system to provide minimum levels of benefit for the poor.
• Support international agencies to reduce poverty in Third World countries.

1. What are the implications for managers?
2. How does the letter relate to the various managerial functions?

INTERNATIONAL CASE 3-2
TO STAY OR NOT TO STAY IN SOUTH AFRICA[36]

Many executives of large multinational corporations face a dilemma involving economic, social, political, and ethical issues. One question many firms face is whether or not to divest themselves of their holdings in South Africa because of that country's apartheid policies. Arguments are advanced on both sides of the issue.

The arguments *for staying* in South Africa are as follows:

• Foreign companies are a positive force for peaceful change and will benefit blacks.
• Foreign firms should not get involved in social disputes. Their primary objective is to make a reasonable profit within a framework of fair policies.

• The progress blacks have made is to a great extent due to a growing economy to which foreign firms have contributed.
• Higher unemployment of blacks will result from the withdrawal of U.S. companies.
• Foreign divestments will not induce the government to change its policies a great deal, if at all.

The arguments *against staying* in South Africa are as follows:

• So far, companies have had only limited success in changing the poor conditions of blacks.
• Businesses have a responsibility not only toward stockholders but also toward society in general. Con-

sequently, they should not be doing business in a country that pursues a policy of apartheid.

- The turmoil and the economic conditions (recession, falling gold prices, double-digit inflation, and other factors) suggest that it may be in the long-term economic interest of the stockholders to withdraw from South Africa.
- Responsible black leaders realize the potential hardships associated with divestments in the short run, yet many blacks are willing to endure them with the hope of a better future.
- In the long run, South Africa cannot afford being

isolated from most of the world that opposes apartheid, and it will have to change its policies.

While the debate continues, top executives of major multinational corporations are faced with the decision whether to stay or not to stay in that country.

1. If you were the CEO of a major multinational corporation with substantial investments in South Africa, how would you decide? What are your reasons for your decision?
2. What do you think is the morally right decision? Why?

REFERENCES

1. Gerald F. Cavanagh, *American Business Values,* 2d ed. (Englewood Cliffs, N.J.: Prentice-Hall, 1984), p. 126.
2. George A. Steiner, *Business and Society* (New York: Random House, 1975), chap. 5; see also George A. Steiner and John F. Steiner, *Business, Government, and Society,* 6th ed. (New York: McGraw-Hill, 1991).
3. Periodically, *Business Week* publishes a list of new products and scientific innovations; see, for example, "The Best of 1991," *Business Week* (Jan. 13, 1992), pp. 123–139. *The Wall Street Journal* also has special reports such as "Technology," *The Wall Street Journal* (Apr. 6, 1992). See also Lewis M. Branscomb, "Does America Need a Technology Policy?" *Harvard Business Review* (March–April 1992), pp. 24–31.
4. See, for example, Emily T. Smith, Vicki Cahan, Naomi Freundlich, James E. Ellis, and Joseph Weber, "The Greening of Corporate America," *Business Week* (Apr. 23, 1990), pp. 96–103.
5. Ronald Henkoff, "Is Greed Dead?" *Fortune* (Aug. 14, 1989), pp. 40–49. See also James B. Stewart, *Den of Thieves* (New York: Simon & Schuster, 1991).
6. See Kai Erikson, "Toxic Reckoning: Business Faces a New Kind of Fear," *Harvard Business Review* (January–February 1990), pp. 118–126.
7. See Gerald D. Keim and Carl P. Zeithaml, "Corporate Political Strategy and Legislative Decision Making: A Review and Contingency Approach," *Academy of Management Review* (October 1986), pp. 828–843.
8. Peter F. Drucker, "The Mystery of the Business Leader," *The Wall Street Journal* (Sept. 29, 1987).
9. Howard R. Bowen, *Social Responsibilities of the Businessman* (New York: Harper & Brothers, 1953).
10. John L. Paluszek, *Business and Society: 1976–2000* (New York: AMACOM, 1976), in George A. Steiner, John B. Miner, and Edmund R. Gray, *Management Policy and Strategy,* 3d ed. (New York: The Macmillan Company, 1986), pp. 38–39. See also Archie B. Carroll, "A Three-Dimensional Conceptual Model of Corporate Performance," *Academy of Management Review* (October 1979), pp. 497–505; Richard E. Wokutch, "Corporate Social Responsibility Japanese Style," *Academy of Management Executive* (May 1990), pp. 56–74.

11. Keith Davis and William C. Frederick, *Business and Society,* 5th ed. (New York: McGraw-Hill Book Company, 1984), p. 564; see also William Frederick, Keith Davis, and James E. Post, *Business and Society,* 6th ed. (New York: McGraw-Hill Book Company, 1988).

12. Edwin Epstein, realizing not only the differences but also a great deal of overlap among business ethics, corporate social responsibility, and corporate social responsiveness, combines the three in his new concept "Corporate Social Policy Process." For a detailed discussion, see Edwin M. Epstein, *Beyond Business Ethics, Corporate Social Responsibility, and Corporate Social Responsiveness: An Introduction to the Corporate Social Policy Process,* Business and Public Policy Working Paper No. BPP-17 (University of California, Berkeley, Business School, July 1986).

13. Steven N. Brenner and Earl A. Molander, "Is the Ethics of Business Changing?" *Harvard Business Review* (January–February 1977), pp. 57–71.

14. For a discussion of mission statements, see John A. Pearce II and Fred David, "Corporate Mission Statements: The Bottom Line," *Academy of Management Executive* (May 1987), pp. 109–115.

15. Bowen, *Social Responsibilities of the Businessman* (1953), pp. 155–156.

16. See also Meinolf Dierkes and Ariane Berthoin Antal, "Whither Corporate Social Reporting: Is It Time to Legislate?" *California Management Review* (Spring 1986), pp. 106–121.

17. Raymond A. Bauer and Dan H. Fenn, Jr., "What Is a Corporate Social Audit?" *Harvard Business Review* (January–February 1973), p. 38.

18. Steiner et al., *Management Policy and Strategy* (1986), p. 47.

19. Social Responsibility Disclosure—1977 Survey of *Fortune* 500 Annual Reports (Cleveland, Ohio: Ernst & Ernst, 1977).

20. Manuel G. Velasquez, *Business Ethics* (Englewood Cliffs, N.J.: Prentice-Hall, 1982), p. 7.

21. Clarence D. Walton (ed.), *The Ethics of Corporate Conduct* (Englewood Cliffs, N.J.: Prentice-Hall, 1977), p. 6; see also La Rue Tone Hosmer, *The Ethics of Management* (Homewood, Ill.: Richard D. Irwin, 1987).

22. For research in ethics, see William A. Kahn, "Toward an Agenda for Business Ethics Research," *Academy of Management Review* (April 1990), pp. 311–328.

23. The discussion in this section is based on Gerald F. Cavanagh, Dennis J. Moberg, and Manuel Velasquez, "The Ethics of Organizational Politics," *Academy of Management Review* (July 1981), pp. 363–374, and has been used with their permission. See also Manuel Velasquez, Dennis J. Moberg, and Gerald F. Cavanagh, "Organizational Statesmanship and Dirty Politics: Ethical Guidelines for the Organizational Politician," *Organizational Dynamics* (Autumn 1983), pp. 65–80, and Gerald F. Cavanagh and Arthur F. McGovern, *Ethical Dilemmas in the Modern Corporation* (Englewood Cliffs, N.J.: Prentice-Hall, 1988).

24. Cavanagh, Moberg, and Velasquez, "The Ethics of Organizational Politics" (1981), p. 369.

25. For additional information, see Terence R. Mitchell and William G. Scott, "America's Problems and Needed Reforms: Confronting the Ethic of Personal Advantage," *The Executive* (August 1990), pp. 23–35.

26. Much of this discussion is based on James Weber, "Institutionalizing Ethics into the Corporation," *MSU Business Topics* (Spring 1981), pp. 47–52, and Theodore V. Purcell, S.J., and James Weber, *Institutionalizing Corporate Ethics: A Case History* (New York: The Presidents Association, The Chief Executive Officers' Division of American Management Association, 1979), Special Study No. 71.

27. Source: Public Law 96-303, July 3, 1980.

28. Weber, "Institutionalizing Ethics into the Corporation" (1981).

29. Brenner and Molander, "Is the Ethics of Business Changing?" (1977), p. 63.

30. Cavanagh, *American Business Values* (1984), chap. 5; Bruce Nussbaum and Alex Beam, "Remaking the Harvard B-School," *Business Week* (Mar. 24, 1986), pp. 54–58.

31. Saul W. Gellerman, "Why 'Good' Managers Make Bad Ethical Choices," *Harvard Business Review* (July–August 1986), pp. 85–90.

32. For ethics training, see Susan J. Harrington, "What Corporate America Is Teaching about Ethics," *Academy of Management Executive* (February 1991), pp. 21–30.

33. See Rogene A. Buchholz, *Business Environment and Public Policy,* 3d ed. (Englewood Cliffs, N.J.: Prentice-Hall, 1989), chap. 19.

34. Walton, *The Ethics of Corporate Conduct* (1977), chap. 7.

35. The case is based on a variety of sources, including Laurie McGinley, "Roman Catholic Bishops Soften Tone of Letter Calling for Action on Poverty," *The Wall Street Journal* (Oct. 7, 1985); "Catholic Social Teaching and the U.S. Economy: First Draft—Bishops' Pastoral," *Origins* (Nov. 15, 1984), pp. 337–383. See also *Second Draft—Pastoral Letter on Catholic Social Teaching and the U.S. Economy* (Oct. 7, 1985). After lengthy discussions, the 115-page letter *Economic Justice for All: Catholic Social Teaching and the U.S. Economy* was approved in November 1986; Oliver F. Williams, "Catholic Social Teaching and the U.S. Economy," in George A. Steiner and John F. Steiner, *Business, Government, and Society,* 5th ed. (New York: Random House, 1988), pp. 382–391. See also Mary Jo Bane and David T. Ellwood, "Is American Business Working for the Poor?" *Harvard Business Review* (September–October 1991), pp. 58–66.

36. John Nielsen, "Time to Quit South Africa?" *Fortune* (Sept. 30, 1985), pp. 18–23; Jonathan Kapstein, John Hoerr, and Elizabeth Weiner, "Leaving South Africa," *Business Week* (Sept. 23, 1985), pp. 104–112; Julian Redfearn, "The Sullivan Principles and U.S. Firms in South Africa," in Steiner et al., *Management Policy and Strategy* (1986), pp. 921–931; David T. Beaty and Oren Harari, "South Africa: White Managers, Black Voices," *Harvard Business Review* (July–August 1987), pp. 98–105; Steiner and Steiner, *Business, Government, and Society,* 5th ed. (1988), pp. 629–639.

Chapter 4

"Labor-management ties are essential, or the Japanese will beat our brains out."[1]

Mario Cuomo

Global and Comparative Management

Chapter Objectives

After reading this chapter, you should be able to:

1. Discuss the nature and purpose of international business and multinational corporations (MNCs).
2. Recognize differences in managing in selected countries.
3. Describe managerial practices in Japan and Theory Z.
4. Explain how managerial functions are carried out in the international environment.
5. Describe the modified Koontz model of comparative management, which separates environmental factors and enterprise functions from management fundamentals.

Chapter 3 focused on the external factors in the domestic environment. The constraining factors on managing are likely to be more severe for international firms. Executives operating in a foreign country need to learn a great deal about the country's educational, economic, legal, and political systems and especially its sociocultural environment.

The first section in this chapter deals with international management and the role of multinational corporations. Then the environmental impact on managing in selected countries is examined, with special attention given to Japanese managerial practices. This is followed by a discussion that shows how the managerial functions of planning, organizing, staffing, leading, and controlling are carried out by international business corporations. Finally, the focus is on comparative management. A model for the study of comparative management is introduced.

INTERNATIONAL MANAGEMENT AND MULTINATIONAL CORPORATIONS

The study of **international management** focuses on the operation of international firms in host countries. It is concerned with managerial issues related to the flow of people, goods, and money, with the ultimate aim being to manage better in situations that involve crossing national boundaries.

The environmental factors that affect domestic firms usually are more critical for international corporations operating in foreign countries. As illustrated in Table 4-1, managers involved in international business are faced with many factors that are different from those of the domestically oriented firm. Managers have to interact with employees who have different educational and cultural backgrounds and value systems; they also must cope with different legal, political, and economic factors. Thus, these environments understandably influence the way managerial and enterprise functions are carried out.

TABLE 4-1 DOMESTIC AND INTERNATIONAL ENTERPRISES: CHARACTERISTICS AND PRACTICES		
The environment	Domestic enterprise (industrialized country)	International enterprise
Educational environment:		
1. Language (spoken, written, official)	One	Multiple
2. Education system (quality, level, extent)	No or little constraint	Great constraint
Sociocultural/ethical environment:		
1. Values, attitudes (toward achievement, risk taking, scientific method, work)	Homogeneous	Heterogeneous
2. Social organization (authority, status, roles, institutions, mobility, social systems)	Similar	Different
Political-legal environment:		
1. Political orientation (power, ideologies)	Country-centered	Transnational
2. Legal environment (laws, codes, regulations)	Fairly uniform	Different
3. National sovereignties	One	Many
4. Government policies, regulations	Same	Different
Economic environment:		
1. Economic development (underdeveloped, industrialized)	At similar stages	At different stages
2. Economic system (capitalistic, mixed, Marxist)	Similar	Different

The Nature and Purpose of International Business

Although business has been conducted on an international scale for many years, international business has gained greater visibility and importance in recent years because of the growth of large multinational corporations. **International businesses** engage in transactions across national boundaries. These transactions include the transfer of goods, services, technology, managerial knowledge, and capital to other countries.

The interaction of a firm with the host country can take many forms, as illustrated in Figure 4-1. One is the *exportation* of goods and services. Another is a *licensing agreement* for producing goods in another country. The parent company may also engage in *management contracts* that provide for operating foreign companies. Still another form of interaction is the *joint venture* with a firm in the host country. Finally, multinationals may set up wholly owned *subsidiaries* or *branches* with production facilities in the host country. Thus, in developing a global strategy, an international firm has many options.[2]

The contact between the parent firm and the host country is affected by several factors; some are unifying, while others can cause conflicts.

Unifying effects.   Unifying influences occur when the parent company provides and shares technical and managerial know-how, thus assisting the host company in the development of human and material resources. Moreover, the parent corporation and the firm in the host country may find it advantageous to be integrated into a

FIGURE 4-1

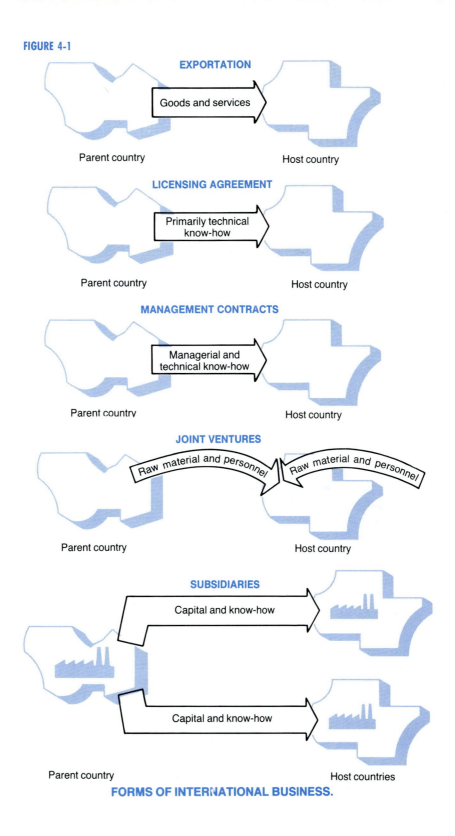

FORMS OF INTERNATIONAL BUSINESS.

global organization structure. Whatever the interaction, policies must provide for equity and result in benefits for both the parent firm and the host company. Only then can one expect a long-lasting relationship.

Potentials for conflict.   Many factors can cause conflicts between the parent firm and the host country. Nationalistic self-interest may overshadow the benefits obtained through cooperation. Similarly, sociocultural differences can lead to breakdowns in communication and subsequent misunderstandings. Also, a large multinational firm may have such overpowering economic effects on a small country that the host country feels overwhelmed. Some international corporations have been charged with making excessive profits, hiring the best local people away from local firms, and operating contrary to social customs. The international corporation must develop social and diplomatic skills in its managers in order to prevent such conflicts and to resolve those that unavoidably occur.

Multinational Corporations

Multinational corporations (MNCs) have their headquarters in one country but their operations in many countries. Of the ten largest global corporations, ranked by 1990 sales, six are American, one is British, one is British/Dutch, one is Japanese, and one is Italian.[3] The ten are (1) General Motors, (2) Royal Dutch/Shell Group (Britain/Netherlands), (3) Exxon, (4) Ford Motor Company, (5) International Business Machines (IBM), (6) Toyota (Japan), (7) IRI (Italy—government-owned), (8) British Petroleum (Britain), (9) Mobil, and (10) General Electric.

From ethnocentric to geocentric orientation.   In its early stages, international business was conducted with an **ethnocentric** outlook; that is, the orientation of the foreign operation was based on that of the parent company.[4] The **polycentric** attitude, on the other hand, is based on the notion that it is best to give the foreign subsidiaries, staffed by local nationals, a great deal of managerial freedom. It is assumed that nationals have the best understanding of the local environment. **Regiocentric** orientation favors the staffing of foreign operations on a regional basis. Thus, a European view may be composed of British, French, German, and Italian influences. The modern multinational corporation has a **geocentric** orientation. This means that the total organization is viewed as an interdependent system operating in many countries. The relationships between headquarters and subsidiaries are collaborative, with communication flowing in both directions. Furthermore, key positions are filled by managers of different nationalities. In short, the orientation of the multinational corporation is truly international and goes beyond a narrow nationalistic viewpoint.[5]

Advantages of multinationals.   Multinational corporations have several advantages over firms that have a domestic orientation. Obviously, the MNC can take advantage of business opportunities in many different countries. It can also raise money for its operations throughout the world. Moreover, multinational firms benefit by being able to establish production facilities in countries where their products can

An example of a global corporation with a geocentric organization is ABB Asea Brown Boveri, the result of a merger between the Swiss Brown and Boveri Company and Swedish Asea. The company's core businesses are electric power, mass transportation, and environmental controls, as well as process automation. This company really has no "home" country. While the headquarters is in Zurich, Switzerland, only 100 of the 240,000 employees work there. The CEO, Percy Barnevik, and only one-fourth of the board are Swedish. In a sense, the financial system is American because the data are compiled in U.S. dollars. This truly global corporation is guided by the motto "Think global and act local." In other words, this company combines a global approach with paying attention to the local needs and demands. This firm may become a model for future global organizational arrangements.

be produced most effectively and efficiently. Companies with worldwide operations sometimes have access to natural resources and materials that may not be available to domestic firms. Finally, the large MNCs can recruit managers and other personnel from a worldwide labor pool.

Challenges for the multinationals.   The advantages of multinational operation must be weighed against the challenges and risks associated with operating in foreign environments. One problem is the increasing nationalism in many countries. Years ago, developing countries lacked managerial, marketing, and technical skills. Consequently, they welcomed the multinationals. But the situation is changing, with people in developing countries acquiring those skills. In addition, countries have not only become aware of the value of their natural resources but also become more skilled in international negotiations. Finally, multinationals must maintain good relations with the host country, a task that may prove difficult because governments frequently change and corporations must deal with, and adapt to, these changes.

From Multinational to Global, or Transnational, Corporations

Just operating in different countries is not enough for large corporations. Nor is the establishment of manufacturing plants in several countries (as Exxon and General Motors have done) sufficient to be competitive in the world market. The shift is toward the **global, or transnational, corporation,** *which views the whole world as one market.* This means, however, that a corporation also has to adapt to national and even local needs. American Express, for example, has an overall advertising strategy—"Membership has its privileges"—but it adjusts its message for individual countries and even specific cities. In Japan, the basic message translates to "Peace of mind only for members."[7]

Domestic markets have become too small. Developing a drug may cost several hundred million dollars and may take more than 10 years. To recover the cost requires selling the drug in a world market. Moreover, global companies have to keep abreast of technological developments around the world. Ford Motor Company decided in the latter half of the 1980s to become a global corporation. Previous attempts to build the "world car" (named the Escort) were not very successful. However, the use of modern communication technology, such as teleconferencing, and reorganization establishes now a much closer link with its European operations. While Ford is aiming at becoming a global corporation, it has no plants in Japan. To compensate for this void, Ford bought a 25 percent share in Mazda. Moreover, the company has another project with Japanese Nissan, which designs a minivan to be built by Ford.

While many firms are aiming at becoming global, only a few have really done so. It requires developing products with the whole world in mind, especially the markets in North America, Asia, and Western Europe. Similarly, strategic decisions must take into account the whole world, but tactics must be adapted to the national and local environments. In staffing, opportunities must be opened for nonnationals to move into upper-management ranks. Finally, strategic alliances may need to be formed with companies in countries the global corporation cannot enter.

INTERNATIONAL MANAGEMENT IN SELECTED COUNTRIES*

It is interesting to know some of the differences in managerial practices in selected countries.[8] This discussion, however, is illustrative rather than comprehensive, and it is based on generalizations. There are, for example, great differences among U.S. managers; the same holds true for managers in other countries. Furthermore, a society is not static, and changes do occur over time. For instance, the traditional authoritarian style of German managers is slowly giving way to a more participative approach.

France: "Le Plan" and the "Cadre"

In France, government planning on a national scale (legal-political environment factor) helps coordinate the plans of individual industries and companies (managerial function of planning). The government's aim is to utilize most effectively the country's resources and to avoid expansion in uneconomic areas. Although government planning—which is also extended to regional areas—is carried out by relatively few, but competent, people, cooperation and assistance are provided by other government departments, employers' organizations, unions, and consumers.

---

* For a detailed discussion of managerial practices in Japan and the People's Republic of China, see the part closings "Global Planning" (following Chapter 8), "Global Organizing" (following Chapter 12), "Global Staffing" (following Chapter 15), "Global Leading" (following Chapter 19), and "Global Controlling" (following Chapter 23).

The plan, which is generally revised every 5 years, attempts to obtain economic growth, price stability, a balance in foreign payments, and a favorable employment situation. Managers, then, are not only constrained by "Le Plan" but also aided by it, since it produces a great deal of information upon which they can draw for their own enterprises.

At times, the plan becomes a global strategy helping specific industries.[9] For example, the French government attempts to integrate the electronics industry into a whole so that it can overcome its weaknesses in information processing, consumer electronics, microelectronics, and automation. To implement the strategy, the government plans to support several national projects, such as speech synthesis, mini- and microcomputers, and large mainframe computers. Clearly, there is a close relationship between government planning and firms, especially those that are owned and directly aided by the government.

In a recent discussion, Jean-Louis Barsoux and Peter Lawrence noted not only the close relationship between government and industry but also the impact of the elite universities' *grandes écoles* on forming the French managerial mind, which is considered essential for managing in both government and business organizations.[10] These schools supply the "cadre," the managerial elite. Moreover, the schools' connections are vital for managerial success. What is valued in these managers is analytical ability, independence, and proficiency in synthesizing facts. While written communication is considered very important, oral communication is de-emphasized. These managers exhibit intellectual ability rather than action. Rationality, problem solving, and numerical analysis are important for obtaining high managerial posts in government as well as business. Indeed, it is not unusual for managers to work for both alternately.

The French managerial model also has drawbacks. It may limit managers to dealing with nonquantifiable and "nonrational" data and to responding quickly to changes in the environment, and it may not result in the selection of the best managers because school ties are more important than performance. Although the managerial characteristics may also be limiting in terms of obtaining a global outlook, French managers, in general, are quite supportive of the European Community 1992 (EC 1992) program. They see it as an opportunity to restructure the New Europe.

Germany: Authority and Codetermination

In the past, and to a lesser extent today, the German cultural environment favored reliance on authority in directing the work force, although it was often benevolent authoritarianism (managerial function of leading). Even today, while managers may show concern for subordinates, they also expect obedience.

It is almost a paradox that, on the one hand, the managerial style is characterized by considerable use of authority, while, on the other hand, labor, by law, is represented by and actively involved in managing large corporations. In 1951 a law was passed that provided for **codetermination,** which requires labor membership in the supervisory board and the executive committee of certain large corporations. Furthermore, a labor director is elected as a member of the executive committee.[11] This position is a difficult one. Labor directors supposedly must represent the interests of the employees and, at the same time, must make managerial decisions that are in the best interest of the enterprise.

Korean Management

Japanese management receives a great deal of attention, partly because of the economic success of Japanese companies. The Republic of Korea (South Korea, referred to here as Korea) has also shown remarkable economic growth, but its management practices are less well known. It would be incorrect to assume that Korean management is simply an extension of Japanese management. It is not, although there are some cultural and structural similarities, such as the dominance of powerful conglomerate companies.

In Japan, managers emphasize group harmony and cohesion, expressed in the concept of *wa;* the Korean concept of *inhwa* also translates into harmony, but with less accent on group values. Korean organizations are quite hierarchical, with family members occupying key positions. Beyond blood relationships, the factors affecting hiring decisions often include the school attended or being from the same geographic region as the top person. The leadership style can best be described as top-down, or autocratic/paternalistic. This approach enables the firm to adjust quickly to the demands in the environment by issuing commands. Lifetime employment does not prevail. Indeed, the labor turnover rates are high when compared with the low rates in Japan. Turnover is primarily attributable to people quitting their job rather than being dismissed. All in all, Korean management is different from both Japanese and U.S. management practices.[12]

Selected Factors Influencing Managing in Other Countries[13]

Managing in *Australia* is influenced by that country's moralistic stance and its emphasis on political and social values, achievement, and risk taking.

Italian managers are operating in an environment of low tolerance for risks. Italians are very competitive, but at the same time they like group decision making.

Management in *Austria* (and *Germany*) is characterized by self-realization and leadership. Independence and competitiveness are valued. The tolerance for risk taking is rather low.

In *Britain*, security is important, and so are resourcefulness, adaptability, and logic. Similarly, individualism is also highly valued.

Preparing Foreign Managers for Work in the United States

With the increasing investment of foreign firms in the United States, more attention must be given to the integration of managers and workers from other countries into American society.[14] This need is highlighted by the fact that the number of intercompany transferees more than tripled from the late 1970s to the mid-1980s. The Japanese, for example, often find it difficult to be outspoken and direct in their interactions with their colleagues and especially with their superiors. People from Arabian countries usually find American teaching methods too impersonal.

Various approaches have been used to reduce culture shock. These include special programs about corporate life in the United States, as well as instruction in English, books, and movies; even tax advice is given to the newcomers. Some companies have found the buddy system useful for making the foreigner feel comfortable in the new environment. In this approach an American looks after the needs of the newcomer. Other firms use role playing to demonstrate alternative types of managerial behavior. Because of their cultural background, Japanese managers usually find it rather difficult to conduct an American-style performance review that focuses on results.

In the past, training and development focused on preparing U.S. managers and workers for overseas assignments. Increasingly, firms are realizing that they need to help foreigners reduce the culture shock they may experience upon coming to America.

JAPANESE MANAGEMENT AND THEORY Z[15]

Japan, one of the leading industrial nations in the world, has adopted managerial practices that are quite different from those of economically advanced countries in the Western world. The discussion below deals with two common Japanese practices: lifetime employment and consensus decision making. This is followed by a discussion of Theory Z. In the closing sections of Parts 2 to 6 of this book, other managerial practices in Japan are discussed and compared with those in the United States and the People's Republic of China.

Lifetime Employment

Important features of Japanese management practice are lifelong employment for permanent employees (related to the staffing function), great concern for the individual employee, and emphasis on seniority. Typically, employees spend their working life with a single enterprise, which in turn provides employees with security and a feeling of belonging. This practice brings the culturally induced concept of *wa* (harmony) to the enterprise, resulting in employee loyalty and close identification with the aims of the company.

However, it also adds to business costs, because employees are kept on the payroll even though there may be insufficient work. Consequently, firms are beginning to question the practice of lifelong employment. Indeed, changes appear to be in the making,[16] but they are slow—very slow. What is often overlooked, however, is that this permanent employment practice is used primarily by large firms. In fact, it is estimated that the job security system applies to only about one-third of the labor force.[17]

Closely related to lifelong employment is the seniority system, which has provided privileges for older employees who have been with the enterprise a long time. But there are indications that the seniority system may be superseded by a more open approach that provides opportunities for advancement for young people. For example, the relatively new Sony Corporation has team leaders (a point is made of not calling them supervisors) who are often young women of 18 or 19. There is little age difference between them and the operators they lead.

Decision Making in Japan

The managerial practice of decision making in Japan is also considerably different from that in the United States. It is built on the concept that change and new ideas come primarily from below. Thus, lower-level employees prepare proposals for higher-level personnel. Supervisors, rather than simply accepting or rejecting the proposals, tactfully question them, make suggestions, and encourage subordinates. If necessary, proposals are sent back to the initiator for more information. Still, in major decisions top management retains its power.

Japanese management, then, uses decision making by consensus to deal with everyday problems; lower-level employees initiate an idea and submit it to the next higher level, until it reaches the desk of the top executive. If the proposal is approved, it is returned to the initiator for implementation. Although the decision-making process is time-consuming, the implementation of the decision—because of the general consensus at various levels of management—is swift and does not require additional "selling."

An important characteristic of Japanese decision making is the large amount of effort that goes into defining the question or problem; there is a great deal of communication *before* a decision is actually made. American managers are often accused of making decisions before defining the problem. In contrast, Japanese management makes a decision only after long discussions of the issue.

In summary, Japanese managerial practice still emphasizes (although changes are occurring) lifetime employment, concern for the individual, seniority, and a sense of loyalty to the firm. Furthermore, in decision making there is open communication among people at different levels of the organizational hierarchy, a great deal of collaboration, and a recognition of mutual dependence.

Theory Z[18]

In **Theory Z,** selected Japanese managerial practices are adapted to the environment of the United States. This approach is practiced by companies such as IBM, Hewlett-Packard, and the diversified retail company Dayton-Hudson.[19] One of the characteristics of Type Z organization, as suggested by Professor William Ouchi, is an emphasis on the interpersonal skills that are needed for group interaction. Yet despite the emphasis on group decision making, responsibility remains with the individual (which is quite different from the Japanese practice, which empha-sizes collective responsibility). There is also an emphasis on informal and demo-cratic relationships based on trust. Yet the hierarchical structure still remains intact, as illustrated by IBM, where not only goals but also authority, rules, and discipline guide corporate behavior.[20]

Participative management facilitates the free flow of information needed to reach a consensus. Formal planning and objectives are important, but numerical measures are not overly emphasized. Instead, a corporate philosophy and corporate values guide managerial actions. People are seen as whole human beings, not simply as factors in production. In short, Theory Z companies selectively use some Japanese managerial practices but make adjustments for the environment prevailing in the United States.

Japanese Companies Operating in the United States[21]

In an attempt to demonstrate the effectiveness of Japanese managerial approaches, success stories of Japanese companies operating in the United States are often cited. Workers at Sony's television plant in San Diego are said to produce as well as workers in Japan. But other cases are not quite as convincing. YKK, Inc., a manufacturer of zippers, has experienced labor-management confrontations similar to those experienced by U.S. companies. At Sanyo's television and microwave plant in Forrest City, Arkansas, a violent strike resulted in bitterness and mistrust.[22] At any rate, the trend of Japanese firms investing in manufacturing facilities in the United States is probably going to continue.

International Perspective

Bridgestone Tire Company[23]

The Bridgestone Corporation, a Japanese tire firm that took over the Firestone Tire & Rubber Company plant in Tennessee, was able not only to smooth the stormy labor relations that had plagued the company for years but also to improve both productivity and quality. Some of the methods used to achieve these results were indeed rather traditional. They included investing in new equipment, setting high quality standards, and using a disciplined managerial approach that required employees to work harder and to give up some seniority provisions, thus allowing the company to fill key positions with the most suitable employees. Moreover, employees were also asked to participate in decisions that affected them and their jobs. For example, workers, not just inspectors, now have responsibility for the quality of the products. And this was done with the cooperation of the union. Bridgestone also used a management-by-objectives approach that is built on the concept of self-control and self-direction.

While the early successes were remarkable, the company encountered problems in the 1990s that actually started earlier. In 1988, General Motors virtually eliminated Firestone as a tire supplier. The 1989–1990 car production decrease hurt not only Firestone/Bridgestone but the tire industry in general. Expansion plans had to be changed. Still, Bridgestone works hard to improve product quality. Changes have also been initiated in management. Managers who had their offices at headquarters were moved to open offices close to the production line.

THE MANAGERIAL FUNCTIONS IN INTERNATIONAL BUSINESS

There is evidence that management fundamentals are applicable in different countries. However, the practice of carrying out the managerial functions of planning, organizing, staffing, leading, and controlling differs considerably in domestic and international enterprises, as shown in Table 4-2.

Planning in the Multinational Corporation

Planning requires setting objectives and then selecting strategies, policies, programs, and procedures for achieving them. A critically important activity for the MNC is the assessment of opportunities and threats in the external environment. This is a complex task even for a domestic enterprise, but it becomes much more intricate when many different, ever-changing world markets must be scanned.

External threats and opportunities must be matched with the internal strengths and weaknesses of the firm. For example, a poor educational system makes it difficult to find qualified personnel. Similarly, cultural orientation toward time will affect planning. Specifically, cultural attitudes that emphasize a short time perspective will not be conducive to long-range planning.[24] Finally, political and economic instability in a country makes it difficult to forecast and will discourage long-term commitment of resources.

Even large multinational companies may find it difficult to compete in the world market. Therefore, they form global strategic partnerships (GSPs).[25] General

TABLE 4-2 MANAGING DOMESTIC AND INTERNATIONAL ENTERPRISES

Managerial functions	Domestic enterprise (industrialized country)	International enterprise
Planning:		
Scanning the environment for threats and opportunities	National market	Worldwide market
Organizing:		
1. Organization structure	Structure for domestic operations	Global structure
2. View of authority	Similar	Different
Staffing:		
1. Sources of managerial talent	National labor pool	Worldwide labor pool
2. Manager orientation	Often ethnocentric	Geocentric
Leading:		
1. Leadership and motivation	Influenced by similar culture	Influenced by many different cultures
2. Communication lines	Relatively short	Network with long distances
Controlling:		
Reporting system	Similar requirements	Many different requirements

Motors formed a joint venture with Toyota to produce cars at the Fremont plant in California.[26] American Telephone and Telegraph Company shares technology with Olivetti and Philips,[27] large multinational corporations in Europe. Kodak works with a Japanese company to produce some of its cameras. Clearly, success of the GSPs will depend on balancing cooperation with competitiveness among the firms.

Organizing the Multinational Corporation

Organization structures are established to achieve corporate objectives. A company can select from a great variety of structures.[28] An enterprise may, for example, establish a vice-presidential position at corporate headquarters with responsibility for the international division. An alternative is to organize according to geographic areas. For example, managers may be put in charge of regions such as North America, Latin America, Europe, Africa, and the Far East. Still another way of grouping organizational activities is according to product lines. For instance, at corporate headquarters, managers may be put in charge of a product line that is marketed worldwide. The truly multinational firm may integrate domestic and international business into a global structure that gives similar importance to domestic and foreign business activities.

Each structure has advantages and limitations, as discussed in Chapter 10. It is important to realize that for the large multinational corporation any one structure may be insufficient. Consequently, different organizational designs may have to be mixed, depending on the environmental and task demands.

International Perspective

What GE Learned in France

Even the most brilliant strategic move may be thwarted by the organization culture.[29] GE learned this lesson when it acquired Cie. Generale de Radiologie (CGR), the French medical equipment maker, in order to gain a foothold in this field in Europe. The clash of organization cultures soon became apparent. GE's culture is influenced by its CEO, John F. Welch, Jr., who emphasizes hard work, self-reliance, and profit orientation. This philosophy is in contrast to the culture in the formerly government-owned, sedate company. Moreover, the fact that most key managerial positions were staffed by Americans was resented.

An apparently minor incident created major problems. In a training session, French and other European managers were asked to wear colorful GE shirts with the slogan "Go for One." The French participants felt that this requirement was humiliating. Moreover, the display in English of the company slogan was resented by the French employees. In another situation, GE managers with the attitude "we have the best methods" wanted to install a new financial-reporting system. Again there was resistance. Reducing the work force to turn the uncompetitive firm around caused further problems. The lesson to be learned is that acquiring companies with different organization cultures requires careful planning and even more careful implementation.

Staffing in the Multinational Corporation[30]

The positions identified in the organization structure must be filled by qualified persons. This involves staffing.

Sources of managerial talent.
Managers of the MNC can be classified in three ways. First, managers may be nationals selected from the country in which the head-quarters is located. These expatriates (with *home-country nationality*) are chosen to represent and manage the enterprise abroad. These managers, because of their experience, are usually familiar with the parent company's policies and operations.

Second, a firm may select managers who are *nationals of the host country*. These managers are familiar with the country's environment, its education system, its culture, its legal and political processes, and its economic environment. They usually also know local customers, suppliers, government officials, behavioral characteristics of employees, and the public in general.

The third group of managerial personnel consists of *third-country nationals*. These are managers who have a nationality that is different from the parent company country or the host country. Such managers may have gained experience by working at the company headquarters as well as in different countries. Thus, they would have developed behavioral flexibility that eases their adaptation to different cultures. These managers may be truly transcultural.

Factors affecting the trend in staffing multinational corporations.
Each of the three sources of managers has advantages and disadvantages, and a firm may use a variety of combinations. A few factors that influence the trend in staffing MNCs are worth noting. First, the cost of sending U.S. managers abroad has increased, partly owing to the declining value of the U.S. dollar in the 1970s and in 1986. Second, people in the host countries are now better prepared to assume responsible managerial positions. While conducting management development programs in Singapore, Hong Kong, and Taipei, one of the authors found that the quality of middle managers measured up to that of their counterparts in the United States. Finally, employing nationals of the host country can improve relations with that country. Therefore, as far as American firms are concerned, the trend is toward employing more host-country nationals than managers from the parent company.[31]

Leading in the Multinational Corporation

Leading involves motivating and communicating. It requires exerting leadership by inducing employees to contribute to enterprise objectives.

Motivating and leading demand an understanding of employees and their cultural environment. For instance, participative management may work well in one country but may cause confusion among employees in another country with a tradition of autocratic rule.

Communication is often a problem in multinational firms with subsidiaries and affiliates in countries where different languages are spoken. Even a firm with operations in a country where English is the primary language may encounter communication problems because of the distance between headquarters and the subsidiary. But new communications technology has greatly improved the transmission of information. Still, a telephone call is not quite the same as a visit and a person-to-person discussion.

Controlling in the Multinational Corporation

Controlling—the measurement and correction of performance to ensure that events conform to plans—is an essential managerial function that is influenced by several environmental factors unique to international enterprises. First, revenues, costs, and profits are measured in different currencies. Second, the ratios between currencies are subject to considerable fluctuations. Third, accounting practices and financial reporting often differ from country to country. For example, accounting procedures may have to satisfy the demands of tax authorities of the host country as well as the government of the parent firm. The procedures must also satisfy stockholders in various countries, agencies in charge of regulating securities, and banks. In addition, procedures must be suitable to meet the internal requirements of the firm. Developing a procedure that meets all these demands at the same time is extremely difficult. Finally, and partly owing to the complex nature of measurement, there is a time lag in the measurement of performance that may delay detecting deviations from standards and initiating corrective action. Computers, however, have done much to speed up the process. All in all, then, these few examples indicate that controlling the international corporation is considerably more difficult than monitoring a domestic operation.

COMPARATIVE MANAGEMENT

Comparative management is defined as *the study and analysis of management in different environments and the reasons that enterprises show different results in various countries.*[32] Management is an important element in economic growth and in the improvement of productivity.

Management as a Critical Element in Economic Growth

In light of the increasing concern for economic growth, it is natural for social scientists to look for underlying causes of that growth.[33] Why does one country have a higher per capita national income than another? Or why do productivity increases differ in various countries?

Concern for productivity and economic growth.[34] Because of the disparity in national incomes and the problems caused in much of the world by incomes that do not allow for adequate subsistence, let alone the raising of cultural standards, the attention of world leaders and development economists has naturally turned to the need for increasing productivity.[35]

The necessities of economic development were thought to be the transfer of technology, education, and capital. But as important as these are, it is now recognized that advanced managerial know-how is essential and often overlooked as an element responsible for growth and improved productivity.[36]

Although one must grant that pure technical knowledge is necessary for economic growth, such knowledge is fairly easy to transfer between countries, and no nation holds a monopoly on it for very long. Even a technological development as sophisticated as that of the atomic bomb, whose secrecy was closely protected by the United States, became known in Russia, France, China, and elsewhere in less than two decades. Most advances in technology are neither as complex nor as well guarded, and so their transfer is not likely to be difficult, particularly when one realizes that in any country only a few people need to have this knowledge to make it available for use.

On the other hand, cultural factors such as the level of education and, in particular, knowledge of skills have an important impact on economic progress. Also, cultural variables such as the desire for the products and services can be significant. Similar constraints on economic progress are a large number of political factors, such as fiscal policy, labor regulations, business restrictions, and foreign policy. But even with these and other constraints that may limit managerial excellence, qualified managers can do much to bring economic progress to a society by identifying constraints and by designing a managerial approach or technique to take them into account.

International Perspective

Porter's Competitive Advantage of Nations[37]

Michael Porter, a Harvard Business School professor, questions the economic theory of comparative advantage. He suggests four sets of factors that contribute to a nation's well-being. The first set pertains to factor conditions such as a nation's resources, its labor costs, and the skills and education of its people. The second set consists of the demand conditions of a nation, such as the market size, the way products may be advertised, and the degree of consumer sophistication. The third set of factors in Porter's model concerns the suppliers. A company prospers when supporting companies are located in the same area. The fourth factor set consists of the firm's strategy and structure as well as rivalry among the competitors.

The combination of the four sets of factors leads to competitive advantage. When only two sets are favorable, competitive advantage usually cannot be sustained. On the other hand, the availability of resources is not always necessary. Japan, for example, lacks natural resources, yet the country prospers. In fact, economic hardship may stimulate economic activity and success, as illustrated by Japan and Germany after World War II. However, these two countries have consumers who demand sophisticated products of high quality. Similarly, Japanese and German companies have good relationships with their suppliers. They also benefit from good educational systems and a skilled labor force.

> Despite the cooperation among Japanese companies on certain levels, they are also fiercely competitive.
>
> Porter offers various suggestions for making the United States more competitive. They include measures such as allowing banks to own equity in firms (as in Germany), prohibiting alliances and mergers among leading competitors, allowing selective investment tax credits to stimulate innovation, making the filing of unwarranted lawsuits more difficult,[38] and promoting rivalry among competitors.

The need for management theory and practice.   The United States has generally been recognized as an early leader in the development of management know-how. The value of the M.B.A. degree is increasingly recognized around the world. Many U.S. schools offer M.B.A. degrees abroad. For example, the University of San Francisco offers an Executive M.B.A. program in Hong Kong for managers from the People's Republic of China.

Although U.S. managers now look increasingly to Japan for improving productivity, the Japanese still send many of their managers to business schools in the United States.[39] Most scholars regard the issue of comparative management as one of transferring American, and perhaps Japanese, management knowledge and practice to developed and less developed countries. It is interesting to note that, in the past, European managers did not look toward Japan for managerial leadership; rather, they adopted traditional American practices such as strategic planning, decentralization of decision making, and incentive systems.[40] More recently, however, German and American car companies have been using the Japanese managerial model in setting up their plants in former East Germany. What is needed for economic progress and improved productivity is a way of coordinating human resources for achievement of the mission of the enterprise. This demands sound management theory and practice, irrespective of their national origin.

A New Management Frontier?

In the past, many countries looked to the United States for answers for their economic and managerial development. Increasingly, however, a number of Asian countries are turning their attention to the Japanese model.[41] The French writer Jean-Jacques Servan-Schreiber, who at one time had high praise for American managerial approaches, now thinks that some of the Asian nations, through the use of microtechnology, will play an increasingly important role in business. While there is still the search for economic solutions to development,[42] the need for managerial know-how becomes evident. The rapid economic developments in places such as Hong Kong, Singapore, South Korea, and Taiwan need to be accompanied by more systematic approaches to managing. Although relatively little empirical research on management in these countries exists today,[43] the well-attended business and management conferences in Pacific Basin countries may give an indication of research in the future.

The Modified Koontz Model of Comparative Management[44]

In comparing management in various countries, Professors Richard N. Farmer and Barry M. Richman—two pioneers in comparative management—emphasized that environments external to the firm do affect management practices.[45] These authors were the first to identify the critical elements in the management process and to evaluate their operation in firms in different cultures. They also described the environmental factors they considered to have a significant impact on the management process and managerial excellence. These factors, viewed as constraints, are classified as (1) educational variables, (2) sociocultural and ethical variables, (3) legal and political variables, and (4) economic variables.* How these environmental factors (abbreviated as "Ed," "Sc," "Lp," and "Ec" in Table 4-3) may influence the managerial functions (Pl, Or, St, Le, Co) and enterprise functions (En, Pr, Ma, Fi) is illustrated by the arrows in Table 4-3.

The importance of nonmanagerial factors.   Management knowledge does not by any means encompass all the knowledge that is utilized in an enterprise. The specialized knowledge, or science, in such basic areas as engineering, production, marketing, and finance is essential to enterprise operation. Many enterprises have been successful, despite poor management, because of brilliant marketing, strong engineering, well-designed and well-operated production facilities, or astute financing.[46] Excellence in management will ultimately make the difference between continued success and decline. Yet it is still true that enterprises may, for a time, succeed entirely through nonmanagerial factors.

A new approach to comparative management.   Enterprise activities fall into two broad categories, managerial and nonmanagerial. Either or both can be the causal factors—at least to some degree—for enterprise excellence. Also, nonmanagerial activities will be affected by the relevant underlying science or knowledge, just as managerial activities will be affected by the underlying management science. Both types of activities will be affected by the availability of human and material resources and by the constraints and influences of the external environment, whether these are educational, political and legal, economic, technological, or sociocultural/ethical.

If the factors affecting enterprise excellence and the role of the underlying management science are to be brought to light more clearly than has been done, then a model of the kind shown in Figure 4-2 is needed.

---

* One could add technological factors, but it is relatively easy to transfer technology. Therefore, technology is often very similar in developed countries. However, in the comparison of developed and less developed countries, the impact of technology on the managerial and enterprise functions must be considered.

TABLE 4-3 THE IMPACT OF EXTERNAL FACTORS ON MANAGERIAL AND ENTERPRISE FUNCTIONS AND ACTIVITIES

Functions and activities	Environmental factors			
	Educational (Ed)	Sociocultural-ethical (Sc)	Legal-political (Lp)	Economic (Ec)
Managerial functions				
Planning (Pl) (Objectives, strategies, policies, programs, procedures, decision making)	Ed → Pl	**Japan:** Consultation in decision making; upward flow of decisions	**France:** Planning within guidelines by government (Le Plan)	Ec → Pl
Organizing (Or) (Structure, roles, grouping of activities, authority and responsibility, coordination)	Ed → Or	**Japan:** authority often based on seniority; respect for age	**Germany:** codetermination; worker representation on supervisory board and executive committee	Ed → Or
Staffing (St) (Work-force requirements, selection, appraisal, compensation, training)	**Japan:** Education determines career; good schools are essential for success	**Japan:** Lifelong employment	**Germany:** Labor participates in major staffing decisions in major firms	Ec → St
Leading (Le) (Motivation, leadership, communication)	Ed → Le	**Japan:** Loyalty to the firm **Germany:** Benevolent-authoritarian leadership	Lp → Le **Germany:** Laws requiring companies to put worker representatives on supervisory board and executive committee	Ec → Le
Controlling (Co) (Standards, measurement, correction)	Ed → Co	**Japan:** Participation in quality control circles	Lp → Co	Ec → Co
Enterprise functions				
Engineering, research, and development (En)	Ed → En	Sc → En	Lp → En	Ec → En
Production (Pr)	Ed → Pr	**Japan:** Group information in quality circles	Lp → Pr	**Japan** and **Germany:** Emphasis on productivity
Marketing (Ma)	Ed → Ma	Sc → Ma	Lp → Ma	Ec → Ma
Finance (Fi)	Ed → Fi	Sc → Fi	Lp → Fi	**Japan:** Banks facilitate debt financing

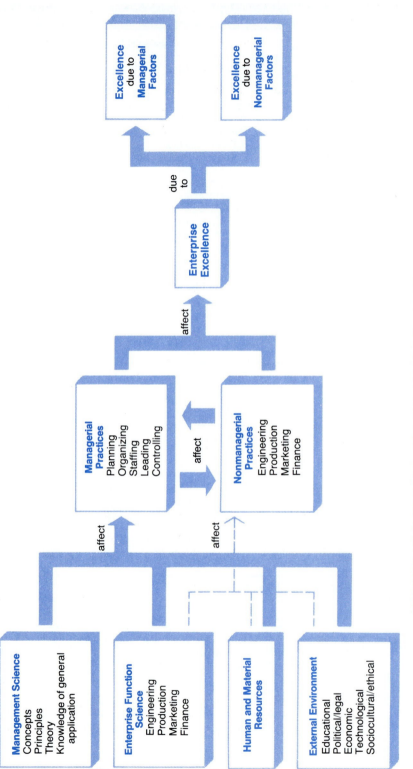

FIGURE 4-2

MODIFIED KOONTZ MODEL FOR ANALYZING COMPARATIVE MANAGEMENT.

Adapted from Harold Koontz, "A Model for Analyzing the Universality and Transferability of Management," *Academy of Management Journal* (December 1969), pp. 415–429.

This model is far more complex than those used by previous researchers in the field of comparative management. It is also believed to be far more accurate and realistic. If the purpose of researchers is to study comparative management, something like this must be prepared in order to understand and see the elements of universality in management.

Rather than viewing factors in the environment simply as "constraints"—a term that has a negative connotation—it is preferable to consider them as environmental "factors"; they may be either constraints or opportunities. For example, in the economic category of factor endowments, a country may be short on capital but rich in natural resources. Similarly, some laws may be restrictive for conducting business, but others may be favorable. Therefore, environment restraints could become opportunities in certain situations.

Increasingly, managers need to adopt a global perspective in leading their enterprises. This requires an understanding of managerial practices in various countries. The proposed model of comparative management helps identify the factors that contribute to managerial and organizational excellence.

SUMMARY

International businesses extend their operations across national boundaries. The educational, sociocultural/ethical, political-legal, and economic environments have a particular impact on international enterprises. Multinational corporations (MNCs) have developed different orientations for operating in foreign countries, ranging from ethnocentric (the foreign operation is based on the parent company's views) to geocentric (the organization is viewed as an interdependent system operating in many countries; that is, it is truly international).

Managerial practices differ in various countries. In France, for example, government planning greatly influences the planning and direction of enterprises. In Germany, the use of authority and the concept of codetermination shape managerial practices. In Korea, managerial practices developed that are different from those in Japan and the United States. American organizations have to be concerned not only about preparing their managers for working abroad but also about preparing foreign managers for working in the United States.

Japanese managerial practices differ greatly from those in the United States. Theory Z, which involves selected Japanese managerial practices, has been adopted by some U.S. companies.

While management fundamentals are applicable in different countries, the practice of carrying out the managerial functions differs in domestic and international enterprises. For example, in an international enterprise, planning is done with a worldwide market in mind. The organization is characterized by a global structure. In staffing, personnel are drawn from a worldwide labor pool. In leading, the many cultural differences are taken into account. And in controlling, the different requirements (for example, for tax purposes) of the various countries must be taken into account.

Comparative management is the study and analysis of management in different environments and the reasons that enterprises show different results in various countries. Management is a critical element for achieving economic growth. Management fundamentals (concepts, theory, and principles) are fairly universal. But the application of the fundamentals differs greatly in various countries; it is the know-how involved in applying knowledge that is different. To overcome some of the limitations of traditional comparative management models, the modified Koontz model is introduced.

KEY IDEAS AND CONCEPTS FOR REVIEW

International business
Exportation
Licensing
Management contract
Joint venture
Subsidiaries
Multinational corporation
Ethnocentric orientation
Polycentric orientation
Regiocentric orientation
Geocentric orientation
Global corporation
Management practices in France

Management practices in Germany
Management practices in Korea
Management practices in Japan and
  Theory Z
Managerial functions in multinational
  corporations
Comparative management
Impact of environmental factors on
  enterprises
Management theory and practice
Modified Koontz model of comparative
  management

FOR DISCUSSION

1. What advantages do multinational corporations have? What challenges must they meet? Give examples.
2. What are some key characteristics of French, German, Korean, and Japanese management practices?
3. What is Theory Z?
4. Compare the ways the managerial functions are carried out in domestic and multinational corporations. Select five differences and discuss their importance.
5. Do you think the managerial concepts and practices applied in the United States can be transferred to England, France, Germany, or any country you know? Explain.

EXERCISES/ACTION STEPS

1. Contact a foreign firm operating in the United States, and interview one or more managers. How do the managerial practices in the U.S. operation differ from those in the firm's home country? Does the firm use host country or parent company managers?
2. From your knowledge of any foreign country, outline the major elements of its culture that would, in your judgment, influence managerial practices in that country.

CASES

INTERNATIONAL CASE 4-1
HONDA MOVES TO THE UNITED STATES[47]

Honda has debunked the auto industry's claim that "nobody can make an economy car in the United States at a profit." Not only is Honda's plant in Marysville, Ohio, profitable, it is said, but its cars are as well built as those made in Japan.

Since Honda holds only a relatively small share of the Japanese car market (in 1990 it ranked fourth in Japan, behind Mitsubishi), it needed an outlet to grow. In the early 1970s, when gas became scarce and expensive, Honda introduced its fuel-efficient cars in the United States. Strong demand and growing trade friction convinced Honda that it needed to repeat the strategy that worked for its motorcycles: build a U.S. operation. The first cars rolled out in 1983—the year quotas became effective. In 1985, Honda outsold both Nissan and Toyota and became the fourth largest car manufacturer in the United States.

The Marysville plant is not demonstrably more automated than American factories, but it works differently. All employees are treated as equals. Workers are chosen for their team skills as well as their expertise. A quarter of the first employees spent up to 3 months in Honda's plant in Japan. When they returned, they taught their coworkers how to assemble cars in teams.

New workers spend several weeks practicing on training cars before they are assigned to a team. Team members trade jobs and learn as many tasks as they can. Team leaders check the quality of the work and help the team in any way they can (solving problems, replacing an absent member, and so on).

Honda attributes its success to workers who are willing to work hard for the company. The "equal partnership" gives employees a stake in the company. Mr. Honda believes that all employees are equally important. Everyone, including the plant manager, wears coveralls and shares the facilities (same lunchroom, washrooms, parking). All employees can help make decisions. Initially, workers were surprised that their supervisors asked them for advice.

The workers are very proud of their work. They like working at Honda, even though they earn roughly 20 percent less than other U.S. autoworkers. Honda's labor costs are about 60 percent lower than the industry average because it has a lower overhead per worker.

Honda expects suppliers to establish the same quality standards it uses. It was willing to help U.S. parts suppliers that did not meet them. Those who insisted that Honda could simply return defective parts were replaced by Japanese suppliers. Some of them have built plants near Marysville, which, in turn, has helped Honda minimize inventory.

Although most U.S. manufacturers barely break even on compacts, Honda earns a handsome profit on each car, and it sells every car it makes. And while this is only half the profit Honda earns on the cars it imports from Japan, it expects the difference to narrow as the workers in the U.S. plant learn to be more efficient.

Now that the company is well established in the U.S. car market, Honda plans to double its U.S. capacity and build luxury cars, which should be more profitable than the less expensive cars. Honda attempts to avoid problems from its low-cost image by selling its luxury cars under another name—Acura—through different dealerships. Far from importing the large, old-fashioned Japanese luxury cars, Honda is developing "European-style" models specifically for the U.S. market. European styling has two advantages: It appeals to the growing number of young professionals, and the cars are small enough that they can be built on Honda's existing compact-car production lines.

1. Why did Honda build a plant in the United States (what were the objectives)? How is the plant in the United States affecting the company in Japan? What problems or advantages might the U.S. operation give Honda in the future?

2. Why was Honda able to build economy cars in the

United States when American car manufacturers could not? What advantages does Honda have over the American companies?

3. How much of Honda's success is due to its policies? How much is due to nonmanagerial factors?

INTERNATIONAL CASE 4-2
WOMAN CEO MANAGES BY THE TEXTBOOK[48]

The demand for managers with an international background is great. Consider Marisa Bellisario, one of the most sought-after executives in Europe in 1984. She was the first woman to head a major industrial firm in Italy, the state-controlled ITALTEL Societa Italiana. This company is the biggest Italian firm making telecommunications equipment. Bellisario's background, however, is international. After receiving her degree in economics and business administration from Turin University, she worked at Olivetti in the electronics division. When Olivetti sold its data processing unit to General Electric, she spent time in Miami working on GE's worldwide marketing strategy for computers. She left GE to head corporate planning at Olivetti. As the CEO at ITALTEL, she turned the company around, showing a small profit. (The firm had experienced huge losses in the past.) Her managerial approach has been characterized as "straight out of the textbook," and companies such as GTE Corporation, IBM, AT&T, and other European and Japanese firms are interested in recruiting her.

1. Why was Ms. Bellisario a much-sought-after CEO? What was her career path?
2. What special problems may she have encountered as a woman heading a major company in Italy?
3. If she was successful managing by the textbook, why do some managers still think that management cannot be taught?

REFERENCES

1. John Hoerr, "What Mario Wants: Supply Side for Workers," *Business Week* (Apr. 11, 1988), p. 79.
2. An increasing number of overseas ventures combine direct investment, licensing, and trade. Farok J. Contractor, "A Generalized Theorem for Joint-Venture and Licensing Negotiations," *Journal of International Business Studies* (Summer 1985), pp. 23–50.
3. Sara Hammes and Richard S. Teitelbaum, "The Global 500—How They Performed in 1990," *Fortune* (July 29, 1991), pp. 238–245.
4. David A. Heenan and Howard V. Perlmutter, *Multinational Organization Development* (Reading, Mass.: Addison-Wesley Publishing Company, 1979), chap. 2.
5. Robert B. Reich, "Who Is Them?" *Harvard Business Review* (March–April 1991), pp. 77–88.
6. Based on a presentation at the 10th Annual International Conference "Strategic Bridging" held in Stockholm, Sept. 24–27, 1990, and William Taylor, "The Logic of Global Business: An Interview with ABB's Percy Barnevik," *Harvard Business Review* (March–April 1991), pp. 91–105.
7. Jeremy Main, "How to Go Global—and Why," *Fortune* (Aug. 28, 1989), pp. 70–76.
8. See also Richard M. Hodgetts and Fred Luthans, *International Management* (New York: McGraw-Hill, 1991).

9. "France—An Electronics Plan with Global Ambitions," *Business Week* (May 31, 1982), p. 39.

10. Jean-Louis Barsoux and Peter Lawrence, "The Making of a French Manager," *Harvard Business Review* (July–August 1991), pp. 58–67.

11. See Simcha Ronen, *Comparative and Multinational Management* (New York: John Wiley & Sons, 1986), chap. 9; David Heenan, *The Re-United States of America* (Reading, Mass.: Addison-Wesley Publishing Company, 1983), chap. 1.

12. For more information on Korean management, see Jon P. Alston, "Wa, Guanxi, and Inhwa: Managerial Principles in Japan, China, and Korea," *Business Horizons* (March–April 1988), pp. 26–31; S. M. Lee and S. Yoo, "The K-Type Management: A Driving Force for Korean Prosperity," *Management International Review* (April 1987), pp. 68–77; T. W. Kang, *Is Korea the Next Japan?* (New York: The Free Press, 1989).

13. See Ronen, *Comparative and Multinational Management* (1986). See also the extensive studies by Geert Hofstede, such as "The Cultural Relativity of Organizational Practices and Theories," *Journal of International Business Studies*, vol. 14, no. 2 (1983), pp. 75–90, and "Motivation, Leadership and Organization: Do American Theories Apply Abroad?" *Organizational Dynamics*, no. 9 (1983), pp. 42–63; Klaus Macharzina and Wolfgang H. Staehle (eds.), *European Approaches to International Management* (Hawthorne, N.J.: Walter de Gruyter, 1986); Gary Clyde Hufbauer (ed.), *Europe 1992—An American Perspective* (Washington, D.C.: The Brookings Institution, 1990).

14. "American Culture Is Often a Puzzle for Foreign Managers in the U.S.," *The Wall Street Journal* (Feb. 12, 1986); Jerry Buckley, "We Learned That Them May Be Us," *U.S. News & World Report* (May 9, 1988), pp. 48–57; William J. Holstein, Pete Engardio, and Dan Cook, "Will Sake and Sour Mash Together," *Business Week* (July 14, 1986), pp. 53–55.

15. For a critique, see Jeremiah J. Sullivan, "A Critique of Theory Z," *Academy of Management Review* (January 1983), pp. 132–142.

16. Masayoshi Kanabayashi, "In Japan, Employees Are Switching Firms for Better Work, Pay," *The Wall Street Journal* (Oct. 11, 1988).

17. Tai K. Oh, "Japanese Management—A Critical Review," *Academy of Management Review* (January 1976), pp. 14–25.

18. See also John E. Rehfeld, "What Working for a Japanese Company Taught Me," *Harvard Business Review* (November–December 1990), pp. 167–176.

19. This discussion is based on William G. Ouchi, *Theory Z* (Reading, Mass.: Addison-Wesley Publishing Company, 1981).

20. "Life at IBM—Rules and Discipline and Praise Shape IBMer's Taut World," *The Wall Street Journal* (Apr. 8, 1982), pp. 1, 14.

21. For a discussion of Japanese influence on American politics and business and some recent frictions between Japan and the United States, see Pat Choate, "Political Advantage: Japan's Campaign for America," *Harvard Business Review* (September–October 1990), pp. 87–103; see also the debate of this article by various authors in "Is Japan 'Buying' U.S. Politics?" *Harvard Business Review* (November–December 1990), pp. 184–200; Akio Morita and Shintaro Ishihara, *Japan That Can Say "No,"* published in Japan by Kobunsha (1989). No English version of this book is available at this time. For a discussion of the book, see David MacEachron, "America: Don't Take 'No' for an Answer," *Harvard Business Review* (March–April 1990), pp. 178–188; the book is also discussed in *Business Week* (Oct. 23, 1989), pp. 78–80, and in Akio Morita, "Racism Underlies Trade Friction," *Fortune* (Jan. 28, 1991), pp. 101–102.

22. John A. Byrne, "At Sanyo's Arkansas Plant the Magic Isn't Working," *Business Week* (July 14, 1986), pp. 51–52.

23. "The Japanese Manager Meets the American Worker," *Business Week* (Aug. 20, 1984), pp. 128–129; Zachary Schiller and Roger Scheffler, "So Far, America Is a Blowout for Bridgestone," *Business Week* (Aug. 6, 1990), pp. 62–63.

24. Institutional investors may have a short time perspective. See Samuel B. Graves and Sandra A. Waddock, "Institutional Ownership and Control: Implications for Long-Term Corporate Strategy," *Academy of Management Executive* (February 1990), pp. 75–83.

25. Howard V. Perlmutter and David A. Heenan, "Cooperate to Compete Globally," *Harvard Business Review* (March–April 1986), pp. 136–152; Jonathan B. Levine and John A. Byrne, "Corporate Odd Couples," *Business Week* (July 21, 1986), pp. 100–105.

26. Doron P. Levin, "GM-Toyota Venture Will Test Ability of Workers in U.S. to Match Japanese," *The Wall Street Journal* (Apr. 5, 1985); William J. Holstein, "Japan, U.S.A.," *Business Week* (July 14, 1986), pp. 45–46.

27. For additional strategies of Philips, see Jonathan Kapstein, "The Big Two of Consumer Electronics: Squeezed—but Fighting Back," *Business Week* (Dec. 30, 1985), pp. 62–64.

28. See also Ronen, *Comparative and Multinational Management* (1986), chap. 8; Paul W. Beamish, J. Peter Killing, Donald J. Lecraw, and Harold Crookell, *International Management* (Homewood, Ill.: Richard D. Irwin, 1990), chap. 6.

29. Mark M. Nelson and E. S. Browning, "GE's Culture Turns Sour at French Unit," *The Wall Street Journal* (July 31, 1990).

30. For a human resource management model, see R. Hal Mason and Robert S. Spich, *Management—An International Perspective* (Homewood, Ill.: Richard D. Irwin, 1987), chap. 8.

31. For cross-cultural training, see J. Stewart Black and Mark Mendenhall, "Cross-Cultural Training Effectiveness: A Review and a Theoretical Framework for Future Research," *Academy of Management Review* (January 1990), pp. 113–136.

32. Richard N. Farmer, in Joseph W. McGuire (ed.), *Contemporary Management—Issues and Viewpoints* (Englewood Cliffs, N.J.: Prentice-Hall, 1974), p. 302.

33. For a discussion of the Economic Development Model, see Karen Paul and Robert Barbato, "The Multinational Corporation in the Less Developed Country: The Economic Development Model versus the North-South Model," *Academy of Management Review* (January 1985), pp. 8–14.

34. See also Michael E. Porter, *The Competitive Advantage of Nations* (New York: The Free Press, 1990); excerpts from the book are in the *Harvard Business Review* (March–April 1990), pp. 73–93.

35. The concern for productivity is shown by the many books on this subject. Rusty S. Byrne reviews eleven such books in the *Harvard Business Review* (September–October 1981), pp. 36–42. In addition, the author discusses newsletters and articles dealing with productivity. Robert N. Mefford found that in a multinational firm operating thirty plants in Europe, Australia, Canada, Latin America, and Asia, the most important factors influencing productivity were managerial performance, the skills of the workers, and the aspect of learning by doing. See his article "Determinants of Productivity Differences in International Manufacturing," *Journal of International Business Studies* (Spring 1986), pp. 63–82.

36. Peter F. Drucker, "Low Wages No Longer Give Competitive Edge," *The Wall Street Journal* (Mar. 16, 1988).

37. Michael E. Porter, "Why Nations Triumph," *Fortune* (Mar. 12, 1990), pp. 94–108; Michael E. Porter, *The Competitive Advantage of Nations* (New York: The Free Press, 1990), especially chap. 3. For a discussion of today's demands of wealthier and more sophisticated consumers see Koh Sera, "Corporate Globalization: A New Trend," *The Academy of Management Executive* (February 1992), pp. 89–96.

38. Now several *Fortune* 500 companies, such as General Mills, sign contracts only with those firms which agree to solve conflicts through a minitrial, mediation, or an alternative dispute resolution (ADR). This may save a company impressive legal costs in solving disputes with customers, suppliers, or employees. It is said that such procedures saved the FDIC $3 million in 1990. For a discussion, see, for example, James F. Henry, "Built-in Protection against Litigation Blues," *The Wall Street Journal* (July 22, 1991).

39. Japanese management practices are discussed earlier in this chapter.

40. "Europe's New Managers—Going Global with a U.S. Style," *Business Week* (May 24, 1982), pp. 116–122.

41. David A. Heenan, *The Re-United States of America* (Reading, Mass.: Addison-Wesley Publishing Company, 1983).

42. Sam C. Hsieh, "A Sequential and Integrated Approach to Economic Development," *Proceedings of the Academy of International Business Southeast Asia Regional Conference, Taipei*, 1986.

43. Dexter C. Dunphy, "The Comparative Study of Managerial Behavior in Eastasia and the West," in Ryine T. Hsieh and Steven A. Scherling (eds.), *Proceedings of the Academy of International Business Southeast Asia Regional Conference, Taipei*, 1986.

44. See also Harold Koontz, "A Model for Analyzing the Universality and Transferability of Management," in Harold Koontz, Cyril O'Donnell, and Heinz Weihrich (eds.), *Management—A Book of Readings*, 5th ed. (New York: McGraw-Hill Book Company, 1980), pp. 88–97.

45. Richard N. Farmer and Barry M. Richman, *Comparative Management and Economic Progress* (Homewood, Ill.: Richard D. Irwin, 1965); Barry M. Richman, "Empirical Testing of a Comparative and International Management Research Model," *Proceedings of the 27th Annual Meeting of the Academy of Management* (Dec. 27–29, 1967), pp. 34–65. Another pioneer and major contributor to comparative management is Professor Negandhi. See Anant R. Negandhi and B. D. Estafen, "A Research Model to Determine the Applicability of American Management Know-How in Differing Cultures and/or Environments," *Academy of Management Journal* (December 1967), pp. 309–318.

46. See, for example, Thomas F. O'Boyle, "German Technology Gains on U.S., Japan," *The Wall Street Journal* (Dec. 15, 1986); Peter F. Drucker, "What We Can Learn from the Germans," *The Wall Street Journal* (Mar. 6, 1986).

47. The case is based on a variety of sources, including W. J. Hampton, "Detroit Beware: Japan Is Ready to Sell Luxury," *Business Week* (Dec. 9, 1985), p. 118; "Here Comes Honda" (interview with Tetsuo Chino), *Barron's* (Dec. 2, 1985), p. 13; Thomas Hout, Michael E. Porter, and Eileen Rudden, "How Global Companies Win Out," *Harvard Business Review* (September–October 1982), pp. 98–108; Faye Rice, "America's New No. 4 Automaker—Honda," *Fortune* (Oct. 28, 1985), p. 30; Stewart Toy, Neil Gross, and James B. Treece, "The Americanization of Honda," *Fortune* (Apr. 25, 1988), pp. 90–96; Clay Chandler and Paul Ingrassia, "Just as U.S. Firms Try Japanese Management, Honda Is Centralizing," *The Wall Street Journal* (Apr. 11, 1991).

48. "ITALTEL's New Chief Gets What She Wants," *Business Week* (Apr. 30, 1984), p. 51; Robert Ball, "Italy's Most Talked-About Executive," *Fortune* (Apr. 2, 1984), pp. 99–102; Marisa Bellisario, "The Turnaround at ITALTEL," *Long Range Planning*, vol. 18, no. 6 (1985), pp. 21–24.

The Basis of Global Management

Management transcends national boundaries. In Chapter 1, the emphasis was on viewing organizations as open systems that interact with the external environment. But the external environment is not limited by national boundaries. Indeed, modern managers have to operate in a global environment. Even firms operating in one country will be affected by international competitive forces. U.S. companies will have to compete more vigorously not only with Pacific Rim companies but also with those belonging to the twelve member nations of the European Community.

The European Community 1992 (EC 1992) program will dramatically change competitive strategies. In Chapter 2, the contributions to management thought of many management scholars and practitioners were highlighted. Many of these contributors were born in the United States, but others, such as Henri Fayol, Hugo Münsterberg, and Max Weber, were born abroad. Still, relatively little has been written about managerial practices in Europe. As the EC 1992 program moves the countries closer toward a unified Europe, more attention is now being paid to the opportunities and threats in Europe. Consequently, the New Europe, with its 340-plus million people, will be discussed in this closing for Part 1, which emphasizes environmental changes in the external environment.

INTERNATIONAL FOCUS:
THE NEW EUROPE: PREPARING FOR THE NEXT DECADE[1]

"Europe 1992" was the year for the completion of the first stage of European economic ties. The EC 1992 program will cause dramatic shifts in economic power. Some see the new program as the New Europe, while others, especially outsiders, see it as a fortress that could provide serious challenges to other countries, including the United States.[2] In order to compete effectively, U.S. and Asian businesses must prepare now for the New Europe.

The Nature of the European Community 1992

The Commission of the European Communities is working on some 300 legislative actions for removing trade barriers and creating an internal market.[3] The desired effects of the new measures are to (1) increase market opportunities, (2) escalate competition within the EC, and (3) boost competition from companies outside the EC. The abolition of transnational trade restrictions and the relaxation of border controls will have a considerable impact on U.S. companies doing business in Europe. Moreover, strong European companies will become formidable competitors in the U.S. market.

The Objective of EC 1992

The objective of the EC 1992 program is to create a single market through the removal of trade barriers, one that will allow the free movement of goods, people, services, and capital.[4] The changes will go beyond economic interests and will encompass many social forces as well; educational degrees, for example, will be affected. The Council of Ministers submitted a directive that would recognize diplomas of higher education across national boundaries.[5] This would make it easier for professionals to work in different countries. It is clear, then, that the EC is more than an economic community; it is a state of mind with political power.[6] At the same time, one may expect less government interference in economic activities.

The Effects of EC 1992 on Selected Countries

The twelve-member European Community consists of Belgium, Denmark, France, Germany, Greece, Ireland, Italy, Luxembourg, the Netherlands, Portugal, Spain, and the United Kingdom. Certain European countries—Austria, Finland, Iceland, Norway, Sweden, and Switzerland—do not belong to the EC.[7] These six countries have been grouped into the European Free Trade Association (EFTA) for more than 25 years. They preferred their independence over being aligned with the EC. They have obtained many of the EC benefits without incurring the costs of belonging. But many of these EFTA countries are concerned about their economic future; they are worried that the new European Community may leave them behind. In fact, Austria, Norway, Sweden, and Turkey have already applied for EC membership or are considering doing so. Denmark is the only Nordic country belonging to the EC. Other Nordic countries have used Denmark as a bridge for doing business with EC members.[8]

When Spain joined the EC, it had problems of inefficiencies and technical backwardness.[9] But all this has changed. During the period 1986–1988, Spain had the fastest growth in gross domestic product in Europe, and Spaniards enjoyed an unprecedented increase in their standard of living. Domestic and foreign investments increased dramatically; for example, foreign investment increased 81 percent in 1987 and continued into 1988.[10] The gradual elimination or reduction of trade barriers may open the floodgate for new products to that country. It has been estimated that multinational marketers control about 50 percent of the total food sales in Spain. Predictions are that Spain will show the fastest growth among the EC countries.[11] But all is not well in Spain. Industry restructuring led to its highest unemployment rate—around 20 percent. Still, 1992 has special meanings (besides the EC program) for Spaniards because of events such as the Olympics in Barcelona, the World's Fair in Seville, and the 500th anniversary of Columbus's voyage to the New World.

France may be the country best prepared for 1992.[12] On the other hand, Spain and Portugal may benefit most, partly because of their open market and their low labor costs. French Premier Michel Rocard is concerned about competition from Germany and Holland.[13] But he also recognizes the benefits of the new EC and is looking forward to increased travel with fewer restrictions. The French people in general are very optimistic about 1992.

Great Britain appears to have a relatively low commitment to the goals of 1992, largely owing to the positions of the unions and politicians. The United Kingdom is benefiting greatly from the Japanese fear of getting locked out of the European market. The British are welcoming investments by the Japanese, who feel comfortable with the English language. Thus in the year ending March 1988, the Japanese invested almost four times as much in Britain as in France, Germany, and Italy combined.[14] This, in turn, caused frictions between former Prime Minister Margaret Thatcher and her European partners. The Japanese were even able to gain nonstrike agreements and flexible work rules from the British labor unions. The Japanese managerial model is considered by many British firms as a key to productivity. Many of them have adopted management techniques such as quality control and just-in-time inventory systems. At any rate, the New Europe will provide challenges for companies around the world. The implications of the New Europe will be discussed throughout this book.

GLOBAL CAR INDUSTRY CASE:
THE CAR MARKET IN THE NEW EUROPE[15]

The European car market is at a crossroads—and the European Community 1992 (EC 1992) program is the reason. Certain European countries, especially Italy and France, had their car market protected from Japanese cars. The question is how EC 1992, which calls for the elimination of trade barriers, will affect European carmakers.

In 1988 and 1989, European manufacturers had excellent sales. Italian Fiat, French Peugeot-Citroen, and German Volkswagen did very well in Europe, the largest market in the world. In the luxury class, Mercedes and BMW maintained a strong market position. However, both firms will be challenged by Japanese upscale models: Nissan's Infiniti and Toyota's Lexus. The German carmakers can hardly argue for Japanese import restrictions unless they are willing to risk constraints from the Japanese, who enjoy the luxury of driving BMW and Mercedes cars in their own country.

But other car manufacturers argued before the EC Commission for indefinite transition rules as 1992 approached. At that time, Italy had established the most stringent barriers to Japanese imports by limiting them to 1 percent of the Italian market. Similarly, France restricted imports of Japanese cars to 3 percent of the total market. In 1988, Italy's car manufacturers Alfa Romeo, Fiat, and Lancia registered 60 percent of the home market, and Peugeot and Renault had over 60 percent of the French market. EC countries other than Italy and France are less restrictive in respect to Japanese car imports. The elimination of all trade barriers would increase the Japanese share of the car market, which has been protected by a variety of overt and covert trade barriers.

There is no agreement on which companies would benefit most from a free market. While some think that Fiat, Peugeot-Citroen, and Volkswagen would gain the most, others suggest that Ford, General Motors, and Volkswagen would be the winners. Ford may indeed be in a unique position. Several years ago, the company began integrating its twenty-two plants in the various EC countries into a truly European firm. In turn, this integrated network resulted in increased productivity, making Ford cars competitive in the car market.

Japanese carmakers traditionally have marketed their cars in Europe by exporting them. Concerned about EC barriers, Japanese firms are positioning themselves to circumvent import restrictions and other indirect barriers such as local content requirements. Toyota, for example, is setting up a manufacturing plant in Great Britain, although the company may have to meet an 80 percent European-parts content requirement. Honda is building a factory in Swindon, England, which, in turn, could increase Honda's European market share. Nissan Motor Corporation has even more ambitious plans for building a factory in northern England, where it has been assembling cars since 1986. Mazda is No. 4 in Japan. But the company is formulating a global strategy through alliances around the world. Cooperation is particularly strong with the Ford Motor Company, which owns 24 percent of Mazda. In fact, 24 percent of cars with the Ford nameplate are made by Mazda. Mazda also has business ties with the Japanese company Suzuki and with France's Citroen. In the meantime, Mazda is shopping for other European partners.

Japanese carmakers will find that it will be more difficult to penetrate the market in Europe than it was in America. Lee Iacocca, Chrysler's CEO, stated in an interview: "Europe has gone to school in (on) the U.S. They will not allow the Japanese to do what they've done here, getting nearly 35 percent of the industry in a decade. There will be competition, but it will be honest competition."

Answer the questions below, or role-play this case.

1. If you were an Italian or French representative, how would you argue before the EC Commission for special rules restricting Japanese imports to Italy?
2. What would be your position before the EC Commission if you were a representative of Great Britain, where many Japanese firms have invested heavily and there is also a strong domestic car industry?

3. As a representative of Germany, what position would you take before the EC Commission?

4. How would you argue your case as a representative of the Japanese car industry?

REFERENCES

1. This section is based on Heinz Weihrich's article in *Academy of Management Executive* (May 1990), pp. 7–18. See also Michael Silva and Bertil Sjoegren, *Europe 1992 and the New World Power Game* (New York: John Wiley & Sons, 1990).

2. Richard A. Melcher, Gregory L. Miles, Gail Schares, Frank J. Comes, and William J. Holstein, "Will the New Europe Cut U.S. Giants Down to Size?" *Business Week* (Dec. 12, 1988), pp. 54–58.

3. Jeremy Thorn, "Exporting: The Community Melting Pot," *Industrial Marketing Digest* (Third Quarter 1988), pp. 51–57; Richard C. Longworth, "The Road to 1992—What a Long, Difficult Trip It's Been," *Europe* (January–February 1992), pp. 6–7.

4. Richard Bailey, "Europe 1992—Dismantling the Barriers: It's Later Than We Think," *Accountancy* (August 1988), pp. 76–77.

5. Josephine Carr, "Contrary to the Spirit of 1992?" *International Financial Law Review* (August 1988), pp. 10–12.

6. Nicholas Colchester, "Europe's Internal Market," *Economist* (July 9, 1988), pp. 5–44.

7. Jules Arbose, "The Anxious 'Little Fish' of Europe," *International Management* (June 1987), pp. 24–33.

8. Kaj Ahlmann, "1992 and the Nordic Countries," *ReActions* (1988), pp. 10, 13.

9. Philip Sington, "A Nation Prepares for 1992," *Euromoney* (June 1988), pp. 2–3; Anonymous, "Catalonia: Spain's Big Battalion," *Euromoney* (April 1988), pp. 1–3.

10. Marina Specht, "Multinationals Eye Spain," *Advertising Age* (Oct. 17, 1988), p. 38.

11. Brian Dumaine, "Buying a Euro-Stake That Will Thrive on the Happenings of 1992," *Fortune* (Jan. 30, 1989), pp. 37–38.

12. John Liscio, "Europe 1992: A Truly Common Market?" *Barron's* (Oct. 3, 1988), pp. 8–9, 20–36.

13. Axel Krause, "Member State Report: France," *Europe* (September 1988), pp. 32–34, 46. France claims that it has Europe's best managed economy, according to Reginald Dale, "France—Pushing to Become the E.C.'s Economic Leader," *Europe* (January–February 1992), pp. 35–38.

14. Richard A. Melcher, Mark Maremont, Amy Borrus, and Thane Peterson, "The Japanese Are Coming—and Thatcher Is All Smiles," *Business Week* (Feb. 20, 1989), pp. 46–47.

15. Richard E. Melcher, "Ford Is Ready to Roll in the New Europe," *Business Week* (Dec. 12, 1988), p. 60; Joann S. Lublin, "Toyota's Plan to Build Cars in Europe Adds to Pressures in Competitive Market," *The Wall Street Journal* (Jan. 30, 1989); Thane Peterson and Amy Borrus, "Japanese Carmakers Flash Their Cash at the EC," *Business Week* (Feb. 13, 1989), pp. 43–46; Keir B. Bonine, "Europe's Carmakers Gear Up for 1992," *Europe* (October 1989), pp. 30–32; Carla Rapoport, "Mazda's Bold New Global Strategy," *Fortune* (Dec. 17, 1990), pp. 109–113; Lee Iacocca's quote is from David J. Morrow, "Iacocca Talks on What Ails Detroit," *Fortune* (Feb. 12, 1990), p. 72; Alex Taylor III, "BMW and Mercedes Make Their Move," *Fortune* (Aug. 12, 1991), pp. 56–63.

PART 2

Planning

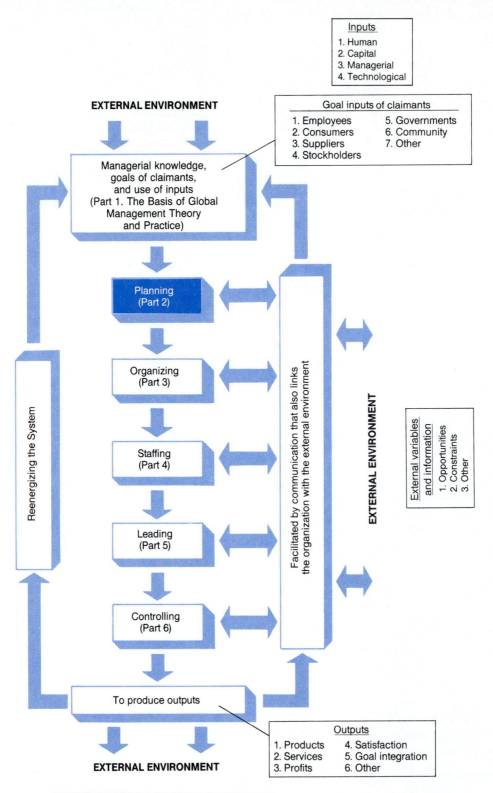

Inputs
1. Human
2. Capital
3. Managerial
4. Technological

Goal inputs of claimants
1. Employees   5. Governments
2. Consumers   6. Community
3. Suppliers   7. Other
4. Stockholders

EXTERNAL ENVIRONMENT

Managerial knowledge,
goals of claimants,
and use of inputs
(Part 1. The Basis of Global
Management Theory
and Practice)

Planning
(Part 2)

Organizing
(Part 3)

Staffing
(Part 4)

Leading
(Part 5)

Controlling
(Part 6)

Reenergizing the System

Facilitated by communication that also links
the organization with the external environment

EXTERNAL ENVIRONMENT

External variables
and information
1. Opportunities
2. Constraints
3. Other

To produce outputs

Outputs
1. Products   4. Satisfaction
2. Services   5. Goal integration
3. Profits   6. Other

EXTERNAL ENVIRONMENT

SYSTEMS APPROACH TO MANAGEMENT

Chapter 5

The Nature and Purpose of Planning

> Planning is a process which begins with objectives; defines strategies, policies, and detailed plans to achieve them; which establishes an organization to implement decisions; and includes a review of performance and feed-back to introduce a new planning cycle.[1]
>
> George A. Steiner

Chapter Objectives

After reading this chapter, you should be able to:

1. Understand what managerial planning is and why it is important.
2. Identify and analyze the various types of plans and show how they relate to one another.
3. Outline and discuss the logical steps in planning and see how these steps are essentially a rational approach to setting objectives and selecting the means of reaching them.
4. Gain an appreciation for the basic principle underlying the determination of how far in the future to plan and how to build desirable flexibility into plans to meet future uncertainties at the lowest cost.
5. Learn the importance of reviewing plans periodically to make sure that they are up to date in light of any new developments.

You are now familiar with basic management theory and have been introduced to the five essential managerial functions: planning, organizing, staffing, leading, and controlling. Chapters 5 to 8 focus on planning and form Part 2 of the book.

In designing an environment for the effective performance of individuals working together in groups, a manager's most essential task is to see that everyone understands the group's purposes and objectives and its methods of attaining them. If group effort is to be effective, people must know what they are expected to accomplish. This is the function of planning. It is the most basic of all the managerial functions. **Planning** involves selecting missions and objectives and the actions to achieve them; it requires decision making, that is, choosing from among alternative future courses of action. Plans thus provide a rational approach to achieving preselected objectives. Planning also strongly implies managerial innovation, as will be discussed in Chapter 8.

Planning bridges the gap from where we are to where we want to go. It makes it possible for things to occur that would not otherwise happen. Although we can seldom predict the exact future and although factors beyond our control may interfere with the best-laid plans, unless we plan, we are leaving events to chance. Planning is an intellectually demanding process; it requires that we consciously determine courses of action and base our decisions on purpose, knowledge, and considered estimates.

THE NATURE OF PLANNING

We can highlight the essential nature of planning by examining its four major aspects: (1) its contribution to purpose and objectives, (2) its primacy among the manager's tasks, (3) its pervasiveness, and (4) the efficiency of resulting plans.

118

The Contribution of Planning to Purpose and Objectives

Every plan and all its supporting plans should contribute to the accomplishment of the purpose and objectives of the enterprise. This concept derives from the nature of the organized enterprise, which exists for the accomplishment of group purpose through deliberate cooperation.

The Primacy of Planning

As you can see in Figure 5-1, since managerial operations in organizing, staffing, leading, and controlling are designed to support the accomplishment of enterprise objectives, planning logically precedes the execution of all the other managerial functions. Although in practice all the functions mesh as a system of action, planning is unique in that it involves establishing the objectives necessary for all group efforts. Besides, a manager must plan in order to know what kinds of organization relationships and personal qualifications are needed, along which course subordinates are to be led, and what kind of control is to be applied. And, of course, all the other managerial functions must be planned if they are to be effective.

Planning and *controlling* are inseparable—the Siamese twins of management (see Figure 5-2). Any attempt to control without plans is meaningless, since there

FIGURE 5-1

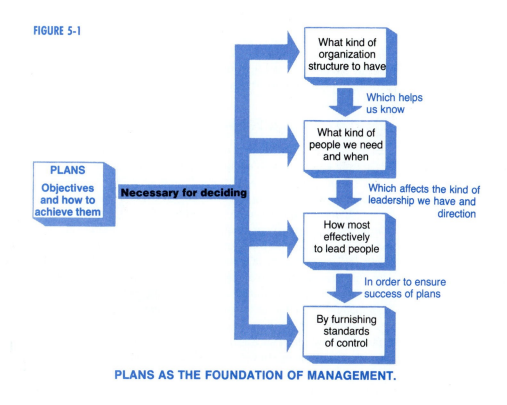

PLANS AS THE FOUNDATION OF MANAGEMENT.

FIGURE 5-2

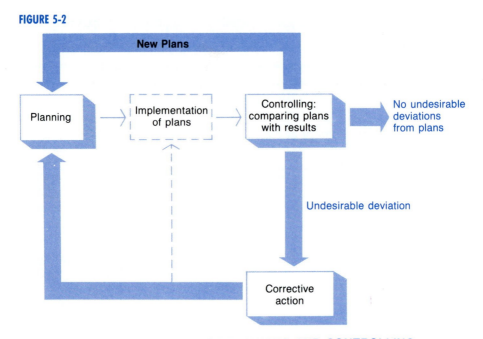

CLOSE RELATIONSHIP OF PLANNING AND CONTROLLING.

is no way for people to tell whether they are going where they want to go (the result of the task of control) unless they first know where they want to go (part of the task of planning). Plans thus furnish the standards of control.

The Pervasiveness of Planning

Planning is a function of all managers, although the character and breadth of planning will vary with each manager's authority and with the nature of the policies and plans outlined by superiors. If managers are not allowed a certain degree of discretion and planning responsibility, they are not truly managers.

   If we recognize the pervasiveness of planning, we can more easily understand why some people distinguish between policy-making (the setting of guidelines for decision making) and administration, or between the "manager" and the "administrator" or "supervisor." One manager, because of his or her authority or position in the organization, may do more planning—or more important planning—than another, or the planning of one may be more basic than that of another and applicable to a larger portion of the enterprise. However, all managers—from presidents to first-level supervisors—plan. Even the head of a road gang or a factory crew plans in a limited area under fairly strict rules and procedures. It is interesting that in studies of work satisfaction, a principal factor in the success of supervisors at the lowest organization level was found to be the extent of their ability to plan.

Perspective

Planning at GM, K-Mart, and RCA

Although all managers plan, the work schedule of the first-line supervisor differs from the strategic plan developed by top managers. Roger Smith, the chief executive officer at General Motors, planned the grand strategy of producing small cars in Japan and Korea. Chairman Fauber of K-Mart, a retail chain known for its no-frills discount stores, planned to "upscale" the operation by offering a wider selection and higher-margin apparel. Thornton Bradshaw of the RCA Corporation redirected strategy, moving the company away from videodiscs and selling businesses not directly related to the company's main purpose. He focused instead on the company's strengths in communication satellites and radar display systems produced for the Navy. While top executives plan the general direction of the firm, managers at all levels must prepare their plans so that they contribute to the overall aims of the organization.

The Efficiency of Plans

The effectiveness of a plan pertains to the degree to which it achieves the purpose or objectives. The **efficiency** of a plan, on the other hand, refers to its contribution to the purpose and objectives, offset by the costs and other factors required to formulate and operate it. A plan may enhance the attainment of objectives, but at an unnecessarily high cost. Plans are efficient if they achieve their purpose at a reasonable cost, when cost is measured not only in terms of time or money or production but also in the degree of individual and group satisfaction.

Many managers have followed plans whose costs were greater than the revenue that could be obtained. For example, one airline acquired certain aircraft with costs exceeding revenues. Companies have also tried to sell products that were unacceptable to the market; an example is an auto manufacturer that tried to capture a market by emphasizing engineering without making competitive advances in style. Plans can even make it impossible to achieve objectives if they make enough people in an organization dissatisfied or unhappy. The new president of a company that was losing money attempted to reorganize and cut expenses quickly by wholesale and unplanned layoffs of key personnel. The resulting fear, resentment, and loss of morale led to productivity that was so much lower as to defeat the new executive's objective of eliminating losses and making profits. Some attempts to install management appraisal and development programs have also failed because of group resentment of the methods used, regardless of the basic soundness of the programs.

TYPES OF PLANS

The failure of some managers to recognize that there are several types of plans has often caused difficulty in making planning effective. It is easy to see that a major program, such as one to build and equip a new factory, is a plan. But a number of other courses of future action are also plans. Keeping in mind that a plan encompasses any course of future action, we can see that plans are varied. They are classified here as (1) purposes or missions, (2) objectives or goals, (3) strategies, (4) policies, (5) procedures, (6) rules, (7) programs, and (8) budgets.

Purposes or Missions

The **mission,** or **purpose** (the terms are often used interchangeably), identifies the basic function or task of an enterprise or agency or any part of it. Every kind of organized operation has, or at least should have if it is to be meaningful, a purpose or mission. In every social system, enterprises have a basic function or task that is assigned to them by society. For example, the purpose of a business generally is the production and distribution of goods and services. The purpose of a state highway department is the design, building, and operation of a system of state highways. The purpose of the courts is the interpretation of laws and their application. The purpose of a university is teaching and research. And so on.

Although we do not do so, some writers distinguish between purposes and missions. While a business, for example, may have a social purpose of producing and distributing goods and services, it can accomplish this by fulfilling a mission of producing certain lines of products. The missions of an oil company, like Exxon, are to search for oil and to produce, refine, and market petroleum and a wide variety of petroleum products, from diesel fuel to chemicals. The mission of the Du Pont Company has been expressed as "better things through chemistry," and Kimberly-Clark (noted for its Kleenex trademark) regards its business mission as the production and sale of paper and paper products. In the 1960s, the mission of NASA was to get a person to the moon before the Russians. Hallmark, which has expanded its business beyond greeting cards, defines its mission as "the social expression business."[2] It is true that in some businesses and other enterprises, the purpose or mission often becomes fuzzy. For example, many of the conglomerates have regarded their mission as **synergy,*** which is accomplished through the combination of a variety of companies.

People sometimes think that the mission of a business, as well as its objective, is to make a profit. It is true that every kind of enterprise must have, as we pointed out in Chapter 1, a "surplus"—in business, a "profit"—goal or objective if it is to survive and do the task society has entrusted to it. But this basic objective is accomplished by undertaking activities, going in clearly defined directions, achieving goals, and accomplishing a mission.

Objectives or Goals

Objectives, or **goals** (the terms are used interchangeably in this book), are the ends toward which activity is aimed. They represent not only the end point of

---

* The concept of synergy can be expressed simply as a situation in which 2 plus 2 becomes equal to 5, or in which the whole is greater than the sum of the parts.

planning but also the end toward which organizing, staffing, leading, and controlling are aimed. While enterprise objectives are the basic plan of the firm, a department may also have its own objectives. Its goals naturally contribute to the attainment of enterprise objectives, but the two sets of goals may be entirely different. For example, an objective of a business might be to make a certain profit by producing a given line of home entertainment equipment, while a goal of the manufacturing department might be to produce the required number of television sets of a given design and quality at a given cost. These objectives are consistent, but they differ in that the manufacturing department alone cannot ensure the accomplishment of the company's objective.

Strategies

For years the military used the word "strategies" to mean grand plans made in light of what it was believed an adversary might or might not do. While the term "strategies" still usually has a competitive implication, managers increasingly use it to reflect broad areas of an enterprise operation. In this book, **strategy** is defined as the determination of the basic long-term objectives of an enterprise and the adoption of courses of action and allocation of resources necessary to achieve these goals.

Thus, a company has to decide what kind of business it is going to be in. Is it a transportation or a railroad company? Is it a container or a paper box manufacturer? The firm also has to decide on its growth goal and its desired profitability. A strategy might include such major policies as marketing directly rather than through distributors, or concentrating on proprietary products, of having a full line of autos, as General Motors decided to have many years ago.

The purpose of strategies, then, is to determine and communicate, through a system of major objectives and policies, a picture of the kind of enterprise that is envisioned. Strategies do not attempt to outline exactly how the enterprise is to accomplish its objectives, since this is the task of countless major and minor supporting programs. But they furnish a framework for guiding thinking and action. Their usefulness in practice and their importance in guiding planning do, however, justify the separation of strategies as a type of plan for the purpose of analysis.

Policies

Policies also are plans in that they are general statements or understandings that guide or channel thinking in decision making. Not all policies are "statements"; they are often merely implied from the actions of managers. The president of a company, for example, may strictly follow—perhaps for convenience rather than as policy—the practice of promoting from within; the practice may then be interpreted as policy and carefully followed by subordinates. In fact, one of the problems of managers is to make sure that subordinates do not interpret as policy minor managerial decisions that are not intended to serve as patterns.

Policies define an area within which a decision is to be made and ensure that the decision will be consistent with, and contribute to, an objective. Policies help decide issues before they become problems, make it unnecessary to analyze the same situation every time it comes up, and unify other plans, thus permitting managers to delegate authority and still maintain control over what their subordinates do. For example, a certain railroad has the policy of acquiring industrial land to replace all company acreage sold along its right-of-way. This policy permits the manager of the land department to develop acquisition plans without continual reference to top management; at the same time, it furnishes a standard of control.

Policies ordinarily exist on all levels of the organization and range from major company policies through major department policies to minor policies applicable to the smallest segment of the organization. They may be related to functions such as sales and finance or merely to a project such as the design of a new product to meet a specified competition.

There are many types of policies. Examples include policies of hiring only university-trained engineers, encouraging employee suggestions for improved cooperation, promoting from within, conforming strictly to a high standard of business ethics, setting competitive prices, and insisting on fixed, rather than cost-plus, pricing.

Since policies are guides to decision making, it follows that they must allow for some discretion. Otherwise, they would be rules. Too often, policies are interpreted as a kind of "ten commandments" that leaves no room for discretion. Although discretion, in some instances, is quite broad, it can be exceedingly narrow. For example, a policy of buying from the lowest of three qualified bidders leaves to discretion only the question of which bidders are qualified; a requirement that goods be bought from a certain supplier, regardless of price or service, would, however, be a rule.

Perspective

A Company's Policy Manual

To see how policies are often *misunderstood*, let us look at examples from a company's policy manual. In each case, there is room for a person in a decision-making capacity to use discretion.

Gifts from suppliers.   Except for token gifts of purely nominal or advertising value, no employee shall accept any gift or gratuity from any supplier at any time. [*What is "token" or "nominal"?*]

Entertainment.   No officer or employee shall accept favors or entertainment from an outside organization or agency which are substantial enough to cause undue influence in the selection of goods or services for the company. [*What is "substantial" or "undue"?*]

Outside employment.   It is improper for any employee to work for any company customers, or for any competitors, or for any vendors or suppliers of goods or services to the company [*this is actually more like a rule because it allows no* *discretion*]; outside employment is further prohibited if it (1) results in a division of loyalty to the company or a conflict of interest, or (2) interferes with or adversely affects the employee's work or opportunity for advancement in the company. [*What is meant by "division of loyalty," "conflict of interest," and "adversely"?*]

Pricing. Territorial division managers may each establish such prices for the products under their individual control as they deem to be in the division's interest, so long as (1) these prices result in gross profit margins for any line of products which are consistent with the approved profit plan, (2) price reductions will not result in detrimental effects on prices of similar products of another company division in another state or country, and (3) prices meet the legal requirements of the state or country in which the prices are effective. [*What are "consistent profit margins," "detrimental effects," and "legal requirements"?*]

Policy is a means of encouraging discretion and initiative, but within limits. The amount of freedom will naturally depend on the policy and in turn will reflect position and authority in the organization. The president of a company with a policy of aggressive price competition has a broad area of discretion and initiative in which to interpret and apply this policy. The district sales manager (who reports to the regional sales manager) abides by the same basic policy, but the interpretations made by the president, the vice president for sales, and the regional sales manager become derivative policies that might narrow the district manager's scope to the point of being, for example, only wide enough to approve a special sale price not exceeding a 10 percent reduction to meet competition (see Figure 5-3).

Making policies consistent and integrated enough to realize enterprise objectives is difficult for many reasons. First, policies are too seldom defined in writing, and their exact interpretations are too little known. Second, the very delegation of authority that policies are intended to implement leads, through its decentralizing influence, to widespread participation in policy-making and interpretation, with almost certain variations among individuals. Third, it is not always easy to control policy because actual policy may be difficult to ascertain, and intended policy may not always be clear.

Procedures

Procedures are plans that establish a required method of handling future activities. They are chronological sequences of required actions. They are guides to action, rather than to thinking, and they detail the exact manner in which certain activities must be accomplished.

Procedures often cut across department lines. For example, in a manufacturing company, the procedure for handling orders will almost certainly involve the

FIGURE 5-3

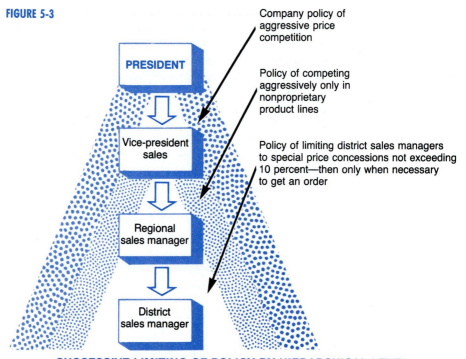

Company policy of
aggressive price
competition

Policy of competing
aggressively only in
nonproprietary
product lines

Policy of limiting district sales managers
to special price concessions not exceeding
10 percent—then only when necessary
to get an order

PRESIDENT

Vice-president
sales

Regional
sales manager

District
sales manager

SUCCESSIVE LIMITING OF POLICY BY HIERARCHICAL LEVEL.

sales department (for the original order), the finance department (for acknowledgment of receipt of funds and for customer credit approval), the accounting department (for recording the transaction), the production department (for the order to produce goods or authority to release them from stock), and the traffic department (for determination of shipping means and route).

A few examples illustrate the relationship between procedures and policies. Company policy may grant employees vacations; procedures established to implement this policy will provide for scheduling vacations to avoid disruption of work, setting methods and rates of vacation pay, maintaining records to assure each employee of a vacation, and spelling out the means for applying for a vacation. A company may have a policy of shipping orders quickly; particularly in a large company, careful procedures will be necessary to ensure that orders are handled in a specific way. Company policy may require the public relations department to clear its employees' public utterances; to implement this policy, managers must establish procedures for obtaining clearance with minimum inconvenience and delay.

Rules

Rules spell out specific required actions or nonactions, allowing no discretion.[3] They are usually the simplest type of plan.

People frequently confuse rules with policies or procedures. Rules are unlike procedures in that they guide action without specifying a time sequence. In fact, a procedure might be looked upon as a sequence of rules. A rule, however, may or may not be part of a procedure. For example, "No smoking" is a rule quite unrelated to any procedure; but a procedure governing the handling of orders may incorporate the rule that all orders must be confirmed the day they are received. This rule allows no deviation from a stated course of action and in no way interferes with the rest of the procedure for handling orders. It is comparable to a rule stating that all fractions of weight of over half an ounce are to be counted as a full ounce or that receiving inspection must count or weigh all materials against the purchase order. The essence of a rule is that it reflects a managerial decision that some certain action must—or must not—be taken.

Be sure you can distinguish rules from policies. The purpose of policies is to guide decision making by marking off areas in which managers can use their discretion. Although rules also serve as guides, they allow no discretion in their application. Many companies and other organizations think they have policies when they really have spelled-out rules. The result is confusion as to when people may use their own judgment, if at all. This can be dangerous. Rules and procedures, by their very nature, are designed to repress thinking; we should use them only when we do not want people in an organization to use their discretion.

Perspective
Procedures and Rules Imposed by the Outside

At times, rules and procedures are implemented because of unfavorable publicity. General Dynamics, one of the largest defense contractors, has been accused of some improprieties.[4] In order not to be suspended from bidding on defense contracts, the company had to agree to a list of rules and procedures imposed by the Defense Department.

These new requirements are designed to prevent the shifting of costs from one contract to another. For example, workers have to prepare and sign their own time cards. The supervisor has to check each card; if one is incorrectly filled out, the worker involved has to make the correction, which then has to be initialed by the worker and the boss. The original entry must not be erased so that it can be checked later. Also, General Dynamics was required to establish tight rules for charging overhead expenses. Employees are not allowed to accept gifts—not even a pen or a calendar.

Thus, rules and procedures can be imposed by an important customer and are examples not only of planning but also of controlling, showing the close relationship between the two functions.

Programs

Programs are a complex of goals, policies, procedures, rules, task assignments, steps to be taken, resources to be employed, and other elements necessary to carry out a given course of action; they are ordinarily supported by budgets. They may be as major as an airline's program to acquire a $400 million fleet of jets or a 5-year program to improve the status and quality of its thousands of supervisors. Or they may be as minor as a program formulated by a single supervisor to improve the morale of workers in the parts-manufacturing department of a farm machinery company.

A primary program may call for many supporting programs. In the case of the airline mentioned above, the program for investing in new jets, involving many millions of dollars for the purchase of the aircraft and the necessary spare parts, requires many supporting programs if the investment is to be properly used. A program for providing the maintenance and operating bases with spare parts and components must be developed in detail. Special maintenance facilities must be prepared and maintenance personnel trained. Pilots and flight engineers must also be trained, and if the new jets mean a net addition to flying hours, flight personnel must be recruited. Flight schedules must be revised and ground station personnel trained to handle the new airplanes and their schedules as service is expanded to new cities in the airline's system. Advertising programs must give adequate publicity to the new service. Plans to finance the aircraft and provide for insurance coverage must be developed.

These and other programs must be devised and implemented before any new aircraft are received and placed in service. Furthermore, all these programs call for coordination and timing, since the failure of any part of this network of supporting plans means delay for the major program as well as unnecessary costs and loss of profits. Some programs, particularly those involving the hiring and training of personnel, can be accomplished too soon as well as too late; needless expense results from employees' being available and trained before their services are required.

Budgets

A **budget** is a statement of expected results expressed in numerical terms. It may be referred to as a "numberized" program. In fact, the financial operating budget is often called a "profit plan." A budget may be expressed in financial terms; in terms of labor-hours, units of product, or machine-hours; or in any other numerically measurable term. It may deal with operations, as the expense budget does; it may reflect capital outlays, as the capital expenditures budget does; or it may show cash flow, as the cash budget does.

Since budgets are also control devices, we reserve our principal discussion of them for Chapter 21, which is on control techniques. However, making a budget is clearly planning. The budget is the fundamental planning instrument in many companies. A budget forces a company to make in advance—whether for a week or for 5 years—a numerical compilation of expected cash flow, expenses and revenues, capital outlays, or labor- or machine-hour utilization. The budget is necessary for control, but it cannot serve as a sensible standard of control unless it reflects plans.

Although a budget usually implements a program, it may in itself be a program. One company in difficult financial straits installed an elaborate budgetary control program designed not only to control expenditures but also to instill cost consciousness in management. In fact, one of the major advantages of budgeting is that it makes people plan; because a budget is in the form of numbers, it forces precision in planning.

Budgets vary considerably in accuracy, detail, and purpose. Some budgets vary according to the organization's level of output; these are called **variable, or flexible, budgets.** Government agencies often develop **program budgets** in which the agency (and each department within the agency) identifies goals, develops detailed programs to meet the goals, and estimates the cost of each program. To prepare an effective program budget, a manager must do some fairly detailed and thorough planning.

Still another type, which is really a combination of the variable budget and the program budget, is the **zero-base budget.** A manager using this approach thinks of the goals and the programs needed to achieve them as a "work package," as though the programs were started from scratch, or "base zero."

STEPS IN PLANNING

Although the steps in planning are presented here in connection with major programs, such as the acquisition of a plant or a fleet of jets or the development of a product, managers would follow essentially the same steps in any other thorough planning. Since minor plans are usually simpler, some of the steps would be more easily accomplished, but the practical steps listed below, and diagrammed in Figure 5-4, are of general application. In practice, however, managers must study the feasibility of possible courses of action at each stage. For example, in establishing objectives, it is necessary to have some idea about the premises underlying the plans. An ambitious objective of increasing sales by 200 percent may be unrealistic in an environment with a projected economic recession. Similarly, feedback is also essential. In formulating supportive plans, there may be a need to reevaluate and change the overall objectives set earlier. Also, a discriminating manager obviously would not use $100 worth of time to make a decision worth 50 cents, but it is shocking to see 50 cents' worth of time used to make a planning decision involving millions of dollars.

1. Being Aware of Opportunities

Although it precedes actual planning and is therefore not strictly a part of the planning process, an awareness of opportunities* in the external environment as well as within the organization is the real starting point for planning. All managers

---

* The word "problems" might be used instead of "opportunities." However, a state of disorder or confusion and a need for a solution to achieve a given goal can more constructively be regarded as an opportunity. In fact, one very successful and astute company president does not permit his colleagues to speak of problems; they must speak only of opportunities.

should take a preliminary look at possible future opportunities and see them clearly and completely, know where they stand in light of their strengths and weaknesses, understand what problems they wish to solve and why, and know what they expect to gain. Setting realistic objectives depends on this awareness. Planning requires a realistic diagnosis of the opportunity situation.

Today, IBM is the leader among U.S. computer firms. But this was not always the case. In fact, the challenges posed by competitors in the 1950s were corporate-life-threatening. The IBM story of the 1950s is an illustration of how problems can become opportunities.

When IBM sold its first computer in 1953, it was in a rather weak competitive position. The first computer was even called "IBM's Univac," indicating its strong resemblance to Univac, which was created by Remington Rand, a company that was ahead in the field by 4 years. The Census Bureau, an important customer, opted for Univac over the IBM equipment. The greatest fears were of the powerful companies General Electric (which was six times the size of IBM) and RCA (which was twice the size). As is so often the case, crises and problems became opportunities. In a lengthy meeting, Thomas J. Watson, Jr., and his top managers decided to make IBM a winner in the commercial market. The decision was followed by hard work by the sales force (which knew very little about computers at that time), the technical experts, and senior executives.

Although Univac may have had the competitive edge in hardware, Watson believed that a strong sales force and systems expertise were crucial to success. Customer satisfaction and service became essential pillars in IBM's later success. Had the competition had the foresight to recruit key personnel from IBM, the company would have been in trouble. When IBM eventually delivered the System 360, it became the standard for major customers. The rest of the IBM success story is history, illustrating that a company with weaknesses (hardware, size), facing threats from strong competitors (Remington Rand, GE, RCA), can build on its strengths (vision, service, sales) to become a success.

2. Establishing Objectives

The second step in planning is to establish objectives for the entire enterprise and then for each subordinate work unit. This is to be done for the long term as well as for the short range. Objectives specify the expected results and indicate the end points of what is to be done, where the primary emphasis is to be placed, and what is to be accomplished by the network of strategies, policies, procedures, rules, budgets, and programs.

Enterprise objectives give direction to the major plans, which, by reflecting these objectives, define the objective of every major department. Major department

FIGURE 5-4

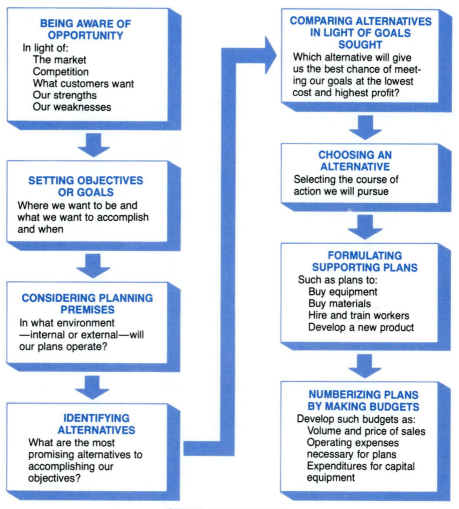

STEPS IN PLANNING.

objectives, in turn, control the objectives of subordinate departments, and so on down the line. In other words, objectives form a hierarchy. The objectives of lesser departments will be more accurate if subdivision managers understand the overall enterprise objectives and the derivative goals. Managers should also have the opportunity to contribute their ideas for setting their own goals and those of the enterprise.

3. Developing Premises

The third logical step in planning is to establish, circulate, and obtain agreement to utilize critical planning premises such as forecasts, applicable basic policies, and existing company plans. They are *assumptions* about the environment in which the plan is to be carried out. It is important for all the managers involved in planning to agree on the premises. In fact, the major **principle of planning premises** is this: *The more thoroughly individuals charged with planning understand and agree to utilize consistent planning premises, the more coordinated enterprise planning will be.*

Forecasting is important in premising: What kinds of markets will there be? What volume of sales? What prices? What products? What technical developments? What costs? What wage rates? What tax rates and policies? What new plants? What policies with respect to dividends? What political or social environment? How will expansion be financed? What are the long-term trends?

Managers have a number of sources to draw from when preparing a forecast for their enterprise. The government publishes a wealth of information that can be useful. Here are just a few examples: *Business Cycle Developments, Survey of Current Business*, and *Economic Indicators*. Most large banks publish newsletters on current economic conditions, often on a monthly basis. *Business Week* magazine prepares outlooks for specific industries. Many universities, such as UCLA, make national and regional economic forecasts. Managers interested in long-term trends will find John Naisbitt's book *Megatrends* useful.[6]

Because the future is so complex, it would not be profitable or realistic to make assumptions about every detail of the future environment of a plan. Therefore, premises are, as a practical matter, limited to assumptions that are critical, or strategic, to a plan, that is, those which most influence its operation.

4. Determining Alternative Courses

The fourth step in planning is to search for and examine alternative courses of action, especially those not immediately apparent. There is seldom a plan for which reasonable alternatives do not exist, and quite often an alternative that is not obvious proves to be the best.

The more common problem is not finding alternatives but reducing the number of alternatives so that the most promising may be analyzed. Even with mathematical techniques and the computer, there is a limit to the number of alternatives that can be thoroughly examined. The planner must usually make a preliminary examination to discover the most fruitful possibilities.

5. Evaluating Alternative Courses

After seeking out alternative courses and examining their strong and weak points, the next step is to evaluate the alternatives by weighing them in light of premises and goals. One course may appear to be the most profitable, but it may require a large cash outlay and have a slow payback; another may look less profitable but may involve less risk; still another may better suit the company's long-range objectives.

If the only objective were to maximize immediate profits in a certain business, if the future were not uncertain, if cash position and capital availability were not worrisome, and if most factors could be reduced to definite data, this evaluation would be relatively easy. But since planners typically encounter many uncertainties, problems of capital shortage, and various intangible factors, evaluation is usually very difficult, even with relatively simple problems. A company may wish to enter a new product line primarily for purposes of prestige, but the forecast may show a financial loss; even so, the question is still open as to whether the loss is worth the gain in prestige.

There are so many alternative courses in most situations and so many variables and limitations to be considered that evaluation can be exceedingly difficult. Because of these complexities, the newer methodologies and applications of operations research and analysis discussed in Chapters 21 and 22 are helpful. Indeed, it is at this step in the planning process that operations research and mathematical as well as computing techniques have their primary application to the field of management.

6. Selecting a Course

This is the point at which the plan is adopted—the real point of decision making. Occasionally, an analysis and evaluation of alternative courses will disclose that two or more are advisable, and the manager may decide to follow several courses rather than the one best course.

7. Formulating Derivative Plans

When a decision is made, planning is seldom complete, and a seventh step is indicated. Derivative plans are almost invariably required to support the basic plan.

8. Numberizing Plans by Budgeting

After decisions are made and plans are set, the final step in giving them meaning, as was indicated in the discussion of types of plans, is to numberize them by converting them into budgets. The overall budgets of an enterprise represent the sum total of income and expenses, with resultant profit or surplus, and the budgets of major balance sheet items such as cash and capital expenditures. Each department or program of a business or some other enterprise can have its own budgets, usually of expenses and capital expenditures, which tie into the overall budget.

If done well, budgets become a means of adding together the various plans and also set important standards against which planning progress can be measured. Budgets will be discussed in connection with managerial control in Chapter 21.

Applying the Planning Steps in Preparing for College

The steps can be applied to most planning situations. High school students probably follow these steps to some degree when planning for college. First, they are aware of opportunities to attend college and the opportunities derived from a college education. Then they set objectives in a variety of areas, such as the area of study and the completion of the degree within 4 years. They also develop planning premises. Thus, they may make the assumption that scholarships are available or that they may have to work while attending college. Some students may assume that they want to stay in the same area or the same state, while others may want to study abroad. In each situation, there are usually several alternatives available that should then be carefully evaluated. Thus, students may assess the advantages and disadvantages of applying for admission at different schools. After receiving several acceptance letters, the students have to select the appropriate college. This is an important decision point. After making a choice, they need to formulate derivative plans, which may include selecting housing, moving to the new location, or finding a job near the college. Then the students need to numberize their plans by converting them into budgets, which may include tuition, moving and housing costs, clothing and entertainment expenses, and so on.

These steps do not always follow the same sequence. For example, when evaluating the alternative courses, one may have to go back and make new assumptions for the various alternatives. Or one may develop different courses of action on the basis of different assumptions. One course may be based on the assumption of obtaining a scholarship, another course on the premise that one has to work through college. Clearly, then, planning is not a linear process but a reiterative one.

THE PLANNING PROCESS:
A RATIONAL APPROACH TO GOAL ACHIEVEMENT

As indicated by the planning steps above, planning is a rational approach to accomplishing objectives. The process can be illustrated as shown in Figure 5-5. In this diagram, progress (toward more sales, higher profits, lower costs, and so forth) is on the vertical axis, and time is on the horizontal axis. Here x indicates where we are (at t_0, or "time zero") and y where we want to be at a future time (at t_n). In short, we are at x and want to go to y. Often we do not have all the data, but we start planning anyway. We may even have to start our planning study at x_1 (at t_{-n}). The line xy is the decision path.

If the future were completely certain, the line xy would be relatively easy to draw. However, in actuality, a myriad of factors may push us away from or toward the desired goal. These are the planning premises. Again, because we cannot forecast or consider everything, we try to develop our path from x to y in light of the most critical premises.

The essential logic of planning applies regardless of the time interval between t_0 and t_n, whether it is 5 minutes or 20 years. However, the clarity of premises, the attainability of goals, and the simplification of planning are almost certain to be inversely related to the time span. That is, if the time span is long, premises may be unclear, goals may be more difficult to achieve, and other planning complexities may be great.

FIGURE 5-5

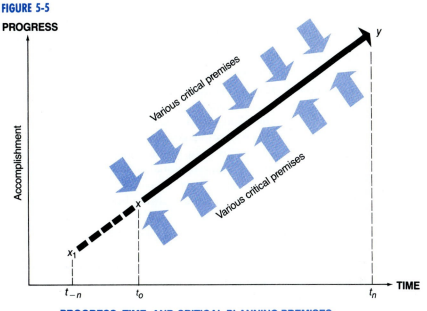

PROGRESS, TIME, AND CRITICAL PLANNING PREMISES.

Decision making may be the easiest part of planning, although it involves techniques of evaluation and considerable skill in applying them. The real difficulties arise primarily in sharpening and giving meaning to objectives and critical premises, seeing the nature and relationships of the strengths and weaknesses of alternatives, and communicating goals and premises to those throughout the enterprise who must plan.

The Planning Period

Shall plans be for a short period or a long one? How shall short-range plans be coordinated with long-range plans? These questions suggest multiple horizons of planning—in some cases, planning a week in advance may be ample, and in others, the desirable period may be a number of years. Even within the same firm at the same time, various planning periods may exist for various matters.

The Commitment Principle

Some criteria must be used in selecting the time range for company planning. The key to choosing the right planning period seems to lie in the **commitment principle:** *Logical planning encompasses a future period of time necessary to fulfill, through a series of actions, the commitments involved in decisions made today.*

We can readily grasp the logic of planning far enough in the future to foresee, as well as possible, the recovery of capital sunk into a building or a machine. Since capital is the lifeblood of an enterprise and is normally limited in relation to the firm's needs, its expenditure must be accompanied by a reasonable possibility of recovering it, plus a return on investment, through operations. For example, when Lever Brothers sank $35 million into a new factory on the West Coast, it decided, in effect, that the detergent business would permit the recovery of this investment over a period of time. If this period was 20 years, then logically the plans should have been based on a 20-year projection of business. Of course, the company might have introduced some flexibility and reduced its risk (as it did) by spending extra funds to make the plant modifiable for other purposes.

But a company can make noncost commitments that have various time frames. For example, it may commit itself to a personnel policy of promoting people from within the organization rather than hiring them from the outside. A company, therefore, may commit itself for varying lengths of time to things that are not always immediately measurable in dollars or any other currency.

What the commitment principle implies.   The commitment principle implies that long-range planning is not really planning for future decisions but, rather, planning for the future impact of today's decisions. In other words, a decision is a commitment, normally of funds, direction of action, or reputation. And decisions lie at the core of planning. While studies and analyses preceded decisions, any type of plan implies that some decision has been made. Indeed, a plan does not really exist as such until a decision has been made. Knowing this, the astute manager will recognize the validity of gearing longer-term considerations to present decisions. To do otherwise is to overlook the basic nature of both planning and decision making.

International Perspective

Making Commitments in the Republics of the Disintegrated Former Soviet Union[7]

Planning requires commitment to a course of action. While the breakup of the Soviet Union provides many opportunities for Western businesses, committing resources for investments is risky. With former President Gorbachev's reforms, many promising opportunities are developing. Instead of dealing with one central government, companies can make business deals with any of the fifteen republics; this, in turn, may reduce red tape. Kazakhstan and Azerbaijan are negotiating directly with Chevron. Many republics are in urgent need of road and telephone systems. AT&T, for example, negotiated a deal with the Republic of Armenia, which has a population of more than 3 million. One Western diplomat commented on the situation in the Soviet Union as follows: "Opportunities like this come up maybe once in a century."

Yet the attempted coup in 1991 to topple the then President Gorbachev showed how volatile the political situation is. Clearly, managers must weigh the opportunities against the risks involved in making commitments. Still, one U.S. executive advised: "If U.S. companies wait until all the problems are solved, somebody else will get the business." Indeed, many European companies (for example, Alcatel of France, Fiat of Italy, and Daimler-Benz of Germany) are making bold moves to do business in the republics that once made up the Soviet

Union. On the other hand, some major U.S. firms such as American Express, BankAmerica Corp., Caterpillar, Coca-Cola, Du Pont, General Electric, General Motors, IBM, Levi Strauss, McDonald's, PepsiCo, Procter & Gamble, and Xerox already have established business relationships in the republics of the former U.S.S.R. Making commitments in an uncertain environment is risky. Neglecting to take advantage of opportunities is also risky.

Application of the commitment principle. There is no uniform or arbitrary length of time for which a company should plan or for which a given program or any of its parts should be planned. An airplane company embarking on a new commercial jet aircraft project should probably plan this program for at least 12 years ahead, with 5 or 6 years for engineering and development and at least as many more years for production and sales, in order to recoup total costs and make a reasonable profit. An instrument manufacturer with a product already developed might need to plan revenues and expenses only 6 months ahead, since this period may represent the cycle of raw-materials purchasing, production, inventorying, and sales. But the same company might wish to see much further into the future before assuming a lease for specialized manufacturing facilities, undertaking a program of management training, or developing and promoting a new product. Other examples, showing that different planning areas require different time periods, are illustrated in Figure 5-6.

Coordination of Short- and Long-Range Plans

Often short-range plans are made without reference to long-range plans. This is plainly a serious error. The importance of integrating the two types can hardly be overemphasized, and no short-run plan should be made unless it contributes to the achievement of the relevant long-range plan. Much waste arises from decisions about immediate situations that fail to consider their effect on more remote objectives.

Sometimes short-range decisions not only fail to contribute to a long-range plan but actually impede, or require changes in, the long-range plan. For example, if a small company accepts a large order without reckoning the effect of the order on its capacity to produce or its supply of cash, this decision may so hamper the company's future ability to finance a systematic expansion that changes may be required in its long-range program. Or, in another company, small additions to the plant (which may be urgently needed) may utilize vacant property so haphazardly as to thwart the land's longer-range use as the site for a large new plant. In other instances, the decision of a plant superintendent to discharge workers without adequate cause may interfere with the company's long-range objective of developing a fair and successful personnel program. The short-range decision of Sewell Avery, chairman of Montgomery Ward, to curtail expansion of the business after

FIGURE 5-6

EXAMPLE OF KINDS OF COMMITMENTS FOR A MANUFACTURING FIRM

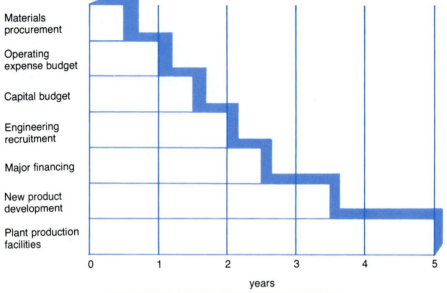

Materials
procurement

Operating
expense budget

Capital budget

Engineering
recruitment

Major financing

New product
development

Plant production
facilities

0   1   2   3   4   5

years

PLANNING AREAS AND TIME PERIODS.
Various management decision areas typically involve planning ahead for differing periods of time. These periods also vary according to the kind of business. For example, a large public utility may plan new power-production plants twenty-five or thirty years into the future, whereas a small garment manufacturer may plan new production facilities only one year ahead.

World War II because he believed that a serious recession was at hand interfered with the long-range program of enhancing the profitability of the company.

Responsible managers should continually review and revise immediate decisions to determine whether they contribute to long-range programs, and subordinate managers should be regularly briefed on long-range plans so that they will make decisions consistent with the company's long-range goals. It is far easier to do this than to correct inconsistencies, especially since short-term commitments tend to lead to further commitments along the same line.

SUMMARY

Planning involves selecting missions and objectives and the actions to achieve them. Planning requires decision making, that is, choosing from among alternative future courses of action. Planning and controlling are closely interrelated, although they are discussed separately in this book.

There are many types of plans, such as purposes or missions, objectives or goals, strategies, policies, procedures, rules, programs, and budgets. Once aware of opportunities, a manager plans rationally by establishing objectives, making assumptions (premises) about the present and future environment, finding and evaluating alternative courses of action, and choosing a course to follow. Next, the manager must make supporting plans and devise a budget. These activities must be carried out with attention to the total environment.

According to the commitment principle, plans should cover a period of time that is long enough to fulfill commitments involved in decisions made today. Short-range plans must, of course, be coordinated with long-range plans.

KEY IDEAS AND CONCEPTS FOR REVIEW

Planning	Rule
Primacy of planning	Program
Pervasiveness of planning	Budget
Efficiency of plans	Variable, or flexible, budget
Purpose or mission	Program budget
Objectives or goals	Zero-base budget
Strategy	Planning steps
Policy	Commitment principle
Procedure	

FOR DISCUSSION

1. "Planning is looking ahead, and control is looking back." Comment.
2. If planning involves a rational approach to selected goals, how can goals or objectives be a type of plan?
3. Draw up a statement of policy, and devise a brief procedure that might be useful in implementing it. Are you sure your policy is not a rule?
4. If all decisions involve commitments and if the future is always uncertain, how can a manager guard against costly mistakes?
5. Using as an example a planning decision with which you are familiar, show to what extent, and how, the commitment principle applies to it.
6. "Planning theory illustrates the open-system approach to management." Comment.

EXERCISES/ACTION STEPS

1. Taking a planning problem that is now facing you, proceed to deal with it in accordance with the planning steps outlined in this chapter.
2. Interview a manager in your area, and ask about the planning process (i.e., the steps in planning).

CASES

CASE 5-1
EASTERN ELECTRIC CORPORATION

Margaret Quinn, the president of Eastern Electric Corporation, one of the large electric utilities operating in the eastern United States, had long been convinced that effective planning in the company was absolutely essential to success. For more than 10 years she had tried to get a company planning program installed without seeing much result. Over this time she had consecutively appointed three vice presidents in charge of planning and, although each had seemed to work hard at the job, she noticed that individual department heads kept going their own ways. They made decisions on problems as they came up, and they prided themselves on doing an effective job of "fighting fires."

But the company seemed to be drifting, and individual decisions of department heads did not always jibe with each other. The executive in charge of regulatory matters was always pressing state commissions to allow higher electric rates without having very much luck, since the commissions felt that costs, although rising, were not justified. The head of public relations was constantly appealing to the public to understand the problems of electric utilities, but electric users in the various communities felt that the

utility was making enough money and that the company should solve its problems without raising rates. The vice president in charge of operations, pressed by many communities to expand electric lines, to put all lines underground to get rid of unsightly poles and lines, and to give customers better service, felt that costs were secondary to keeping customers off his back.

When a consultant called in at the request of Ms. Quinn looked over the situation, he found that the company really was not planning very well. The vice president of planning and his staff were working hard making studies and forecasts and submitting them to the president. There they stopped, since all the department heads looked on them as impractical paperwork that had no importance for their day-to-day operations.

1. If you were the consultant, what steps would you suggest to get the company to plan effectively?
2. What advice would you give the company as to how far in the future to plan?
3. How would you suggest to the president that your recommendations be put into effect?

CASE 5-2
PLANNING AND CONTROL AT APPLE COMPUTER[8]

Apple Computer, Inc., enjoyed a phenomenal early success after it was founded in 1977 by Steve Wozniak, the technical expert, and Steve Jobs, the marketing genius.

However, success did not last for very long, partly because of the introduction of the IBM Personal Computer. In the early 1980s, in the view of some observers, Apple needed tighter control and a more professional approach to managing. John Sculley was lured from the Pepsi-Cola Company to give Apple a new direction.

To bring the company under control, Sculley employed cost-cutting measures to improve its profitability. At the same time, however, research and development expenditures were increased so that the company could remain a technological leader in the field. However, later he was accused of spending not enough on research and development and too much on advertising. The firm was also reorganized to reduce duplication of efforts, to lower the break-even point, and to reduce friction among the departments. To improve its effectiveness and efficiency, Apple introduced new reporting procedures. Furthermore, considerable efforts were made to control the inventory level, which is a serious problem in the personal-computer industry. These measures, combined with a successful strategy (Apple's Macintosh computer is making inroads into business corporations that are dominated by IBM) and helped by the popularity of desktop publishing, resulted in an increase of over 150 percent in earnings in the 1986 fiscal year.

1. What is the relationship between planning and controlling?
2. What other types of plans can be used for controlling the organization?

REFERENCES

1. George A. Steiner, *Top Management Planning* (London: The Macmillan Company, 1969), p. 7.
2. William L. Glueck and Lawrence R. Jauch, *Business Policy and Strategic Management* (New York: McGraw-Hill Book Company, 1984), chap. 2.
3. See also F. Neil Brady, "Rules for Making Exceptions to Rules," *Academy of Management Review* (July 1987), pp. 436–444.
4. Ford S. Worthy, "Mr. Clean Charts a New Course at General Dynamics," *Fortune* (Apr. 28, 1986), pp. 70–76.
5. "The Greatest Capitalist in History," *Fortune* (Aug. 31, 1987), pp. 24–35; Philip H. Dorn, "The Song Remains the Same," *Datamation* (February 1984), pp. 105–110.
6. John Naisbitt, *Megatrends* (New York: Warner Books, 1982).
7. Paul Hofheinz, "Let's Do Business," *Fortune* (Sept. 23, 1991), pp. 62–68; Richard A. Melcher, Mark Ivey, Jonathan B. Levine, David Greising, and Joyce Barnathan, "For Investors, 'After One Step Backward, It's Two Steps Forward,' " *Business Week* (Sept. 2, 1991), pp. 28–29; Paul Hofheinz, "Russia Starts All Over Again," *Business Week* (Jan. 13, 1992), pp. 60–61.
8. Deborah C. Wise, "Can John Sculley Clean Up the Mess at Apple?" *Business Week* (July 29, 1985), pp. 70–71; Deborah C. Wise, "Apple, Part 2: The No-Nonsense Era of John Sculley," *Business Week* (Jan. 27, 1986), pp. 96–98; Katherine M. Hafner and Geoff Lewis, "Apple's Comeback," *Business Week* (Jan. 19, 1987), pp. 84–89; Brian O'Reilly, "Apple Finally Invades the Office," *Fortune* (Nov. 9, 1987), pp. 52–64; Brenton R. Schlender, "Shedding His Shyness, John Sculley Promotes Apple—and Himself," *The Wall Street Journal* (Aug. 18, 1988); Brian O'Reilly, "Growing Apple Anew for the Business Market," *Fortune* (Jan. 4, 1988), pp. 36–37.

Objectives

Management by objectives is viewed in a larger context than that of a mere appraisal procedure. It regards appraisal as only one of several sub-systems operating within a larger system of goal-oriented management.[1]
George S. Odiorne

Chapter Objectives

After reading this chapter, you should be able to:

1. Explain the nature of objectives.
2. Outline the evolving concepts in management by objectives (MBO) and explain the systems approach to MBO.
3. Analyze the process of managing and appraising by objectives.
4. Show how verifiable objectives can be set for different situations.
5. Describe the benefits of MBO.
6. Recognize the weaknesses of MBO and ways to overcome them.

In Chapter 5 **objectives** were defined as the important ends toward which organizational and individual activities are directed. Since writers and practitioners make no clear distinction between the terms "goals" and "objectives," they are used interchangeably in this book. Within the context of the discussion it will become clear whether they are long-term or short-term, broad or specific. The emphasis in this chapter is on **verifiable** objectives; that is, at the end of the period it should be possible to determine whether or not the objective has been achieved. The goal of every manager is to create a surplus (in business organizations this means profits). Clear and verifiable objectives facilitate measurement of the surplus as well as the effectiveness and efficiency of managerial actions.

THE NATURE OF OBJECTIVES

Objectives state end results, and overall objectives need to be supported by sub-objectives. Thus, objectives form a hierarchy as well as a network. Moreover, organizations and managers have multiple goals that are sometimes incompatible and may lead to conflicts within the organization, within the group, and even within individuals. A manager may have to choose between short-term and long-term performance, and personal interests may have to be subordinated to organizational objectives.

A Hierarchy of Objectives

As Figure 6-1 shows, objectives form a hierarchy, ranging from the broad aim to specific individual objectives. The zenith of the hierarchy is the socioeconomic purpose of society, such as requiring the organization to contribute to the welfare of the people by providing goods and services at a reasonable cost. Then there is the mission or the purpose of the business, which might be to furnish convenient, low-cost transportation for the average person. The stated mission might be to produce, market, and service automobiles. As you will notice, the distinction between purpose and mission is a fine one, and therefore many writers and practi-

FIGURE 6-1

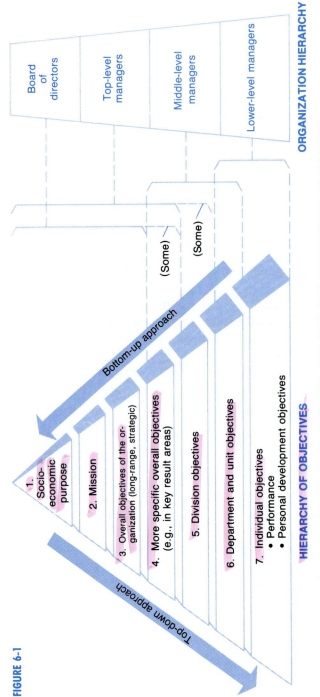

HIERARCHY OF OBJECTIVES

RELATIONSHIP OF OBJECTIVES AND THE ORGANIZATIONAL HIERARCHY.

Adapted from H. Weihrich and J. Mendleson, *Management: An MBO Approach* (Dubuque, Iowa: Wm. C. Brown Co., 1978), p. xi. Used with permission.

tioners do not differentiate between the two terms. At any rate, these aims are, in turn, translated into general overall objectives and strategies (which will be discussed in Chapter 7), such as designing, producing, and marketing reliable, low-cost, fuel-efficient automobiles.

The next level of the hierarchy contains more specific objectives, such as those in the **key result areas.** These are the areas in which performance is essential for the success of the enterprise. Some examples of objectives for key result areas are the following: to obtain a 10 percent return on investment by the end of calendar year 1993 (profitability); to increase the number of units of product X by 7 percent without an increase in cost or a reduction of the current quality level by June 30, 1993 (productivity).

The objectives have to be further translated into division, department, and unit objectives down to the lowest level of the organization.

Perspective	
Key Result Areas According to Drucker	Although there is no complete agreement on what the key result areas of a business should be—and they may differ for various enterprises—Peter F. Drucker suggests the following: market standing, innovation, productivity, physical and financial resources, profitability, manager performance and development, worker performance and attitude, and public responsibility.[2] More recently, however, two other key result areas have become of strategic importance: service and quality. These topics will be discussed later in this book.

The Process of Setting Objectives and the Organizational Hierarchy[3]

As Figure 6-1 indicates, managers at different levels in the organizational hierarchy are concerned with different kinds of objectives. The board of directors and top-level managers are very much involved in determining the purpose, the mission, and the overall objectives of the firm, as well as the more specific overall objectives in the key result areas. Middle-level managers, such as the vice president or manager of marketing or the production manager, are involved in the setting of key-result-area objectives, division objectives, and department objectives. The primary concern of lower-level managers is setting objectives of departments and units as well as of their subordinates. Although individual objectives, consisting of performance and development goals, are shown at the bottom of the hierarchy, managers at higher levels also should set objectives for their own performance and development.

There is some controversy about whether an organization should use the top-down or the bottom-up approach in setting objectives, as indicated by the arrows in Figure 6-1. In the top-down approach upper-level managers determine the objectives for subordinates, while in the bottom-up approach subordinates initiate the setting of objectives for their positions and present them to their superior.

Proponents of the top-down approach suggest that the total organization needs direction through corporate objectives provided by the chief executive officer (in conjunction with the board of directors). Proponents of the bottom-up approach, on the other hand, argue that top management needs to have information from lower levels in the form of objectives. In addition, subordinates are likely to be highly motivated by, and committed to, goals that they initiate. Personal experience has shown that the bottom-up approach is underutilized but that either approach alone is insufficient. Both are essential, but the emphasis should depend on the situation, including such factors as the size of the organization, the organizational culture, the preferred leadership style of the executive, and the urgency of the plan.

A Network of Objectives

Both objectives and planning programs normally form a network of desired results and events. If goals are not interconnected and if they do not support one another, people very often pursue paths that may seem good for their own department but may be detrimental to the company as a whole.

Goals and plans are seldom linear; that is, when one objective has been accomplished, it is not neatly followed by another, and so on. Goals and programs form an interlocking network. Figure 6-2 depicts the network of contributing programs (each of which has appropriate objectives) that constitute a typical new product program. Each of the programs could itself be broken down into an interlocking network. Thus, the product research program presented in Figure 6-2 as a single event might involve a network of such goals and programs as the development of a preliminary schematic design, the development of a breadboard model (such as a design that focuses on the product's function but disregards its appearance), the simplification of electronic and mechanical elements, and the packaging design.

Managers must make sure that the components of the network "fit" one another. Fitting is a matter not only of having the various programs carried out but also of timing their completion, since undertaking one program often depends on first completing another.

It is easy for one department of a company to set goals that may seem entirely appropriate for it, only to find itself operating at cross-purposes with another department. The manufacturing department may see that its goals are best served by long production runs, but this might interfere with the marketing department's desire to have all products in the line readily available or with the finance department's goal of maintaining investment in inventory at a certain low level.

Organizational studies by Gordon Donaldson showed that companies too often set goals that are unrealistic without recognizing the many constraining factors such as the economic condition or the moves by competitors.[4] Moreover, setting the company's financial goals is a continuing process in which conflicting priorities must be balanced. In fact, managers too often see the objectives from their own perspective—on the basis of their self-interest—without understanding the total network of aims.

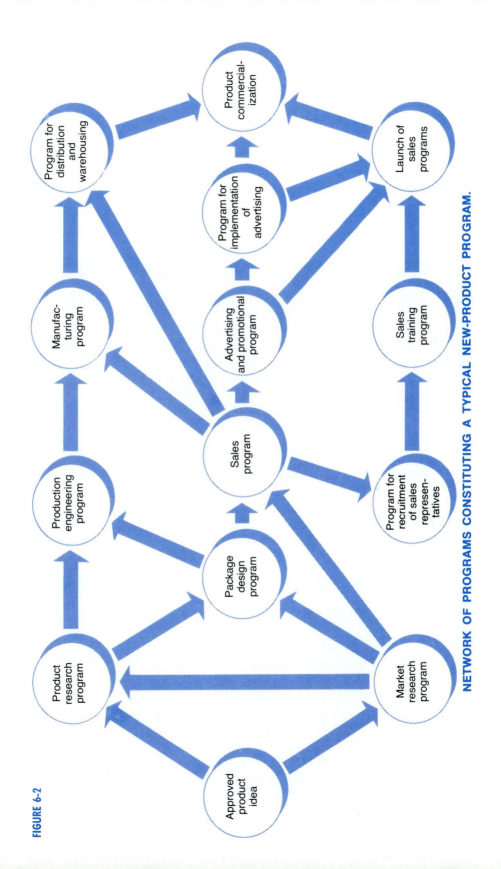

FIGURE 6-2

NETWORK OF PROGRAMS CONSTITUTING A TYPICAL NEW-PRODUCT PROGRAM.

It is bad enough when goals do not support and interlock with one another. It may be catastrophic to the overall operation when they interfere with one another. What is needed is what one executive described as a matrix of mutually supportive goals.

A Multiplicity of Objectives

Aims are, of course, numerous. Even the mission and broad major objectives of an enterprise are normally multiple, as shown in the Perspective below.

Perspective

Examples of Overall Objectives, or Aims, of a Business

A business might include the following among its overall objectives:

- Obtaining a certain rate of profit and return on investment
- Emphasizing research to develop a continuing flow of proprietary products
- Developing public stock ownership
- Financing primarily by earnings plowback and bank debt
- Distributing products in foreign markets
- Ensuring competitive prices for superior products
- Achieving a dominant position in an industry
- Adhering to the values of the society in which it operates

Similarly, to say that a university's mission is education and research is not enough. It would be much more accurate (but still not verifiable) to list the overall objectives, as shown in the next Perspective.

Perspective

Overall Objectives of a University

The overall objectives of a university might be the following:

- Attracting highly qualified students
- Offering basic training in the liberal arts and sciences as well as in certain professional fields
- Granting the Ph.D. degree to qualified candidates
- Attracting highly regarded professors
- Discovering and organizing new knowledge through research
- Operating as a private school supported principally through tuition and gifts of alumni and friends.

Likewise, at every level in the hierarchy of objectives, goals are likely to be multiple. Some people think that a manager cannot effectively pursue more than a few objectives, perhaps two to five. The argument is that too many objectives tend to dilute the drive needed for their accomplishment and may unduly highlight minor objectives to the detriment of major ones.

There is something to that position, but two to five objectives seem too arbitrary and too few. It is true that minor goals should not be given the status of important objectives unless a lower-level job is involved. It would hardly be useful for an upper-level manager to occupy his or her time with such lesser objectives as greeting callers, attending meetings, and answering correspondence. There are certain things that any manager is expected to do, and they need not be made into specific and special objectives. Goals are not conceived of as dealing with every facet of a person's job; they should not be confused with activities.

Even if routine matters are excluded, it seems that there is no definite number of objectives. To be sure, if there are so many that none receives adequate attention, planning will be ineffective. At the same time, managers might pursue simultaneously as many as ten or fifteen significant objectives. However, it would be wise to state the relative importance of each objective. At any rate, the number depends on how much the managers will do themselves and how much they can assign to subordinates, thereby limiting their role to one of assigning, supervising, and controlling.

EVOLVING CONCEPTS IN MANAGEMENT BY OBJECTIVES[5]

Management by objectives (MBO) is now practiced around the world. Yet, despite its wide applications, it is not always clear what is meant by MBO. Some still think of it as an appraisal tool; others see it as a motivational technique; still others consider MBO a planning and control device. In other words, definitions and applications of MBO differ widely, and it is therefore important to highlight the evolving concepts.[6] First, however, MBO should be defined. **Management by objectives** is a comprehensive managerial system that integrates many key managerial activities in a systematic manner and that is consciously directed toward the effective and efficient achievement of organizational and individual objectives. This view of MBO as a system of managing is not shared by all. Some still define MBO in a very narrow, limited way.

Early Impetus to MBO

No one person can be called the originator of an approach that emphasizes objectives. Common sense has told people for many centuries that groups and individuals expect to accomplish some end results. However, certain individuals have long placed emphasis on management by objectives and, by doing so, have speeded its development as a systematic process.

One of these is Peter F. Drucker.[7] In 1954 he acted as a catalyst by emphasizing that objectives must be set in all areas where performance affects the health of the enterprise. He laid down a philosophy that emphasizes self-control and self-direction. About the same time, if not earlier, the General Electric Company was using elements of MBO in its reorganization efforts to decentralize managerial decision making. The company implemented this philosophy of appraisal by identifying key result areas and undertaking considerable research on the measurement of performance.

Emphasis on Performance Appraisal

In 1957, in his classic article in the *Harvard Business Review,* Douglas McGregor, a major contributor to the behavioral sciences, criticized traditional appraisal programs that focused on personality trait criteria for evaluating subordinates.[8] In the traditional approach, managers are required to pass judgment on the personal worth of subordinates. Consequently, McGregor suggested a new approach to appraisal based on Drucker's concept of management by objectives. Specifically, subordinates assume the responsibility of setting short-term objectives for themselves, and then they review those objectives with their superior. Of course, the superior has veto power over those objectives, but in the appropriate environment it will hardly need to be used.

Performance is then evaluated against the present objectives, primarily by the subordinates themselves. In this new approach, which encourages self-appraisal and self-development, the emphasis is where it ought to be: on performance rather than on personality. The manager, acting as a coach, elicits the active involvement of subordinates in the appraisal process, which leads to commitment and creates an environment for motivation.

Emphasis on Short-Term Objectives and Motivation

Researchers, consultants, and practitioners have long recognized the importance of individual goal setting. Early studies at the University of Maryland found that performance was higher when people had specific objectives than when they were simply asked to do their best.[9] Furthermore, high levels of intentions were associated with high levels of performance.[10] One of the early field studies on an MBO program, as well as a follow-up study, found "a significant upward movement in the overall average level of goals."[11] Also, an improvement in the attainment of goals and a continuing increase in productivity were noted in this firm. However, productivity had tapered off when the follow-up study was made. Although goal setting is not the only factor in motivating employees, it is an important one (other factors are incentives, participation, and autonomy).[12] Certainly, goal setting as a motivational technique is not restricted to business but is also useful in public organizations. The general vagueness of objectives in many public organizations is a challenge for managers, but there is evidence that this is a challenge that can be met.[13]

Inclusion of Long-Range Planning in the MBO Process

In MBO programs that emphasize performance appraisal and motivation, the focus tends to be on short-term objectives. This orientation, unfortunately, may result in undesirable managerial behavior. For example, a production manager, in an effort to reduce maintenance costs, may neglect the necessary expenses for keeping the machines in good working order. The breakdown of machinery may not be evident at first, but it can result in costly repairs much later. In an effort to show a good return on investment in a given year, the nurturing of good customer relations may be neglected. Similarly, a manager may not invest in new products that would take several years before contributing to profit. Recognizing these shortcomings, many organizations now include long-range and strategic planning in MBO programs.

The Systems Approach to MBO

Management by objectives has undergone many changes; it has been used in performance appraisal, as an instrument for motivating individuals, and, more recently, in strategic planning. But there are still other managerial subsystems that can be integrated into the MBO process; they include design of organizational structures, portfolio management, management development, career development, compensation programs, and budgeting. These various managerial activities need to be integrated into a system. For example, the late George Odiorne, the most vocal spokesperson for MBO, considered it to be a system of managerial leadership. Others discuss the systematic relationships of MBO and many other key managerial activities in different environments.[14]

One of the early research studies that investigated MBO as a comprehensive system of managing indicates that most key managerial activities can and should be integrated with the MBO process. The degree of integration, however, differs for individual activities. It was found, for example, that the highest degree of integration of MBO with managerial functions was in controlling, planning, and directing. But several key managerial activities in staffing and organizing also were well integrated into the MBO process. These findings suggest that MBO, to be effective, has to be viewed as a comprehensive system. In short, it must be considered a way of managing, and not an addition to the managerial job.[15]

THE PROCESS OF MANAGING BY OBJECTIVES

The practical importance of objectives in management can best be seen by summarizing how successful managing by objectives works in practice.[16] Figure 6-3 graphically portrays this process. Ideally, the process starts at the top of an organization and has the active support of the chief executive, who gives direction to the organization. It is not essential that objective setting start at the top, however. It can start at the division level, at the marketing-manager level, or even lower. For example, in one company the system was first started in a division where it was carried down to the lowest level of supervision with an interlocking network

FIGURE 6-3

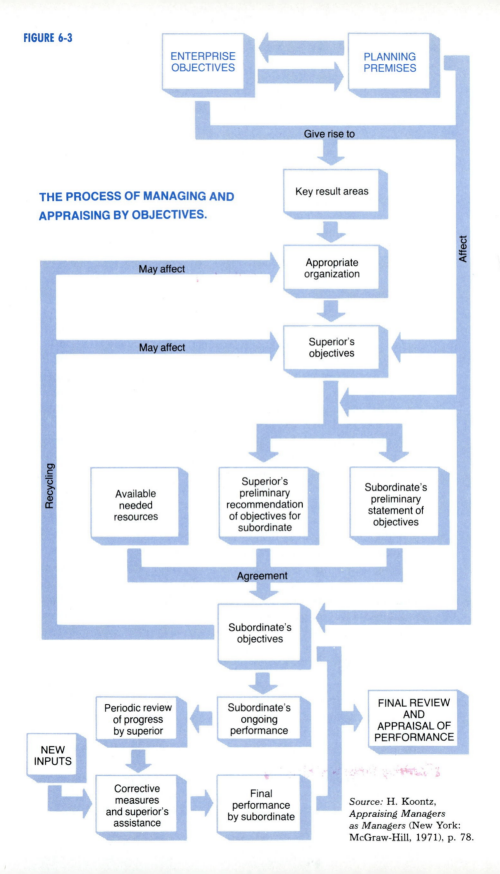

THE PROCESS OF MANAGING AND APPRAISING BY OBJECTIVES.

ENTERPRISE OBJECTIVES

PLANNING PREMISES

Give rise to

Affect

Key result areas

May affect

Appropriate organization

May affect

Superior's objectives

Recycling

Available needed resources

Superior's preliminary recommendation of objectives for subordinate

Subordinate's preliminary statement of objectives

Agreement

Subordinate's objectives

Periodic review of progress by superior

Subordinate's ongoing performance

FINAL REVIEW AND APPRAISAL OF PERFORMANCE

NEW INPUTS

Corrective measures and superior's assistance

Final performance by subordinate

Source: H. Koontz, *Appraising Managers as Managers* (New York: McGraw-Hill, 1971), p. 78.

of goals. Under the personal leadership and tutelage of the division general manager, it succeeded in the areas of profitability, cost reduction, and improved operations. Soon, some other division managers and the chief executive became interested in, and attempted to implement, similar programs. In another case, the head of an accounting section developed a system for his group; his success not only earned him recognition (and promotion) but also served as the starting point for a companywide program.

As in all other kinds of planning, one of the critical needs in MBO is the development and dissemination of consistent planning premises. No manager can be expected to set goals or establish budgets without guidelines.

Setting Preliminary Objectives at the Top

Given appropriate planning premises, the first step in setting objectives is for the top manager to determine what he or she perceives to be the purpose or mission and the more important goals of the enterprise for a given period ahead. These goals can be set for any period—a quarter, a year, 5 years, or whatever is appropriate in given circumstances. In most instances, objectives are set to coincide with the annual budget or the completion of a major project. But this is not necessary and often is not desirable. Certain goals should be scheduled for accomplishment in a much shorter period and others in a much longer period. Also, as one proceeds down the organizational hierarchy, the length of time set for accomplishing goals typically tends to get shorter. It is seldom feasible or wise for first-level supervisors, for example, to set many annual goals, since their goal span on most operating matters, such as cost or scrap reduction, rearrangement of facilities, or the institution of special personnel programs, is short (most of these goals may be accomplished in weeks or months).

The goals set by the superior are preliminary, based on an analysis and judgment as to what can and should be accomplished by the organization within a certain period. This requires taking into account the company's strengths and weaknesses in light of available opportunities and threats. These goals must be regarded as tentative and subject to modification while the entire chain of verifiable objectives is worked out by subordinates. It is usually not advisable to force objectives on subordinates, since force can scarcely give rise to a sense of commitment. Most managers also find that the process of working out goals with subordinates reveals problems they should deal with and opportunities they were not previously aware of.

When setting objectives, the manager also establishes measures of goal accomplishment. If verifiable objectives are developed, these measures, whether in sales dollars, profits, percentages, cost levels, or program execution, will normally be built into the objectives.

Clarifying Organizational Roles

The relationship between expected results and the responsibility for attaining them is often overlooked. Ideally, each goal and subgoal should be one particular person's clear responsibility. Analysis of an organization's structure, however, often reveals that the responsibility is vague and that clarification or reorganization is needed. Sometimes it is impossible to structure an organization so that a given objective is someone's personal responsibility. In setting goals for launching a new product, for example, the managers of research, marketing, and production must carefully coordinate their activities. Their separate functions can be centralized by putting a product manager in charge. If this is not desirable, at least the specific parts of each coordinating manager's contribution to the program goal can and should be clearly identified.

Setting Subordinates' Objectives

After making sure that subordinate managers have been informed of pertinent general objectives, strategies, and planning premises, the superior can then proceed to work with subordinates in setting their objectives. The superior asks what goals the subordinates believe they can accomplish, in what time period, and with what resources. They will then discuss some preliminary thoughts about what goals seem feasible for the company or department.

The superior's role at this point is extremely important. Questions that she or he should ask include: What can you contribute? How can we improve your operation to help me improve mine? What stands in the way; what obstructions keep you from a higher level of performance? What changes can we make? How can I help? It is amazing how many things can be identified that might obstruct performance and how many constructive ideas can be drawn from the experience and knowledge of subordinates.

Perspective
Objective Setting at Chrysler

At the beginning of each quarter, Lee Iacocca, the CEO at Chrysler Corporation, meets with all subordinates who report directly to him. They discuss plans and objectives until they reach agreements. These agreements are written down in terms of verifiable objectives for the coming quarter. Subordinates have much freedom to pursue their aims. Of course, the ways to achieve results have to be ethical, and they have to be within the company's policies. During the quarter, Iacocca is available to assist, advise, and coach his subordinates. At the next quarterly meeting, performance is measured against previously set objectives, and people are held accountable for their performance. By using this approach, Lee Iacocca is clear about the contributions he can anticipate from his subordinates, and they, in turn, know what is expected of them.

Superiors must also be patient counselors, helping their subordinates develop consistent and supportive objectives and being careful not to set goals that are impossible to achieve. It is human nature to believe that anything can be accomplished a year hence but that much less can be done next week. And one of the things that can weaken a program of managing by objectives is to allow managers to set unrealistic objectives.

At the same time, having subordinates set goals does not mean that people can do whatever they want to do. Superiors must listen to, and work with, their subordinates, but in the end they must take responsibility for approving subordinates' goals. The superior's judgment and final approval must be based on what is reasonably attainable with "stretch" and "pull," what is fully supportive of upper-level objectives, what is consistent with the goals of other managers in other functions, and what is consistent with the longer-run objectives and interests of the department and the company.

One of the major advantages of carefully setting up a network of verifiable goals and a requirement for doing so effectively is tying in the need of capital, materials, and human resources at the same time. All managers at all levels require these resources to accomplish their goals. By relating these resources to the goals themselves, superiors can better see the most effective and most economical way of allocating them. It helps to avoid the bane of any upper-level manager's existence: "nickel and diming" by subordinates who need "one more" technician or "one more" piece of equipment, requests that are easy for them to "sell" to their boss and difficult for the superior to refuse.

Recycling Objectives

Objectives can hardly be set by starting at the top and dividing them up among subordinates. Nor should they be started from the bottom. A degree of recycling is required. Recycling is indicated by the arrows in Figures 6-1 and 6-3. Top managers may have some idea of what their subordinates' objectives should be—but they will almost certainly change these preconceived goals as the contributions of the subordinates come into focus. Thus, setting objectives is not only a joint process but also an interactive one. For example, a sales manager may realistically set a goal to achieve product sales that are much higher than what top management has believed possible. In this event, the goals of the manufacturing and finance departments will surely be affected.

HOW TO SET OBJECTIVES

Without clear objectives, managing is haphazard. No individual and no group can expect to perform effectively and efficiently unless there is a clear aim. Table 6-1 illustrates some objectives and how they can be restated in a way that allows measurement.

Quantitative and Qualitative Objectives[17]

To be measurable, objectives must be verifiable. This means that one must be able to answer the following question: At the end of the period, how do I know if the

TABLE 6-1   EXAMPLES OF NONVERIFIABLE AND VERIFIABLE OBJECTIVES

Nonverifiable objectives	Verifiable objectives
1. To make a reasonable profit	1. To achieve a return on investment of 12% at the end of the current fiscal year
2. To improve communication	2. To issue a two-page monthly newsletter beginning July 1, 1994, involving not more than 40 working hours of preparation time (after the first issue)
3. To improve productivity of the production department	3. To increase production output by 5% by December 31, 1994, without additional costs and while maintaining the current quality level
4. To develop better managers	4. To design and conduct a 40-hour in-house program on the "fundamentals of management," to be completed by October 1, 1994, involving not more than 200 working hours of the management development staff and with at least 90% of the 100 managers passing the exam (specified)
5. To install a computer system	5. To install a computerized control system in the production department by December 31, 1994, requiring not more than 500 working hours of systems analysis and operating with not more than 10% downtime during the first 3 months nor 2% thereafter

objective has been accomplished? For example, the objective of making a reasonable profit can at best indicate whether the company made a profit or had a loss (see Table 6-1), but it does not state how much profit is to be made. Also, what is reasonable to the subordinate may not be at all acceptable to the superior. In the case of such a disagreement, it is, of course, the subordinate who loses the argument. In contrast, a return on investment of 12 percent at the end of the current fiscal year can be measured; it answers these questions: How much or what? When?

At times it is more difficult to state results in verifiable terms. This is especially true for staff personnel and also in government. For example, installing a computer system is an important task, but "to install a computer system" is not a verifiable goal. But suppose the objective is "to install a computerized control system (with certain specifications) in the production department by December 31, 1994, with an expenditure of not more than 500 working hours." Then, goal accomplishment can be measured. Moreover, quality can also be specified (in terms of computer downtime).

Setting Objectives in Government[18]

The need of managing by objectives in government has been recognized by Frederic V. Malek, a former special assistant to the President and one of the driving forces in the implementation of MBO in the federal government.[19] He stated: "If the executive branch of government is to be managed effectively, it clearly needs a system for setting priorities, pinpointing responsibility for their achievement, requiring follow-through, and generating enough feedback that programs can be monitored and evaluated from the top." The MBO program initiated in the federal government in the early 1970s indeed had some success. For example, the Department of Health, Education, and Welfare set an objective for training 35,000 welfare recipients and placing them in meaningful jobs, an objective that seemed almost impossible to achieve. The goal was not only achieved but also exceeded; 40,000 welfare recipients were trained and placed on payrolls.

To be sure, the management of government has some special problems. Many expenditures are uncontrollable because they are mandated by law. There is also the tendency to perpetuate ineffective programs for political reasons, and congressional members have a political rather than a managerial orientation. Finally, the traditional budgeting process is not conducive to managerial productivity.

Improving the operation of the federal government, and other governments as well, requires:

1. Identifying ineffective programs by comparing performance with preestablished objectives
2. Using zero-base budgeting (a topic to be discussed later, in Chapter 21)
3. Applying MBO concepts for measuring individual performance
4. Preparing short- and long-range objectives and plans
5. Installing effective controls
6. Designing sound organization structures with clear responsibilities and decision-making authority at appropriate levels
7. Developing and preparing government officials for managerial responsibilities

Thus, the setting of objectives, as in MBO programs, not only is essential for making line managers in business organizations more effective but also is equally important for improving the performance of staff personnel and public administrators.

Guidelines for Setting Objectives

Setting objectives is indeed a difficult task. It requires intelligent coaching by the superior and extensive practice by the subordinate. The guidelines shown in Table 6-2 will help managers in setting their objectives.

The list of objectives should not be too long, yet it should cover the main features of the job. As this chapter has emphasized, objectives should be verifiable and should state what is to be accomplished and when. If possible, the quality desired and the projected cost of achieving the objectives should be indicated. Furthermore, objectives should present a challenge, indicate priorities, and promote personal and professional growth and development. These and other criteria for good objectives are summarized in Table 6-2. Testing objectives against the criteria shown in the checklist is a good exercise for managers and aspiring managers.

TABLE 6-2   CHECKLIST FOR MANAGER OBJECTIVES

If the objectives meet the criterion, write "+" in the box at the right of the statement. If they do not, mark "−" in the box.

1. Do the objectives cover the main features of my job?   ☐

2. Is the list of objectives too long? If so, can I combine some objectives?   ☐

3. Are the objectives verifiable; that is, will I know at the end of the period whether or not they have been achieved?   ☐

4. Do the objectives indicate:
    (a) Quantity (how much)?   ☐
    (b) Quality (how well, or specific characteristics)?   ☐
    (c) Time (when)?   ☐
    (d) Cost (at what cost)?   ☐

5. Are the objectives challenging, yet reasonable?   ☐

6. Are priorities assigned to the objectives (ranking, weighing, etc.)?   ☐

7. Does the set of objectives also include:
    (a) Improvement objectives?   ☐
    (b) Personal development objectives?   ☐

8. Are the objectives coordinated with those of other managers and organizational units?   ☐
    Are they consistent with objectives of my superior, my department, the company?   ☐

9. Have I communicated the objectives to all who need to be informed?   ☐

10. Are the short-term objectives consistent with long-term aims?   ☐

11. Are the assumptions underlying the objectives clearly identified?   ☐

12. Are the objectives expressed clearly, and are they in writing?   ☐

13. Do the objectives provide for timely feedback so that I can take any necessary corrective steps?   ☐

14. Are my resources and authority sufficient for achieving the objectives?   ☐

15. Have I given the individuals who are expected to accomplish objectives a chance to suggest their objectives?   ☐

16. Do my subordinates have control over aspects for which they are assigned responsibility?   ☐

BENEFITS AND WEAKNESSES OF MANAGEMENT BY OBJECTIVES AND SOME RECOMMENDATIONS

Although goal-oriented management is now one of the most widely practiced managerial approaches, its effectiveness is sometimes questioned. Faulty implementation is often blamed, but another reason is that MBO may be applied as a mechanistic technique focusing on selected aspects of the managerial process without integrating them into a system.

A review of 185 studies showed that it is rather difficult to evaluate the true effectiveness of MBO.[20] For one, MBO is defined and practiced differently by various organizations. For some it means simply goal setting, while for others it is a comprehensive system of managing. Also, effectiveness is not easy to define, and an increase or decrease in performance may be due to factors other than MBO. It may take 2 to 5 years to implement an MBO program, and during that time many factors other than the program can influence the operation of the firm. As pointed out several years ago—and it is still true today—if a goal-oriented management approach is to produce results, it has to be adapted to the specific situation.[21]

Nevertheless, one can learn from experience and research by taking a realistic view and analyzing some of the benefits and weaknesses of MBO.

Benefits of Management by Objectives

As pointed out earlier, there is considerable evidence, much of it from laboratory studies, that shows the motivational aspects of clear goals. But there are other benefits.

Improvement of managing.   All the advantages of management by objectives can be summarized by saying that it results in greatly improved management. Objectives cannot be established without planning, and results-oriented planning is the only kind that makes sense. Management by objectives forces managers to think about planning for results, rather than merely planning activities or work. To ensure that objectives are realistic, MBO also requires that managers think of the way they will accomplish results, the organization and personnel they will need to do so, and the resources and assistance they will require. Also, there is no better incentive for control and no better way to know the standards for control than having a set of clear goals.

Clarification of organization.   Another major benefit of managing by objectives is that it forces managers to clarify organizational roles and structures. To the extent possible, positions should be built around the key results expected of the people occupying them.

Companies that have effectively embarked on MBO programs have often discovered deficiencies in their organization. Managers often forget that to get results, they must delegate authority according to the results they expect. As an executive of Honeywell is reported to have said: "There are two things that might also be considered fundamental creed at Honeywell: decentralized management is needed to make Honeywell work and management by objectives is needed to make decentralization work."

Encouragement of personal commitment.   One of the great advantages of management by objectives is that it encourages people to commit themselves to their goals. No longer are people just doing work, following instructions, and waiting for guidance and decisions; they are now individuals with clearly defined purposes. They have had a part in actually setting their objectives; they have had an opportunity to put their ideas into planning programs; they understand their area of discretion—their authority—and they have been able to get help from their superiors to ensure that they can accomplish their goals. These are the elements that make for a feeling of commitment. People become enthusiastic when they control their own fate.

Development of effective controls.   In the same way that management by objectives sparks more effective planning, it also aids in developing effective controls. Recall that control involves measuring results and taking action to correct deviations from plans in order to ensure that goals are reached. As will be explained in Chapter 20, on the system and process of management control, one of the major problems is knowing what to watch; a clear set of verifiable goals is the best guide.

Weaknesses of Management by Objectives

With all its advantages, a system of management by objectives has a number of weaknesses. Most are due to shortcomings in applying the MBO concepts.

Failure to teach the philosophy of MBO.   As simple as management by objectives may seem, managers who would put it into practice must understand and appreciate a good deal about it. They, in turn, must explain to subordinates what it is, how it works, why it is being done, what part it will play in appraising performance, and, above all, how participants can benefit. The philosophy is built on concepts of self-control and self-direction that are aimed at making managers professionals.

Failure to give guidelines to goal setters.   Management by objectives, like any other kind of planning, cannot work if those who are expected to set goals are not given needed guidelines. Managers must know what the corporate goals are and how their own activities fit in with them. If corporation goals are vague, unreal, or inconsistent, it is virtually impossible for managers to tune in with them.

Managers also need planning premises and a knowledge of major company policies. People must have some assumptions as to the future, some understanding of policies affecting their areas of operation, and an awareness of the objectives and programs with which their goals interlock in order to plan effectively. Failure to fill these needs can result in a fatal vacuum in planning.

Difficulty of setting goals.   Truly verifiable goals are difficult to set, particularly if they are to have the right degree of stretch or pull, quarter in and quarter out, year in and year out. Goal setting may not be much more difficult than any other kind of effective planning, although it will probably take more study and work to establish verifiable objectives that are formidable but attainable than to develop many other plans, which tend only to lay out work to be done. Participants in MBO programs report at times that the excessive concern with economic results puts pressure on individuals that may encourage questionable behavior.[22] To reduce the probability of selecting unethical means for achieving results, top management must agree to reasonable objectives, clearly state behavioral expectations, and give high priority to ethical behavior, rewarding it as well as punishing unethical activities.

Emphasis on short-run goals. In most MBO programs, managers set goals for the short term, seldom for more than a year and often for a quarter or less. There is clearly a danger of emphasizing the short run, perhaps at the expense of the longer range. This means, of course, that superiors must always assure themselves that current objectives, like any other short-run plan, are designed to serve longer-range goals.

Danger of inflexibility. Managers often hesitate to change objectives. Although goals may cease to be meaningful if they are changed too often and do not represent a well-thought-out and well-planned result, it is nonetheless foolish to expect a manager to strive for a goal that has been made obsolete by revised corporate objectives, changed premises, or modified policies.

Other dangers. There are some other dangers and difficulties in management by objectives. In their desire to make goals verifiable, people may overuse quantitative goals and attempt to use numbers in areas where they are not applicable, or they may downgrade important goals that are difficult to state in terms of end results. A favorable company image may be the key strength of an enterprise, yet it is difficult to state this in quantitative terms. Sometimes managers fail to use objectives as a constructive force, even with the full participation and assistance of their superiors. There is also the danger of forgetting that managing involves more than goal setting.

Difficulties may also arise in applying goal-oriented planning in a very dynamic and complex environment. In human services delivery systems it was noted that MBO was rejected because of difficulties in (1) converting broad organizational objectives into more detailed organizational unit objectives, (2) measuring performance and providing feedback, (3) determining what is meritorious performance and rewarding individuals accordingly, (4) stating long-term objectives that are congruent with short-term goals, and (5) adjusting to the fast-changing environment.[23]

But even with the difficulties and dangers of managing by objectives in certain situations, this system emphasizes in practice the setting of goals long known to be an essential part of planning and managing.

SUMMARY

Objectives are the end points toward which activities are aimed. Objectives are verifiable if it is possible, at the end of the period, to determine whether or not they have been accomplished.

Objectives form both a hierarchy—reaching from corporate purposes and missions down to individual goals—and a network as they are reflected in interlocking programs. Managers can best determine the number of objectives they should realistically set for themselves by analyzing the nature of the job and how much they can do themselves and how much they can delegate. In any case, managers should know the relative importance of each of their goals.

Management by objectives (MBO) has been widely used for performance appraisal and employee motivation, but it is really a system of managing. The MBO process consists of setting goals at the highest level of the organization, clarifying the specific roles of those responsible for achieving the goals, and setting and modifying objectives for subordinates. Goals can be set for line managers as well as for staff personnel. Goals can be qualitative or quantitative.

Among its other benefits, MBO results in better managing, often forces managers to clarify the structure of their organizations, encourages people to commit themselves to their goals, and helps develop effective controls.

Some of its weaknesses are that managers sometimes fail to explain the philosophy of MBO (which emphasizes self-control and self-direction) to subordinates and give them guidelines for their goal setting. In addition, goals themselves are difficult to set, tend to be short-run, and may become inflexible despite changes in the environment of plan operations. People, in their search for verifiability, may overemphasize quantifiable goals.

KEY IDEAS AND CONCEPTS FOR REVIEW

Objectives

Hierarchy of objectives

Key result areas

Network of objectives

Evolving concepts in management by
  objectives (MBO)

Systems approach to managing by
  objectives

MBO process

Quantitative objectives

Qualitative objectives

Verifiability

Objective setting in government

Benefits of MBO

Weaknesses of MBO

Recommendations for improving MBO

FOR DISCUSSION

1. To what extent do you believe that managers you have known in business or elsewhere have a clear understanding of their objectives? If, in your opinion, they do not, how would you suggest that they go about setting them?
2. Some people object to defining long-term goals because they think it is impossible to know what will happen over a long period. Do you believe this is an intelligent position to take? Why or why not?
3. Take any program of any kind that you would like to see accomplished, and draw up a network of contributing programs and goals that would be necessary for its accomplishment.
4. "The only planning tool we need in this company is the budget. If everyone meets his or her budget, we need nothing else, and management by objectives would be an unnecessary frill." Comment.

5. Although many business enterprises have talked about and introduced MBO programs, the actual record of performance under these programs has been poor. Why?
6. Do you believe that managing by objectives could be introduced in a government agency? A university? A college fraternity or sorority?
7. What are your five most important personal objectives? Are they long- or short-range? Are the objectives verifiable?
8. In your organization, what does your superior expect from you in respect to the level of performance? Is it stated in writing? If you wrote your job objective on a sheet of paper and your boss wrote down what he or she expects of you, would the two be consistent?

EXERCISES/ACTION STEPS

1. Make a list of goals you wish to achieve in the next 5 years. Are they verifiable? Are they attainable?
2. In this chapter, the overall objectives of a university were identified. Develop overall objectives for your university, objectives for your college, and objectives for the various departments in your college. Show how these objectives are interrelated to form a network.

CASES

CASE 6-1
DEVELOPING VERIFIABLE GOALS

The division manager had recently heard a lecture on management by objectives. His enthusiasm, kindled at that time, tended to grow the more he thought about it. He finally decided to introduce the concept and see what headway he could make at his next staff meeting.

He recounted the theoretical developments in this technique, cited the advantages to the division of its application, and asked his subordinates to think about adopting it.

It was not as easy as everyone had thought. At the next meeting, several questions were raised. "Do you have division goals assigned by the president to you for next year?" the finance manager wanted to know.

"No, I do not," the division manager replied. "I have been waiting for the president's office to tell me what is expected, but they act as if they will do nothing about the matter."

"What is the division to do, then?" the manager of production asked, rather hoping that no action would be indicated.

"I intend to list my expectations for the division," the division manager said. "There is not much mystery about them. I expect $30 million in sales; a profit on sales before taxes of 8 percent; a return on investment of 15 percent; an ongoing program in effect by June 30, with specific characteristics I will list later, to develop our own future managers; the completion of development work on our XZ model by the end of the year; and stabilization of employee turnover at 5 percent."

The staff was somewhat stunned that their superior had thought through to these verifiable objectives and stated them with such clarity and assurance. They were also surprised about his sincerity in wanting to achieve them.

"During the next month I want each of you to

translate these objectives into verifiable goals for your own functions. Naturally they will be different for finance, marketing, production, engineering, and administration. However you state them, I will expect them to add up to the realization of the division goals."

1. Can a division manager develop verifiable goals, or objectives, when they have not been assigned to

him or her by the president? How? What kind of information or help do you believe is important for the division manager to have from headquarters?
2. Was the division manager setting goals in the best way? What would you have done?

INTERNATIONAL CASE 6-2
SCANDINAVIAN AIRLINES SYSTEM[24]

The Scandinavian Airlines System (SAS) originated when the airlines of Sweden, Norway, and Denmark formed a consortium. During the 1970s competition became fierce and resulted in a loss of market share, deterioration of service, and reduced profitability. The external environment was marked by high fuel prices and rising costs, a decrease in demand for air service, and price wars.

To help SAS recover from this slump, Jan Carlzon, the CEO, undertook drastic decentralization in 1981. The use of top-down authority was replaced by open communication and by the transfer of greater decision power to personnel close to the customers. Furthermore, service quality standards were set at a high level. While the rest of the industry was stagnant, Carlzon turned the company around by "filling seats." *Air Transport World* elected SAS "Airline of the Year."

What, then, accounted for the airline's turnaround? Detailed rules and regulations inhibiting frontline personnel were reviewed and changed. Frontline people received 2 to 3 days' training so that they could respond better to customers' needs. Carlzon gave customer relations and services high priority. The previous top-down approach in communication inhibited creativity, initiative, and prompt action of frontline personnel. The new company philosophy emphasized that personnel in all divisions and at all levels have to support personnel close to the customers.

To make intelligent decisions, employees throughout the company need to be informed. Carlzon spends a great deal of time communicating the goals and strategies of SAS in a way that is understandable to all employees—managers as well as nonmanagers. For example, one of SAS's strategies is to become

known as "the businessman's strategy" (with rather high fares), with upgraded service, on-time performance, good food, and comfort. Less emphasis is placed on the leisure traveler, with lower fares and reduced service.

To implement the strategy, management by objectives is used. The 1987 Annual Report states: "SAS's organization is based on management by objectives and decentralized profit responsibility." The role of the managers is not only to give direction but also to give responsibility for the means of achieving the ends to subordinates. The managers are supporters and advisers rather than autocratic bosses.

For the future, SAS has two important goals: (1) to become the most efficient airline in Europe by 1992 and (2) to be one of the five major airlines in Europe after 1995.

A keystone in SAS's *global* strategy is to form strategic alliances. In fact, SAS sought partners before such alliances became popular. The first attempts to forge alliances failed. The proposed 1986 merger with Belgian World Airlines, Sabena, failed because of legal complexities. An attempt to take over British Caledonian Airways Ltd. was blocked by British Airways PLC. And the Peronist party of Argentina blocked the deal with Aerolineas Argentinas.

Undeterred by early failures, Carlzon pursued his alliances strategy in order to make SAS competitive with larger European airlines such as Lufthansa (German), British Airways, and KLM (Dutch). Carlzon realized that in the larger EC 1992 environment (Sweden is not a member of the European Community), when many of the trade barriers will fall, SAS will need alliances. One such arrangement was made with Thai Airways International (1987) to coordinate services in Bangkok, Copenhagen, and Stockholm. Similarly, the 1988 agreement with Texas Air, the parent company of Continental Airlines, gives SAS access to the Newark, New Jersey, airport in the United States. In 1988, SAS also bought a stake in Airlines of Britain Holdings. An agreement to exchange equities with Swissair was reached in 1989. In the same year, alliances were made with All Nippon Airways (Japanese), Lan-Chile, Canadian Airlines International, and Finnair to gain access to airline hubs in Tokyo, Latin America, Toronto, and Helsinki. But critics question whether SAS's strategy will work or whether SAS is simply wasting money on other airlines it cannot control.

1. In a geographically dispersed company such as SAS, how can you decentralize without losing control?
2. How would you set verifiable objectives in these areas: (1) on-time arrival, (2) customer satisfaction, and (3) company success? Set objectives in other key result areas.
3. Are Carlzon's philosophy and the organizational culture conducive to a management-by-objectives program?
4. Are top-down and bottom-up managing incongruent?
5. Do you think that the strategic alliances with many different airlines will work?

REFERENCES

1. George S. Odiorne, *Management by Objectives* (New York: Pitman Publishing Corp., 1965), p. v.
2. Peter F. Drucker, *The Practice of Management* (New York: Harper & Brothers, 1954), p. 63.
3. Parts of this discussion are based on Heinz Weihrich, *Management Excellence—Productivity through MBO* (New York: McGraw-Hill Book Company, 1985), chap. 4.
4. Gordon Donaldson, "Financial Goals and Strategic Consequences," *Harvard Business Review* (May–June 1985), pp. 57–66.
5. See also George Odiorne, Heinz Weihrich, and Jack Mendleson (eds.), *Executive Skills—A Management by Objectives Approach* (Dubuque, Iowa: Wm. C. Brown Company, 1980).
6. For a detailed discussion of the history of MBO, see George S. Odiorne, "MBO: A Backward Glance," *Business Horizons* (October 1978), pp. 14–24. An excellent discussion of the early history of MBO is by Ronald G. Greenwood, "Management by Objectives: As Developed by Peter Drucker, Assisted by Harold Smiddy," *Academy of Management Review* (April 1981), pp. 225–230.
7. For his original discussion of managing by objectives, see Drucker, *The Practice of Management* (1954), pp. 121–136. In conversation with Harold Koontz, Drucker gave credit for the concept to the late Harold E. Smiddy, then of General Electric. See also Greenwood, "Management by Objectives" (April 1981), pp. 225–230.
8. Douglas McGregor, "An Uneasy Look at Performance Appraisal," *Harvard Business Review* (May–June 1957), pp. 89–94. In even more recent writings the emphasis in MBO is still on goal setting and appraisal, as shown by Mark L. McConkie, "A Clarification of the Goal Setting and Appraisal Process in MBO," *Academy of Management Review* (January 1979), pp. 29–40.
9. Edwin A. Locke and Judith F. Bryan, "Performance Goals as Determinants of Level of Performance and Boredom," *Journal of Applied Psychology* (April 1967), pp. 120–130.
10. Edwin A. Locke, "The Relationship of Intentions to Level of Performance," *Journal of Applied Psychology* (February 1966), pp. 60–66.

11. Anthony P. Raia, "A Second Look at Management Goals and Controls," *California Management Review* (Summer 1966), pp. 49–58.

12. Edwin A. Locke, "The Ubiquity of the Technique of Goal Setting in Theories of and Approaches to Employee Motivation," *Academy of Management Review* (July 1978), pp. 594–601.

13. Heinz Weihrich, "The Application of Management by Objectives in Government," *Faculty Working Paper MG 76-3* (Tempe, Ariz.: Arizona State University, 1976).

14. Anthony P. Raia, *Managing by Objectives* (Glenview, Ill.: Scott, Foresman and Company, 1974); Dale D. McConkey, *MBO for Nonprofit Organizations* (New York: AMACOM, American Management Association, 1975); George L. Morrisey, *Management by Objectives and Results in the Public Sector* (Reading, Mass.: Addison-Wesley Publishing Company, 1976).

15. Heinz Weihrich, "A Study of the Integration of Management by Objectives with Key Managerial Activities and the Relationship to Selected Effectiveness Measures," doctoral dissertation, University of California, Los Angeles, 1973.

16. Some of the material in this section is drawn from Harold Koontz, *Appraising Managers as Managers* (New York: McGraw-Hill Book Company, 1971), chaps. 3–4.

17. For computerized goal setting at Cypress Semiconductor, see T. J. Rogers, "No Excuses Management," *Harvard Business Review* (July–August 1990), pp. 84–98.

18. See also M. A. Mark, "Productivity Measurement of Government Services—Federal, State, and Local," *White House Conference on Productivity*, Panel Background Papers, 1983.

19. This discussion is based on Malek's book *Washington's Hidden Tragedy* (New York: The Free Press, 1978), chaps. 7–9. It provides one of the best insights into the operation of MBO in the federal government.

20. Jack N. Kondrasuk, "Studies in MBO Effectiveness," *Academy of Management Review* (July 1981), pp. 419–430.

21. Heinz Weihrich, "An Uneasy Look at the MBO Jungle—Toward a Contingency Approach to MBO," *Management International Review*, vol. 16, no. 4 (1976), pp. 103–109.

22. Charles D. Pringle and Justin G. Longenecker, "The Ethics of MBO," *Academy of Management Review* (April 1982), pp. 305–312.

23. Mark A. Covaleski and Mark W. Dirsmith, "MBO and Goal Directedness in a Hospital Context," *Academy of Management Review* (July 1981), pp. 409–418.

24. A variety of sources have been used, including SAS's Annual Report (1987); Jan Carlzon, *Moments of Truth* (New York: Perennial Library, 1989); Amanda Bennett, "SAS's 'Nice Guy' Is Aiming to Finish First," *The Wall Street Journal* (Mar. 2, 1989); Jonathan Kapstein and Mark Maremont, "Can SAS Keep Flying with the Big Birds?" *Business Week* (Nov. 27, 1989), pp. 142–146.

Strategic management is an exciting process that allows an organization to be proactive rather than reactive in shaping its own future.[1]

Fred R. David

Strategies, Policies, and Planning Premises

Chapter Objectives

After reading this chapter, you should be able to:

1. Explain the nature and purpose of strategies and policies.
2. Describe the strategic planning process.
3. Understand the TOWS Matrix and the Business Portfolio Matrix.
4. Describe the major kinds of strategies and policies.
5. Identify Porter's generic strategies.
6. Make recommendations for the effective implementation of strategies.
7. Discuss the nature and types of premises and forecasts.
8. Understand how to make premising effective.

Today most business enterprises engage in strategic planning, although the degrees of sophistication and formality vary considerably. Conceptually, strategic planning is deceptively simple: Analyze the current and expected future situation, determine the direction of the firm, and develop means for achieving the mission. In reality, this is an extremely complex process that demands a systematic approach for identifying and analyzing factors external to the organization and matching them with the firm's capabilities.

Planning is done in an environment of uncertainty. No one can be sure what the external as well as the internal environment will be even next week, much less several years from now. Therefore, people make assumptions or forecasts about the anticipated environment. Some of the forecasts become assumptions for other plans. For example, the gross national product forecast becomes the assumption for sales planning, which in turn becomes the basis for production planning, and so on.

In this chapter you will learn about (1) the nature and purpose of strategies and policies; (2) the strategic planning process, which identifies the critical aspects of formulating a strategy; (3) the TOWS Matrix, a tool for systematically integrating external and internal factors; (4) the Business Portfolio Matrix, a tool for allocating resources; (5) the major kinds of strategies and policies; (6) three generic strategies; and (7) the means for effectively implementing strategies. Since plans are made in an environment of uncertainty, you will also learn (8) about premising and forecasting and (9) how to make premising effective.

THE NATURE AND PURPOSE OF STRATEGIES AND POLICIES

Strategies and policies are closely related. Both give direction, both are the framework for plans, both are the basis of operational plans, and both affect all areas of managing.

Strategy and Policy

The term "strategy" (which is derived from the Greek word *strategos*, meaning "general") has been used in different ways. Authors differ in at least one major aspect about *strategies*. Some writers focus on both the end points (purpose, mission, goals, objectives) and the means of achieving them (policies and plans). Others emphasize the means to the ends in the strategic process rather than the ends per se. As pointed out in Chapter 5, **strategy** refers to the determination of the purpose (or mission) and the basic long-term objectives of an enterprise, and the adoption of courses of action and allocation of resources necessary to achieve these aims. Therefore, objectives (discussed in Chapter 6) are a part of strategy formulation.

Since ends have already been discussed (Chapter 6), let us turn our attention now to the means of achieving them, including the situation analysis. It is assumed that the purpose of the enterprise has already been established yet is subject to change after an evaluation of the situation.

Policies are general statements or understandings that guide managers' thinking in decision making. They ensure that decisions fall within certain boundaries. They usually do not require action but are intended to guide managers in their commitment to the decision they ultimately make.

The essence of policy is discretion. Strategy, on the other hand, concerns the direction in which human and material resources will be applied in order to increase the chance of achieving selected objectives.

Certain major policies and strategies may be essentially the same. A policy of developing only those new products that fit into a company's marketing plan or one of distributing only through retailers may be an essential element of a company's strategy for new product development or marketing. One company may have a policy of growth through the acquisition of other companies, while another may have a policy of growing only by expanding present markets and products. While these are policies, they are also essential elements of major strategies. Perhaps one way to draw a meaningful distinction is to say that policies will guide a manager's thinking in decision making—if a decision is to be made—while a strategy implies the commitment of resources in a given direction.

The Key Function: Giving Direction to Plans

The key function of strategies and policies is to unify and give direction to plans. In other words, they influence the course along which an enterprise is trying to go. But, standing alone, they do not ensure that an organization will, in fact, go where it wants to go.

The Guide: Furnishing the Framework for Plans

Strategies and policies help managers plan by guiding operating decisions and often premaking them. The **principle of the strategy and policy framework** is, then, that *the more strategies and policies are clearly understood and implemented in practice, the more consistent and effective will be the framework for enterprise* *plans*. For example, if a company has a major policy of developing only new products that fit its marketing organization, it will avoid wasting energy and resources on new products that do not meet this test.

The Need for Operational Planning: Tactics

To be effective, strategies and policies must be put into practice by means of plans, increasing in detail until they get down to the nuts and bolts of operations. **Tactics, then, are the action plans through which strategies are executed.** Strategies must be supported by effective tactics.

The Effect on All Areas of Managing

Since strategies and policies affect planning, they also greatly affect other areas of managing. For example, major strategies and policies will naturally influence organization structure and, through this, other functions of the manager. In his extraordinary analysis of the history of some of the nation's largest companies, Alfred Chandler, Jr., depicts in detail how strategy affected organization structure.[2] In the Du Pont Company, the organization around product lines, with centralized control, followed the strategy of product diversification. General Motors had essentially the same situation. In Du Pont, the strategy of diversification was dictated by the need to use resources made surplus by the post–World War I decline in the explosives business. In General Motors, on the other hand, the strategy was one of integration and expansion of a large, disparate group of companies acquired by W. C. Durant in his formation of the company during the two decades before 1920. While the strategies of these two companies were based on different premises and situations, they led to essentially the same organization structures.

THE STRATEGIC PLANNING PROCESS

Although specific steps in the formulation of a strategy may vary, the process can be built, at least conceptually, around the key elements shown in Figure 7-1.

Inputs

The various organizational *inputs*, including the goal inputs of the claimants, were discussed in Chapter 1 and need no elaboration.

Enterprise Profile

The *enterprise profile* is usually the starting point for determining where the company is and where it should go. Thus, top managers determine the basic purpose of the enterprise and clarify the firm's geographic orientation, such as whether it should operate in selected regions, in all states in the United States, or even in different countries. In addition, managers assess the firm's competitive situation.

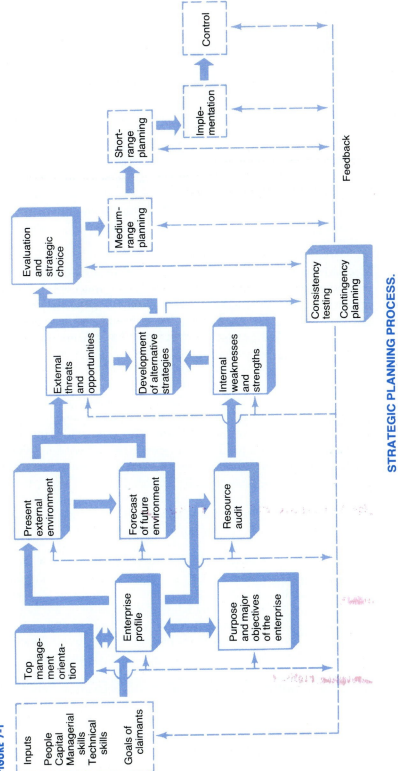

FIGURE 7-1

STRATEGIC PLANNING PROCESS.

Adapted from Heinz Weihrich, "The TOWS Matrix: A Tool for Situational Analysis," *Long-Range Planning*, vol. 15, no. 2 (1982), pp. 54–66.

Top managers get paid for making tough decisions, and many of their decisions are strategic for the future of the company. Let us look at some examples of decisions that altered the course of the company.[3]

General Motors.   Roger Smith of General Motors saw the opportunities in the high-tech field and their importance for GM. Consequently, he decided to acquire Electronic Data Systems Corp., a large data processing company. But the resistance to the merger of these two companies (with very different organizational cultures) by GM's staff was substantial. Long-established organizations do not change easily, and Roger Smith learned a great deal about the difficulty of making dramatic changes.

Gould Inc.   William Ylvisaker, the former CEO at Gould Inc., changed the firm from a manufacturer of car batteries and electrical equipment to a high-tech electronics firm. This new direction required a change in personnel; half of Gould's management committee left the company. Making such drastic decisions requires a strong-willed person; Ylvisaker was named one of the ten toughest corporate managers by *Fortune* magazine.

Warner-Lambert.   When Ward Hagan wanted to restructure Warner-Lambert, he had to streamline the drug company. This required selling the eyeglass manufacturer American Optical (a loser) as well as Entenmann, a profitable bakery firm. To give a new direction to the firm, Hagan employed the consulting services of McKinsey & Co. to teach its managers strategic planning. To be sure, nobody can predict the long-term future with great accuracy, but strategic planning forces managers to think critically and analytically about the future. The company sent 500 of its managers to a program that trained them in critical thinking. To demonstrate the importance of strategic thinking, the company rewarded managers who utilized the technique with promotions.

Rolm Corporation.   Rolm Corporation was concerned about its dependence on military customers, which led to a search for related product lines. Despite a thorough search, the results were at first disappointing. Persistence and a continuing search led to the development of digital switching equipment that was more advanced than that of Rolm's competitors. Some risk-taking decisions turned out to be right and made the company a giant in its field before the firm was acquired by IBM and later by Siemens, a German firm.

Orientation of Top Managers

The enterprise profile is shaped by people, especially *top managers*, and their *orientation* is important for formulating the strategy. They set the organizational climate, and they determine the direction of the firm. Consequently, their values, their preferences, and their attitudes toward risks have to be carefully examined because they have an impact on the strategy.

Purpose and Major Objectives

The *purpose* (or mission) and the major *objectives* are the end points toward which the activities of the enterprise are directed. Since the previous chapter dealt with these topics at length, additional discussion here is unnecessary.

External Environment

The present and future *external environment* must be assessed in terms of threats and opportunities. The evaluation focuses on economic, social, political, legal, demographic, and geographic factors. In addition, the environment is scanned for technological developments, for products and services on the market, and for other factors necessary in determining the competitive situation of the enterprise.

Internal Environment

Similarly, the firm's *internal environment* should be audited and evaluated in respect to its resources and its weaknesses and strengths in research and development, production, operations, procurement, marketing, and products and services. Other internal factors that are important for formulating a strategy and should be assessed include human resources and financial resources, as well as the company image, the organization structure and climate, the planning and control system, and relations with customers.

Development of Alternative Strategies

Strategic *alternatives* are developed on the basis of an analysis of the external and internal environment. An organization may pursue many different kinds of strategies. It may *specialize* or *concentrate*, as the Korean Hyundai Company did by producing lower-priced cars (in contrast to General Motors, for example, which has a complete product line ranging from inexpensive to luxury cars).

Alternatively, a firm may *diversify*, extending the operation into new and profitable markets. K-Mart formed Specialty Retailing Groups, which include stores such as Walden Book Company, Inc.; Builders Square, Inc.; Designer Depot; and Pay Less Drug Stores Northwest, Inc.

Still another strategy is to go *international* and expand the operation into other countries. The multinational firms discussed in Chapter 4 provide many examples. The same chapter examines *joint ventures*, which may be an appropriate strategy for some firms. They are especially suitable for big undertakings in which firms have to pool their resources, as illustrated by the joint venture of General Motors and Toyota to produce small cars in California.

Under certain circumstances, a company may have to adopt a *liquidation* strategy by terminating an unprofitable product line or even dissolving the firm, as illustrated by the Savings & Loan Associations, especially in the 1990s. But in some cases liquidation may not be necessary; a *retrenchment* strategy may be appropriate. In such a situation the company may curtail its operation temporarily.

These are just a few examples of possible strategies. In practice, companies, especially large ones, pursue a combination of strategies.

Evaluation and Choice of Strategies

The various strategies have to be carefully *evaluated* before the *choice* is made. Strategic choices must be considered in light of the risks involved in a particular decision. Some profitable opportunities may not be pursued because a failure in a risky venture could result in bankruptcy of the firm. Another critical element in choosing a strategy is timing. Even the best product may fail if it is introduced to the market at an inappropriate time. Moreover, the reaction of competitors must be taken into consideration. When IBM reduced the price of its PC computer in reaction to the sales success of Apple's Macintosh computer, firms producing IBM-compatible computers had little choice but to reduce their prices as well. This illustrates the interconnection of the strategies of several firms in the same industry.

Medium- and Short-Range Planning, Implementation, and Control

Although not a part of the strategic planning process (and therefore shown by broken lines in Figure 7-1), *medium-* and *short-range planning* as well as the *implementation* of the plans must be considered during all phases of the process. *Control* must also be provided for monitoring performance against plans. The importance of *feedback* is shown by the loops in the model.

Consistency and Contingency

The last key aspect of the strategic planning process is testing for *consistency* and preparing for *contingency plans*. Both topics will be discussed later in this chapter.

THE TOWS MATRIX: A MODERN TOOL FOR ANALYSIS OF THE SITUATION

Today, strategy designers have been aided by a number of matrixes showing the relationships of critical variables. For example, the Boston Consulting Group developed the Business Portfolio Matrix, which will be discussed later. More recently, the TOWS Matrix© has been introduced for analyzing the situation.[4]

FIGURE 7-2

Internal factors / External factors	Internal strengths (S) e.g., strengths in management, operations, finance, marketing, R&D, engineering	Internal weaknesses (W) e.g., weaknesses in areas shown in the box of "strengths"
External opportunities (O) (Consider risks also) e.g., current and future economic conditions, political and social changes, new products, services, and technology	SO Strategy: Maxi-Maxi Potentially the most successful strategy, utilizing the organization's strengths to take advantage of opportunities	WO Strategy: Mini-Maxi e.g., developmental strategy to overcome weaknesses in order to take advantage of opportunities
External threats (T): e.g., lack of energy, competition, and areas similar to those shown in the "opportunities" box above	ST Strategy: Maxi-Mini e.g., use of strengths to cope with threats or to avoid threats	WT Strategy: Mini-Mini e.g., retrenchment, liquidation, or joint venture

THE TOWS MATRIX FOR STRATEGY FORMULATION.

The TOWS Matrix has a wider scope, and it has different emphases from those of the Business Portfolio Matrix. The former does not replace the latter. The TOWS Matrix is a conceptual framework for a systematic analysis that facilitates matching the external threats and opportunities with the internal weaknesses and strengths of the organization.

It has been common to suggest that companies identify their strengths and weaknesses, as well as the opportunities and threats in the external environment. But what is often overlooked is that combining these factors may require distinct strategic choices. To systematize these choices, the TOWS Matrix has been proposed; "T" stands for threats, "O" for opportunities, "W" for weaknesses, and "S" for strengths. The TOWS model starts with the threats because in many situations a company undertakes strategic planning as a result of a perceived crisis, problem, or threat.

Four Alternative Strategies

Figure 7-2 presents the four alternative strategies of the TOWS Matrix.* The strategies are based on the analysis of the external environment (threats and opportunities) and the internal environment (weaknesses and strengths).

---

* Although the emphasis is on strategies in this discussion, similar analyses can be made for developing the more detailed tactics/action plans.

1. The WT strategy (in the lower right-hand corner) aims to minimize both weaknesses and threats. It may require that the company, for example, form a joint venture, retrench, or even liquidate.

2. The WO strategy attempts to minimize the weaknesses and maximize the opportunities. Thus, a firm with certain weaknesses in some areas may either develop those areas within the enterprise or acquire the needed competencies (such as technology or persons with needed skills) from the outside, making it possible to take advantage of opportunities in the external environment.

3. The ST strategy is based on the organization's strengths to deal with threats in the environment. The aim is to maximize the former while minimizing the latter. Thus, a company may use its technological, financial, managerial, or marketing strengths to cope with the threats of a new product introduced by its competitor.

4. The most desirable situation is one in which a company can use its strengths to take advantage of opportunities (the SO strategy). Indeed, it is the aim of enterprises to move from other positions in the matrix to this one. If they have weaknesses, they will strive to overcome them, making them strengths. If they face threats, they will cope with them so that they can focus on opportunities.

Time Dimension and the TOWS Matrix

So far, the factors displayed in the TOWS Matrix pertain to analysis at a particular point in time. However, external and internal environments are dynamic: Some factors change over time, while others change very little. Because of the dynamics

FIGURE 7-3

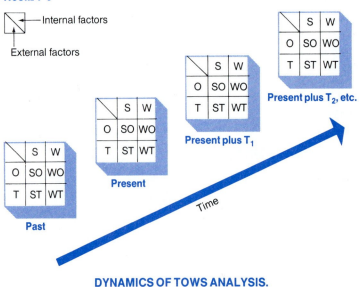

DYNAMICS OF TOWS ANALYSIS.

in the environment, the strategy designer must prepare several TOWS Matrixes at different points in time, as shown in Figure 7-3. Thus, one may start with a TOWS analysis of the past, continue with an analysis of the present, and, perhaps most important, focus on different time periods (T_1, T_2, etc.) in the future.

THE PORTFOLIO MATRIX: A TOOL FOR ALLOCATING RESOURCES

The Business Portfolio Matrix was developed by the Boston Consulting Group (BCG).[5] Figure 7-4, a simplified version of the matrix, shows the linkages between the growth rate of the business and the relative competitive position of the firm, identified by the market share. Businesses in the "question marks" quadrant, with a weak market share and a high growth rate, usually require cash investment so that they can become "stars," the businesses in the high-growth, strongly competitive position. These kinds of businesses have opportunities for growth and profit. The "cash cows," with a strong competitive position and a low growth rate, are usually well established in the market, and such enterprises are in the position of making their products at a low cost. Therefore, the products of these enterprises provide the cash needed for their operation. The "dogs" are businesses with a low growth rate and a weak market share. These businesses are usually not profitable and generally should be disposed of.

The Portfolio Matrix was developed for large corporations with several divisions that are often organized around strategic business units (a topic to be

FIGURE 7-4

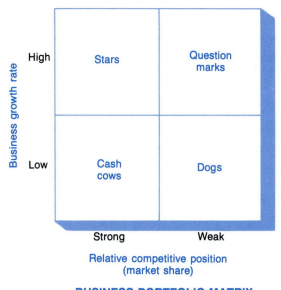

BUSINESS PORTFOLIO MATRIX.

Adapted from *The Product Portfolio Matrix,* copyright © 1970, the Boston Consulting Group, Inc.

discussed in Chapter 10). While portfolio analysis was popular in the 1970s, it is not without its critics, who contend that it is too simplistic. Also, the growth-rate criterion has been considered insufficient for the evaluation of an industry's attractiveness. Similarly, the market share as a yardstick for estimating the competitive position may be inadequate.[6]

MAJOR KINDS OF STRATEGIES AND POLICIES

For a business enterprise (and, with some modification, for other kinds of organizations as well), the major strategies and policies that give an overall direction to operations are likely to be in the following areas:*

Growth

Growth strategies give answers to such questions as these: How much growth should occur? How fast? Where? How should it occur?[7]

Finance

Every business enterprise and, for that matter, any nonbusiness enterprise must have a clear strategy for financing its operations. There are various ways of doing this and usually many serious limitations.

Organization

Organizational strategy has to do with the type of organizational pattern an enterprise will use. It answers practical questions—for example: How centralized or decentralized should decision-making authority be? What kinds of departmental patterns are most suitable? How should staff positions be designed? Naturally, organization structures furnish the system of roles and role relationships that helps people accomplish objectives.

Personnel

There can be many major strategies in the area of human resources and relationships. They deal with such topics as union relations, compensation, selection, hiring, training, and appraisal, as well as with special matters such as job enrichment.

Public Relations

Strategies in this area can hardly be independent; they must support other major strategies and efforts. They must also be designed in light of the company's type

---

* Although the term "strategies" is used in this section, some may be policies; there is a great deal of overlap between the two, as mentioned earlier in this chapter.

of business, its closeness to the public, and its susceptibility to regulation by government agencies. In any area, strategies can be developed only if the right questions are asked. While no set of strategies can be formulated that will fit all organizations and situations, certain key questions will help any company discover what its strategies should be. The right questions will lead to answers. As examples, some key questions are presented below for two major strategic areas: products or services and marketing. With a little thought, you can devise key questions for other major strategic areas.

Products or Services

A business exists to furnish products or services. In a very real sense, profits are merely a measure—although an important one—of how well a company serves its customers. New products or services, more than any other single factor, determine what an enterprise is or will be.

The key questions in this area can be summarized as follows:

What is our business?

Who are our customers?

What do our customers want?

How much will our customers buy and at what price?

Do we wish to be a product leader?

Do we wish to develop our own new products?

What advantages do we have in serving customer needs?

How should we respond to existing and potential competition?

How far can we go in serving customer needs?

What profits can we expect?

What basic form should our strategy take?

Marketing

Marketing strategies are designed to guide managers in getting products or services to customers and in encouraging customers to buy. Marketing strategies are closely related to product strategies; they must be interrelated and mutually supportive. As a matter of fact, Peter Drucker regards the two basic business functions as innovation (for example, the creation of new goods or services) and marketing. A business can scarcely survive without at least one of these functions and preferably both.

The key questions that serve as guides for establishing a marketing strategy are these:

Where are our customers, and why do they buy?

How do our customers buy?

How is it best for us to sell?

Do we have something to offer that competitors do not?

Do we wish to take legal steps to discourage competition?

Do we need, and can we supply, supporting services?

What are the best pricing strategy and policy for our operation?

How can we best serve our customers?

INDUSTRY ANALYSIS AND GENERIC COMPETITIVE STRATEGIES BY PORTER[8]

Professor Michael Porter at Harvard has suggested that strategy formulation requires an analysis of the industry (that is, of its attractiveness) and the company's position within that industry. This analysis becomes the basis for the generic strategies.

Industry Analysis

In the analysis of the industry, Porter identified five forces: (1) the competition among companies, (2) the threat of new companies entering the market, (3) the possibility of using substitute products or services, (4) the bargaining power of suppliers, and (5) the bargaining power of the buyers or customers. On the basis of the industry analysis, a company may adopt generic strategies. These strategies are generic because they may be suitable on a broad level of different kinds of organizations. Any enterprise, however, may use more than one strategy.

Overall Cost Leadership Strategy

This strategic approach aims at reductions in cost, based to a great extent on experience. Thus, the emphasis may be on keeping a close watch on costs in areas such as research and development, sales, and service. The objective is for a company to have a low cost structure compared with that of its competitors. This strategy often requires a large relative market share and cost-efficient facilities, as illustrated by the well-publicized Lincoln Electric Company, which produces arc welding equipment and supplies. Another example may be the low-cost Ivory soap sold in a broad market.

Differentiation Strategy

A company following a differentiation strategy attempts to offer something unique in the industry in respect to products or services. Porsche sports cars are indeed special; so is the Caterpillar Company, which is known for its prompt service and availability of spare parts. In the broad consumer market, Dial soap is differentiated from other brands of soap by the use of deodorants.

Focused Strategies

A company adopting a focused strategy (low-cost or differentiation) concentrates on special groups of customers, a particular product line, a specific geographic region, or other aspects that become the focal point of the firm's efforts. Rather than serving the total market with its products or services, an enterprise may emphasize a specific segment of the market. This may be accomplished by a low-cost strategy, differentiation, or both. Porter illustrates the *focused low-cost strategy* with the example of La Quinta Inns, which operate in a certain region of the United States and appeal to traveling businesspeople, such as salespeople. The *focused differentiation strategy* may be exemplified by Cray Research Inc., which specializes in very powerful and sophisticated computers. The differentiation allows the company to charge premium prices.

In general, a company needs to choose a generic strategy and should not "get stuck in the middle." A company that gets stuck in the middle needs to decide on a low-cost strategy in a broad or narrow market or offer a differentiated (that is, unique) product or service in a broad or narrow market.

EFFECTIVE IMPLEMENTATION OF STRATEGIES

Strategic planning, to be effective, must go beyond the allocation of resources to achieve organizational objectives. It must be accompanied by strategic thinking that also includes designing an appropriate organization structure, an effective management information system, a budgeting system to facilitate the accomplishment of strategic objectives, and a reward system that supports the strategy.

Strategic Planning Failures and Some Recommendations

Let us look first at some of the reasons why strategic planning may fail and then consider what can be done to improve such planning.

One study attributed strategic planning failures to the following factors:[9]

1. Managers are inadequately prepared for strategic planning.
2. The information for preparing the plans is insufficient for planning for action.
3. The goals of the organization are too vague to be of value.
4. The business units (a distinct form of organization that will be discussed in Chapter 10) are not clearly identified.
5. The reviews of the strategic plans of the business units are not done effectively.
6. The link between strategic planning and control is insufficient.

Strategic planning is the job of line managers, especially those at the top of the organization. These managers may be assisted by staff planners, particularly in large companies. But in order to do an effective job, line managers must be coached in strategic planning.

The overall strategic plan needs to be supplemented by specific action plans. This, in general, requires the contributions of line managers from different functional departments, such as research and development, engineering, production, marketing, financing, and personnel, to plan for the people required to carry out the plan. But integrating the various functional groups is not easy. Thus, companies have set up a task force, with heavy representation of middle managers, to cut across the functional barriers.

Goals and objectives, to be meaningful, have to be more than platitudes such as "achieving excellence." The degree of specificity depends on the level in the hierarchy of objectives, as pointed out in Chapter 6.

When organizations become too large, they are frequently broken down into strategic business units (SBUs). These units are expected to operate as if they were relatively independent businesses. But it is important that the boundaries of the different SBUs be correctly drawn. Otherwise, strategic planning may be difficult.

Consider, for example, a large organization with many SBUs, each having its own strategic plan, each competing with the others for scarce resources, each making overly optimistic projections for its own strategic plan. Conflicts are bound to arise at the corporate level. It is indeed an art of the top executive to integrate these strategic plans into a meaningful whole that serves the interest of the total organization. SBUs will be discussed in greater detail in Chapter 10, on departmentation.

Plans are the basis for control. Without plans no control is possible. Too often strategic plans and budgets are in conflict. Too often budgets are based on last year's budgets rather than on the strategic plan. Too often budgets are prepared without a specific action plan to implement the strategy. Strategic plans can also be thwarted by a compensation system that rewards short-term results at the expense of the long-term health of the organization.

From this discussion it is clear that strategic planning needs to be integrated with the total managerial process, such as the organization structure; the appraisal, reward, and motivational system; and the controls used to measure performance against objectives. This is just another illustration that effective management requires a systems approach that recognizes the interdependence of the managerial activities.

International Perspective

GM's Strategy[10]

Strategies have become increasingly complex and internationally oriented. Take General Motors, which has been threatened by foreign competitors, especially the Japanese. For decades, GM had a "do-it-yourself" strategy. But now some GM cars are made by rival Asian companies such as Suzuki Motors Company and Isuzu Motors Ltd. of Japan. In addition, GM engaged in a joint venture with Toyota Motor Corporation to produce subcompacts in California. Equally surprising is GM's strategic move into nonautomotive businesses such as information processing and robotics. To implement this strategy, GM bought Electronic Data Systems Corporation and engaged in a joint venture with the Japanese robot maker Fanuc Ltd. But a change in strategy usually requires a reorganization, and GM reorganized its organization structure that had served the company well for over 60 years.

Successful Implementation of Strategies

It is one thing to develop clear and meaningful strategies. It is another matter, and one of very great practical importance, to implement strategies effectively.[11] If strategic planning is to be successful, certain steps must be taken to implement it. Following are eight recommendations that should be considered by managers who wish to put their strategies to work.

1. Communicating strategies to all key decision-making managers. It does little good to formulate meaningful strategies unless they are communicated to all those managers who are in a position to make decisions on programs and plans designed to implement them. Nothing has been communicated unless it is clear to the receiver. Strategies may be clear to the executive committee members and the chief executive who participated in developing them. However, strategies should be communicated in writing, and top executives and their subordinates must make sure that everyone involved in implementing strategies understands them.

2. Developing and communicating planning premises. The importance of planning premises will be stressed later in this chapter. Managers must develop premises critical to plans and decisions, explain them to all those in the decision-making chain, and give instructions to develop programs and make decisions in line with them. Too few organizations do this. But if premises do not include key assumptions about the environment in which plans will operate, decisions are likely to be based on personal assumptions and predilections. This will almost certainly lead to a collection of uncoordinated plans.

3. Ensuring that action plans contribute to and reflect major objectives and strategies. Action plans are tactical or operational programs and decisions, major or minor, that take place in various parts of an organization. If they do not reflect desired objectives and strategies, the result will be vague hopes or useless intentions. If care is not taken in this area, strategic planning is not likely to have a bottom-line impact, that is, to have an important effect on company profits.

There are various ways of making sure that action plans contribute to major goals. If every manager understands strategies, all managers can certainly review the recommendations of staff advisers and line subordinates to see that they contribute and are consistent. It might even be a good idea for major decisions to be reviewed by an appropriate small committee, such as one including a manager's superior, the superior's superior, and a staff specialist. Budgets should also be reviewed with objectives and strategies in mind.

4. Reviewing strategies regularly.   Even carefully developed strategies may cease to be suitable if conditions change. Therefore, they should be reviewed from time to time, certainly not less than once a year for major strategies and perhaps more often. Financial performance alone is an insufficient indicator of company success and may, indeed, be misleading. The strategy review may require scanning the external environment for new opportunities and threats and reevaluating internal strengths and weaknesses. In the external environment, for example, new competitors may enter the market, or substitute products or services may be introduced. Moreover, new suppliers may enter the market, or traditional ones may exit. Similarly, traditional buyers of goods and services may cease to exist, and new ones may emerge. In short, the competitive situation may be changed by new forces requiring a regular review of strategies.

5. Developing contingency strategies and programs.   If considerable change in competitive factors or other elements in the environment may occur, strategies for such contingencies should be formulated. No one, of course, can wait to make plans until a future environment is certain. Even if there is considerable uncertainty and events may occur that make a given set of objectives, strategies, or programs obsolete, a manager has no choice but to proceed on the most credible set of premises he or she can come up with at a given time. But even then, one need not be totally unprepared if certain possible contingencies do occur. Contingency plans can provide a degree of preparation.

6. Making the organization structure fit planning needs.   The organization structure, with its system of delegations, should be designed to help managers accomplish goals and make the decisions necessary to put plans into effect. If possible, one person should be responsible for the accomplishment of each goal and for the implementation of strategies to achieve this goal. In other words, end-result areas and key tasks should be identified and assigned to single positions as far down the organization structure as is feasible. Since such an assignment sometimes cannot be made, there may be no alternative but to utilize a form of matrix organization, a type of organization structure that will be discussed in Chapter 10. If this is done, however, the responsibilities of the various positions in the matrix should be clearly defined.

The role of staff analyst in an organization structure should be so defined as to make it clear that the job of people in a staff position is to advise. Staff studies and recommendations then enter the decision system at the various points where decisions are actually made. Unless they do so, the end result will be independent staff work of no value for planning.

7. Continuing to emphasize planning and implementing strategy.   Even if an organization has a workable system of objectives and strategies and their implementation, the system can easily fail unless responsible managers continue to stress the nature and importance of these elements. This process may seem tedious and unnecessarily repetitive, but it is the best way to make sure that members of an organization learn about them. Teaching does not necessarily mean conducting seminars; rather, much of the teaching can take place in the day-to-day interaction between superiors and subordinates.

8. Creating a company climate that forces planning. People tend to allow problems and crises of today to interfere with effective planning for tomorrow. The only way to ensure that planning will be done is to develop strategies carefully and to take pains to implement them.

PREMISING AND FORECASTING

One of the essential and often overlooked steps in effective and coordinate planning is premising, which is the establishment of, and the agreement by managers and planners to utilize, consistent assumptions critical to plans under consideration. **Planning premises** are defined as the anticipated environment in which plans are expected to operate. They include assumptions or forecasts of the future and known conditions that will affect the operation of plans. Examples are prevailing policies and existing company plans that control the basic nature of supporting plans.

A distinction should be drawn between forecasts that are planning premises and forecasts that are translated into future expectancies, usually in financial terms, from actual plans developed. For example, a forecast to determine future business conditions, sales volume, or political environment furnishes premises on which to develop plans. However, a forecast of the costs or revenues from a new capital investment translates a planning program into future expectations. In the first case, the forecast is a prerequisite of planning; in the second case, the forecast is a result of planning.

At the same time, plans themselves and forecasts of their future effects often become premises for other plans. The decision by an electric utility company to construct a nuclear generating plant, for example, creates conditions that give rise to premises for transmission line plans and other plans necessarily dependent on the generating plant being built.

ENVIRONMENTAL FORECASTING[12]

If the future could be forecast with accuracy, planning would be relatively simple. Managers would need only to take into account their human and material resources and their opportunities and threats, compute the optimum method of reaching their objective, and proceed with a relatively high degree of certainty toward it. In practice, forecasting is much more complicated.

Values and Areas of Forecasting

Forecasting has values aside from its use. First, the making of forecasts and their review by managers compel thinking ahead, looking to the future, and providing for it. Second, preparation of the forecast may disclose areas where necessary control is lacking. Third, forecasting, especially when there is participation throughout the organization, helps to unify and coordinate plans. By focusing attention on the future, it assists in bringing a singleness of purpose to planning.

The environmental areas that are frequently chosen for making forecasts usually include the (1) economic, (2) social, (3) political/legal, and (4) technological environments, which were discussed in Chapters 3 and 4.

Forecasting with the Delphi Technique

One of the attempts to make technological forecasting more accurate and meaningful is the use of the Delphi technique.[13] This technique, developed by Olaf Helmer and his colleagues at the RAND Corporation, has a degree of scientific respectability and acceptance. A typical process of the Delphi technique is as follows:

1. A panel of experts on a particular problem area is selected—usually from both inside and outside the organization.
2. The experts are asked to make (anonymously, so that they will not be influenced by others) a forecast as to what they think will happen, and when, in various areas of new discoveries or developments.
3. The answers are compiled, and the composite results are fed back to the panel members.
4. With this information at hand (but still with individual anonymity), further estimates of the future are made.
5. This process may be repeated several times.
6. When a convergence of opinion begins to evolve, the results are then used as an acceptable forecast.

Note that the purpose of the successive opinions and feedback is not to force the experts to compromise but, rather, by bringing additional informational inputs to bear, to make opinions more informed. It is thus hoped, and experience has verified this hope, that an informed consensus among experts will be arrived at.

THE SALES FORECAST: KEY PLAN AND PREMISE

Even though its use has been noteworthy in business, the idea of basing planning on a forecast of the market has much in common with nonbusiness enterprises. Certainly, a university must be concerned in its planning with its student "market," a government welfare department must gear its plans to meet expected caseloads, and church plans must be influenced by the number of communicants expected in an area.

The Nature and Use of the Sales Forecast

The **sales forecast** is a prediction of expected sales, by product and price, for a number of months or years. It is, then, a kind of pro forma sales portion of the traditional income statement for the future.

The sales forecast is the key to internal planning. Business and capital outlays and policies of all kinds are made for the purpose of maximizing profits from expected sales. Although there are some enterprises that need to pay scant attention to sales (for example, the small-city water company or the government defense contractor with a long-term order that has little chance of being canceled or modified), it is a rare business that can overlook the market for long. Even the farmer, who, operating under price supports, may have a guaranteed market for a certain product for a coming year, can hardly ignore market influences as they affect succeeding years or alternative crops.

Smaller companies often make the mistake of believing that sales forecasts are too expensive and of overlooking the variety of sources of data available at little or no cost. The purchasing agent, members of the sales staff, the treasurer, and the production manager are among those who may possess bits and pieces of information that, gathered together, could make an acceptable forecast. Moreover, the wide range of information available from government and industry sources is neither difficult nor expensive to obtain.

Methods of Sales Forecasting

Methods utilized in sales forecasting may generally be classified as (1) the jury of executive opinion method, (2) the sales force composite method, (3) the users' expectation method, (4) statistical methods, and (5) deductive methods.

Jury of executive opinion method. The jury of executive opinion method is perhaps the oldest and simplest method of making sales forecasts, since it merely combines and averages the views, many of which may be little more than hunches, of top managers. In most cases, the final estimate is an opinion of the president, based on a consideration of the opinions of other officers; in other cases, the poll of opinion leads to a rough kind of average estimate. In some cases, the process amounts to little more than group guessing; in other cases, it involves the careful judgment of experienced executives who have studied the underlying factors that influence their company's sales.

This method has the advantage of ease and simplicity; it allows for the pooling of experience and judgment, and it need not require the preparation of elaborate economic studies and statistics. An advantage not often cited is that by forcing top managers to make an estimate, it may put pressure on them to develop pertinent data. On the other hand, such a method has serious drawbacks; for example, forecasts may be based on opinion rather than on facts and analyses.

Sales force composite method. One of the commonly used methods of sales forecasting is to obtain from salespeople and sales managers their combined view as to expected sales. The usual technique is to ask salespeople to forecast sales for their districts and have these estimates reviewed by regional sales managers and then by the head-office sales manager. Sometimes salespeople are given guides in the form of company planning premises as to business conditions in general, and often the salespeople's estimates are reviewed by the product specialists, such as the company brand, sales, and advertising managers.

This method is based on the belief that those closest to the sales picture have the best knowledge of the market. Other advantages ascribed to this method are that it places forecasting, initially at least, in the hands of those who must make good on the forecast; it gives a broad sample that makes the total forecast more valid; and it allows an easy breakdown by product, customer, or territory.

On the other hand, the sales force composite method suffers from the fact that salespeople and often even sales executives are apt to be poor forecasters for any period except the immediate future, since they tend to give primary weight to present conditions. Where forecasts are desired for more than the short range, sales personnel normally are at a loss to make sound forecasts because of lack of knowledge of basic social, political, and economic trends. Moreover, under certain conditions—particularly where the forecasts are used for quota purposes—sales personnel are inclined to be pessimistic, while in other instances—especially when salespeople want more liberal allowances for expenses, promotion, or advertising—they are inclined to be rather optimistic.

At the same time, most companies have found that forecasts submitted by the sales organization are useful and valuable inputs for the company forecasting effort. It has been found that when the sales force composite method is properly cross-checked, it furnishes surprisingly good forecasts. Checking methods include a review by head-office marketing and sales experts and a constant check by salespeople of their estimates of past performance against actual results.

Users' expectation method.   Many companies, particularly those serving industrial customers in industries composed of a small number of companies or where a few large companies are dominant, find it useful to base their forecasts on expected purchases by these customers. Clearly, if a company can obtain an adequate and reliable information sample of what its customers will buy, even though the actual orders are not in hand, it will have a good basis upon which to develop a sales forecast.

The users' expectation method has clear advantages where other ways of forecasting are inadequate or where the company cannot make a systematic forecast on its own, such as in small companies with limited resources for forecasting, in cases of new products where the market is known, or in instances where a supplier is dependent on the plans of major customers. This method is obviously difficult to use in cases where customers are numerous, not easily located, or uncooperative. It is also subject to the difficulty of assessing customer expectations accurately, since the best of these assessments are usually estimates of needs, not commitments.

Statistical methods.   The most generally relied upon approach to sales forecasting is the application of various statistical methods. As mathematical techniques have improved and the computer has come into wider use, so have statistics. These statistical methods may be divided into (a) analysis of trends and cycles, (b) correlation analysis, and (c) use of mathematical formulas or models.

Trends and cycles. In approaching forecasting through an analysis of **trends and cycles,** the analyst summarizes a pertinent series of data that reflects dollar or unit sales, units per thousand population, or other basic indicators of sales volume. On the basis of these data the forecast is projected by extrapolation. This analysis is based on the assumption that "what is past is prologue" and that a trend will continue unless something happens to it. It is then up to the analyst to judge whether that "something" will happen. In fact, it is important to the user of a forecast to know whether it represents a mere projection of past trends or a real forecast of what the forecaster expects will happen.

Correlation analysis. One of the widely used statistical methods is **correlation analysis,** the measurement of the relationship between company sales and one or more other factors.* What is usually desired is a close correlation between sales and some broad national index that can be used with a reasonable degree of accuracy, such as gross national product, national income, or consumers' disposable income. Such correlation, whether direct or with a lag or lead of a given time period, can give a company a useful and highly reliable basis for sales forecasting.

Virtually every forecaster has found some accurate correlations in using this method. Many companies have found that their sales, aside from industry sales, bear a close relationship to some national index. The problem for the forecaster is, of course, to study the various relationships, with their leads and lags, to find one or more that serve as indicators of the company's sales.

Mathematical formula or model. The third statistical method, one that usually grows out of finding either a trend or correlation analysis relationships, is to develop a **mathematical formula** to depict the relationship of a number of variables to the company's sales. Often, sales for an individual company are subject to a number of variables. If the relationship of these can be ascertained with reasonable accuracy or if credible assumptions can be made to fill in statistical gaps, a mathematical model very useful to the forecaster can be constructed.

Limitations of statistical methods. Although statistical methods are good for sales forecasting from the standpoint of reliability, they are often subject to certain drawbacks. They require research and the use of statistically trained help, which may be costly. It is not always possible to find reliable trends, correlations, or mathematical relationships. Many defense subcontractors have found, for example, that their sales potential is closely related to such vague factors as defense strategy, the course of a conflict, individual program expenditure level, and advances in the art of the industry, none of which bears a reliable correlation with predictable national or industry data. There is also a danger that managers may rely too

---

* Correlation analysis is used to determine many other kinds of relationships. As a method of sales forecasting, it is just one example.

heavily on statistical relationships and the results implied and thereby miss significant changes that intelligent judgment would have appraised. In any statistical method, it must be realized that the past is used only as a basis for prediction and that the future does not necessarily reflect the past.

Deductive methods.   No forecaster should overlook the opportunity to apply judgment and draw intelligent deductions from facts and relationships. Generally, what is involved is finding out what the present situation is, where the sales are, and why and then analyzing deductively, with resort to both objective factors and subjective judgment, the factors underlying sales. Although the indications so developed may be put into a mathematical model or merely left as an imprecisely correlated conglomeration of facts and value judgments, they are often a useful check on results arrived at through more scientific methods.

After all, the state of the art of forecasting is such that an independent, and often apparently intuitive, appraisal of the sales picture by an intelligent and experienced brain is still an input that no forecaster should overlook. This method has sometimes been referred to as the "lost horse" technique, a label based on the old gag about the best way to find a lost horse: Go to where the horse was last seen and ask yourself where you would go if you were a horse.

Combination of Methods

In practice, there is a tendency to combine sales forecasting methods. This is as it should be. The importance of the final forecast for all aspects of company planning makes desirable a forecast system in which every possible input can be utilized. What warms forecasters' hearts and gives them a feeling of reliability is finding that several different forecast indicators, based on independent approaches and data, all point to the same result. And even if they do not, the disparity may serve as a warning that a single approach may have overlooked an essential factor.

EFFECTIVE PREMISING

Since so many failures occur in planning and planning coordination through poor premising, special attention should be given to this step in planning. It is difficult to identify the factors in a future environment that will affect a manager's plans. But it is also difficult, once these factors have been identified, to achieve practical implementation of consistent and meaningful planning premises. Effective premising is a four-part process.

1. Selection of the premises that bear materially on the programs.   There are many premises that are of strategic importance to one enterprise but not to another. Thus, top managers of every enterprise, and to a certain extent every manager within it, should select their own premises. This basic question should be asked and answered: What factors in the environment, whether external or internal, will influence most the course of plans for which I am responsible?

2. Development of alternative premises for contingency planning. Since the future cannot be predicted with great certainty, managers should develop plans given different assumptions.

3. Verification of the consistency of premises. One way of ensuring that premises are consistent is to have each planning staff at headquarters and divisional levels recommend its crucial planning premises, applicable to an enterprise or a division, to the appropriate top executive. Having the top executive approve these premises, usually after consultation with his or her staff, will ensure that the assumptions selected and formulated will be the ones on which the enterprise or division is willing to stake its future.

4. Communication of the premises. One of the first requirements of effective premise communication is to analyze all managers' "need to know," interpreting this broadly rather than narrowly, and to make sure that premises important for their planning are made available to them. Some companies have found it wise to develop and disseminate to those who need it a manual of planning premises, incorporating assumptions with wide application to planning. Such a manual will, of course, be kept current as premises change. In addition, whenever a budget proposal or program recommendation is requested and whenever a major program assignment is made, superiors should develop and distribute supplementary planning premises for managers reporting to them.

Strategies and policies, then, give direction to the enterprise and provide a framework for developing tactics and other action plans. Meaningful premises facilitate consistency and coordination of plans.

SUMMARY

There are different definitions of strategy. A comprehensive one refers to the determination of the purpose (or mission) and the basic long-term objectives of an enterprise and the adoption of courses of action and allocation of resources necessary to achieve these aims. Policies are general statements or understandings that guide managers' thinking in decision making. Both strategies and policies give direction to plans. They provide the framework for plans and serve as a basis for the development of tactics and other managerial activities.

The strategic planning model shows how the process works. It identifies the critical elements of this process and indicates how they relate to each other. The TOWS Matrix is a modern tool for analyzing the threats and opportunities in the external environment and the relationships to the organization's (internal) weaknesses and strengths. The Portfolio Matrix is a tool for allocating resources, linking the business growth rate with the relative competitive position (measured by market share) of the firm.

Major kinds of strategies and policies need to be developed in areas such as growth, finance, organization, personnel, public relations, products or services, and marketing. Professor Porter identified three generic competitive strategies related to overall cost leadership, differentiation, and focus.

To implement strategies effectively, managers must communicate the strategies and planning premises to all who should know them and must make sure that the plans contribute to and reflect the strategies and goals they serve. Managers must also review strategies regularly, develop contingency strategies, and be sure that the organization structure of the enterprise fits its planning program. Managers need to make learning about planning and implementing strategy an ongoing process.

Planning premises are the anticipated environment. They include assumptions or forecasts of the future and known conditions. One approach to forecasting is the Delphi technique, developed by the RAND Corporation. The various kinds of sales forecasting methods include the jury of executive opinion, the sales force composite, the users' expectation, statistical, and deductive methods. Effective premising requires proper selection of premises, development of alternative premises for contingency planning, provision for consistency, and communication of the planning premises.

KEY IDEAS AND CONCEPTS FOR REVIEW

Strategies	Major kinds of strategies
Policies	Three generic strategies by Porter
Principle of strategy and policy framework	Requirements for successful implementation of strategies
Key elements in the strategic planning process	Planning premises
TOWS Matrix by Weihrich	Delphi technique
Portfolio Matrix by the Boston Consulting Group	Sales forecast
	Five methods of sales forecasting
	Requirements for effective premising

FOR DISCUSSION

1. How can you distinguish between strategies and policies?
2. Are strategies and policies as important in a nonbusiness enterprise (such as a labor union, the State Department, a hospital, or a city fire department) as they are in a business? Why and how?
3. Why are contingency strategies important?
4. Choose an organization you know and identify its strengths and weaknesses. What are its special opportunities and threats in the external environment?
5. How would you make an organizational appraisal of your college or university? What kind of "business" is the school in?
6. How can strategies be implemented effectively?
7. Identify major premises that, in your judgment, the Ford Motor Company would need in order to forecast its sales of automobiles for the next 2 years.
8. How would you make premising effective?

EXERCISES/ACTION STEPS

1. Read two articles in magazines such as *Fortune* or *Business Week* that deal with strategy. List the strengths and weaknesses of the company as well as the opportunities and threats faced by the firm.
2. Take a major decision problem facing you, and outline the more critical planning premises surrounding it. How many of these are matters of knowledge, and how many are matters of forecast? How many are qualitative, and how many are quantitative? How many are within your control?

CASES

CASE 7-1
AMERICAN FLIES HIGH[14]

American Airlines aims high. Among U.S. airlines, it had the greatest share of passenger traffic and the best operating margin in 1988. It is well poised to face the future by planning to acquire a large fleet of McDonnell-Douglas planes. Moreover, it intends to share its highly successful SABRE (which stands for Semi-Automated Business Research Environment) reservation system with Delta Airlines.

A part of American's success is due to the leadership of its chairman, Robert L. Crandall. His strategy has been to grow from within. While this approach has been highly successful, it may also have contributed to forgoing the opportunity to purchase Pan Am's routes to the Far East, which were acquired by United Airlines. This may inhibit American's plan for expansion in the Asian market because it is difficult to obtain landing rights at Narita's airport in Japan. Thus, Crandall is considering other airline hubs such as airports in Seoul or Taipei. American is also expanding rapidly in the European market in cities such as Paris, Lyons, London, Manchester, Brussels, and Stockholm. It is estimated that the market growth is going to be higher in Europe, Latin America, and especially Asia. The strategy of internal growth is different from that of Texas Air, which grew through acquisitions, or United Airlines, which aimed at becoming a comprehensive travel-service organization.

Crandall's strategy is not only directed toward external opportunities but also supported by internal changes. While criticism has been voiced against the dominance of the SABRE reservation system, American intends to blunt this criticism by selling a share to Delta Airlines before the government takes action. This reservation system has become so important that Crandall commented in a speech: "So the question might be—if we are forced to divest—which do we sell, SABRE or the airline?" Not only is the jet fleet going to be modernized, but the firm also is installing a computer system aimed at tracking lost luggage and reducing the number of late plane arrivals. Organizationally, American is delegating more authority to the local operations. A program to elicit ideas for improvements resulted in savings of $41 million. Even the smallest improvement can result in great organizationwide savings.

Unions have been pacified through a program to share over $120 million with the employees. But in 1990, the pilots' union pressed for wage increases. A growing enterprise also provides opportunities for rapid promotion, which result in employees' satisfaction. But the idea of relating performance to pay has met resistance from the unions. Mechanics and pilots also want to have a greater share of the company's success. While American is flying high, an economic recession could change all that.

1. What were the key success factors at American Airlines?
2. How would a recession affect the company, and what could be done about that?

INTERNATIONAL CASE 7-2
OPPORTUNITIES AND THREATS IN FORMER EAST GERMANY AFTER THE UNIFICATION[15]

The fast-moving events in Eastern Europe, particularly in former East Germany, demand attention. The unification of Germany provides opportunities in former East Germany; but opportunities are accompanied by risks. Companies that want to strategically penetrate this market need to understand the opportunities and threats.

Opportunities in former East Germany.   The unification of Germany is providing business opportunities. As was expected, West German firms were the first to take advantage of them. American multinationals are following. However, middle- and small-sized U.S. firms need to reevaluate the opportunities in former East Germany, the focus of this case.

West German firms may appear to have an advantage in moving into East Germany. These companies have a free-market orientation which is similar to that of U.S. firms. But U.S. businesses may be more flexible in taking advantage of the opportunities than some West German firms, which have been accused of wanting to sell in East Germany but hesitating to make major investments. In response to this criticism, Siemens, the electronics giant, plans to invest over $600 million in East Germany. This is the boldest step taken by any company so far. West Germany's Standard Elektrik Lorenz plans to modernize large parts of the antiquated telephone system in East Germany.

Financial institutions have been quite aggressive in expanding into East Germany. The Deutsche Bank, the largest German bank, plans a network of 250 branches in East Germany. The Dresdner Bank, which originated in East Germany, is also opening several new offices. The big insurance company Allianz acquired a 51 percent interest in the East German Staatliche Versicherung, the formerly state-owned insurance company. Although Allianz does not expect profits from this venture (now called Deutsche Versicherungs AG, or DVAG) for at least the next 5 years, the long-term insurance opportunities are good. For example, most of the 129 East German *Kombinates* (industrial conglomerates) are facing liability exposures. In the past, these companies did not have such liability risks.

Some other firms that have taken strategic initiatives may serve as models for U.S. enterprises. Volkswagen (VW) already has an engine project with VEB IFA-Kombinat Personenkraftwagen in Karl-Marx-Stadt (East Germany). Moreover, VW set up a venture in Zwickau to produce fifty Polo-class (small) cars. The aim is eventually to produce 250,000 vehicles per year. In the meantime, VW is organizing the marketing of IFA (East German) cars, VWs, Audis, and SEATs (produced by VW's Spanish unit) in East Germany.

BMW, the maker of quality and luxury cars, has a different strategy. The firm was invited into a cooperative arrangement with BMW's original plant in Eisenach, East Germany. After World War II, this company produced the much maligned Wartburg model. BMW politely rejected the offer. The Eisenach plant uses four times as many people to produce cars as the BMW plant in West Germany. Eberhard von Kuenheim, BMW's chairman, commented: "The plant looks like a picture of our plants in 1928, with no renovation." Instead of investing in existing companies, BMW plans to invest in small start-up companies to produce components and tools.

American companies, especially those which have been operating in Europe for some time, are also seizing the opportunities. General Motors (GM) is heading to East Germany, where the land is relatively cheap and the demand for cars is great. The company plans to assemble the Opel Vectra in Eisenach. In the food sector, McDonald's intends to open 100 restaurants. Likewise, Coca-Cola will expand to East Germany, where it is already well known, primarily through West German TV advertising.

Woolworth wanted to be the first American general merchandise store in East Germany, started slowly in 1990, and moved more rapidly in 1991. Woolworth's chairman, Harold Sells, stated: "East Germany will be our No. 1 priority." Woolworth has a long tradition in Germany. It opened its first store there in 1927 and now has 286 stores in West Germany. Older people in East Germany remember the company name very well. After the opening of the iron curtain, Woolworth stores in West Germany's border towns did a brisk business with East Germans.

Woolworth may be a pioneer in penetrating Eastern Europe, and Toys 'R' Us may be following this example by opening stores in East Germany.

While multinational companies find it relatively easy to enter the East German market, smaller companies may find it more difficult to take advantage of the business opportunities. Still, opportunities are there. In the past, most manufacturing and servicing was done by the *Kombinates,* the state-owned firms. Now, however, these *Kombinates* are being split up and transformed into more than 8000 companies. The goal of the newly created Trust is to make them privately owned firms. Some, however, will not survive in the new competitive environment of the free market. By supplying management know-how, U.S. companies may find investment opportunities appealing.

East Germany may be attractive to U.S. firms because it has a convertible currency and a favorable tax structure. Furthermore, it has a Western-oriented tax system. Perhaps most important, there is a great need to rebuild the country with most support coming from West Germany. East German economic standards have to be brought up to those of West Germany very quickly, even at a very high cost. Thus, U.S. firms may take advantage of the opportunities in housing, construction, retail stores, transportation, telecommunications, tourism, energy, and the rehabilitation of the environment.

Opportunities must be seen in light of risks. Research and development (R&D) is a case in point. There is an oversupply of scientists, a valuable resource, that may be tapped by companies. On the other hand, the research laboratories and the measuring instruments for conducting research are outdated by Western standards. There is also the danger of scientists moving to the West. To inhibit the "brain drain," the West German government encourages scientists to remain by providing attractive wages. Another attraction is that East German researchers will be connected to the American data bank Dialog, which enables them to draw scientific knowledge from the Western world. Clearly, East Germany provides opportunities as well as threats for entering companies, not only those from West Germany and other EC countries but also American firms.

Threats and risks in former East Germany. Even with strong financial support from the West, East Germany faces problems. For one, the economic forecasts are built on rather optimistic assumptions. Western investments in plants and equipment may not come as fast as expected. Productivity, which is estimated to be 20 to 30 percent below that of West Germany, needs to be improved. The infrastructure is in very poor condition, and the polluted environment does not attract Westerners to work in East Germany. Yet, qualified managers are badly needed.

Perhaps the most difficult adjustment will be required in the mentality of the people who lived for 45 years in a centrally planned, bureaucratic economy. The question is whether East Germans can adapt quickly to the free-market economy. Certainly, some people are afraid of the accompanying uncertainties. Will people be willing to accept individual responsibility in an economy in which the state will not be the provider? In the new environment, performance counts, not Communist-party membership. Indeed, insecurity is the concomitant of capitalism. Following the economic union, many workers will be laid off. Many firms simply cannot compete with the West and need to be shut down. Moreover, the image of poor quality makes current East German products unattractive. Management skills will be needed to focus on the profit objective, not to get a cushioned budget allocation from the former central government. The goal is not only to produce but also to produce what the customers want—and European customers are demanding quality at a reasonable price.

Although the long-term future of a united Germany provides many opportunities, the short-term problems need to be solved. Companies, whether from the 12 EC countries or the United States, must be willing to make a long-term commitment to reap the benefits from a strategic move into East Germany. Thoughtful commitment can be very beneficial for companies. The strategic decision whether or not to enter the East German market may have to be made now.

1. Draw a TOWS Matrix as discussed in this chapter, and list the opportunities and threats a company may encounter in East Germany.
2. Take a multinational company (e.g., PepsiCo, Ford Motor Company) with which you are familiar, and identify its strengths and weaknesses. List them in a TOWS Matrix.
3. Develop alternative strategies, such as SO, WO, ST, and WT, as discussed in this chapter.

REFERENCES

1. Fred R. David, *Fundamentals of Strategic Management* (Columbus, Ohio: Merrill Publishing Co., 1986), p. 4.

2. Alfred D. Chandler, Jr., *Strategy and Structure* (Cambridge, Mass.: The M.I.T. Press, 1962). In this excellent historical study, the author analyzes the history of Du Pont, General Motors, Standard Oil Company (New Jersey), and Sears, Roebuck and shows how in each case organization structure followed and reflected strategy. See also Alfred D. Chandler, Jr., "The Enduring Logic of Industrial Success," *Harvard Business Review* (March–April 1990), pp. 130–140.

3. Myron Magnet, "How Top Managers Make a Company's Toughest Decision," *Fortune* (Mar. 18, 1985), pp. 52–57. See also Roger Evered, "The Strategic Decision Process," in Don Hellriegel and John W. Slocum, Jr. (eds.), *Management in the World Today* (Reading, Mass.: Addison-Wesley Publishing Company, 1975).

4. This discussion and the accompanying figures have been adapted from Heinz Weihrich, "The TOWS Matrix—A Tool for Situational Analysis," *Long Range Planning,* vol. 15, no. 2 (1982), pp. 54–66.

5. Bruce D. Henderson, "The Experience Curve Revisited" (Boston Consulting Group, undated); Barry Hedly, "Strategy and the 'Business Portfolio,' " *Long Range Planning* (February 1977), pp. 9–15; Bruce D. Henderson, "The Application and Misapplication of the Experience Curve," *Journal of Business Strategy* (Winter 1984).

6. Charles W. Hofer and Dan E. Schendel, *Strategy Formulation: Analytical Concepts* (St. Paul: West Publishing Company, 1978); Richard G. Hamermesh and Roderick E. White, "Manage beyond Portfolio Analysis," *Harvard Business Review* (January–February 1984), pp. 103–109.

7. See John A. Pearce II and James W. Harwey, "Concentrated Growth Strategies," *Academy of Management Executive* (February 1990), pp. 61–68.

8. Michael E. Porter, "How Competitive Forces Shape Strategy," *Harvard Business Review* (March–April 1979), pp. 137–145. See also by the same author, *Competitive Strategy* (New York: The Free Press, 1980); *Competitive Advantage* (New York: The Free Press, 1985); *The Competitive Advantage of Nations* (New York: The Free Press, 1990).

9. Daniel H. Gray, "Uses and Misuses of Strategic Planning," *Harvard Business Review* (January–February 1986), pp. 89–97.

10. See also Gene Bylinsky, "Japan's Robot King Wins Again," *Fortune* (May 25, 1987), pp. 53–58.

11. Much of this is drawn from Harold Koontz, "Making Strategic Planning Work," *Business Horizons* (April 1976), pp. 37–47; see also Donald C. Hambrick and Albert A. Cannella, Jr., "Strategy Implementation as Substance and Selling," *Academy of Management Executive* (November 1989), pp. 278–285.

12. For an excellent discussion of the various approaches to forecasting, see Spyros Makridakis and Steven C. Wheelwright, "Forecasting: Issues and Challenges for Marketing Management," in Harold Koontz, Cyril O'Donnell, and Heinz Weihrich, *Management: A Book of Readings,* 5th ed. (New York: McGraw-Hill Book Company, 1980), pp. 136–151.

13. See also Frederick J. Parente, Janet K. Anderson, Patrick Myers, and Thomas O'Brien, "An Examination of Factors Contributing to Delphi Accuracy," *Journal of Forecasting,* vol. 3, no. 2 (1984), pp. 173–182.

14. Kevin Kelly, Todd Mason, Christopher Power, and James E. Ellis, "American Aims for the Sky," *Business Week* (Feb. 20, 1989), pp. 54–56; remarks by Robert L. Crandall

before the Cooperative Users of Recognition Equipment 1985 Conference (Dallas, June 18, 1985); Kenneth Labich, "American Takes on the World," *Fortune* (Sept. 24, 1990), pp. 40–48.

15. This case is based on Heinz Weihrich, "Europe 1992 and a Unified Germany: Opportunities and Threats for U.S. Firms," *Academy of Management Executive* (February 1991), pp. 93–96. The information is based on a variety of sources, including Timothy Aeppel, "Siemens Unveils East German Investment Plan," *The Wall Street Journal* (June 28, 1990); Don Lewis, "East Germans Seek Insurance Advice," *Business Insurance* (June 11, 1990), pp. 29–30; *Annual Report 1989, Volkswagen AG* (issued Apr. 4, 1990), p. 17; quote by Eberhard von Kuenheim in Philip Revzin and Timothy Aeppel, "BMW to Invest in Small Plants in East Europe," *The Wall Street Journal* (Apr. 23, 1990); quote by Harold Sells in Francine Schwadel, "Woolworth Is Bargaining on Return to East Germany," *The Wall Street Journal* (June 20, 1990); Sam Starobin, "Opportunity in Germany," *New England Business* (June 1990), pp. 14, 16; James L. Robb, "Special Report: Commercial Opportunities in the GDR" (East Germany), *Business America* (June 18, 1990), p. 11; Igor Reichlin, "From Two Germanys, One Dynamo?" *Business Week* (June 15, 1990), pp. 124–126; Eugene T. Yon, "Corporate Strategy and the New Europe," *Academy of Management Executive* (Aug. 1990), pp. 61–65. See also Herbert Henzler, "Managing the Merger: A Strategy for the New Germany," *Harvard Business Review,* January–February 1992, pp. 24–29.

Making decisions is, on one hand, one of the most fascinating manifestations of biological activity and, on the other hand, a matter of terrifying implications for the whole human race.

C. West Churchman[1]

Decision Making

Chapter Objectives

After reading this chapter, you should be able to:

1. Analyze decision making as a rational process, with special attention given to evaluating alternatives in light of the goals sought.
2. Develop alternative courses of action with due consideration of the limiting factor.
3. Select alternatives on the basis of experience and experimentation, as well as research and analysis.
4. Differentiate between programmed and nonprogrammed decisions.
5. Understand the differences between decisions made under conditions of certainty, uncertainty, and risk.
6. Select from among alternatives, using risk analysis, decision trees, and preference theory.
7. Evaluate the importance of decision making.
8. Recognize the utility of decision support systems (DSSs).
9. Understand the importance of creativity and innovation in managing.
10. Apply the systems approach to decision making.

choose the best alternative?

Decision making is defined as the selection of a course of action from among alternatives; it is the core of planning. A plan cannot be said to exist unless a decision—a commitment of resources, direction, or reputation—has been made. Until that point, there are only planning studies and analyses. Managers sometimes see decision making as their central job because they must constantly choose what is to be done, who is to do it, and when, where, and occasionally even how it will be done. Decision making is, however, only a step in planning, even when it is done quickly and with little thought or when it influences action for only a few minutes. It is also part of everyone's daily living. A course of action can seldom be judged alone, because virtually every decision must be geared to other plans. The stereotype of the finger-snapping, button-pushing managerial mogul fades as the requirements of systematic research and analysis preceding a decision come into focus.

THE IMPORTANCE AND LIMITATIONS OF RATIONAL DECISION MAKING

In the discussion of the steps in planning in Chapter 5, decision making was considered a major part of planning. As a matter of fact, given an awareness of an opportunity and a goal, the decision process is really the core of planning. Thus, in this context, the process leading to making a decision might be thought of as (1) premising, (2) identifying alternatives, (3) evaluating alternatives in terms of the goal sought, and (4) choosing an alternative, that is, making a decision.

Although this chapter emphasizes the logic and techniques of choosing a course of action, the discussion will show that decision making is really one of the steps in planning.

Rationality in Decision Making

It is frequently said that effective decision making must be rational. But what is rationality? When is a person thinking or deciding rationally?

People acting or deciding rationally are attempting to reach some goal that cannot be attained without action. They must have a clear understanding of alternative courses by which a goal can be reached under existing circumstances and limitations. They also must have the information and the ability to analyze and evaluate alternatives in light of the goal sought. Finally, they must have a desire to come to the best solution by selecting the alternative that most effectively satisfies goal achievement.

People seldom achieve complete rationality, particularly in managing.[2] In the first place, since no one can make decisions affecting the past, decisions must operate for the future, and the future almost invariably involves uncertainties. In the second place, it is difficult to recognize all the alternatives that might be followed to reach a goal; this is particularly true when decision making involves opportunities to do something that has not been done before. Moreover, in most instances, not all alternatives can be analyzed, even with the newest available analytical techniques and computers.

Limited, or "Bounded," Rationality

A manager must settle for limited rationality, or "bounded" rationality. In other words, limitations of information, time, and certainty limit rationality, even though a manager tries earnestly to be completely rational. Since managers cannot be completely rational in practice, they sometimes allow their dislike of risk—their desire to "play it safe"—to interfere with the desire to reach the best solution under the circumstances. Herbert Simon[3] has called this **satisficing,** that is, picking a course of action that is satisfactory or good enough under the circumstances. Although many managerial decisions are made with a desire to "get by" as safely as possible, most managers do attempt to make the best decisions they can within the limits of rationality and in light of the size and nature of the risks involved.

We will now consider the steps of the decision-making process in detail.

Perspective

Compaq vs. IBM[4]

In 1986 Compaq announced a new personal computer model, the Deskpro 386. The new model was based on Intel's 80386 chip, which was considerably faster than the one in the IBM AT model. The decision to market this new computer in 1986 was rather risky and based on incomplete information. It also was a departure from Compaq's past strategy, which had proved to be very successful. Previously, Compaq had followed IBM standards by making a computer that used IBM software.

But with the Deskpro 386, Compaq assumed the lead over the corporate giant IBM, which was expected to market a computer based on the 80386 technology in 1987.

What, then, was Compaq's dilemma? On the one hand, the company had a head start over its major competitor and gained a considerable market share. On the other hand, the new IBM could have included some proprietary features that would have made the Deskpro 386 incompatible with IBM's computer. Moreover, the success of a personal computer depends to a large extent on its software (programs). Thus, software writers may not have been willing to invest their efforts until it was clear that the Compaq computer was indeed truly compatible with the one IBM planned to introduce. The executives at Compaq had to make a tough decision. They did—and they succeeded.

In 1991, Compaq again faced difficult decisions. Compaq was the leader in the formation with twenty other computer companies of the Advanced Computing Environment (ACE), whose aim it is to set standards for the Reduced Instruction Set Computing (RISC). The ACE group hopes to convince software makers to create programs that can challenge companies such as IBM and Sun Microsystems Inc. that have been using RISC. Will Compaq succeed in challenging the "giants"?

THE SEARCH FOR ALTERNATIVES

Assuming that we know what our goals are and agree on clear planning premises, the first step of decision making is to develop alternatives. There are almost always alternatives to any course of action; indeed, if there seems to be only one way of doing a thing, that way is probably wrong. If we can think of only one course of action, clearly we have not thought hard enough.

The ability to develop alternatives is often as important as being able to select correctly from among them. On the other hand, ingenuity, research, and common sense will often unearth so many choices that all of them cannot be adequately evaluated. The manager needs help in this situation, and this help, as well as assistance in choosing the best alternative, is found in the concept of the limiting or strategic factor.

A **limiting factor** is something that stands in the way of accomplishing a desired objective. Recognizing the limiting factors in a given situation makes it possible to narrow the search for alternatives to those that will overcome the limiting factors. The **principle of the limiting factor** is as follows: *By recognizing and overcoming those factors that stand critically in the way of a goal, the best alternative course of action can be selected.*

EVALUATION OF ALTERNATIVES

Once appropriate alternatives have been found, the next step in planning is to evaluate them and select the one that will best contribute to the goal. This is the point of ultimate decision making, although decisions must also be made in the other steps of planning—in selecting goals, in choosing critical premises, and even in selecting alternatives.

Quantitative and Qualitative Factors

In comparing alternative plans for achieving an objective, people are likely to think exclusively of **quantitative factors.** These are factors that can be measured in numerical terms, such as time or various fixed and operating costs. No one would question the importance of this type of analysis, but the success of the venture would be endangered if intangible, or qualitative, factors were ignored. **Qualitative, or intangible, factors** are those that are difficult to measure numerically, such as the quality of labor relations, the risk of technological change, or the international political climate. There are all too many instances in which an excellent quantitative plan was destroyed by an unforeseen war, a fine marketing plan was made inoperable by a long transportation strike, or a rational borrowing plan was hampered by an economic recession. These illustrations point out the importance of giving attention to both quantitative and qualitative factors when comparing alternatives.

To evaluate and compare the intangible factors in a planning problem and make decisions, managers must first recognize these factors and then determine whether a reasonable quantitative measurement can be given them. If not, they should find out as much as possible about the factors, perhaps rate them in terms of their importance, compare their probable influence on the outcome with that of the quantitative factors, and then come to a decision. This decision may give predominant weight to a single intangible.

Such a procedure allows the manager to make decisions on the basis of the weight of the total evidence. It does involve fallible personal judgments; however, few managerial decisions can be so accurately quantified that judgment is unnecessary. Decision making is seldom simple. It is not without justification that the successful executive has been cynically described as a person who guesses right.

Marginal Analysis

Evaluating alternatives may involve utilizing the techniques of **marginal analysis** to compare additional revenues arising from additional costs. Where the objective is to maximize profits, this goal will be reached, as elementary economics teaches, when the additional revenues and additional costs are equal. In other words, if the additional revenues of a larger quantity are greater than its additional costs, more profits can be made by producing more. However, if the additional revenues of the larger quantity are less than its additional costs, a larger profit can be made by producing less.

Marginal analysis can be used in comparing factors other than costs and revenues. For example, to find the best output of a machine, inputs could be varied against outputs until the additional input equals the additional output. This would then be the point of maximum efficiency of the machine. Or the number of subordinates reporting to a manager might conceivably be increased to the point at which additional savings in costs, better communication and morale, and other factors equal additional losses in effectiveness of control, leadership, and similar factors.

Cost Effectiveness Analysis

An improvement on, or variation of, traditional marginal analysis is cost effectiveness, or cost benefit, analysis. **Cost effectiveness analysis** seeks the best ratio of benefits and costs; this means, for example, finding the least costly way of reaching an objective or getting the greatest value for given expenditures.

In its simplest terms, cost effectiveness analysis is a technique for choosing the best plan when the objectives are less specific than sales, costs, or profits. For example, a defense objective may be deterring or repelling an enemy attack, a social objective may be reducing air pollution or retraining the unemployed, and a business objective may be participating in social objectives through a program of training unemployables.

Nonquantifiable objectives can sometimes be given some fairly specific measures of effectiveness. In a program with the general objective of improving employee morale, for example, a company can measure effectiveness by such verifiable factors as employee turnover, absenteeism, and volume of grievances and can supplement these measurements with such subjective inputs as the judgments of qualified experts.

The major features of cost effectiveness analysis are that it focuses on the results of a program, helps weigh the potential benefits of each alternative against its potential cost, and involves a comparison of the alternatives in terms of the overall advantages.

Although the decision on cost effectiveness involves the same steps as any other planning decision, its major distinguishing features are the following:

1. Objectives are normally oriented to output or end result and are usually not precise.
2. Alternatives ordinarily represent total systems, programs, or strategies for meeting objectives.
3. The measures of effectiveness must be relevant to objectives and set in terms as precise as possible, although some may not be subject to quantification.
4. Cost estimates may include nonmonetary as well as monetary costs.
5. Decision standards, while definite but not usually as specific as cost or profit, may include achieving a given objective at the lowest cost, achieving it with the resources available, or providing for a trade-off of cost for effectiveness, particularly in light of the claims of other programs.

SELECTING AN ALTERNATIVE: THREE APPROACHES

When selecting among alternatives, managers can use three basic approaches: (1) experience, (2) experimentation, and (3) research and analysis. (See Figure 8-1.)

FIGURE 8-1

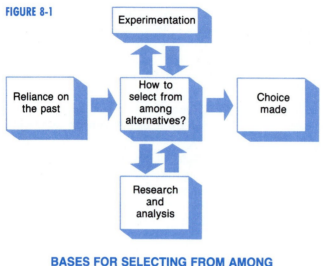

**BASES FOR SELECTING FROM AMONG
ALTERNATIVE COURSES OF ACTION.**

Experience

Reliance on past experience probably plays a larger part than it deserves in decision making. Experienced managers usually believe, often without realizing it, that the things they have successfully accomplished and the mistakes they have made furnish almost infallible guides to the future. This attitude is likely to be more pronounced the more experience a manager has had and the higher in an organization he or she has risen.

To some extent, experience is the best teacher. The very fact that managers have reached their position appears to justify their past decisions. Moreover, the process of thinking problems through, making decisions, and seeing programs succeed or fail does make for a degree of good judgment (at times bordering on intuition). Many people, however, do not profit by their errors, and there are managers who seem never to gain the seasoned judgment required by modern enterprise.

Relying on past experience as a guide for future action can be dangerous, however. In the first place, most people do not recognize the underlying reasons for their mistakes or failures. In the second place, the lessons of experience may be entirely inapplicable to new problems. Good decisions must be evaluated against future events, while experience belongs to the past.

On the other hand, if a person carefully analyzes experience, rather than blindly following it, and if he or she distills from experience the fundamental reasons for success or failure, then experience can be useful as a basis for decision analysis. A successful program, a well-managed company, a profitable product promotion, or any other decision that turns out well may furnish useful data for such distillation. Just as scientists do not hesitate to build upon the research of others and would be foolish indeed merely to duplicate it, managers can learn much from others.

Experimentation

An obvious way to decide among alternatives is to try one of them and see what happens. Experimentation is often used in scientific inquiry. People often argue that it should be employed more often in managing and that the only way a manager can make sure some plans are right—especially in view of the intangible factors—is to try the various alternatives and see which is best.

The experimental technique is likely to be the most expensive of all techniques, especially if a program requires heavy expenditures of capital and personnel and if the firm cannot afford to vigorously attempt several alternatives. Besides, after an experiment has been tried, there may still be doubt about what it proved, since the future may not duplicate the present. This technique, therefore, should be used only after considering other alternatives.

On the other hand, there are many decisions that cannot be made until the best course of action can be ascertained by experiment. Even reflections on experience or the most careful research may not assure managers of correct decisions. This is nowhere better illustrated than in the planning of a new airplane.

Perspective

Experimentation in Building an Airplane

An airplane manufacturer may draw from personal experience and that of other plane manufacturers and new plane users. Engineers and economists may make extensive studies of stress, vibration, fuel consumption, speed, space allocation, and other factors. But all these studies do not answer every question about the flight characteristics and economics of a successful plane; therefore, some experimentation is almost always involved in the process of selecting the right course to follow. Ordinarily, a first-production, or prototype, airplane is constructed and tested, and on the basis of these tests, production airplanes are made according to a somewhat revised design.

Experimentation is used in other ways. A firm may test a new product in a certain market before expanding its sale nationwide. Organizational techniques are often tried in a branch office or plant before being applied over an entire company. A candidate for a management job may be tested in the job during the incumbent's vacation.

Research and Analysis

One of the most effective techniques for selecting from alternatives when major decisions are involved is research and analysis. This approach means solving a problem by first comprehending it. It thus involves a search for relationships among the more critical of the variables, constraints, and premises that bear upon the goal sought. It is the pencil-and-paper (or, better, the computer-and-printout) approach to decision making.

Solving a planning problem requires breaking it into its component parts and studying the various quantitative and qualitative factors. Study and analysis are likely to be far cheaper than experimentation. The hours of time and reams of paper used for analyses usually cost much less than trying the various alternatives. In manufacturing airplanes, for example, if careful research did not precede the building and testing of the prototype airplane and its parts, the resulting costs would be enormous.

A major step in the research-and-analysis approach is to develop a model simulating the problem. Thus, architects often make models of buildings in the form of extensive blueprints or three-dimensional renditions. Engineers test models of airplane wings and missiles in a wind tunnel. But the most useful simulation is likely to be a representation of the variables in a problem situation by mathematical terms and relationships. Conceptualizing a problem is a major step toward its solution. The physical sciences have long relied on mathematical models to do this, and it is encouraging to see this method being applied to managerial decision making.

One of the most comprehensive research-and-analysis approaches to decision making is operations research. Since this is an important tool for production and operations management, it will be discussed more fully in Chapter 22.

PROGRAMMED AND NONPROGRAMMED DECISIONS

A distinction can be made between programmed and nonprogrammed decisions. A **programmed decision,** as shown in Figure 8-2, is applied to structured or routine problems. Lathe operators have specifications and rules that tell them whether the part they made is acceptable, has to be discarded, or should be reworked. Another example of a programmed decision is the reordering of standard inventory items. (In fact, there is a formula for doing this, which will be discussed in Chapter 22.) This kind of decision is used for routine and repetitive work; it

FIGURE 8-2

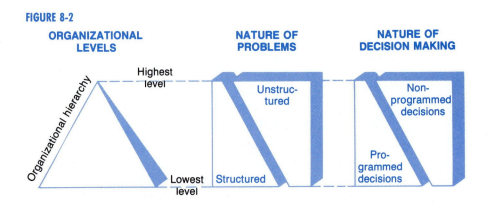

NATURE OF PROBLEMS AND DECISION MAKING IN THE ORGANIZATION.

relies primarily on previously established criteria. It is, in effect, decision making by precedent.

Nonprogrammed decisions are used for unstructured, novel, and ill-defined situations of a nonrecurring nature. Examples are the introduction of the Macintosh computer by Apple Computer, Inc., the development of the four-wheel-drive passenger car by Audi, and the marketing of a small video camera by Kodak. In fact, strategic decisions, in general, are nonprogrammed decisions, since they require subjective judgments.

Most decisions are neither completely programmed nor completely nonprogrammed; they are a combination of both. As Figure 8-2 indicates, most nonprogrammed decisions are made by upper-level managers; this is because upper-level managers have to deal with unstructured problems.[5] Problems at lower levels of the organization are often routine and well structured, requiring less decision discretion by managers and nonmanagers.

DECISION MAKING UNDER CERTAINTY, UNCERTAINTY, AND RISK

Virtually all decisions are made in an environment of at least some uncertainty.[6] However, the degree will vary from relative certainty to great uncertainty. There are certain risks involved in making decisions.

In a situation involving certainty, people are reasonably sure about what will happen when they make a decision. The information is available and is considered to be reliable, and the cause and effect relationships are known.

In a situation of uncertainty, on the other hand, people have only a meager database, they do not know whether or not the data are reliable, and they are very unsure about whether or not the situation may change. Moreover, they cannot evaluate the interactions of the different variables. For example, a corporation that decides to expand its operation in a strange country may know little about the country's culture, laws, economic environment, and politics. The political situation may be so volatile that even the experts cannot predict a possible change in government.

In a risk situation, factual information may exist, but it may be incomplete. To improve decision making, one may estimate the objective probabilities of an outcome by using, for example, mathematical models.[7] On the other hand, subjective probability, based on judgment and experience, may be used. Fortunately, there are a number of tools available that help managers make more effective decisions.

MODERN APPROACHES TO DECISION MAKING UNDER UNCERTAINTY

A number of modern techniques improve the quality of decision making under the normal conditions of uncertainty. Among the most important of these are (1) risk analysis, (2) decision trees, and (3) preference theory.

Risk Analysis

All intelligent decision makers dealing with uncertainty like to know the size and nature of the risk they are taking in choosing a course of action. One of the deficiencies in using the traditional approaches of operations research for problem solving is that many of the data used in a model are merely estimates and others are based on probabilities. The ordinary practice is to have staff specialists come up with "best estimates." However, new techniques have been developed that give a more precise view of risk.

Virtually every decision is based on the interaction of a number of important variables, many of which have an element of uncertainty but, perhaps, a fairly high degree of probability. Thus, the wisdom of launching a new product might depend on a number of critical variables: the cost of introducing the product, the cost of producing it, the capital investment that will be required, the price that can be set for the product, the size of the potential market, and the share of the total market that it will represent.

For a new-product investment program, the range of probabilities for a return on investment might be based on different estimates, as follows:

Rate of return, %	0	10	15	20	25	30	35	40
Probability of achieving at least this rate	.90	.80	.70	.65	.60	.50	.40	.30

In other words, there is a 90 percent (.90) chance that the rate of return (or the rate at which the company earns money from its investment) will be at least zero, an 80 percent (.80) chance that it will be at least 10 percent, and so on.

Given such data as these, a manager is better able to assess the probability of accomplishing a best estimate and can see the chances of success that he or she might have if a lower rate of return would be sufficient.

Decision Trees

One of the best ways to analyze a decision is to use a so-called decision tree. **Decision trees** depict, in the form of a "tree," the decision points, chance events, and probabilities involved in various courses that might be undertaken. A common problem occurs in business when a new product is introduced. Managers must decide whether to install expensive permanent equipment to ensure production at the lowest possible cost or to undertake cheaper, temporary tooling that will involve a higher manufacturing cost but lower capital investments and will result in smaller

FIGURE 8-3

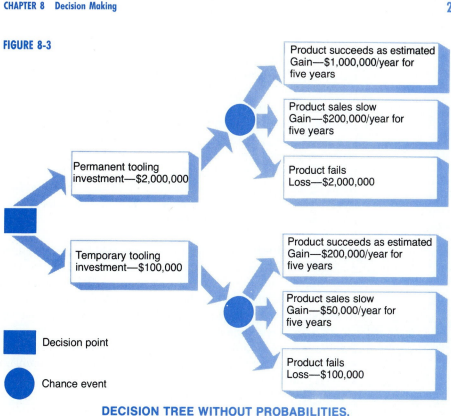

Product succeeds as estimated
Gain—$1,000,000/year for
five years

Product sales slow
Gain—$200,000/year for
five years

Product fails
Loss—$2,000,000

Permanent tooling
investment—$2,000,000

Temporary tooling
investment—$100,000

Product succeeds as estimated
Gain—$200,000/year for
five years

Product sales slow
Gain—$50,000/year for
five years

Product fails
Loss—$100,000

Decision point

Chance event

DECISION TREE WITHOUT PROBABILITIES.

losses if the product does not sell as well as estimated. In its simplest form, a tree showing the decisions a manager faces in this situation might be similar to that in Figure 8-3.

The decision tree approach makes it possible to see at least the major alternatives and the fact that subsequent decisions may depend on events in the future. By incorporating the probabilities of various events in the tree, managers can also comprehend the true probability of a decision's leading to the desired results. The "best estimate" may really turn out to be quite risky. One thing is certain: Decision trees and similar decision techniques replace broad judgments with a focus on the important elements in a decision, bring out into the open premises that are often hidden, and disclose the reasoning process by which decisions are made under uncertainty.

Preference Theory

Preference, or **utility, theory** is based on the notion that individual attitudes toward risk will vary: Some individuals are willing to take only smaller risks than those indicated by probabilities ("risk averters"), and others are willing to take greater risks ("gamblers"). While referred to here as "preference theory," this technique is more classically called "utility theory." Purely statistical probabilities, as applied to decision making, rest on the assumption that decision makers will follow them. In other words, it might seem reasonable that if there were a 60 percent chance of a decision's being the right one, a person would take it. This is not necessarily true, however; since the risk of being wrong is 40 percent, the individual might not wish to take this risk. Managers avoid risk, particularly if the penalty for being wrong is severe, whether it be in terms of monetary loss, reputation, or job security. If this seems doubtful, consider the likelihood, on a personal basis, of risking, say, $40,000 on the 60 percent chance of making $100,000, realizing that there is still a 40 percent chance of losing $40,000. People might readily risk $4 on a chance of making $10, and gamblers have been known to risk much more on a smaller chance of success.

Attitudes toward risk.   In order to give probabilities practical meaning in decision making, it is necessary to understand the individual decision maker's aversion to, or acceptance of, risk. This varies not only with the individual but also with the size of the risk, the level of the manager in an organization, and the source of the funds involved (are they personal, or do they belong to the company?).

Higher-level managers are accustomed to taking larger risks than are lower-level managers, and their decision areas tend to involve larger elements of risk. A company president may have to take great risks in launching a new product, selecting an advertising program, or choosing a vice president, while a first-level supervisor's risk taking may be limited to hiring or promoting semiskilled workers or approving vacation schedules for subordinates.

Also, the same top managers who may make a decision involving risks of millions of dollars for a company in a given program with a chance of success of, say, 75 percent would not be likely to do that with their own personal fortunes, at least not unless their fortunes were very large. Moreover, the same manager willing to take a 75 percent risk in one case might not be willing to do so in another. Furthermore, a top executive might "go for" a large advertising program for which the chance of success is 70 percent but might decide against an investment in plant and equipment unless the probability of success were higher. In other words, attitudes toward risk vary with events, as well as with people and positions.

Personal risk or preference curves.   While not much is known about personal attitudes toward risk, two things are certain: Some people are risk averters in some situations and gamblers in others, and some people have by nature a high aversion to risk while others have a low one. Typical personal risk or preference curves may be drawn as in Figure 8-4. This graph shows both risk averter's and gambler's curves, as well as what is referred to as a "personal" curve. The latter, of course, implies that most of us are gamblers when small stakes are involved but that we soon become risk averters when the stakes rise.

Most managers (understandably influenced by the dangers of failure) tend to be risk averters to some extent and do not in fact play the averages. Therefore, statistical probabilities are not good enough for practical decision making.

FIGURE 8-4

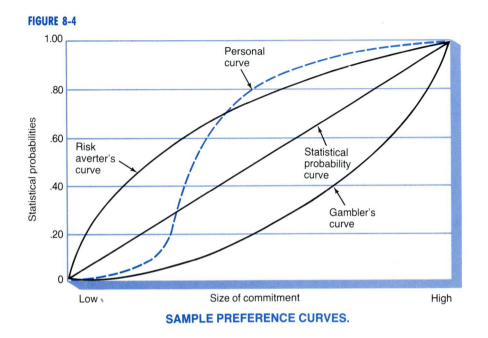

SAMPLE PREFERENCE CURVES.

Although perhaps too many managers are risk averters and thereby miss opportunities, few are players of pure statistical averages, at least in important decisions. Therefore, individual preference curves could be substituted for statistical probabilities in decision trees. This can be done, at least roughly, by assessing a person's willingness to take risks in a variety of real or imaginary situations and by developing an individual preference curve for that person. Even if this is not done systematically, those of us who receive recommendations on courses of action from subordinates gain an important advantage if we are aware of the effect of our subordinates' attitudes toward risk in making decisions or decision recommendations.

EVALUATING THE IMPORTANCE OF A DECISION

Since managers not only must make correct decisions but also must make them as needed and as economically as possible, and since they must do this often, guidelines to the relative importance of decisions are useful. Decisions of lesser importance do not require thorough analysis and research, and they may even be safely delegated without endangering an individual manager's basic responsibility. The importance of a decision also depends on the extent of responsibility, and so what may be of practically no importance to a corporation president may be of great importance to a section head.

If a decision commits the enterprise to a heavy expenditure of funds or to an important personnel program, such as a program for management appraisal and training, or if the commitment can be fulfilled only over a long period, such as by the construction of a new chemical plant, it should be subjected to suitable attention at an upper level of management.

Some plans can be easily changed, some have built into them the possibility of a future change of direction, and others involve action that is difficult to reverse. Clearly, decisions that involve inflexible courses of action must be more carefully evaluated than decisions that can be easily changed.

If goals and premises are fairly certain, a decision resting on them tends to be less difficult and to require less judgment and analysis than it would if the goals and premises were highly uncertain.

If the goals, inputs, restrictions, and variables can be accurately measured, as with definite inputs in a production machine shop, the importance of the decision, other things remaining the same, tends to be less than if the inputs were difficult to quantify, as in pricing a new consumer product or deciding on its style.

In situations where the impact of a decision on people is great, its importance is high. A doctor's mistake in a hospital can be fatal to a patient. No one making a decision that affects other people can afford to overlook the needs of those people who accept the decision.

DECISION SUPPORT SYSTEMS

Decision support systems (DSSs) use computers to facilitate the decision-making process of semistructured tasks. These systems are designed not to replace managerial judgment but to support it and to make the decision process more effective. Decision support systems also help managers react quickly to changing needs.[8] It is clear, then, that the design of an effective system requires a thorough knowledge of how managers make decisions.

The availability of minicomputers and microcomputers, as well as of communication networks, makes it possible to access and utilize a great deal of information at low cost. Thus, DSS gives managers an important tool for decision making under their own control.

Although there are similarities between management information systems (MISs) and DSSs, there are also differences. Traditionally, the designers of MIS were technical experts, and managers (who had to make the decisions) had only minor inputs. In contrast, DSS focuses on the decision-making process and on managers, who, in cooperation with the technical professionals, design the system suitable for a particular position. Managers, having access to databases in DSSs, can manipulate data and explore the effectiveness of alternative courses of action. These and other differences between MIS and DSS are shown in Table 8-1.

Now many software programs are available for microcomputers. There is a great variety of ready-made software for word processing, graphics, decision support, spreadsheets, and databases, and there are packages that integrate various software programs. Managers can be overwhelmed by the many choices of programs that aid the decision-making process. What was formerly done by hand can now be shown in a computer spreadsheet. The great advantage of computerizing

TABLE 8-1 COMPARISONS BETWEEN MIS AND DSS	
MIS	**DSS**
Focus on structured tasks and routine decisions (e.g., use of procedures, use of decision rules)	Focus on semistructured tasks, requiring managerial judgment
Emphasis on data storage	Emphasis on data manipulation
Often only indirect access to data by managers	Direct data access by managers
Reliance on computer expert	Reliance on manager's own judgment
Access to data possibly requiring a wait for manager's turn	Direct access to computer and data
MIS manager not completely understanding the nature of the decision	Manager knowing decision environment
Emphasis on efficiency	Emphasis on effectiveness

Sources: Peter G. W. Keen and Michael S. Scott Morton, *Decision Support Systems—An Organizational Perspective* (Reading, Mass.: Addison-Wesley Publishing Company, 1978); Ronald R. Wood, "The Personal Computer: How It Can Increase Management Productivity," *Financial Executive* (February 1984); Ernest A. Kallman and Leon Reinharth, *Information Systems for Planning and Decision Making* (New York: Van Nostrand Reinhold, 1984).

the information is that the data can be manipulated and many reports can be generated with little effort to highlight the information wanted.

CREATIVITY AND INNOVATION

An important factor in managing people is creativity. A distinction can be made between creativity and innovation. The term **creativity** usually refers to the ability and power to develop new ideas. **Innovation,** on the other hand, usually means the use of these ideas. In an organization, this can mean a new product, a new service, or a new way of doing things. Although this discussion centers on the creative process, it is implied that organizations not only generate new ideas but also translate them into practical applications.

The Creative Process

The creative process is seldom simple and linear. Instead, it generally consists of four overlapping and interacting phases: (1) unconscious scanning, (2) intuition, (3) insight, and (4) logical formulation.[9]

The first phase, *unconscious scanning,* is difficult to explain because it is beyond consciousness. This scanning usually requires an absorption in the problem, which may be vague in the mind. Yet managers working under time constraints often make decisions prematurely rather than dealing thoroughly with ambiguous, ill-defined problems.

The second phase, *intuition,* connects the unconscious with the conscious. This stage may involve a combination of factors that may seem contradictory at first. For example, in the 1920s Donaldson Brown and Alfred Sloan of General Motors conceived the idea of a decentralized division structure with centralized control—concepts that seem to contradict each other. Yet the idea makes sense when one recognizes the underlying principles of (1) giving responsibility for the operations to the general manager of each division and (2) maintaining centralized control in headquarters over certain functions. It took the intuition of two great corporate leaders to see that these two principles could interact in the managerial process.

Intuition needs time to work. It requires that people find new combinations and integrate diverse concepts and ideas. Thus, one must think through the problem. Intuitive thinking is promoted by several techniques such as brainstorming and synectics, which will be discussed shortly.

Insight, the third phase of the creative process, is mostly the result of hard work. For example, many ideas are needed in the development of a usable product, a new service, or a new process. What is interesting is that insight may come at times when the thoughts are not directly focused on the problem at hand. Moreover, new insights may last for only a few minutes, and effective managers may benefit from having paper and pencil ready to make notes of their creative ideas.

The last phase in the creative process is *logical formulation* or *verification.* Insight needs to be tested through logic or experiment. This may be accomplished by continuing to work on an idea or by inviting critiques from others. Brown and Sloan's idea of decentralization, for example, needed to be tested against organizational reality.

Techniques to Enhance Creativity

Creativity can be taught.[10] Creative thoughts are often the fruits of extensive efforts, and several techniques are available to nurture those kinds of thoughts, especially in the decision-making process. Some techniques focus on group interactions; others focus on individual actions. As illustrative of the various techniques, two popular ones are brainstorming and synectics.

Brainstorming.   One of the best-known techniques for facilitating creativity has been developed by Alex F. Osborn, who has been called "the father of brainstorming."[11] The purpose of this approach is to improve problem solving by finding new and unusual solutions. In the brainstorming sessions, a multiplication of ideas is sought. The rules are as follows:

1. No ideas are ever criticized.
2. The more radical the ideas are, the better.
3. The quantity of idea production is stressed.
4. The improvement of ideas by others is encouraged.

Brainstorming, which emphasizes group thinking, was widely accepted after its introduction. However, the enthusiasm was dampened by research which showed that individuals could develop better ideas working by themselves than they could working in groups. Additional research, however, showed that in some situations the group approach may work well. This may be the case when the information is distributed among various people or when a poorer group decision is more acceptable than a better individual decision that, for example, may be opposed by those who have to implement it. Also, the acceptance of new ideas is usually greater when the decision is made by the group charged with its implementation.[12]

Synectics.   Originally known as the Gordon technique (named after its creator, William J. Gordon), this system was further modified and became known as synectics.[13] In this approach, the members of the synectics team are carefully selected for their suitability to deal with the problem, which may involve the entire organization.

The leader of the group plays a vital role in this approach. In fact, only the leader knows the specific nature of the problem. This person narrows and carefully leads the discussion without revealing the actual problem itself. The main reason for this approach is to prevent the group from reaching a premature solution to the problem. The system involves a complex set of interactions from which a solution emerges—frequently the invention of a new product.

Limitations of Traditional Group Discussion

Although the techniques of brainstorming and synectics may result in creative ideas, it would be incorrect to assume that creativity flourishes only in groups. Indeed, the usual group discussion can inhibit creativity.[14] For example, group members may pursue an idea to the exclusion of other alternatives. Experts on a topic may not be willing to express their ideas in a group for fear of being ridiculed. Also, lower-level managers may be inhibited in expressing their views in a group with higher-level managers. Pressures to conform can discourage the expression of deviant opinions. The need for getting along with others can be stronger than the need for exploring creative but unpopular alternatives to the solution of a problem. Finally, because they need to arrive at a decision, groups may not make the effort of searching for data relevant to a decision.

Perspective

How 3M Fosters Innovation[15]

Companies have different strategies to foster innovation. At Johnson & Johnson, autonomous operating units are encouraged to innovate. The organization culture allows failure to occur. At Rubbermaid, 30 percent of its sales are derived from products that are less than 5 years old. Hewlett-Packard encourages researchers to spend 10 percent of their time on their pet projects, and Merck allocates time and resources to its researchers for working on high-risk products with a potential for high payouts. Dow Corning and General Electric engage in joint projects with customers to develop new products. One of the masters in innovation is Minnesota Mining & Manufacturing (3M).

The organizational environment of 3M fosters creative thinking and a tolerance for new ideas. In 1988, more than 30 percent of its sales came from products that were less than 5 years old. How does 3M do it? For one, the company operates with few rules. Anything that hampers innovation, such as excessive planning or intolerance of mistakes, is eliminated. On the other hand, information sharing is greatly encouraged. Although financial measures act as a control, the real control comes from among peers who review each other's work. Salaries and promotions are linked to the development and commercialization of products. Moreover, the innovator gets an opportunity to manage his or her new product.

The typical process is as follows: When a person in the organization has an idea for a new product, he or she forms a team consisting of individuals from the functional areas, such as the technical department, manufacturing, marketing, sales, and, at times, finance. The team works on the product design, production, and marketing. Moreover, various uses of the product are explored. Team members are rewarded for the success of the product.

Corporate guidelines foster innovation. For example, the 25 percent rule states that one-fourth of a division's sales should come from products that are less than 5 years old. The 15 percent rule allows a person to spend 15 percent of his or her time on a product-related pet project. Rules or guidelines are rather simple: Develop a tolerance for failure; reward those who have a good product idea and who can form an effective action team to promote the product; establish close relationships with customers; share technology with others in the company; keep the project alive by allocating time or financial grants; keep the divisions small.

This approach at 3M has been successful. But the company realizes that it faces new challenges, especially from the Japanese. Thus, the chairman and CEO, Jake Jacobson, plans to continue cost cutting without harming innovation. While in the past, many of the more than 60,000 products, ranging from Scotch tape (invented in 1929) to the very successful yellow Post-it note pads, were relatively small items, the new direction is to develop bigger products and to expand overseas. The future will tell whether innovation will continue to be a key success factor for 3M.

The Creative Manager

All too often it is assumed that most people are noncreative and have little ability to develop new ideas. This assumption, unfortunately, can be detrimental to the organization, for in the appropriate environment virtually all people are capable of being creative, even though the degree of creativity varies considerably among individuals.

Generally speaking, creative people are inquisitive and come up with many new and unusual ideas; they are seldom satisfied with the status quo. Although intelligent, they not only rely on the rational process but also involve the emotional aspects of their personality in problem solving. They appear to be excited about solving a problem, even to the point of tenacity. Creative individuals are aware of themselves and capable of independent judgment. They object to conformity and see themselves as being different.

It is beyond question that creative people can make great contributions to an enterprise. At the same time, however, they may also cause difficulties in organizations. Change—as any manager knows—is not always popular. Moreover, change frequently has undesirable and unexpected side effects. Similarly, unusual ideas, pursued stubbornly, may frustrate others and inhibit the smooth functioning of an organization. Finally, creative individuals may be disruptive by ignoring established policies, rules, and regulations.

As a result, the creativity of most individuals is probably underutilized in many cases, despite the fact that unusual innovations can be of great benefit to the firm. However, individual and group techniques can be effectively used to nurture creativity, especially in the area of planning. But creativity is not a substitute for managerial judgment. It is the manager who must determine and weigh the risks involved in pursuing unusual ideas and translating them into innovative practices.

THE SYSTEMS APPROACH AND DECISION MAKING*

Decisions cannot usually be made, of course, in a closed-system environment. As already emphasized, many elements of the environment of planning lie outside the enterprise. In addition, every department or section of an enterprise is a subsystem of the entire enterprise; managers of these organizational units must be responsive to the policies and programs of other organizational units and of the total enterprise. Moreover, people within the enterprise are a part of the social system, and their thinking and attitudes must be taken into account whenever a manager makes a decision.

Furthermore, even when managers construct a closed-system model, as they may do with operations research decision models, they do so simply to have a workable program to solve. But in so doing, they make certain assumptions as to environmental forces that heavily influence their decision, they enter inputs into their calculations as they are or appear to be at any given time, and they change the construction of their model when forces and developments beyond its boundaries so require.

---

* Decision making is also influenced by personal values and the organization culture. These concepts are discussed in Chapter 12. Similarly, the impact of groups on decision making is elaborated in Chapter 18.

FIGURE 8-5

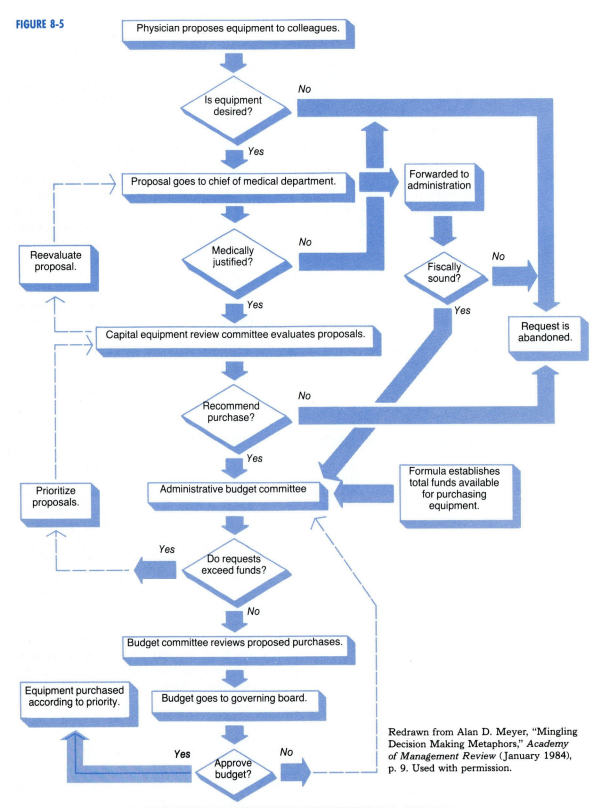

Redrawn from Alan D. Meyer, "Mingling Decision Making Metaphors," *Academy of Management Review* (January 1984), p. 9. Used with permission.

FLOWCHART FOR INVESTMENT DECISIONS IN A HOSPITAL.

A decision system can become very complex. The flow diagram of information for proposed investments is shown in Figure 8-5.[16]

Now imagine the many other decisions that have to be made in a hospital pertaining to the well-being of patients, providing the basis for fiscal soundness, and balancing the interests of trustees, administrators, and physicians. More recently, some hospitals began thinking strategically by making decisions that related the hospital's strengths and weaknesses to opportunities and threats in the external environment within the framework of its mission. While it might be difficult to diagram all the various decision processes, and one could be overwhelmed by its complexity, the systems nature of decision making must be recognized. The hospital, it should be kept in mind, cannot be a closed system but must serve the needs of the community of which it is a part.

Saying that managers take into account the various elements in the system environment of their problem does not mean, however, that they abdicate their role as decision makers. Someone must select a course of action from among alternatives, taking into account events and forces in the environment of a decision. It is often not feasible, or advisable, to democratize the decision process to the extent that for all decisions a vote is taken from subordinates or the many other persons who may have some immediate or remote interest in the decision. At some point a decision has to be made.

SUMMARY

Decision making is the selection of a course of action from among alternatives; it is the core of planning. Managers must make choices on the basis of limited, or bounded, rationality. That is, they must make decisions in light of everything they can learn about a situation, which may not be everything they should know. "Satisficing" is a term sometimes used to describe picking a course of action that is satisfactory under the circumstances.

Because there are almost always alternatives—usually many—to a course of action, managers need to narrow them down to those few that deal with the limiting factors. These are the factors that stand in the way of achieving a desired objective. Alternatives are then evaluated in terms of quantitative and qualitative factors. Other techniques for evaluating alternatives include marginal analysis and cost effectiveness analysis. Experience, experimentation, and research and analysis come into play in making decisions.

Programmed and nonprogrammed decisions are different. The former are suited for structured or routine problems. These kinds of decisions are made especially by lower-level managers and nonmanagers. Nonprogrammed decisions, on the other hand, are used for unstructured and nonroutine problems and are made especially by upper-level managers.

Some modern approaches to decision making are risk analysis (which assigns mathematical probabilities to the outcomes of decisions), decision trees (which illustrate the decision points, chance events, and probabilities of various courses of action), and preference theory (which takes into account managers' willingness to take certain risks).

The factors that determine the importance of a decision are the size of the commitment, the flexibility or inflexibility of plans, the certainty or uncertainty of goals and premises, the degree to which variables can be measured, and the impact on people.

Decision support systems (DSSs) use computers to help the decision-making process of semistructured tasks. These systems help managers to make better decisions; they are not a substitute for managerial judgment.

Creativity, the ability and power to develop new ideas, is important for effective managing. Innovation is the use of these ideas. The creative process consists of four overlapping phases: (1) unconscious scanning, (2) intuition, (3) insight, and (4) logical formulation. Two popular techniques for enhancing creativity are brainstorming and synectics.

Finally, decisions must be made with the recognition that organizations are open systems, interacting with the environment.

KEY IDEAS AND CONCEPTS FOR REVIEW

Decision making	Risk analysis
Limited, or bounded, rationality	Decision trees
Satisficing	Preference, or utility, theory
Principle of the limiting factor	Factors for evaluating a decision
Quantitative factors	Decision support systems (DSSs)
Qualitative factors	Creativity
Marginal analysis	Innovation
Cost effectiveness analysis	Creative process
Three approaches to selecting alternatives	Brainstorming
Programmed decisions	Synectics
Nonprogrammed decisions	Systems approach to decision making

FOR DISCUSSION

1. Why is experience often referred to not only as an expensive basis for decision making but also as a dangerous one? How can a manager make the best use of experience?
2. In a decision problem you now know of, how and where would you apply the principle of the limiting factor?
3. Identify five decision problems, and recommend programmed or nonprogrammed decisions. If the examples are from an organizational setting, did they occur at upper or lower levels?
4. Draw a decision tree for a decision problem you face.
5. "Decision making is the primary task of the manager." Comment.
6. How does risk aversion affect your own life? Given a situation, draw your preference curve.

7. Think of a problem that was creatively solved. Did the solution come from group discussion, or was it the result of an individual effort? Reconstruct the phases of the creative process.

EXERCISES/ACTION STEPS

1. Your boss offers you a promotion to a position in a location your family does not like. Make the necessary assumptions, and then state how and what you would decide.
2. Interview a manager of a local company, and obtain information about the decision-making process in the organization. Discuss with him or her the concept of bounded rationality, and see if it applies to the manager.

CASES

CASE 8-1
OLYMPIC TOY COMPANY

"I expect all the managers in my department to act completely rationally in every decision they make," declared Eleanor Johnson, vice president for marketing for the Olympic Toy Company. "Every one of us, no matter what his or her position, is hired to be a professional rationalist, and I expect all of us not only to know what they are doing and why but to be right in their decisions. I know that someone has said that a good manager needs only to be right in more than half of his or her decisions. But that is not good enough for me. I would agree that you may be excused for occasionally making a mistake, especially if it is a matter beyond your control, but I can never excuse you for not acting rationally."

"I agree with your idea, Eleanor," said Jill Goldberg, her advertising manager, "and I always try to be rational and logical in my decisions. But would you mind helping me be sure of this by explaining just what 'acting rationally' is?"

1. Explain how the vice president for marketing might describe what is involved in making rational decisions.
2. If Jill Goldberg then declares that there is no way she can be completely rational, what would you suggest as a reply?

INTERNATIONAL CASE 8-2
GOING GLOBAL: NO SURE WAY TO SUCCESS FOR FEDERAL EXPRESS[17]

Driven both by his desire to be number one and by the saturated U.S. market, Frederick Smith, CEO and founder of Federal Express, seized the opportunity by expanding his delivery service to Europe. His aim was to become a dominant international force. But competing abroad with entrenched European com-petitors and the necessity of complying with the many foreign regulations caused many unexpected problems, which resulted in considerable losses for Federal Express. In Europe's multifaceted political and cultural environments with many local regulations, Federal was forced to acquire local companies. Yet, the heavy investments in local European companies were not accompanied by corresponding increases in sales. But Smith defended his European expansion by saying: "You have to put the network in place before you can offer the product."

Federal's innovative electronic transmission service, Zap Mail, failed because of the increased popularity of facsimile (FAX) machines among businesses and individuals. Speedy FAX transmissions reduce the need for express delivery services. Federal Express spent some $350 million developing and promoting Zap Mail before it was discontinued in 1986. In package delivery, United Parcel Service (UPS), which is introducing overnight delivery, is also proving to be a formidable competitor in both the American and European markets. UPS's brown trucks are now a common sight in Europe.

There are also constraining factors in the Pacific Basin. Japan, for example, places restrictions on air delivery of heavy packages. Consequently, Federal Express has to operate flights in which only a fraction of the capacity of the airplanes is used. As the world becomes a global market, Federal also has to face tough competition from companies such as Japan's Nippon Cargo Airlines, America's DHL Worldwide Express, and TNT of Australia.

In an attempt to become a truly global company, Federal Express purchased Tiger International Airlines. This acquisition extends Federal's routes to Japan, London, and Brussels, as well as to Seoul, Hong Kong, Bangkok, Singapore, Manila, and Australia. Flying Tigers also serves South American cities such as Rio de Janeiro, São Paulo, and Buenos Aires. With the extended routes to Paris, Frankfurt, and Dubai, Federal Express (through the acquisition of Tiger International) now spans the globe.

But the over $800 million purchase of Tiger was risky. Integrating the two organizational cultures may prove to be a formidable task. Federal's entrepreneurial culture is quite different from that of the unionized Tiger company. Moreover, Tiger's important customer, UPS, is one of Federal's competitors. As Mr. Smith ponders the opportunities, he also is aware of the risks and constraints.

1. What are Mr. Smith's most pressing issues, and what should he do?
2. What threats and opportunities do you see for Federal Express in Europe during the 1990s?

REFERENCES

1. C. West Churchman, "The Myth of Management," in Michael T. Matteson and John M. Ivancevich (eds.), *Management Classics*, 3d ed. (Plano, Texas: Business Publications, 1986), p. 371.
2. See James G. March and Herbert A. Simon, *Organizations* (New York: John Wiley & Sons, 1958, 1966).
3. March and Simon, *Organizations* (1958, 1966), p. 169.
4. Bro Uttal, "Compaq Bids for PC Leadership," *Fortune* (Sept. 29, 1986), pp. 30–32; Jo E. Davis and Geoff Lewis, "Compaq Is Trying to Steal a March on IBM," *Business Week* (Sept. 22, 1986), p. 30; Edward Warner, "Compaq Introduces 386 PC, Challenges IBM to Match It," *InfoWorld* (Sept. 15, 1986), pp. 1, 8; Jo Ellen Davis and Geoff Lewis, "Who's Afraid of IBM?" *Business Week* (June 29, 1987), pp. 68–74; Jim Bartimo, "Compaq Plots Strategy to Widen Its Horizons beyond a Niche in PCs," *The Wall Street Journal* (Apr. 10, 1991).
5. Weston H. Agor, "How Top Executives Use Their Intuition to Make Important Decisions," *Business Horizons* (January–February 1986), pp. 49–53.
6. Strategic decision making often involves a great deal of uncertainty. See Charles R. Schwenk, "Cognitive Simplification Processes in Strategic Decision-Making," *Strategic Management Journal* (April–June 1984), pp. 111–128; Agor, "How Top Executives Use Their Intuition" (1986), pp. 49–53.

7. See also Jitendra V. Singh, "Performance, Slack, and Risk Taking in Organizational Decision Making," *Academy of Management Journal* (September 1986), pp. 562–585.

8. Steven Alter, *Decision Support Systems: Current Practice and Continuing Challenges* (Reading, Mass.: Addison-Wesley Publishing Company, 1980), p. xi.

9. Much of the discussion of the creative process is based on Michael B. McCaskey, *The Executive Challenge—Managing Change and Ambiguity* (Marshfield, Mass.: Pitman Publishing, 1982), chap. 8.

10. Emily T. Smith, "Are You Creative? Research Shows Creativity Can Be Taught—and Companies Are Listening," *Business Week* (Sept. 30, 1985), pp. 80–84.

11. Alex F. Osborn, *Applied Imagination,* 3d rev. ed. (New York: Charles Scribner's Sons, 1963).

12. Irvin Summers and David E. White, "Creativity Techniques: Toward Improvement of the Decision Process," *Academy of Management Review* (April 1976), pp. 99–107.

13. William J. Gordon, "Operational Approach to Creativity," *Harvard Business Review* (November–December 1956), pp. 41–51; William J. Gordon, *Synectics* (New York: Harper & Brothers, 1961).

14. George S. Steiner, John B. Miner, and Edmund R. Gray, *Management Policy and Strategy,* 3d ed. (New York: The Macmillan Company, 1986), pp. 174–177; Andre L. Delbecq, Andrew H. Van de Ven, and David H. Gustafson, *Group Techniques for Program Planning* (Glenview, Ill.: Scott, Foresman and Company, 1975).

15. Russel Mitchell, "Masters of Innovation," *Business Week* (Apr. 10, 1989), pp. 58–63.

16. Alan D. Meyer, "Mingling Decision Making Metaphors," *Academy of Management Review* (January 1984), pp. 6–17.

17. This case is based on a variety of sources, including Dean Foust, Jonathan Kapstein, Pia Farrell, Peter Finch, and Chris Power, "Mr. Smith Goes Global," *Business Week* (Feb. 13, 1989), pp. 66–72; Peter Waldman and James R. Schiffman, "Federal Express Profit Falls 54%; Takeover Cited," *The Wall Street Journal* (Sept. 22, 1989); Philip Hastings, Martin Savery, Gary Gimson, and Simon Tan, "Express Services: A Struggle for World Domination," *Asian Business* (May 1989), pp. 66–71; Peter Waldman, "Federal Express Faces Problems Overseas," *The Wall Street Journal* (July 20, 1990).

Summary of Major Principles, or Guides, for Planning

Perhaps the best way to summarize Part 2, on planning, is to list some of the major principles, or guidelines, that may be used in planning. While others might be added, the most essential guiding principles are those listed below.

The Purpose and Nature of Planning

The purpose and nature of planning may be summarized by reference to the following principles.

Principle of contribution to objectives. The purpose of every plan and all supporting plans is to promote the accomplishment of enterprise objectives.

Principle of objectives. If objectives are to be meaningful to people, they must be clear, attainable, and verifiable.

Principle of primacy of planning. Planning logically precedes all other managerial functions.

Principle of efficiency of plans. The efficiency of a plan is measured by the amount it contributes to purpose and objectives as offset by the costs required to formulate and operate it and by unsought consequences.

The Structure of Plans

Two major principles dealing with the structure of plans can go far in tying plans together, making supporting plans contribute to major plans, and ensuring that plans in one department harmonize with those in another.

Principle of planning premises. The more thoroughly the individuals who are charged with planning understand and agree to utilize consistent planning premises, the more coordinated enterprise planning will be.

Principle of the strategy and policy framework. The more strategies and policies are clearly understood and implemented in practice, the more consistent and effective will be the framework of enterprise plans.

The Process of Planning

Within the process of planning, there are four principles that help in the development of a practical science of planning.

Principle of the limiting factor. In choosing among alternatives, the more accurately individuals can recognize and solve for those factors which are limiting or critical to the attainment of the desired goal, the more easily and accurately they can select the most favorable alternative.

The commitment principle. Logical planning should cover a period of time in the future necessary to foresee as well as possible, through a series of actions, the fulfillment of commitments involved in a decision made today.

Principle of flexibility. Building flexibility into plans will lessen the danger of losses incurred through unexpected events, but the cost of flexibility should be weighed against its advantages.

Principle of navigational change. The more that planning decisions commit individuals to a future path, the more important it is to check on events and expectations periodically and redraw plans as necessary to maintain a course toward a desired goal.

The commitment principle and the principles of flexibility and navigational change are aimed at a contingency approach to planning. Although it makes sense to forecast and draw plans far enough into the future to be reasonably sure of meeting commitments, often it is impossible to do so, or the future is so uncertain that it is too risky to fulfill those commitments.

The principle of flexibility deals with that ability to change which is built into plans. The principle of navigational change, on the other hand, implies reviewing plans from time to time and redrawing them if this is required by changed events and expectations. Unless plans have built-in flexibility, navigational change may be difficult or costly.

Global Planning

This part closing focuses on the global dimension of planning. First, managerial practices in Japan, the United States, and the People's Republic of China are discussed.[1] Second, opportunities, threats, and competitive battles in the New Europe are identified. Finally, the global car industry case focuses on the German Daimler-Benz company.

PLANNING PRACTICES IN JAPAN, THE UNITED STATES, AND THE PEOPLE'S REPUBLIC OF CHINA[2]

The level of productivity is of great concern to all nations. In recent years, many U.S. enterprises have looked to Japan to find the answer to the productivity crisis in the United States. On the other hand, many Japanese scholars attend universities in the United States to learn about management. Japan's phenomenal success in increasing productivity is often attributed to its managerial approach.[3] There is an abundance of literature on both U.S. and Japanese management. One such book even made the best-seller list,[4] and there are other books[5] and many more articles. But the literature on Chinese management is very sparse. Since Japan and the United States present contrasting managerial approaches, Chinese managers probably could adopt aspects from either approach to make their enterprises more effective and efficient. The purpose of this discussion is to compare and contrast the Japanese and U.S. managerial models and to evaluate them with current practices used by *large, state-owned enterprises in the People's Republic of China,* which will be referred to as *China.*

This section focuses on planning, as summarized in the accompanying table.[6] The discussions in Parts 3, 4, 5, and 6 of this book are on organizing, staffing, leading, and controlling. At the outset, a word of caution is in order. It is obvious that not all American firms are managed the same way as discussed in this text. The same is true for Japanese and Chinese managerial practices.

Planning in Japan

In Japan, planning is greatly aided by the cooperation between government and business. After World War II, Japan developed policies for economic growth and strength as well as international competitiveness. These policies harmonized monetary and fiscal policies within the industrial structure. In this kind of relatively economic predictability, environment planning is less risky. Planning is choosing the purpose and objectives of the organization as a whole or a part of it and selecting the means to achieve those ends; it requires making decisions. The Japanese, in general, have a longer-term orientation in planning than American managers. There are several reasons. In Japan, for example, banks are the primary providers of capital, and their interest is in the long-term health of the enterprises.

Planning in the United States

In contrast, U.S. managers are often under pressure by stockholders to show favorable financial ratios each time they report them. This, unfortunately, may not

COMPARISONS OF JAPANESE, U.S., AND CHINESE PLANNING		
Japanese management	**U.S. management**	**Chinese management**
1. Long-term orientation	1. Primarily short-term orientation	1. Long-term and short-term orientation (5-year plan and annual plan)
2. Collective decision making (*ringi*) with consensus	2. Individual decision making	2. Decision making by committees; at the top, often individual
3. Involvement of many people in preparing and making the decision	3. Involvement of a few people in making the decision and "selling" it to persons with divergent values	3. Top-down; participation at lower levels
4. Flow of critical decisions from top to bottom and back to top; flow of non-critical decisions often from bottom to top (In either case, emphasis is on consensus.)	4. Decisions initiated at the top, flowing down	4. Top-down—initiated at the top
5. Slow decision making; fast implementation of the decision	5. Fast decision making; slow implementation requiring compromise, often resulting in suboptimal decisions	5. Slow decision making; slow implementation (But now changes are taking place.)

encourage investments that have a payout in the more distant future. Also, Americans usually stay in their managerial positions only a relatively short time, and so a myopic decision can seldom be traced to the manager who had made it but in the meantime was promoted or even changed companies. Japanese managers usually do have a longer-term orientation in their strategic planning efforts than their counterparts in the United States.

Planning in China

In China, the situation is quite different. Most of the enterprises are state-owned, and it is only more recently that some private firms have come into existence. In our comparison, however, we focus only on the former. In these enterprises, both long- and short-term plans are prepared. The 5-year plan is prepared at the top (the State Planning Commission), while more detailed plans are made at lower levels. The orientation is to meeting objectives and achieving the assigned plan rather than to being successful in the market. While strategy formulation may not be practiced widely in a formal manner, strategic thinking in military terms is a part of the Chinese culture. The book *Bing-Fa* is one of the most complete books on military strategy. Thus, certain principles may be applied by managers in dealing with Western corporations. For example, the best strategy is considered to be that of winning without a war. The next best one is to win through alliances. There is also the difficulty of integrating organizational and personal goals because the achievement of organizational objectives has little bearing on individual benefits.

Decision Making in Japan

One of the most interesting aspects of Japanese management is the way decisions are made. In a typical organization, several levels are involved in making a decision. Actually, the most important part of the process is the understanding and the analysis of the problem and the development of various alternative solutions. Critical decisions may flow from top management to lower levels and back to the top. Noncritical decisions may originate at the bottom and be submitted to top managers. The final authority for making a decision still rests with top management. But before a proposal reaches the executive's desk, the problem and the possible solutions have been discussed at various levels in the organizational hierarchy. Top management still has the option to accept or reject a decision. But it is more likely that a decision will be returned to subordinates for further study rather than being rejected outright.

A proposal is confirmed through the *ringi* process. The *ringi-sho* is a proposal document prepared by a staff member. This paper is circulated among various managers before it goes to top management for formal approval. The document, which is usually initialed by those involved in or affected by the decision, elicits the cooperation and participation of many people. This, in turn, assures that the problem or the decision is examined from different perspectives. That this decision-making process is time-consuming is obvious. But after a consensus is reached, the implementation of the plan is rather swift because of the understanding of the plan, the clarification of the problem, the evaluation of the different alternatives, and the involvement of those people who will implement the decision. But the sharing of decision power and responsibilities can also result in a problem in that no one feels individually responsible for the decision.

Decision Making in the United States

In U.S. organizations, decisions are made primarily by individuals, and usually only a few people are involved. Consequently, after a decision has been made, it has to be sold to others, often to people with different values and different perceptions of what the problem really is and how it should be solved. In this way, the making of a decision is rather fast, but its implementation is very time-consuming and requires compromises with those managers holding different viewpoints. The result is that the decision which is eventually implemented may be suboptimal because of the compromises necessary to appease those with divergent opinions. It is true that decision responsibility can be traced to individuals as long as they are in the same position, but at the same time this may result in a practice of finding "scapegoats" for wrong decisions. All in all, in U.S. companies, decision power and responsibility are vested in designated individuals, while in Japan, many people share both decision power and responsibility.

Decision Making in China

In China, major decisions are made by individuals at the top, but many people are involved in operational decisions.[7] Lower-level managers have very little authority to make decisions. Decision making through the central planning bureau is under the direct control of the state. This, unfortunately, results in a lack of flexibility in the implementation of the decisions. Although there is a realization of the need to change, managers in the upper echelons of the hierarchy resist reforms because reform would mean giving up some of the privileges they have as officials.

The managerial practices of organizing in Japan, the United States, and China are discussed in Part 3.

INTERNATIONAL FOCUS:
PLANNING IN THE NEW EUROPE

While EC 1992 is viewed by some companies as a threat, the removal of barriers within the European Community provides many opportunities for U.S. companies. An example of such a threat was the May 24, 1989, vote by the European Parliament to require European broadcasters to make a majority of their entertainment programming European productions (in the past, 70 percent of such programs were from the United States).[8] A ruling such as this gives the Parliament power similar to that of the legislative branch of governments. Although the

Parliament cannot initiate legislation, it has veto power over many decisions by the European Community. On the other hand, the EC Parliament in Strasbourg has no taxing authority, and this diminishes its power. Still, it has been estimated that about half of German legislation is based on EC directives.

The Opportunities

The EC provides many opportunities. It is expected that the unification will boost productivity, cut costs, and encourage strategic alliances. It has been estimated that the integration of the markets will result in an increase of 5 percent of the EC gross domestic product.[9] The United States, the largest commercial partner in the EC market with over 340 million people, can expect to increase its sales.[10]

In recent years, many U.S. multinational companies have become leaner and more efficient. International Business Machines (IBM), a major force in Europe, recently closed five plants and cut its work force by 20,000 in anticipation of the challenges in the 1990s.[11] Many of the remaining people have been reassigned for the company's emphasis on software development. Without excessive cost burdens, many U.S. firms such as IBM are ready to take advantage of the European challenge. In fact, some U.S. multinational corporations may be better prepared for 1992 than some European firms. They may find it easier to adapt to the idea of a European market because they have operated in various countries for a long time, and for them removal of the border barriers will enhance their operations.

Ford Motor Company may be in a better position to take advantage of the new economic environment than some of its European competitors. While companies such as Volkswagen in Germany, Peugeot and Renault in France, and Fiat in Italy do lead in their own country, Ford is well established in many European countries with its many plants.[12] In fact, Ford began many years ago to integrate its companies in the various countries into a truly European firm. While operating in many countries, Ford realized the need for tailoring its product designs according to local needs. Moreover, having an integrated network results in increased productivity. The firm is so optimistic about the developments leading up to the New Europe that it plans to spend over $7 billion to strengthen its position in Europe.

Take the fast-delivery service. As the U.S. market for overnight and same-day delivery becomes saturated, firms are seeking opportunities in Europe. The route between Europe and the United States is already heavily served by Federal Express.[13] However, the real opportunity for this company may be the intra-European expansion. United Parcel Service (UPS), another U.S. company in the delivery service, already plays a dominant role in Europe and will be greatly aided by the free movement of goods. Even if national barriers do not completely fall, fewer customs restrictions will greatly expand business activities.

The H. J. Heinz Company expects to spend up to $1 billion on plant renewal, marketing, and acquisitions in order to strengthen its position in soups, beans, ketchup, and baby food.[14] The aim is to make Heinz's ketchup as well known as Coca-Cola, according to the company's chairman. Heinz is optimistic despite having to face competitors such as Unilever and Nestle, companies that are substantially bigger.

Caterpillar, the maker of construction equipment and earth-moving machinery, is well established with its five factories in Europe. The company holds a 35 to 40 percent share in the heavy-equipment market.[15] Caterpillar also expects to benefit from the New European market. So far, different standards and specifications have made it difficult to produce efficiently. Big projects, such as the tunnel under the English Channel, as well as the building of roads in Spain, Portugal, and France, provide this company with good opportunities. However, the opportunities are counterbalanced by competitive threats, not only from European firms but especially from Komatsu of Japan.

Major U.S. firms, in general, really have not been very good at exporting goods to Europe. Their strengths are in direct investments, as shown by the few examples. A single market will benefit them. However, for firms not yet established in Europe, EC 1992 poses major threats.

Threats and Battles

There is considerable concern that the free market will be all but free to outsiders.[16] Some see in the frequently used terms (called "Eurospeak") such as "nurturing industries," "transitional rules," and "reciprocity" veiled protections against outsiders. Some Europeans are afraid that the early beneficiaries of EC 1992 may be U.S. and Japanese companies through their marketing and manufacturing strengths. To counteract the outside threats, EC countries are trying to strengthen the areas in which they are weak, such as research and development in aeronautics and information technology. Moreover, the telecommunications companies are forming strategic alliances.

Battles are shaping up in a variety of areas:

In computers. Political pressure is being exerted on U.S. and Japanese firms to conduct more research and production in Europe.

In financial services. There may be restrictions placed on banks and security firms unless foreign countries grant reciprocal rights.

In telecommunications. Attempts are being made to favor local suppliers of telecommunications equipment and to keep their European monopolies in telephone and data transmission services.

Similar EC restrictions are being pushed in consumer electronics, the media, public works,[17] textiles, and footwear. It is also probable that internal subsidies and quotas may continue in agriculture, fisheries, textiles, and steel.

The Different Impacts of the EC on Industries

If the EC adheres to stated policies, there will be opportunities for outsiders in industries such as electronics and telecommunications and in the service sector. Some firms, concerned about protective policies, are playing it safe and reorienting strategies by, for example, making strategic alliances with European companies.[18]

Electronics and telecommunications.   The aim of the EC policy is to give EC members equal opportunity to sell, among other products, telecommunications equipment. So far, indigenous manufacturers in Europe have had their market protected. Although innovation often originates with small firms, they are usually not prepared to serve the huge market. Manufacturers from the Far East and the United States, on the other hand, have had experience in competing in large markets. Because research in high technology is expensive, high volume may be required to obtain certain economies of scale.[19] It is understandable that European electronics firms are very concerned about catching up with the Americans and Japanese.[20] In 1987, for example, the estimated trade deficit of the EC high-technology industry was $10 billion. In contrast, the United States had an estimated surplus of $1.3 billion and the Japanese $8.6 billion. Indeed, there is the fear of a trade war in this industry.

The EC Commission is aware of the special situation of the telecommunications equipment and service sector, as shown by its Green Paper. The paper reviews the rapid pace of technological diversification, new ways of accessing information, the demand for effective communication, and the positioning of multinational corporations that pose a competitive challenge to Europeans.[21]

The service sector.   There is considerable concern among U.S. managers as to how EC 1992 will affect the service sector. More than 55 directives, supplemented by other regulations, will affect the service sector.[22] The categories of the service directives pertain to (1) financial services, such as insurance, banking, and mortgage credit, (2) transportation, (3) miscellaneous services in medicine, engineering, and tourism, and (4) activities crossing the various services.

German banks have had considerable experience in operating in many countries. There has already been a concentration in financial services. These banks may provide the expertise needed for small companies to take advantage of the larger integrated market.[23]

The airline industry is also being deregulated. Rather than engaging in mergers, airlines probably will be integrated into a network tying together selected carriers.[24] For example, Scandinavian Airlines System (SAS) has cooperation agreements with British Midland. Dutch KLM has a stake in Northwestern and plans to buy into the Belgian airline SABENA. To have access to the Asian market, KLM plans to join a cargo venture with Singapore Airlines. Major purchases, however, have been largely restricted to domestic airlines.[25] British Airways, for example, bought British Caledonian, Swissair acquired 40 percent of Crossair (Swiss), and KLM bought a share of Transavia. The new cooperation among airlines is further illustrated by the two computer reservation systems—Galileo and Amadeus—to which many European airlines are linked. One step toward deregulation has already been taken by providing more flexibility in establishing fares. On the other hand, airlines are the pride of their country (most countries require national ownership and control of the airlines), and one may not see many mergers and acquisitions as in other industries. At any rate, U.S. airlines can expect greater challenges from their European competitors.

Technology and mergers.   The EC 1992 program has already stimulated many mergers and acquisitions in the technology industry. Perhaps an even more important impact will come from the rapid pace of technological developments.[26] Technology does not wait for structural and political changes. Since only strong firms will survive, the need to share costly research and a global marketing network may force mergers and acquisitions even more so than political forces.

Several U.S. companies are trying to get a foothold in the European food and consumer sectors, which were protected in the past.[27] The General Electric Company (of the United States) plans to merge with the unrelated company with the same name in the United Kingdom, with the aim of linking their electrical equipment, medical, and consumer groups. Although Europeans, aided by the low value of the U.S. dollar, have been buying U.S. companies at a frantic pace, there is much opposition to very big American acquisitions in Europe. So far, there has not yet been a successful U.S. takeover that amounted to over $1 billion. Thus, for many U.S. firms the more viable avenue may be to obtain partial holdings through joint ventures, especially in the defense industry, telecommunications, and financial services. With the many barriers, the acquisition opportunities are limited, thus driving up the prices for these takeover candidates.

EC members are also discussing merger control.[28] The existing merger regulations often require dealing with several national authorities, resulting in a good deal of duplication. Currently, completing a merger is very time consuming. The aim of the new regulations is to provide greater clarity and certainty in legal matters and facilitate speedy decisions.

GLOBAL CAR INDUSTRY CASE: HOW CAN DAIMLER-BENZ PREPARE FOR THE TWENTY-FIRST CENTURY?[29]

The traditionally small Japanese cars are now supplemented by Japanese luxury models such as Lexus and Infinity to compete with European cars made by BMW and Mercedes. The Japanese Toyota and Nissan companies are targeting luxury car markets not only in the United States but also in Europe. Fearing that a "Fortress Europe" may evolve from the European Community 1992 (EC 1992) program, the Japanese have developed a strategy to establish themselves in the European market by setting up manufacturing plants in England with the encouragement of the former Japanese-friendly Thatcher government. One interesting question is how European carmakers will respond to the Japanese threat.

Daimler's Profile in 1990

Daimler-Benz was commonly known for its Mercedes cars, which have the image of engineering excellence. Yet, the company faces fierce competition from Japanese carmakers. In addition, this traditional car company has been undergoing dramatic changes, venturing into nondefense and defense electronics. Consequently, Daimler has to wrestle with fundamental questions such as the following:

What *is* our business?

Who are our customers?

What do our customers want?

What *should* our business be?

Although in the past, Daimler was known primarily for its Mercedes-Benz luxury cars, buses, and trucks, this has been changing. For one, Mercedes has expanded its car model range so that its domain includes the market for smaller cars. Much more dramatic has been the recent diversification into electronics and aerospace. In 1989, Daimler was divided into three operating groups: Cars and trucks are in the Mercedes-Benz unit; electronics not related to defense is in the AEG unit; and defense electronics and military aerospace are in the DA (Deutsche Aerospace) group. In 1990, a fourth group was set up: the DEBIT (Daimler-Benz Interservices AG), which focuses on financial services, marketing, software systems, and other services. The plan is to become one of the biggest service groups in Europe, if not in the world. The common threads integrating the business units are high technology and the development and creative application of new materials.

While it was relatively easy to identify the primary customers for luxury cars, the task became much more complex with the creation of the four operating units. Marketing consumer goods and services and dealing with the government in defense contracts require very different approaches to market penetration. The wants and needs of the divergent customer groups are quite different. Although the four operating groups are designed to work in a fairly autonomous manner, at some point the very divergent organizational cultures and management systems need to be integrated—a difficult task indeed.

Purpose or Mission of Daimler

In the past, it was relatively easy to identify Daimler's purpose when the company's aim was to produce cars that were "engineered like no other car in the world." Now, with four operating divisions, this task is much more difficult. Automobiles will remain the primary sector; producing and distributing high-quality luxury cars is still the main purpose. However, with the acquisition of the aerospace group Messerschmitt-Boelkow-Blohm GmbH (MBB), Daimler became one of the leading defense contractors. While this purchase seemed a wise strategic move at that time, the recent developments in Eastern Europe and the thawing between East and West suggest that the once profitable defense contracts may be curtailed.

Edzard Reuter's vision of Daimler is that it will be "an integrated transportation company, in vehicles, railroads and aircraft." Reuter wants Daimler to be a global company yet remain flexible to cope with the dynamic changes. Through the entrance into new fields, the company aims to gain access to new information technologies, new materials, and systems knowledge. The top priority will still be to build the best automobiles in the world, although by the end of the decade the company will play an important role in aerospace, electronics, and factory automation.

The Need to Formulate a Strategy

Daimler realizes the need for a systematic analysis of its strengths, weaknesses, opportunities, and threats as the basis for formulating a strategy. The analysis of the external environment identified these factors:

External threats. Daimler faces several threats. The easing of tensions between East and West reduces the need for military hardware. Thus, Daimler's defense unit may fall on hard times in the 1990s. But the focus will be on the automobile sector.

In Europe, and indeed around the world, the German BMW firm is Daimler's major competitor. While in the past, BMW's strength was in smaller cars, the Series 5 and 7 cars compete directly with Mercedes's middle- and upper-class luxury cars. The recent agreement of cooperation between the French Renault and Swedish Volvo carmakers reduces their development costs and makes their cars more competitive with Mercedes in the European market. Moreover, Volvo plans a joint project with Mitsubishi for making cars in a plant 70 miles from Amsterdam, Holland. American manufacturers have a strategy of their own. In order to gain access to the Mercedes-BMW–dominated luxury market, Ford acquired the British Jaguar Company. Similarly, General Motors formed a strategic alliance with Swedish Saab-Scania.

Even greater threats to Mercedes are the recently introduced Japanese luxury cars Lexus and Infiniti by Toyota and Nissan, respectively. Comparisons have shown that the Japanese cars are on a par with those by BMW and Mercedes. The traditional rival is, of course, BMW. That company is a threat to Mercedes not only in the European market but also in Japan, where the appetite for European luxury cars has increased. Mercedes engaged in a cooperative agreement with the Japanese Mitsubishi company. The ties between the two companies go beyond the interest in cars; they extend to electronics and aerospace. For example, the aim is to produce jointly a 75-seat aircraft. Collaboration in the defense sector, however, has been ruled out. The combination of these two giant companies makes the competition shudder.

Another threat for Mercedes consists of laws and regulations governing emissions. Diesel engines, Mercedes's traditional strength, have come under attack by environmentalists. Moreover, car buyers' preferences have been shifting from the sluggish diesel-powered vehicles to gasoline engines.

External opportunities. The robust economies in the Pacific Rim countries have increased the demand for luxury cars. Moreover, European countries such as Spain, which will profit greatly from the EC 1992 program, provide good opportunities for Mercedes. While there is a great demand for automobiles in Eastern Europe, the initial demand is likely to be for low-priced cars because of the shortage of hard currency. In the future, however, as the economies improve, the demand for luxury cars is likely to increase.

In Eastern Europe, especially former East Germany, there are opportunities for acquiring supplier companies. Daimler, with its strong financial position, has good opportunities for purchasing those companies. However, the concern is that the company may harm its quality image by producing cars in the eastern part of Germany, which in the past produced the Wartburg and Trabant, cars of very low quality.

Increasingly, electronic components are used in cars for fuel injection, brakes, and a variety of other applications. In the future, developments in the electronics and information technologies will become even more important for automobiles.

Internal weaknesses.   One of the weaknesses of Mercedes is the high cost structure. In Germany, the factory hourly wage is $21, but it is $17.50 in Japan and $16.90 in the United States. Germans work 38 hours per week; the Japanese, 42 hours; and Americans, 40 hours. West Germans also have many more holidays than workers in any other industrialized country except Italy. Germany has 30 holidays, Japan has 11, and the United States has 12. Although these figures are for the countries and not the automotive industry, they give, nevertheless, an important insight as to why the costs of automobile production are so high for Mercedes.

The size of Daimler and its bureaucratic structure are potential weaknesses; and so is the venturing into nonautomotive businesses. Past successes of Daimler can make the organization complacent. The long time it takes to develop a new model may be an indication of that.

Internal strengths.   With $12 billion available and the strong backing of the Deutsche Bank, Germany's largest bank, Daimler-Benz is in a strong financial position. Moreover, the high-priced SL roadster has a backlog of orders of several years. Critical in the production line is the new S-Class model, which is expected to sell for over $70,000 in the United States; some models even go up to $100,000 or more. Another Mercedes strength is the company's location near its suppliers. The geographic proximity facilitates close cooperation and shortens the time for transporting parts. Mercedes will also benefit from the high-technology strengths of the acquired companies because the new car models use electronics for many functions, such as antilock brakes and fuel and ignition controls.

The Strategic Fit

One key aspect of strategic planning is the testing for *consistency* of the various elements of the plan. Some observers question Daimler's wisdom in venturing outside the traditional automotive business through the acquisitions of the defense companies and the AEG appliance firm. Also, the cooperation between Daimler and Mitsubishi may be hindered by the difference in organization cultures. The orderly German bureaucratic organization structure appears to be inconsistent with the group-oriented managerial approach of the Japanese.

Summary of the Daimler Case

As Daimler-Benz moves toward the twenty-first century, it will have to make some strategic choices. Its mission has changed from being an automotive company to being an integrated transportation company, defense contractor, and consumer appliances manufacturer. In the past, the focus was on the Mercedes unit, which now faces fierce competition from Japanese carmakers in the luxury market. The TOWS Matrix (discussed in Chapter 7), an analytical tool that can be used to identify a firm's strengths and weaknesses and the relationships to external opportunities and threats, can also be used to develop four distinct strategies for Daimler-Benz. These choices must be made in light of risks and also must be congruent with the vision of the CEO, Edzard Reuter. Daimler must prepare now for the competitive global car market.

1. Use the TOWS Matrix to identify Daimler's strengths and weaknesses. Prepare a matrix as shown in Figure 7-2 (in Chapter 7), and fill in Daimler-Benz's strengths and weaknesses in the appropriate boxes.
2. Identify external opportunities and threats, and note them in the TOWS Matrix.
3. Develop alternative strategies (SO, ST, WO, and WT), write them in the appropriate boxes, and make strategic choices.
4. What do you think of the acquisitions of non-car-related companies?
5. What will be the competitive position of Daimler against BMW, Infiniti, Lexus, and other luxury automobiles in the year 2000?

REFERENCES

1. See also James A. Wall, Jr., "Managers in the People's Republic of China," *Academy of Management Executive* (May 1990), pp. 19–32.
2. Sources of information are also given in note 6 below. In addition, see Lu Zu-Wen, "The Evolution of Business Management in the Mainland of China Paves the Way for Opening to the Outside World," *Proceedings of the Academy of International Business Southeast Asia Regional Conference, Taipei*, vol. 2 (June 26–28, 1986), pp. 16–18; and Quian Jiaju, "The Primary Stage of Socialism," *China Reconstructs* (March 1988), pp. 15–18.
3. In the past, low wage rates were often cited as a reason for the success of Japanese firms. However, with the rise of the Japanese yen and the fact that the labor cost component of products is becoming increasingly less important, managerial competence is becoming even more crucial. Peter F. Drucker, "Low Wages No Longer Give Competitive Edge," *The Wall Street Journal* (Mar. 16, 1988).
4. W. G. Ouchi, *Theory Z* (Reading, Mass.: Addison-Wesley Publishing Company, 1981).
5. For example, see R. T. Pascale and A. G. Athos, *The Art of Japanese Management* (New York: Simon & Schuster, 1981); Ezra F. Vogel, *Japan as Number One* (New York: Harper & Row, Publishers, 1979).
6. Information for the tables in the closing sections for Parts 2 to 6 is based on a variety of sources. Japanese managerial practices have been widely discussed in the literature and at professional meetings such as the Japanese–United States Business Conference

held in Tokyo, Japan, April 4–8, 1983; the Pan-Pacific Conference held in Honolulu, Hawaii, March 26–28, 1984, in Seoul, Korea, May 13–15, 1985, and in Taipei, Taiwan, May 17–20, 1987. See also Janet Goff, "Japanese Management in Historical Perspective," *Japan Quarterly* (July 1990), pp. 369ff.; Fred Luthans, Harriette S. McCaul, and Nancy G. Dodd, "Organizational Commitment: A Comparison of American, Japanese, and Korean Employees," *Academy of Management Journal* (March 1985), pp. 213–219; Richard E. Wokutch, "Corporate Social Responsibility Japanese Style," *Academy of Management Executive* (May 1990), pp. 56–74; Ikujiro Nonaka and Johny K. Johansson, "Japanese Management: What about the 'Hard' Skills?" *Academy of Management Review* (April 1985), pp. 181–191; Ronald Sheldon and Brian Kleiner, "What Japanese Management Techniques Can (or Should) Be Applied by American Managers," *Industrial Management* (May–June 1990), pp. 17–19; William G. Ouchi and Alfred M. Jaeger, "Type Z Organization: Stability in the Midst of Mobility," *Academy of Management Review* (April 1978), pp. 305–314; Peter F. Drucker, "Behind Japan's Success," *Harvard Business Review* (January–February 1981); Lee Smith, "Japan's Autocratic Manager," *Fortune* (Jan. 7, 1985), pp. 56–65; Hirotake Takeuchi, "Productivity: Learning from the Japanese," *California Management Review* (Summer 1981), pp. 5–20; Amy Borrus, "Can Japan's Giants Cut the Apron Strings?" *Business Week* (May 14, 1990), pp. 105–106; John Lie, "Is Korean Management Just Like Japanese Management?" *Management International Review,* vol. 30, no. 2 (Second Quarter 1990), pp. 113–118; Christine Nielsen Specter and Janet Stern Solomon, "The Human Resource Factor in Chinese Management Reform," *International Studies of Management and Organization* (Spring–Summer 1990), pp. 15ff.; Yeshimichi Yamashita, "Japanese Executives Face Life Out of the Nest," *The Wall Street Journal* (Nov. 16, 1991); Thomas F. O'Boyle, "Two Worlds—Under Japanese Bosses, Americans Find Work Both Better and Worse," *The Wall Street Journal* (Nov. 27, 1991).

Information was also gathered during visits to Japan and from research conducted with Japanese managers operating in the United States. The authors acknowledge the contributions and assistance of Professor Richard Babcock, at the University of San Francisco, and many Chinese scholars and managers, especially Ms. Jie and Mr. Zhijian Yang.

7. See also John S. Henley and Mee Kau Nyaw, "Introducing Market Forces into Managerial Decision Making in Chinese Industrial Enterprises," *Journal of Management Studies,* vol. 23 (1986), pp. 635–656.

8. Blanca Riemer, "The European Parliament Gets Its Act Together," *Business Week* (June 12, 1989), pp. 44–49, and Gerard de Selys, "Europe's Audiovisual Challenge," *Europe* (April 1989), pp. 28–30.

9. Francine Lamoriello, "Completing the Internal Market by 1992: The EC's Legislative Program for Business," *Business America* (Aug. 1, 1988), pp. 4–7.

10. William C. Verity, "U.S. Business Needs to Prepare Now for Europe's Single Internal Market," *Business America* (Aug. 1, 1988), pp. 2–3.

11. Geoff Lewis, "Is the Computer Business Maturing?" *Business Week* (Mar. 6, 1989), pp. 68–78.

12. Richard E. Melcher, "Ford Is Ready to Roll in the New Europe," *Business Week* (Dec. 12, 1988), p. 60.

13. Kevin Willmott, "Carriers Jostling for Their 1992 Positions," *Euromoney* (July 1988), pp. 4–10. So far, the international business has been costly to Federal Express. See Dean Foust, Jonathan Kapstein, Pia Farrell, Peter Finch, and Chris Power, "Mr. Smith Goes Global," *Business Week* (Feb. 13, 1989), pp. 66–72.

14. Gregory L. Miles, Frank J. Comes, and Ellen Wallace, "Heinz Squares Off against Its Archrival," *Business Week* (Dec. 12, 1988), p. 58.

15. Brian Bremner, "Cat's Fight to Stay King of the Jungle," *Business Week* (Dec. 12, 1988), p. 58.

16. Blanca Riemer, Joyce Heard, and Thane Peterson, "Laying the Foundation for a Great Wall of Europe," *Business Week* (Aug. 1, 1988), pp. 40–41.

17. Susan Lee, "An Impossible Dream?" *Forbes* (July 25, 1988), pp. 78–83.

18. Martyn Chase, "Borderless Europe: Promise and Pitfalls for U.S. Firms," *Electronic Business* (Oct. 15, 1988), pp. 46–48.

19. Sherry Buchanan, "Inside the Fortress: Europe after 1992," *Electronic Business* (Oct. 15, 1988), pp. 38–43.

20. Jack Gee, "1992: Supplying Electronics to 320 Million Europeans," *Electronic Business* (Sept. 15, 1988), pp. 16–18.

21. Edgar Carl Law, "1992—The Pivotal Year for European Telecommunications," *Business Communications Review* (July–August 1988), pp. 70–72.

22. Brant W. Free, "The EC Single Internal Market: Implications for U.S. Service Industries," *Business America* (Aug. 1, 1988), pp. 10–11.

23. Ulrich Ramm, "Proven Skills Match Challenge of 1992," *Asian Finance* (Sept. 15, 1988), pp. 74–77.

24. Jeffrey M. Lenorovitz, "Airlines Will Cooperate, Not Merge, after Deregulation of Europe in 1992," *Aviation Week & Space Technology* (Sept. 5, 1988), pp. 133, 135.

25. David Black, "Europe's Airlines Gear Up for 1992," *Europe* (July–August 1989), pp. 30–31, 55.

26. Georg Krneta, "The Technology Kicker: M&A Stimulus beyond 1992," *Mergers & Acquisitions* (September–October 1988), pp. 57–60.

27. Joann S. Lublin, "American Takeovers Soaring in Europe as Firms Position Themselves for 1992," *The Wall Street Journal* (Jan. 17, 1989).

28. Peter D. Sutherland, "Approaching a Showdown on European Merger Control," *Mergers & Acquisitions* (September–October 1988), pp. 61–64.

29. The framework of this case is based in part on Heinz Weihrich, "The TOWS Matrix—A Tool for Situational Analysis," *Long Range Planning* (April 1982), pp. 52–64, and information in the case was drawn from a variety of sources, including the following: Shawn Tully, "Now Japan's Autos Push into Europe," *Fortune* (Jan. 29, 1990), pp. 96–106; Timothy Aeppel and Terence Roth, "Thaw in Cold War Stymies Daimler-Benz," *The Wall Street Journal* (Apr. 3, 1990); William E. Casey and Terence Roth, "Chairman Sees Daimler-Benz on Right Track," *The Wall Street Journal* (May 11, 1990); E. S. Browning, "Renault, Volvo Agree to Enter into Alliance," *The Wall Street Journal* (Feb. 26, 1990); Jonathan Kapstein, Stewart Toy, and John Rossant, "Why Renault Feels Safer Buckling Up with Volvo," *Business Week* (Mar. 12, 1990), pp. 53–54; Jonathan Kapstein and Stewart Toy, "Mitsubishi Is Taking a Back Road into Europe," *Business Week* (Nov. 19, 1990), p. 64; Alex Taylor III, "Here Come Japan's New Luxury Cars," *Fortune* (Aug. 14, 1989), pp. 62–66; "Daimler-Benz, Mitsubishi Group Discuss Expanding Business Ties beyond Autos," *The Wall Street Journal* (Mar. 7, 1990); Igor Reichlin and Gail E. Schares, "What's Haunting West German Unions: East Germans," *Business Week* (May 21, 1990), p. 60; Robert Neff and William J. Holstein, "Mighty Mitsubishi Is on the Move," *Business Week* (Sept. 24, 1990), pp. 98–110; Edzard Reuter, Vom Geist der Wirtschaft (Stuttgart, Germany: Deutsche Verlags-Anstalt, 1986). In 1993 Daimler begins assembling Mercedes cars in Mexico: see Alex Taylor III, "Another Lap for Mercedes Chief," *Fortune* (Apr. 20, 1992), p. 185.

Organizing

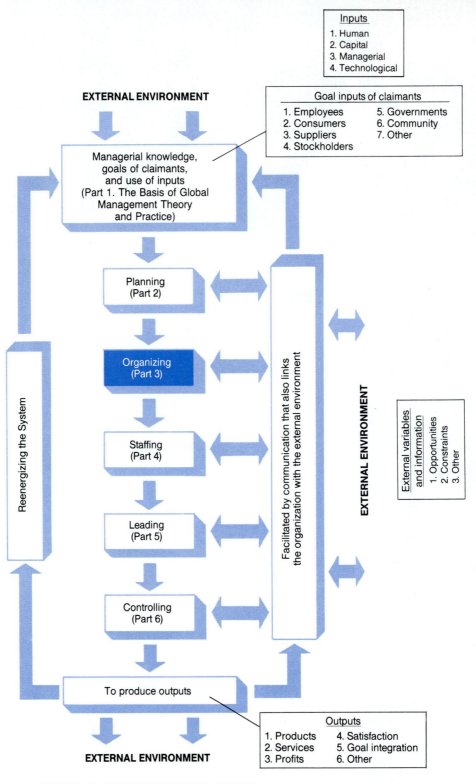

Inputs
1. Human
2. Capital
3. Managerial
4. Technological

EXTERNAL ENVIRONMENT

Goal inputs of claimants
1. Employees   5. Governments
2. Consumers   6. Community
3. Suppliers   7. Other
4. Stockholders

Managerial knowledge,
goals of claimants,
and use of inputs
(Part 1. The Basis of Global
Management Theory
and Practice)

Planning
(Part 2)

Organizing
(Part 3)

Staffing
(Part 4)

Leading
(Part 5)

Controlling
(Part 6)

Reenergizing the System

Facilitated by communication that also links
the organization with the external environment

EXTERNAL ENVIRONMENT

External variables
and information
1. Opportunities
2. Constraints
3. Other

To produce outputs

EXTERNAL ENVIRONMENT

Outputs
1. Products   4. Satisfaction
2. Services   5. Goal integration
3. Profits   6. Other

SYSTEMS APPROACH TO MANAGEMENT

> The typical large business 20 years hence will have fewer than half the levels of management of its counterpart today, and no more than a third the managers.[1]
>
> Peter F. Drucker

The Nature of Organizing and Entrepreneuring

Chapter Objectives

After reading this chapter, you should be able to:

1. Realize that the purpose of an organization structure is to establish a formal system of roles that people can perform so that they may best work together to achieve enterprise objectives.
2. Understand the meaning of "organizing" and "organization."
3. Draw a distinction between formal and informal organization.
4. Show how organization structures and their levels are due to the limitations of the span of management.
5. Recognize that the exact number of people a manager can effectively supervise depends on a number of underlying variables and situations.
6. Describe the nature of entrepreneuring and intrapreneuring.
7. Demonstrate the logic of organizing and its relationship to other managerial functions.
8. Make clear that the application of structural organization theory must necessarily take situations into account.

It is often said that good people can make any organization pattern work. Some even assert that vagueness in organization is a good thing in that it forces teamwork, since people know that they must cooperate to get anything done. However, there can be no doubt that good people and those who want to cooperate will work together most effectively if they know the parts they are to play in any team operation and the way their roles relate to one another. This is as true in business or government as it is in football or in a symphony orchestra. Designing and maintaining these systems of roles is basically the managerial function of organizing.

For an **organizational role** to exist and be meaningful to people, it must incorporate (1) verifiable objectives, which, as indicated in Part 2, are a major part of planning; (2) a clear idea of the major duties or activities involved; and (3) an understood area of discretion or authority so that the person filling the role knows what he or she can do to accomplish goals.[2] In addition, to make a role work out effectively, provision should be made for supplying needed information and other tools necessary for performance in that role.

It is in this sense that we think of **organizing** as (1) the identification and classification of required activities, (2) the grouping of activities necessary to attain objectives, (3) the assignment of each grouping to a manager with the authority (delegation) necessary to supervise it, and (4) the provision for coordination horizontally (on the same or a similar organizational level) and vertically (for example, corporate headquarters, division, and department) in the organization structure.

An organization structure should be designed to clarify who is to do what tasks and who is responsible for what results, to remove obstacles to performance caused by confusion and uncertainty of assignment, and to furnish decision-making and communications networks reflecting and supporting enterprise objectives.

"Organization" is a word many people use loosely. Some would say it includes all the behavior of all participants. Others would equate it with the total system of social and cultural relationships. Still others refer to an enterprise, such as the United States Steel Corporation or the Department of Defense, as an "organization." But for most practicing managers, the term **organization** implies a *formalized intentional structure of roles or positions*. In this book, the term is generally used in reference to a formalized structure of roles, although it is sometimes used to denote an enterprise.

What does "intentional structure of roles" mean? In the first place, as already implied in the definition of the nature and content of organizational roles, people working together must fill certain roles. In the second place, the roles people are asked to fill should be intentionally designed to ensure that required activities are done and that activities fit together so that people can work smoothly, effectively, and efficiently in groups. Certainly, most managers believe they are organizing when they establish such an intentional structure.

FORMAL AND INFORMAL ORGANIZATION

Many writers on management distinguish between formal and informal organization. Both types are found in organizations as shown in Figure 9-1. Let us look at them in more detail.

Formal Organization[3]

In this book, generally, **formal organization** means the intentional structure of roles in a formally organized enterprise. Describing an organization as "formal," however, does not mean there is anything inherently inflexible or unduly confining about it. If a manager is to organize well, the structure must furnish an environment in which individual performance, both present and future, contributes most effectively to group goals.

Formal organization must be flexible. There should be room for discretion,

FIGURE 9-1

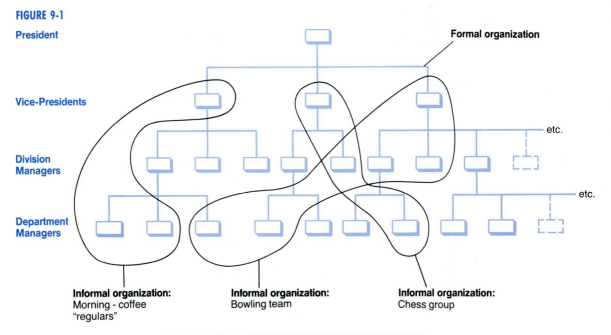

THE FORMAL AND INFORMAL ORGANIZATION.

for advantageous utilization of creative talents, and for recognition of individual likes and capacities in the most formal of organizations. Yet individual effort in a group situation must be channeled toward group and organization goals.

Although the attainment of goals must be the reason for any cooperative activity, we must look further for principles to guide the establishment of effective formal organization. These principles—summarized at the end of Part 3—pertain to the unity of objectives and organizational efficiency.

Informal Organization

Chester Barnard, author of the management classic *The Functions of the Executive*, described informal organization as any joint personal activity without conscious joint purpose, even though contributing to joint results.[4] Thus, the informal relationships established in the group of people playing chess during lunchtime may aid in the achievement of organizational goals. It is much easier to ask for help on an organization problem from someone you know personally, even if he or she may be in a different department, than from someone you know only as a name on an organization chart. More recently, Keith Davis of Arizona State University, who has written extensively on the topic and whose definition will be used in this book, described the **informal organization** as "a network of personal and social relations not established or required by the formal organization but arising spontaneously as people associate with one another."[5] Thus, informal organizations—relationships not appearing on an organization chart—might include the machine-shop group, the sixth-floor crowd, the Friday evening bowling gang, and the morning-coffee "regulars."

ORGANIZATIONAL DIVISION: THE DEPARTMENT

One aspect of organizing is the establishment of departments. The word **department** designates *a distinct area, division, or branch of an organization over which a manager has authority for the performance of specified activities*. A department, as the term is generally used, may be the production division, the sales department, the West Coast branch, the market research section, or the accounts receivable unit. In some enterprises, departmental terminology is loosely applied; in others, especially large ones, a stricter terminology indicates hierarchical relationships. Thus, a vice president may head a division; a director, a department; a manager, a branch; and a chief, a section.

ORGANIZATION LEVELS AND THE SPAN OF MANAGEMENT*

While the purpose of organizing is to make human cooperation effective, the reason for levels of organization is the limitations of the span of management. In other

* In much of the literature on management, this is referred to as the "span of control." Despite the widespread use of this term, in this book "span of management" will be used, since the span is one of management and not merely of control, which is only one function of managing.

words, organization levels exist because there is a limit to the number of persons a manager can supervise effectively, even though this limit varies depending on situations.[6] The relationships between the span of management and the organizational levels are shown in Figure 9-2. A wide span of management is associated with few organizational levels; a narrow span, with many levels.

Choosing the Span

In every organization, it must be decided how many subordinates a superior can manage. Students of management have found that this number is usually four to

FIGURE 9-2

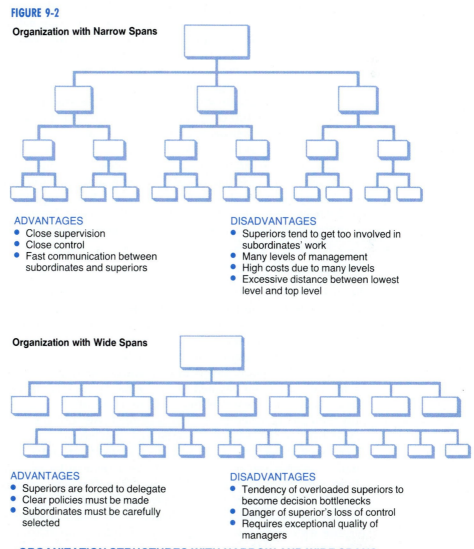

Organization with Narrow Spans

ADVANTAGES
- Close supervision
- Close control
- Fast communication between subordinates and superiors

DISADVANTAGES
- Superiors tend to get too involved in subordinates' work
- Many levels of management
- High costs due to many levels
- Excessive distance between lowest level and top level

Organization with Wide Spans

ADVANTAGES
- Superiors are forced to delegate
- Clear policies must be made
- Subordinates must be carefully selected

DISADVANTAGES
- Tendency of overloaded superiors to become decision bottlenecks
- Danger of superior's loss of control
- Requires exceptional quality of managers

ORGANIZATION STRUCTURES WITH NARROW AND WIDE SPANS.

eight subordinates at the upper levels of organization and eight to fifteen or more at the lower levels. For example, the prominent British consultant Lyndall Urwick found "the ideal number of subordinates for all superior authorities . . . to be four," while "at the lowest level of organization, where what is delegated is responsibility for the performance of specific tasks and not for the supervision of others, the number may be eight or twelve."[7] Others find that a manager may be able to supervise as many as twenty to thirty subordinates.

In a survey of 100 large companies made by the American Management Association, the number of executives reporting to the presidents varied from one to twenty-four, and only twenty-six presidents had six or fewer subordinates; the median number was nine.[8] In forty-one smaller companies surveyed, twenty-five of the presidents supervised seven or more subordinates, and the most common number was eight. Comparable results were found in other studies.

In a very real sense, none of these studies is truly indicative of the actual span of management. For one thing, they measure the span only at or near the top of an enterprise. This is hardly typical of what the span may be throughout the enterprise, particularly since every organizer has experienced tremendous pressure for having a large number of the functions report to the top executives. It is probable that spans below the top executive are much narrower. Indeed, a study of more than 100 companies of all sizes revealed a much narrower span in the middle levels of management than at the top.

In addition, the fact that apparently well-managed companies have, among them and certainly within them, widely varying spans indicates that merely counting the numbers in existing spans is not enough to establish what a span *ought* to be. This is true even if it could be assumed that, through trial and error, each company has reached the best number. That might prove only that underlying conditions vary (this will be discussed later in the chapter).

Problems with Organization Levels

There is a tendency to regard organization and departmentation as ends in themselves and to gauge the effectiveness of organization structures in terms of clarity and completeness of departments and department levels. The division of activities into departments and hierarchical organization and the creation of multiple levels are not completely desirable in themselves.

In the first place, levels are *expensive*. As they increase, more and more effort and money are devoted to managing, because of the additional managers, the staffs to assist them, and the necessity of coordinating departmental activities, plus the costs of facilities for the personnel. Accountants refer to such costs as "overhead," or "burden," or "general and administrative," in contrast to so-called direct costs. Real production is accomplished by factory, engineering, or sales employees, who are, or could logically be accounted for as, "direct labor." Levels above the "firing line" are predominantly staffed with managers whose cost it would be desirable to eliminate, if that were possible.

In the second place, departmental levels *complicate communication*. An enterprise with many levels has greater difficulty communicating objectives, plans, and policies downward through the organization structure than does a firm in which the top manager communicates directly with employees. Omissions and misinterpretations occur as information passes down the line. Levels also complicate communication from the "firing line" to the commanding superiors, which is every bit as important as downward communication. It has been well said that levels are "filters" of information.

Finally, numerous departments and levels *complicate planning and control.* A plan that may be definite and complete at the top level loses coordination and clarity as it is subdivided at lower levels. Control becomes more difficult as levels and managers are added; at the same time the complexities of planning and difficulties of communication make this control more important.

Operational-Management Position: A Situational Approach

The classical school approach to the span of management deals with specifying numbers of subordinates for an effective span. Actual experience does support the classical school opinion that at upper and top levels the span is from three to seven or eight subordinates. However, more recent operational-management theorists have taken the position that there are too many underlying variables in a management situation for us to specify any particular number of subordinates that a manager can effectively supervise. Thus the **principle of the span of management** states that *there is a limit to the number of subordinates a manager can effectively supervise, but the exact number will depend on the impact of underlying factors.*

In other words, the dominant current guideline is to look for the causes of limited span in individual situations rather than to assume that there is a widely applicable numerical limit. Examining what consumes the time of managers in their handling of superior-subordinate relationships and ascertaining devices that can be used to reduce these time pressures will be not only a helpful approach for determining the best span in individual cases but also a powerful tool for finding out what can be done to extend the span without destroying effective supervision. There can be no argument that the costs of levels of supervision make it highly desirable for every individual manager to have as many subordinates as can be effectively supervised.

FACTORS DETERMINING AN EFFECTIVE SPAN

The number of subordinates a manager can effectively manage depends on the impact of underlying factors. Aside from such personal capacities as comprehending quickly, getting along with people, and commanding loyalty and respect, the most important determinant is a manager's ability to reduce the time he or she spends with subordinates. This ability naturally varies with managers and their jobs, but several factors materially influence the number and frequency of such contacts and therefore the span of management (see Table 9-1).

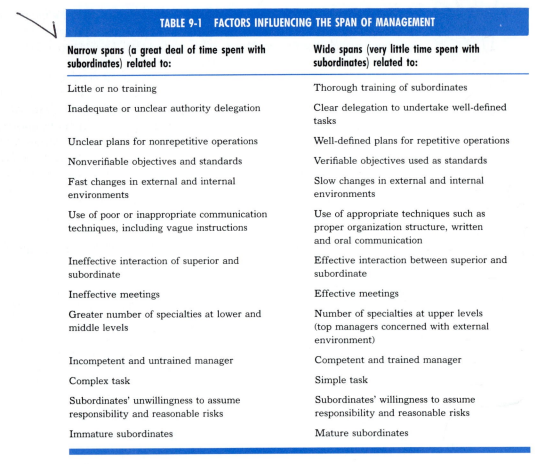

TABLE 9-1 FACTORS INFLUENCING THE SPAN OF MANAGEMENT	
Narrow spans (a great deal of time spent with subordinates) related to:	**Wide spans (very little time spent with subordinates) related to:**
Little or no training	Thorough training of subordinates
Inadequate or unclear authority delegation	Clear delegation to undertake well-defined tasks
Unclear plans for nonrepetitive operations	Well-defined plans for repetitive operations
Nonverifiable objectives and standards	Verifiable objectives used as standards
Fast changes in external and internal environments	Slow changes in external and internal environments
Use of poor or inappropriate communication techniques, including vague instructions	Use of appropriate techniques such as proper organization structure, written and oral communication
Ineffective interaction of superior and subordinate	Effective interaction between superior and subordinate
Ineffective meetings	Effective meetings
Greater number of specialties at lower and middle levels	Number of specialties at upper levels (top managers concerned with external environment)
Incompetent and untrained manager	Competent and trained manager
Complex task	Simple task
Subordinates' unwillingness to assume responsibility and reasonable risks	Subordinates' willingness to assume responsibility and reasonable risks
Immature subordinates	Mature subordinates

Training of Subordinates

The better the training of subordinates, the fewer the number of necessary superior-subordinate relationships. Well-trained subordinates require not only less of their managers' time but also less contact with their managers.

Training programs increase in new and more complex industries. Managers in the railroad industry, for example, would—because the technology does not change much—tend to be more completely trained than those in the aerospace industry. The rapid changes in policy and procedures in the complex electronics and missile industries would increase training problems.

Clarity of Delegation of Authority

Although training enables managers to reduce the frequency and extensiveness of time-consuming contacts, the principal cause of the heavy time burdens of superior-subordinate relationships is to be found in poorly conceived and confused organization. The most serious symptom of poor organization affecting the span of management is inadequate or unclear authority delegation. If a manager clearly delegates authority to undertake a well-defined task, a well-trained subordinate can get it done with a minimum of the manager's time and attention. But if the subordinate's task is not one that can be done, if it is not clearly defined, or if the subordinate does not have the authority to undertake it effectively, either the task will not be performed or the manager will have to spend a disproportionate amount of time supervising and guiding the subordinate's efforts.

Clarity of Plans

Much of the character of a subordinate's job is defined by the plans to be put into effect. If these plans are well defined, if they are workable, if the authority to undertake them has been delegated, and if the subordinate understands what is expected, little of a supervisor's time will be required. Such is often the case with a production supervisor responsible for largely repetitive operations. Thus, in one large-volume work-clothing manufacturer's plant, production supervisors operated satisfactorily with as many as thirty subordinates.

On the other hand, if plans cannot be drawn accurately and subordinates must do much of their own planning, they may require considerable guidance. However, if the superior has set up clear policies to guide decisions and has made sure they are consistent with the operations and goals of the department, and if the subordinate understands them, there will certainly be fewer demands on the superior's time than there would be if these policies were indefinite, incomplete, or not understood.

Use of Objective Standards

A manager must find out, either by personal observation or through the use of objective standards, whether subordinates are following plans. Obviously, good objective standards, revealing with ease any deviations from plans, enable managers to avoid many time-consuming contacts and to direct attention to exceptions at points critical to the successful execution of plans.

Rate of Change

Certain enterprises change much more rapidly than others. The rate of change is an important determinant of the degree to which policies can be formulated and the stability of policies maintained. It may explain the organization structure of companies—railroad, banking, and public utility companies, for example—operating with wide spans of management or, on the other hand, the very narrow span of management used by General Eisenhower during World War II.

The effect of slow change on policy formulation and on the training of subordinates is dramatically shown in the organization of the Roman Catholic Church. This organization, in terms of durability and stability, can probably be regarded as the most successful in the history of Western civilization. Yet the organization levels are few: In most cases bishops report directly to the Pope and parish pastors to bishops, although in some instances bishops report to archbishops. Thus, there are generally very few levels in this worldwide organization and a consequent wide span of management at each level. Even though it is probably too broad, this extraordinarily wide span is apparently tolerable, partly because the bishops possess a high degree of training and, even more, because the rate of change in the Church has been slow. Changes in procedures or policies are developments of decades, and major objectives have remained the same for almost 2000 years.

Communication Techniques

The effectiveness with which communication techniques are used also influences the span of management. Objective standards of control are a kind of communications device, but many other techniques reduce the time spent with subordinates.

If every plan, instruction, order, or direction has to be communicated by personal contact and every organization change or staffing problem has to be handled orally, a manager's time will obviously be heavily burdened. Some executives use "assistant-to" positions or administrative staff personnel as a communications device to help them solve their problems with key subordinates. Written recommendations by subordinates, summarizing important considerations, frequently speed decision making. Some busy top executives widen their span of management by insisting on a summary presentation of written recommendations, even when these involved enormously important decisions. A carefully reasoned and presented recommendation helps an executive reach a considered decision in minutes when even the most efficient conference would require an hour.

An ability to communicate plans and instructions clearly and concisely also tends to increase a manager's span. The subordinate who, after leaving a superior's office or receiving instructions, is still in doubt about what is wanted or what has been said is sure to request further meetings sooner or later. The subordinate's job is greatly facilitated by superiors who can express themselves well. A manager's casual, easy style may please subordinates, but when this easiness degenerates into confusion and wasted time, it sharply reduces the effective span of management and often lowers morale as well.

Amount of Personal Contact Needed

In many instances, face-to-face meetings are necessary. Many situations cannot be completely handled with written reports, memorandums, policy statements, planning documents, or other communications that do not involve personal contact. An executive may find it valuable and stimulating to subordinates to meet and discuss problems in the give-and-take of a conference. Some problems are of such political delicacy that they can be handled only in face-to-face meetings. This is also true when it comes to appraising people's performance and discussing it with them. And there are other situations in which the best way of communicating a problem, instructing a subordinate, or "getting a feel" for how people really think on some matter is to spend time in personal contact.

One wonders, however, whether the high percentage of executive time spent in meetings and committees might be reduced somewhat by better training, better policy-making and planning, clearer delegation, more thorough staff work, better control systems and objectives standards, and, in general, better application of sound principles of management. One wonders, also, whether much of the time spent in personal contact might not be much better spent in thought and study.

At the other extreme, many companies seem somewhat unaware of how newer personnel techniques affect first-line supervisors, many of whom appear to have spans of management far beyond their abilities to handle them. Merit ratings, insurance programs, grievance procedures, and other personnel matters now requiring supervisors' time in face-to-face relationships have reduced their traditionally wide spans. This is not to say that these innovations are not worth their cost, but span-of-management limitations must be evaluated in light of these factors. Perhaps the point has been reached at which first-level supervisors, with a traditionally large number of people reporting to them, are the most overworked of all managers.

Variation by Organization Level

Several research projects have found that the size of the most effective span differs by organization level. In one major study, the researchers developed and tested a model to take this variable into account and found that the degree of specialization by individuals ("person specialization") was the most important variable affecting span, although technology and size were also tested, since previous research had concentrated on these.[9] The study revealed that (1) when a greater number of specialties were supervised, effective spans were narrower at lower and middle levels of organization but were increased at upper levels, primarily because top-level managers were most concerned with the interface of the enterprise with its external environment, strategic planning, and major policy matters; (2) routineness (lack of variety of work) of an operation appeared to have little effect at any level; and (3) size (in terms of personnel) had little effect at lower levels but a positive effect at middle levels.

Actually, this study is consistent with the impact of variables outlined above. It found what many practitioners have long known: Neither size nor technology has much to do with an effective span at upper levels of an organization, although the variables outlined in this section do have a significant influence.

Other Factors

Besides the factors discussed above, there are others that affect the span of management. For example, a manager who is competent and well trained can effectively supervise more people than one who is not. Furthermore, simple tasks may allow for a wider span than tasks that are complex and include a great variety of activities. Still other factors favor a wider span of management, such as the positive attitudes of subordinates toward the assumption of responsibility, as well as their willingness to take reasonable risks. Similarly, with more mature subordinates, the superior may delegate more authority, thus widening the span.

Need for Balance

There can be no doubt that despite the desirability of flat organization structure, the span of management is limited by real and important restrictions. Managers may have more subordinates than they can manage effectively, even though they delegate authority, carry on training, formulate plans and policies clearly, and adopt efficient control and communication techniques. It is equally true that as an enterprise grows, the span-of-management limitations force an increase in the number of levels simply because there are more people to supervise.

What is required is more precise balancing, in a given situation, of all pertinent factors. Widening spans and reducing the number of levels may be the answer in some cases; the reverse may be true in others. One must balance all the costs of adopting one course or the other, not only the financial costs but also costs in morale, personal development, and attainment of enterprise objectives. In a military organization, perhaps the attainment of objectives quickly and without error would be most important. On the other hand, in a department store operation, the long-run objective of profit may be best served by forcing initiative and personal development at the lower levels of the organization.

AN ORGANIZATIONAL ENVIRONMENT FOR ENTREPRENEURING AND INTRAPRENEURING

At times, special organizational arrangements need to be made for fostering and utilizing entrepreneurship. Frequently, **entrepreneurship** is thought to apply to managing small businesses,[10] but some authors expand the concept so that it applies also to large organizations and to managers carrying out entrepreneurial roles through which they initiate changes to take advantage of opportunities.[11] Although it is common to seek the "entrepreneurial personality," Peter Drucker suggested that this search may not be successful.[12] Instead, one should look for commitment to systematic innovation, which is a specific activity of entrepreneurs. The essence of entrepreneurship is innovation, goal-oriented change to utilize the enterprise's potential. As entrepreneurs, managers try to improve the situation.

The Intrapreneur and the Entrepreneur

Gifford Pinchot makes a distinction between the intrapreneur and the entrepreneur. Specifically, an **intrapreneur** is a person who focuses on innovation and creativity and who transforms a dream or an idea into a profitable venture by operating *within* the organizational environment. In contrast, the **entrepreneur** is a person who does similar things, but *outside* the organizational setting.[13] Entrepreneurs have the ability to see an opportunity; to obtain the necessary capital, labor, and other inputs; and to put together an operation successfully. They are willing to take the personal risk of success and failure. Other authors do not make a distinction between entrepreneur and intrapreneur. In this book the term "entrepreneur" designates an enterprising person working either within or outside the organization.

Creating an Environment for Entrepreneurship

Since it is a managerial responsibility to create an environment for the effective and efficient achievement of group goals, managers must promote opportunities for entrepreneurs to utilize their potential for innovation. Entrepreneurs take personal risks in initiating change, and they expect to be rewarded for their efforts. The taking of even reasonable risk will, at times, result in eventual failure, but this must be tolerated. Finally, entrepreneurs need some degree of freedom to pursue their ideas; this, in turn, requires that sufficient authority be delegated. The personal risks for the entrepreneur outside the organization (the individual who has his or her own business) are of a different kind. Failure may mean bankruptcy.

Innovative persons often have ideas that tend to run contrary to what is considered "conventional wisdom." It is quite common that these individuals are not well liked by their colleagues and that their contributions are often not sufficiently appreciated. It is, therefore, not surprising that entrepreneurs leave large companies and start their own businesses. When Steve Wozniak could not get his dream of building a small computer fulfilled at Hewlett-Packard, he left that prestigious firm to form—together with another entrepreneur, Steve Jobs— Apple Computer. Progressive companies, such as IBM or 3M, consciously try to develop an organizational environment that promotes entrepreneurship within the company.

Becoming an entrepreneur is fashionable.[14] Several universities teach entrepreneurship. The Wharton School in Philadelphia has an entrepreneurial center. Some people do not want to work for a big company; rather, they want to be their own boss and live the life they want. In the 1980s, many employees lost their job and consequently started their own business. Some companies even provided support so that these new firms could become suppliers. Women seem to be attracted to entrepreneurship. Feeling discriminated at work in companies, some go on their own. Important requirements for becoming an entrepreneur are self-confidence, a willingness to work hard, experience with the product, a good general education, and some money to start.

Innovation and Entrepreneurship

When hearing about innovation and entrepreneurship, one thinks immediately of the success stories of people such as Steven Jobs of Apple Computer and Ross Perot of Electronic Data Systems (acquired by General Motors). It may be an appealing thought to get rich and get rich quick, often by establishing new companies.[15] Entrepreneurs have creative ideas; they use their management skills and resources to meet identifiable needs in the marketplace. If successful, an entrepreneur can become wealthy.

Peter Drucker suggests that innovation applies not only to high-tech companies but equally to low-tech, established businesses. Worthwhile innovation is not a matter of sheer luck; it requires systematic and rational work, well organized and managed for results.[16]

What does entrepreneurship imply? It suggests dissatisfaction with how things are and an awareness of a need to do things differently. Innovation comes about because of some of the following situations:

1. The unexpected event, failure, or success
2. The incongruous—what is assumed and what really is
3. The process or task that needed improvement
4. Changes in the market or industry structure
5. Changes in demographics
6. Changes in meaning or in the way things are perceived
7. Newly acquired knowledge

Innovations based solely on bright ideas may be very risky and are, at times, not successful. General Electric's ambitious plans for the "factory of the future" may have been a costly mistake.[17] These plans may have been based on unrealistic forecasts and GE's unrealistic expectations to automate industry. The concept of the new factory expressed the wish of the chairperson, who wanted to promote entrepreneurship in an organization that was known to be highly structured.

The most successful innovations are often the mundane ones. Take the Japanese, who make minor innovations (providing, for example, little conveniences that customers like) in their cars or in their electronic equipment.[18] James Brian Quinn found in his research that successful large companies are listening carefully to the needs of their customers. They establish teams that search for creative alternatives to serve their customers—but within a limiting framework and with clear goals in mind.[19]

Perspective

Post-it Note Pads[20]

Even in companies with a policy of promoting entrepreneurship and innovation, the development of new products requires perseverance to transform an idea into reality.

Art Fry, the inventor of Post-it note pads, was singing in a church choir. The bookmarks placed in his hymnal fell out after the first church service, making it difficult to find the relevant pages for the second service. The need was clear: An adhesive paper slip that could be easily removed without damaging the page. However, developing an adhesive with appropriate stickiness was not an easy task. In the past, the 3M Company, where Art Fry worked, was known for providing products with great adhesion. For Art's purpose, however, a material was needed that not only had sufficient adhesion but also could be removed. The 3M laboratory did not provide much help in the research and development of such a product. Nor did the marketing department think a great deal of this idea. But being an inventor as well as an innovator, Art Fry pursued his goal with great perseverance. The result was the Post-it note pads, which turned out to be a very profitable product for 3M.

THE STRUCTURE AND PROCESS OF ORGANIZING[21]

Looking at organizing as a process requires that several fundamentals be considered. In the first place, the structure must reflect objectives and plans, because activities derive from them. In the second place, it must reflect the authority available to an enterprise's management. Authority in a given organization is a socially determined right to exercise discretion; as such, it is subject to change.

In the third place, an organization structure, like any plan, must reflect its environment. Just as the premises of a plan may be economic, technological, political, social, or ethical, so may be those of an organization structure. It must be designed to work, to permit contributions by members of a group, and to help people gain objectives efficiently in a changing future. In this sense, a workable organization structure can never be static. There is no single organization structure that works best in all kinds of situations. An effective organization structure depends on the situation.

In the fourth place, since the organization is staffed with people, the groupings of activities and the authority relationships of an organization structure must take into account people's limitations and customs. This is not to say that the structure must be designed around individuals instead of around goals and accompanying activities. But an important consideration is the kinds of people who are to staff it.

The Logic of Organizing

There is a fundamental logic to organizing, as shown in Figure 9-3. Although steps 1 and 2 are actually part of planning, the organizing process consists of the following six steps:

1. Establishing enterprise objectives
2. Formulating supporting objectives, policies, and plans
3. Identifying and classifying the activities necessary to accomplish these
4. Grouping these activities in light of the human and material resources available and the best way, under the circumstances, of using them
5. Delegating to the head of each group the authority necessary to perform the activities
6. Tying the groups together horizontally and vertically, through authority relationships and information flows

Some Misconceptions

Organizing does not imply any extreme occupational specialization, which in many instances makes labor uninteresting, tedious, and unduly restrictive. There is nothing in organization itself that dictates this. To say that tasks should be specific is not to say they must be limited and mechanical. Whether they should be broken down into minute parts—as on a typical assembly line—or be defined broadly enough to encompass the design, production, and sale of a machine is for the organizer to consider in light of the results desired. In any organization, jobs can

FIGURE 9-3

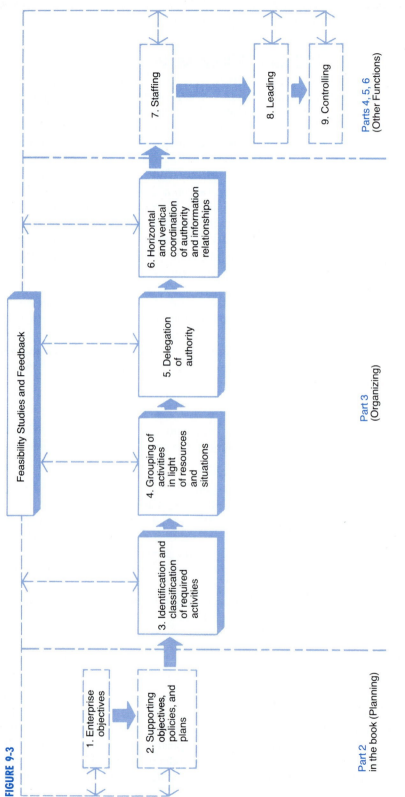

ORGANIZING PROCESS.

be defined to allow little or no personal leeway or the widest possible discretion. One must not forget that there is no best way to organize and that the application of structural organization theory must take into account the situation.

BASIC QUESTIONS FOR EFFECTIVE ORGANIZING

It is useful to analyze the managerial function of organizing by raising and answering the following questions:

1. What determines the span of management and hence the levels of organization? (answered in this chapter)
2. What determines the basic framework of departmentation, and what are the strengths and weaknesses of the basic forms? (answered in Chapter 10)
3. What kinds of authority relationships exist in organizations? (answered in Chapter 11)
4. How should authority be dispersed throughout the organization structure, and what determines the extent of this dispersion? (answered in Chapter 11)
5. How should the manager make organization theory work in practice? (answered in Chapter 12)

The answers to these questions form a basis for a theory of organizing. When considered along with similar analyses of planning, staffing, leading, and controlling, they constitute an operational approach to management.

SUMMARY

The term "organization" is often used loosely. Formal organization is the intentional structure of roles. Informal organization is a network of personal and social relations neither established nor required by formal authority but arising spontaneously. "Span of management" refers to the number of people a manager can effectively supervise. A wide span of management results in few organizational levels, and a narrow span results in many levels. There is no definite number of people a manager can always effectively supervise; the number depends on several underlying factors. These include the degree of training of subordinates that is required and possessed, the clarity of authority delegation, the clarity of plans, the use of objective standards, the rate of change, the effectiveness of communication techniques, the amount of personal contact needed, and the level in the organization.

Intrapreneurs and entrepreneurs focus on innovation and creativity. It is the manager's responsibility to create an environment that promotes entrepreneurship.

The steps in organizing include formulating objectives and supporting objectives, policies, and plans to achieve the ends (strictly speaking, this is carried out in planning); identifying and classifying activities; grouping these activities; delegating authority; and coordinating authority as well as information relationships.

KEY IDEAS AND CONCEPTS FOR REVIEW

Organizational role

Organizing

Formal organization

Informal organization

Department

Principle of the span of management

Factors determining the span of
   management

Entrepreneuring

Intrapreneuring

Innovation and entrepreneurship

Logical steps of organizing

Basic questions for effective organizing

FOR DISCUSSION

1. Since people must occupy organization positions, and since an effective organization depends on people, it is often said that the best organization arises when a manager hires good people and lets them do a job in their own way. Comment.
2. A formal organization is often conceived of as a communications system. Is it? How?
3. Construct a diagram depicting the formal organization of an enterprise or activity with which you are familiar. How does this organization chart help or hinder the establishment of an environment for performance?
4. Using the same enterprise or activity as in question 3, chart the informal organization. Does it help or hinder the formal organization? Why?
5. Urwick and other writers seem to say that at top levels the number of persons in the span of management should not exceed six. However, approximately 750 bishops and some 1200 other persons have reported directly to the Pope. At one time in the Bank of America organization, over 600 bank managers reported to the chief executive officer. How do you square these facts with the idea that there is a limit to the number of subordinates a manager can supervise?
6. When you become a manager, what criteria will you favor to determine your span?

EXERCISES/ACTION STEPS

1. Organize a family picnic using the steps suggested in this chapter.
2. Interview a manager in your community, and ask him or her how many subordinates he or she has. Are different numbers of subordinates supervised at the top, the middle, and the bottom of the organizational hierarchy? What really determines the span of management in this organization? Do you think the span is appropriate for the enterprise?

CASES

CASE 9-1
MEASUREMENT INSTRUMENTS CORPORATION

William B. Richman, president of the Measurement Instruments Corporation, was explaining his organization arrangements to the board of directors. His organization chart is shown in Figure 9-4.

FIGURE 9-4

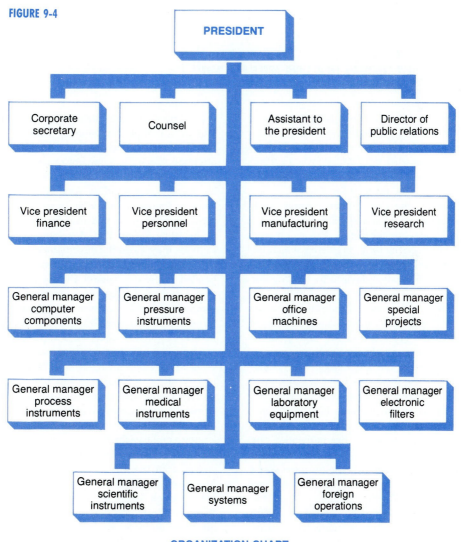

ORGANIZATION CHART
MEASUREMENT INSTRUMENTS CORPORATION

When asked by a board member whether he thought he had too many people reporting to him, Mr. Richman replied: "I do not believe in the traditional principle of span of control, or span of management, that managers should have only four or five persons reporting to them. This is what makes waste and bureaucracy. All my subordinates are good people and know what they are doing. All can reach me readily with their problems when they have them. All feel close to the top because they are close to the top. Moreover, I want to know firsthand how every person is doing and to detect any weakness or errors as soon as possible. Furthermore, if a store manager at Sears, Roebuck can have twenty-five to thirty persons reporting to him, I ought to be able to handle nineteen. In addition, too few reporting to a manager doesn't give him enough to do, and I assume that you hired me to give the company my full time."

1. How would you respond to Mr. Richman's arguments?
2. If you were a member of the board of directors, what would you suggest Mr. Richman do?

INTERNATIONAL CASE 9-2
CAN THE NEW EXECUTIVE TEAM TURN APPLE AROUND?[22]

At Apple Computer, the third revolution may be in the making. In 1977, Apple led the personal computer revolution, and this was followed in 1984 by the introduction of the user-friendly Macintosh. In 1990, the new management team of Sculley and Spindler devised a new low-price strategy for Apple.

John Sculley, the CEO, stated: "Apple works best with its back against the wall." This probably was true in Apple's roller coaster history. But will it work in the 1990s? Starting in 1989, problems, which had their inception earlier, began to show. The 1988 organizational decentralization devised by Sculley during his sabbatical leave did not work. Although the company's Pacific Rim and European operations flourished, the delegation of daily decision making to the four presidents created rivalries and organizational confusion. Sculley called 1990 the worst year of his business life. Apple lost market share. High operating margins and the lavish life of managers with many perks contributed to the fact that the Mac computer was very costly and became less competitive against IBM compatibles. High managerial turnover and low morale contributed to the perception that Apple lacked a vision for the future. In the 1980s, Apple made progress in entering the business sector, but the original customers (individuals, schools, and small businesses) turned from the high-priced Macs to the much less expensive IBM compatibles. With the introduction of Microsoft's Window 3.0 software, which made IBM compatibles more user-friendly, it became evident that Apple was in trouble.

This crisis laid the foundation for the third revolution, a strategy initiated by Sculley and his new No. 2 executive, Michael Spindler. Sculley turned his attention to the development of new technology. Engineers were skeptical because Sculley, an architect by training, was hired by Apple from Pepsi-Cola because of his marketing skills. Despite his limited technical expertise, it is said that he devotes 70 percent of his time to product development. His systems thinking may speed the development of new products.

Michael Spindler, a German executive who headed Apple's successful European operation, took over sales, marketing, manufacturing, and corporate communication. His extensive experience in electronics was with Siemens, Intel, and Digital Equipment before he joined Apple in Europe. His managerial style was different from previous managerial approaches at Apple's Cupertino, California, headquarters. With an emphasis on disciplined planning and control, he initiated tighter budgets and attempted to eliminate organizational politics while at the same time stressing teamwork. The new Sculley-Spindler strategy emphasizes low prices to lure back the original customers (individuals, schools, and small businesses) with the introduction of three new products. Moreover, more attention will be given to laptop and notebook computers. A cooperative arrangement with Sony and Toshiba is even considered for manufacturing these portable computers. Finally, resources are allocated for the development of a new operating system and applications programs.

Drastically reducing the prices of Apple's new model line is also a risky strategy. Will those customers who switched to IBM compatibles be attracted by the lower prices and return to the user-friendly Mac? Apple managers certainly hope that the new strategy ushers in the third revolution. Perhaps one of the critical decisions is whether Apple should be a consumer or business products firm.

1. What do you think about the ups and downs of Apple?

2. Is Sculley's background in architecture and marketing suitable for a technically oriented company? Why or why not?

3. Do Spindler's European background and his more structured approach work in a company that was used to a loose organization structure?

4. Should Apple become a business- or consumer-focused company? Or can the company serve both businesses and consumers and schools?

REFERENCES

1. Peter F. Drucker, "The Coming of the New Organization," *Harvard Business Review* (January–February 1988), p. 45.
2. See also Allen I. Kraut and Patricia R. Pedigo, "The Role of the Manager: What's Really Important in Different Management Jobs," *Academy of Management Executive* (November 1989), pp. 286–293.
3. See also Elliott Jaques, "In Praise of Hierarchy," *Harvard Business Review* (January–February 1990), pp. 127–133.
4. Chester I. Barnard, *The Functions of the Executive* (Cambridge, Mass.: Harvard University Press, 1938, 1964).
5. Keith Davis and John Newstrom, *Human Behavior at Work* (New York: McGraw-Hill Book Company, 1985), p. 308.
6. See also Harold Koontz, "Making Theory Operational: The Span of Management," in Harold Koontz, Cyril O'Donnell, and Heinz Weihrich (eds.), *Management—A Book of Readings*, 5th ed. (New York: McGraw-Hill Book Company, 1980), pp. 232–240.
7. Lyndall Urwick, "Axioms of Organization," *Public Administration Magazine* (London; October 1955), pp. 348–349. However, in other writings, Urwick modified this position by saying, "No person should supervise more than five, or at the most, six, direct subordinates *whose work interlocks.*" See *Notes on the Theory of Organization* (New York: American Management Association, 1952), p. 53.
8. As summarized in *Business Week* (Aug. 18, 1951), pp. 102–103. Healey found similar variations in his study of 409 manufacturing companies in Ohio, although the median was six subordinates. See J. H. Healey, *Executive Coordination and Control* (Columbus: Ohio State University Press, 1956), p. 66.
9. Robert D. Dewar and Donald P. Simet, "A Level Specific Prediction of Spans of Control Examining the Effects of Size, Technology, and Specialization," *Journal of the Academy of Management* (March 1981), pp. 5–24.
10. Ricky W. Griffin, *Management* (Boston: Houghton Mifflin Company, 1984), chap. 22.
11. Henry Mintzberg, *The Nature of Managerial Work* (New York: Harper & Row, 1973), chap. 4; James Brian Quinn, "Managing Innovation: Controlled Chaos," *Harvard Business Review* (May–June 1985), pp. 73–84. Entrepreneurship has also been extended to public organizations. See Ravi Ramamurti, "Public Entrepreneurs: Who They Are and How They Operate," *California Management Review* (Spring 1986), pp. 142–158.
12. Peter F. Drucker, "The Discipline of Innovation," *Harvard Business Review* (May–June 1985), pp. 67–72. See also Peter F. Drucker, "A Prescription for Entrepreneurial Management," *Industry Week* (Apr. 19, 1985), pp. 33–40.

13. Gifford Pinchot III, *Intrapreneuring* (New York: Harper & Row, 1985).

14. Jeremy Main, "A Golden Age for Entrepreneurs," *Fortune* (Feb. 12, 1990), pp. 120–125.

15. For a critical review of some books on entrepreneurship, see David E. Gumpert, "Stalking the Entrepreneur," *Harvard Business Review* (May–June 1986), pp. 32–36.

16. Peter F. Drucker, *Innovation and Entrepreneurship—Practices and Principles* (New York: Harper & Row, 1985); Peter F. Drucker, "The Discipline of Innovation," *Harvard Business Review* (May–June 1985), pp. 67–72; John W. Wilson, "The New Economy According to Drucker," *Business Week* (June 10, 1985), pp. 10–12; and Everett Groseclose, "A Management Sage's Shibboleths for Success," *The Wall Street Journal* (Oct. 7, 1985).

17. Peter Petre, "How GE Bobbled the Factory of the Future," *Fortune* (Nov. 11, 1985), pp. 52–63.

18. More recently, Japan has been breaking with tradition and now begins funding of basic research. See Stephen K. Yoder, "Going Crazy in Japan," *The Wall Street Journal*, A Special Report on Technology in the Workplace (Nov. 10, 1986).

19. James B. Quinn, "Managing Innovation: Controlled Chaos," *Harvard Business Review* (May–June 1985), pp. 73–84.

20. The Post-it story has been reported in various sources, including the videotape "In Search of Excellence"; Pinchot, *Intrapreneuring* (1985); Lester C. Krogh, "Can the Entrepreneurial Spirit Exist within a Large Company?" *3M: An Executive Message*, delivered at the Conference Board, Conference on Research and Development, New York (Apr. 25, 1984); and Brian Dumaine, "Ability to Innovate," *Fortune* (Jan. 29, 1990), pp. 43–46.

21. For a discussion of designing organizations, see David P. Hanna, *Designing Organizations for High Performance* (Reading, Mass.: Addison-Wesley, 1988), and Robert E. Quinn and Kim S. Cameron (eds.), *Paradox and Transformation—Toward a Theory of Change in Organization and Management* (Cambridge, Mass.: Ballinger, 1988).

22. The case is based on a variety of sources, including Barbara Buell, Jonathan B. Levine, and Neil Gross, "Apple: New Team, New Strategy," *Business Week* (Oct. 15, 1990), pp. 86–96; Barbara Buell, in ibid., p. 92; and Brenton R. Schlender, "Yet Another Strategy for Apple," *Fortune* (Oct. 22, 1990), pp. 81–87.

Chapter 10

If we are to respond to wildly altered business and economic circumstances, we need entirely new ways of thinking about organizations.[1]

Tom Peters

Organizational Structure: Departmentation

Chapter Objectives

After reading this chapter, you should be able to:

1. Identify the basic patterns of traditional departmentation and analyze their advantages and disadvantages.
2. Analyze matrix organizations and outline the steps that can be taken to avoid the dangers of disunity of command.
3. Understand the modern departmentation according to strategic business units (SBUs).
4. Recognize that there is no single best pattern of departmentation to use and that responsible managers must select patterns that will assist in accomplishing enterprise objectives in light of the particular situation.

The limitation on the number of subordinates that can be directly managed would restrict the size of enterprises if it were not for the device of **departmentation.** Grouping activities and people into departments makes it possible to expand organizations—at least in theory—to an indefinite degree. Departments, however, differ with respect to the basic patterns used to group the activities. The nature of these patterns, developed out of logic and practice, and their relative merits will be dealt with in the following sections.

At the outset, it must be emphasized that there is no single best way of departmentizing that is applicable to all organizations or to all situations. The pattern used will depend on given situations and on what managers believe will yield the best results for them in the situation they face.

DEPARTMENTATION BY SIMPLE NUMBERS

Departmentation by simple numbers was once an important method in the organization of tribes, clans, and armies. Although it is rapidly falling into disuse, it still may have certain applications in modern society.

The simple-numbers method of departmentizing is achieved by tolling off persons who are to perform the same duties and putting them under the supervision of a manager. The essential fact is not what these people do, where they work, or what they work with; it is that the success of the undertaking depends only on the number of people involved in it.

Even though a quick examination may impress an investigator with the number of people departmentized on a human resource basis, the usefulness of this organizational device has declined with each passing century. For one thing, technology has advanced, demanding more specialized and different skills. In the United States, the last stronghold of common labor was agriculture, and even here it is restricted more and more to the harvesting of fewer and fewer crops as farming operations become larger and more specialized.

A second reason for the decline of departmentizing purely by numbers is that groups composed of specialized personnel are frequently more efficient than those based merely on numbers. The reorganization of the defense forces of the United States on this basis is a case in point. People skilled in the use of different types of weapons have been combined into single units. For example, the addition of artillery and tactical air support to the traditional infantry division makes it a much more formidable fighting unit than it would be if each were organized separately.

A third and long-standing reason for the decline of departmentation by numbers is that it is useful only at the lowest level of the organization structure. As soon as any factor other than pure human power becomes important, the simple-numbers basis of departmentation fails to produce good results.

DEPARTMENTATION BY TIME

One of the oldest forms of departmentation, generally used at lower levels of the organization, is grouping activities on the basis of time. The use of shifts is common in many enterprises where for economic, technological, or other reasons the normal workday will not suffice. Examples of this kind of departmentation can be found in hospitals, where around-the-clock patient care is essential. Similarly, the fire department has to be ready to respond to emergencies at any time. But there are also technological reasons for the use of shifts. A steel furnace, for example, cannot be turned on and off at will; the process of making steel is continuous and requires workers to work in three shifts.

Advantages

These few examples indicate a number of advantages of departmentation by time. First, services can be rendered that go beyond the typical 8-hour workday, often extending to 24 hours a day. Second, it is possible to use processes that cannot be interrupted, those that require a continuing cycle. Third, expensive capital equipment can be used more than 8 hours a day when workers in several shifts use the same machines. Fourth, some people—students attending classes during the day, for instance—find it convenient to work at night.

Disadvantages

Departmentation by time also has disadvantages. First, supervision may be lacking during the night shift. Second, there is the fatigue factor; it is difficult for most people to switch, for instance, from a day shift to a night shift and vice versa. Third, having several shifts may cause problems in coordination and communication. In a hospital, for example, nurses from different shifts attending the same patient may not be familiar with the patient's particular problems. In a factory, the night shift may not clean up the machines to be used by the day shift people. Fourth, the payment of overtime rates can increase the cost of the product or service.

DEPARTMENTATION BY ENTERPRISE FUNCTION

Grouping activities in accordance with the functions of an enterprise—functional departmentation—embodies what enterprises typically do. Since all enterprises undertake the creation of something useful and desired by others, the basic enterprise functions are production (creating utility or adding utility to a good or service), selling (finding customers, patients, clients, students, or members who will agree to accept the good or service at a price or for a cost), and financing (raising and collecting, safeguarding, and expending the funds of the enterprise). It has been logical to group these activities into such departments as engineering, production, sales or marketing, and finance. Figure 10-1 shows a typical functional grouping for a manufacturing company.

Often, these particular functional designations do not appear in the organization chart. First, there is no generally accepted terminology: A manufacturing enterprise employs the terms "production," "sales," and "finance"; a wholesaler is concerned with such activities as "buying," "selling," and "finance"; and a railroad is involved with "operations," "traffic," and "finance."

A second reason for the variance of terms is that basic activities often differ in importance: Hospitals have no selling departments; churches, no production departments. This does not mean that these activities are not undertaken; rather, they are unspecialized or of such minor importance that they are combined with other activities.

A third reason for the absence of sales, production, or finance departments on many organization charts is that other methods of departmentation may have been deliberately selected. Those responsible for the enterprise may decide to organize on the basis of product, customer, territory, or marketing channel (the way goods or services reach the user).

Functional departmentation is the most widely employed basis for organizing activities and is present in almost every enterprise at some level in the organization structure. The characteristics of the selling, production, and finance functions of enterprises are so widely recognized and thoroughly understood that they are the basis not only of departmental organization but also, most often, of departmentation at the top level.

Coordination of activities may be achieved through rules and procedures, various aspects of planning (for example, goals and budgets), the organizational hierarchy, personal contacts, and sometimes liaison departments. Such a department may be used between engineering and manufacturing to handle design or change problems.[2]

Advantages

The most important advantage of functional departmentation is that it is a logical and time-proven method. It is also the best way of making certain that the power and prestige of the basic activities of the enterprise will be defended by the top managers. This is an important consideration among functional managers, for they see on every side the encroachments of staff and service groups, which sometimes

FIGURE 10-1

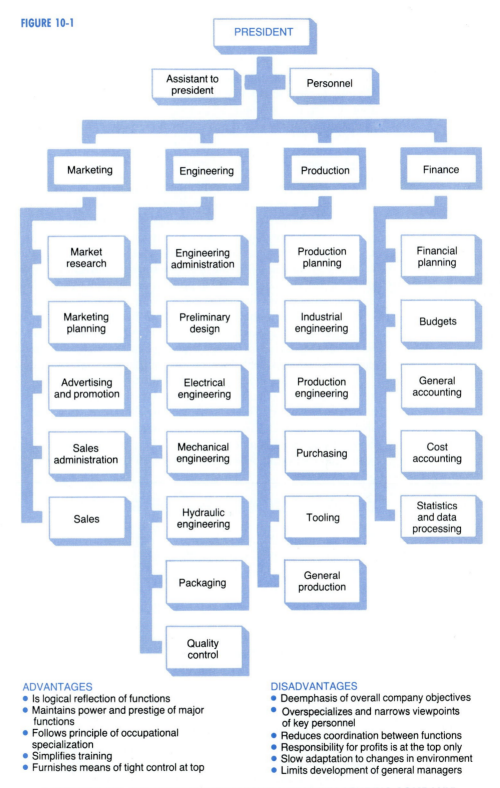

PRESIDENT

Assistant to president

Personnel

Marketing
- Market research
- Marketing planning
- Advertising and promotion
- Sales administration
- Sales

Engineering
- Engineering administration
- Preliminary design
- Electrical engineering
- Mechanical engineering
- Hydraulic engineering
- Packaging
- Quality control

Production
- Production planning
- Industrial engineering
- Production engineering
- Purchasing
- Tooling
- General production

Finance
- Financial planning
- Budgets
- General accounting
- Cost accounting
- Statistics and data processing

ADVANTAGES
- Is logical reflection of functions
- Maintains power and prestige of major functions
- Follows principle of occupational specialization
- Simplifies training
- Furnishes means of tight control at top

DISADVANTAGES
- Deemphasis of overall company objectives
- Overspecializes and narrows viewpoints of key personnel
- Reduces coordination between functions
- Responsibility for profits is at the top only
- Slow adaptation to changes in environment
- Limits development of general managers

A FUNCTIONAL ORGANIZATION GROUPING (MANUFACTURING COMPANY).

threaten the security of the principal line executives. Another advantage is that functional departmentation follows the principle of occupational specialization and thereby facilitates efficiency in the utilization of people. Still other advantages are that it simplifies training and, because the top managers are responsible for the end results, furnishes a means of tight control at the top.

Disadvantages

In spite of the advantages of functional departmentation, there are times when the claims of other methods seem even stronger. The size of the geographic area over which an enterprise operates may call for territorial grouping of activities; the production or purchase of numerous product lines, or of products designed for certain buyer classifications, may call for grouping along product or customer lines. In addition, functional departmentation may tend to de-emphasize overall enterprise objectives. Accountants, production experts, and salespeople, working in specialized departments, often have problems seeing the business as a whole, and coordination among them is frequently difficult to achieve. They develop attitudes and other behavior patterns involving loyalty to a functional department and not to the enterprise as a whole. Such "walls" between functional departments are common, and considerable effort is required to break them down.

Another disadvantage is that only the chief executive officer can be held responsible for profits. In small firms, this is all right, but in large firms the burden becomes too heavy for one person to bear. Also, this kind of departmentation makes it difficult to adapt quickly to environmental changes.[3] Finally, the functionally organized company is not the best training ground for general managers, who need certain knowledge and experience in all enterprise functions.

DEPARTMENTATION BY TERRITORY OR GEOGRAPHY

Departmentation based on territory is rather common in enterprises that operate over wide geographic areas. In this case, it may be important that activities in a given area or territory be grouped and assigned to a manager, for example, as shown in Figure 10-2.

Extent of Use

Territorial departmentation is especially attractive to large-scale firms or other enterprises whose activities are physically or geographically dispersed. However, a plant may be local in its activities and still assign the personnel in its security department on a territorial basis, placing two guards, for example, at each of the south and west gates. Department stores assign floorwalkers on this basis, and it is a common way to assign janitors, window washers, and the like. Business firms resort to this method when similar operations are undertaken in different geographic areas, as in automobile assembling, chain retailing and wholesaling, and oil refining. Many government agencies—the Internal Revenue Service, the Federal Reserve Board, the federal courts, and the Postal Service, among others—

FIGURE 10-2

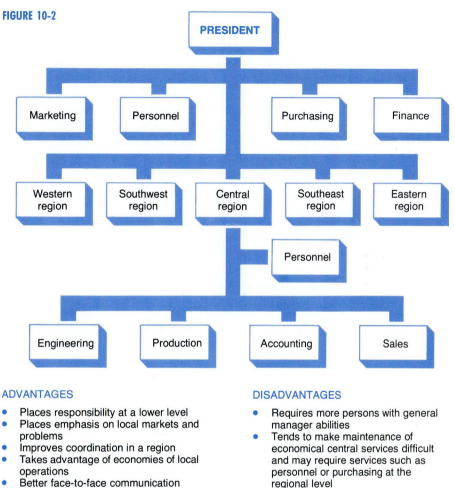

ADVANTAGES

- Places responsibility at a lower level
- Places emphasis on local markets and problems
- Improves coordination in a region
- Takes advantage of economies of local operations
- Better face-to-face communication with local interests
- Furnishes measurable training ground for general managers

DISADVANTAGES

- Requires more persons with general manager abilities
- Tends to make maintenance of economical central services difficult and may require services such as personnel or purchasing at the regional level
- Increases problem of top management control

A TERRITORIAL, OR GEOGRAPHIC, ORGANIZATION GROUPING (MANUFACTURING COMPANY).

adopt this basis of organization in their efforts to provide like services simultaneously across the nation. Territorial departmentation is most often used in sales and in production; it is not used in finance, which is usually concentrated at the headquarters.

Advantages

Departmentation by territory, or geography, offers a number of advantages. It places responsibility at a lower level, encourages local participation in decision making, and improves coordination of activities in a region. Managers can give special attention to the needs and problems of local markets. Thus, they may recruit local salespeople who are familiar with the special situation in the area. Moreover, these salespeople can spend more time selling and less time traveling.

Production may also be organized on a territorial basis by establishing plants in particular regions. This can reduce transportation costs and delivery time. Moreover, labor rates may be lower in certain regions, and producing things locally may create jobs and goodwill in the local community.

Geographic departmentation improves face-to-face communication with local people. Also, since the manager in a territory has to carry out many different functional and managerial activities, this type of organization provides a good training ground for general managers.

Disadvantages

There are also disadvantages in organizing territorially. This kind of departmentation requires more persons with general managerial abilities, and a shortage of them is often a factor limiting the growth of an enterprise. Moreover, geographic departmentation tends to lead to duplication of services. Thus, managers of a territory want to have their own purchasing, personnel, accounting, and other services—services that are also carried out in the home office. This duplication, naturally, can be costly. Finally, geographic departmentation may increase the problem of control by top managers at the headquarters, who may find it difficult to monitor the activities of the departments located in various territories.

CUSTOMER DEPARTMENTATION

Grouping activities so that they reflect a primary interest in customers is common in a variety of enterprises. Customers are the key to the way activities are grouped when each of the different things an enterprise does for them is managed by one department head. The industrial sales department of a wholesaler that also sells to retailers is a case in point. Business owners and managers frequently arrange activities on this basis to cater to the requirements of clearly defined customer groups, and educational institutions offer regular and extension courses to serve different groups of students.

There are difficult decisions to be made in separating some types of customer departments from product departments. For example, in the great central cash markets for agricultural products, the loan officers of commercial banks frequently specialize in fruit, vegetables, or grain, even to the point where an individual officer will make loans only on wheat or oranges. This is a case of customer departmentation, since loan service is provided by type of customer. Figure 10-3 illustrates a typical customer departmentation in a large bank.

Advantages

Customer departmentation can address the special and widely varied needs of customers for clearly defined services. The manufacturer that sells to both whole-

FIGURE 10-3

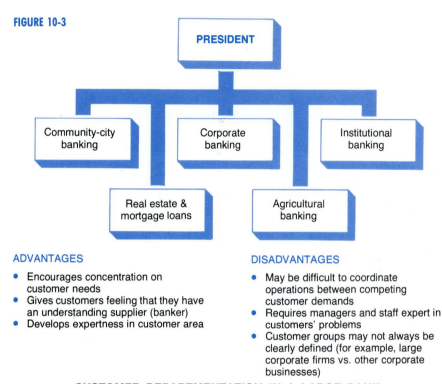

ADVANTAGES

- Encourages concentration on customer needs
- Gives customers feeling that they have an understanding supplier (banker)
- Develops expertness in customer area

DISADVANTAGES

- May be difficult to coordinate operations between competing customer demands
- Requires managers and staff expert in customers' problems
- Customer groups may not always be clearly defined (for example, large corporate firms vs. other corporate businesses)

CUSTOMER DEPARTMENTATION IN A LARGE BANK.

salers and industrial buyers frequently can meet their special needs by setting up separate departments. This kind of departmentation demonstrates the company's willingness to understand the business of its clients. At the same time, the company supplying the product or service gains expertise in the businesses of its customers.

Nonbusiness groups follow similar practices. The extension services of universities, such as night-school divisions, are arranged, with respect to time, subject matter, and sometimes instructors, to appeal to an entirely different group of students than those who attend the university on a full-time day basis. The operations of a United Way drive are arranged on the basis of different "customer" classifications. And departments of the federal government are set up to care for farmers, businesspeople, industrial workers, the elderly, and other specific groups.

Disadvantages

Customer departmentation is not without certain drawbacks. There is, for instance, the difficulty of coordination between customer departments, and those organized on other bases, with constant pressure from the managers of customer departments for special treatment. Moreover, customer departmentation requires managers and staff specialists familiar with the customers' situations. In addition, differentiation among the various customer groups (for example, large corporations versus medium-size firms) might be difficult.

Another disadvantage is the possibility of underemployment of facilities and labor-specialized workers in customer groups. In recession periods, some customer groups (for example, machine-tool buyers) may all but disappear; in expansion periods, unequal development of customer groups and demands is characteristic.

PROCESS OR EQUIPMENT DEPARTMENTATION

Manufacturing firms often group activities around a process or a type of equipment. Such a basis of departmentation can be found in paint or electroplating process grouping or in the arrangement in one plant area of punch presses or automatic screw machines. In this kind of departmentation, people and materials are brought together in order to carry out a particular operation. Figure 10-4 illustrates such an organizational arrangement.

One common example of equipment departmentation is the electronic data processing department. As installations for data processing have become expensive and complex, with ever-increasing capacities, they have tended to be organized in a separate department. Most large and even medium-size companies have such departments. In some cases, computer stations connected to an enterprise's central computer (or to an outside one on a time-sharing or leasing basis), minicomputers, and electronic desktop computers have tended to slow the growth of centralized computer departments. However, major data processing departments will unquestionably continue to exist and to be placed fairly high in the organization structure.

DEPARTMENTATION BY PRODUCT

Grouping activities on the basis of products or product lines has been growing in importance in multiline, large-scale enterprises. It can be seen as an evolutionary process. Typically, companies and other enterprises adopting this form of departmentation were organized by enterprise function. With the growth of the firm, production managers, sales and service managers, and engineering executives encountered problems of size. The managerial job became complex, and the span of management limited the managers' ability to increase the number of immediate subordinate managers. At this point, reorganization on a product division basis became necessary. This structure permits top management to delegate to a division executive extensive authority over the manufacturing, sales, service, and engineering functions that relate to a given product or product line and to exact a considerable degree of profit responsibility from each of these managers. Figure 10-5 shows an example of a typical product organization grouping for a manufacturing company.[4]

Advantages

Product or product line is an important basis for departmentation because it facilitates the use of specialized capital (for example, a press for molding car bodies), promotes a certain type of coordination, and permits the maximum use of personal

FIGURE 10-4

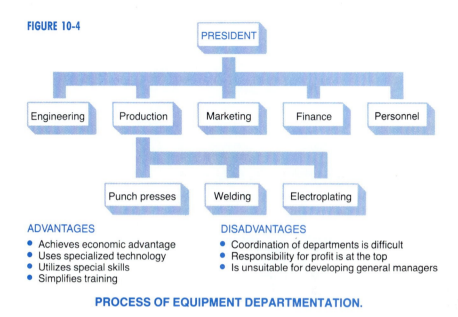

ADVANTAGES
- Achieves economic advantage
- Uses specialized technology
- Utilizes special skills
- Simplifies training

DISADVANTAGES
- Coordination of departments is difficult
- Responsibility for profit is at the top
- Is unsuitable for developing general managers

PROCESS OF EQUIPMENT DEPARTMENTATION.

skills and specialized knowledge. For example, the sales effort of a particular person may be most effective when confined to lubricants, or conveyors, or power plants, each of which is best sold by an expert thoroughly familiar with the product. For companies whose potential volume of business is high enough to justify fully employing such salespeople, the advantages of product departmentation are significant. If production of an item, or closely related items, is on a scale sufficient to warrant fully specialized facilities, strong pressure may be felt for product departmentation in order to realize economic advantages in manufacturing, assembly, or handling. Note also that this kind of departmentation permits growth and diversity of products and services offered by the firm.

If it is important for activities relating to a particular product to be coordinated, then product departmentation may be preferred. Better timing and customer service can thus sometimes be provided. If sales and engineering efforts are also located in the plant, cooperation with production can be exceptionally good. However, other factors, which will be considered later, may reduce this advantage.

Finally, profit responsibility can be exacted from product department managers. When such executives supervise the sales, production, engineering, service, and cost functions, they may be held responsible for certain profit goals. Along with the managers of other similarly organized groups, they have the responsibility of producing a profit, and this enables top managers to evaluate more intelligently the contribution of each product line to total profit. Moreover, this kind of departmentation provides a measurable training ground for general managers.

Some Notes of Caution

In considering these advantages, however, it is essential to avoid oversimplification. Product-line managers may be saddled with heavy overhead costs, allocated from

FIGURE 10-5

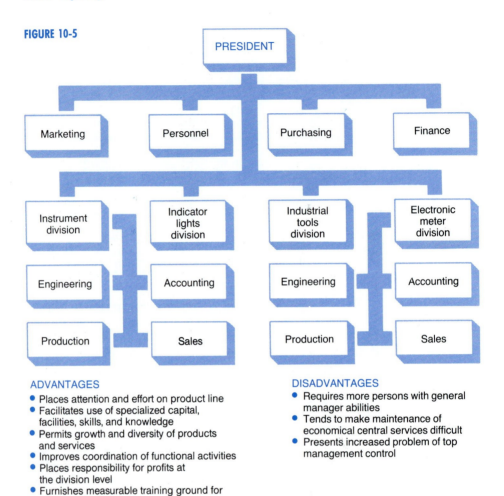

ADVANTAGES
- Places attention and effort on product line
- Facilitates use of specialized capital, facilities, skills, and knowledge
- Permits growth and diversity of products and services
- Improves coordination of functional activities
- Places responsibility for profits at the division level
- Furnishes measurable training ground for general managers

DISADVANTAGES
- Requires more persons with general manager abilities
- Tends to make maintenance of economical central services difficult
- Presents increased problem of top management control

A PRODUCT ORGANIZATION GROUPING (MANUFACTURING COMPANY).

the expense of operating the headquarters office, perhaps a central research division, and, frequently, many central service divisions. Product managers understandably resent being charged with costs over which they have no control.

Disadvantages

The disadvantages of product departmentation are similar to those of territorial departmentation. They include the necessity of having available more persons with general managerial abilities, the dangers of increased costs through duplication of central service and staff activities, and the problem of maintaining top-management control. The latter is especially important because a product division manager is, to a very great extent, in the same position as the chief executive of a single-product-line company. Enterprises that operate with product divisions must have enough decision making and control at the headquarters level to ensure that the entire enterprise does not disintegrate.

MATRIX ORGANIZATION[5]

Another kind of departmentation is matrix or grid organization, or project or product management. As will be explained later, however, pure project management need not imply a grid or matrix. The essence of **matrix organization** normally is the combining of functional and project or product patterns of departmentation in the same organization structure. As shown in Figure 10-6, which depicts matrix organization in an engineering department, there are functional managers in charge of engineering functions and an overlay of project managers responsible for the end product. While this form has been common in engineering and in research and development, it has also been widely used, although seldom drawn as a matrix, in product marketing organization.

This kind of organization occurs frequently in construction (for example, building a bridge), in aerospace (for example, designing and launching a weather satellite), in marketing (for example, planning and executing an advertising campaign for a major new product), in the installation of an electronic data processing system, or in management consulting firms in which professional experts work together on a project.[6]

Why Matrix Management Is Used

As companies and customers have become increasingly interested in end results, that is, in the final product or completed project, there has been pressure to establish responsibility for ensuring such end results. Of course, this could be accomplished by organizing along traditional product department lines. This is often done, even in engineering, where a project manager is put in charge of all the engineering and support personnel necessary to accomplish an entire project. This kind of organization is depicted in Figure 10-7.

But pure project organization may not be feasible for a number of reasons. For example, the project may not be able to utilize certain specialized engineering personnel or equipment full time: a solid-state physicist may be needed only occasionally, or the project may need only part-time use of an expensive environmental test laboratory or a prototype shop. Also, the project may be of relatively short duration. Although there is no logical reason why an organization structure should not be changed daily or monthly, there is the practical reason that people, particularly highly trained professionals, simply may not tolerate the insecurity of frequent organization change. Another reason why pure project organization may not be feasible is that highly trained professionals (and some that are not so highly trained) generally prefer to be allied organizationally with their professional group. They feel more at home in the functional department; they feel that their professional reputation and advancement will be better served by belonging to such a

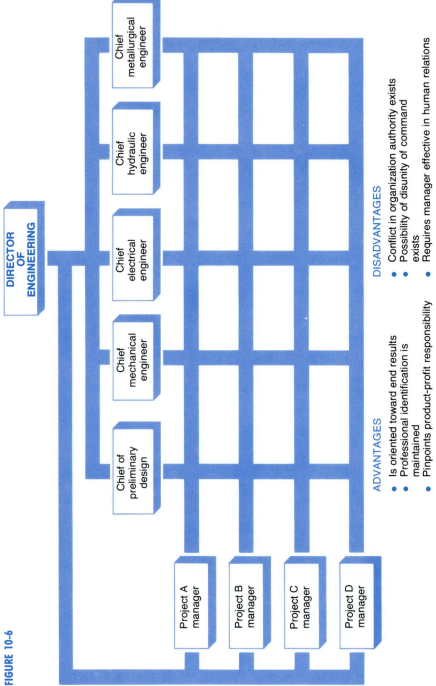

FIGURE 10-6

ADVANTAGES

- Is oriented toward end results
- Professional identification is maintained
- Pinpoints product-profit responsibility

DISADVANTAGES

- Conflict in organization authority exists
- Possibility of disunity of command exists
- Requires manager effective in human relations

MATRIX ORGANIZATION IN ENGINEERING.

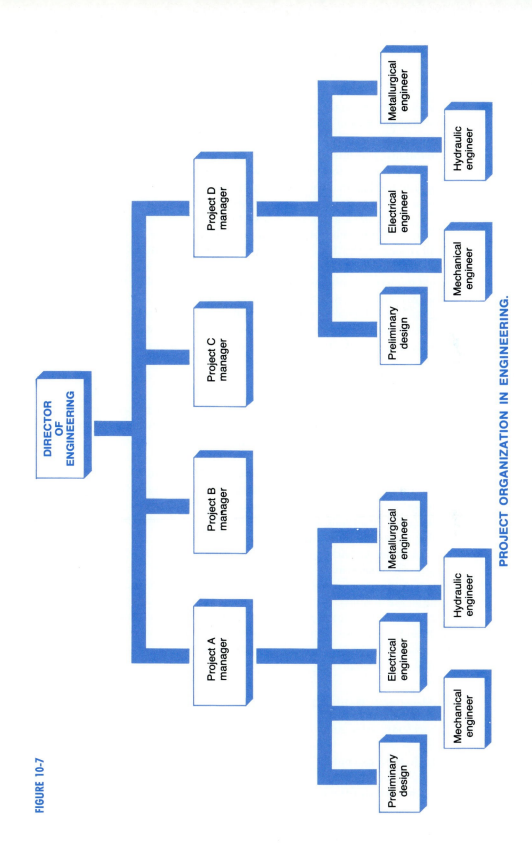

FIGURE 10-7

PROJECT ORGANIZATION IN ENGINEERING.

group than by being allied with a project; and they believe that their superiors, if they are professionals in the same field, will be more likely to appreciate their expertise at times of salary advances, promotions, or layoffs. These feelings ordinarily exist not only among engineers and scientists but also among lawyers, accountants, and university professors.

The reasons for the existence of a matrix organization in commercial or industrial product management may be somewhat different. In a soap and detergent company, for example, the top management may want individual responsibility for profit to exist for a given product or brand. If the company had only one product or brand, there would obviously be no problem; the chief executive would have profit responsibility. If the company could organize through the use of an integrated (research, marketing, manufacturing) product division, then the division manager would have profit responsibility. But where, as in a multiproduct soap and detergent company, technology and economics dictate that the company can hardly have separate manufacturing facilities or sales forces for each product, the way to get a degree of profit responsibility is to overlay, in some way, a product manager with responsibility for profit for a given brand or product.

Variations in Practice

There are many variations of the project or product manager role. In some cases, the project or product managers have no authority to tell any functional department to do anything; they may be only information gatherers, keeping tabs on how their project or product is proceeding and reporting to a top executive when significant deviations from plans occur. In other cases, they might be persuaders, using knowledge and personal persuasiveness to get results. Obviously, these roles have some very serious drawbacks, particularly if the manager without any organization power whatsoever is actually held responsible for end results. No wonder that turnover among those who hold such positions has been high!

Another variation in practice is simply to draw a grid or matrix, like that in Figure 10-6, showing certain managers in charge of functional departments and others in charge of projects or products. This grid is usually intended to represent a pure case of dual command. The results are predictable. If something goes wrong with a project or product, it is often difficult for a top superior to know who is at fault and where the difficulties really lie. Also, in such cases, there tend to arise the usual friction, buck-passing, and confusion one would expect to result from disunity of command.

Problems with Matrix Management

Let us summarize some typical problems found in matrix management.[7]

1. A state of conflict exists between functional and project managers, as both compete for limited resources (for example, financial and human). Moreover, members of the project team may encounter role ambiguity.

2. Role conflict, role ambiguity, and role overload may result in stress for the functional and project managers as well as for the team members.
3. An imbalance of authority and power, as well as horizontal and vertical influence of the project and functional managers, can also lead to problems in matrix organizations.[8] If, for example, the functional manager has too much power, work on a particular project may receive a low priority, thereby delaying its completion. An imbalance of authority in favor of the project manager, on the other hand, may result in inefficiencies. The functional manager, for example, may frequently be required to change the machine setup to accommodate work on various projects.
4. Because of the potential conflicts, managers may want to protect themselves against blame by putting everything in writing, which increases administration costs.
5. Matrix organization requires many time-consuming meetings.[9]

Guidelines for Making Matrix Management Effective[10]

Matrix management can be made more effective by following these guidelines:

1. Define the objectives of the project or task.
2. Clarify the roles, authority, and responsibilities of managers and team members.
3. Ensure that influence is based on knowledge and information, rather than on rank.
4. Balance the power of functional and project managers.
5. Select an experienced manager for the project who can provide leadership.
6. Undertake organization and team development.
7. Install appropriate cost, time, and quality controls that report deviations from standards in a timely manner.
8. Reward project managers and team members fairly.

STRATEGIC BUSINESS UNITS (SBUs)

More recently, companies have been using an organizational device generally referred to as a **strategic business unit** (SBU). SBUs are distinct little businesses set up as units in a larger company to ensure that a certain product or product line is promoted and handled as though it were an independent business. One of the earlier users of this organizational device was the General Electric Company. This special organization unit was introduced to ensure that each product or product line of the hundreds offered by the company would receive the same attention as it would if it were developed, produced, and marketed by an independent company. In some cases companies have also used the device for a major product line. Occidental Chemical Company, for example, used it for such products as phosphates, alkalies, and resins.[11]

To be called an SBU, a business unit must meet specific criteria. An SBU, for example, must (1) have its own mission, distinct from the mission of other SBUs, (2) have definable groups of competitors, (3) prepare its own integrative plans, fairly distinct from those of other SBUs, (4) manage its resources in key areas, and (5) have a proper size—neither too large nor too small.[12] Obviously, in practice it might be difficult to define SBUs that meet all of these criteria.

For each SBU a manager (usually a "business manager") is appointed with responsibility for guiding and promoting the product from the research laboratory through product engineering, market research, production, packaging, and marketing and with bottom-line responsibility for its profitability.[13] Thus, an SBU is given its own mission and goals, as well as a manager who, with the assistance of a full-time or part-time staff (people from other departments assigned to the SBU on a part-time basis), will develop and implement strategic and operating plans for the product. The organization of a typical SBU, that for phosphates in the Occidental Chemical Company, is shown in Figure 10-8. Note that reporting to the business manager for phosphates are all the functions that would be found necessary in a separate company.

Obviously, the major benefit of utilizing an SBU organization is to provide assurance that a product will not get "lost" among other products (usually those with larger sales and profits) in a large company. It preserves the attention and energies of a manager and staff whose job it is to guide and promote a product or product line. It is thus an organizational technique for preserving the entrepreneurial attention and drive so characteristic of the small company. In fact, it is an excellent means of promoting entrepreneurship, which is likely to be so lacking in the large company.[14]

Perspective

Restructuring at AT&T[15]

After the 5 years that it took to break up the Bell System, AT&T's long-distance market share dropped from about 84 percent to 68 percent. The company has restructured since the breakup, establishing business units divided into several groups headed by group executives.

There are a variety of reasons for the decentralized decision making. One of them is to give lower-level managers profit responsibility for their units. Moreover, it is hoped that the new structure will reduce battles over cost allocations. For example, in the past the research and development cost allocation resulted in considerable discord among various organizational units.

Reorganization, however, may cause problems with customers and suppliers. They are concerned that the contact persons within AT&T too often change; this stands in the way of developing more permanent business relationships.

At any rate, organization structures must be reviewed from time to time so that the organization not only works smoothly internally but also responds to the changing needs in the external environment.

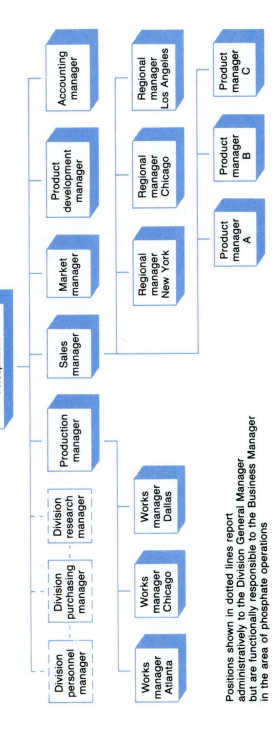

FIGURE 10-8

GENERAL MANAGER
Industrial Chemicals

BUSINESS MANAGER
Phosphates

Division personnel manager

Division purchasing manager

Division research manager

Production manager

Works manager Atlanta

Works manager Chicago

Works manager Dallas

Sales manager

Market manager

Product development manager

Accounting manager

Regional manager New York

Regional manager Chicago

Regional manager Los Angeles

Product manager A

Product manager B

Product manager C

Positions shown in dotted lines report
administratively to the Division General Manager
but are functionally responsible to the Business Manager
in the area of phosphate operations

**TYPICAL STRATEGIC BUSINESS UNIT ORGANIZATION
IN A LARGE INDUSTRIAL CHEMICAL COMPANY.**

ORGANIZATION STRUCTURES FOR THE GLOBAL ENVIRONMENT

Organization structures differ greatly for enterprises operating in the global environment. The kind of structure depends on a variety of factors, such as the degree of international orientation and commitment. A company, for example, may begin internationalizing its operation by simply creating at its headquarters an international department, headed by an export manager. As the company expands its international operation, foreign subsidiaries and later international divisions may be established in various countries, reporting to a manager in charge of global operation at headquarters or possibly the CEO. With additional growth of the international operations, several countries may be grouped into regions, such as Africa, Asia, Europe, and South America. Furthermore, the European division (and other divisions as well) may then be divided into groups of countries—for example, the European Community countries, non-EC countries (such as Austria, Sweden, Norway, and Switzerland), and Eastern European countries (such as Czechoslovakia, Poland, and Hungary).

While the focus above was on international geographic structures, companies may also choose functional or process departmentation in addition to the geographic pattern. For example, an oil company may subdivide the functional group for exploration according to the regions, such as exploration in Alaska or exploration in the Persian Gulf. Similarly, the functional groups of refining and marketing may be subdivided into the various regions. Clearly, petroleum products may be marketed in different areas than those where exploration or production takes place.

CHOOSING THE PATTERN OF DEPARTMENTATION

There is no one best way of departmentizing that is applicable to all organizations and all situations.[16] Managers must determine what is best by looking at the situation they face—the jobs to be done and the way they should be done, the people involved and their personalities, the technology employed in the department, the users being served, and other internal and external environmental factors in the situation. However, if they know the various departmentation patterns, and the advantages, disadvantages, and dangers of each, practicing managers should be able to design the organization structure most suitable for their particular operations.[17]

The Aim: Achieving Objectives

Departmentation is not an end in itself but is simply a method of arranging activities to facilitate the accomplishment of objectives. Each method has its advantages and disadvantages. Consequently, the process of selection involves a consideration of the relative advantages of each pattern at each level in the organization structure. In all cases, the central question concerns the type of organizational environment that the manager wishes to design and the situation being faced. The preceding discussion of the alternative methods of departmentation showed that each method yields certain gains and involves certain costs.

Mixing Types of Departmentation

Another point to be highlighted concerns the mixing of types of departmentation within a functional area. For example, a wholesale drug firm has grouped the buying and selling activities relating to beverages in one product department, but it has grouped, on the same level, all other selling activities on a territorial basis. A manufacturer of plastic goods has territorialized both the production and the sale of all its products except dinnerware, which is itself a product department. A functional department manager may, in other words, employ two or more bases for grouping activities on the same organizational level. Such practices may be justified on logical grounds: The objective of departmentation is not to build a rigid structure, balanced in terms of levels and characterized by consistency and identical bases, but to group activities in the manner that will best contribute to achieving enterprise objectives. If a variety of bases does this, there is no reason why managers should not take advantage of the alternatives before them.

The logic of this view is frequently ignored by those who design organization structures. For some reason, possibly to make an organization chart look pretty or to maintain control, specialists often insist that all departmentized activities below the primary level of organization be grouped in exactly the same manner. For instance, the organization structure of the Internal Revenue Service at the regional and district levels is essentially the same, despite tremendous variation in district sizes.

International Perspective

Organizational Structure at Unilever

Unilever, the Anglo-Dutch multinational corporation, has a top-management team consisting of the chairperson and two vice chairpersons. The executive officers are grouped into (1) functional areas: personnel, finance, commercial, research, controller, and treasurer, (2) product groups: food and drinks, detergents, frozen products, chemicals, personal products, agribusinesses, and edible fats and dairy products, and (3) geographic regions: Europe, East Asia and the Pacific, North America, Latin America, and Central Asia.

SUMMARY

The grouping of activities and people into departments makes organizational expansion possible. Departmentation can be done by simple numbers, by time, by enterprise function, by territory or geography, by the kinds of customers served, and by the process or equipment required. Relatively new kinds of departmentation are the product organization grouping, matrix or grid organization, project organization, and the strategic business unit (SBU). Organization structures for the global environment may vary greatly, ranging from an export department at the headquarters to regional groupings, with many variations in between. In addition, companies may have one or more functionally organized groupings within an individual region.

There is no single best way to organize; the most appropriate pattern depends on various factors in a given situation. These factors include the kind of job to be done, the way the task must be done, the kinds of people involved, the technology, the people served, and other internal and external considerations. At any rate, the selection of a specific departmentation pattern should be done so that organizational and individual objectives can be achieved effectively and efficiently. Accomplishing this goal often requires mixing forms of departmentation.

KEY IDEAS AND CONCEPTS FOR REVIEW

Departmentation by simple numbers
Departmentation by time
Departmentation by enterprise function
Departmentation by territory or
   geography
Customer departmentation

Process or equipment departmentation
Departmentation by product
Matrix organization (or grid, or project,
   or product)
Strategic business units (SBUs)

FOR DISCUSSION

1. Some sociologists tell us that organization structuring is a social invention. What do you think they mean? Do they imply that there is a "right" or "wrong" way to organize? What test of whether an organization structure is "right" would you suggest?
2. If you were the president of a company that was organized along functional lines and a consultant suggested that you organize along territorial or product lines, what might concern you in following this recommendation?
3. Why do you think that many large companies have organized along product lines (e.g., General Motors and Du Pont), while other large companies have territorial departments (e.g., Prudential Life Insurance Company)?
4. Why do most large department store and supermarket chains organize their stores on a territorial basis and then organize the internal store units by products? Give examples from your own experience.
5. Why do most small companies use functionally organized departments?
6. Why are so many federal government agencies organized primarily on a territorial basis?
7. Do you see any reasons why managing by objectives may result in increased use of matrix organizational structures?
8. How does this chapter illustrate a situational approach to management?

EXERCISES/ACTION STEPS

1. Divide the class into groups of four or five students (depending on class size). Assign one pattern of departmentation to each group (assign two to each if the class is small). The groups should discuss (a) the nature of the assigned departmentation, (b) companies that use this departmental arrangement, (c) the advantages of the departmentation, and (d) the disadvantages of the departmentation.

2. Select a company and identify the departmentation pattern (or patterns) used by the enterprise. Draw an organization chart for the firm. Why do you think the company selected the type of departmentation it did? Would you recommend a different departmentation arrangement? State your reasons for your recommendation.

CASES

CASE 10-1
AGRICULTURAL FERTILIZER DIVISION OF THE NORTHERN CHEMICAL CORPORATION

At the end of a busy day, a group of middle-level managers of the Agricultural Fertilizer Division of the Northern Chemical Corporation gathered to reflect on their problems. The headquarters of Northern Chemical had recently set up a central data processing department in Houston, where all the corporation's data processing would be done for its various divisions located throughout the United States. At that time, the data processing equipment of every division had been taken away; each division headquarters office was given a terminal connected to Houston, and each division was required to get any report processing it needed from the Houston facility.

The headquarters of the Agricultural Fertilizer Division was located in Sacramento, California. This division had long concentrated on developing and selling fertilizers to the large agricultural growers in the West and on distributing its garden and house plant fertilizers to stores throughout the country. It had been very successful, with sales growing rapidly and profits even faster. But the line managers of the division were quite unhappy about not being able to have their own computer facilities to give them the analyses and reports they needed.

Bill Jacobs, production planning and control supervisor, was particularly disturbed about the change to centralized data processing. "There is no way," said Jacobs, "that I can plan our products, especially with our many products and customers and the demands of our large growers for good service, if Houston runs our programs. The people there do not always have the data needed in their data bank, and, by the time I get it worked out with them, I have lost much valuable time."

Barry Hill, district sales manager for Northern California, was even unhappier. He pointed out that he often needed to run productivity and profitability studies for large growers and that he could not do so unless the division had a computer operation in its own offices in Sacramento. "The growers will never understand why I cannot make these analyses for them quickly, nor will they understand why they must be made in Houston; they will soon tell me that there are other companies that can serve their needs," moaned Hill.

"You do have a problem," said Mona Fredericks, head of statistical analyses and reports in the division controller's office. "But yours is a small one compared with mine. I have to get many special and regular reports to headquarters, to the division managers, and to all you people in sales, market research, product development, and production. You always want them right away and in the form you can use most easily. How can I do that for you now?"

The frustration reached its peak when Joe Morey, cost control supervisor, startled the group by saying: "Did you know that all the departments in our division are being charged fees each month for Houston's services and that these are higher than the costs when we each had our own little computer system?"

1. Do you agree that these people have a serious problem?
2. If you were one of them, what would you do about it?
3. If you were to view this purely as an organization problem, what conclusions would you draw and what suggestions would you make?

INTERNATIONAL CASE 10-2
SIEMENS, THE SLEEPING GIANT[18]

Siemens, the over-140-year-old German giant, is loaded with cash. The company generates its revenues from energy and automation, nuclear power, PBXs (private branch exchanges) and computers, telecommunication and security systems, medical equipment, electrical and automotive products, and a variety of other sources. There is some concern that the proliferation of products may be detrimental.

The company's some 365,000 employees will face a different environment in the future through the EC 1992 program, which eliminated trade barriers for the twelve member states of the European Community. In the past, Siemens benefited from profitable state contracts. For example, the company sold cordless telephones to the state at a price eight times higher than the price of Japanese products.

The goal of the CEO, Karl-Heinz Kaske, is to transform the sleeping organization into an aggressive multinational corporation battling with companies such as AT&T in the field of telecommunications and with General Electric in factory automation. The key building block in the new strategy is microelectronics. Indeed, the company spent more on research and development than its competitors, yet it lags behind many of them in profit margins.

To prepare for the new competitive environment, the company started reorganization. In 1988 two layers of management were eliminated, and the following year the seven operating divisions were transformed into fifteen (later reduced to thirteen) organizational units with separate sales and marketing personnel. This should speed up, for example, the approval of new products. Unprofitable lines are being shut down, an approach very uncommon in German industries. Managers who expected lifetime employ-

ment are concerned. Telecommunications, which lost over $100 million a year, will be compared with the medical unit, which showed an annual growth rate of 17 percent.

In the past, the corporate culture placed a high value on technology but de-emphasized marketing. This is changing. Siemens is redirecting its focus on market share not only within Europe but also in the United States and Japan—two very important markets.

The power of Central Research was reduced by giving more responsibility to the business units to do the application-driven research; Central Research now focuses on basic research. Furthermore, business units not only have more responsibility for research but also are held more accountable for their costs. Actually, Siemens can look back at over 140 years of innovations. Here are some examples: The pointer telegraph was patented in 1847, the first electric railway in 1879, the world's first telex network in 1938, the world's first high-performance laser printer in 1977, and the first European-built 1-megabit chips in 1988. However, the organization structure that was appropriate in the past may not serve the future competitive, global market.

1. How can one demonstrate to the cash-rich organization that change is necessary.
2. What kind of organization structure would you recommend to Siemens to help it prepare for a future strongly influenced by the EC 1992 program and the competitive U.S. market?
3. How should research and development activities be organized?

REFERENCES

1. Tom Peters, "Restoring American Competitiveness: Looking for New Models of Organizations," *Academy of Management Executive* (May 1988), p. 103.
2. Jay R. Galbraith, "Matrix Organization Designs: How to Combine Functional and Project Forms," in Harold Koontz, Cyril O'Donnell, and Heinz Weihrich (eds.), *Management: A Book of Readings*, 5th ed. (New York: McGraw-Hill Book Company, 1980), pp. 292–300.
3. Thomas J. Peters and Robert H. Waterman, Jr., *In Search of Excellence* (New York: Harper & Row, 1982).
4. Product management is also used in nonmanufacturing companies. See, for example, Robert B. Fetter and Jean L. Freeman, "Diagnosis Related Groups: Product Line Management within Hospitals," *Academy of Management Review* (January 1986), pp. 41–54.
5. See also Christopher A. Bartlett and Sumantra Ghoshal, "Matrix Management: Not a Structure, a Frame of Mind," *Harvard Business Review* (July–August 1990), pp. 138–145.
6. John M. Stewart, "Making Project Management Work," in Harold Koontz and Cyril O'Donnell (eds.), *Management: A Book of Readings*, 2d ed. (New York: McGraw-Hill Book Company, 1968), pp. 202–213; Kenneth Knight, in Koontz, O'Donnell, and Weihrich, *Management* (1980), pp. 301–312.
7. Based primarily on Knight, in *Management* (1980).
8. Although not directly related to matrix organization, an interesting discussion of power relationships can be found in Fernando Bartolome and Andre Laurent, "The Manager: Master and Servant of Power," *Harvard Business Review* (November–December 1986), pp. 77–81.
9. For additional information on limitations of matrix management, see Robert A. Pitts and John D. Daniels, "Aftermath of the Matrix Mania," *Columbia Journal of World Business* (Summer 1984), pp. 48–54.
10. Stewart, in *Management* (1968); Knight, in *Management* (1980); Jay Galbraith, *Designing Complex Organizations* (Reading, Mass.: Addison-Wesley Publishing Company, 1973), chap. 5. See also William H. Hoffmann, "Strategy Matrix," *Managerial Planning* (May–June 1985), pp. 4–9, 75.
11. For a discussion of SBUs, see W. K. Hall, "SBUs: Hot, New Topic in the Management of Diversification," *Business Horizons* (February 1978), pp. 13–23.
12. Frederick W. Gluck, "A Fresh Look at Strategic Management," *Journal of Business Strategy* (Fall 1985), pp. 4–19.
13. For a discussion of the effective use of business units, see Boris Yavitz and William H. Newman, "What the Corporation Should Provide Its Business Units," *Journal of Business Strategy* (Summer 1982), pp. 14–19.
14. For a critique of SBUs, see, for example, C. K. Prahalad and Gary Hamel, "The Core Competence of the Corporation," *Harvard Business School* (May–July 1990), pp. 79–91.
15. Janet Guyon, "AT&T to Break Main Businesses into Small Units," *The Wall Street Journal* (Feb. 17, 1989).
16. An argument for using relatively simple organizational forms, even for multinational companies, has been made after a study of four Swedish firms by Gunnar Hedlund, "Organization In-Between: The Evolution of the Mother-Daughter Structure of Managing Foreign Subsidiaries in Swedish MNCs," *Journal of International Business Studies* (Fall 1984), pp. 109–122.

17. For an interesting review of books on organizing, see P. H. Ginyer, "Designing Effective Organizations—Book Review Article," *Long Range Planning* (April 1984), pp. 151–156.

18. The case is based on a variety of sources, including Gail Schares, John J. Keller, Thane Peterson, and Mark Marmont, "Siemens: A Plodding Giant Starts to Pick Up Speed," *Business Week* (Feb. 20, 1989), pp. 136–138; Karl Heinrich Ruessmann, "The Second Shock," *Manager Magazine* (February 1991); Barbara N. Berkman, "Rebuilding the House of Siemens on a Worldwide Foundation," *Electronic Business* (Aug. 6, 1990), pp. 28–32; Teri Sprackland, "Siemens Buys Big to Profit Little in the U.S.," *Electronic Business* (Aug. 6, 1990), pp. 34–35; Gail E. Schares, Jonathan B. Levine, and Peter Coy, "The New Generation at Siemens," *Business Week* (March 9, 1992), pp. 46–48.

Delegation of authority must be real. It includes not only what a superior says to his/her subordinate, but also the way in which he/she acts.[1]

John G. Staiger

Line/Staff Authority and Decentralization

Chapter Objectives

After reading this chapter, you should be able to:

1. Understand the nature of authority and power.
2. Distinguish between line and staff, realizing their nature as relationships rather than positions or people.
3. Explain the nature and use of functional authority as a mixture of line and staff.
4. Discuss the nature of centralization, decentralization, and delegation of authority.
5. Explain the factors that generally determine the degree of decentralization.
6. Recognize the importance of obtaining balance in the centralization and decentralization of authority.

Now that the patterns of departmentation have been discussed, it is time to consider another essential question: What kind of authority is found in an organizational structure? The question has to do with the nature of authority relationships—the problem of line and staff. This chapter will also deal with the question: How much authority should be delegated? The answer concerns decentralization of authority. Without authority—the power to exercise discretion in making decisions—properly placed in managers, various departments cannot become smoothly working units harmonized for the accomplishment of enterprise objectives. Authority relationships, whether vertical or horizontal, are the factors that make organization possible, facilitate departmental activities, and bring coordination to an enterprise.

AUTHORITY AND POWER

Before concentrating on the authority in organization, it will be useful to distinguish between authority and power. **Power,** a much broader concept than authority, is the ability of individuals or groups to induce or influence the beliefs or actions of other persons or groups.[2] **Authority** in organization is the right in a position (and, through it, the right of the person occupying the position) to exercise discretion in making decisions affecting others. It is, of course, one type of power, but power in an organization setting.

Although there are many different **bases of power,** the power of primary concern in this book is *legitimate* power.[3] It normally arises from position and derives from our cultural system of rights, obligations, and duties whereby a "position" is accepted by people as being "legitimate." In a privately owned business, authority of position arises primarily from the social institution (a "bundle of rights") of private property. In government, this authority arises basically from the institution of representative government. A traffic officer who gives you a traffic ticket gets the power to do so because we have a system of representative government in which we have elected legislators to make laws and provide for their enforcement.

Power may also come from the *expertness* of a person or a group. This is the power of knowledge. Physicians, lawyers, and university professors may have considerable influence on others because they are respected for their special knowledge. Power may further exist as *referent* power, that is, influence that people or groups may exercise because people believe in them and their ideas. Thus, Martin Luther King had very little legitimate power, but by the force of his personality, his ideas, and his ability to preach, he strongly influenced the behavior of many people. Likewise, a movie star or a military hero might possess considerable referent power.

In addition, power arises from the ability of some people to grant rewards. Purchasing agents, with little position power, might be able to exercise considerable influence through their ability to expedite or delay a much-needed spare part. Likewise, university professors have considerable *reward* power; they can grant or withhold high grades.

Coercive power is still another type. Although closely related to reward power and normally arising from legitimate power, it is the power to punish, whether by firing a subordinate or withholding a merit increase.

While organization authority is the power to exercise discretion in decision making, it almost invariably arises from the power of position, or legitimate power.[4] When people speak of authority in managerial settings, they are usually referring to the power of positions. At the same time, other factors, such as personality and style of dealing with people, are involved in leadership.[5]

LINE AND STAFF CONCEPTS

Much confusion has arisen both in the literature and among managers as to what "line" and "staff" are; as a result, there is probably no area of management that causes more difficulties, more friction, and more loss of time and effectiveness. Yet line and staff relationships are important as an organizational way of life, and the authority relationships of members of an organization must necessarily affect the operation of the enterprise.

One widely held view of line and staff is that line functions are those that have direct impact on the accomplishment of the objectives of the enterprise. On the other hand, staff functions are those that help the line persons work most effectively in accomplishing the objectives. The people who hold to this view almost invariably classify production and sales (and sometimes finance) as line functions and purchasing, accounting, personnel, plant maintenance, and quality control as staff functions.

The confusion arising from such a concept is immediately apparent. It is argued that purchasing, for example, merely helps in achieving the main goals of business because unlike the production departments, such as painting or parts assembly, it is not directly essential. But is purchasing really any less essential than production departments to the achievement of company objectives? Is it not possible for the company to store up painted or assembled parts and get along without these departments for a while, just as it could get along for a while without purchasing? And could not the same question be asked about other so-called staff and service departments, such as accounting, personnel, and plant maintenance? There is probably nothing that could stop the satisfactory production and sale of most manufactured goods more completely than the failure of quality control.

The Nature of Line and Staff Relationships[6]

A more precise and logically valid concept of line and staff is that they are simply a matter of relationships. Line authority gives a superior a line of authority over a subordinate.[7] It exists in all organizations as an uninterrupted scale or series of steps. Hence, the **scalar principle** in organization: *The clearer the line of authority from the ultimate management position in an enterprise to every subordinate position, the clearer will be the responsibility for decision making and the more effective will be organization communication.* In many large enterprises, the steps are long and complicated, but even in the smallest, the very fact of organization introduces the scalar principle.

It therefore becomes apparent from the scalar principle that **line** authority is that relationship in which a superior exercises direct supervision over a subordinate—an authority relationship in direct line or steps.

The nature of the **staff** relationship is advisory. The function of people in a pure staff capacity is to investigate, research, and give advice to line managers.

Perspective

Line or Staff? What Is Your Career Goal?

The goal of many M.B.A. graduates is to work in staff positions, using their analytical skills to advise line managers. It has been reported that in 1985 over a third of Harvard's M.B.A. graduates chose such a career.[8] In earlier years, this percentage was even higher.

In the 1980s, partly owing to the economy and the competitive pressure, the situation was changing as many large companies reduced their staff. For example, the task of strategy formulation was carried out more frequently by the line managers, who also had to implement the strategy, rather than by the strategic planners in headquarters. Consequently, people who used to plan, advise, and analyze business situations moved into line positions in which they were required to set priorities, make decisions, and motivate people to contribute to the aims of the enterprise.

While some staff personnel made an effective transition into line positions, others failed. One of the problems these "newcomers" encountered was the resentment of the "old-time" managers, who saw the positions they had aspired to taken by former staff. Clearly, line work is different from staff tasks. Having real authority for executing decisions can be exciting, but not everyone can make the transition. Thus, aspiring managers should carefully analyze their strengths, weaknesses, and motivations before choosing their career paths.

Line and Staff Relationships or Departmentation?[9]

Some managers and writers regard line and staff as types of departments. Although a department may stand in a predominantly line or staff position with respect to other departments, line and staff are distinguished by *authority relationships* and not by what people do.

For example, one may think of the public relations department, to the extent that it is primarily advisory to the top executives, as a staff department. But within the department are line relationships; the director will stand in a line authority position with respect to his or her immediate subordinates. On the other hand, the vice president in charge of production may head what is clearly and generally known as a line department. His or her job is not primarily advisory to the chief executive officer. If, however, the vice president counsels the chief executive on overall company production policy, the relationship becomes one of staff.

When one looks at an organization structure as a whole, the general character of line and staff relationships for the total organization emerges. Certain departments are predominantly staff in their relationship to the entire organization; other departments are primarily line.

Figure 11-1 shows a simplified organization chart of a manufacturing company. The activities of the director of research and the director of public relations are apt to be mainly advisory to the mainstream of corporate operations and are consequently often considered staff activities. The finance, production, and sales departments, with activities generally related to the main corporate functions, are ordinarily considered line departments.

Although it is often convenient and even correct to refer to one department as a line department and to another as a staff department, their activities do not so characterize the departments. Line and staff are characterized by relationships and not by departmental activities.

FUNCTIONAL AUTHORITY

Functional authority *is the right that is delegated to an individual or a department to control specified processes, practices, policies, or other matters relating to activities undertaken by persons in other departments.* If the principle of unity of command were followed without exception, authority over these activities would be exercised only by their line superiors. But numerous reasons—including a lack of special knowledge, a lack of ability to supervise processes, and the danger of diverse interpretations of policies—explain why these managers are occasionally not allowed to exercise this authority. In such cases, line managers are deprived of some authority. It is delegated by their common superior to a staff specialist or to a manager in another department. For example, a company controller is ordinarily given functional authority to prescribe the system of accounting throughout the company, but this specialized authority is really a delegation from the chief executive.

Functional authority is not restricted to managers of a particular type of department. It may be exercised by line, service, or staff department heads, but more

FIGURE 11-1

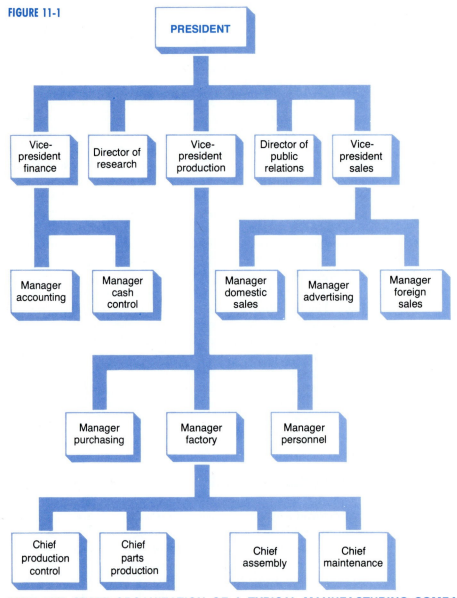

LINE AND STAFF ORGANIZATION OF A TYPICAL MANUFACTURING COMPANY.

often by the latter two because service and staff departments are usually composed of specialists whose knowledge becomes the basis for functional controls.

Delegation of Functional Authority

One can better understand functional authority by thinking of it as *a small slice of the authority of a line superior*. A corporation president, for example, has complete authority to manage a corporation, subject only to limitations placed by such superior authority as the board of directors, the corporate charter and bylaws, and government regulations. In the pure staff situation, the advisers on personnel, accounting, purchasing, or public relations have no part of this line authority, their duty being merely to offer counsel. But when the president delegates to these advisers the right to issue instructions directly to the line organizations, as shown in Figure 11-2, that right is called "functional authority."

The four staff and service executives have functional authority over the line organizations with respect to procedures in the fields of accounting, personnel,

FIGURE 11-2

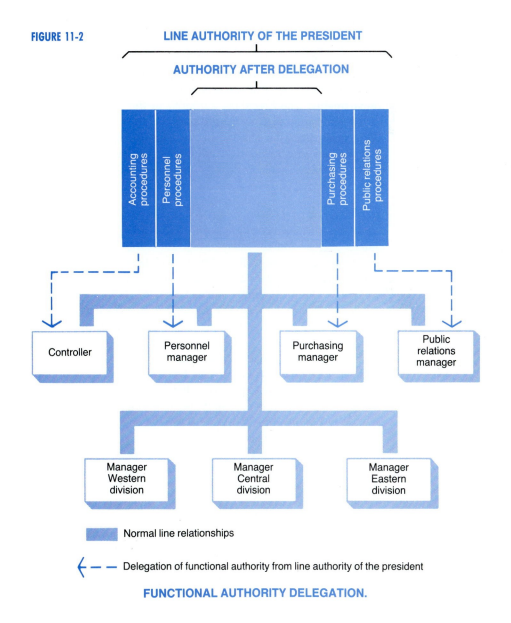

LINE AUTHORITY OF THE PRESIDENT

AUTHORITY AFTER DELEGATION

Accounting procedures

Personnel procedures

Purchasing procedures

Public relations procedures

Controller

Personnel manager

Purchasing manager

Public relations manager

Manager Western division

Manager Central division

Manager Eastern division

Normal line relationships

Delegation of functional authority from line authority of the president

FUNCTIONAL AUTHORITY DELEGATION.

purchasing, and public relations. What has happened is that the president, feeling it is unnecessary to clear such specialized matters personally, has delegated line authority to staff assistants (or managers) to issue their own instructions to the operating department. Of course, subordinate managers can use the same device, as in the case of a factory superintendent who delegates to cost, production control, and quality control supervisors the functional authority to prescribe procedures for the operating supervisors.

Restricting the Area of Functional Authority

Functional authority should be carefully restricted. A purchasing manager's functional authority, for example, is generally limited to setting the procedures for divisional or departmental purchasing and does not include telling departments what they can purchase or when. When these managers conduct certain purchasing activities that relate to the whole company, they are acting as heads of service departments. The functional authority of the personnel manager over the general line organization is likewise ordinarily limited to prescribing procedures for handling grievances, for sharing in the administration of wage and salary programs, and for handling vacation schedules and similar matters.

BENEFITS OF STAFF

There are, of course, many important benefits in using staff. The necessity of having the advice of well-qualified specialists in various areas of an organization's operations can scarcely be overestimated, especially as operations become more complex. The U.S. Army learned this the hard way in 1898: In the Spanish-American War, troops were sent into Cuba in woolen uniforms despite the tropical heat and were expected to take territory, although they lacked accurate road and topographic maps.

Today, staff advice is far more critical for business, government, and other enterprises than it was in the past. Operating managers are now faced with making decisions that require expert knowledge in economic, technical, political, legal, and social areas. Moreover, it may be necessary, in many instances where highly specialized knowledge is required, to give specialists some functional authority to make decisions for their bosses.

Another major advantage of staff is that these specialists may be allowed the time to think, to gather data, and to analyze, whereas their superiors, busy managing operations, cannot do so. It is a rare operating manager, especially at top levels, who has the time, or will take the time, to do those things that a staff assistant can do so well.

Therefore, not only can the staff help line managers to be effective, but as problems grow more complex, staff analysis and advice are becoming an urgent necessity. Moreover, despite the dangers of multiple command, functional authority delegated to staff specialists is often imperative.

LIMITATIONS OF STAFF

Although staff relationships are usually necessary to an enterprise and can do much to make it successful, the nature of staff authority and the difficulty of understanding it lead to certain problems in practice.

Danger of Undermining Line Authority

Operating managers often view staff personnel with skepticism. Too frequently, a president brings in staff executives, clothes them with authority (frequently very vague), and commands all other managers to cooperate. The proposals of staff specialists are received by the president with enthusiasm, and pressure is brought to bear upon the managers involved to put them into effect. What is actually taking place here is that the authority of department managers is being undermined; yet, grudgingly and resentfully, the proposals will be accepted because all will recognize the high tide of the staff specialists' prestige. A continuation of this situation might harm or even destroy operating departments. Capable managers, not willing to submit to indignity or wait until the tide ebbs, might resign; or they might put the matter bluntly to their boss—fire the staff specialists or get along without the line managers!

Operating departments represent the main line of the enterprise, and their managers gain a degree of indispensability. If staff advisers forget that they are to counsel and not to order, if they overlook the fact that their value lies in the extent to which they strengthen line managers, and if—worse yet—they undermine line authority, they risk becoming expendable. If there is an expendable person in an organization, it is likely to be the staff assistant.

Lack of Staff Responsibility

Advisory departments only propose a plan; others must make the decision to adopt the plan and put it into operation. This creates an ideal situation for shifting blame for mistakes. The staff will claim that it was a good plan and that it failed because the operating manager was unqualified, uninterested, or intent on sabotage. The manager who must make the plan work will claim that it was a poor plan hatched by inexperienced and impractical theorists.

Thinking in a Vacuum

The argument that a staff position gives planners time to think is appealing, but it overlooks an important point: Because staff people do not implement what they recommend, it is possible that staff may think in a vacuum. The alleged impracticality of staff recommendations often results in friction, loss of morale, and even sabotage.

Another weakness in the suggestion that planners must be set off from line departments in order to think is the implication that operating managers are without creative ability. They may, indeed, be without specialized knowledge, but this can be furnished by able staff assistants. Good operating managers can analyze plans, see long-range implications, and spot fatal weaknesses as well as, and sometimes better than, most staff assistants.

Managerial Problems

Few would deny the importance of maintaining unity of command. It is not easy for a department head to be responsible to two or more people; at the worker level, it may be disastrous to attempt multiple responsibility. Some disunity in command may be unavoidable, since functional authority relationships are often unavoidable. But managers should remain aware of the difficulties of multiple authority and should either limit it—even with the loss of some uniformity or of the fruits of specialization—or carefully clarify it.

Furthermore, too much staff activity may complicate a line executive's job of leadership and control. A corporation president may be so busy dealing with the recommendations of a large number of staff assistants and straightening twisted lines of authority that time and attention may not be available for operating departments. Similarly, a business may become so intent on making policies and setting procedures that there is little time left to make instruments or provide transportation service.

DECENTRALIZATION OF AUTHORITY

The previous sections focused on the kinds of authority relationships, such as line, staff, and functional authority. This section emphasizes the dispersion of authority in the organization.

The Nature of Decentralization

Organization authority is merely the discretion conferred on people to use their judgment to make decisions and issue instructions. **Decentralization** is the tendency to disperse decision-making authority in an organized structure. It is a fundamental aspect of delegation; to the extent that authority is not delegated, it

FIGURE 11-3

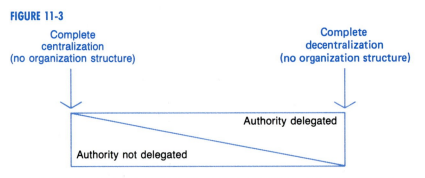

CENTRALIZATION AND DECENTRALIZATION AS TENDENCIES.

is centralized. How much should authority be concentrated in or dispersed throughout the organization? There could be absolute centralization of authority in one person, but that implies no subordinate managers and therefore no structured organization. Some decentralization exists in all organizations. On the other hand, there cannot be absolute decentralization, for if managers delegated all their authority, their status as managers would cease, their position would be eliminated, and there would, again, be no organization. Centralization and decentralization are tendencies, as indicated in Figure 11-3.

Different Kinds of Centralization

The term "centralization" has several meanings:

1. **Centralization of performance** pertains to geographic concentration; it characterizes, for example, a company operating in a single location.
2. **Departmental centralization** refers to concentration of specialized activities, generally in one department. For example, maintenance for a whole plant may be carried out by a single department.
3. **Centralization as an aspect of management** is the tendency to restrict delegation of decision making. A high degree of authority is held at or near the top by managers in the organizational hierarchy.

Decentralization as a Philosophy and Policy

Decentralization implies more than delegation: It reflects a philosophy of organization and management. It requires careful selection of which decisions to push down into the organization structure and which to hold near the top, specific policymaking to guide the decision making, proper selection and training of people, and adequate controls. A policy of decentralization affects all areas of management and can be looked upon as an essential element of a managerial system. In fact, without it, managers could not use their discretion to handle the ever-changing situations they face.

DELEGATION OF AUTHORITY*

As simple as delegation of authority appears to be, studies have shown that many managers fail because of poor delegation. Delegation is necessary for an organization to exist. Just as no one person in an enterprise can do all the tasks necessary for accomplishing a group purpose, so is it impossible, as an enterprise grows, for one person to exercise all the authority for making decisions. As explained in Chapter 9, there is a limit to the number of persons managers can effectively supervise and make decisions for. Once this limit has been passed, authority must be delegated to subordinates, who will make decisions within the area of their assigned duties.

---

* Some authors discuss the concept of "empowerment" in connection with delegation.

How Authority Is Delegated

Authority is delegated when a superior gives a subordinate discretion to make decisions. Clearly, superiors cannot delegate authority they do not have, whether they are board members, presidents, vice presidents, or supervisors.

The **process of delegation** involves (1) determining the results expected from a position, (2) assigning tasks to the position, (3) delegating authority for accomplishing these tasks, and (4) holding the person in that position responsible for the accomplishment of the tasks. In practice, it is impossible to split this process, since expecting a person to accomplish goals without giving authority to achieve them is unfair, as is delegating authority without knowing the end results for which it will be used. Moreover, since the superior's responsibility cannot be delegated, a boss must hold subordinates responsible for completing their assignments.

Splintered Authority

Splintered authority exists wherever a problem cannot be solved or a decision made without pooling the authority of two or more managers. For example, the superintendent of plant A may see an opportunity to reduce costs through a minor modification in her procedures and those in plant B, but her authority cannot encompass the change. But if the superintendents of the two plants can agree on the change (and if it affects no other managers), all they need to do is pool their authority and make the decision. Individually, their authority is said to be "splintered." In day-to-day operations of any company, there are many cases of splintered authority. Many managerial conferences are held because of the necessity of pooling authority to make a decision.

Such problems could be handled by merely referring the decision upward until it reaches a person with the authority to make it unilaterally. In the case of the two plant superintendents, it might lie within the authority of the vice president in charge of manufacturing. In many cases, the splinters of authority, although far down in the organization, exist in departments that have a common superior only in the office of the president.

One of the authors observed the solution of a problem involving a Western railroad whose headquarters was in Chicago. The problem was relatively minor, but a decision on it in Los Angeles required the consolidated authority of the traffic department, the operating department, and the public relations department. It could have been referred up the line by each of the managers to the president's office, where sufficient authority for making the decision was concentrated. But if such decisions were always handled by upward reference, the president's office would be swamped. In this case, the managers of the three departments in the Los Angeles office met briefly, pooled their delegated authority, and quickly made the decision.

Splintered authority cannot be wholly avoided in making decisions. However, recurring decisions on the same matters may be evidence that authority delegations have not been properly made and that some reorganization is required.

Recovery of Delegated Authority

A manager who delegates authority does not permanently dispose of it; delegated authority can always be regained. Reorganization inevitably involves some recovery and redelegation of authority. In a shuffle in an organization, rights are recovered by the responsible head of the firm or a department and then redelegated to managers of new or modified departments; the head of a new department may receive the authority formerly held by other managers. For example, when a reorganization takes quality control responsibility away from a works manager and assigns it to a new manager of quality control who will report to the vice president in charge of manufacturing, the vice president has recovered some of the authority formerly delegated to the works manager and has redelegated it, with or without modification, to the new quality control executive.

THE ART OF DELEGATION

Most failures in effective delegation occur not because managers do not understand the nature and principles of delegation but because they are unable or unwilling to apply them.[10] Delegation is, in a way, an elementary act of managing. Yet studies of managerial failures almost invariably find that poor or inept delegation is at or near the top of the list of causes. Much of the reason lies in personal attitudes toward delegation.

Personal Attitudes toward Delegation

Although charting an organization and outlining managerial goals and duties will help in making delegations, and knowledge of the principles of delegation will furnish a basis for it, certain personal attitudes underlie real delegation.

Receptiveness.   An underlying attribute of managers who will delegate authority is a willingness to give other people's ideas a chance. Decision making always involves some discretion, and a subordinate's decision is not likely to be exactly the one a superior would have made. The manager who knows how to delegate must have a minimum of the "NIH (not invented here) factor" and must be able not only to welcome the ideas of others but also to help others and to compliment them on their ingenuity.

Willingness to let go.   A manager who will effectively delegate authority must be willing to release the right to make decisions to subordinates. A major fault of some managers who move up the executive ladder—or of the pioneer who has built a large business from the small beginning of, say, a garage machine shop—is that they want to continue to make decisions for the positions they have left. Corporate presidents and vice presidents who insist on confirming every purchase or approving the appointment of every laborer or secretary do not realize that doing so takes their time and attention away from far more important decisions.

If the size or complexity of the organization forces delegation of authority, managers should realize that there is a "law of comparative managerial advantage," somewhat like the law of comparative economic advantage that applies to nations. Well known to economists and logically sound, the law of comparative economic advantage states that a country's wealth will be enhanced if it exports what it produces most efficiently and imports what it produces least efficiently, even though it could produce the imported goods more cheaply than any other nation. Likewise, managers will enhance their contributions to the firm if they concentrate on tasks that contribute most to the firm's objectives and assign to subordinates other tasks, even though they could accomplish them better themselves.

Willingness to let others make mistakes.

Although no responsible manager would sit idly by and let a subordinate make a mistake that might endanger the company or the subordinate's position in the company, continual checking on the subordinate to ensure that no mistakes are ever made will make true delegation impossible. Since everyone makes mistakes, a subordinate must be allowed to make some, and their cost must be considered an investment in personal development.

Serious or repeated mistakes can be largely avoided without nullifying delegation or hindering the development of a subordinate. Patient counseling, asking leading or discerning questions, and carefully explaining the objectives and policies are some of the methods available to the manager who would delegate well. None of these techniques involves discouraging subordinates with intimidating criticism or harping on their shortcomings.

Willingness to trust subordinates.

Superiors have no alternative to trusting their subordinates, for delegation implies a trustful attitude between them. This trust is sometimes hard to come by. A superior may put off delegation with the thought that subordinates are not yet experienced enough, that they cannot handle people, that they have not yet developed judgment, or that they do not appreciate all the facts bearing on a situation. Sometimes these considerations are true, but then a superior should either train subordinates or else select others who are prepared to assume the responsibility. Too often, however, bosses distrust their subordinates because they do not wish to let go, are threatened by subordinates' successes, do not delegate wisely, or do not know how to set up controls to ensure proper use of the authority.

Willingness to establish and use broad controls.

Since superiors cannot delegate responsibility for performance, they should not delegate authority unless they are willing to find means of getting feedback, that is, of assuring themselves that the authority is being used to support enterprise or department goals and plans. Obviously, controls cannot be established and exercised unless goals, policies, and plans are used as basic standards for judging the activities of subordinates. More often than not, reluctance to delegate and to trust subordinates comes from the superior's inadequate planning and understandable fear of loss of control.

Guides for Overcoming Weak Delegation

The following practical guides will facilitate successful delegation:

1. *Define assignments and delegate authority in light of results expected.* Or, to put it another way, grant sufficient authority to make possible the accomplishment of goal assignments.
2. *Select the person in light of the job to be done.* Although the good organizer will approach delegation primarily from the standpoint of the task to be accomplished, in the final analysis staffing as a part of the total system of delegation cannot be ignored.
3. *Maintain open lines of communication.* Since the superior does not delegate all authority or abdicate responsibility, and since managerial independence therefore does not exist, decentralization should not lead to insulation. There should be a free flow of information between superior and subordinate, furnishing the subordinate with the information needed to make decisions and to interpret properly the authority delegated. Delegations, then, do depend on situations.
4. *Establish proper controls.* Because no manager can relinquish responsibility, delegations should be accompanied by techniques for ensuring that the authority is properly used. But if controls are to enhance delegation, they must be relatively broad and be designed to show deviations from plans, rather than interfering with routine actions of subordinates.
5. *Reward effective delegation and successful assumption of authority.* Managers should be ever-watchful for means of rewarding both effective delegation and effective assumption of authority. Although many of these rewards will be monetary, the granting of greater discretion and prestige—both in a given position and by promotion to a higher position—is often even more of an incentive.

FACTORS DETERMINING THE DEGREE OF DECENTRALIZATION OF AUTHORITY

Managers cannot ordinarily be for or against decentralization of authority. They may *prefer* to delegate authority, or they may like to make all the decisions.

Although the temperament of individual managers influences the extent of authority delegation, other factors also affect it. Most of them are beyond the control of individual managers. Managers may resist their influence, but no successful manager can ignore them.

Costliness of the Decision

Perhaps the overriding factor determining the extent of decentralization is, as in other aspects of policy, costliness. As a general rule, the more costly the action to be decided on, the more probable it is that the decision will be made at the upper levels of management. Cost may be reckoned directly in dollars and cents or in such intangibles as the company's reputation, its competitive position, or employee morale. Thus, an airline's decision to purchase airplanes will be made at the top levels, while the decision to purchase desks may be made in the second or third echelon of an operating department. Quality control in drug manufacturing, where a mistake might endanger lives, to say nothing of the company's reputation, would normally report to a high level, while quality inspection in widget manufacturing might report to a much lower one.

The fact that the cost of a mistake affects decentralization is not necessarily based on the assumption that top managers make fewer mistakes than subordinates. They *may* make fewer mistakes, since they are probably better trained and in possession of more facts, but the controlling reason is the weight of responsibility. Delegating authority is not delegating responsibility; superiors are still responsible for the organizational activities of their subordinates. Therefore, managers typically prefer not to delegate authority for crucial decisions.

The need for top control depends on the area of decision. In the typical large business, top managers may reasonably feel that they cannot delegate authority over the expenditure of capital funds. The financial aspects of General Motors' operations are centralized under an executive vice president, who reports to the chairperson or vice chairperson of the board of directors rather than to the president. This is an example of the importance of centralization in the area of finance.

Desire for Uniformity of Policy

Those who value consistency above all invariably favor centralized authority, since this is the easiest road to such a goal. They may wish to ensure that customers will be treated alike with respect to quality, price, credit, delivery, and service; that the same policies will be followed in dealing with suppliers; or that public relations policies will be standardized.

Uniform policy also has certain internal advantages. For example, standardized accounting, statistics, and financial records make it easier to compare relative efficiencies of departments and keep down costs. The administration of a union contract is facilitated by uniform policy with respect to wages, promotions, vacations, dismissals, and similar matters. Taxes and government regulation entail fewer worries and less chance of error with uniform policies.

Yet many enterprises go to considerable lengths to make sure that some policies will not be completely uniform. Many companies encourage variety in all except major matters, hoping that out of such nonuniformity may come managerial innovation, progress, competition among organizational units, improved morale and efficiency, and a supply of promotable managers.

Size and Character of the Organization

The larger the organization, the more decisions to be made, and the more places in which they must be made, the more difficult it is to coordinate them. These complexities of organization may require that policy questions be passed up the line and discussed not only with many managers in the chain of command but also with many managers at each level, since horizontal agreement may be as necessary as vertical clearance.

Slow decisions—slow because of the number of specialists and managers who must be consulted—are costly. To minimize this cost, authority should be decentralized wherever feasible. Indeed, the large enterprise that prides itself on the right kind of decentralization may differ widely among companies, depending largely on the quality of the management.

The costs of large size may be reduced by organizing an enterprise into several units, such as product or territorial divisions. Efficiency may be increased by making the unit small enough for its top executives to be near the point where decisions are made. This makes speedy decisions possible, keeps executives from spending time coordinating their decisions with many others, reduces the amount of paperwork, and improves the quality of decisions by reducing them to manageable proportions.

Also important in determining size is the character of a unit. For decentralization to be thoroughly effective, a unit must possess a certain economic and managerial self-sufficiency. Functional departments, such as sales or manufacturing or engineering, cannot be independent units, while product or territorial departments of the same size can be, encompassing as they do nearly all the functions of an enterprise. It therefore follows that if the uneconomic aspects of size are to be reduced, it is preferable to departmentize along product, territorial, or distribution channel lines.

In the zeal to overcome the disadvantages of size by reducing the size of the decision-making unit, certain shortcomings of decentralization should not be overlooked. When authority is decentralized, a lack of policy uniformity and of coordination may follow. The branch, product division, or other self-sufficient unit may be so preoccupied with its objectives as to lose sight of those of the enterprise as a whole.

History and Culture of the Enterprise

Whether authority will be decentralized frequently depends on the way the business has been built. Those enterprises which, in the main, expand from within—such as Marshall Field and Company and International Harvester Company—show a marked tendency to keep authority centralized, as do those which expand under the direction of their owner-founders. The Ford Motor Company was, under its founder, an extraordinary case of centralized authority; Henry Ford, Sr., prided himself on having no organizational titles in the top management except that of president and general manager, insisting, to the extent he could, that every major decision in that vast company be made by himself.

On the other hand, enterprises that result from mergers and consolidations are likely to show, at least at first, a definite tendency to retain decentralized authority, especially if the unit acquired is already operating profitably. To be sure, this tendency not to rock the boat may be politically inspired rather than based purely on managerial considerations. Certainly, the claim to independence of the once independent units is especially strong, and many years may have to pass before the chief executive of the consolidated company dares to reduce materially the degree of decentralization.

In some cases, the first influence of a merger or an acquisition may be toward increased centralization. If the controlling group wishes to put in its own management or take immediate advantage of the economies of combined operation, the requirements of policy uniformity and quick action may necessitate centralization.

Management Philosophy

The character and philosophy of top executives have an important influence on the extent to which authority is decentralized. Sometimes top managers are despotic, tolerating no interference with the authority they jealously hoard. At other times, top managers keep authority not merely to gratify a desire for status or power but because they simply cannot give up the activities and authority they enjoyed before they reached the top or before the business expanded from an owner-manager shop.

In many cases, top managers may see decentralization as a way of organizational life that takes advantage of the innate desire of people to create, to be free, and to have status. Many successful top managers find in it a means to promote the desire for freedom to economic efficiency, much as the free enterprise system has been responsible for this country's remarkable industrial progress.

Retaining efficiency and discipline while allowing people to express themselves, to exercise initiative, and to have some voice in the affairs of the organization is the greatest problem organizations, especially large ones, have to solve.

Desire for Independence

Individuals and groups often desire a degree of independence from bosses who are far away. It is not at all unusual for West Coast divisions or subsidiaries of companies headquartered in New York to feel somewhat hostile toward directives coming from headquarters managers who are believed not to know West Coast conditions.

Individuals may become frustrated by delay in getting decisions, by long lines of communication, and by the great game of passing the buck. This frustration can lead to dangerous loss of good people, to jockeying by the office politician, and to an attitude of "not rocking the boat" by the less competent seeker of security.

Availability of Managers

A real shortage of managers would limit decentralization of authority, since in order to delegate, superiors must have qualified managers to whom to give authority. But too often the scarcity of good managers is used as an excuse for centralizing authority; executives who complain that they have no one to whom they can delegate authority are often trying to magnify their own value to the firm or are confessing a failure to develop subordinates.

There are also executives who believe that a firm should centralize authority because it will then need very few good managers. One difficulty is that the firm that so centralizes authority may not be able to train managers to take over the duties of the top executives, and external sources must then be relied on to furnish necessary replacements.

The key to safe decentralization is adequate training of managers. By the same token, decentralization is perhaps the most important key to training. Many large firms whose size makes decentralization a necessity consciously push decision making down into the organization for the purpose of developing managers; they feel that the best training is actual experience. Since this policy usually carries with it chances for mistakes by a novice, it is good practice to limit, at least initially, the importance of the decisions so delegated.

Control Techniques

Another factor affecting the degree of decentralization is the state of development of control techniques. A good manager at any level of the organization cannot delegate authority without having some way of knowing whether it will be used properly. Because some managers do not know how to control, they are unwilling to delegate authority. They may think that it takes more time to correct a mistake than to do the job themselves.

Improvements in statistical devices, accounting controls, the use of computers, and other techniques have helped make possible the current trend toward considerable managerial decentralization. Even the most ardent supporters of decentralization, such as General Motors, Du Pont, and Sears, could hardly take so favorable a view without adequate techniques to show managers, from the top down, whether performance is conforming to plans. To decentralize is not to lose control, and to push decision making down into the organization is not to walk away from responsibility.

Decentralized Performance

Decentralized performance refers to *the situation where the managers of an enterprise are dispersed over a geographic area.* The reason for decentralized performance is basically a technical matter depending on such factors as the economies of division of labor, the opportunities for using machines, the nature of the work to be performed (a railroad has no choice but to spread its performance), and the location of raw materials, labor supply, and customers. This geographic decentralization influences the degree of decentralization of authority.

Authority tends to be decentralized when performance is decentralized, if for no other reason than that the absentee manager is unable to manage, although there are exceptions. For example, some of the large chain store enterprises are characterized by widely decentralized performance, and yet the local manager of a store may have little or no authority over pricing, advertising and merchandising methods, inventory and purchasing, and product line, all of which may be controlled from a central or regional office. The head of a local manufacturing plant of a large organization may have little authority beyond the right to hire and fire, and even then action may be limited by company policy and procedure and by the authority of a centralized personnel department. At the same time, the decentralization of performance limits the ability to centralize authority. The most dictatorial top manager of a national organization based in New York cannot supervise the San Francisco plant as closely as if it were adjacent to the home office.

It does not necessarily follow, however, that when performance is centralized, authority has to be centralized. You may have a company in one location in which authority is greatly decentralized because of the top executive's attitude toward delegation. Nevertheless, in a one-plant situation, authority centralization would be easier than if the company had many plants in distant locations.

Business Dynamics: The Pace of Change

The pace of change of an enterprise also affects the degree to which authority may be decentralized. If a business is growing fast and facing complex problems of expansion, its managers, particularly those responsible for top policy, may be forced to make a large share of the decisions. But, strangely enough, this very dynamic condition may force these managers to delegate authority and take a calculated risk on the costs of error. Generally, this dilemma is resolved in the direction of delegation, and in order to avoid delegation to untrained subordinates, close attention is given to rapid formation of policies and the acceleration of training in management. An alternative often adopted is to slow the rate of change, including the cause of fast change, expansion. Many top managers have found that the critical factor limiting their ability to meet change and expand a business or some other enterprise is the lack of trained personnel to whom authority may be delegated.

In old, well-established, or slow-moving businesses, there is a natural tendency to centralize or recentralize authority. When few major decisions must be made, the advantages of uniform policy and the economies of having a few well-qualified persons make the decisions cause authority to be centralized. In slow-moving businesses too much centralization may carry danger. New discoveries, vigorous competition from an unexpected source, and political change are only a few of the factors that might introduce conditions requiring change. An overcentralized firm may not be able to meet a situation as well as if authority were decentralized.

Environmental Influences

The factors determining the extent of decentralization that we have dealt with so far are largely factors within the enterprise. However, the economics of decentralization of performance and the character of change include elements well beyond the control of an enterprise's managers. In addition, there are definite external forces affecting the extent of decentralization. Among the most important of these are governmental controls, national unionism, and tax policies.

Government regulation of many facets of business policy makes decentralization difficult and sometimes impossible. If prices are regulated, sales managers cannot be given much real freedom in determining them. If materials are allocated and restricted, purchasing and factory managers are not free to buy or use any they might wish. If labor may be asked to work only a limited number of hours at a given rate of pay, the local division manager cannot freely set hours and wages.

Top management itself no longer has authority over many aspects of policy and cannot, therefore, delegate authority it does not have. Much authority in areas controlled by government action could still be decentralized. But managers often do not dare trust subordinates to interpret government regulations, especially since the penalties and the public criticism for breaking laws are so serious and since interpretation of most laws is a matter for the specialist.

In the same way, the rise of national unions in the past decades has had a centralizing influence on business. So long as department or division managers can negotiate the terms of a labor contract by dealing either with local unions or with employees directly, authority to negotiate may be delegated by top management to these subordinates. But where, as is increasingly the case, a national union enters into a collective bargaining contract with headquarters management, with the terms of the contract applicable to all workers of a company wherever they are located, a company cannot chance decentralization of certain decision making any more than it can in the case of government controls.

The tax systems of the national, state, and local governments have had a marked regulatory effect on business. The tax collector, especially the federal tax collector, sits at the elbow of every executive who makes a decision involving funds. The impact of taxation is often a policy-determining factor that overshadows such traditional business considerations as plant expansion, marketing policies, and economical operations. Uniformity of tax policy becomes of primary importance to company management. This spells centralization because managers without appropriate tax advice cannot be expected to make wise decisions. It may even require a central tax department acting not only in an advisory capacity and as a tax service agency but also with a high degree of functional authority over matters with tax implications.

RECENTRALIZATION OF AUTHORITY[11] AND BALANCE AS THE KEY TO DECENTRALIZATION[12]

At times an enterprise can be said to recentralize authority—to centralize authority that was once decentralized. **Recentralization** is normally not a complete reversal of decentralization, for the authority delegations are not wholly withdrawn by the managers who made them. The process is a centralization of authority over a certain type of activity or a certain kind of function, wherever in the organization it may be found.

To avoid pitfalls, any program for decentralization of authority must take into consideration the advantages and limitations summarized in Table 11-1.

As noted earlier, strong forces favor the practice of decentralization. At the same time, extensive decentralization is not to be blindly undertaken. Perhaps the principal problem of decentralization is loss of control. No enterprise can decen-

TABLE 11-1   ADVANTAGES AND LIMITATIONS OF DECENTRALIZATION

Advantages of decentralization

1. Relieves top management of some burden of decision making and forces upper-level managers to let go.
2. Encourages decision making and assumption of authority and responsibility.
3. Gives managers more freedom and independence in decision making.
4. Promotes establishment and use of broad controls which may increase motivation.
5. Makes comparison of performance of different organizational units possible.
6. Facilitates setting up of profit centers.
7. Facilitates product diversification.
8. Promotes development of general managers.
9. Aids in adaptation to fast-changing environment.

Limitations of decentralization

1. Makes it more difficult to have a uniform policy.
2. Increases complexity of coordination of decentralized organizational units.
3. May result in loss of some control by upper-level managers.
4. May be limited by inadequate control techniques.
5. May be constrained by inadequate planning and control systems.
6. Can be limited by the availability of qualified managers.
7. Involves considerable expenses for training managers.
8. May be limited by external forces (national labor unions, governmental controls, tax policies).
9. May not be favored by economies of scale of some operations.

tralize to the extent that its existence is threatened and the achievement of its goals is frustrated. If organizational disintegration is to be avoided, decentralization must be tempered by selective centralization in certain major policy areas. The company with well-balanced decentralization will probably centralize decisions at the top on such things as financing, overall profit goals and budgeting, major facilities and other capital expenditures, important new product programs, major marketing strategies, basic personnel policies, and the development and compensation of managerial personnel.

The achievement of balance is perhaps one of the greatest accomplishments of Alfred Sloan in his management of General Motors (GM) over the years. Although practicing and preaching decentralization, he and his top management team realized that no department or division could be given complete freedom. As a result, within GM, despite its large size, authority has been retained at the very top for major policy and program decisions on matters affecting the soundness and success of the entire company. Through decentralization, however, once major program and strategy decisions have been made at the top, the countless decisions involving their execution are made by operating divisions.

SUMMARY

There are a number of different bases of power. Power can be legitimate, expert, referent, reward, or coercive. There are also various ways to conceptualize line and staff. Generally, line and staff are characterized by relationships and not by people or departments. Line authority is that relationship in which a superior exercises direct supervision over subordinates. The staff relationship, on the other hand, consists of giving advice and counsel. Functional authority is the right to control *selected* processes, practices, policies, or other matters in departments other than a person's own. Functional authority is a small slice of a line manager's authority and should be used sparingly.

Using staff has benefits as well as limitations, such as the danger of undermining line and the lack of responsibility of staff. There are also the possibilities of making impractical recommendations and undermining the unity of command.

Another important concept is decentralization, which is the tendency to disperse decision-making authority. Centralization, on the other hand, is the concentration of authority. It may refer to geographic concentration, departmental centralization, or the tendency to restrict delegation of decision making. The process of delegation of authority includes determining the results to be achieved, assigning tasks, delegating authority for accomplishing the tasks, and holding people responsible for results.

Delegation, which is an art, is influenced by personal attitudes. In addition, practical guides exist that can help managers overcome weak delegation. Decentralization is influenced by many other factors a manager should recognize when determining the degree of authority delegation. Previously decentralized authority may be recentralized. Balance is the key to proper decentralization.

KEY IDEAS AND CONCEPTS FOR REVIEW

Power
Authority
Bases of power
Scalar principle
Line
Staff
Functional authority
Limitations of staff
Decentralization
Centralization

Process of delegation
Splintered authority
Attitudes toward delegation
Guides for overcoming weak delegation
Factors determining the degree of decentralization
Decentralized performance
Recentralization
Advantages and limitations of decentralization

FOR DISCUSSION

1. What are the kinds of power exercised in your organization or school?
2. Why has there been a conflict between line and staff for so long and in so many companies? Can this conflict be removed?
3. Take as examples a number of positions in any kind of enterprise (business, church, government, etc.). Classify each as line or staff.
4. If the task of a person in a purely staff position is to offer advice, how can an individual receiving this advice make sure that it is independent, well researched, and realistic?
5. How many cases of functional authority in organization have you seen? Analyzing a few, do you agree that they could have been avoided? If avoidance had been possible, would you have eliminated them? If they could not have been avoided or if you had not wanted to eliminate them, how would you remove most of the difficulties that might arise?
6. If you were asked to advise a young college graduate who has accepted a staff position as assistant to a factory manager, what suggestions would you make?
7. Why is poor delegation of authority often found to be the most important cause of managerial failure?
8. In many foreign countries where companies have grown from within and are often family-owned, very little authority is decentralized. What do you think would explain this? What effect does it have?
9. If you were a manager, would you decentralize authority? State several reasons for your answer. How would you make sure that you did not decentralize too much?
10. Should authority be pushed down in an organization as far as it will go?

EXERCISES/ACTION STEPS

1. Interview a line manager and a staff person at a local company. Ask them what they like and dislike about their jobs. Reflect on the interviews, and ask yourself whether a line position or a staff one is the major aim of your career plan.
2. Interview two line managers about their views on delegation. Do they think that their superior delegates sufficient authority to them? Also inquire how they feel about delegating authority to their subordinates.

CASES

CASE 11-1
ABC AIRLINES

The president of ABC Airlines, seeing that costs were getting out of control as the company grew, brought in as an assistant a brilliant young man who was a certified public accountant. The assistant was told about the company's problem of rising costs and was asked for his help in solving the problem.

The new assistant gathered a staff of high-quality industrial engineers, financial analysts, and recent top graduates from one of the nation's best-known graduate schools of business administration. After laying out the company's problem, he assigned them to investigate cost problems and management methods in the airline's operations, maintenance, engineering, and sales departments. After a number of studies, the president's assistant found many sources of inefficiency in the various departments and initiated a number of changes in operating practices. In addition, he made many reports to the president outlining in detail the inefficiencies his staff had found and the measures being taken to correct them. These reports also showed, with ample supporting detail, the millions of dollars that his actions were saving the company.

Just as these cost saving programs were being implemented, the vice presidents in charge of operations, maintenance, engineering, and sales descended on the president and insisted that the assistant be discharged.

1. Why should the assistant, who was doing so well, be so much resented by the vice presidents? What went wrong?
2. Assuming that the findings of the assistant and his staff were accurate, what should have been done by the president, the assistant, the vice presidents, and others to make these findings useful?

INTERNATIONAL CASE 11-2
FORD'S GLOBAL STRATEGY: CENTERS OF EXCELLENCE[13]

In 1986 Ford passed its bigger competitor, General Motors, with earnings of $3.3 billion. Ford's market share is about 20 percent. But success, in many instances, may be only temporary, and Ford's chairman, Donald E. Petersen, is concerned about complacency. Indeed, the company has to work hard to maintain its reputation for stylish, aerodynamic cars and high quality.

Under the former leadership of Henry Ford II, the company was very centralized. But Petersen's plan is to make Ford an integrated global enterprise. Thus, a great deal of authority for the development of specific models or components is now centralized in the company's various technical centers around the world rather than in Detroit. Under this plan, a car or its components are developed in the technical center with the best expertise in a particular field, anywhere in the world. This could save the company a lot of money by avoiding duplication in development and reducing tooling costs. For example, Ford of Europe, located in England, is the center for developing the platform for the new model that will replace the European Sierra and the American Tempo and Topaz. Ford will sell the new cars in Europe and in the United States. Similarly, in Japan Mazda (Ford owns

25 percent of the company), which has much experience in building small cars, will be the center for developing the platform for the car that will replace the Escort. The North American center of excellence will focus on midsize cars. Similar centers are planned for major components such as transmissions and engines. While these centers of excellence develop platforms and key components, exterior and interior styling will be the responsibility of companies in the various regions.

The concept of the centers of excellence may seem promising, yet a previous attempt in the early 1980s to build a "world car" in Europe failed. It is said that the American car, the Escort, shared only one part with its European counterpart, namely a seal in the water pump.

1. What do you think of Ford's overall decentralization with centralized authority for the development of specific cars and components at the technical centers?
2. Why does Ford think that the concept of having centers of excellence located in various parts of the world will be the correct organization structure for the twenty-first century?

REFERENCES

1. John G. Staiger, "What Cannot Be Decentralized," in Harold Koontz, Cyril O'Donnell, and Heinz Weihrich (eds.), *Management: A Book of Readings,* 5th ed. (New York: McGraw-Hill Book Company, 1980), p. 319.

2. The concept of power has been widely discussed in the literature. See, for example, the thorough discussion by Gerald R. Salancik and Jeffrey Pfeffer, "Who Gets Power—and How They Hold On to It: A Strategic-Contingency Model of Power," in David A. Nadler, Michael L. Tushman, and Nina G. Hatvany (eds.), *Managing Organizations—Readings and Cases* (Boston: Little, Brown and Company, 1982), pp. 385–399.

3. John R. P. French, Jr., and Bertram Raven, "The Bases of Social Power," in Walter E. Natemeyer (eds.), *Classics of Organizational Behavior* (Oak Park, Ill.: Moore Publishing Company, 1978), pp. 198–210.

4. But authority patterns may vary with culture. See Trudy Heller, "Changing Authority Patterns: A Cultural Perspective," *Academy of Management Review* (July 1985), pp. 488–495.

5. For a research study on the topic of power, see Anthony T. Cobb, "An Episodic Model of Power: Toward an Integration of Theory and Research," *Academy of Management Review* (July 1984), pp. 482–493.

6. For an interesting discussion of line and staff relationships in large organizations, see Jerome Wilkenfield, "Managing Staff Functions in a Large Corporation," *Management Review* (June 1986), pp. 41–44.

7. It has been suggested that as formal authority diminishes, it must be replaced by influence. See Bernard Keys and Thomas L. Case, "How to Become an Influential Manager," *Academy of Management Executive* (November 1990), pp. 38–51.

8. Jeff Bailey, "Where the Action Is: Executives in Staff Jobs Seek Line Positions," *The Wall Street Journal* (Aug. 12, 1986); see also David Wessel, "Do as I Do: More Consultants Quit Profession to Start New Businesses," *The Wall Street Journal* (Oct. 15, 1986).

9. Hall L. Logan, "Line and Staff: An Obsolete Concept?" in Koontz, O'Donnell, and Weihrich, *Management* (1980), pp. 322–325.

10. See also Charles D. Pringle, "Seven Reasons Why Managers Don't Delegate," *Management Solutions* (November 1986), pp. 26–30.

11. For a discussion of recentralizing the information systems organization, see Ernest M. Von Simson, "The 'Centrally Decentralized' IS Organization," *Harvard Business Review* (July–August 1990), pp. 158–162.

12. See also John G. Staiger, "What Cannot Be Decentralized," in Koontz, O'Donnell, and Weihrich, *Management* (1980), pp. 319–321.

13. The case is based on a variety of sources, including James B. Treece et al., "Can Ford Stay on Top?" *Business Week* (Sept. 28, 1987), pp. 78–86.

Effective Organizing and Organizational Culture

Managing corporate transformations ultimately means changing behavior and culture.[1]

Michael Beer

Chapter Objectives

After reading this chapter, you should be able to:

1. Recognize some common mistakes made in organizing.
2. Avoid mistakes in organizing by planning.
3. Show how organizing can be improved by maintaining flexibility and by making staff more effective.
4. Avoid conflict by clarifying the organization structure and ensuring an understanding of organizing.
5. Promote and develop an appropriate organization culture.
6. Recognize that effective organizing depends on the situation.

Organizing involves developing an intentional structure of roles for effective performance. Organizing requires a network of decision and communication centers for coordinating efforts toward group and enterprise goals. To work, an organization structure must be understood, and principles must be put into practice. As emphasized at the outset, in organizing, as elsewhere in managing, there is no one best way. What works will always depend on the specific situation.

SOME MISTAKES IN ORGANIZING

Despite their obvious nature and their interference with personal and enterprise goals, the persistence of certain mistakes in organizing is striking evidence of the difficulty of managing, the lack of sophistication of managers, or both.

Failure to Plan Properly

It is not unusual to find an enterprise continuing with a traditional organization structure long after its objectives, plans, and external environment have changed. For example, a company may keep its product research department under the control of the manufacturing division long after the business environment has changed from being production-oriented (as in a typical sellers' market) to being marketing-oriented (as in a typical buyers' market). Or a company may continue its functional organization structure when product groupings and the need for integrated, decentralized profit responsibility demand decentralized product divisions.

Also, a company may need managers of a kind not currently available or, just as likely, may find that certain managers have not grown with the company or do not fit current needs. Small, growing businesses often make the mistake of assuming that original employees can grow with the company, only to find that a good engineering designer, made a vice president of engineering, cannot fill the larger role of the engineering chief or that a once adequate production superintendent cannot head a larger manufacturing department.

Another guideline for planning involves properly organizing around people. Organization structure must normally be modified to take people into account, and there is much to be said for trying to take full advantage of employee strengths and weaknesses. But managers organizing primarily around people overlook several facts. In the first place, managers organizing in this way cannot be assured that all bases will be covered and all the necessary tasks will be undertaken. In the second place, there is the danger that different people will desire to do the same things, resulting in conflict or multiple command. In the third place, people have a way of coming and going in an enterprise—through retirement, resignation, promotion, or death—which makes organizing around them risky and their positions, when vacated, hard to describe accurately and to fill adequately.

Such mistakes occur when an enterprise fails to plan properly toward a future materially different from the past or present. By looking forward, a manager should determine what kind of organization structure will best serve future needs and what kinds of people will best serve an organization.

Failure to Clarify Relationships

The failure to clarify organization relationships, probably more than any other mistake, accounts for friction, politics, and inefficiencies. Since both the authority and the responsibility for action are critical, lack of clarity about them means lack of knowledge of the parts that members are to play on an enterprise team. This does not imply the need for detailed job descriptions or the possibility that people cannot operate as a team. Although some enterprise leaders have prided themselves on having a team of subordinates without specified tasks and authority lines, any sports coach could tell them that such a team is likely to be a group of jealous, insecure, buck-passing individuals jockeying for position and favor.

Failure to Delegate Authority

A common complaint in organization life is that managers are reluctant to push decision making down into the organization. In some businesses where uniformity of policy is necessary and decision making can be handled by one or a few managers, there may be neither the need nor the desire to decentralize authority. But decision-making bottlenecks, excessive referral of small problems to upper echelons, overburdening of top executives with detail, continual "fire fighting" and "meeting of crises," and underdevelopment of managers in the lower levels of organization give evidence that failing to delegate authority to the proper extent is decidedly a mistake.

Failure to Balance Delegation

Another mistake made in organizing is failure to maintain balanced delegation. In other words, some managers—in their zeal for decentralization—may push decision making too far down in the organization. It may reach down to the very bottom of the structure, and a system of independent organizational satellites may develop.

Even when it is not taken to this extreme, excessive delegation may cause organization failures.

As we pointed out in the chapter on decentralization, top managers must retain some authority, particularly over decisions that have companywide impact, and at least enough to review the plans and performance of subordinates. Managers must not forget that there is some authority they should not delegate. Nor should they overlook the fact that they must maintain enough authority to ensure that when they do delegate authority to a subordinate, it will be used in the way and for the purposes intended.

Confusion of Lines of Authority with Lines of Information

The problems and costs of levels of organization and departmentation can be reduced by opening wide the channels of information. Unless information is confidential (and businesses and government, as well as other enterprises, overuse this classification), there is no reason why lines of information should follow lines of authority. In other words, relevant information should be widely available to people at all levels of the organization. Information gathering should be separated from decision making, since only the latter requires managerial authority. Enterprises often force lines of information to follow lines of authority when the only reason for following a chain of command is to preserve the integrity of decision-making authority and the clarity of responsibility.

Granting Authority without Exacting Responsibility

A significant cause of mismanagement is assignment of authority without holding a person responsible. Authority delegation is not responsibility delegation; superiors remain responsible for the proper exercise of authority by their subordinates. Any other relationship would lead to organizational chaos. But all those to whom authority is delegated must be willing to be held responsible for their actions.

Holding People Responsible Who Do Not Have Authority

A common complaint of subordinates is that superiors hold them responsible for results without giving them the authority to accomplish them. Some of these complaints are unjustified and based on a misunderstanding of the fact that subordinates can seldom have unlimited authority in any area because their actions must be coordinated with those of people in other positions and must conform to policy. Subordinates often see their jobs as all-encompassing and forget that their authority must be limited to their own departments and must be within controlling policy guidelines.

Too often, however, complaints are justified; managers, sometimes without realizing they are doing so, hold subordinates responsible for results they have no power to accomplish. This does not happen so frequently where organization lines and duties have been clearly set forth, but where a structure of roles is unclear or confused, it does occur.

Careless Application of the Staff Device

There are many valid reasons for using a staff assistant or staff specialist and even building entire advisory departments. However, there is the danger that staff people will be used by their superiors to undermine the authority of the very managers they are intended merely to advise.

There is an ever-present danger that top managers may surround themselves with staff specialists and become so preoccupied with the specialists' work that they exclude from their schedule the time and attention needed for their line subordinates; or they may assign problems to their staff that would be more appropriately assigned to line managers.

In other instances, staff personnel exercise line authority that has not been delegated to them. It is easy to understand the impatience of staff specialists who see clearly how a situation should be handled, while the line officer in charge of it seems to be slow and clumsy. The very quality that makes staff specialists valuable—specialized knowledge—also makes them impatient of command. Yet if they were to exercise authority without clear delegation, they would be not only undermining the authority of the responsible line official but also breaking down the unity of command.

Misuse of Functional Authority

Perhaps even more dangerous to good managing are the problems arising from undefined and unrestricted delegation of functional authority. This is especially common because the complexities of a modern enterprise often create instances where it is desirable to give a predominantly staff or service department functional authority over activities in other parts of the organization.

In the search for economies of specialization and for advantages of technically expert opinion, managers often unduly exalt staff and service departments at the expense of the operating department. Many line officers—from the vice president in charge of operations to a first-level supervisor—feel, with justice, that the business is being run by the staff and service departments through their exercise of functional authority. The personnel department, for example, may hire workers for line departments on the basis of psychological test results without consulting with the managers of the line departments.

Multiple Subordination

The principal danger of too much functional authority is the breakdown of unity of command. We have only to look at the various departments of a typical medium-size or large business to see how such a breakdown occurs. The controller prescribes accounting procedures throughout the company. The purchasing director prescribes how and where purchases are to be made. The personnel manager dictates (often according to union contracts or government regulations) how employees shall be classified for pay purposes, how vacations shall be scheduled, and how many hours are to be worked. The traffic manager controls the routing of all freight. The general counsel insists that all contracts bear his or her approval and be made in the prescribed form. The public relations director requires that all public utterances of managers and other employees be cleared or meet a prescribed policy line. And the tax director reviews all program decisions for clearance on their tax aspects.

Thus, with all these staff and service specialists having some degree of line authority over other parts of the organization, plus similar groups in divisions and regions, operating managers find themselves subject to the direction of a number of people with functional authority in addition to their principal superiors, who usually have the final decision concerning their pay scales and chances for promotion. It is no wonder that many managers, especially those at lower levels where there are so many functional authorities, feel frustrated.

Misunderstanding of the Function of Service Departments

Service departments are often looked upon as being rather unconcerned with the accomplishment of major enterprise objectives, when they are, in fact, just as immediately concerned as any operating department would be. Sometimes people, particularly those in so-called line departments, regard a service department as relatively unnecessary and unimportant and therefore something to be ignored when possible.

On the other hand, many service departments mistakenly look upon their function as an end unto itself rather than a service to other departments. Thus, a purchasing department may not realize that its purpose is to purchase efficiently items ordered by authorized departments; or a statistics department may forget that it exists to furnish data desired by others rather than to produce reports of its own choosing.

Perhaps the greatest misuse of service departments is summed up in the words "efficient inefficiency." When managers establish service departments, looking more to cost savings than to the efficiency of the entire enterprise, a highly "efficient" service may do an inefficient job of servicing. For example, little is gained in setting up a low-cost central recruiting section if the employees recruited do not meet organization needs.

Overorganization and Underorganization

Overorganization usually results from failure to put into practice the idea that the structure of the enterprise is merely a system for making possible the efficient performance of people. Managers unduly complicating the structure by creating too many levels ignore the fact that efficiency demands that managers supervise as many subordinates as they can. Narrow spans may reflect a misunderstanding of the span-of-management principle, managerial inability to minimize the time requirements of necessary human relationships, or lack of time to manage—a lack often caused by poor assignments and authority delegations. Likewise, the multiplication of staff and service activities or departments may be caused by inadequate delegation to line subordinates and the tendency to regard service specialization and efficiency so narrowly that larger enterprise operations are overlooked.

Managers also overorganize by appointing unnecessary line assistants (for example, assistant or deputy managers). Having a line assistant is justified when managers wish to devote their time to matters outside their department, during their long absences from the office, when they wish to delegate line authority in a given area such as engineering, or during a limited training period for a subordinate to whom full managerial status is soon to be given. Otherwise, the separation of managers from their other subordinates and the confusion as to who is really the superior that results from this practice lead us to conclude that it should be undertaken carefully and sparingly.

Sometimes, excessive procedures are confused with overorganization. Overorganization—particularly if interlaced with functional authority—can lead to excessive procedures. But much of the red tape often blamed on overorganization really results from poor planning. The failure to regard procedures as plans—and to treat them with the respect given other kinds of plans—often results in bewilderingly complex and even unnecessary procedures.

Similarly, too many committees, sapping the time and energies of managers and their staffs, are often blamed on overorganization rather than on poor organization (particularly when committees make decisions better made by individuals). An excess of committees often results from having authority delegated to too many positions or from vague delegation. Such an excess may actually point to underorganization.

AVOIDING MISTAKES IN ORGANIZING BY PLANNING

As with the other functions of managing, establishment of objectives and orderly planning are necessary for good organization. As Urwick said in his classic book, "Lack of design (in organization) is illogical, cruel, wasteful, and inefficient."[2] It is illogical because good design, or planning, must come first, whether one speaks of engineering or social practice. It is cruel because "the main sufferers from a lack of design in organization are those individuals who work in an undertaking." It is wasteful because "unless jobs are clearly put together along lines of functional specialization, it is impossible to train new men (or women) to succeed to positions as the incumbents are promoted, resign or retire." And it is inefficient because if management is not based on principles, it will be based on personalities, with the resultant rise of company politics, for "a machine will not run smoothly when fundamental engineering principles have been ignored in construction."

Planning for the Ideal

The search for an ideal organization to reflect enterprise goals under given circumstances is the impetus to planning. The search entails charting the main lines of organization, considering the organizational philosophy of the enterprise managers (for example, whether authority should be centralized as much as possible or whether the company should divide its operations into semi-independent product or territorial divisions), and sketching out consequent authority relationships. The ultimate form established, like all other plans, seldom remains unchanged, and continuous remolding of the ideal plan is normally necessary. Nevertheless, an ideal organization plan constitutes a standard, and by comparing the present structure with it, enterprise leaders know what changes should be made when possible.

An organizer must always be careful not to be blinded by popular notions in organizing, because what may work in one company may not work in another. Principles of organizing have general application, but the background of each company's operations and needs must be considered in applying these principles. Organization structure needs to be tailor-made.

Modification for the Human Factor

If available personnel do not fit into the ideal structure and cannot or should not be pushed aside, the only choice is to modify the structure to fit individual capabilities, attitudes, or limitations. Although this modification may seem like organizing around people, in this case one is first organizing around the goals to be met and activities to be undertaken and only then making modifications for the human factor. Thus, planning will reduce compromising the necessity for principle whenever changes occur in personnel.

Advantages of Organization Planning

Planning the organization structure helps determine future personnel needs and required training programs. Unless it knows what managerial personnel will be needed and what experience should be demanded, an enterprise cannot intelligently recruit people and train them.

Furthermore, organization planning can disclose weaknesses. Duplication of effort, unclear lines of authority, overlong lines of communication, excessive red tape, and obsolete practices show up best when desirable and actual organization structures are compared.

AVOIDING ORGANIZATIONAL INFLEXIBILITY

One basic advantage of organization planning is the avoidance of organizational inflexibility. Many enterprises, especially those which have been in operation for many years, become too rigid to meet the first test of effective organization structure: the ability to adapt to a changing environment and meet new contingencies. This resistance to change can cause considerable loss of efficiency in organizations.

Signs of Inflexibility

Some older companies provide ample evidence of inflexibility: an organization pattern that is no longer suited to the times, a district or regional organization that could be either abolished or enlarged because of improved communications, or a structure that is too highly centralized for an enlarged enterprise requiring decentralization.

Avoiding Inflexibility through Reorganization

Although reorganization is intended to respond to changes in the enterprise environment, there may be other compelling reasons for reorganization. Those related to the business environment include changes in operations caused by the acquisition or sale of major properties, changes in product line or marketing methods, business cycles, competitive influences, new production techniques, labor union policy, government regulatory and fiscal policy, and the current state of knowledge about organizing. New techniques and principles may become applicable, such as developing managers by allowing them to manage decentralized semi-independent units of a company. Or new methods may come into use, such as gaining adequate financial control with a high degree of decentralization.

Moreover, a new chief executive officer and new vice presidents and department heads are likely to have some definite organizational ideas of their own. Shifts may be due merely to the desire of new managers to make changes based on ideas formulated through previous experience or to the fact that their personalities and methods of managing require a changed organization structure.

Furthermore, reorganization may be caused by demonstrated deficiencies in an existing structure. Some of these arise from organizational weaknesses: excessive spans of management, an excessive number of committees, lack of uniform policy, slow decision making, failure to accomplish objectives, inability to meet schedules, excessive costs, or a breakdown of financial control. Other deficiencies may stem from inadequacies of managers. Lack of knowledge or skill on the part of a manager who for some reason cannot be replaced may be avoided by organizing in a way that moves much of the authority for decision making to another position.

Personality clashes between managers also may be solved by reorganization. Staff-line conflicts may develop to such an extent that they can be resolved only by reorganization.

Perspective

Restructuring IBM[3]

Even well-managed companies restructure their organization from time to time. Indeed, reorganization may be a sign of good management when it is done to adapt to changes in the environment. The realization of the need for change underlies IBM's 1988 reorganization.

When IBM's performance was not as good as expected, chairman John Akers decided that it was time for restructuring. One problem was that decisions which should have been made by the marketing and main product groups were referred upward to the management committee. Another concern was the company's ineffectiveness in identifying market niches and responding quickly with new products to fill the needs of customers. Moreover, the old structure often resulted in conflicts among various groups, such as battles among marketing groups over rival products.

To overcome these problems, IBM responded in several ways. For one, major tasks were assigned and authority delegated to lower levels, resulting in what might be considered mini IBM companies. Personal computers, for example, were combined with the typewriter division. Similarly, the midrange computer group was combined with the large mainframe computer unit. Although the mainframe computer is still the market leader, its market share has been eroding, for some of its computing functions are now carried out by midsize computers.

A major reorganization requires a change in managerial positions and personnel. Terry Lautenbach, known for his problem-solving ability, has been given the responsibility of overseeing the six new marketing and main product groups. Some time ago, *Fortune* magazine noted the difficulties women encounter in trying to move into top managerial positions in U.S. corporations. At IBM, however, the reshuffling placed Ms. Ellen Hancock in one of the most powerful positions held by a woman in a U.S. firm.

The Need for Readjustment and Change

In addition to pressing reasons for reorganization, there is a certain need for moderate and continuing readjustment merely to keep the structure from becoming stagnant. "Empire building" (that is, building up a large organization so that the manager appears to be more important) is not so attractive when all those involved know that their positions are subject to change. As a company president told his subordinates: "Don't bother to build any empires, because I can assure you that you won't be in the same position three years from now." Some managers, realizing that an organization structure must be a living thing, make structural changes merely to accustom subordinates to change.

Perspective

Managing for the 1990s at United Technologies[4]

How can one turn a company with over 180,000 employees around, a company that suffered from a reputation of poor service and customers deserting in droves to competitors? Certainly, such a crisis situation is a stimulus for change. Such a change came when Bob Daniell took over the reign at United Technologies Corp. (UTC) in 1986. It was a change from the autocratic managerial approach of his predecessor to a participative style. The Pratt & Whitney division of United Technologies serves as an example. How did Daniell turn the company around? For one, he is a listener and a team builder. Moreover, he lets his managers participate in the decision-making process and empowers his workers. This means doing away with blame fixing and replacing it with real problem solving. It also means eliminating excessive organizational levels and getting closer to the customers. But changes do not come without effort. They require investing in employees and training them for the challenging task of managing.

Much can be said for developing a tradition of change. People who are used to change tend to accept it without the frustration and demoralization that result when the need for reorganization is allowed to reach the stage at which change must be revolutionary. On the other hand, a company that is continually undertaking major reorganization may damage morale, and its employees may spend much of their time wondering what will happen to them because of organizational changes.

MAKING STAFF WORK EFFECTIVE

The line-staff problem is not only one of the most difficult that organizations face but also the source of an extraordinarily large amount of inefficiency. Solving this problem requires great managerial skill, careful attention to principles, and patient teaching of personnel.

Understanding Authority Relationships

Managers must understand the nature of authority relationships if they want to solve the problems of line and staff. As long as managers regard line and staff as groups of people or groupings of activities (for example, service departments), confusion will result. Line and staff are authority relationships, and many jobs have elements of both. The line relationship involves making decisions and acting on them. The staff relationship, on the other hand, implies the right to assist and counsel. In short, the line may "tell," but the staff must "sell" (its recommendations).

Making Line Listen to Staff

If staff counsel and advice are justifiable at all, it is because of the need for assistance either from experts or from those freed from more pressing duties to give such assistance. Obviously, if staff help is not used, it would make sense to abolish it. Line managers should realize that competent staff assistants offer suggestions to aid and not to undermine or criticize. Although line-staff friction may stem from ineptness or overzealousness on the part of staff people, trouble also arises when line executives too carefully guard their authority and resent the very assistance they need.

Line managers should be encouraged or required to consult with staff. Enterprises would do well to adopt the practice of compulsory staff assistance wherein the line must listen to staff. At General Motors, for example, product division managers consult with the headquarters staff divisions before proposing a major program or policy to the top executive or the finance committee. They may not be required to do so, but they are likely to find that this practice results in smoother sailing for their proposals; and if they can present a united front with the staff division concerned, there will unquestionably be a better chance for the adoption of their proposals.

Keeping Staff Informed

Common criticisms of staff are that specialists operate in a vacuum, fail to appreciate the complexity of the line manager's job, and overlook important facts in making recommendations. To some extent, these criticisms are warranted, because specialists cannot be expected to know all the fine points of a manager's job. Specialists should take care that their recommendations deal only with matters within their competence, and operating managers should not lean too heavily on a recommendation if it deals only with part of a problem.

Many criticisms arise because staff assistants are not kept informed on matters within their field. Even the best assistant cannot advise properly in such cases. If line managers fail to inform their staff of decisions affecting its work or if they do not pave the way—through announcements and requests for cooperation—for staff to obtain the requisite information on specific problems, the staff cannot function as intended. In relieving their superiors of the necessity for gathering and analyzing such information, staff assistants largely justify their existence.

Requiring Completed Staff Work

Many staff persons overlook the fact that in order to be most helpful, their recommendations should be complete enough to make possible a simple positive or negative answer by a line manager. Staff assistants should be problem solvers and not problem creators. They create problems for managers when their advice is indecisive or vague, when their conclusions are wrong, when they have not taken into account all the facts or have not consulted the persons seriously affected by a proposed solution, or when they do not point out to superiors the pitfalls as well as the advantages of a recommended course of action.

Completed staff work implies presentation of a clear recommendation based on full consideration of a problem, clearance with persons importantly affected, suggestions about avoiding any difficulties involved, and, often, preparation of the paperwork—letters, directives, job descriptions, and specifications—so that a manager can accept or reject the proposal without further study, long conferences, or unnecessary work. Should a recommendation be accepted, thorough staff work provides line managers with the machinery to put it into effect. People in staff positions who learn to do these things can find themselves highly valued and appreciated.

Making Staff Work as a Way of Organizational Life

An understanding of staff authority lays the foundation for an organizational way of life. Wherever staff is used, its responsibility is to develop and maintain a climate of favorable personal relations. Essentially, the task of staff assistants is to make responsible line managers "look good" and to help them do a better job. A staff assistant should not attempt to assume credit for an idea. Not only is this a sure way of alienating line teammates who do not like being shown up by a staff assistant, but operating managers who accept ideas actually bear responsibility for implementation of the proposals.

Even under the best of circumstances, it is difficult to coordinate line and staff authority, for people must be persuaded to cooperate. Staff persons must gain and hold the confidence of their coworkers. They must keep in close touch with operating departments, know their managers and staffs, and understand their problems. They must, through precept and example, convince their line teammates that their prime interest is the welfare of operating managers, and they must downgrade their own contributions while embellishing those of the persons they assist. People in a staff capacity have succeeded in their role when line executives seek their advice and ask them to study their problems.

Companies also employ the outside assistance of professional firms. Consultants, for example, may provide advice for line managers. The relationships between line and outside staff are similar to those discussed above. However, outside assistance is often only for a limited time, and it is even more difficult to hold outside staff accountable, especially when those staff people are not involved in the implementation of their recommendations.

AVOIDING CONFLICT BY CLARIFICATION

A major reason for conflict in organizations is that people do not understand their assignments and those of their coworkers. No matter how well conceived an organization structure may be, people must understand it to make it work. Understanding is aided materially by the proper use of organization charts, accurate job descriptions, the spelling out of authority and informational relationships, and the introduction of specific goals for specific positions.

Organization Charts

Every organization structure, even a poor one, can be charted, for a chart merely indicates how departments are tied together along the principal lines of authority. It is therefore somewhat surprising to find top managers occasionally taking pride in the fact that they do not have an organization chart or, if they do have one, feeling that the chart should be kept a secret.

Advantages. A prominent manufacturer once said that although he could see some use for an organization chart for his factory, he had refused to chart the organization above the level of factory superintendent. His argument was that charts tend to make people overly conscious of being superiors or inferiors, tend to destroy team feeling, and give persons occupying a box on the chart too great a feeling of "ownership." Another top executive once said that if an organization is left uncharted, it can be changed more easily and that the absence of a chart also encourages a competitive drive for higher executive positions on the part of the uncharted middle-management group.

These reasons for not charting organization structures are clearly unsound. Subordinate-superior relationships exist not because of charting but, rather, because of essential reporting relationships. As for a chart's creating a too-comfortable feeling and causing a lack of drive on the part of those who have "arrived," these are matters of top leadership—of reorganizing whenever the enterprise environment demands, of developing a tradition of change, and of making subordinate managers continue to meet adequate, well-understood standards of performance. Managers who believe team spirit can be produced without clearly spelling out relationships are fooling themselves and preparing the way for politics, intrigue, frustration, buck-passing, lack of coordination, duplicated effort, vague policy, uncertain decision making, and other evidences of organizational inefficiency.

Since a chart maps lines of decision-making authority, sometimes merely charting an organization can show inconsistencies and complexities and lead to their correction. A chart also reveals to managers and new personnel how they tie into the entire structure.

Limitations.   Organization charts are subject to important limitations. In the first place, a chart shows only formal authority relationships and omits the many significant informal and informational relationships. Figure 12-1 shows many, but not nearly all, of the informal and informational relationships found in a typical organized enterprise. It shows also the major line, or formal, relationships. It does not show how much authority exists at any point in the structure. While it would be interesting to chart an organization with lines of different widths to denote formal authority of varying degrees, authority is not subject to such measurement. And if the multiple lines of informal relationships and of communication were drawn, they would so complicate a chart that it could not be understood.

Many charts show structures as they are supposed to be or used to be, rather than as they really are. Managers hesitate or neglect to redraft charts, forgetting that organization structures are dynamic and that charts should not be allowed to become obsolete.

Another difficulty with organization charts is that individuals may confuse authority relationships with status. The staff officer reporting to the corporation president may be shown at the top of the organization chart, while a regional line officer may be shown one or two levels lower. Although good charting attempts to make levels on the chart conform to levels of enterprise importance, it cannot always do so. This problem can be handled by clearly spelling out authority relationships and by using that best indicator of status—salary and bonus levels. No one is likely, for example, to hear that the general manager of Chevrolet in General Motors feels a sense of inferiority because his position on the chart is below that of the company secretary.

Position Descriptions

Every managerial position should be defined. A good position description informs everyone of the incumbent's responsibilities. A modern position description is not a detailed list of all the activities an individual is expected to undertake, and it certainly does not specify how to undertake them. Rather, it states the basic function of the position, the major end-result areas for which the manager is responsible, and the reporting relationships involved. The description also makes

FIGURE 12-1

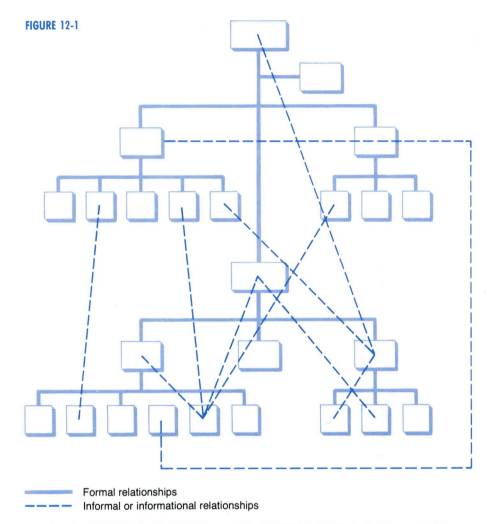

▬▬▬▬   Formal relationships
- - - -   Informal or informational relationships

THE FORMAL AND INFORMAL OR INFORMATIONAL ORGANIZATION.

reference to the current chart of approval authorizations to clarify the position's authority, and it states the set of verifiable objectives for the end-result areas.

Position descriptions have many benefits. As jobs are analyzed, duties and responsibilities are brought into focus and areas of overlapping or neglected duties come to light. Forcing people to consider what should be done and who should do it is more than worth the effort. Further benefits of job descriptions include the guidance they provide in training new managers, in drawing up candidate requirements, and in setting salary levels. Finally, as a means of control over organization, the position description furnishes a standard against which to judge whether a position is necessary and, if so, what its organization level and exact location in the structure should be.

ENSURING UNDERSTANDING OF ORGANIZING

All the members of an enterprise must understand the structure of their organization in order for that structure to work. This requires teaching. Also, since formal organization is supplemented by informal organization, members of an enterprise must understand the general workings of informal as well as formal organization.

Teaching the Nature of Organizing

Many soundly conceived organization plans fail because organization members do not understand them. A well-written organization manual—containing a statement of organization philosophy, programs, charts, and an outline of job descriptions—goes far toward making organizing understandable. If an organization structure is put into written words and charts, it has a better chance of being clear than if it is not. However, because even the best-written words and charts do not always clearly convey the same meaning to every reader, effective managers cannot stop with written clarification. They must teach those in their operation the meaning of the organization structure, their position in it, and the relationships involved.

Managers may do this by individual coaching, by adding staff or special meetings, or by simply watching how the structure works. If subordinates pass decisions up the line that they should be making themselves, managers can take this opportunity to clarify authority. Likewise, if communication among members of a group seems to be inadequate, managers can look for causes in either a poorly conceived or a poorly understood organization structure. Too many group meetings or too much committee work is a signal for managers to do some investigating. Thus, managers are obligated continually to teach the fundamentals of organizing, for if they do not, their enterprise or department is likely to fail.

Recognizing the Importance of Informal Organization and the Grapevine

Another way of making the formal organization work effectively is to recognize and take full advantage of informal organization. The nature of informal organizations and their distinction from formal organizations were discussed in Chapter 9. Many informal organizations arise from the formal organization in which they operate. They include interrelationships that are not usually charted, such as the unwritten rules of organizational conduct, the way to "learn the ropes," the people in an enterprise who have power not implied by or coming from an organization position, and gossip. One of the best-known examples of an important informal organization, one which seems to exist in every department and organization, is the "grapevine."

The grapevine.   Informal organization tends to exist when members of a formal organization (perhaps a company department) know one another well enough to pass on information—sometimes only gossip—that is in some way connected with the enterprise. In the typical enterprise—whose members spend many hours a day deriving material security and status, as well as social satisfaction, from the grapevine—the desire for information concerning the organization and its people is strong enough that such information is rapidly transmitted between persons who know and trust one another.

The grapevine, of course, thrives on information not openly available to the entire group, whether because that information is regarded as confidential, or because formal lines of communication are inadequate to spread it, or because it is of the kind, like much gossip, that would never be formally disclosed. Even managers who conscientiously inform employees through company bulletins or newspapers never so completely or quickly disclose all information of interest as to make the grapevine purposeless.

Since all forms of informal organization serve essential human communication needs, the grapevine is inevitable and valuable. Indeed, an intelligent top manager would probably be wise to feed it accurate information, since it is very effective for quick communication. There is much to be said for a manager's getting a place—personally or through a trusted staff member or secretary—on the company grapevine.

Benefits.   Informal organization brings a kind of cohesiveness to formal organization. It imparts to members of a formal organization a sense of belonging, status, self-respect, and satisfaction. Many managers, understanding this fact, consciously use informal organizations as channels of communication and molders of employee morale.

PROMOTING AN APPROPRIATE ORGANIZATION CULTURE[5]

The effectiveness of an organization is also influenced by the organization culture, which affects the way the managerial functions of planning, organizing, staffing, leading, and controlling are carried out. Illustrations of organization culture are listed in Table 12-1. Given the choice, most people would probably prefer to work in an organization such as environment B, in which one can participate in the decision-making process, one is evaluated on the basis of performance criteria rather than on the basis of friendship, one has open communication channels in all directions, and one has the opportunity to exercise a great deal of self-control. In their search for excellent companies, Thomas Peters and Robert Waterman, the authors of a best-selling book on management, found that the dominance of a coherent culture characterized these organizations.[6]

But the recognition of the importance of corporate culture is not new at all (although some management gurus want you to believe it is).[7] Over 2000 years ago, in 431 B.C., Pericles in ancient Greece eloquently urged the Athenians, who were at war with the Spartans, to adhere to values such as those inherent in democracy: informality in communication, the importance of individual dignity, and promotion based on performance. Pericles realized that the underlying values might mean victory or defeat. These values are not so different from those espoused by many U.S. companies.

TABLE 12-1 ILLUSTRATIONS OF ORGANIZATION CULTURE AND MANAGEMENT PRACTICE	
Environment A	**Environment B**
Planning	
Goals are set in an autocratic manner.	Goals are set with a great deal of participation.
Decision making is centralized.	Decision making is decentralized.
Organizing	
Authority is centralized.	Authority is decentralized.
Authority is narrowly defined.	Authority is broadly defined.
Staffing	
People are selected on the basis of friendship.	People are selected on the basis of performance criteria.
Training is in a narrowly defined specialty.	Training is in many functional areas.
Leading	
Managers exercise directive leadership.	Managers practice participative leadership.
Communication flow is primarily top-down.	Communication flow is top-down, bottom-up, horizontal, and diagonal.
Controlling	
Superiors exercise strict control.	Individuals exercise a great deal of self-control.
Focus is on financial criteria.	Focus is on multiple criteria.

Defining Organization Culture

As it relates to organizations, **culture** is the general pattern of behavior, shared beliefs, and values that members have in common.[8] Culture can be inferred from what people say, do, and think within an organizational setting. It involves the learning and transmitting of knowledge, beliefs, and patterns of behavior over a period of time, which means that an organization culture is fairly stable and does not change fast.[9] It often sets the tone for the company and establishes implied rules for the way people should behave. Many slogans give a general idea of what a particular company stands for.[10] Here are some examples:

For General Electric, it is "Progress is our most important product."

American Telephone & Telegraph Company is proud of its "universal service."

Delta Airlines describes its internal climate with the slogan "the Delta family feeling."

Du Pont makes "better things for better living through chemistry."

KLM Royal Dutch Airlines wants to be known as "the reliable airline." Its president, Jan F.A. de Soet, stated that KLM is not a flamboyant airline. Instead, the organization culture reflects the Dutch dislike of ostentation.[11]

Similarly, IBM wants to be known for its service, Sears for quality and price, Caterpillar for its 24-hour parts service, Polaroid for its innovation, Maytag for its reliability, and so on. Indeed, the orientation of these companies, often expressed in slogans, contributed to the successful conduct of their businesses.

The Influence of the Leader on Organization Culture

Managers, especially top managers, create the climate for the enterprise. Their values influence the direction of the firm. Although the term "value" is used differently, a **value** can be defined as a fairly permanent belief about what is appropriate and what is not that guides the actions and behavior of employees in fulfilling the organization's aims. Values can be thought of as forming an ideology that permeates everyday decisions.

In many successful companies, value-driven corporate leaders serve as role models, set the standards for performance, motivate employees, make the company special, and are a symbol to the external environment.[12] It was Edwin Land, the founder of Polaroid, who created a favorable organizational environment for research and innovation. It was Jim Treybig of Tandem, in the Silicon Valley near San Francisco, who made it a point to emphasize that every person is a human being and deserves to be treated accordingly. It was William Cooper Procter of Procter & Gamble who ran the company with the slogan "Do what is right." It was Theodore Vail of AT&T who addressed the needs of customers by emphasizing service. It was Du Pont's CEO Woolard who initiated the Adopt a Customer program, through which workers are encouraged to visit their customers monthly to find out their needs and concerns. The organization culture created by corporate leaders can result in managerial functions being carried out in quite different ways.

While the CEO must indicate the direction, some contend that change must come from the bottom of the organization.[13] At Du Pont's Towanda plant in Pennsylvania, people are organized in self-directing teams. Employees have a great deal of freedom to set their own schedules, solve their own problems, and even participate in selecting coworkers. Indicative of this culture is that managers are called facilitators rather than superiors.

Changing a culture may take a long time, even 5 to 10 years. It demands changing values, symbols, myths, and behavior. It may require first understanding the old culture, identifying a subculture in the organization, and rewarding those living this culture. Rewards do not have to be in financial terms. In Sharp's factory in Japan, top performers are rewarded by becoming members of the "gold badge" team, which reports directly to the president. At any rate, CEOs must symbolize the culture they want to promote.

Perspective

General
Motors'
Mission
and Culture

General Motors' chairman, Roger B. Smith, is attempting to change the company's culture.[14] One of the major tasks is to merge GM's culture with the very different ones of its newly acquired firms, such as the high-tech aerospace firm Hughes Aircraft Company and the computer services company Electronic Data Systems (EDS), headed by the colorful, action-oriented entrepreneur Ross Perot.[15] While GM emphasized bureaucratic processes and procedures, EDS focused on achieving results in a militarylike fashion. While decision making was slow at GM and risk taking usually not rewarded, Hughes, being at the forefront of technology, continuously had to scan the environment for new developments and opportunities, making decisions that, at times, involved a great deal of risk.

To give direction to the divergent cultures, Smith distributes "culture cards" that state the company's mission: "The fundamental purpose of General Motors is to provide products and services of such quality that our customers will receive superior value, our employees and business partners will share our success, and our stockholders will receive a sustained, superior return on their investment."[16]

A clear vision of a common purpose elicits commitment. Moreover, when people participate in the decision-making process and exercise self-direction and self-control, they feel committed to their own plans. But espoused values need to be reinforced through rewards and incentives, ceremonies, stories, and symbolic actions.[17]

CONTINGENCIES IN ORGANIZING

Throughout this book we have emphasized that to be effective, organizations must adapt to the specific requirement of the situation. Major contributions toward a contingency, or situational, theory of organizing have been made by researchers in the United States and abroad. We will briefly examine some studies and their major contributions.

Studies by Burns and Stalker

Tom Burns and G. M. Stalker investigated the relationship between management practices and characteristics of the external environment.[18] Specifically, they interviewed key persons in twenty English and Scottish companies and developed a conceptual scheme with two different systems of management practices. One system was called "mechanistic" and the other "organic."[19]

The **mechanistic management system** appears to be appropriate for relatively stable organization environments. This system is characterized by, among other things, specialized differentiation of tasks, by individuals viewing their tasks as being distinct from the whole, by precisely defined rights and obligations, by a hierarchical structure, by vertical interactions between the superior and the subordinates, and by having instructions and decisions come from the superior.

The **organic management system,** on the other hand, is characterized by individual performance based on knowledge of the task of the whole concern, continued redefinition of tasks through interaction with others, and a great deal of lateral interaction and consultation. This system, it is suggested, is more suitable for coping with unstable and changing conditions and unpredictable problems.

Studies by Woodward

The studies of 100 British firms conducted by Joan Woodward indicate that there is a relationship between organization design and different types of technology.[20] This researcher classified the enterprises into three groups according to increasing degrees of technological complexity: (1) small-batch and unit production, making such items as special purpose equipment or custom-made products; (2) large-batch and mass production, as, for example, in the manufacture of items produced in large quantities on the assembly line; and (3) process or continuous-flow production, such as that found in chemical firms and oil refineries.

The findings suggest that the more successful firms in the large-batch and mass production category were organized in a manner similar to what Burns and Stalker described as mechanistic.

On the other hand, the small-batch and unit production firms, as well as the process or continuous-flow production firms, were more effective with organic structures. In short, the Woodward research suggests that to be effective, organization design is contingent on production technology.

Studies by Lawrence and Lorsch

Building on the studies by Woodward and Burns and Stalker, the research by Paul R. Lawrence and Jay W. Lorsch focused on the relative stability of environments. Organizations with changing environments demand greater **differentiation,** a term defined as *"the difference in cognitive and emotional orientation among managers in different functional departments."*[21] A company in the plastics industry, for example, working in a dynamic environment, requires considerable differentiation. Such an organization also has a great need for **integration,** a term defined as *"the quality of the state of collaboration that exists among departments that are required to achieve unity of effort by the demands of the environment."*[22] Thus, more unstable environments call for more organic types of organization, using, for example, teams that cut across functions in order to integrate activities.

On the other hand, more stable environments demand less differentiation, and the means for integration may differ from those in dynamic environments. For example, Lawrence and Lorsch found that a company in the container industry with a relatively stable environment was effective in using more mechanistic organizational arrangements such as a managerial hierarchy.

SUMMARY

Organizing involves developing an intentional structure of roles for effective performance. Many mistakes in organizing can be avoided by first planning the ideal organization for goal achievement and then making modifications for the human or other situational factors. Organization planning identifies staffing needs and helps overcome staffing deficiencies. It also discloses duplication of effort, unclear authority and communication lines, and obsolete ways of doing things. An effective organization remains flexible and adjusts for changes in the environment.

To make staff work effective, it is important to teach the authority relationships, to make line listen to staff people, and to keep staff informed. Furthermore, effectiveness demands that staff persons prepare complete recommendations and that the utilization of staff become a way of organizational life.

Organizational conflict can be reduced by the use of organization charts and position descriptions. Organizing is improved by teaching its nature and by recognizing the informal organization and the grapevine. Moreover, effective enterprises develop and nurture an appropriate organization culture.

Effective organizations adapt to the situation. Three contingency approaches to organizing were identified. Burns and Stalker discussed the mechanistic and the organic management systems. Woodward classified enterprises into (1) small-batch and unit production, (2) large-batch and mass production, and (3) process or continuous-flow production. Lawrence and Lorsch focused on the relative stability of environments and discussed organizations in terms of differentiation and integration.

KEY IDEAS AND CONCEPTS FOR REVIEW

Avoiding mistakes in organizing by
    planning
Avoiding organizational inflexibility
Effective staff work
Avoiding conflict by clarification
Organization charts
Position description
Understanding of organizing
Informal organization
The grapevine

Organization culture
Values
Mechanistic management system
Organic management system
Small-batch and unit production
Large-batch and mass production
Process or continuous-flow production
Differentiation
Integration

FOR DISCUSSION

1. Many psychologists have pointed to the advantages of "job enlargement," that is, assigning tasks that are not so specialized that an individual loses a sense of doing things that are meaningful. Assuming that managers wish to limit specialization of tasks and "enlarge" jobs, can they do so and still apply the basic principles of organizing? How?

2. Taking an organized enterprise with which you have some familiarity, can you find any of the deficiencies that commonly occur in organization structures?

3. It is sometimes stated that the typical organization chart is undemocratic in that it emphasizes the superiority and inferiority of people and positions. Comment.

4. What, in your judgment, makes an organization structure "good"? How do "good" organization structures support leadership?

5. What would you need to know to plan an organization structure? How far ahead should you plan it? How would you go about making such a plan?

6. Take an organization you know and discuss its culture. Is the culture helping or hindering the organization with respect to the achievement of its goals? In what ways?

EXERCISES/ACTION STEPS

1. Visit a company in your area that is considered a model of effective management. Get any information on this company that gives you some insight into the operation. What makes this organization excellent? Would you like to work for this enterprise? Why, or why not?

2. Gather information on a company that is considered poorly managed. If it is a local company, talk to people and read the newspaper. If the firm is not in your area, gather the information from magazines (e.g., *Fortune, Forbes, Business Week*) and newspapers (e.g., *The Wall Street Journal*). What are some of the problems? What would you recommend to make this firm more effective? Present your findings and your recommendations to the class.

CASES

CASE 12-1
ORGANIZATION CULTURE AT IBM[23]

Everyone at IBM is expected to follow three fundamental principles: Respect individuals, strive for excellence, and provide the best service. Thomas Watson founded a patriarchy to instill these principles. His successors have maintained them in the face of rapid growth and changing technology by moving toward a more entrepreneurial system.

One way top management shows its respect for individuals is by treating all employees as equals. IBM hires employees for life. No one will lose his or her job unless he or she consistently fails to meet clear standards or violates the ethics code. There is no distinction between white-, blue-, and pink-collar workers. Many employees will move through line and staff positions over the course of their career. All em-

ployees are encouraged to continue their education and prepare themselves for promotions. Almost all middle- and upper-level positions are filled by existing IBM employees.

New employees undergo up to 9 months of training to prepare them for their job and to indoctrinate them in the IBM philosophy. Those who stay rapidly adapt to the corporate culture by dressing conservatively, engaging in competition and team sports, attending various company events, and embracing other aspects of corporate life. Another mark of respect for the individual is the attention top management pays to employee suggestions. The firm has a tradition of open doors at the highest levels. At least once a year, employees discuss matters important to them with their managers. In turn, managers publicly respond to all comments received in suggestion boxes. A suggestion program rewards ideas that reduce costs or improve products or quality control. Between 1975 and 1984, IBM paid workers almost $60 million for suggestions that saved the company $300 million.

Top management monitors employee morale through questionnaires and roundtable discussions at all levels. It holds branch and division managers accountable for any problems and actively helps them improve morale. Most employees are happy being a part of the IBM family and stay with the company for their entire professional life.

IBM is well known for dependable service. Top management emphasizes its commitment to service by focusing on the people who provide that service: the marketing representatives. Most of the top executives, including Thomas Watson, the former CEO, began their career as salespeople.

Representatives are given full responsibility for pleasing customers. If representatives lose an account, the original sales commission for that account is deducted from their salary. It is not surprising that the representatives spend much of their time helping customers to maintain their system.

Distinction at IBM is based on merit. The system is designed to foster achievers. Managers establish realistic goals and exuberantly reward employees when they reach them. Almost 25 percent of the employees get bonuses, many receive gifts or a dinner for two, and they receive frequent praise.

The merit system is most obvious in the sales force. Annual sales quotas are set so that approximately 80 percent of the sales representatives will meet them. The representatives' monthly sales are posted on bulletin boards. Managers are expected to help subordinates to meet their goals. Those who achieve their quota join the "100% Club." They attend a lavish three-day annual celebration. The 10 percent of the sales representatives who have the highest sales join the "Golden Circle" and celebrate their success at a posh resort. Those who consistently fail to meet quotas are dismissed.

The competition is tempered by a rigorously enforced code of ethics and team spirit. No matter what their levels, managers depend on their teams' efforts for successes. Because the teams are small, managers can give extensive personal attention to their subordinates. In addition, the sales branches hold monthly rallies to review progress and reward top performers.

As IBM grew, the organization became a vast bureaucracy. Growth has spawned many rules and controls. The hierarchy in such a large organization may slow down communication between departments. Thus, despite their immediate superior's attention to their professional needs, some employees feel insignificant and do not know the direction of the company.

IBM's customer orientation helped the firm to respond rapidly to changes in the market despite the bureaucracy. When personal computers became popular, top management realized it had ignored a product its customers wanted. To get a personal computer on the market fast, top management bypassed its bureaucracy by forming an independent business unit (IBU). The vice president and his team were freed from other duties so that they could devote their full attention to developing, manufacturing, and marketing the IBM personal computer (PC) without interference from the rest of the organization.

The PC team made several revolutionary decisions, including buying components from other companies, using "open architecture" so other companies could provide software and compatible equipment, and distributing the PC through computer stores. Previously, IBM had insisted on providing all computer services and equipment itself, and its technical specifications had been jealously guarded secrets.

IBM now exploits opportunities in telecommunications, robotics, electronics, scientific instrumentation, and computer software by buying into existing companies or forming IBUs. It has also moved toward decentralization, giving individuals more autonomy without relinquishing its founder's basic philosophy.

Since John Akers became chairman, changes have been occurring in the organization culture, exemplified by the slogan "Just say no." This means that employees should resist unnecessary requests from upper-level managers. In the past, many decisions had to be approved by several persons at higher levels. To reduce the unnecessary bureaucracy, decision making is pushed to lower levels, and staff personnel are reassigned to line positions.

1. What is IBM's culture? How does it affect employees? What symbols, traditions, and norms typify IBM?
2. How has the culture changed? How did it help or hinder IBM's adaptation to the external environment?
3. What problem could acquisitions and IBUs create? How should IBM integrate them?

INTERNATIONAL CASE 12-2
RESTRUCTURING AT KOREA'S DAEWOO[24]

Daewoo was founded in 1967 by its hardworking, relentlessly driven chairman, Kim (surname) Woo-Choong. After its initial success in exporting textiles, the company expanded into trade, autos, machinery, consumer electronics, construction, heavy shipping, computers, telephones, and financial services, becoming Korea's fourth largest business group. The company became, for example, a textile supplier for Sears, Christian Dior, Calvin Klein, and London Fog. Daewoo also engaged in a joint venture with General Motors to build the Le Mans car. However, labor and other problems limited the car shipments.

Chairman Kim's philosophy of hard work and the value placed in people were important factors in the firm's success. However, in the late 1980s and early 1990s, the company faced several problems. For one, Kim was concerned that with the increasing prosperity of Koreans, the work force might lose the spirit of hard work. Moreover, there was a growing discontent among the younger workers and a lessening of motivation.

Through Kim's hands-off approach to managing, some of the companies in the Daewoo business group went out of control. For example, in the unprofitable heavy shipping industry, he noticed many unnecessary expenses. The elimination of company-sponsored barbershops saved the company $8 million a year.

In general, Daewoo's work force is young and well educated. In contrast to similar positions in many other Korean companies, top positions at Daewoo are occupied by managers with no family ties.

Although Daewoo is a major company with its 91,000 employees, it is not dominant in any one industry. The strategy of being a supplier for major foreign companies, such as Caterpillar, General Motors, and Boeing, may have led to bypassing opportunities for becoming a major marketer of its own brands. Now, in the 1990s, Kim is also looking at opportunities in Europe; for example, he formed a joint venture with a distribution company in France.

The massive restructuring has already had some positive effects. Kim sold some steel, financial, and real estate units. The hands-off managerial style has been replaced by a hands-on style, resulting in recentralization. Managers were "retired" or otherwise let go. Thousands of positions were also eliminated.

Things were looking better in 1991. The company lost money in 1988 and 1989 but made some profit in 1990 partly because of the sale of some major assets. The joint venture with GM registered a healthy growth. The company was also optimistic about the future of the new compact car Espero. Still, in the early 1990s, Daewoo has had to cope with the strong Korean currency, its labor costs, Japanese competition, and recessions in various countries in which it operates.

1. What are the advantages and disadvantages of a hands-off, decentralized management approach?
2. How can Daewoo stay competitive with the Japanese?
3. What are some of the controllable and uncontrollable factors in this case? How should Mr. Kim respond to those factors?

REFERENCES

1. Michael Beer, "Revitalizing Organizations: Change Process and Emergent Model," *Academy of Management Executive* (February 1987), p. 51.
2. Lyndall Urwick, *The Elements of Administration* (New York: Harper & Row, 1944), p. 38.
3. Michael W. Miller and Paul B. Carroll, "IBM Unveils a Sweeping Restructuring in Bid to Decentralize Decision-Making," *The Wall Street Journal* (Jan. 29, 1988).
4. Todd Vogel, "Where 1990s-Style Management Is Already Hard at Work," *Business Week* (Oct. 23, 1989), pp. 92–100.

5. See also Taylor Cox, Jr., "The Multicultural Organization," *Academy of Management Executive* (May 1991), pp. 34–47.

6. Thomas J. Peters and Robert H. Waterman, Jr., *In Search of Excellence* (New York: Harper & Row, 1982).

7. John K. Clemens, "A Lesson from 431 B.C.," *Fortune* (Oct. 13, 1986), pp. 161–164.

8. Vijay Sathe, "Some Action Implications of Corporate Culture: A Manager's Guide to Action," *Organizational Dynamics* (Autumn 1983), pp. 4–23; S. R. Luce, "Managing Corporate Culture," *Canadian Business Review* (Spring 1984), pp. 40–43; Stanley M. Davis, "Corporate Culture and Human Resource Management: Two Keys to Implementing Strategy," *Human Resource Planning,* vol. 6, no. 3 (1983), pp. 159–167; Edgar H. Schein, "What You Need to Know about Organizational Culture," *Training and Development Journal* (January 1986), pp. 30–33.

9. B. Littal, "The Corporate Culture Vultures," *Fortune* (Oct. 17, 1983), pp. 66–72.

10. Terrence E. Deal and Allan A. Kennedy, *Corporate Cultures* (Reading, Mass.: Addison-Wesley Publishing Company, 1982), chap. 2.

11. Susan Carey, "Quiet KLM: Agile, Aggressive, Profitable," *The Wall Street Journal* (July 14, 1989).

12. For a classification of values, see Yoash Wiener, "Forms of Value Systems: A Focus on Organizational Effectiveness and Cultural Change and Maintenance," *Academy of Management Review* (October 1988), pp. 534–545.

13. Brian Dumaine, "Creating a New Company Culture," *Fortune* (Jan. 15, 1990), pp. 127–131.

14. David E. Whiteside, "Roger Smith's Campaign to Change the GM Culture," *Business Week* (Apr. 7, 1986), pp. 84–85; Russell Mitchell, "How General Motors Is Bringing Up Ross Perot's Baby," *Business Week* (Apr. 14, 1986), pp. 96–100; Melinda Grenier Guiles, "GM's Smith Presses for Sweeping Changes, but Questions Arise," *The Wall Street Journal* (Mar. 14, 1985). Partly owing to cultural differences, Ross Perot parted with General Motors.

15. Walter Guzzardi, Jr., "The U.S. Business Hall of Fame," *Fortune* (Mar. 14, 1988), pp. 144–145.

16. Clemens, "A Lesson from 431 B.C." (1986), p. 164.

17. James M. Kouzes, David F. Caldwell, and Barry Z. Posner, "Organizational Culture: How It Is Created, Maintained, and Changed," presentation by the authors, 1983.

18. Tom Burns and G. M. Stalker, *The Management of Innovation* (London: Tavistock Publications, 1961).

19. For additional discussion, see Patrick E. Connor, "Organization Structure and Design," in James E. Rosenzweig and Fremont E. Kast (eds.), *Modules in Management* (Chicago: SRA, Science Research Associates, 1984).

20. Joan Woodward, *Industrial Organization: Theory and Practice* (London: Oxford University Press, 1965), especially chap. 5.

21. Paul R. Lawrence and Jay W. Lorsch, *Organization and Environment* (Homewood, Ill.: Richard D. Irwin, 1969), p. 11.

22. Lawrence and Lorsch, *Organization and Environment* (1969), p. 11.

23. This case is based on a variety of sources, including the following: P. H. Dorn, "The Song Remains the Same," *Datamation* (February 1984), pp. 105–110; L. W. Foster, "From Darwin to Now: The Evolution of Organizational Strategies," *Journal of Business Strategy* (Spring 1985), pp. 94–98; B. Jeffery, "With a Little Help from Some Friends," *Datamation* (February 1984), pp. 147–150; D. Kneal, J. Marcom, Jr., and Randall Smith, "IBM: Behind the Monolith—A Special Report," *The Wall Street Journal* (Apr. 7, 1986), pp. 19–22; L. Luciano, "Seeing the Future Work at IBM," *Money* (November

1985); Peter D. Petre, "Meet the Lean, Mean New IBM," *Fortune* (June 13, 1983), p. 69; T. Sweeny, "Corporate Culture," *San Francisco Business* (February 1986), p. 6; Jo Ellen Davis and Geoff Lewis, "Who's Afraid of IBM?" *Business Week* (June 29, 1987), pp. 68–74; "The Greatest Capitalist in History," *Fortune* (Aug. 31, 1987), pp. 24–35; Michael W. Miller and Paul B. Carroll, "New Big Blue—Akers's Drive to Mend IBM Is Shaking Up Its Vaunted Traditions," *The Wall Street Journal* (Nov. 11, 1988).

24. The case is based on a variety of sources, including Laxmi Nakarmi, "At Daewoo, A 'Revolution' at the Top," *Business Week* (Feb. 18, 1991), pp. 68–69. The assistance of Professor Dong-Sung Cho of Seoul National University, who, together with Professor J. Aguilar, wrote the Harvard Business School case Daewoo Group (1984), is greatly appreciated.

Summary of Major Principles, or Guides, for Organizing

Although the science of organizing has not yet developed to the point at which its principles are infallible laws, there is considerable agreement among management scholars and practitioners about a number of them. These principles are truths (or are believed to be truths) of general applicability, although their application is not precise enough to give them the exactness of the laws of pure science. They are more in the nature of essential criteria for effective organizing. The most essential guiding principles of organizing are summarized in this section.

The Purpose of Organizing

The purpose of organizing is to aid in making objectives meaningful and to contribute to organizational efficiency.

Principle of unity of objectives. An organization structure is effective if it enables individuals to contribute to enterprise objectives.

Principle of organizational efficiency. An organization is efficient if it is structured to aid the accomplishment of enterprise objectives with a minimum of unsought consequences or costs.

The Cause of Organizing

The basic cause of organization structure is the limitation of the span of management. If there were no such limitation, an unorganized enterprise might have only one manager.

Span-of-management principle. In each managerial position, there is a limit to the number of persons an individual can effectively manage, but the exact number will depend on the impact of underlying variables.

The Structure of Organization: Authority

Authority is the cement of organization structure, the thread that makes it possible, the means by which groups of activities can be placed under a manager and coordination of organizational units can be promoted. It is the tool by which a manager is able to exercise discretion and create an environment for individual performance. Some of the most useful principles of organizing are related to authority.

Scalar principle. The clearer the line of authority from the ultimate management position in an enterprise to every subordinate position, the clearer will be the responsibility for decision making and the more effective will be organization communication.

Principle of delegation by results expected. Authority delegated to all individual managers should be adequate to ensure their ability to accomplish results expected.

Principle of absoluteness of responsibility. The responsibility of subordinates to their superiors for performance is absolute, and superiors cannot escape responsibility for the organization activities of their subordinates.

Principle of parity of authority and responsibility. The responsibility for actions cannot be greater than that implied by the authority delegated, nor should it be less.

Principle of unity of command. The more complete an individual's reporting relationships to a single superior, the smaller the problem of conflicting instructions and the greater the feeling of personal responsibility for results.

Authority-level principle. Maintenance of intended delegation requires that decisions within the authority of individual managers should be made by them and not be referred upward in the organization structure.

The Structure of Organization: Departmentized Activities

Organization involves the design of a departmental framework. Although there are several principles in this area, one is of major importance.

Principle of functional definition. The more a position or a department has a clear definition of the results expected, activities to be undertaken, and organization authority delegated and has an understanding of authority and informational relationships with other positions, the more adequately the responsible individual can contribute toward accomplishing enterprise objectives.

The Process of Organizing

The various principles of authority delegation and of departmentation are fundamental truths about the process of organizing. They deal with phases of the two primary aspects of organizing—authority and activity groupings. There are other principles that deal with the process of organizing. It is through their application that managers gain a sense of proportion or a measure of the total organizing process.

Principle of balance.   In every structure there is a need for balance. The application of principles or techniques must be balanced to ensure the overall effectiveness of the structure in meeting enterprise objectives.

The principle of balance is common to all areas of science and to all functions of the manager. The inefficiencies of broad spans of management must be balanced against the inefficiencies of long lines of communication. The losses from multiple command must be balanced against the gains from expertness and uniformity in delegating functional authority to staff and service departments. The savings of functional specialization in departmentalizing must be balanced against the advantages of establishing profit-responsible, semi-independent product or territorial departments. It is apparent, once again, that the application of management theory depends on the specific situation.

Principle of flexibility.   The more that provisions are made for building flexibility into an organization structure, the more adequately an organization structure can fulfill its purpose.

Devices and techniques for anticipating and reacting to change must be built into every structure. Every enterprise moves toward its goal in a changing environment, both external and internal. The enterprise that develops inflexibilities, whether these are resistance to change, too complicated procedures, or too firm departmental lines, is risking the inability to meet the challenges of economic, technical, biological, political, and social changes.

Principle of leadership facilitation.   The more an organization structure and its delegations of authority enable managers to design and maintain an environment for performance, the more they will help the leadership abilities of those managers.

Since managership depends to a great extent on the quality of leadership of those in managerial positions, it is important for the organization structure to do its part in creating a situation in which a manager can most effectively lead. In this sense, organizing is a technique of promoting leadership. If the authority allocation and the structural arrangements create a situation in which heads of departments tend to be looked upon as leaders and in which their task of leadership is aided, organization structuring has accomplished an essential task.

Global Organizing

This part closing is about global organizing. First, the managerial practices in Japan, the United States, and China are discussed. Second, the international focus is on the study of quality service in Europe, the United States and Canada, and Japan. Third, a global car industry case is presented.

ORGANIZING PRACTICES IN JAPAN, THE UNITED STATES, AND THE PEOPLE'S REPUBLIC OF CHINA[1]

In the Part 2 closing, the managerial planning practices in Japan, the United States, and China were compared. In this part closing, a similar analysis is done for the managerial function of organizing, as summarized in the table on page 348.

Organizing involves setting up a structure to coordinate human efforts so that people can contribute effectively and efficiently to the aims of the enterprise. This requires determining roles, responsibilities, and accountability.

Organizing in Japan

In Japanese companies, largely owing to the search for consensus in decision making, the emphasis is on collective responsibility and accountability. Individual responsibilities, then, are implied rather than explicitly defined. Although this may discourage placing the blame for an incorrect decision on individuals, it also can create a great deal of uncertainty. In fact, the organization structure is rather ambiguous, and the de-emphasis on formal authority promotes informality and

COMPARISONS OF JAPANESE, U.S., AND CHINESE ORGANIZING*		
Japanese management	**U.S. management**	**Chinese management**
1. Collective responsibility and accountability	1. Individual responsibility and accountability	1. Collective and individual responsibility
2. Ambiguous decision responsibility	2. Clear and specific decision responsibility	2. Attempts to introduce the "factory responsibility system"
3. Informal organization structure	3. Formal, bureaucratic organization structure	3. Formal, bureaucratic organization structure
4. Well-known common organization culture and philosophy; competitive spirit toward other enterprises	4. Lack of common organization culture; identification with profession rather than with company	4. Identification with the company but no competitive spirit

* Sources of information are given in note 6 in the Part 2 closing References.

egalitarianism. Another characteristic found in Japanese firms is a common organizational culture and philosophy, placing a high value on unity and harmony within the organization. At the same time, there is a competitive spirit toward other enterprises. Organizational change is accomplished by changing processes, with the aim of maintaining harmony among those affected. Also, the change agent (OD consultant) is virtually always an employee of the company.

Organizing in the United States

Organizations in the United States emphasize individual responsibility, with efforts to clarify and make explicit who is responsible for what. Often specific job descriptions clarify the nature and extent of individual responsibilities. Indeed, many organizations, especially those operating in a stable environment, have been rather successful in using the formal, bureaucratic organization structure. As far as the climate is concerned, not many managers make special efforts to create a commonly shared organization culture. This may indeed be difficult because professionals—managers as well as technical people—often have a closer identification with their profession than with a particular company. In addition, the work force often consists of people with different values derived from a diverse heritage. Many American firms have a high employee turnover rate, which is partly due to the great mobility of the people in this country. With a relatively short duration of employment with any one company, the loyalty toward the company is at times rather low. Organizational change is often accomplished by changing goals instead of processes. But organizations using change agents with a behavioral science orientation may focus on interpersonal processes to reduce conflicts and improve performance. In the United States it is quite common to employ organization development consultants from outside the firm, which is almost never done in Japan.

Organizing in China

Chinese managerial practices are very much influenced by the fact that the enterprises are owned by the state and guided by government officials. This results in a bureaucratic organization structure that does not respond well to changes in the environment. Such a structure may not have been crucial in the past (although it is ineffective) because managers did not have to respond to competing organizations. While factory managers, as individuals, are expected to achieve the yearly plan, on lower levels the notion of a vague collective responsibility prevails. Within the formal, bureaucratic structure the relationships among people are rather informal. The person heading the organization is not always the one in power. Personal connections, family relationships, and seniority are frequently more important than formal authority.

Recently, attempts have been made through the "factory responsibility system" to delegate more authority to lower levels. In fact, factories are allowed to make profits. However, these profits derived from special activities are specially taxed.[2] As in Japan, one can find strong organization cultures in Chinese enterprises. Research indicates that the degree of identification with the enterprise may vary greatly. But a low degree of commitment to the company does not result in frequent organizational changes because it is very difficult to change jobs among state-owned organizations. Also, there is a lack of competitive spirit among employees, as can be found in the United States.

INTERNATIONAL FOCUS: ORGANIZING FOR QUALITY SERVICE IN EUROPE, THE UNITED STATES, AND JAPAN[3]

Service excellence will be one of the key success factors in the global competitive environment. John Humble, with the support of the Management Centre Europe and its parent company, the American Management Association, as well as the Japanese Management Association, conducted a landmark international study on service. A total of 3375 top and middle managers took part in the study: 1300 Europeans, almost the same number of Americans and Canadians, and nearly 800 Japanese. While differences among the Europeans, Americans and Canadians, and Japanese were found, all seem to agree on the importance of superior service.

In this study, the concept of "service" is used in a broad sense. It applies to the external and internal philosophy, policies, procedures, and selected other elements.

Overall Findings

These are the findings in a nutshell: Over 90 percent of those who participated in the study think that service will become more important in the next 5 years. Perhaps even more important for managers is that almost 80 percent of the respondents think that improving the quality of service is going to be "the key to competitive success." Providing superior service is not limited to top- or lower-level management positions; 92 percent of the respondents stated that it is one of the key responsibilities of any position.

Customer Satisfaction

A more detailed analysis of the study shows some interesting results. When the respondents were asked about the importance of service 5 years ago and the importance in the next 5 years, the Japanese attached much more importance to service than either the Europeans or the Americans. Some of the reasons for giving importance to service are that (1) it is a major differentiating factor, (2) competition is fiercer, and (3) customers are more demanding than in the past.

There are a variety of means for improving service, including discussions with the sales force, regular customer–senior management meetings, market research of potential customers, and customer questionnaires. On all criteria, the Japanese scored higher than the Europeans and Americans.

In measuring the degree of customer satisfaction, a variety of methods are used. The Japanese scored higher than the Europeans and Americans on all criteria. There are some interesting differences between the U.S. and European respondents (percentages shown in parentheses). The methods for measuring satisfaction include personal visits by salespeople and managers, analysis of customer complaints, focus meetings with customer groups, employment of independent professionals, the use of questionnaires (Europe, 65 percent; United States, 97 percent), and toll-free telephone services (Europe, 39 percent; United States, 51 percent). Somewhat puzzling is how the Japanese measure customer satisfaction. When asked whether or not the companies have quantified performance standards, only 36 percent of the Japanese said "yes" (Europeans, 59 percent; Americans, 58 percent), and 53 percent of the Japanese sample answered "no" (Europeans, 32 percent; Americans, 38 percent). The other respondents answered "don't know." It appears, then, that the Japanese have more feel for customer service than hard data.

Organizing for Service Excellence

In organizing for superior service, respondents from the three areas said that bureaucracy often gets in the way of eliminating barriers. A very interesting finding is the degree of authority given to managers to satisfy customers. Specifically, when respondents were asked "In your organization, do you personally have the authority to use your own judgment to satisfy the customer?" 84 percent in the United States and 68 percent in Europe said "yes" but only 34 percent in Japan. This clearly indicates the individualistic approach to managing in America versus the group approach aiming at consensus in Japan.

Implications of the Survey

The survey findings have important implications. Managers and nonmanagers need to pay more attention to service in order to stay competitive. Training is one answer. Another is to observe the competitors' approaches to servicing their customers. Moreover, customer satisfaction must be systematically monitored. Perhaps most important, an improved customer service commitment must be a major part of everyone's job (for example, included as a performance standard) and an integral aspect of the company's strategic plan.

GLOBAL CAR INDUSTRY CASE: HOW THE LEXUS WAS BORN[4]

One of the greatest examples of global competition is in the car industry. As the Japanese gained market share in America, U.S. carmakers required the Japanese to self-impose quotas on cars exported to the States. This encouraged Japanese firms not only to establish their plants in the United States but also to build bigger and more luxurious cars to compete against the higher-priced U.S. cars and the expensive European cars such as the Mercedes and the BMW.

One such Japanese car is the Lexus, by Toyota. This car is aimed at those who would like to buy a Mercedes or BMW but cannot afford either. With a sticker price of $35,000, the Lexus was substantially less expensive than the comparable European imports.

In 1983, Toyota set out to develop the best car in the world—measured against the Mercedes and the BMW. The aim was to produce a quiet, comfortable, and safe car that could travel at 150 mph and still avoid the gas-guzzler tax imposed on cars getting less than 22.5 miles per gallon. This seemed to be an idea of conflicting goals; that is, cars being fast seemed irreconcilable with cars being, at the same time, fuel-efficient. To meet these conflicting goals, each subsystem of the car had to be carefully scrutinized, improved whenever possible, and integrated with the total design. The first version of the 32-valve V-8 engine did not meet the fuel economy requirement. The engineers applied a problem-solving technique called "thoroughgoing counter measures at the source." This means an attempt to improve every component until the design objectives are achieved. Not only the engine but also the transmission and other parts underwent close scrutiny to make the car meet U.S. fuel requirements.

The approach to achieve quality is different from that of German car manufacturers. The latter use relatively labor-intensive production processes. In contrast, Toyota's advanced manufacturing technology aims at high quality through automation requiring only a fraction of the work force used by German carmakers. Indeed, this strategy, if successful, may be the secret weapon to gain market share in the luxury car market.

In the development of the Lexus, each aspect of the car was carefully studied with the consumer in mind. The car body and the rear heck, for example, were meticulously designed and tested for air drag. The cars of competitors serving as benchmarks were thoroughly studied. Similarities of the Lexus with the Mercedes and BMW are unmistakable. The name Lexus, by the way, was carefully chosen. Several potential names consisting of nonsense words were selected by the computer. Lexus, it was thought, conveyed a sense of luxury.

To market the car, Toyota established a separate dealer network, an approach taken previously by Nissan to sell its Acura cars. Again, painstaking effort was applied in designing the showrooms and training mechanics. For the introduction of the car, reporters were flown to Germany, where they had the opportunity to compare the Lexus with Jaguars, BMWs, and Mercedes cars on the autobahn, which has no speed limit. After six years in the making, the $500 million car was finally born. What will the future hold for the Lexus?

European carmakers are naturally concerned about the coming invasion of Japanese luxury cars. Mercedes and BMW not only have to compete in the U.S. market but also may face threats of a Japanese invasion on the Continent as the European Community of 1992 moves toward a global automobile market.

1. Could U.S. manufacturers apply the same approach as Toyota to build such a car? Why, or why not? What might be some obstacles?
2. Do you think that the Lexus can obtain an image similar to that of the BMW and Mercedes cars?
3. Prepare a profile of the potential buyer of the Lexus.
4. What should Mercedes and BMW do to counteract the Japanese threat in the United States and in Europe?

REFERENCES

1. Sources of information are given in note 6 in the Part 2 closing References.
2. John R. Schermerhorn, Jr., "Organizational Features of Chinese Industrial Enterprise: Paradoxes of Stability in Times of Change," *Academy of Management Executive* (November 1987), pp. 345–349.
3. Based on the research conducted by John Humble and Domenico Fanelli, "Service— The New Competitive Edge" (Brussels: Management Centre Europe, not dated). The research began in 1988 and continued until 1989. Excerpts summarized with permission of John Humble.
4. Miscellaneous sources were used, including Alex Taylor III, "Here Come Japan's New Luxury Cars," *Fortune* (Aug. 14, 1989), pp. 62–66; Wendy Zellner, "Two Days in Boot Camp—Learning to Love Lexus," *Business Week* (Sept. 4, 1989), p. 87; Mark Landler and Wendy Zellner, "No Joyride for Japan," *Business Week* (Jan. 15, 1990), pp. 20–21; "Mercedes-Benz Unit in U.S. to Unveil Car Priced under $30,000 (by staff reporter), *The Wall Street Journal* (Aug. 31, 1990).

PART **4**

Staffing

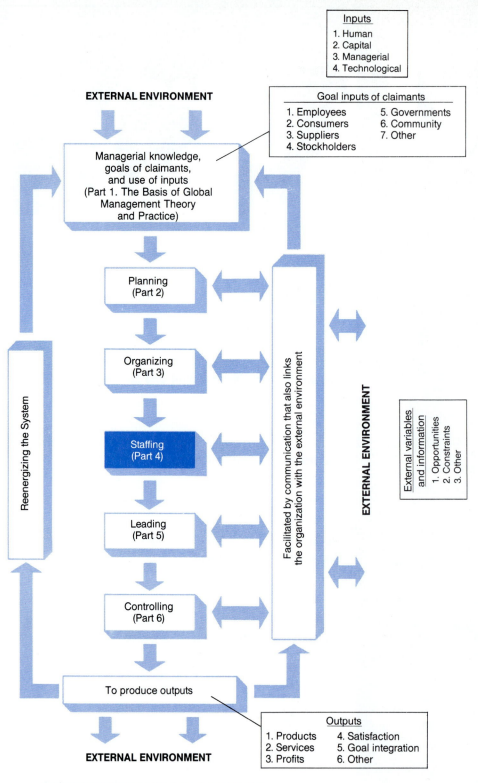

SYSTEMS APPROACH TO MANAGEMENT

Chapter 13

Human Resource Management and Selection

Technological, economic, and social changes are causing organizations to depend more and more on human resources to accomplish their objectives.[1]

Lloyd Baird and Ilan Meshoulam

Chapter Objectives

After reading this chapter, you should be able to:

1. Define the managerial function of staffing and explain what it means to be a manager.
2. Describe the systems approach to human resource management.
3. Explain the management inventory and the factors in the external and internal environment affecting staffing.
4. Explain the policy of open competition and ways to make staffing more effective.
5. Summarize important aspects of the systems approach to manager selection.
6. Analyze position requirements, important characteristics of job design, and characteristics needed by managers.
7. Describe the process of matching manager qualifications with position requirements.
8. Discuss the orientation and socialization process for new employees.

Few executives would argue with the fact that people are vital for the effective operation of a company. Managers often say that people are their most important asset. Yet the "human assets" are virtually never shown on the balance sheet as a distinct category, although a great deal of money is invested in the recruitment, selection, and training of people. It is for this reason that the late Rensis Likert and his colleagues suggested maintaining accounts of the valuable human assets. They refer to this process as "human resource accounting."[2] This approach is not without its problems,[3] and there is even conflict among management experts, between the proponents of human resource accounting and the financial people who have to develop the system for measuring the human assets.[4] What is important here is the recognition that staffing is a crucial function of managers, one that may well determine the success or failure of an enterprise.

This chapter begins with a definition of the managerial function of staffing and an explanation of what it means to be a manager, then introduces an overview of the systems approach to human resource management, and concludes with a discussion of the various aspects of selecting the right person.

DEFINITION OF STAFFING

The managerial function of **staffing** is defined as *filling, and keeping filled, positions in the organization structure*. This is done by identifying work-force requirements, inventorying the people available, and recruiting, selecting, placing, promoting, appraising, planning the careers of, compensating, and training or otherwise developing both candidates and current jobholders so that they can accomplish their tasks effectively and efficiently.* It is clear that staffing must be closely linked to organizing, that is, to the setting up of intentional structures of roles and positions.

Many writers on management theory discuss staffing as a phase of organizing. In this book, however, staffing is identified as a separate managerial function for several reasons. First, the staffing of organizational roles includes knowledge and

* Another term now frequently used for the managerial function of staffing is "human resource management."

approaches not usually recognized by practicing managers, who often think of organizing as just setting up a structure of roles and give little attention to filling these roles. Second, making staffing a separate function facilitates placing an even greater emphasis on the human element in selection, appraisal, career planning, and manager development. Third, an important body of knowledge and experience has been developed in the area of staffing. The fourth reason for separating staffing is that managers often overlook the fact that staffing is their responsibility—not that of the personnel department. To be sure, this department provides valuable assistance, but it is the job of managers to fill the positions in their organization and keep them filled with qualified people.

DEFINING THE MANAGERIAL JOB

Complete agreement does not exist as to what exactly constitutes the job of a manager. In fact, the nature of managerial tasks has been studied from several different perspectives.[5] One group of writers, known as the *great man school,* studied successful managers and described their behaviors and habits. Although the stories about these people are interesting, the authors usually do not provide an underlying theory to explain the success of their subjects. Other writers—primarily economists—focus on the *entrepreneurial* aspects of managing. Their main concern is profit maximization, innovation, risk taking, and similar activities. Yet another group of writers emphasizes *decision making,* especially the kinds of decisions that cannot be easily programmed. An additional view of the managerial job draws attention to *leadership,* with an emphasis on particular traits and managerial styles. Closely related to this approach is the discussion about *power* and *influence,* that is, the leader's control of the environment and subordinates. Other writers focus their attention on the *behavior of leaders* by examining the content of the manager's job. Finally, the approach favored by Henry Mintzberg is based on observing the *work activities* of managers.[6] He found through observations of five executives that their work was characterized by brevity, variety, discontinuity, and action orientation. He also noted that executives favor oral communication and that they engage in many activities that link the enterprise with its environment.

It is useful, as already emphasized, to organize the key tasks of managers into the five functions of planning, organizing, staffing, leading, and controlling, which constitute the framework of this book.

THE SYSTEMS APPROACH TO HUMAN RESOURCE MANAGEMENT: AN OVERVIEW OF THE STAFFING FUNCTION

Figure 13-1 shows how the managerial function of staffing relates to the total management system.* Specifically, enterprise plans (discussed in Part 2 of this

* Figure 13-1 is an overview of the staffing function. The variables not discussed in Part 4, but which also focus on staffing, are enclosed with broken lines.

FIGURE 13-1

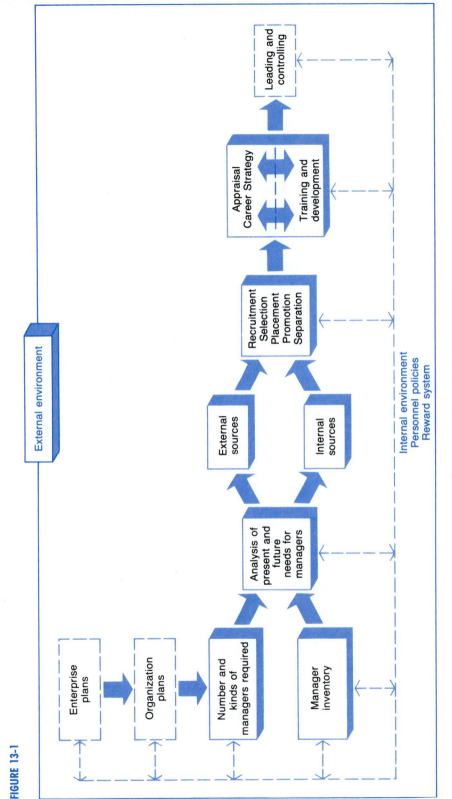

SYSTEMS APPROACH TO STAFFING.

book) become the basis for organization plans (Part 3), which are necessary to achieve enterprise objectives. The present and projected organization structure determines the number and kinds of managers required. These demands for managers are compared with available talent through the management inventory. On the basis of this analysis, external and internal sources are utilized in the processes of recruitment, selection, placement, promotion, and separation.[7] Other essential aspects of staffing are appraisal, career strategy, and training and development of managers.

Staffing, as seen in the model, affects leading and controlling. For instance, well-trained managers create an environment in which people, working together in groups, can achieve enterprise objectives and at the same time accomplish personal goals. In other words, proper staffing facilitates leading (Part 5). Similarly, selecting quality managers affects controlling, for example, by preventing many undesirable deviations from becoming major problems (Part 6).

Staffing requires an open-system approach. It is carried out within the enterprise, which, in turn, is linked to the external environment. Therefore, internal factors of the firm—such as personnel policies, the organizational climate, and the reward system—must be taken into account. Clearly, without adequate rewards it is impossible to attract and keep quality managers. The external environment cannot be ignored either; high technology demands well-trained, well-educated, and highly skilled managers. Inability to meet the demand for such managers may well prevent an enterprise from growing at a desired rate.

Factors Affecting the Number and Kinds of Managers Required

The number of managers needed in an enterprise depends not only on its size but also on the complexity of the organization structure, the plans for expansion, and the rate of turnover of managerial personnel. The ratio between the number of managers and the number of employees does not follow any law. It is possible, by enlarging or contracting the delegation of authority, to modify a structure so that the number of managers in a given instance will increase or decrease regardless of the size of an operation.

Although the need for determining the number of managers required has been stressed here, it is clear that numbers are only part of the picture. Specifically, the qualifications for individual positions must be identified so that the best-suited managers can be chosen. This kind of detailed analysis of position requirements will be discussed later in this chapter.

Determination of Available Managerial Resources: The Management Inventory

It is common for any business, as well as for most nonbusiness enterprises, to keep an inventory of raw materials and goods on hand to enable it to carry on its operations. It is far less common for enterprises to keep an inventory of available human resources, particularly managers, despite the fact that the required number of competent managers is a vital requirement for success. Keeping abreast of the

FIGURE 13-2

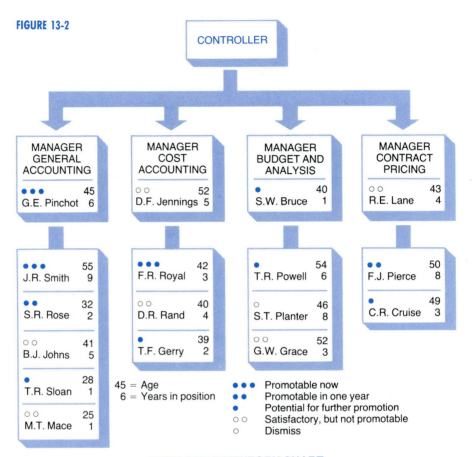

MANAGER INVENTORY CHART.

Note: The age shown on the inventory chart must not be used to discriminate against employees on the basis of their age. (That is illegal.)

management potential within a firm can be done by the use of an inventory chart,* which is simply an organization chart of a unit with managerial positions indicated and keyed as to the promotability of each incumbent.

Figure 13-2 depicts a typical manager inventory chart. At a glance the controller can see where he or she stands with respect to the staffing function. The controller's successor is probably the manager of general accounting, and this person, in turn, has a successor ready for promotion. Supporting that person, in turn, is a subordinate who will be ready for promotion in a year, but below that position are one person who does not have potential and two newly hired employees.

The cost accounting manager represents the all-too-frequent case of a person who is acceptable but not promotable. This individual stands in the way of one

_____
* Another term for "inventory chart" is "management replacement chart."

subordinate who is promotable now. The remaining people in this department represent extremes of nonpromotability and good potential. Overall, the staffing pattern in this department is not satisfactory.

The manager of budget and analysis has considerable development to accomplish before being ready for promotion. There is no immediately promotable successor. To complicate matters, no further potential exists among the remaining two subordinates.

Contract pricing portends some problems. Its manager is not promotable, but there is good potential in the subordinates.

Advantages and Limitations of the Manager Inventory Chart

The manager inventory chart, as seen from the preceding discussion, has certain general advantages:

1. The chart gives an overview of the staffing situation of an organization.
2. Managers who are ready for promotion can now be easily identified. Prompt action in finding a suitable position within the organization may reduce the propensity of managers to seek employment outside the company.
3. The chart also shows the future internal supply of managers by indicating who is promotable in a year or more.
4. Managers who do not perform satisfactorily are identified, and the need for training or replacement is indicated.
5. If the organization has insufficient "depth," recruitment and training plans can be initiated immediately to ensure the future supply of managers.
6. Managers who are close to retirement can be identified, and preparations can be made for their replacement.
7. The chart facilitates the transfer of managers not only to strengthen weak departments but also to broaden the managers' experience.
8. One can identify and prevent the hoarding of promotable people by their immediate superiors, a practice quite common, especially in large enterprises. Naturally, superiors dislike depriving themselves of able subordinates by letting them transfer to other organizational units. But the overall interest of the enterprise is more important than the self-interest of an individual manager.
9. Managers can counsel subordinates about their career paths and relate them to employment opportunities within the company.

Despite its many advantages, the manager inventory chart also has some limitations:

1. The chart does not show to what position the manager may be promotable. If an opening occurs in another organizational unit, the person who is "promotable now" will not necessarily be able to fit this position, since knowledge or skills may be required in specialized areas. A promotable manager in a production department can hardly fill the job of vice president of sales.

2. The data shown on the chart are not sufficient for making a fair assessment of all the capabilities of individuals. It is still necessary to keep records of each individual's skills, performance, and other biographical information.
3. Although the chart is useful for counseling subordinates, it is often not practical to share the information with all employees. Instead, only the top manager of a division or a department may have this information available.
4. It takes time and effort to keep the chart up to date.
5. Upper-level managers may be reluctant to make their charts available to other upper-level managers because they may be afraid they will lose competent subordinates to other organizational units.

Analysis of the Need for Managers: External and Internal Information Sources

As shown in Figure 13-1, the need for managers is determined by enterprise and organizational plans and, more specifically, by an analysis of the number of managers required and the number available as identified through the management inventory. But there are other factors, internal and external, that influence the demand for and supply of managers. The external forces include economic, technological, social, political, and legal factors (which were discussed in Chapters 3 and 4). For example, economic growth may result in increased demand for the product, which requires an expansion of the work force, thus increasing the demand for managers. At the same time, competing companies may also expand and recruit from a common labor pool, thus reducing the supply of managers. One must also consider the trends in the labor market, the demographics, and the composition of the community with respect to knowledge and skills of the labor pool and the attitude toward the company. Information about the long-term trends in the labor market may be obtained from several sources. The U.S. government, for example, publishes the *Monthly Labor Review* and the annual *Manpower Report of the President,* which makes long-term projections. Some trade associations and unions also project the demand for labor.

The data about the need for and the availability of personnel give rise to four demand-and-supply situations, each requiring a different emphasis in personnel actions. This is illustrated in the matrix shown in Figure 13-3.

With a high supply of managers and a high demand, the focus is on selection, placement, and promotion. Consequently, particular efforts are made to match the available managers with enterprise needs most effectively.

A low supply of managers and a high demand requires a different emphasis. If the company favors internal promotions—and many firms do—special emphasis is placed on training and development to enlarge and improve the pool of managers. But this takes time, and planning far in advance of actual needs is essential. Staffing may be based on open competition for available jobs, and managers from outside the firm should also be considered. Thus, recruitment is another option. In a situation with a high demand for managers within the enterprise, chances are that there is also a general demand for managers in the external environment. It is therefore crucial that compensation be competitive. This is important for retaining managers already employed by the enterprise, and it is also essential for recruiting managers.

FIGURE 13-3

PERSONNEL ACTIONS BASED ON MANAGER SUPPLY
AND DEMAND WITHIN THE ENTERPRISE.

A company with a high supply of managers and a low demand has several alternatives available. The firm can change plans to provide for growth, which would increase the demand for managers, and thus take advantage of the managerial assets. The company may also resort to replacement or "outplacement" (a conscious attempt to help managers find and select other suitable employment),[8] layoffs, demotions, or early retirements.

An enterprise with a low supply of managers and a low demand should give special attention to enterprise plans, because this situation indicates a degree of stagnation in the firm. Since developing managers takes a long time, the company should start the process early if there are prospects of growth and of changes in demand for managers in the future.

The demand for and supply of labor must not be viewed from a national or even local perspective. On a broader scale, we find the imbalances of demand and supply increasing.[9] In the past, labor was very much a fixed factor of production. But in several developing countries, such as Taiwan, South Korea, Poland, and Hungary, the demand for qualified labor and managers may increase with their rapid economic development, resulting in labor shortages. The educational level of the global work force is also changing, with the proportion of college graduates increasing in countries such as China and Brazil.

Other Important Aspects in the Systems Approach to Staffing

After the need for managerial personnel has been determined, a number of candidates may have to be *recruited.* (See Figure 13-1.) This involves attracting qualified candidates to fill organizational roles. From these, managers or potential managers are *selected;* this is the process of choosing from among the candidates the most suitable ones. The aim is to *place* people in positions that allow them to utilize their personal strengths and, perhaps, overcome their weaknesses by getting experience or training in those skills in which they need improvement. Finally, placing a manager in a new position within the enterprise often results in a *promotion,* which normally involves more responsibility. Since recruitment, selection, placement, and promotion are complex processes, they will be discussed in greater detail later in this chapter. Similarly, appraisal, career strategy, training, and development will be discussed in the following staffing chapters. The reference to leading and controlling in Figure 13-1 indicates that effective staffing influences these functions.

SITUATIONAL FACTORS AFFECTING STAFFING

The actual process of staffing shown in Figure 13-1 is affected by many environmental factors. Specifically, external factors include the level of education, the prevailing attitudes in society (such as the attitude toward work), the many laws and regulations that directly affect staffing, the economic conditions, and the supply of and demand for managers outside the enterprise.

There are also many internal factors that affect staffing. They include, for example, organizational goals, tasks, technology, organization structure, the kinds of people employed by the enterprise, the demand for and the supply of managers within the enterprise, the reward system, and various kinds of policies. Some organizations are highly structured; others are not. For some positions—such as the position of a sales manager—skill in human relations may be of vital importance, while the same skill may be less critical for a research scientist working fairly independently in the laboratory. Effective staffing, then, requires recognition of many external and internal situational factors, but the focus here is on those that have a particular relevance to staffing.

The External Environment

Factors in the external environment do affect staffing to various degrees. These influences can be grouped into educational, sociocultural, legal-political, and economic constraints or opportunities. For example, the high technology used in many industries requires extensive and intensive education. Similarly, managers in the sociocultural environment in the United States generally do not accept orders blindly; they want to become active participants in the decision-making process. Furthermore, now and in the future, managers will have to be more oriented toward the public than they have been in the past, responding to the public's legitimate needs and adhering to high ethical standards.

The economic environment—including the competitive situation—determines the external supply of, and the demand for, managers. Legal and political constraints require that firms follow laws and guidelines issued by various levels of government. Table 13-1 summarizes major federal laws relating to fair employment that influence the staffing function. The following discussion focuses on equal employment opportunity and the role of women in management, as well as on the staffing of international businesses.

TABLE 13-1 MAJOR FEDERAL LAWS GOVERNING EQUAL EMPLOYMENT OPPORTUNITY (EEO)*		
Major equal employment opportunity laws	**Objectives**	**Jurisdiction**
Equal Pay Act (1963)	Equal pay for equal work regardless of sex	Employers engaged in interstate commerce and most employees of federal, state, and local governments
Title VII of the Civil Rights Act (1964) (as amended in 1972)	EEO for different races, colors, religions, sexes, and national origins	Employers with fifteen or more employees; unions with fifteen or more members; employment agencies; union hiring halls; institutions of higher education; federal, state, and local governments
Age Discrimination in Employment Act (1967) (as amended from age 65 to 70 in 1978)	EEO for ages 40 to 70	Employers with twenty or more employees; unions with twenty-five or more members; employment agencies; federal, state, and local governments
Vocational Rehabilitation Act (1973)	EEO and reasonable affirmative action for handicapped people	Federal government agencies and government contractors with contracts of $2500 or more
Pregnancy Discrimination Act (1978)	EEO during pregnancy	Same as for Civil Rights Act

* New laws and guidelines will be issued in the early 1990s.
Source: Keith Davis and John W. Newstrom, *Human Behavior at Work: Organizational Behavior* (New York: McGraw-Hill Book Company, 1985), p. 402. Used with permission.

Equal employment opportunity.   Several laws have been passed that provide for equal employment opportunity (EEO). The laws prohibit employment practices that discriminate on the basis of race, color, religion, national origin, sex, or age (in specified age ranges).[10] EEO is based on federal, state, and local laws, and these laws impact on staffing. Recruitment and selection for promotion must be in compliance with these laws. This means that managers making decisions in these areas must be knowledgeable about the laws and the way they apply to the staffing function.

Women in management.   In the last decade or so, women have made significant progress in obtaining responsible positions in organizations. Among the reasons for this development are laws governing fair employment practices, changing societal attitudes toward women in the workplace, and the desire of companies to project a favorable image by placing qualified women in managerial positions.[11]

Opportunities for women occupying managerial positions are increasing. But career advancements may depend on the functional area, on the kind of industry, or on particular companies.

Women are likely to be found at upper levels of management in areas such as personnel and public relations. Certain industries provide faster advancement opportunities than others. Financial services institutions, such as banks, and retailing firms, which traditionally employed large percentages of women, also have more women in managerial positions.

Certain companies have more women managers than do other firms. United Airlines, for example, has greatly improved opportunities for women. While 15 percent of managerial positions were held by women in 1980, the figure was 25 percent in 1985. At Bay Banks in Boston, seven of the nineteen top managers are women. Other companies providing good career opportunities for women are General Electric, Federal Express, and Procter & Gamble.

Some of the gains were due to legal actions. But there are other factors, such as the educational revolution.

Evidence indicates that women also have some difficulty making it to the top. For example, no women are major candidates for the position of chief executive officer in the *Fortune* 500 corporations. Discrimination has been given as one reason, according to a *Fortune* article.[13] On the other hand, women's representation on boards of directors is increasing.[14] Nevertheless, the total number of women serving on boards is still rather small.

Staffing in the international environment.   One must look beyond the immediate external environment and recognize the worldwide changes brought about primarily by advanced communication technology and by the existence of multinational corporations.[15] It is not unusual for large international firms to have top-management teams composed of managers of many different nationalities. The geocentric attitude is the basis for viewing the organization as a worldwide entity engaged in global decision making, including staffing decisions.

Companies have three sources for staffing the positions in international operations: (1) managers from the home country of the firm, (2) managers from the host country, and (3) managers from a third country.[16] In the early stages of the development of an international business, managers were often selected from the *home* country. Some of the reasons include the managers' experience at the home office and their familiarity with products, personnel, enterprise goals and policies, and so on. This facilitates not only planning but also control. On the other hand, the home-country national may be unfamiliar with the language or the environment of the foreign country. Moreover, it is usually more expensive to send managers and their families abroad. For the family, it is often difficult to adjust to the new environment of a foreign country. Also, host countries may pressure the parent firm to employ host-country managers.

Managers who are *host-country nationals* do speak the language and are familiar with the country's environment. Employing them is generally less costly, and it may not require relocating them and their families. The problem is that those managers may not be familiar with the firm's products and operations, and thus control may be more difficult.

The other alternative is to employ *third-country nationals,* who often are international career managers. Still, the host country may prefer to have its own nationals in the positions of power. Professor Arvind Phatak has voiced caution in selecting managers from countries that had political conflicts in the past, such as India and Pakistan or Greece and Turkey.[17] There are, of course, many other factors that have to be taken into account when operating abroad, as illustrated in the Perspective on differences in the workweek in various countries.

International Perspective

Workweek Differences in Various Countries

Many Western countries are accustomed to the 5-day workweek. In 1987, the Japanese Parliament put the 40-hour workweek on the books.[18] The Labor-Standard Law, which has been in effect for 40 years, reduces the 48-hour week by 2 hours, with further reductions later on. About two-thirds of the employees have to work on at least two Saturdays during a month. Thus, the new law, which is not expected to have a great immediate impact on the competitive position of Japanese companies, may eventually affect the social and economic life, giving Japanese workers more time to shop and to travel.

In 1986, the workers in Japan averaged 2102 hours of work a year, compared with 1924 hours in the United States and about 1600 in Europe. Long, hard work has been highly valued in the Japanese culture. Japanese workers, for example, get 15 days of paid vacation a year but typically use only half of them. In addition, they get about 17 holidays with pay, which is similar to the number in the United States but far below the number enjoyed by Europeans, who have almost 30 such holidays.

The Internal Environment

The internal factors selected for this discussion concern staffing managerial positions with personnel from within the firm as well as from the outside, determining the responsibility for staffing, and recognizing the need for top-management support in overcoming resistance to change.

Promotion from within.   Originally, promotion from within implied that workers proceeded into frontline supervisory positions and then upward through the organizational structure. Thus, a firm was pictured as receiving a flow of nonmanagerial employees from which future managers emerged. As used to be said in the railroad industry, "When a president retires or dies, we hire a new office worker."

As long as the matter is considered in general terms, there is little doubt that employees overwhelmingly favor a policy of promotion from within. The banning of outsiders places limits on competition for positions and gives employees an established monopoly on managerial openings. Employees come to doubt the wisdom of the policy, however, when they are confronted with a specific case of selection of one of their own for promotion. This feeling is present at all levels of the organization, largely because of jealousy or because of rivalry for promotion. The difficulty becomes most evident when a general manager is being selected from among the sales, production, finance, or engineering managers. Top managers are often inclined to choose the easy way and avoid problems by selecting an outsider.

Perspective

Companies with Policies of Promotion from Within

Many companies advocate promotion from within. For example, William P. Given, when president of the American Brake Shoe Company, wrote, "It is our policy to give our own people the benefit of advancement as openings occur. We believe that unless we have no one who can possibly qualify it is not fair to our people to hire an outsider." Even more emphatic is the position taken by Sears, Roebuck and Company. In a booklet given to prospective employees is this statement: "At Sears the policy of 'promotion from within' is not just a phrase or slogan. It is a fact, insured by specific administrative measures to make sure that it happens." Similarly, Mobil Oil Company states that its policy is to fill all jobs, whenever possible, from within; and Procter & Gamble asserts that it adheres strictly to its policy of promotion from within and that managers are required to train their successors. It is generally known that a good way for a boss to advance is to train subordinates so that they push the boss out of her or his current job. The policy of promotion from within is a part of the total approach to human resources management at Procter & Gamble that includes an intensive selection process, extensive on-the-job training, and a good compensation system.

Promoting from within the enterprise not only has positive values relating to morale, employees' long-run commitment to the company, and the firm's reputation but also permits taking advantage of the presence of potentially fine managers among the firm's employees. However, even though these positive but unmeasurable values are important, executives should not be blind to the dangers of either overemphasizing this source or relying on it exclusively.

A danger presented by a policy of exclusively promoting from within is that it may lead to the selection of persons for promotion who have, perhaps, only imitated their superiors. This is not necessarily a fault, especially if only the best methods, routines, and viewpoints are cultivated, but this is likely to be an unapproachable ideal. The fact is that enterprises often need people from the outside to introduce new ideas and practices. Consequently, there is a good reason to avoid a policy of exclusive promotion from within.

Promotion from within in large companies.   On the other hand, a policy of promotion from within may be quite suitable for a very large company such as Sears, Du Pont, or General Motors. Nevertheless, large business and nonbusiness organizations usually have so many qualified people that promotion from within actually approaches a condition similar to an open-competition policy. Even in these large companies, however, it may be necessary to go outside, as General Motors did when it hired a university professor as vice president to head its environmental control staff.

The policy of open competition.   Managers must decide whether the benefits of a policy of promotion from within outweigh the policy's shortcomings. There are clear-cut reasons for implementing the principle of open competition by opening vacant positions to the best-qualified persons available, whether inside or outside the enterprise. It gives the firm, in the final analysis, the opportunity to secure the services of the best-suited candidates. It counters the shortcomings of a policy of exclusive promotion from within, permits a firm to adopt the best techniques in recruiting managers, and motivates the complacent "heir apparent." To exchange these advantages for the moral advantages attributed to internal promotion would appear questionable.

A policy of open competition is a better and more honest means of ensuring managerial competence than is obligatory promotion from within. However, it does put the managers who use it under a special obligation. If morale is to be protected in applying an open-competition policy, the enterprise must have fair and objective methods of appraising and selecting its people. It should also do everything possible to help people develop so that they can qualify for promotions.

When these requirements are met, it would be expected that every manager making an appointment to a vacancy or a new position would have available a roster of qualified candidates within the entire enterprise. If people know that their qualifications are being considered, if they have been fairly appraised and have been given opportunities for development, they are far less likely to feel a sense of injustice if an opening goes to an outsider. Other things being equal, present employees should be able to compete with outsiders. If a person has the ability for a position, he or she has the considerable advantage of knowing the enterprise and its personnel, history, problems, policies, and objectives. For the superior candidate, the policy of open competition should be a challenge and not a hindrance to advancement.

Responsibility for staffing.   While responsibility for staffing should rest with every manager at every level, the ultimate responsibility is with the chief executive officer and the policy-making group of top executives. They have the duty of developing policy, assigning its execution to subordinates, and ensuring its proper application. Policy considerations, for example, include decisions about the development of a staffing program, the desirability of promoting from within or securing managers from the outside, the sources for candidates, the selection procedure to follow, the kind of appraisal program to use, the nature of manager and organization development, and the promotion and retirement policies to follow.

Line managers should certainly make use of the services of staff members—usually from the personnel department—in recruiting, selecting, placing, promoting, appraising, and training people. In the final analysis, however, it is the manager's responsibility to fill positions with the best-qualified persons.

Need for top-management support in overcoming resistance to effective staffing.   The prestige and power of top management must be brought to bear if staffing is to be effective. Some managers within the organization will resent losing promising subordinates, even though they can make a greater contribution to the enterprise in a different department. Others will resist changes required by managerial and organizational development efforts. There are also those who may be threatened by imaginative and achievement-oriented subordinates. Still others may not see staffing as a pressing matter and may neglect it altogether. To overcome these human tendencies, top-management involvement in staffing is necessary.

SELECTION: MATCHING THE PERSON WITH THE JOB

Plant, equipment, materials, and people do not make a business any more than airplanes, tanks, ships, and people make an effective military force. One other element is indispensable: effective managers. The quality of managers is one of the most important factors determining the continuing success of any organization. It necessarily follows, therefore, that the selection of managers is one of the most critical steps in the entire process of managing. **Selection** is the process of choosing from among candidates, from within the organization or from the outside, the most suitable person for the current position or for future positions.

SYSTEMS APPROACH TO SELECTION: AN OVERVIEW

Since qualified managers are critical to the success of an enterprise, a systematic approach is essential to manager selection and to the assessment of present and future needs for managerial personnel.

An overview of the systems approach to selection is illustrated in Figure 13-4. The variables that are closely related to selection but are not discussed in this section are marked with broken lines in the model. The managerial requirements plan is based on the firm's objectives, forecasts, plans, and strategies. This plan is translated into position and job design requirements which are matched with such individual characteristics as intelligence, knowledge, skills, attitudes, and experience. To meet organizational requirements, managers recruit, select, place, and promote people. This, of course, must be done with due consideration for the internal environment (for example, company policies, supply of and demand for

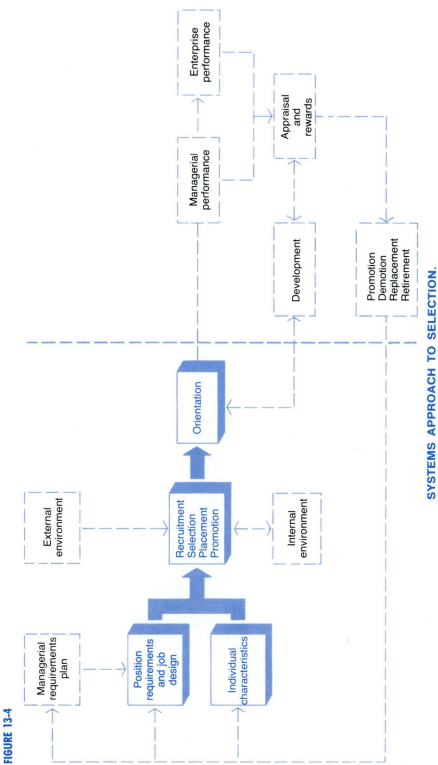

FIGURE 13-4

SYSTEMS APPROACH TO SELECTION.

Variables marked with broken lines are staffing and other activities that are discussed in other chapters.

managers, and the organizational climate) and the external environment (laws, regulations, availability of managers). After people have been selected and placed in positions, they must be introduced to the new job. This orientation involves learning about the company, its operation, and its social aspects.

The newly placed managers then carry out their managerial and nonmanagerial functions (such as marketing), resulting in managerial performance, which eventually determines enterprise performance. Subsequently, managerial performance is appraised, and managers are rewarded. (See Chapter 14.) On the basis of this evaluation, manager and organization development is initiated (Chapter 15). Finally, appraisal may also become the basis for promotion, demotion, replacement, and retirement decisions.

That is the selection model in brief; now each major variable in the model will receive closer attention.

POSITION REQUIREMENTS AND JOB DESIGN

Selecting a manager effectively requires a clear understanding of the nature and purpose of the position which is to be filled. An objective analysis of position requirements must be made, and, as far as possible, the job must be designed to meet organizational and individual needs. In addition, positions must be evaluated and compared so that the incumbents can be treated equitably. Among other factors to consider are the skills required—technical, human, conceptual, and design— since these vary with the level in the organizational hierarchy and the personal characteristics needed by managers. (See Chapter 1.)

Identifying Job Requirements

In identifying job requirements, firms must answer questions such as these: What has to be done in this job? How is it done? What background knowledge, attitudes, and skills are required? Since positions are not static, additional questions may have to be considered: Can the job be done differently? If so, what are the new requirements? Finding answers to these and similar questions requires that the job be analyzed. This can be done through observation, interviews, questionnaires, or even a systems analysis. Thus, a job description, based on job analysis, usually lists important duties, authority-responsibility, and the relationship to other positions. More recently, some firms have also included objectives and expected results in job descriptions.

There is, of course, no foolproof rule for designing managerial jobs. Nevertheless, firms can avoid mistakes by following some guidelines.

Appropriate scope of the job.   A job too narrowly defined provides no challenge, no opportunity for growth, and no sense of accomplishment. Consequently, good managers will be bored and dissatisfied. On the other hand, a job must not be so broad that it cannot be effectively handled. The result will be stress, frustration, and loss of control.

Full-time challenge of the job.   Sometimes managers are given a job that does not require their full time and effort. They are not challenged by their task, and they feel underutilized. Consequently, they often meddle in the work of their subordinates, who then also feel that they do not have sufficient authority and discretion to do their jobs. Some time ago, when a utility company asked for help in solving organizational conflicts, it was found that people did not have full-time jobs; they were quarreling about jobs, duties, and tasks; they were in each other's way. Thus, they channeled their energy against one another instead of toward the aims of the company. The need to design jobs with challenging objectives, duties, and responsibilities should be obvious.

Managerial skills required by job design.   Generally, the design of the job should start with the tasks to be accomplished. The design is usually broad enough to accommodate people's needs and desires. But some writers on management suggest that it may be necessary to design the job to fit the leadership style of a particular person. It may be especially appropriate to design jobs for exceptional persons, in order to utilize their potential. The problem, of course, is that such a position would probably have to be restructured every time a new manager occupied it. The job description, then, must provide a clear idea of the performance requirements for a person in a particular position but must also allow some flexibility so that the employer can take advantage of individual characteristics and abilities.

   Any position description is contingent on the particular job and the organization. For example, in a bureaucratic and fairly stable organization environment, a position may be described in relatively specific terms. In contrast, in a dynamic organization with an unstable, fast-changing environment, a job description may have to be more general and most likely will have to be reviewed more frequently. A situational approach to job descriptions and job designs is called for.

Job Design

People spend a great deal of time on the job, and it is therefore important to design jobs so that individuals feel good about their work. This requires an appropriate job structure in terms of content, function, and relationships.

Design of jobs for individuals and work teams.   The focus of job design can be on the individual position or on work groups.[19] First, individual jobs can be enriched by grouping tasks into natural work units. This means putting tasks that are related into one category and assigning an individual to carry out the tasks. A second related approach is to combine several tasks into one job. For example, rather than having the tasks of assembling a water pump carried out by several persons on the assembly line, workstations can be established with individuals doing the whole task of putting the unit together and even testing it. A third way of enriching the job is to establish direct relationships with the customer or client. A systems analyst may present findings and recommendations directly to the managers involved in the systems change rather than reporting to his or her superior, who would then make the recommendations to top management. Fourth, prompt and specific feedback should be built into the system whenever appropriate. In one retail store, for example, salespersons received the sales figures for each day and summary figures for each month. Fifth, individual jobs can be enriched through vertical job loading, which is increasing individuals' responsibility for planning, doing, and controlling their job.

Similar arguments can be made for improving the design of jobs for work teams.[20] Jobs should be designed so that groups have a complete task to perform. Moreover, teams may be given authority and freedom to decide how well the jobs shall be performed; thus, the groups are given a great deal of autonomy. Within the team, individuals can often be trained so that they can rotate to different jobs within the group. Finally, rewards may be administered on the basis of group performance, which tends to induce cooperation rather than competition among team members.

Factors influencing job design.   In designing jobs, the requirements of the enterprise have to be taken into account. But other factors must be considered in order to realize maximum benefits; they include individual differences, the technology involved, the costs associated with restructuring the jobs, the organization structure, and the internal climate.

People have different needs. Those with unused capabilities and a need for growth and development usually want to have their job enriched and to assume greater responsibility. While some people prefer to work by themselves, others with social needs usually work well in groups. The nature of the task and the technology related to the job must also be considered. While it may be possible for work teams to assemble automobiles, as is done at a Volvo plant in Sweden, it may not be efficient to use the same work design for the high production runs at General Motors in the United States. The costs of changing to new job designs must also be considered. It makes a great deal of difference whether a plant is newly designed or an old plant has to be redesigned and changed to accommodate new job design concepts.

The organization structure must also be taken into account. Individual jobs must fit the overall structure. Autonomous work groups, for example, may work well in decentralized organization, but they may be inappropriate in a centralized structure. Similarly, the organizational climate influences job design. Groups may function well in an atmosphere that encourages participation, job enrichment, and autonomous work, while they may not fit into an enterprise with an autocratic, top-down approach to managerial leadership.

SKILLS AND PERSONAL CHARACTERISTICS NEEDED BY MANAGERS

To be effective, managers need various skills ranging from technical to design. The relative importance of these skills varies according to the level in the organization, as discussed in Chapter 1. In addition, analytical and problem-solving abilities and certain personal characteristics are sought in managers.

Analytical and Problem-Solving Abilities

One of the frequently mentioned skills desired of managers is analytical and problem-solving ability. But as Alan Stoneman, former president of the Purex Corporation, used to say, "We have no problems here; all are opportunities; all a problem should be is an opportunity." In other words, managers must be able to identify problems, analyze complex situations, and, by solving the problems encountered, exploit the opportunities presented. They must scan the environment and identify, through a rational process, those factors that stand in the way of opportunities. Thus, analytical skills should be used to determine the needs of present customers—or potential customers—and then to satisfy those needs with a product or a service. It has been amply demonstrated that this opportunity-seeking approach can mean corporate success. For example, Edwin H. Land of Polaroid filled the needs of people who wanted instant photographs. But problem identification and analysis are not enough. Managers also need the will to implement the solutions they come up with; they must recognize the emotions, needs, and motivations of the people involved in initiating the required change as well as of those who resist change.

Personal Characteristics Needed by Managers

In addition to the various skills that effective managers need, several personal characteristics are also important. They are (1) a desire to manage, (2) the ability to communicate with empathy, (3) integrity and honesty, and (4) the person's experience—his or her past performance as a manager—which is a very significant characteristic.

Desire to manage.   The successful manager has a strong desire to manage, to influence others, and to get results through the team efforts of subordinates. To be sure, many people want the privileges that come with managerial positions, which include high status and salary, but they lack the basic motivation to achieve results by creating an environment in which people are able to work together toward common aims. The desire to manage requires effort, time, energy, and, usually, long hours of work.

Communication skills and empathy.   Another important characteristic of managers is the ability to communicate through written reports, letters, speeches, and discussions. Communication demands clarity, but even more, it demands *empathy*. This is the ability to understand the feelings of another person and to deal with the emotional aspects of communication. Communication skills are important for effective *intragroup communication*, that is, communication with people in the same organizational unit. As one moves up in the organization, however, *intergroup communication* becomes increasingly important. This is communication not only with other departments but also with groups outside the enterprise: customers, suppliers, governments, the community, and, of course, the stockholders in business enterprises.

Integrity and honesty.   Managers must be morally sound and worthy of trust. Integrity in managers includes honesty in money matters and in dealing with others, effort to keep superiors informed, adherence to the full truth, strength of character, and behavior in accordance with ethical standards.

Many of these qualities, and others, have been cited by top executives of major companies. Henry Ford II, former chairperson of Ford Motor Company, mentioned as appealing qualities honesty, candor, and openness. Similarly, Donald M. Kendall, chairperson of PepsiCo, Inc., listed work ethics and integrity as essential characteristics of executives. Noah Dietrich, who ran the Howard Hughes empire for 32 years, identified honesty and candor as the top qualities of his subordinates. His attitude was "I cannot do my job if the executives who report to me do not tell me the truth about their operations."

Past performance as a manager.   Past performance as a manager is probably the most reliable forecast of a manager's future performance. Of course, an assessment of managerial experience is not possible in selecting first-line supervisors from the ranks, since they have not had such experience. But past accomplishments are important considerations in the selection of middle- and upper-level managers. In a survey of *Fortune* 500 companies, most CEOs said that experience within the company was the key to their successful careers.[21]

Procter & Gamble, a traditional American company, had little choice but to go international. In order to stay competitive with companies such as Unilever (Anglo-Dutch) and Kao Corporation (Japanese), P&G was forced to market its products—which include Tide detergent, Secret deodorant, Folgers coffee, Crisco shortening, NyQuil cough syrup, and many other well-known consumer products—on a global basis. It has been estimated that overseas sales, which made up about one-fourth of total sales in the mid-eighties, will be over half of total sales in the early 1990s. In 1984, P&G operated in 27 countries, and 5 years later it did so in 48 countries.

When John Smale was preparing to retire and was looking for a successor, he sought a person with extensive overseas experience. To prepare for and to continue the trend of overseas marketing, P&G selected Edwin Artzt, who had a background in international operations. As group executive of the European Common Market, Artzt developed pan-European marketing in the 1970s, long before the European Community 1992 program was even considered. The Single European market, the objective of EC 1992, with its 340-plus million consumers, is the largest market in the Western world. But Artzt's expansion plans are not restricted to Europe. Indeed, he sees good opportunities for P&G products in the Far East.

Future executives, to be sure, need to develop a global perspective. International experience will become a prerequisite for promotion, not only for P&G but also for many other U.S. firms.

MATCHING QUALIFICATIONS WITH POSITION REQUIREMENTS

After the organizational positions are identified, managers are obtained through recruitment, selection, placement, and promotion. (See the variables in Figure 13-4.) There are basically two sources of managerial personnel: People from within the enterprise may be promoted or transferred, and managers may be hired from the outside. For *internal* promotions, a computerized information system may help to identify qualified candidates. It can be used in conjunction with a comprehensive human resource plan. Specifically, it can be utilized to anticipate staff requirements, new openings, attritions, development needs, and career planning.

There are also several *external* sources available, and the enterprise may use different methods in finding qualified managers. Many employment agencies—public and private—and executive recruiters (sometimes called "headhunters") locate suitable candidates for positions. Other sources for managers are professional associations, educational institutions, referrals from people within the enterprise, and, of course, unsolicited applications from persons interested in the firm.

Recruitment of Managers

Recruiting involves attracting candidates to fill the positions in the organization structure. Before recruiting begins, the position's requirements, which should relate directly to the task, must be clearly identified. This makes it easier to recruit suitable candidates from the outside. Enterprises with a favorable public image find it easier to attract qualified candidates. A company such as IBM (International Business Machines) is well recognized; small firms, which often offer excellent growth and development opportunities, may have to make great efforts to communicate to the applicant the products, services, and opportunities they offer.

Recruitment in the public sector has many similarities to recruitment in the private sector. However, government regulations or policies may demand that managers adhere to special hiring guidelines. For example, legislation may require that potential employees live within a municipality's boundaries. Another difference is that applicants for public sector positions often have to take competitive tests such as civil service examinations, although an increasing number of privately owned enterprises are using written and oral tests as well.

Unfortunately, the selection process in government is not always as objective and rational as it should be, and the practice of making decisions on criteria other than competence is probably not unusual. Frederic V. Malek, a former special assistant to the President and now a business executive himself, reports that it is unthinkable for a major corporation to put a person without considerable managerial experience in charge of 5000 people, yet in government this is not uncommon.[23] Thus, in order to improve the effectiveness and efficiency of government, a better selection process is required.

Information Exchange Contributing to Successful Selection

The exchange of information works two ways in recruitment and selection: An enterprise provides applicants with an objective description of the company and

FIGURE 13-5

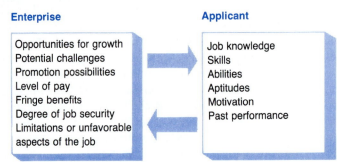

Enterprise	Applicant
Opportunities for growth Potential challenges Promotion possibilities Level of pay Fringe benefits Degree of job security Limitations or unfavorable aspects of the job	Job knowledge Skills Abilities Aptitudes Motivation Past performance

EXCHANGE OF INFORMATION IN SELECTION OF MANAGERS.

the position, while the applicants provide information about their capabilities. (See Figure 13-5.)

Business and other organizations attempt to project a favorable image, stress opportunities for personal growth and development, highlight potential challenges, and indicate promotion possibilities. They also convey information about pay, fringe benefits, and, perhaps, job security. This can, of course, be overdone, raising unrealistic expectations in the applicant. In the long run, there may be undesirable side effects resulting in low job satisfaction, high turnover, and unfulfilled dreams. Certainly, the enterprise should present itself in an attractive light, yet the opportunities should be discussed in a factual and realistic manner, covering limitations and even unfavorable aspects of the job.

On the other hand, management should elicit from all the applicants an objective demonstration of their knowledge, skills, abilities, aptitudes, motivation, and past performance. A number of techniques and instruments can reveal this information (they will be discussed later in the chapter). To be sure, the collection of data about an applicant can go too far and can become an invasion of privacy. The managerial candidate will tolerate only a reasonable amount of interviewing, testing, and disclosure of personal information. Clearly, managers must exercise restraint and request information that is essential and relevant to the job.

Selection, Placement, and Promotion[24]

Selecting a manager is choosing from among the candidates the one who best meets the position requirements. Since the selection may be for a specific job opening or for future managerial requirements, there are two approaches to filling organizational positions. In the *selection approach*, applicants are sought to fill a position with rather specific requirements; in the *placement approach*, the strengths and weaknesses of the individual are evaluated, and a suitable position is found or even designed.

Promotion is a change within the organization to a higher position that has greater responsibilities and requires more advanced skills. It usually involves higher status and an increase in pay. The various facets of selection generally apply also to promotion, which may be a reward for outstanding performance or a result of the firm's desire to better utilize an individual's skills and abilities. Promotions may be a reward for past performance, but only if there is evidence of potential competency. Otherwise, persons may be promoted to a level at which they are incompetent.

While some observers paint a gloomy picture for the baby-boomers, others look more optimistically into the future. About half of the U.S. labor force is now under 35, and these men and women will be determining the success of enterprises and, on a broader scale, the well-being of the country.

Demographics suggest that there may be an oversupply of managers. Yet the salaries of the young managers have not been eroded. Some factors, such as decentralization of organizations, have increased the demand for general managers. On the other hand, the extensive use of computers may have a particular impact on middle managers, as the discussion on management information systems (Chapter 21) will show. It seems likely that the competition for managerial jobs is going to increase.

What kind of work force will these managers lead? *Fortune* magazine interviewed about 100 workers across the country and found that they are very much aware of the economic—including the Japanese—challenges. At the same time, they are willing to adapt. In fact, they are eager to learn new skills, are willing to relocate, and are open to changing jobs if necessary. The vitalization of industry will depend to a great extent on the young work force: managers and nonmanagers alike.

The Peter Principle

Errors in selection are possible, perhaps even common. According to Laurence J. Peter and Raymond Hall, authors of *The Peter Principle*, managers tend to be promoted to the level of their incompetence.[26] Specifically, if a manager succeeds in a position, this very success may lead to promotion to a higher position, often one requiring skills that the person does not possess. Such a promotion may involve work that is over the manager's head. While the possibility of individual growth must not be overlooked, the Peter Principle can serve as a warning not to take the selection and promotion process lightly.

Donald Burr, the founder of the no-frills People Express Airlines, has been hailed by some for his unorthodox managerial style. The company grew at a phenomenal rate between 1980 and 1986, when it was sold to Texas Air after experiencing huge losses. Many reasons have been given for the fall of People Express: overextending itself by buying Frontier Airlines, taking on major airlines by competing on "their" routes, undercutting of airfares by much stronger competitors, and using an inappropriate managerial style. Personnel policies gave employees a great deal of freedom, and job rotation provided them with many learning opportunities. But upon reflection, Burr thinks now that his strict policy of *promotion from within* was a mistake. Because of the fast growth, people had to be promoted to positions where they had to assume more responsibilities than they were ready for. In other words, they were promoted to the level of their incompetence. But attracting experienced and competent managers from the outside at Burr's pay of $75,000 a year would have been difficult.

Responsibility for Selection

The final decision in the selection of a person for a new position should rest with the candidate's prospective superior; only then can the selector be held accountable for the performance of the chosen candidate. It is also advisable to get the opinions of others, especially those with whom the candidate will have working relationships. In addition, the superior of the selector should be involved, approving, rather than actually making, the selection decision. This gives additional assurance that the selecting manager is choosing people on the basis of adequate qualifications and potential for growth rather than on the basis of friendships.

SELECTION PROCESS, TECHNIQUES, AND INSTRUMENTS

This section presents an overview of the selection process, followed by a discussion of a number of instruments and techniques, including interviews, tests, and the assessment center. For good selection, the information about the applicant should be both *valid* and *reliable*. When people ask if data are **valid,** they raise this question: Are the data measuring what they are supposed to be measuring? In selection, validity is the degree to which the data predict the candidate's success as a manager. The information should also have a high degree of **reliability,** a term that refers to the accuracy and consistency of the measurement. For example, a reliable test, if repeated under the same conditions, would give essentially the same results.

The Selection Process

There are some variations of the specific steps in the selection process. For example, the interview of a candidate for a first-level supervisory position may be relatively simple when compared with the rigorous interviews for a top-level executive. Nevertheless, the following broad outline is indicative of the typical process.

First, the selection criteria are established, usually on the basis of current—and sometimes future—job requirements. These criteria include such items as education, knowledge, skills, and experience. Second, the candidate is requested to complete an application form (this step may be omitted if the candidate for the position is from within the organization). Third, a screening interview is conducted to identify the more promising candidates. Fourth, additional information may be obtained by testing the candidate's qualifications for the position. Fifth, formal interviews are conducted by the manager, his or her superior, and other persons within the organization. Sixth, the information provided by the candidate is checked and verified. Seventh, a physical examination may be required. Eighth, on the basis of the results of previous steps, the candidate is either offered the job or informed that he or she has not been selected for the position. Let us examine some parts of the selection process in greater detail.

Interviews

Virtually every manager hired or promoted by a company is interviewed by one or more people. Despite its general use, the interview is considerably distrusted as a reliable and valid means for selecting managers. Various interviewers may weigh or interpret the obtained information differently. Interviewers often do not ask the right questions. They may be influenced by the interviewee's general appearance, which may have little bearing on job performance. They also frequently make up their minds early in the interview, before they have all the information necessary to make a fair judgment.

Several techniques can be used to improve the interviewing process and overcome some of these weaknesses. First, interviewers should be trained so that they know what to look for. For example, in interviewing people from within the enterprise, they should analyze and discuss past records. They should study the results achieved as well as the way key managerial activities were performed. Chapter 14, on appraisal, shows in greater detail how this can be done. When selecting managers from outside the firm, interviewers find that these data are more difficult to obtain, and they usually get them by checking with the listed references.

Second, interviewers should be prepared to ask the right questions. There are structured, semistructured, and unstructured interviews. In an *unstructured* interview, an interviewer may say something like "Tell me about your last job." In the *semistructured* interview, the manager follows an interview guide but may also ask other questions. In a *structured* interview, the interviewer asks a set of prepared questions, such as the following:

What were your specific duties and responsibilities in your last job?

What did you achieve in this job, and how does this compare with the normal output for this job?

Who could be asked to verify these achievements?

To what extent were these achievements due to your efforts?

What were the contributions of other people?

Who are they?

What did you like and dislike about your job?

What innovations did you make in your job?

Why do you want to change your job?

A third way to improve selection is to conduct multiple interviews utilizing different interviewers. Thus, several people can compare their evaluations and perceptions. However, not all interviewers should vote in selecting a candidate; rather, they should provide additional information for the manager who will be responsible for the final decision.

Fourth, the interview is just one aspect of the selection process. It should be supplemented by data from the application form, the results of various tests, and the information obtained from persons listed as references. Reference checks and letters of recommendation may be necessary to verify the information given by the applicant. For a reference to be useful, the person must know the applicant well and give a truthful and complete assessment of the applicant. Many people are reluctant to provide complete information, and so an applicant's strong points are often overemphasized, while his or her shortcomings may be glossed over. The Privacy Act of 1974 and related legislation and judicial rulings have made it even more difficult to obtain objective references. Under the Privacy Act, the applicant has a legal right to inspect letters of reference unless this right is waived. This is one of the reasons that teachers are sometimes reluctant to make objective and accurate job referrals for their students.

Tests

The primary aim of testing is to obtain data about the applicants that help predict their probable success as managers. Some of the benefits from testing include finding the best person for the job, obtaining a high degree of job satisfaction for the applicant, and reducing turnover. The most commonly used tests can be classified as follows:

1. **Intelligence tests** are designed to measure mental capacity and to test memory, speed of thought, and ability to see relationships in complex problem situations.
2. **Proficiency and aptitude tests** are constructed to discover interests, existing skills, and potential for acquiring skills.
3. **Vocational tests** are designed to show a candidate's most suitable occupation or the areas in which the candidate's interests match the interests of people working in those areas.
4. **Personality tests** are designed to reveal candidates' personal characteristics and the way candidates may interact with others, thereby giving a measure of leadership potential.

Tests have a number of limitations, however. First, competent industrial psychologists agree that tests are not accurate enough to be used as the sole measure of candidates' characteristics but must be interpreted in the light of each individual's entire history. Second, the test user must know what tests do and what their limitations are. One of the major limitations is uncertainty about whether tests are really applicable; even psychologists are not highly confident that present-day tests are effective in measuring managerial abilities and potentials. Third, before any test is widely used, it should be tried out, if possible on personnel currently employed in an enterprise, to see whether it is valid for employees whose managerial abilities are already known. Fourth, it is also important that tests be administered and interpreted by experts in the field. Finally, tests should not discriminate unfairly and should be consistent with laws and government guidelines.

Assessment Centers

The assessment center is not a location but a technique for selecting and promoting managers. This approach may be used in combination with training. Assessment centers were first used for selecting and promoting lower-level supervisors, but now they are applied to middle-level managers as well. They seem, however, to be inappropriate for top executives. The assessment center technique is not new. It was used by the German and British military in World War II and the American Office of Strategic Services. But its first corporate use in the United States is generally attributed to the American Telephone and Telegraph Company in the 1950s.

Intended to measure how a potential manager will act in typical managerial situations, the usual center approach is to have candidates take part in a series of exercises. During this period they are observed and assessed by psychologists or experienced managers. A typical assessment center will have the candidates do the following:

Take various psychological tests.

Engage in management games in small groups.

Engage in "in-basket" exercises, in which they are asked to handle a variety of matters that they might face in a managerial job.

Participate in a leaderless group discussion of some problem.

Give a brief oral presentation on a particular topic or theme, usually recommending a course of desirable action to a mythical superior.

Engage in various other exercises, such as preparing a written report.

During these exercises, the candidates are observed by their evaluators, who also interview them from time to time. At the end of the assessment center period, each assessor summarizes his or her appraisals of each candidate's performance; then the assessors compare their evaluations, come to conclusions concerning each candidate's managerial potential, and write a summary report on each candidate. These reports are made available to appointing managers for their guidance. They are also often used as guides for management development. In many cases candidates are given feedback on their evaluation; in other cases feedback is given only when candidates request it. Sometimes the summary evaluation as to promotability remains confidential, even though candidates may be informed by assessors about their performance in the various exercises.

Evidence of the usefulness of the assessment center approach—although not conclusive—is encouraging. On the other hand, there is some controversy as to whom, by whom, and under what circumstances this and other tests should be administered and as to who should receive the test results.

Assessment centers do present some problems. First, they are costly in terms of time, especially since many effective programs extend over a 5-day period. Second, training assessors is a problem, particularly in those companies which believe, with some justification, that the best assessors are likely to be experienced line managers rather than trained psychologists. Third, although a number of different exercises are used to cover the kinds of things a manager does, questions have been raised as to whether these exercises are the best criteria for evaluation. An even greater problem exists in determining which evaluation measures should be applied to each exercise. Most assessment centers, being highly oriented to individual and interpersonal behavior under various circumstances, may be overlooking the most important element in selecting managers, especially those about to enter the managerial ranks for the first time. That element is motivation—whether or not a person truly wants to be a manager. To be so motivated, candidates must know what managing is, what it involves, and what is required to be a successful manager. Obviously, motivation is a difficult quality to evaluate. However, by making clear to a candidate what managing involves and requires and then asking the candidate to think this over, the interviewer can give the candidate a good basis on which to determine whether he or she really wants to be a manager.

Limitations of the Selection Process

The diversity of selection approaches and tests indicates that there is no one perfect way to select managers. Experience has shown that even carefully chosen selection criteria are still imperfect in predicting performance. Furthermore, there is a distinction between what persons *can do*, that is, their ability to perform, and what they *will do*, which relates to motivation. The latter is a function of the individual and the environment. For example, a person's needs may be different at various times. The organizational environment also changes. The climate of an enterprise may change from one that encourages initiative to one that restricts it because a new top management introduces a different managerial philosophy. Therefore, selection techniques and instruments are not a sure way to predict what people will do, even though they may have the ability to do it.

Testing itself, especially psychological testing, has limitations. Specifically, the seeking of certain information may be considered an invasion of privacy. In addition, it has been charged that some tests unfairly discriminate against women or members of minority groups. These complex issues are not easily resolved, yet they cannot be ignored when an enterprise is selecting managers.

Still other concerns in selection and hiring are the time and cost involved in making personnel decisions. It is important to identify such factors as advertising expenses, agency fees, costs of test materials, time spent interviewing candidates, costs for reference checks, medical exams, start-up time required for the new manager to get acquainted with the job, relocation, and orientation of the new employee. When recruiting costs are recognized, it becomes evident that turnover can be very expensive to an enterprise.

ORIENTING AND SOCIALIZING NEW EMPLOYEES

The selection of the best person for the job is only the first step in building an effective management team. Even companies that make great efforts in the recruitment and selection process often ignore the needs of new managers after they have been hired. Yet the first few days and weeks can be crucial for integrating the new person into the organization.

Orientation involves the introduction of new employees to the enterprise—its functions, tasks, and people. Large firms usually have a *formal orientation program*, which explains these features of the company: history, products and services, general policies and practices, organization (divisions, departments, and geographic locations), benefits (insurance, retirement, vacations), requirements for confidentiality and secrecy (especially with regard to defense contracts), safety and other regulations. These may be further described in detail in a company booklet, but the orientation meeting provides new employees with an opportunity to ask questions. Although these formal programs are usually conducted by persons from the personnel department, the primary responsibility for orienting the new manager still rests with the superior.

There is another and perhaps even more important aspect of orientation: the socialization of new managers. **Organizational socialization** is defined in several different ways. A global view includes three aspects: acquisition of work skills and abilities, adoption of appropriate role behaviors, and adjustment to the norms and values of the work group.[28] So, in addition to meeting the specific requirements of the job, new managers will usually encounter new values, new personal relationships, and new modes of behavior. They do not know people they can ask for advice, they do not know how the organization works, and they have a fear of being unsuccessful in the new job. All this uncertainty can cause a great deal of anxiety for a new employee, especially a management trainee. Because the initial experience in an enterprise can be very important for future management behavior, the first contact of trainees should be with the best superiors in the enterprise, people who can serve as models for future behavior.

SUMMARY

Staffing means filling positions in the organization structure. It involves identifying work-force requirements, inventorying the people available, and recruiting, selecting, placing, promoting, appraising, planning the careers of, compensating, and training people.

In the systems approach to staffing, enterprise and organization plans become important inputs for staffing tasks. The number and quality of managers required to carry out crucial tasks depend on many different factors. One major step in staffing is to determine the people available by making a management inventory. This can be done by using an inventory chart.

Staffing does not take place in a vacuum; one must consider many situational factors—both internal and external. Staffing requires adherence to equal employment opportunity (EEO) laws so that practices do not discriminate, for example, against minorities or women. Also, one must evaluate the pros and cons of promoting people from within the organization or selecting people from the outside.

In the systems model for selection, the comprehensive managerial requirements plan is the basis for position requirements. In designing jobs, the enterprise must see that the scope of the job is appropriate; that the position involves a full-time, challenging job; and that it reflects required skills. The job structure must be appropriate in terms of content, function, and relationships. Jobs can be designed for individuals or work teams. The importance of technical, human, conceptual, and design skills varies with the level in the organizational hierarchy. The position requirements are matched with the various skills and characteristics of individuals. The matching is important in recruitment, selection, placement, and promotion.

Errors in selection can lead to actualization of the Peter Principle, which states that managers tend to be promoted to the level of their incompetence. Although the advice of several people should be sought, the selection decision should generally rest with the immediate superior of the candidate for the position.

The selection process may include interviews, various tests, and the use of assessment centers. To avoid dissatisfaction and employee turnover, companies must ensure that new employees are introduced to and integrated with other persons in the organization.

KEY IDEAS AND CONCEPTS FOR REVIEW

Staffing

Systems approach to human resource
   management

Management inventory

Situational factors affecting staffing

Equal employment opportunity (EEO)

Women in management

Promotion from within

Policy of open competition

Systems approach to selection

Position and job requirements

Job design

Recruitment

Selection

Placement

Promotion

Peter Principle

Validity

Reliability

Selection process

Kinds of tests

Assessment centers

Orientation and socialization

FOR DISCUSSION

1. Why is the function of staffing seldom approached logically? Briefly describe the systems approach to staffing. How is staffing related to other managerial functions and activities?
2. List and evaluate external factors affecting staffing. Which ones are most critical today? Explain.

3. What are the key characteristics of a manager inventory chart? Discuss the advantages and disadvantages of such a chart.

4. What are the dangers and difficulties in applying a policy of promotion from within? What is meant by a policy of open competition? Do you favor such a policy? Why, or why not?

5. What is the systems approach to selection of managers? Why is it called a systems approach? How does it differ from other approaches?

6. What are some of the factors that are important in designing individual jobs and jobs for work teams? Which ones seem most important to you? Why?

7. The Peter Principle has been widely quoted in management circles. What do you think of it? Do you think that it could ever apply to you? Does it mean that all chief executives are incompetent? Explain.

8. What is an assessment center? How does it work? Would you like to participate in such a center? Why, or why not?

EXERCISES/ACTION STEPS

1. Select an organization you know, and evaluate the effectiveness of the enterprise's recruitment and selection of people. How systematically are these and other staffing activities carried out?

2. Go to the library and research the background of successful CEOs. You may begin by looking at *Fortune* magazine or reading the biography of Lee Iacocca, the CEO at Chrysler. What makes the CEOs successful?

CASES

CASE 13-1
BELDEN ELECTRONICS COMPANY

The Belden Electronics Company (BEC) has an excellent national as well as international reputation, and its employees are proud to work for the firm. But the company demands complete loyalty from its employees and even tries to influence their behavior and appearance after work.

Christine Sharp, a bright young woman who had been working for BEC for over 10 years, was highly respected by her colleagues and did a fine job as a divisional sales manager. It was generally agreed that she had excellent potential for advancement. For 2 months Ms. Sharp had been dating Frank Simmons, who worked in the electronics division of a competing company. One day, Ralph Schmidt, Christine's boss, approached her about this matter, stating that there might be a possible conflict of interest in her association with an employee of the competitor. He made it clear that BEC has an unwritten policy that demands (and rewards) complete loyalty from all its employees.

Shortly after this emotional confrontation with her boss, Ms. Sharp was transferred to a nonmanagerial position without any loss in pay. She also noted that even her friends at BEC tried to avoid her. But Ms. Sharp felt very strongly that the company had no business suggesting whom she could and could not see after working hours; as a result, she quit her job.

1. Can a company demand loyalty to the extent indicated in the case? Would your answer be different if Ms. Sharp had access to important company trade secrets?

2. What would you have done in Ms. Sharp's position?

3. What would you have done in the supervisor's position?

INTERNATIONAL CASE 13-2
JOB DESIGN AT VOLVO IN SWEDEN[29]

Job design receives considerable attention abroad as well as in the United States. At the Volvo truck assembly plant in Sweden, work teams have a great deal of autonomy. For example, these teams choose their own supervisor, assign the work among themselves, set their own outputs within specified limits, and assume responsibility for quality control. In Kalmar, Sweden, Volvo designed an auto plant for teams of fifteen to twenty-five employees; each team handles a specific major task. Still, absenteeism remains high at 17 percent, only slightly below the absenteeism rate at the assembly line plant in Gothenburg (19 to 20 percent). Almost a third of its well-educated work force leaves the company every year. To cope with these kinds of problems, Volvo set up a new plant in Uddevalla, Sweden, which reduced the absenteeism rate to 8 percent.

The new Uddevalla plant, built with governmental assistance (generous tax write-offs) and union cooperation, has been in full operation since 1989. It is seen by some as the death of the automobile assembly line. Teams of seven to ten hourly workers assemble four cars per shift. Volvo claims that in this new plant, cars are produced with fewer work hours and with a higher quality than in other plants. However, Volvo does not give specific productivity figures.

The Uddevalla plant consists of six assembly sites with eight teams, each one made up of seven to ten workers. Each team has an ombudsperson but no traditional supervisor. Workers receive 16 weeks of training before working on the cars. This is followed by 16 months of on-the-job training.

To be sure, the plant's production capacity is much smaller than that of U.S. plants; the production goal for 1991 was 40,000 cars, while the average at traditional plants was 120,000. The workstations are well designed for a comfortable working position, with a minimum of stretching or bending required by the workers. Moreover, they are relatively quiet and well lit.

The new plant gained worldwide attention. Reporters from all over the world, especially from Japan, visited the plant. Carmakers from the United States, as well as unions, converged at Uddevalla. But skeptics maintain that the new work design will not result in the productivity levels required for mass production as it is practiced in Japan and the United States.

1. Why do you think Volvo experimented with the team approach?
2. Do you think the team approach will work in the United States? Why, or why not?
3. If U.S. car companies did away with the assembly line, what would have to be done to make the team approach work?

REFERENCES

1. Lloyd Baird and Ilan Meshoulam, "Managing Two Fits of Strategic Human Resource Management," *Academy of Management Review* (January 1988), pp. 116–128. This quote is based on the work by N. Tichy, C. J. Fombrun, and M. A. DeVanna, "Strategic Human Resource Management," *Sloan Management Review*, vol. 23, no. 2, pp. 47–64.

2. Rensis Likert, *The Human Organization: Its Management and Value* (New York: McGraw-Hill Book Company, 1967), chap. 9.

3. For a detailed discussion of problems, see Phil H. Mirvis and Barry A. Macy, "Human Resource Accounting: A Measurement Perspective," *Academy of Management Review* (April 1976), pp. 74–83.

4. J. D. Powell, H. A. Sciullo, and G. Mattson, "Human Resource Accounting: Why the Delay?" *Journal of Management* (Fall 1976), pp. 25–31.

5. For a comprehensive review, see Henry Mintzberg, *The Nature of Managerial Work* (New York: Harper & Row, 1973), chap. 2; see also Harry S. Jonas III, Ronald E. Fry, and Suresh Srivastva, "The Office of the CEO: Understanding the Executive Experience," *Academy of Management Executive* (August 1990), pp. 36–48.

6. Henry Mintzberg, "The Manager's Job: Folklore and Fact," *Harvard Business Review* (July–August 1975), pp. 49–61.

7. See also Thomas J. Condon and Richard H. Wolff, "Procedures That Safeguard Your Right to Fire," *Harvard Business Review* (November–December 1985), pp. 16–18.

8. Since job security cannot always be guaranteed, outplacement may be a way of helping employees. See the discussion with Peter F. Drucker in "Advice from the Dr. Spock of Business," *Business Week* (Sept. 28, 1987), pp. 61–65.

9. William B. Johnston, "Global Work Force 2000: The New World Labor Market," *Harvard Business Review* (March–April 1991), pp. 115–127.

10. See, for example, David G. Scalise and Daniel J. Smith, "Legal Update: When Are Job Requirements Discriminatory?" *Personnel* (March 1986), pp. 41–48.

11. See also Gary N. Powell, "One More Time: Do Female and Male Managers Differ?" *Academy of Management Executive* (August 1990), pp. 68–75.

12. Karen Blumenthal, "Room at the Top," *The Wall Street Journal,* special report (Mar. 24, 1986); Irene Pave, "A Woman's Place Is at GE, Federal Express, P&G . . . ," *Business Week* (June 23, 1986). See also Karen Pennar and Edward Mervosh, "Women at Work," *Business Week* (Jan. 28, 1985), pp. 80–85; Richard J. Herrnstein, "Are Women Workers Different?" *Fortune* (Apr. 1, 1985), pp. 177–180.

13. Susan Fraker, "Why Women Aren't Getting to the Top," *Fortune* (Apr. 16, 1984), pp. 40–45.

14. Clare Ansberry, "Board Games," *The Wall Street Journal,* special report (Mar. 24, 1986).

15. See also Simcha Ronen, *Comparative and Multinational Management* (New York: John Wiley & Sons, 1986), chap. 12.

16. Anant R. Negandhi, *International Management* (Boston: Allyn and Bacon, 1987), chap. 8.

17. Arvind V. Phatak, *International Dimensions of Management* (Boston: Kent Publishing Company, 1983), p. 92. For more information, see the third edition of the book, 1992.

18. Larry Armstrong, "Why Tokyo Is Tinkering with the Treadmill," *Business Week* (Sept. 28, 1987), pp. 45–48.

19. This discussion of job design is based in part on David A. Nadler, J. Richard Hackman, and Edward E. Lawler III, *Managing Organizational Behavior* (Boston: Little, Brown and Company, 1979), chap. 5.

20. Nadler et al., *Managing Organizational Behavior* (1979).

21. Maggie McComas, "Atop the Fortune 500: A Survey of the C.E.O.s," *Fortune* (Apr. 28, 1986), pp. 26–31.

22. Zachary Schiller, "P&G's Worldly New Boss Wants a More Worldly Company,"*Business Week* (Oct. 30, 1989), pp. 40–41; Brian Dumaine, "P&G Rewrites the Marketing Rules," *Fortune* (Nov. 6, 1989), pp. 34–48; Zachary Schiller, "No More Mr. Nice Guy at P&G— Not by a Long Shot," *Business Week* (Feb. 3, 1992), pp. 54–56.

23. Frederic V. Malek, *Washington's Hidden Tragedy* (New York: The Free Press, 1978), p. 68.

24. For discussions of affirmative actions, see R. Roosevelt Thomas, Jr., "From Affirmative Action to Affirming Diversity," *Harvard Business Review* (March–April 1990), pp. 107–117; Dorothy P. Moore and Marsha Hass, *Academy of Management Executive* (February 1990), pp. 84–90.

25. Myron Magnet, "Baby-Boom Executives Are Making It," *Fortune* (Sept. 2, 1985), pp. 22–28; and Michael Brody, "Meet Today's Young American Worker," *Fortune* (Nov. 11, 1985), pp. 90–98.

26. Laurence J. Peter and Raymond Hall, *The Peter Principle* (New York: Bantam Books, 1969). See also Laurence J. Peter, *The Peter Pyramid: Or Will We Ever Get the Point?* reviewed by Peter Shaw, "A Management Guru Peters Out," *The Wall Street Journal* (Jan. 24, 1986).

27. John A. Byrne, "Donald Burr May Be Ready to Take to the Skies Again," *Business Week* (Jan. 16, 1989), pp. 74–75.

28. Daniel C. Feldman, "The Multiple Socialization of Organization Members," *Academy of Management Review* (April 1981), pp. 309–318.

29. Information has been drawn from a variety of sources, including Jonathan Kapstein and John Hoerr, "Volvo's Radical New Plant: 'The Death of the Assembly Line'?" *Business Week* (Aug. 28, 1989), pp. 92–93.

Performance Appraisal and Career Strategy

Both the organization and the individual employee want the performance appraisal to meet particular objectives. In some cases these objectives or goals are compatible, but in many cases they are not.[1]

Michael Beer

Chapter Objectives

After reading this chapter, you should be able to:

1. Recognize the importance of effectively appraising managers.
2. Identify the qualities that should be measured in appraising managers.
3. Show that traditional trait appraisals have not been effective.
4. Present a system of managerial appraisal based on evaluating performance against verifiable objectives and performance as a manager.
5. Describe the team approach to evaluation.
6. Recognize the rewards and stress of managing.
7. Identify important aspects of career planning.

Managerial appraisal has sometimes been referred to as the Achilles' heel of managerial staffing, but it is probably a major key to managing itself. It is the basis for determining who is promotable to a higher position. It is also important to management development, because if a manager's strengths and weaknesses are not known, it is difficult to determine whether development efforts are aimed in the right direction. Appraisal is, or should be, an integral part of a system of managing. Knowing how well a manager plans, organizes, staffs, leads, and controls is really the only way to ensure that those occupying managerial positions are actually managing effectively. If a business, a government agency, a charitable organization, or even a university is to reach its goals effectively and efficiently, ways of accurately measuring management performance must be found and implemented.

There are other reasons why effective managerial appraisal is important. One of the most compelling arises from the provisions of Title VII of the Civil Rights Act of 1964 (as amended) and the regulations of the Equal Employment Opportunity Commission and the Office of Federal Contract Compliance. These agencies have been highly critical of many appraisal programs, finding that they often result in discrimination, particularly in areas of race, age, and sex. Courts have supported the federal agencies in their insistence that to be acceptable, an appraisal program must be reliable and valid.[2] That these are rigorous standards is apparent.

Effective performance appraisal should also recognize the legitimate desire of employees for progress in their professions. One way to integrate organizational demands and individual needs is through career management, which can be a part of performance appraisal, as this chapter will explain.

THE PURPOSES AND USES OF APPRAISAL

Appraisals serve different organizational and individual needs. Some important studies are discussed below.

The Conference Board Study[3]

An extensive study by The Conference Board showed that the *objectives* of appraisals, based on the frequency mentioned, were (1) management development, (2) performance appraisal, (3) performance improvement, (4) compensation, (5) potential identification, (6) feedback, (7) work-force planning, and (8) communication.

However, when respondents were asked how the companies *used* appraisals, the ranking differed: (1) performance feedback, (2) compensation administration, (3) promotion decisions, (4) identification of management development needs, (5) work-force planning, and (6) validation of selection procedures.

The differences between the stated objectives of appraisals and the way they were used may be an important reason for the dissatisfaction with appraisals that was indicated by some of the personnel managers participating in this study. Note also that the objectives and uses of appraisals have a different orientation. In determining compensation, or often even in evaluating performance, superiors assume the role of judges. In contrast, when the aim is to develop subordinates, managers need to be counselors, helpers, and teachers.

The General Electric Studies

Some of the best-known studies on performance appraisals were done at the General Electric Company.[4] The findings of the initial study showed that (1) criticism had a negative impact on goal accomplishment, (2) praise had little effect, (3) specific goals improved performance, (4) critical appraisal resulted in defensiveness and inferior performance, (5) coaching should be done on a day-to-day basis rather than once a year, (6) joint objective setting, not criticism, improved performance, (7) meetings with the primary purpose of improving performance should not be conducted at the same time that salary or promotion is being considered, and (8) subordinates' participation in setting objectives improved performance.

In light of the findings, General Electric developed a new appraisal program called "Work Planning and Review" (WP&R). This new approach emphasized frequent discussions of performance without summary ratings. Furthermore, salary actions were discussed at separate meetings. Finally, problem solving and joint objective setting were emphasized. The experience at General Electric suggests that the two purposes of performance appraisal should be separated because if the appraisal is used as the basis for salary action, the superior assumes the role of a judge, while in the attempt to motivate employees, the manager takes the role of a coach. It is through recognizing the split roles in performance appraisal and by setting specific goals mutually agreed on by the superior and the subordinates that productivity can be improved.

THE PROBLEM OF MANAGEMENT APPRAISAL

Managers have long been reluctant to appraise subordinates. However, in an activity as important as managing, there should be no reluctance to measure performance as accurately as possible. In almost all kinds of group enterprises, whether in work or in play, performance has usually been rated in some way. Moreover, most people, particularly people of ability, want to know how well they are doing.

It is difficult to believe that the controversy, the misgivings, and even the disillusionment that are still so widespread with respect to managerial performance appraisal have come from the practices of measuring and evaluating. Rather, it appears that they have arisen from the things measured, the standards used, and the way measurement is done.

Managers can understandably take exception, feel unhappy, or resist when they believe that they are evaluating, or being evaluated, inaccurately or against standards that are inapplicable, inadequate, or subjective. However, some light and hope have emerged in the past 30 years and offer promise of making evaluation effective. The interest in evaluating managers by comparing actual performance against preset verifiable objectives or goals is a development of considerable potential.[5]

Even appraisal against verifiable objectives is not enough. It needs to be supplemented by an appraisal of managers as managers. Still, neither system is without difficulties and pitfalls, and neither can be operated by simply adopting the technique and doing the paperwork. More must be done. In the first place, it is essential that managing by verifiable objectives, as explained in Chapter 6, be a way of life in an enterprise. In the second place, managers need not only a clear understanding of the managerial job and the fundamentals underlying it but also an ability to apply these fundamentals in practice.

CHOOSING THE APPRAISAL CRITERIA

The appraisal should measure performance in accomplishing goals and plans as well as performance as a manager. No one wants a person in a managerial role who appears to do everything right as a manager but who cannot turn in a good record of profit making, marketing, controllership, or whatever the area of responsibility may be. Nor should one be satisfied to have a "performer" in a managerial position who cannot operate effectively as a manager. Some star performers may have succeeded through no fault of their own.

Performance in Accomplishing Goals

In assessing performance, systems of appraising against verifiable preselected goals have extraordinary value. Given consistent, integrated, and understood planning designed to reach specific objectives, probably the best criteria of managerial performance relate to the ability to set goals intelligently, to plan programs that will accomplish those goals, and to succeed in achieving them. Those who have operated under one variation of this system often claim that these criteria are inadequate and that elements of luck or other factors beyond the manager's control are taken into account when arriving at any appraisal. But in too many cases, managers who achieve results owing to sheer luck are promoted, and others, who do not achieve expected results because of factors beyond their control, are blamed for failures. Thus, appraisal against verifiable objectives is, by itself, insufficient.

Performance as Managers

The system of measuring performance against preestablished objectives should be supplemented by an appraisal of a manager *as a manager*. Managers at any level also undertake nonmanagerial duties, and these cannot be overlooked. The primary purpose for which managers are hired and against which they should be measured, however, is their performance as managers—that is, they should be appraised on the basis of how well they understand and undertake the managerial functions of planning, organizing, staffing, leading, and controlling. The standards to use in this area are the fundamentals of management, but first some traditional appraisal programs should be examined.

TRADITIONAL TRAIT APPRAISALS

For many years, managers have been evaluated against standards of personal traits and work characteristics. Typical trait-rating evaluation systems may list ten to fifteen personal characteristics, such as ability to get along with people, leadership, analytical competence, industry, judgment, and initiative. The list may also include such work-related characteristics as job knowledge, ability to carry through on assignments, production or cost results, and success in seeing that plans and instructions are carried out. At least until recent years, personal traits have far outnumbered work-related characteristics. On the basis of these standards, the rater appraises subordinates, rating them from unacceptable to outstanding.

Weaknesses of Trait Appraisal

Managers resist doing this type of evaluation or tend to go through the paperwork without knowing exactly how to rate. Even in firms that have made earnest attempts to "sell" such programs, to indoctrinate managers, and to train them in the meaning of traits so that they can improve their appraisal ability, few managers can or will evaluate properly.

One practical problem of the trait approach to appraisal is that because trait evaluation cannot be objective, serious and fair-minded managers do not wish to utilize their obviously subjective judgment on a matter as important as performance. And employees who receive less than the top rating almost invariably feel that they have been dealt with unfairly.

Another problem is that the basic assumption of trait appraisals is open to question. The connection between performance and possession of specific traits is doubtful. What is evaluated tends to be outside of—separated from—a manager's actual operations. Trait appraisal substitutes someone's opinion of an individual for what that individual really does.

Many managers look upon trait rating as only a paperwork exercise that must be done because someone has ordered it. When people have this attitude, they go through the paperwork and tend to make ratings as painless (for the subordinate and themselves) as possible. Consequently, they tend not to be very discriminating. It is interesting, but hardly surprising, that a study of ratings of U.S. Navy officers several years ago came up with an arithmetical paradox: Of all officers rated over a period of time, some 98.5 percent were outstanding or excellent, and only 1 percent were average!

Trait criteria are at best nebulous. Raters are dealing with a blunt tool, and subordinates are likely to be vague about what qualities they are being rated on. In the hands of most practitioners, trait appraisal is a crude device, and since raters are painfully aware of this, they are reluctant to use it in a manner that would damage the careers of their subordinates. One of the principal purposes of appraisal is to provide a basis on which to discuss performance and plan for improvement. But trait evaluations provide few tangible things to discuss, little on which participants can agree as fact, and therefore little mutual understanding of what is required to obtain improvement.

Attempts to Strengthen Trait Rating

As the deficiencies of trait rating have come to be recognized, a number of changes and additions have been introduced. Some are aimed at making the traits more comprehensible to raters. In a rating form used by a well-known business corporation, a person's "judgment" is defined as his or her capability to distinguish the significant from the less significant in arriving at sound conclusions. Likewise, attempts are made to give meanings to various grades under each category.

Often, too, trait and work-quality forms are supplemented by open-ended evaluations in which, without specific guidance, appraisers are asked to supply whatever evidence on performance they feel is pertinent. Sometimes, also, this approach is used for the entire appraisal. Appraisers may be given a broad outline to guide them; for example, they may be asked for comments under such categories as operations, organization, personnel, and finance, and they may be asked specifically to consider such things as quality, quantity, time required to complete work, customer relations, and subordinate employee morale. Although these categories are helpful, experience has shown that they do not greatly improve the quality of ratings.

Attempts have also been made to improve the effectiveness of the rating process. In some systems, subordinates are required to rate themselves, and superiors must compare their own ratings with those made by subordinates. In other instances, the superior's superior is asked to rate the former's subordinate or at least to carefully review the evaluation made by the immediate superior. Sometimes, a rater is forced by an appraisal system to rank subordinates from the best to the least able. In still other cases, rating has been done through the use of critical incidents that are assumed to give meaning to the grades given. These incidents are important events or decisions critical for effective performance in a particular job. Such incidents may represent outstanding or unsatisfactory performance.

These and other devices have been used to offset the disadvantages of trait rating. They have helped, but they cannot overcome the fact that traits and work qualities are subjective and are not necessarily correlated with what a manager's job really is.

APPRAISING MANAGERS AGAINST VERIFIABLE OBJECTIVES

One widely used approach to managerial appraisal is the system of evaluating managerial performance against the setting and accomplishing of verifiable objectives. As was noted in Chapter 6, a network of meaningful and attainable objectives is basic to effective managing. This is simple logic, since people cannot be expected to accomplish a task with effectiveness or efficiency unless they know what the end points of their efforts should be. Nor can any organized enterprise in business or elsewhere be expected to do so.

The Appraisal Process

Once a program of managing by verifiable objectives is operating, appraisal is a fairly easy step. Supervisors determine how well managers set objectives and how well they have performed against them. In cases where appraisal by results has failed or been disillusioning, the principal reason is that managing by objectives was seen only as an appraisal technique. The system is not likely to work if used only for this purpose. Management by objectives must be a way of managing, a way of planning, as well as the key to organizing, staffing, leading, and controlling. When this is the case, appraisal boils down to whether or not managers have established adequate and reasonably attainable objectives and how they have performed against them in a certain period.

Look at the system of managing and appraising by objectives in Figure 6-3 (page 152). As the figure shows, appraising is merely a last step in the entire process.

There are other questions too. Were the goals adequate? Did they call for "stretched" (high but reasonable) performance?* These questions can be answered only through the judgment and experience of a person's superior, although this judgment can become sharper with time and experience, and it may be even more objective if the superior can use the goals of other managers in similar positions for comparison.

In assessing the accomplishment of goals, the evaluator must take into account such considerations as whether the goals were reasonably attainable in the first

---

* For additional questions, see the checklist in Table 6-2.

place, whether factors beyond a person's control unduly helped or hindered the person in accomplishing goals, and what the reasons for the results were. The reviewer should also note whether an individual continued to operate against obsolete goals when situations changed and revised goals were called for.

Three Kinds of Reviews

The simplified model of performance appraisal shown in Figure 14-1 indicates three kinds of appraisals: (1) a comprehensive review, (2) progress or periodic reviews, and (3) continuous monitoring.

There is general agreement that a *formal comprehensive appraisal* should be conducted at least once a year, but some people suggest that such discussions should take place more frequently. Some enterprises do all the reviews within a short period of time each year, while others schedule the appraisals throughout the year, often at the employment anniversary. A case could be made against any rigid schedule of annual performance reviews. Instead, it may be argued, with good reason, that performance should be reviewed, for example, after the completion of a major project. Obviously, no universally applicable suggestion can be made about the time frame for the formal comprehensive review. It depends on the nature of

FIGURE 14-1

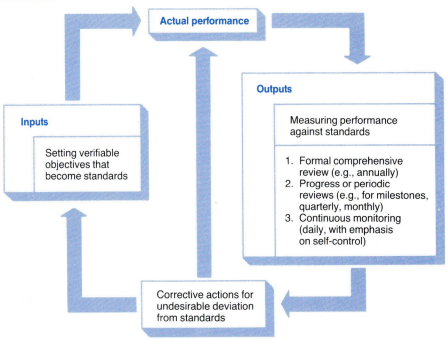

THE APPRAISAL PROCESS.

Redrawn from Heinz Weihrich, *Management Excellence: Productivity through MBO* (New York: McGraw-Hill Book Company, 1985), p. 125.

the task, past company practices, and other situational factors. Once, twice, or even three times may be appropriate for a particular organization or a person who is new in a job.

What is important is that the formal comprehensive reviews be supplemented by frequent *progress* or *periodic reviews*. These reviews can be short and relatively informal, but they help identify problems or barriers that hinder effective performance. They also keep communication open between the superior and subordinates. Furthermore, priorities can be rearranged and objectives can be renegotiated if warranted by changed situations. It surely is inappropriate to pursue obsolete or even unsuitable objectives that were agreed on in an environment of uncertainties.

Finally, there is *continuous monitoring* of performance. With this system, when performance deviates from plans, one does not have to wait for the next periodic review to correct it. The superior and the subordinate discuss the situation immediately so that corrective actions can be taken at once in order to prevent a small deviation from developing into a major problem.

Strengths of Appraisal against Verifiable Objectives

The strengths of appraising against accomplishment of objectives are almost the same as those of managing by objectives. Both are part of the same process, both are basic to effective managing, and both are means of improving the quality of managing.

In the area of appraising, there are special and important strengths. Appraising on the basis of performance against verifiable objectives has the great advantage of being operational. Appraisals are not apart from the job that managers do but are a review of what they actually did as managers.

There are always questions of how well a person did; of whether goals were missed or accomplished, and for what reasons; and of how much in the way of goal attainment should be expected. But information about what a person has done, measured against what that individual agreed was a reasonable target, is available. This information furnishes strong presumptions of objectivity and reduces the element of pure judgment in appraisal. Besides, the appraisal can be carried on in an atmosphere in which superiors work cooperatively with subordinates rather than sitting in judgment of them.

Weaknesses of Appraisal against Verifiable Objectives

As noted in Chapter 6, there are certain weaknesses in the implementation of managing by objectives. These, of course, apply with equal force to appraisal. One of them is that it is entirely possible for persons to meet or miss goals through no fault of their own. Luck often plays a part in performance. For example, a new product's acceptance may be far beyond expectations, and its success will make a marketing manager look exceptionally good, even though the quality of the marketing program and its implementation might actually be poor. Or an unpredictable cancellation of a major military contract might make the record of a division manager look unsatisfactory.

Most evaluators will say that they always take uncontrollable or unexpected factors into account in assessing goal performance, and to a very great extent they do. But it is extremely difficult to do so. In an outstanding sales record, for example, how can anyone be sure how much was due to luck and how much to competence? Outstanding performers are rated highly, at least as long as they perform. Nonperformers can hardly escape having a cloud cast over them.

With its emphasis on accomplishing operating objectives, the system of appraising against these may overlook needs for individual development. Goal attainment tends to be short-run in practice. Even if longer-range goals are put into the system, seldom are they so long-range as to allow for adequate long-term development of managers. Managers concerned primarily with results might be driven by the system to take too little time to plan, implement, and follow through with programs required for their development and that of their subordinates.

On the other hand, since managing by objectives gives better visibility to managerial needs, development programs can be better pinpointed. If individual development is to be ensured, goals in this area should be specifically set.

From an appraisal as well as an operating management point of view, perhaps the greatest deficiency of management by objectives is that it appraises operating performance only. Not only is there the question of luck, mentioned previously, but also there are other factors to appraise, notably an individual's *managerial* abilities. This is why an adequate appraisal system must appraise performance as a manager as well as performance in setting and meeting goals.

A SUGGESTED PROGRAM: APPRAISING MANAGERS AS MANAGERS

The most appropriate standards to use for appraising managers as managers are the fundamentals of management. It is not enough to appraise a manager broadly, evaluating only performance of the basic functions of the manager; appraisal should go further.

The best approach is to utilize the basic techniques and principles of management as standards. If they are basic, as they have been found to be in a wide variety of managerial positions and environments, they should serve as reasonably good standards. As crude as they may be, and even though some judgment may be necessary in applying them to practice, they give the evaluator some benchmarks for measuring how well subordinates understand and are following the functions of managing. They are definitely more specific and more applicable for evaluations than such broad standards as work and dress habits, cooperation, intelligence, judgment, and loyalty. They at least focus attention on what may be expected of a manager *as a manager*. And when used in conjunction with appraisal of the performance of plans and goals, they can help remove much of the weakness in many management appraisal systems.

In brief, the program involves classifying the functions of the manager as done in this book and then dealing with each function by a series of questions. The questions are designed to reflect the most important fundamentals of managing in each area. Although the total list of key questions, the form used, the system of ratings, and the instructions for operating the program are too extensive to be treated in this book,[6] some sample "checkpoints" are presented below.

Perspective

Sample Questions for Appraising Managers as Managers

In the area of *planning,* a manager's rating would be determined through questions such as the following. Does the manager:

- Set for the departmental unit both short-term and long-term goals in verifiable terms that are related in a positive way to those of superiors and of the company?
- In choosing from among alternatives, recognize and give primary attention to those factors which are limiting or critical to the solution of a problem?
- Check plans periodically to see whether they are consistent with current expectations?

In the area of *organizing,* questions such as the following are asked. Does the manager:

- Delegate authority to subordinates on the basis of results expected of them?
- Refrain from making decisions in that area once authority has been delegated to subordinates?
- Regularly teach subordinates, or otherwise make sure that they understand, the nature of line and staff relationships?

In the three other areas of managing—staffing, leading, and controlling—evaluators ask similar questions. In all, there are seventy-three checkpoints.

Semantics has always been a problem in management. Therefore, it is wise to use a standard book on management (such as this one) and refer to the pages that correspond to the questions.[7] This approach leads to a fair degree of managerial development.

Managers are rated on how well they perform the activities. The scale used is from 0 for "inadequate" to 5 for "superior." To give the numerical ratings more rigor, each rating is defined. For example, "superior" means "a standard of performance which could not be improved under any circumstances or conditions known to the rater."

To further reduce subjectivity and to increase the discrimination among performance levels, the program requires that (1) in the comprehensive annual appraisal, incident examples be given to support certain ratings, (2) the ratings be reviewed by the superior's superior, and (3) the raters be informed that their own evaluation will depend in part on how well they discriminate on the ratings of performance levels when evaluating their subordinates. Obviously, objectivity is enhanced by the number (seventy-three) and the specificity of the checkpoint questions.

Advantages of the New Program

Experience with this program in a multinational company showed certain advantages. By focusing on the essentials of management, this method of evaluation gives operational meaning to what management really is. Also, the use of a standard reference text for interpretation of concepts and terms removes many of the semantic and communication difficulties so commonly encountered. Such things as variable budgets, verifiable objectives, staff, functional authority, and delegation take on consistent meaning. Likewise, many management techniques become uniformly understood.

The system, furthermore, has proved to be a tool for management development; in many cases, it has brought to managers' attention certain basics that they may have long disregarded or not understood. In addition, it has been found useful in pinpointing areas in which weaknesses exist and to which development should be directed. Finally, as intended, the program acts as a supplement to, and a check on, appraisal of managers' effectiveness in setting and achieving goals. If a manager has a record of outstanding performance in goal accomplishment but is found to be a less-than-average manager, those in charge will look for the reason. Normally, one would expect a truly effective manager to be effective also in meeting goals.

Weaknesses of the New Program

There are, however, a number of weaknesses or shortcomings in the approach. It applies only to managerial aspects of a given position and not to such technical qualifications as marketing or engineering abilities that might also be important. These, however, can be weighed on the basis of goals selected and achieved. There is also the apparent complexity of the seventy-three checkpoints; rating on all of them does take time, but the time is well spent.

Perspective

Performance Appraisal: An Illustration

One utility company that had used the management-by-objectives approach successfully in its appraisal program found it desirable to supplement the program with a performance appraisal based on common management responsibilities. The form used for this evaluation, shown in Table 14-1, was based on the ideas discussed above, but it has been greatly simplified. Although the program covers all the managerial functions, the number of managerial activities graded has been substantially reduced from the seventy-three suggested above. The program provides for frequent performance review so that corrective actions can be taken without delay. Note that this approach focuses on individual development; if performance of an activity either requires improvement or is unsatisfactory, this weakness, as well as plans for overcoming it, must be documented.

Perhaps the major shortcoming in appraising managers as managers is the subjectivity involved. As we mentioned earlier, some subjectivity in rating each checkpoint was found to be unavoidable. However, the program still has a high degree of objectivity and is far more objective than appraisal of managers only on the broader areas of the managerial functions. At least the checkpoints are specific and pertain to the essentials of managing.

A TEAM EVALUATION APPROACH[8]

More recently, another approach to performance appraisal has been introduced. The criteria selected for evaluation are, in part, similar to those above and include planning, decision making, organizing, coordinating, staffing, motivating, and controlling. But other factors, such as selling skills, may also be included.

The appraisal process involves the person being evaluated and consists of the following steps:

- Selection of job-related criteria
- Development of examples of observable behavior
- Selection of four to eight raters (peers, associates, other supervisors, and, naturally, the immediate superior)
- Preparation of the rating forms applicable to the job
- Completion of the forms by the raters
- Integration of the various ratings
- Analysis of the results and preparation of the report

This approach has been used not only for appraisal but also for the selection of people for promotion and for personnel development, and even for dealing with alcoholism.

The advantages suggested by the originators of this approach include a rather high degree of accuracy in appraising people by obtaining several inputs rather than input from the superior only. The program can be used to identify raters' biases (for example, rating others consistently high or low, or giving such ratings to certain groups of people, such as women or those belonging to minority groups). The persons being rated apparently consider this approach quite fair, since they are involved in selecting evaluation criteria as well as the raters. It also allows comparing individuals with each other. Although this approach has been used by a variety of enterprises, additional assessments seem necessary.

REWARDS AND STRESS OF MANAGING

Managers are different; they have different needs, desires, and motives. The essentials of motivation will be discussed in Chapter 16. The concern here is with some of the general and financial rewards, as well as the stressful aspects, of managing.

TABLE 14-1 PERFORMANCE APPRAISAL: COMMON MANAGEMENT RESPONSIBILITIES

Name	Rated by		Date

To be completed and included as part of the overall appraisal for all unit positions and above who have authority and responsibility for managing human resources.

Needs improvement or Unsatisfactory progress as well as corrective plans must be documented in REMARKS.

Importance weight assigned to Common Management Responsibilities

Performance Rating				
Out-stand-ing	Super-ior	Fully compe-tent	Needs improve-ment	Unsat-isfac-tory
5	4	3	2	1

1. Planning:

   A. Develops and implements effective plans that contain verifiable and realistic goals and objectives.

   B. Plans include long-range considerations.

   C. Establishes specific quantitative/qualitative work goals or standards to be achieved by subordinates.

   REMARKS:

2. Organization / Staffing:*

   A. Organizes and staffs consistent with a thorough understanding of job responsibilities.

   B. Identifies changes in job responsibilities and effects changes in Position Information Questionnaires.

   C. Selects qualified personnel to fill vacancies.

   REMARKS:

3. Delegation / Control:

   A. Delegates authority and maintains control consistent with expectations.

   B. Control techniques and standards reflect plans and satisfy budget compliance as well as report exceptions in a timely way.

   C. Controls provide for optimizing resource utilization.

   REMARKS:

Performance Progress Review												
Month												
J	F	M	A	M	J	J	A	S	O	N	D
A											
B											
C											

4. Decision Making / Directing:
   A. Accepts responsibility for making decisions.
   B. Decisions are timely and consistent with plans, programs, and policies.
   C. Qualifies decisions by considering all points of view (subordinates, peer, superior).
   D. Problem solving is effective.
   REMARKS:

5. Administration:
   A. Administration of policies and procedures.
   B. Contributes effectively to corporate goals such as Affirmative Action, Safety, EEOC, Minority Contractor, etc.
   C. Sets and administers effective disciplinary standards.
   REMARKS:

6. Compensation:
   A. Administration of Performance Planning and Appraisal Program.
   B. Performance appraisal is based on job-related criteria.
   C. Salary administration is fair, equitable, and consistent with corporate wage and salary administration guidelines.
   D. Performance Planning and Appraisal is used as an effective motivating tool and morale builder.
   E. Communicates Performance Planning and Appraisal program and expected results to subordinates effectively.
   REMARKS:

7. Human Resource Development:
   A. Provides for subordinate training and development and assists motivated subordinates to prepare for additional responsibility.
   B. Human resource planning and career development procedures are current and realistic.
   C. Subordinates' developmental needs are specifically documented.
   D. Succession plans written for all subordinates.
   E. Actively pursues own personal plan for career development and/or improvement as agreed to with immediate supervisor.
   REMARKS:

Code:

☑	Fully meeting expectations or better
⊙	Needs improvement
Ū	Unsatisfactory

* The "Performance Progress Review" and "Performance Rating" boxes have been omitted for the managerial responsibilities that follow.

405

Rewards of Managing

Since managerial candidates differ widely in age, economic position, and level of maturity, they want many things, but these usually include opportunity, power, and income. Most managerial candidates desire the opportunity for a progressive career that provides depth and breadth of managerial experience. Related to this is the challenge found in meaningful work. Most people, but perhaps managers in particular, want to feel that they have the power to make a significant contribution to the aims of an enterprise and even to society.

In addition, managers want to be, and should be, rewarded for their contributions, although the size of the financial rewards has been criticized. The International Perspective specifies the compensation of executives in various countries.

International Perspective

Are U.S. CEOs Overpaid and Other U.S. Managers Underpaid?

The CEOs in the United States are paid substantially more than those in many European and Pacific Basin countries.[9] In 1987, the CEOs of 24 U.S. firms received over $5 million in pay, and about 300 CEOs earned over $1 million. Jack Welch of General Electric earned over $12,500,000 in compensation, compared with $930,000 for Karl Heinz Kaske, the head of Siemens in Germany. Anders Scharp at Electrolux in Sweden received $437,000 in compensation and Ichiro Shinji of JVC (Victor Company of Japan) $290,000. In the automobile industry there are similar disparities. While Lee Iacocca received $17,656,000 in compensation in 1987 from Chrysler, the CEO at Daimler-Benz in Germany got $1,200,000, the Honda CEO in Japan got $450,000, and the head of Peugeot in France got $250,000.

Even with the weak dollar, CEOs in the United States earned, in the latter part of the 1980s, about 40 percent more than those in Japan, more than twice as much as those in Great Britain, and about 3.5 times as much as top managers in Australia. Moreover, in U.S. firms in the late 1980s, the compensation of CEOs, on the average, was about 14 times that of college graduates entering their companies; in Japan, it was 10 times as much; and in Australia, 4 times as much.[10]

One recent study found that the typical salary for entry-level managers is rather low in the United States. The salary for such managers is $46,800 in Germany and $41,500 in Japan, and in the United States it is $32,300, which is still higher than in Britain ($26,000). However, these comparisons must be seen in light of taxes paid. Thus, this study concludes that the take-home pay of Americans still buys more goods and services than that of entry-level managers in the countries studied.[11]

Professors Gerald Cavanagh and Arthur McGovern point out that traditionally, executive performance was recognized by large salaries and bonuses but that these earnings are becoming increasingly disproportionate to the compensation of others.[12] Ross Perot (also known as the Texas billionaire), the founder of Electronic Data Systems and onetime director at General Motors (GM), criticized the excessive earnings of CEOs at GM, while they were demanding restraint from hourly workers.

A 1991 cover story in *Business Week* raised the question "Are CEOs Paid Too Much?"[13] There is, indeed, a growing concern of employees, investors, and academics that the pay of executives is increasing, even in a recession, when company performance declines. An executive salary considered outrageous in one year becomes the standard the following year.

Not only the amount of pay outrages the critics but also the relation to company performance. During the decade of the 1980s, executive pay rose 212 percent, but earnings per share of the Standard & Poor's (S&P) 500 firms increased only 78 percent. While in 1990, the profits of companies decreased by 7 percent, the pay and other gains of CEOs rose by 7 percent. An extreme example in 1990 is that Chrysler's earnings decreased 79 percent, but the company's chairman, Lee Iacocca, received a 25 percent total pay increase. Pay increases, critics say, are getting out of control.

CEOs' salaries are also disproportionate to the salaries of people in other professions. Compare once more the executive pay increase of 212 percent during the decade of the 1980s, this time with the pay increase of teachers, 95 percent; engineers, 73 percent; and factory workers, only 53 percent. Peter F. Drucker, one of the most respected commentators on management issues, suggested in the 1980s that the CEOs' pay should be not much higher than 20 times that of the lowest-paid employee of the company. In 1980, the CEOs' pay was about 42 times that of the factory worker, but by 1990, it was 85 times higher.[14] Consider another example. In 1990, Stephen Wolf, the chairman of UAL (parent company of United Airlines), earned about 1200 times the pay of a newly hired flight attendant. Drucker suggested that if companies do not reform executive pay, Congress may do it.[15] Indeed, in June 1991, the Securities and Exchange Commission (SEC) testified before the Congress about corporation laws related to the pay of CEOs.[16]

One should not overlook, however, efforts that have been made to link pay to performance and to induce managers to make decisions that are in the long-term interest of the enterprise.[17] At Ford, for example, more emphasis is given to stock grants that reward the achievement of 5-year objectives. These criteria include not only return on equity but also measures such as customer satisfaction, involvement of employees, and product quality. Furthermore, performance is compared with that of competitors. For instance, even though quality may have improved at Ford, if more quality improvements have been made by a competitor, this will be held against Ford's managers if their quality improvements have not been sufficient.

Stress in Managing

Stress is a very complex phenomenon. It is, therefore, no surprise that there is no commonly accepted definition. A widely used working definition is *an adaptive response, mediated by individual differences and/or psychological processes, that* is, a consequence of any external (environmental) action, situation, or event that places excessive psychological and/or physical demands on a person.[18]

Hans Selye, probably the leading authority on the concept of stress, described stress as "the rate of all wear and tear caused by life."[19] Alvin Toffler, the author of Future Shock, said, "Dr. Hans Selye knows more about stress than any other scientist alive."[20]

There are many physical sources of stress, such as work overload, irregular work hours, loss of sleep, loud noises, bright light, and insufficient light. Psychological sources of stress may be due to a particular situation, such as a boring job, inability to socialize, lack of autonomy, responsibility for results without sufficient authority, unrealistic objectives, role ambiguity or role conflict, or a dual-career marriage. But what might be stressful to one person may be less so to another; people react differently to situations.

Stress can have various effects on the individual as well as on the organization. There are the physiological effects that may be linked to a variety of illnesses. Then there are psychological effects such as burnout or boredom. Various kinds of behavior, such as drug and alcohol abuse, inordinate food consumption, accidents, or withdrawal from the stressful situation (absenteeism, excessive labor turnover), may be a reaction to stress. Clearly, not only does the individual suffer, but the organization may also be affected by the turnover or impaired decision making of its managers and nonmanagers alike.

Individuals and organizations have attempted to deal with stress in various ways.[21] Individuals, for example, may try to reduce stress through better management of their time, healthful nutrition, exercise, career planning, a change in jobs, promotion of psychological health, relaxation,[22] meditation, and prayer. Organizations may provide counseling or recreation facilities or may improve the job design by matching the person with the job.

Fitting the Needs of the Individual to the Demands of the Job

Managing, then, offers rewards but also involves stress. An individual aspiring to a managerial position should evaluate both the advantages and the disadvantages of managing before pursuing this career. A proper fit between individual needs and the demands of the task will benefit both the individual and the enterprise. Career management will help to achieve this fit.

FORMULATING THE CAREER STRATEGY[23]

The appraisal of performance should identify the strengths and weaknesses of an individual; this identification can be the starting point for a career plan. The personal strategy should be designed to utilize strengths and overcome weaknesses in order to take advantage of career opportunities. Although there are different approaches to career development, it is considered here as a process of developing a personal strategy that is conceptually similar to an organization strategy. This process is shown in Figure 14-2.

FIGURE 14-2

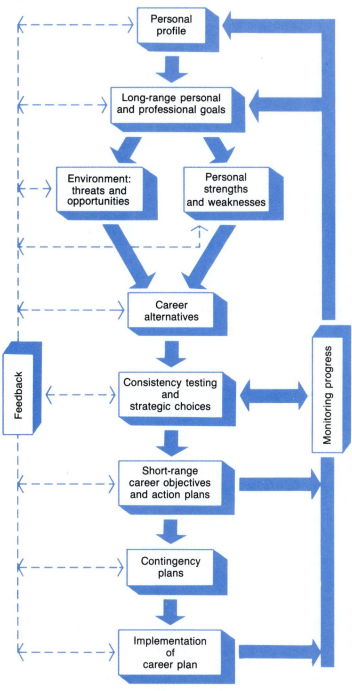

FORMULATION OF CAREER STRATEGY.

1. Preparation of a Personal Profile

One of the most difficult tasks is gaining insight into oneself, yet this is an essential first step in developing a career strategy. Managers should ask themselves: Am I an introvert or an extrovert? What are my attitudes toward time, achievement, work, material things, and change? The answers to these and similar questions and a clarification of values will help in determining the direction of the professional career.

2. Development of Long-Range Personal and Professional Goals

No airplane would take off without a flight plan including a destination. Yet how clear are managers about the direction of their lives? People often resist career planning because it involves making decisions. By choosing one goal, a person gives up opportunities to pursue others; if an individual studies to become a lawyer, she or he cannot become a doctor at the same time. Managers also resist goal setting because uncertainties in the environment cause concern about making commitments. Furthermore, there is the fear of failing to achieve goals, because the nonachievement of objectives is a blow to one's ego.

But by understanding the factors that inhibit goal setting, one can take steps to increase commitment. First, when the setting of performance goals becomes a part of the appraisal process, identifying career goals is easier. Besides, one does not set career goals all at once. Rather, goal setting is a continuing process that allows flexibility; professional goals can be revised in the light of changing circumstances. Another factor that reduces resistance to goal setting is the integration of long-term aims with the more immediate requirement for action. For example, the aim of becoming a doctor makes it easier to study boring subjects that are necessary for the medical degree.

How far in advance should one plan? The answer may be found in the commitment principle discussed in Chapter 5. It states that planning should cover a period of time necessary for the fulfillment of commitments involved in the decision made today. Therefore, the time frame for career planning will differ with the circumstances. For example, if a person wants to become a professor, it is necessary to plan for university studies of 7 to 9 years. On the other hand, if the career goal is to become a taxi driver, the time span is much shorter. At any rate, the long-term aim has to be translated into short-term objectives. Before this is done, it is necessary to make a careful assessment of the external environment, including its threats and opportunities.

3. Analysis of the Environment: Threats and Opportunities

In the analysis of the environment inside and outside the organization, many diverse factors need to be taken into account. They include economic, social, political, technological, and demographic factors; they also include the labor market, competition, and other factors relevant to a particular situation. For example, joining an expanding company usually provides more career opportunities than working for a mature company that is not expected to grow. Similarly, working for a mobile manager means an increased probability that the position of the superior will become vacant; or one might "ride the coattails" of a competent mobile superior by following him or her through a series of promotions up the organizational hierarchy. At any rate, successful career planning requires a systematic scanning of the environment for opportunities and threats.

One has to be concerned not only about the present but also about the future environment. This requires forecasting. Since there are a great many factors that need to be analyzed, planning one's career necessitates being selective and concentrating on those factors critical to personal success.

4. Analysis of Personal Strengths and Weaknesses

For successful career planning, the environmental opportunities and threats must be matched with the strengths and weaknesses of individuals. Capabilities may be categorized as technical, human, conceptual, or design. As Figure 1-2 illustrated, the relative importance of these skills differs for the various positions in the organizational hierarchy, with technical skills being very important on the supervisory level, conceptual skills being crucial for top managers, and human skills being important at all levels.

5. Development of Strategic Career Alternatives

In developing a career strategy, one usually has several alternatives. The most successful strategy would be to build on one's strengths to take advantage of opportunities. For example, if a person has an excellent knowledge of computers and many companies are looking for computer programmers, he or she should find many opportunities for a satisfying career. On the other hand, if there is a demand for programmers, and if an individual is interested in programming but lacks the necessary skills, the proper approach would be a developmental strategy to overcome the weakness and develop the skills in order to take advantage of the opportunities.

It may also be important to recognize the threats in the environment and develop a strategy to cope with them. A person with excellent managerial and technical skills may work in a declining company or industry. The appropriate strategy might be to find employment in an expanding firm or in a growing industry.

6. Consistency Testing and Strategic Choices

In developing a personal strategy, one must realize that the rational choice based on strengths and opportunities is not always the most fulfilling alternative. Although one may have certain skills demanded in the job market, a career in that field may not be congruent with personal values or interests. For example, a person may prefer dealing with people to programming computers. Some may find great satisfaction in specialization, while others prefer to broaden their knowledge and skills.

Strategic choices require trade-offs. Some alternatives involve high risks, others low risks. Some choices demand action now; other choices can wait. Careers that were glamorous in the past may have an uncertain future. Rational and systematic analysis is just one step in the career-planning process, for a choice also involves personal preferences, personal ambitions, and personal values.

7. Development of Short-Range Career Objectives and Action Plans

So far, concern has centered on career direction. But the strategy has to be supported by short-term objectives and action plans, which can be a part of the performance appraisal process. Thus, if the aim is to achieve a certain management position that requires a master of business degree, the short-term objective may be to complete a number of courses. Here is an example of a short-term verifiable objective: to complete the course Fundamentals of Management by May 30 with a grade of A. This objective is measurable, as it states the task to be done, the deadline, and the quality of performance (the grade).

Objectives often must be supported by action plans. Continuing with the example, the completion of the management course may require preparing a schedule for attending classes, doing the homework, and obtaining the support of the spouse, who may suffer because attending classes takes time that might otherwise be spent with the family. It is obvious that the long-term strategic career plan needs to be supported by short-term objectives and action plans.

8. Development of Contingency Plans

Career plans are developed in an environment of uncertainty, and the future cannot be predicted with great accuracy. Therefore, contingency plans based on alternative assumptions should be prepared. While one may enjoy working for a small, fast-growing venture company, it may be wise to prepare an alternative career plan based on the assumption that the venture may not succeed.

9. Implementation of the Career Plan

Career planning may start during the performance appraisal. At that time, the person's growth and development should be discussed. Career goals and personal ambitions can be considered in selecting and promoting and in designing training and development programs.

10. Monitoring Progress

Monitoring is the process of evaluating progress toward career goals and making necessary corrections in the aims or plans. An opportune time for assessing career programs is during the performance appraisal. This is the time not only to review performance against objectives in the operating areas but also to review the achievement of milestones in the career plan. In addition, progress should be monitored at other times, such as at the completion of an important task or project.

Dual-Career Couples

An effective career strategy requires that consideration be given to the career of the spouse. Dual-career couples, with both partners working, sometimes have to make very stressful choices.[24] For example, if both partners have successful careers, the opportunity for a promotion that requires relocation is a particularly painful decision. Merrill Lynch Relocation Management, Inc., conducted a survey of 600 major companies and found that 60 percent of relocations involved dual-career couples. It was estimated that the figure would be 75 percent by 1990.[25]

Some companies are accommodating the special needs of dual-career couples by having a flexible approach to transfers that involve relocation, considering the needs of both partners in career planning, helping to find employment for the spouse either within the company or outside, and providing maternity leave and day-care services for children. With the large number of married women in the work force, an increasing number of companies have recognized the stressful situation of dual-career couples and implemented more flexible policies, career planning, personnel selection, placement, and promotion.

SUMMARY

Appraisal is essential for effective managing. The Conference Board study showed differences between the stated objectives of appraisals and the way they were actually used. These differences may have caused dissatisfaction. In the Work Planning and Review approach to appraisal, General Electric emphasized frequent performance discussions; but performance discussions and salary actions were dealt with at separate meetings.

Appraisal should measure performance in achieving goals and plans and performance as a manager, that is, how well a person carries out key managerial activities. Traditional appraisal methods that attempt to measure personality traits have serious limitations.

An effective method is to appraise managers against verifiable objectives, as exemplified by the discussion of management by objectives (MBO) in Chapter 6. This approach is operational, related to the manager's job, and relatively objective. Still, a person may perform well (or badly) because of luck or factors beyond his or her control. Therefore, the management-by-objectives approach should be supplemented by appraisal of managers as managers, that is, appraisal of how well they perform their key managerial activities.

There are three kinds of reviews: (1) the formal comprehensive appraisal, (2) progress or periodic reviews, and (3) continuous monitoring. In a suggested appraisal program, key managerial activities are presented as checklist questions and grouped under the categories of planning, organizing, staffing, leading, and controlling.

Since managers differ greatly, they look for different rewards, such as opportunity and income. But the job of a manager is also stressful, and this can affect the individual as well as the organization. Therefore, various ways of coping with stress have evolved.

Career planning can be effectively integrated with performance appraisal. Although the specific steps in developing a career strategy may vary, the process is similar to developing an organization strategy. Since dual-career couples are quite common, an effective career strategy must include consideration of the spouse's career.

KEY IDEAS AND CONCEPTS FOR REVIEW

Purposes and uses of appraisal

Work Planning and Review at General Electric

Weaknesses of trait appraisal

Steps in the appraisal process (against verifiable objectives)

Three kinds of reviews

Strengths and weaknesses of appraisal against verifiable objectives

Appraising managers as managers

Advantages and weaknesses of appraising managers as managers

Team evaluation approach

Rewards of managing

Stress

Ten steps in formulating a career strategy

Dual-career couples

FOR DISCUSSION

1. Do you think managers should be appraised regularly? If so, how?
2. What problems may arise from the fact that different managers on the same level appraise differently, some generally rating higher than others?
3. Many firms evaluate managers on such personality factors as aggressiveness, cooperation, leadership, and attitude. Do you think this kind of rating makes sense?
4. An argument has been made in this book for appraising managers on their ability to manage. Should anything more be expected of them?
5. How do you feel about an appraisal system based on results expected and realized? Would you prefer to be appraised on this basis? If not, why not?
6. What is your assessment of the degree of objectivity or subjectivity of the appraisal approaches suggested in this chapter? Can you suggest any further means of making appraisals more objective?
7. On what basis should your performance in college be appraised?
8. What would you say to a student who tells you that he studied at least 4 hours every day in preparation for the midterm exam and still got only a C?
9. Describe the most rewarding and most stressful aspects of your job or your college experience.
10. What is your career goal? Have you developed a plan to achieve your goal? If not, why not?

EXERCISES/ACTION STEPS

1. Interview two managers. Ask them what criteria are used for their performance appraisal. Are the criteria verifiable? Do these managers think that the performance evaluation measures their performance in a fair manner?

2. Develop a career plan for yourself. Identify a personal profile for yourself, and state your long-range personal and professional goals. What are your strengths and weaknesses? Follow the steps explained in this chapter to develop a comprehensive strategic career plan for yourself.

CASES

CASE 14-1
HARDSTONE CORPORATION

William Hardstone, president of the Hardstone Corporation, was interested in putting in a bonus plan for his top managers and their immediate subordinates. The management consultant whom he engaged to help him with the plan strongly recommended that the bonus plan be based on (1) establishing a bonus pool of 8 percent of profits after retaining 12 percent on stockholders' equity plus long-term borrowing, and (2) allocating bonus shares to each person on the basis of position, salary level, and performance on the job.

Mr. Hardstone readily agreed to these principles. The consultant then pointed out that an appraisal of individual performance, as objective as possible, would be a necessary part of such a plan.

Mr. Hardstone agreed but told the consultant: "I don't want any formal plan of appraisal. I had one once, and all that paperwork was meaningless, since everyone was marked 'outstanding' or 'excellent.' I will do my own evaluation and allocate the bonuses to each person. I know how they are all doing and how well they are performing."

1. Do you believe that bonuses should be based, at least in part, on every individual's performance?
2. How would you answer Mr. Hardstone? Is he right, or could he be wrong? What would you suggest?

CASE 14-2
FORESITE INCORPORATED

Carl Fisher was the president of Foresite, Inc., a multidivisional company in the high-technology field. The large company was well known for its technical innovations and the high caliber of its scientists and engineers. But competition was on the increase, and the president realized that the success of the firm depended on effective management. It was felt that planning was one of the very weak areas where improvement was needed. Therefore, the president invited John Weigand, a management consultant, to "look at his company" and to explore alternative ways of improving the organization. At the first meeting considerable trust developed between Fisher and Weigand, and in the course of the discussion it was agreed that any major organization intervention

should be based on facts—that is, on data collected from the organization itself. Weigand began by interviewing three major department heads—Mr. Albani, Mr. Johnson, and Mr. Baker—to get an overview of the firm and the quality of its managers. The president agreed, tentatively, to a long-range systematic organizational development effort. However, the immediate problem was making some selections for key managerial positions.

Managers have to be well versed in all managerial functions, but at this point it was felt that aspects of planning were particularly important. With the guidance of the consultant, Carl Fisher assessed the planning activities of three managers considered for the positions of (1) head of the corporate planning

PERFORMANCE AS A MANAGER

Planning	Florence Albani	Ted Johnson	George Baker
1. Does the manager set for the departmental unit both short-term and long-term goals in verifiable terms (either qualitative or quantitative) that are related in a positive way to those of the superior and the company?	N	3.5	4.5
2. To what extent does the manager make sure that the goals of the department are understood by those who report to him or her?	3.0	3.0	4.0
3. How well does the manager assist those who report to him or her in establishing verifiable and consistent goals for their operations?	3.5	3.0	4.5
4. To what extent does the manager utilize consistent and approved planning premises in planning and see that subordinates do likewise?	4.5	3.5	4.0
5. Does the manager understand the role of company policies in decision making and ensure that subordinates do likewise?	4.5	4.0	4.0
6. Does the manager attempt to solve problems of subordinates by policy guidance, coaching, and encouragement of innovation, rather than by rules and procedures?	4.0	3.0	4.5
7. Does the manager help subordinates get the information they need to assist them in their planning?	4.5	3.5	4.0
8. To what extent does the manager seek out applicable alternatives before making a decision?	4.0	4.0	3.5
9. In choosing from among alternatives, does the manager recognize and give primary attention to those factors which are limiting, or critical, to the solution of a problem?	4.0	N	3.5
10. In making decisions, how well does the manager bear in mind the size and length of commitment involved in each decision?	4.5	4.0	3.5
11. Does the manager check plans periodically to see if they are still consistent with current expectations?	3.0	4.5	4.0
12. To what extent does the manager consider the need for, as well as the cost of, flexibility in arriving at a planning decision?	4.0	4.5	4.5
13. In developing and implementing plans, does the manager regularly consider long-range implications of the decisions along with the short-range results expected?	4.0	4.5	4.0
14. When the manager submits problems to the superior, or when a superior seeks help in solving problems, does he or she submit considered analyses of alternatives (with advantages and disadvantages) and recommended suggestions for solution?	4.0	4.0	3.5
Total number of questions in which ratings are made:	13	13	14
Total score on questions given ratings:	51.5	49.0	56.0
Average of ratings in Planning:	4.0	3.8	4.0

group and (2) division manager. He found useful the appraisal approach developed by Harold Koontz and described in the text.

The instructions for rating candidates for the positions were: In rating each question, give the following marks for each (for each level of rating use only one of two numbers, such as 4.0 or 4.5 for *Excellent;* use no other decimals). The possible marks were:

X = Not applicable to position

N = Not known accurately enough to rate

5.0 = *Superior:* A standard of performance which could not be improved under any circumstances or conditions known to the rater

4.0 or 4.5 = *Excellent:* A standard of performance which leaves little of any consequence to be desired

3.0 or 3.5 = *Good:* A standard of performance above the average and meeting all normal requirements of the position

2.0 or 2.5 = *Average:* A standard of performance regarded as average for the position involved and the people available

1.0 or 1.5 = *Fair:* A standard of performance below normal requirements of the position, but one that may be regarded as marginally or temporarily acceptable

0.0 = *Inadequate:* A standard of performance regarded as unacceptable for the position involved

The results of the evaluations are shown in the table on page 416.

To gain greater confidence in his judgment, Carl Fisher asked two of his vice presidents to rate the three candidates. Their evaluations were consistent with the president's appraisal.

Assume that all three candidates have similar technical and managerial skills besides those in the table and that their performance results are similar.

1. Whom would you select for the position of head of the corporate planning staff? Why?
2. Whom would you choose for the position of division manager?
3. What other factors would you consider in making the selection?
4. What training and development would you recommend for each of the managers?

REFERENCES

1. Michael Beer, "Performance Appraisal: Dilemmas and Possibilities," in Kendrith M. Rowland and Gerald R. Ferris (eds.), *Current Issues in Personnel Management,* 3d ed. (Boston: Allyn and Bacon, 1986), pp. 142–151.
2. For research on the possible rater's bias, see Eileen A. Hogan, "Effects of Prior Expectations on Performance Ratings: A Longitudinal Study," *Academy of Management Journal* (June 1987), pp. 354–368.
3. Robert I. Lazer and Walter S. Wikstrom, *Appraising Managerial Performance: Current Practices and Future Directions* (New York: The Conference Board, 1977).
4. Herbert H. Meyer, Emanuel Kay, and John R. P. French, Jr., "Split Roles in Performance Appraisal," *Harvard Business Review* (January–February 1965), pp. 123–129. See also Herbert H. Meyer, "A Solution to the Performance Appraisal Feedback Enigma," *Academy of Management Executive* (February 1991), pp. 68–76.
5. George S. Odiorne, "Measuring the Unmeasurable: Setting Standards for Management Performance," *Business Horizons* (July–August 1987), pp. 69–75.
6. All the key questions are given in Harold Koontz, *Appraising Managers as Managers* (New York: McGraw-Hill Book Company, 1971), chaps. 5 and 6 and apps. 2–5.
7. This has been done, for example, in the text booklet accompanying the cassette recording program *Measuring Managers: A Double-Barreled Approach,* by Harold Koontz and Heinz Weihrich (New York: American Management Association, 1981).

8. Mark R. Edwards, Walter C. Borman, and J. Ruth Sproull, "Solving the Double Bind in Performance Appraisal: A Saga of Wolves, Sloths, and Eagles," *Business Horizons* (May–June 1985), pp. 59–68; Mark R. Edwards and J. Ruth Sproull, "Team Talent Assessment: Optimizing Assessee Visibility and Assessment Accuracy," *Human Resource Planning* (Autumn 1985), pp. 157–171; Mark R. Edwards and J. Ruth Sproull, "Confronting Alcoholism through Team Evaluation," *Business Horizons* (May–June 1986), pp. 78–83.

9. Shawn Tully, "American Bosses Are Overpaid . . . ," *Fortune* (Nov. 7, 1988), pp. 121–136.

10. Amanda Bennett, "Corporate Chief's Pay Far Outpaces Inflation and the Gains of Staffs," *The Wall Street Journal* (Mar. 28, 1988).

11. Shawn Tully, "Where People Live Best," *Fortune* (Mar. 11, 1991), pp. 44–54.

12. Gerald F. Cavanagh and Arthur F. McGovern, *Ethical Dilemmas in the Modern Corporation* (Englewood Cliffs, N.J.: Prentice-Hall, 1988), chap. 3.

13. John A. Byrne, "The Flap over Executive Pay," *Business Week* (May 6, 1991), pp. 90–96; see also the special issue *The Wall Street Journal Reports—Executive Pay* (Apr. 17, 1991).

14. Other sources cite different figures, such as that the CEO of major Japanese companies earns approximately 17 times the pay of the average worker and about 23 to 25 times that in France and Germany. In comparison, the U.S. CEO earns 53 times in cash rewards the pay of the average worker and 107 times when other compensation is included in the comparison. See Kevin G. Salwen, "Executive Pay May Be Subject to New Scrutiny, *The Wall Street Journal* (May 16, 1991). Some of the figures vary perhaps because of different exchange rates at various times or because in some cases the pay of the lowest-paid factory worker is used, while in other cases the average pay of workers is the basis for comparison.

15. Peter F. Drucker, "Reform Executive Pay or Congress Will," *The Wall Street Journal* (Apr. 24, 1984).

16. Salwen, "Executive Pay" (1991).

17. Amanda Bennett, "More Managers Find Salary, Bonus Are Tied Directly to Performance," *The Wall Street Journal* (Feb. 28, 1986); "Rewarding Executives for Taking the Long View," *Business Week* (Apr. 2, 1984), pp. 99–100, 108.

18. James L. Gibson, John M. Ivancevich, and James H. Donnelly, Jr., *Organizations*, 5th ed. (Plano, Tex.: Business Publications, 1985), p. 220.

19. Hans Selye, *The Stress of Life*, rev. ed. (New York: McGraw-Hill Book Company, 1976), p. viii.

20. Hans Selye, *The Stress without Distress* (New York: New American Library, 1975), book cover.

21. Emily T. Smith, Jody Brott, Alice Cuneo, and Jo Ellen Davis, "Stress: The Test Americans Are Failing," *Business Week* (Apr. 18, 1988), pp. 74–76.

22. See, for example, Herbert Benson, *The Relaxation Response* (New York: Avon Books, 1975).

23. Adapted from Heinz Weihrich, *Management Excellence—Productivity through MBO* (New York: McGraw-Hill Book Company, 1985). See also Douglas T. Hall and Judith Richter, "Career Gridlock: Baby Boomers Hit the Wall," *Academy of Management Executive* (August 1990), pp. 7–22.

24. Julie Connelly, "How Dual-Income Couples Cope," *Fortune* (Sept. 24, 1990), pp. 129–136.

25. Irene Pave, "Move Me, Move My Spouse: Relocating the Corporate Couple," *Business Week* (Dec. 16, 1985), pp. 57–60.

The object of education is to prepare the young to educate themselves throughout their lives.

Robert Maynard Hutchins

Managing Change through Manager and Organization Development

Chapter Objectives

After reading this chapter, you should be able to:

1. Distinguish between manager development, managerial training, and organization development.
2. Discuss the manager development process and training.
3. Describe the various approaches to manager development.
4. Identify changes and sources of conflicts and show how to manage them.
5. Describe the characteristics and process of organization development.

This chapter deals with change. First, the focus is on the change of individuals, specifically, manager development and training. But people do not operate in isolation. Consequently, in the second part of this chapter the emphasis shifts to groups of individuals and organizations.

Excellent executives look to the future and prepare for it. One important way to do this is to develop and train managers so that they are able to cope with new demands, new problems, and new challenges. Indeed, executives have a responsibility to provide training and development opportunities for their employees so that the employees can reach their full potential.[1]

The costs of training represent major investments, so executives are justifiably concerned about the effectiveness of training. It has been estimated that companies spent at least $30 billion in 1988 to educate their work forces.[2] A considerable amount of this money was wasted. It is important that management education be effective and efficient, and therefore this chapter emphasizes the need for a systematic approach to manager and organization development.

The term **manager development** refers to long-term, future-oriented programs and the progress a person makes in learning how to manage. **Managerial training,** on the other hand, pertains to the programs that facilitate the learning process and is mostly a short-term activity to help people to do their jobs better.[3] In this book, **organization development** (OD) is a systematic, integrated, and planned approach to improving the effectiveness of groups of people and of the whole organization or a major organizational unit. Organization development uses various techniques for identifying and solving problems.

Essentially, then, OD focuses on the total organization (or a major segment of it), while manager development concentrates on individuals. These approaches support each other and should be integrated to improve the effectiveness of both the managers and the enterprise.

MANAGER DEVELOPMENT PROCESS AND TRAINING

Before specific training and development programs are chosen, three kinds of needs must be considered. The needs of the organization include such items as the

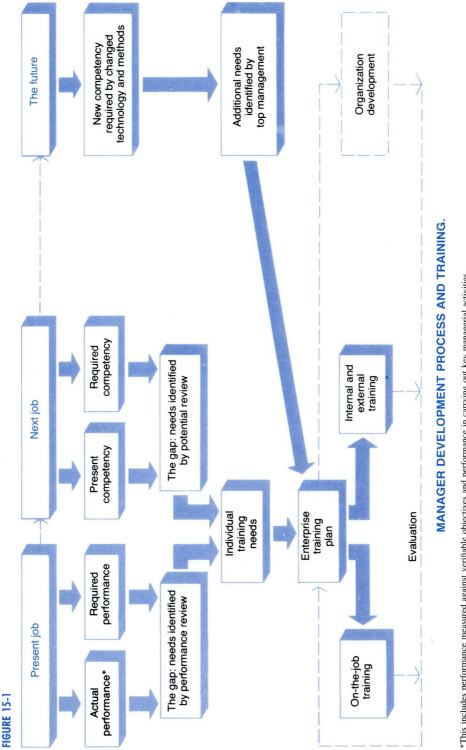

FIGURE 15-1

MANAGER DEVELOPMENT PROCESS AND TRAINING.

*This includes performance measured against verifiable objectives and performance in carrying out key managerial activities.

Adapted from John W. Humble, *Improving Business Results* [Maidenhead, England: McGraw-Hill Book Company (UK), Ltd., 1968].

objectives of the enterprise, the availability of managers, and turnover rates. Needs related to the operations and the job itself can be determined from job descriptions and performance standards. Data about individual training needs can be gathered from performance appraisals, interviews with the jobholder, tests, surveys, and career plans for individuals. Let us look more closely at the steps in the manager development process, focusing first on the present job, then on the next job in the career ladder, and finally on the long-term future needs of the organization. The steps in manager development are depicted in Figure 15-1.

Present Job

Manager development and training must be based on a needs analysis derived from a comparison of actual performance and behavior with required performance and behavior. Such an analysis is shown in Figure 15-2. A district sales manager has decided that the selling of 1000 units is a reasonable expectation, but the actual sales are only 800, 200 units short of the sales target. Analysis of the deviation from the standard might indicate that the manager lacks the knowledge and skills for making a forecast and that conflicts among subordinate managers hinder effective teamwork. On the basis of this analysis, training needs and methods for overcoming the deficiencies are identified. Consequently, the district sales manager enrolls in courses in forecasting and conflict resolution. Furthermore, organization development efforts are undertaken to facilitate cooperation among organization units.

Next Job

As shown in Figure 15-1, a similar process is applied in the identification of the training needs for the next job. Specifically, present competency is compared with the competency demanded by the next job. For instance, a person who has worked mainly in production may be under consideration for a job as a project manager.

FIGURE 15-2

TRAINING NEEDS ANALYSIS.

This position requires training in functional areas such as engineering, marketing, and even finance. This systematic preparation for a new assignment certainly is a more professional approach than simply thrusting a person into a new work situation without training.

Future Needs

Progressive organizations go one step further in their training and development approach; they prepare for the more distant future. This requires that they forecast what new competencies will be demanded by changing technology and methods. For example, energy shortages may again occur, and this requires that managers be trained not only in the technical aspects of energy conservation but also in energy-related long-range planning and creative problem solving. These new demands—created by the external environment—have to be integrated into enterprise training plans that focus on the present and the future. These plans are contingent not only on the training needs but also on the various approaches to manager development that are available.

Perspective

Systematic Training and Development at IBM[4]

At IBM's General Products Division in San Jose, California, efforts are made to integrate training and development with the objectives of the enterprise. Training effectiveness is then measured against preestablished objectives. In addition, training and development activities are coordinated with the human resource plan.

The objective of the educational efforts is to identify the skills needed to do the current job effectively and the skills needed to improve productivity and quality. On the basis of this analysis, a cost-effective curriculum is developed. Instructors are recruited, selected, and prepared to deliver an effective program. The curriculum is frequently evaluated through posttests, surveys, and interviews of trainees by managers. In addition, computer-based testing not only provides information about the readiness of the trainees but also gives feedback about the progress of students. Classroom activities are monitored by auditors and through student feedback. After analysis of the various evaluations, problems are identified and recommendations are made for improvements. All in all, attempts are made to continuously monitor and improve the educational efforts. This certainly is money spent more wisely than by offering and evaluating programs on the basis of their entertainment value, as is so often done by other organizations.

APPROACHES TO MANAGER DEVELOPMENT: ON-THE-JOB TRAINING

Many opportunities for development can be found on the job. Trainees can learn as they contribute to the aims of the enterprise. However, because this approach requires competent higher-level managers who can teach and coach trainees, there are limitations to on-the-job training.

Planned Progression

Planned progression is a technique that gives managers a clear idea of their path of development. Managers know where they stand and where they are going. For example, a lower-level manager may have available an outline of the path from superintendent to works manager and eventually to production manager. The manager then knows the requirements for advancement and the means of achieving it. Unfortunately, there may be an overemphasis on the next job instead of on good performance of present tasks. Planned progression may be perceived by trainees as a smooth path to the top, but it really is a step-by-step approach which requires that tasks be done well at each level.

Job Rotation

The purpose of job rotation is to broaden the knowledge of managers or potential managers. Trainees learn about the different enterprise functions by rotating into different positions. They may rotate through (1) nonsupervisory work, (2) observation assignments (observing what managers do, rather than managing themselves), (3) various managerial training positions, and (4) middle-level "assistant" positions, and there is even (5) unspecified rotation to various managerial positions in different departments such as production, sales, and finance.

The idea of job rotation is good, but there are difficulties. As the term indicates, in some job rotation programs participants do not actually have managerial authority. Instead, they observe or assist line managers, but they do not have the responsibility they would have if they were actually managing. Even in rotations to managerial positions, the participants in the training program may not remain long enough in each position to prove their future effectiveness as managers. Furthermore, when the rotation program is completed, there may be no suitable positions available for the newly trained managers. Despite these drawbacks, if the inherent difficulties are understood by both managers and trainees, job rotation has positive aspects and should benefit trainees.

The Massachusetts Institute of Technology study of Japanese car manufacturing plants in North America showed that they differ greatly in many respects from U.S. plants. For example, it takes 21 hours in the Japanese plants to assemble a car versus 25 hours in U.S. firms. One reason may be the differences in the training of workers: 370 hours in Japanese firms and only 46 hours in U.S. companies. Moreover, the former have only 65 defects per 100 cars compared with 82 for the latter. The work arrangements are also different. Japanese plants in the United States have 71 percent of their workers in teams compared with 17 percent in U.S. plants.

Creation of "Assistant-to" Positions

"Assistant-to" positions are frequently created to broaden the viewpoints of trainees by allowing them to work closely with experienced managers who can give special attention to the developmental needs of trainees. Managers can, among other things, give selected assignments to test the judgment of trainees. As in job rotation, this approach can be very effective when superiors are also qualified teachers who can guide and develop trainees until they are ready to assume full responsibilities as managers.

Temporary Promotions

Individuals are frequently appointed as "acting" managers when, for example, the permanent manager is on vacation, is ill, or is making an extended business trip or even when a position is vacant. Thus, temporary promotions are a developmental device as well as a convenience to the enterprise.

When the acting manager makes decisions and assumes full responsibility, the experience can be valuable. On the other hand, if such a manager is merely a figurehead, makes no decisions, and really does not manage, the developmental benefit may be minimal.

Committees and Junior Boards

Committees and "junior boards," also known as "multiple management," are sometimes used as developmental techniques. These give trainees the opportunities to interact with experienced managers. Furthermore, trainees, usually from the middle, but sometimes from the lower level, become acquainted with a variety of issues that concern the whole organization. They learn about the relationships among different departments and the problems created by the interaction of these organizational units. Trainees may be given the opportunity to submit reports and proposals to the committee or the board and to demonstrate their analytical and conceptual abilities. On the other hand, trainees may be treated in a paternalistic way by senior executives; although trainees are appointed to committees or junior boards, they may not be given opportunities to participate, an omission that might frustrate and discourage them. The program would then be detrimental to their development.

Coaching

On-the-job training is a never-ending process. A good example of on-the-job training is athletic coaching. To be effective, coaching, which is the responsibility of every line manager, must be done in a climate of confidence and trust between the superior and the trainees. Patience and wisdom are required of superiors, who must be able to delegate authority and give recognition and praise for jobs well done. Effective coaches will develop the strengths and potentials of subordinates and help them overcome their weaknesses. Coaching requires time, but if done well, it will save time and money and will prevent costly mistakes by subordinates; thus, in the long run, it will benefit all—the superior, the subordinates, and the enterprise.

APPROACHES TO MANAGER DEVELOPMENT: INTERNAL AND EXTERNAL TRAINING

Besides on-the-job training, there are many other approaches to manager development. These programs may be conducted within the company, or they may be offered externally by educational institutions and management associations, as indicated in Figure 15-1.

Sensitivity Training, T-Groups, and Encounter Groups

Sensitivity training, also called *T-group* ("T" stands for "training"), *encounter group,* or *leadership training,* is a controversial approach to manager development. Although popular in the 1960s and early 1970s, T-groups have lost favor as a managerial training technique in many companies.[6] Still, certain aspects of sensitivity training may be used in team-building efforts. The objectives of sensitivity training generally include (1) better insight into one's own behavior and the way one "appears" to others, (2) better understanding of group processes, and (3) development of skills in diagnosing and intervening in group processes.

Although the sensitivity-training process has many variations, one general characteristic is that people interact and then receive feedback on their behavior from the trainer and other group members, who express their opinions freely and openly. The feedback may be candid and direct: "Jim, I do not get a good feeling when you approach the topic the way you just did. Could we talk about it?"

Jim may accept this comment and resolve to change his behavior. But he may also feel hurt and withdraw from the group. The T-group process may lead to personal anxieties and frustrations, but if properly administered, it can result in collaborative and supportive behavior.

The benefits of sensitivity training must be balanced against the criticisms of the approach.[7] For example, some people may be psychologically harmed because they simply cannot cope with the concurrent invasions of privacy. Owing to the group pressure and group dynamics, participants may reveal more about themselves than they actually intended to. There also is concern that some trainers may not be qualified to conduct sessions that become highly emotional. Finally, the relevancy of the outcomes of sensitivity training to the work situation has been questioned.

Despite the concerns of researchers and observers, certain enterprises do use T-groups in their development efforts. The following guidelines can help to reduce potential harm and increase effectiveness:

1. Participation in T-groups should be voluntary.
2. Participants should be screened, and those who could be harmed (for example, highly defensive people) should be excluded from this experience.
3. Trainers should be carefully evaluated and their competence clearly established.
4. Potential participants should be informed about the goals and process before they commit themselves to sensitivity training.

5. Before using sensitivity training, organizations should clearly identify development and training needs and objectives. Given these needs and objectives, other methods should also be considered.

Conference Programs

Conference programs may be used in internal or external training. During conference programs, managers or potential managers are exposed to the ideas of speakers who are experts in their field. Within the company, people may be instructed in the history of the firm and its purposes, policies, and relationships with customers, consumers, and other groups. External conferences may vary greatly, ranging from programs on specific managerial techniques to programs on broad topics, such as the relationship between business and society.

These programs can be valuable if they satisfy a training need and are thoughtfully planned. A careful selection of topics and speakers will increase the effectiveness of this training device. Furthermore, conferences can be made more successful by including discussions; two-way communication allows participants to ask for clarification of specific topics that are particularly relevant to them.

University Management Programs

Besides offering undergraduate and graduate degrees in business administration, many universities now conduct courses, workshops, conferences, institutes, and formal programs for training managers. These offerings may include evening courses, short seminars, live-in programs, a full graduate curriculum, or even programs custom-designed for the needs of individual companies. Some executive development centers even provide career development assistance with programs designed to fit typical training and development needs of first-line supervisors, middle managers, and top executives.

These university programs expose managers to theories, principles, and new developments in management. In addition, there is usually a valuable interchange of experience among managers who, in similar positions, face similar challenges.

International Perspective

M.B.A. Degrees for Japanese?[8]

Japanese companies—such as Sumito, NEC, and Toshiba—send their employees to U.S. business schools. Dartmouth's Amos Tuck School, for instance, in conjunction with the International University of Japan, offers an M.B.A. degree for Japanese. Students who came were shocked by cultural differences. Being challenged by the professor to state their opinion certainly was a surprise. In Japan, speaking up to the professor is not encouraged, as this could indicate arrogance. Another surprise for the Japanese students was being asked to evaluate the teaching performance of their professors. The U.S. experience may make it difficult for some students to return to their Japanese companies and subordinate their ideas to that of the work group.

Readings, Television, and Video Instructions

Another approach to development is planned reading of relevant and current management literature. This is essentially self-development. A manager may be aided by the training department, which often develops a reading list of valuable books. This learning experience can be enhanced through discussion of articles and books with other managers and the superior.

Increasingly, management and other topics are featured in television programs. For certain programs, college credit can be obtained. Moreover, videotapes on a variety of subjects are available for use in the university or company classroom.

International Perspective

Management Development at China Resources

A rather innovative program for educating Chinese managers has been undertaken by the University of San Francisco (USF). China Resources, one of the largest Chinese trading companies, located in Hong Kong, China, and other places, recognized the need for developing its managers. Consequently, an agreement was reached with USF to offer a manager development program.

Regular M.B.A. classes at USF are videotaped for showing in Hong Kong. The Chinese managers are required to cover the same material as students enrolled in the program at USF. These managers, who are admitted only after very careful screening, are encouraged to request information or additional explanations of concepts taught through fax transmissions. Instructors, in turn, answer these questions, also via fax. Local Chinese instructors also help the manager-students understand the material. Periodically, a USF instructor visits the company's headquarters in Hong Kong to give special lectures, answer questions, and administer exams. Preliminary results of this cost-effective approach are quite encouraging.

Business Simulation, Experiential Exercises, and Expert Systems

Business games and experiential exercises have been used for some time, but the introduction of microcomputers has made these approaches to training and development even more popular. The computer, however, is only one of several tools; many of the exercises do not require any hardware at all.

The great variety of business simulations is best illustrated by the topics discussed at meetings of the Association for Business Simulation and Experiential Learning (ABSEL).[9] The approaches range from behavioral exercises dealing, for example, with attitudes and values to simulations in courses such as marketing, accounting, decision support systems, and business policy and strategic management.

Recently, **expert systems** have received a great deal of attention. They are a subset of artificial intelligence (AI), which involves the use of computers to duplicate the functioning of the brain.[10] AI was initially used for problem solving in games such as checkers and chess. Later it was applied in medicine. Researchers at Stanford developed a knowledge-based system to serve as an "intelligent consultant" to help in the diagnosis and treatment of specific diseases. Similar systems are now being developed to assist managers in making decisions. For example, expert systems are used for checking sales orders, for oil drilling, for monitoring steam turbines at Westinghouse, for credit authorization at American Express, for tax accounting decisions at Coopers & Lybrand, for pricing systems bids at IBM, and for capital investments at Texas Instruments.[11]

Expert systems are an exciting new frontier for training and development, but a great deal of research will have to be done to validate the systems, especially those for unstructured decisions such as in strategic management.

Special Training Programs

Management development must take an open-system approach that responds to the needs and demands of the external environment. Recently, government and industry have become aware of the need for training programs specifically designed for members of minority groups and for individuals who are physically handicapped. Many firms have made special efforts to train these people so that they may utilize their full potential while contributing to the aims of the enterprise.

Companies may also offer special programs on selected subjects. The topic of ethics may be discussed to give the work force guidelines for ethical behavior. The subject of corporate culture may be addressed in either a formal or informal manner. Japanese companies in particular are known for making special efforts to instill the company philosophy in employees to promote a desirable corporate culture.

Evaluation and Transfer

Determining the effectiveness of training programs is difficult. It requires measurements against standards and a systematic identification of training needs and objectives.

In general, developmental objectives include (1) an increase in knowledge, (2) development of attitudes conducive to good managing, (3) acquisition of skills, (4) improvement of management performance, and (5) achievement of enterprise objectives.

If training is to be effective, it is extremely important that the criteria used in the classroom situation resemble as closely as possible the criteria relevant in the working environment. One of the authors observed a T-group that had as its goals openness and frank feedback on each person's conduct in the group. The behavioral change of one of the participants would have had to be rated "excellent" when measured against the T-group criteria. However, when this person attempted to transfer his new values and behavior to the job, he met resistance and outright hostility. Arguments occurred, and as a result, this person had to leave the company. Although the person changed, his boss did not; nor did his coworkers or the total work environment. This illustration shows that manager development requires a situational approach in which training objectives, techniques, and methods are sufficiently congruent with the values, norms, and characteristics of the environment.

MANAGING CHANGE

The forces for change may come from the environment external to the firm, from within the organization, or from the individuals themselves.

Changes That Affect Manager and Organization Development

Several trends, some of them already occurring, will have implications for developing human resources. Here are some illustrations:[12]

1. The increasing use of computers, especially microcomputers, requires that teachers as well as students become computer-literate.
2. Education extends into the adult life. Lifelong learning becomes a necessity, and educational institutions and enterprises must recognize the special educational needs of adults.
3. The proportion of knowledge workers will increase and the need for skill workers will decrease, which may require more training in knowledge, conceptual, and design skills.
4. The shift from manufacturing to service industries requires retraining in preparation for new positions.
5. The choice of educational opportunities will increase. For example, many companies already are conducting their own training programs.[13]
6. There may be greater cooperation and interdependence between the private and the public sectors—at least in some countries, such as Canada.
7. Internationalization will continue, and so managers in different countries must learn to communicate and to adapt to each other. Companies need to train with a global perspective.

There are various ways to respond to these forces. One approach is simply to react to a crisis. Unfortunately, this is usually not the most effective response. Another approach is to deliberately plan the change. This may require new objectives or policies, organizational rearrangements, or a change in leadership style and organization culture.

Techniques for Initiating Change[14]

Organizations may be in a state of equilibrium, with forces pushing for change on the one hand and forces resisting change by attempting to maintain the status quo on the other. Kurt Lewin expressed this phenomenon in his **field force theory,** which suggests that an equilibrium is maintained by *driving* forces and *restraining* forces, as shown in Figure 15-3.[15] In initiating change, the tendency is to increase

FIGURE 15-3

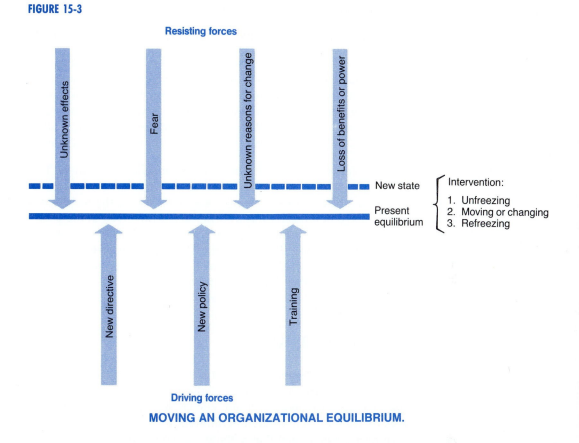

Resisting forces

Unknown effects

Fear

Unknown reasons for change

Loss of benefits or power

New state

Present equilibrium

Intervention:

1. Unfreezing
2. Moving or changing
3. Refreezing

New directive

New policy

Training

Driving forces

MOVING AN ORGANIZATIONAL EQUILIBRIUM.

the driving forces. This may indeed produce some movement, but it usually also increases resistance by strengthening the restraining forces. Another approach, one that is usually more effective, is to reduce or eliminate the restraining forces and then move to a new level of equilibrium. In organizations, therefore, a change in policy is less resisted when those affected by it participate in the change.

The change process involves three steps:[16] (1) unfreezing, (2) moving or changing, and (3) refreezing. The first stage, unfreezing, creates motivation for change. If people feel uncomfortable with the present situation, they may see the need for change. However, in some cases an ethical question may arise regarding the legitimacy of deliberately creating discomfort that may initiate change.

The second stage is the change itself. This change may occur through assimilation of new information, exposure to new concepts, or development of a different perspective.

The third stage, refreezing, stabilizes the change. Change, to be effective, has to be congruent with a person's self-concept and values. If the change is incongruent with the attitudes and behaviors of others in the organization, chances are that the person will revert back to the old behavior. Thus, reinforcement of the new behavior is essential.

Resistance to Change

There are many reasons why people resist change. Here are some examples:

1. What is not known causes fear and induces resistance. An organizational restructuring can leave a person uncertain about its effect on his or her job. People want to feel secure and have some control over the change.
2. Not knowing the reason for the change also causes resistance. In fact, it is often unclear to those affected why the change is necessary at all.
3. Change may also result in a reduction of benefits or a loss of power.

Reduction of resistance can be achieved in many different ways. The involvement of organizational members in planning the change can reduce uncertainty. Communication about proposed changes also helps clarify the reasons or effects of the changes. Some approaches focus on the people involved in the change; others involve changes in organization structure or technology. The sociotechnical systems approach shown in Figure 2-2 in Chapter 2 suggests that effective organization requires consideration of both the social and the technical dimensions in an enterprise. There are many other approaches to improving organizational effectiveness, such as those discussed later in this chapter.

ORGANIZATIONAL CONFLICT

Conflict is a part of organizational life and may occur within the individual, between individuals, between the individual and the group, and between groups. While conflict is generally perceived as dysfunctional, it can also be beneficial because it may cause an issue to be presented in different perspectives. One top executive of a major company maintained that if there was no conflict on an issue, it could not have been sufficiently analyzed, and the final decision on the issue was usually postponed until all aspects were critically evaluated.

Sources of Conflict

There are many potential sources of conflict. Today's organizations are characterized by complex relationships and a high degree of task interdependence that can cause frictions. Moreover, the goals of the parties are often incompatible, especially when the parties compete for limited resources. People also have different values and different perceptions of issues. A production manager, for example, may take the position that streamlining the product line and concentrating on a few products can make the organization more productive, while a sales manager may desire a broad product line that will satisfy diverse customer demands. An engineer may want to design the best product regardless of cost or market demand considerations.

Conflict can arise from other sources as well. There may be conflicts between people in line and staff positions. A superior's autocratic leadership style may cause conflicts. Differing educational backgrounds are potential sources of conflict. Perhaps most often mentioned is lack of communication. Many of these topics are discussed in various chapters of this book.

Managing Conflict

Conflict can be managed in different ways, some focusing on interpersonal relationships and others on structural changes. *Avoidance* of the situation that causes the conflict is an example of an interpersonal approach.[17] Another way of coping with conflict is through *smoothing*, emphasizing the areas of agreement and common goals and de-emphasizing disagreements. A third way is *forcing*, pushing one's own view on others; this, of course, will cause overt or covert resistance. A traditional way of coping with conflict is to *compromise*, agreeing in part with the other person's view or demand.

Attempts can also be made to *change the behavior* of individuals, a very difficult task indeed. At times, it may also be possible to *reassign* an individual to another organizational unit. In many situations, conflicts are resolved by a *person higher up in the organization* who has sufficient authority to decide an issue. The problem is that the loser may attempt to get even with the winner at a later time, thus perpetuating the conflict. In the *problem-solving* approach to organizational conflicts, differences are openly confronted, and the issues are analyzed as objectively as possible.

Another way of coping with conflict is to make structural changes. This means modifying and integrating the *objectives* of groups with different viewpoints. Moreover, the *organization structure* may have to be changed and authority-responsibility relationships clarified. New ways of *coordinating* activities may have to be found. *Tasks* and *work locations* can also be rearranged. In one workroom, for example, machines were placed in a way that prevented conflicting parties from interacting with one another. Often one must not only decide on the necessary changes but also select the appropriate process. For this reason, the next section focuses on organization development.

ORGANIZATION DEVELOPMENT

Organization development, typically shortened to OD, is a systematic, integrated, and planned approach to improving enterprise effectiveness. It is designed to solve problems that decrease operating efficiency at all levels. Such problems may include lack of cooperation, excessive decentralization, and poor communication.

The techniques of OD may involve laboratory training (for example, people communicating in a group situation), managerial-grid training, and survey feedback.[18] Some OD practitioners also use team building, process consultation, job enrichment, organizational behavior modification, job design, stress management, career and life planning, and management by objectives as part of their approach.[19]

The Organization Development Process

Organization development is a situational or contingency approach to improving enterprise effectiveness. Although various techniques are utilized, the process often involves the steps shown in Figure 15-4. An example can illustrate the application of the model.

FIGURE 15-4

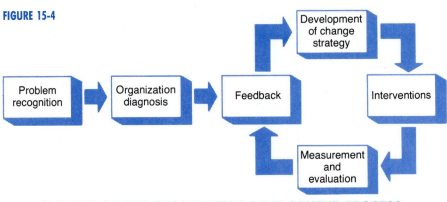

A MODEL OF THE ORGANIZATION DEVELOPMENT PROCESS.

Adapted from H. M. F. Rush, *Organizational Development: A Reconnaissance* (New York: National Industrial Conference Board, Inc., 1973), p. 6. Used by permission.

Consider a firm that experiences certain problems: conflict among organizational units, low morale, customer complaints, and increasing costs (*problem recognition* in the model). The chief executive contacts an OD expert to discuss the situation. The two agree on the necessity of an *organizational diagnosis*. The consultant then collects information from several organizational units, using questionnaires, interviews, and observations. The data are analyzed and prepared for feedback.

The executive confers with other managers and sets up a meeting with them. At the meeting, after some introductory comments, the consultant presents the findings under the headings "relations between departments," "enterprise goals," and "customer relations" (*feedback*). The group then ranks the problems in order of their importance. With the guidance of the consultant, the group discusses the difficulties, identifies the underlying causes, and explores possible solutions.

The role of the consultant is that of a coach facilitating the process. Short lectures and exercises on decision making, team building, and problem solving are integrated into the process. At times, subgroups are established to deal with specific issues. The emphasis is on openness and objectivity. The meeting ends with an agreement on a *change strategy*.

The specific *interventions* may include a change in the organization structure, a more effective procedure for handling customer complaints, and the establishment of a team charged with the responsibility of implementing a cost reduction program. Furthermore, the group agrees to meet again in 3 months to *measure and evaluate* the effectiveness of the OD efforts.

Although three phases complete the OD cycle, the effort does not end. Instead, OD becomes a *continuous process*—planned, systematic, and focused on change—that aims at making the enterprise more effective.

OD in Action

General Motors (GM) used OD to improve the effectiveness of its management system. OD as a long-range, situational effort is based on action research and problem-solving techniques.[20] Scientific analysis was used to identify factors that bore on a particular problem. In light of the findings, improvements were made through interventions such as changes in the job content, the organization structure, and the enterprise environment.

At GM's Oldsmobile division, the OD program reduced absenteeism and turnover; the Chevrolet group improved employee job satisfaction; and the Buick division, using a job enrichment program, increased productivity, reduced petty grievances, improved departmental morale, and facilitated better interpersonal relationships.[21]

Organization development is not restricted to business but is widely practiced in the military, which may be a surprise to those who perceive the military as an autocratic, mechanistic organization with values apparently incompatible with OD technologies.[22] The U.S. Army tried a number of new managerial approaches, including OD, which it named "organizational effectiveness" (OE). Among the techniques employed were team building, goal setting, and developmental efforts based on surveys. These decentralized and flexible OE efforts had the strong support of top management, which may have been an important factor in the effectiveness of the program as perceived by respondents in a study.

The OD efforts in the U.S. Navy emphasized survey feedback. The pilot program, called "command development," was not a spectacular success. Nevertheless, the OD efforts were continued under the name "human resource management" (HRM). This program (summarized in Table 15-1) is quite standardized. Although a high percentage of participants felt positive about the program, others did not like the survey or felt that the process was too time-consuming.

The U.S. Air Force does not have a centralized program but relies on a variety of approaches such as laboratory training, team building, survey feedback, and job enrichment. The results were also mixed. Here, as elsewhere, most claims for the effectiveness of OD are based on testimonials and anecdotes. There is little solid empirical evidence that OD efforts changed the organizations or improved performance.

Although the results of the various kinds of OD efforts in different organizations are mixed, some are encouraging. Still, more research needs to be done in a variety of companies under different conditions to make a definitive evaluation of OD. Today, there is still a major gap in research on the cost and effectiveness of OD efforts. No doubt such research is a complex task, because it is not easy to isolate cause and effect relationships. For instance, improved enterprise performance may be attributable to favorable market conditions and not to OD efforts. However, the great interest in measuring productivity—indicated by several writings[23]—may eventually result in the development of more sophisticated tools for assessing the effects of OD and other managerial approaches.

BRIDGING THE GAP BETWEEN ACADEMIA AND INDUSTRY[24]

In most Western countries there is a lack of cooperation between academic institutions and industry. Except possibly in some technical fields, there is generally a communication gap between industry and academia. But this unnecessary gap

		TABLE 15-1 THE NAVY'S HUMAN RESOURCE MANAGEMENT CYCLE
Time phasing	**Time to conduct**	**Step activity**
Weeks 1–2	1½ days	1. Initial meetings between commanding officer (CO) and consultants
Week 2	½ day	2. Data-gathering planning meetings: Will interview be conducted? What questions? Are additional survey questions desired? Schedule the survey administration
Week 3	1 hour per person	3. Survey administration (mandatory): To all hands
Week 4	As required	4. Conduct interviews (optional)
Week 5	1 day	5. Return survey results to CO: Brief printout format, terms Study and analysis
Weeks 6–7	½ day per working group	6. Survey feedback to work groups (optional): Familiarization with data Source of perceptions? Supervisory self-knowledge Possible solutions/recommendations for action
Weeks 8–9	½ day	7. Action-planning meeting (optional): Develop plans for human resource availability week: OD, equal opportunity, alcohol, drug abuse, and overseas diplomacy
Week 10	1–3 days per group	8. Human resource workshops (optional): Vertical slice of ship or intact work group Modular training packages (standardized series of lectures, films, and exercises on such topics as motivation, communications, MBO, leadership, and race relations)
	2 days	9. Command action-planning workshop (optional): Selected members of crew normally (CO participates part-time) CO approves plan (a command action plan is mandatory)
Week 11	Indefinite	10. Action phase: Implement action plans
Weeks 25–30	½ day	11. Follow-up by consultant: Determine effect of human resource activities through interviews and discussions Meet with CO
Weeks 11–104	As negotiated	12. Follow-on activities (optional): Survey readministered Conduct additional workshops or training activities

Source: D. D. Umstot, "Organization Development Technology and the Military: A Surprising Merger?" *Academy of Management Review*, vol. 5, no. 2 (April 1980), p. 194. Used with permission.

could be narrowed if each side capitalized on its strengths and worked to overcome its weaknesses. The strengths of academics who also consult and of practicing managers are as follows:

Academic teacher/trainer/consultant	Practicing manager
Not influenced by "bad" habits or experience	Extensive hands-on experience
Experience with several companies in different environments	Long-term experience, often with one company
Conceptual orientation	Action orientation

What, then, would be an effective strategy based on the strengths of academicians and managers to make training and development pay off? Here are some suggestions:

1. Academically oriented resource persons need to learn a great deal about the companies they consult with: their products, services, culture, needs, and so on.
2. Manager development plans must be integrated with the aims of the enterprise. Academic trainers and consultants need to be up to date on the company's mission, goals, and new policies. Thus academics and managers can nurture their relationship by trusting and learning from each other.
3. The teacher-trainers must select and train champions within the firm for keeping the program's momentum alive and must conduct follow-up surveys and programs. Continuous reinforcement of new ways of managing is necessary for transferring knowledge and skills from the classroom to the workplace.
4. Teacher-trainers will be more effective if they interview trainees before the program begins. These interviews are best conducted at the workplace of the participants. This not only provides trainers with an understanding of the trainees' environment but also builds trust. It shows the program participants that the teacher-trainer is interested in *their* problems. The program can also be better tailored to the needs of the organization.
5. On the basis of an analysis of organizational and individual needs, a combination of training methods should be selected, such as presentations, skill training, individual consultation, and process consultation. Training and development needs must determine training methods.
6. Training and development must be evaluated on the basis of preselected, verifiable objectives. For example, at IBM's General Products Division, the training programs are frequently evaluated through posttests, surveys, and interviews of trainees by managers, as mentioned earlier in this chapter.[25]

Academicians as well as managers need to cooperate and use their respective strengths to prepare young people for the challenging job of managing.

In order to make business courses more meaningful, many schools invite guest speakers to share their experiences.[26] This creates close ties between business schools and enterprises. Executives become aware of the quality of each school's curriculum, and students may find it advantageous to know about the companies when they are looking for a job. Moreover, executives often serve on advisory boards, which make the schools aware of the needs of the business community. This does not mean, however, that market-driven schools should adopt any management fad.[27] Instead, management education must be broad enough to encompass the teaching of all key managerial activities in planning, organizing, staffing, leading, and controlling.

SUMMARY

Manager development refers to the progress a manager makes in learning how to manage effectively. Frequently, it also pertains to developmental programs. Organization development (OD), on the other hand, is a systematic, integrated, and planned approach to making the whole organization or an organization unit effective.

Good results can be achieved through a systematic approach to manager development and training. On-the-job training includes planned progression, job rotation, creation of "assistant-to" positions, temporary promotions, use of committees and junior boards, and coaching. Manager development may include a variety of internal and external training programs.

There are many sources of conflicts. Ways of managing conflict include avoiding the situation, smoothing, forcing, compromising, changing behavior, reassigning individuals, resolving the conflict at higher levels, and problem solving. Another approach is to make structural changes: modifying objectives, developing new methods of coordination, and rearranging authority-responsibility relationships, tasks, and work locations.

The typical organization development process includes the recognition of problems, the diagnosis of an organization, feedback of information on the organization, the development of a change strategy, interventions, and measurement and evaluation of the change efforts. A number of different OD programs are used to improve organizational effectiveness and efficiency. Academicians and managers must use their respective strengths for effective training and development.

KEY IDEAS AND CONCEPTS FOR REVIEW

Manager development
Managerial training
Organization development (OD)

On-the-job training
Internal and external training and
  development

Manager development process
Sensitivity training
T-groups
Business simulation
Experiential exercises
Expert systems
Field force theory

Sources of organizational conflict
Ways of managing organizational conflict
Organization development process
Strengths of academicians/trainers/
    consultants vs. strengths of practicing
    managers

FOR DISCUSSION

1. It has been argued that firms have an obligation to train and develop all employees with managerial potential. Do you agree? Why, or why not?
2. What are some typical failures in manager development and training? Can you explain these failures? What would you recommend to overcome the shortcomings?
3. Evaluate the advantages and limitations of different approaches to on-the-job training.
4. Evaluate sensitivity training as a technique for training managers. Do you think sensitivity training would make you a better manager? Explain.
5. In the job you now have or the one you expect to have in the future, what kind of coaching and management development would be most beneficial to you?
6. What is an expert system, and how can it help managers make decisions?
7. What are the main characteristics of organization development? How does OD differ from manager development? Do you think OD might work in your organization? Explain why or why not.

EXERCISES/ACTION STEPS

1. Select an organization you know, and analyze its management development efforts.
2. What kinds of conflicts have you experienced in an organization with which you are familiar? What were the causes of the conflicts? What was done, if anything, about resolving these conflicts?

CASES

CASE 15-1
MANAGEMENT EDUCATION AT THE HARVARD BUSINESS SCHOOL[28]

Harvard is one of the leading business schools. Yet there is growing concern about whether the school is moving in the right direction. Harvard's mission has been to educate "general managers and business leaders," but over 50 percent of its graduates took jobs in investment banking and management consulting. Moreover, less than one-fourth of the 1987 M.B.A.s

went into manufacturing companies, and of those, most moved into staff, rather than line, positions.

Investment houses and consulting firms are eager to recruit at Harvard, offering attractive starting salaries. While some critics accuse the students of being greedy, many professors supplement their salaries by teaching in corporations, consulting, appearing as expert witnesses, or serving on corporate boards. While consulting can enhance teaching, there is a maximum time officially allowed for outside activities.

The approach to teaching has also changed. The case approach, for which Harvard is famous, used to stress the role of the general manager. While cases are still used, more analytical tools have become increasingly important. For example, the course Business Policy has changed to Competitive Strategy under the leadership of Professor Michael Porter, who, with a background in economics, uses concepts and theories in making competitive analyses.

Harvard, once known for developing business leaders, now increasingly educates specialists. Most of the students have shown little interest in joining manufacturing firms. Yet manufacturing may be critical for making the United States competitive.

1. Do you think Harvard is moving in the right direction?
2. How does Harvard's approach compare with the one used in your school?

CASE 15-2
CONSULTANT HUGH WILLS[29]

Hugh Wills, a management consultant, was well known through his writings on various management topics. The director of management and organization development at a large, well-managed multinational company became interested in the ideas of Hugh Wills and invited him for a 2-day consultation on a management development strategy for the firm. If the recommendations were perceived as fulfilling the company's developmental needs, a long-term consulting relationship could evolve.

In the past, the company had consulted with professors from several universities. But it was felt that they were too theoretical and that their recommendations had little relevance to the company's needs. A major competitor was also well-managed, but it did not get quite as high a rating on "management quality" in a survey conducted by a professional organization. On the other hand, the competitor had a well-rounded, comprehensive management and organization development program in place. Both firms were considered by far the best-managed companies in the industry.

While thinking about a management development program he might suggest later, Wills considered the integration of the following criteria for effective training and development: (1) Integrate the mission of the organization in the program, (2) design a program based on developmental needs, (3) focus on short-term training and long-term development, (4) select appropriate internal or external teachers, (5) obtain the participation of top managers, and (6) make an evaluation of the costs and benefits.

1. How should Wills prepare for the meeting?
2. Prepare a schedule for the 2-day meeting. To whom should Wills talk, and what should be the subject matter?
3. What are some of the critical factors for a successful meeting?
4. What kind of program would you suggest to meet the six criteria for effective development programs?

REFERENCES

1. See also William Wiggenhorn, "Motorola U: When Training Becomes an Education," *Harvard Business Review* (July–August 1990), pp. 71–83.
2. Harry B. Bernhard and Cynthia A. Ingols, "Six Lessons for the Corporate Classroom," *Harvard Business Review* (September–October 1988), pp. 40–48.

3. Ibid.

4. Van Symons, "A Fine Mesh at IBM," *Training* (April 1987), pp. 49–51.

5. "Measuring the Gap between U.S. and Japanese Auto Makers," *Business Week* (Oct. 8, 1990), p. 83.

6. The more recent use of sensitivity training by General Motors has also been criticized. See Jack Falvey, "Before Spending $3 Million on Leadership, Read This," *The Wall Street Journal* (Oct. 3, 1988).

7. For an evaluation of sensitivity training, see Alan C. Filley, Robert J. House, and Steven Kerr, *Managerial Process and Organizational Behavior*, 2d ed. (Glenview, Ill.: Scott, Foresman and Company, 1976), pp. 498–503.

8. Patricia A. Langan, "Trying to Clone U.S.-Style MBAs," *Fortune* (Oct. 8, 1990), pp. 143–151.

9. Such as the fifteenth annual meeting held in March 1988 in San Diego, California.

10. Norman E. Sondak and Robert O. Briggs, "Expert Systems—The New Business Simulation Tool"; Theodore F. Gautschi and Mohad Prasad, "An Initial Step towards Developing and Using an Expert System with a Business Simulation"; and Marian Sackson and Andrew Varanelli, Jr., "The Use of an Expert System to Develop Strategic Scenarios"; all three articles appeared in Patricia Sanders and Tom Pray (eds.), *Developments in Business Simulation & Experiential Exercises*, Proceedings of the Fifteenth Annual Conference of ABSEL, San Diego, Mar. 16–18, 1988.

11. Dorothy Leonard-Barton and John J. Sviokla, "Putting Expert Systems to Work," *Harvard Business Review* (March–April 1988), pp. 91–98.

12. Based, in part, on Norman B. Wright, "The Revolution around Us: Human Resource Development in the 80's," *Business Quarterly* (Fall 1984), pp. 6–8.

13. Lucia Solorzano, "Why Business Spends Billions Educating Workers," *U.S. News & World Report* (Feb. 10, 1986), pp. 50–51.

14. See also Michael Beer, Russell A. Eisenstat, and Bert Spector, "Why Change Programs Don't Produce Change," *Harvard Business Review* (November–December 1990), pp. 158–166.

15. Kurt Lewin, *Field Theory in Social Science: Selected Theoretical Papers* (New York: Harper & Brothers, 1951).

16. Edgar H. Schein, *Organizational Psychology*, 3d ed. (Englewood Cliffs, N.J.: Prentice-Hall, 1980), chap. 13; D. D. Warrick, *Managing Organization Change and Development* (Chicago: SRA Science Research Associates, 1984).

17. See Robert R. Blake and Jane S. Mouton, *Building a Dynamic Corporation through Grid Organization Development* (Reading, Mass.: Addison-Wesley Publishing Company, 1969), chap. 6.

18. A survey feedback approach was used by Xerox and is discussed by Norman Deets and Richard Morano, "Xerox's Strategy for Changing Management Styles," *Management Review* (March 1986), pp. 31–35.

19. For a discussion of the history of OD and the contributions to the field, see Wendell L. French, "The Emergence and Early History of Organization Development: With Reference to Influences upon and Interactions among Some of the Key Actors," *Group and Organization Studies* (September 1983).

20. This is the purpose of the concept of double-loop learning as discussed by Chris Argyris, "The Executive Mind and Double-Loop Learning," *Organizational Dynamics* (Autumn 1982), pp. 4–22; Chris Argyris, "Double Loop Learning in Organizations," in David A. Kolb, Irwin M. Rubin, and James M. McIntyre (eds.), *Organizational Psychology*, 4th ed. (Englewood Cliffs, N.J.: Prentice-Hall, 1984), pp. 45–58.

21. Stephen P. Robbins, *The Administrative Process* (Englewood Cliffs, N.J.: Prentice-Hall, 1976), pp. 340–345, 347–349.

22. This discussion is drawn from Denis D. Umstot, "Organization Development Technology and the Military: A Surprising Merger?" *Academy of Management Review* (April 1980), pp. 189–201.

23. For more information on improving managerial productivity, see, for example, Paul Mali, *Improving Total Productivity* (New York: John Wiley & Sons, 1978); Heinz Weihrich, *Management Excellence—Productivity through MBO* (New York: McGraw-Hill Book Company, 1985).

24. Based on Heinz Weihrich and Diethard Buehler, "Training for Managers for the Global Market," *Business* (July–August–September 1990), pp. 40–42.

25. Symons, "A Fine Mesh at IBM" (1987).

26. Ed Bean, "By Practicing What It Preaches, Fuqua Wins a Place among Top Business Schools," *The Wall Street Journal* (May 13, 1986).

27. John A. Byrne, "Business Fads: What's In—And Out," *Business Week* (Jan. 20, 1986), pp. 52–61; and Kenneth Dreyfack and John A. Byrne, "When Companies Tell B-Schools What to Teach," *Business Week* (Feb. 10, 1986), pp. 60–61.

28. Walter Kiechel III, "New Debate about Harvard Business School," *Fortune* (Nov. 9, 1987), pp. 34–48.

29. This case is based on a variety of experiences. For additional information, see Karl Heinrich Ruessmann, "Strahlkraft durch Kompetenz," *Manager Magazine* (April 1988), pp. 254–273, and Harry B. Bernhard and Cynthia A. Ingols, "Six Lessons for the Corporate Classroom," *Harvard Business Review* (September–October 1988), pp. 40–48.

Summary of Major Principles, or Guides, for Staffing

There are no universally accepted staffing principles. Nevertheless, those listed below are useful as guidelines for understanding the staffing function. These principles are grouped under the purpose and process of staffing.

The Purpose of Staffing

The purpose of staffing is summarized by the following principles.

Principle of the objective of staffing. The objective of managerial staffing is to ensure that organization roles are filled by those qualified personnel who are able and willing to occupy them.

Principle of staffing. The clearer the definition of organization roles and their human requirements, and the better the techniques of manager appraisal and training employed, the higher the managerial quality.

The first principle stresses the importance of the desire and ability to undertake the responsibilities of management. There is considerable evidence of failure to achieve results when these qualities are lacking. The second principle rests on an important body of knowledge concerning management practices. Those organizations that have no established job definitions, no effective appraisals, and no system for training and development will have to rely on coincidence or outside sources to fill positions with able managers. On the other hand, enterprises applying the systems approach to staffing and human resource management will utilize the potentials of individuals in the enterprise more effectively and efficiently.

The Process of Staffing

The following principles indicate the means for effective staffing.

Principle of job definition. The more precisely the results expected of managers are identified, the more the dimensions of their positions can be defined.

This principle is similar to the principle of functional definition discussed in Part 3, on organizing. Since organizational roles are occupied by people with different needs, these roles must have many dimensions—such as pay, status, power, discretion, and possibility of accomplishment—that induce managers to perform.

Principle of managerial appraisal.   The more clearly verifiable objectives and required managerial activities are identified, the more precise can be the appraisal of managers against these criteria.

The principle suggests that performance should be measured both against verifiable objectives—as in an appraisal approach based on management by objectives—and against standards of performance as managers. The appraisal of managers as managers considers how well the key managerial activities within the functions of planning, organizing, staffing, leading, and controlling are carried out.

Principle of open competition.   The more an enterprise is committed to the assurance of quality management, the more it will encourage open competition among all candidates for management positions.

Violation of this principle has led many firms to appoint managers with inadequate abilities. Although social pressures strongly favor promotion from within the firm, these forces should be resisted whenever better candidates can be brought in from the outside. At the same time, the application of this principle obligates an organization to appraise its people accurately and to provide them with opportunities for development.

Principle of management training and development.   The more management training and development are integrated with the management process and enterprise objectives, the more effective the development programs and activities will be.

This principle suggests that in the systems approach, training and development efforts are related to the managerial functions, the aims of the enterprise, and the professional needs of managers.

Principle of training objectives.   The more precisely the training objectives are stated, the more likely are the chances of achieving them.

The analysis of training needs is the basis for training objectives that give direction to development and facilitate the measurement of the effectiveness of training efforts. This principle brings into focus the contribution that training makes to the purpose of the enterprise and the development of individuals.

Principle of continuing development.   The more an enterprise is committed to managerial excellence, the more it requires that managers practice continuing self-development.

This principle suggests that in a fast-changing and competitive environment, managers cannot stop learning. Instead, they have to update their managerial knowledge continuously, reevaluate their approaches to managing, and improve their managerial skills and performance to achieve enterprise results.

Global Staffing

This part closing is about global staffing. First, as in the two previous part closings of this book, the managerial practices in Japan, the United States, and China are discussed. In this part closing, staffing is highlighted. Second, the international focus is on the German/European model for training and development. Finally, a global car industry case is discussed.

STAFFING PRACTICES IN JAPAN, THE UNITED STATES, AND THE PEOPLE'S REPUBLIC OF CHINA[1]

Staffing requires identifying human resource needs and filling the organization structure, and keeping it filled, with competent people. It is in the management of human resources—besides the decision-making process—that the Japanese and Chinese approaches to managing differ greatly from that of U.S. companies, as shown in the accompanying table.

Staffing in Japan

In Japan, people are hired out of school. For a young man, choosing a company is one of the most important decisions he makes, besides selecting a spouse and a university. After a person has joined a company, there is hardly any opportunity to find employment in another firm. Within the company promotion is rather slow, and for most young people the career paths during the first few years with the company are similar. Still, employees develop a strong identification with the company, which in turn takes care of them. Employees repay with their loyalty.

The performance of employees is evaluated once or twice a year. In addition, their progress is monitored on an informal basis. Working together with others in

COMPARISONS OF JAPANESE, U.S., AND CHINESE STAFFING*

Japanese management	U.S. management	Chinese management
1. Young people hired out of school; hardly any mobility of people among companies	1. People hired out of schools and from other companies; frequent company changes	1. Most hired from school; fewer from other companies
2. Slow promotion through the ranks	2. Rapid advancement highly desired and demanded	2. Slow promotion—but regular salary increases
3. Loyalty to the company	3. Loyalty to the profession	3. Lack of loyalty to both company and profession
4. Performance appraisal once or twice a year common	4. Comprehensive performance evaluation, usually once a year	4. Performance review usually once a year
5. Appraisal of long-term performance	5. Appraisal of short-term results	5. 5-year plan; otherwise, short-term targets
6. Promotions based on long-term performance and other criteria	6. Promotions based primarily on individual performance and often on relatively short-term performance	6. Promotions are supposed to be based on performance, potential ability, and education. But family ties and good relations with top managers are important.
7. Training and development considered a long-term investment	7. Training and development undertaken with hesitation (employee may switch to another firm)	7. Training programs available; state exam administered for managers
8. Lifetime employment common in companies	8. Job insecurity prevailing	8. Job security; virtually lifetime employment

*Sources of information are given in note 6 in the Part 2 closing References.

an office, without walls separating employees and superiors, means that there is little doubt about how well individuals are performing. A more comprehensive performance review is conducted a few years after an employee has entered a firm. With a long-term evaluation, the probability of the influence of luck or misfortune is reduced. What is evaluated are the overall, long-range success and decision capability of the individual. This practice results in linking rewards (such as promotions) to effective long-term performance. Still, the differences in pay increases among young employees after entering a firm are rather small, and rewards are essentially based on group and company performance rather than on individual contributions.

Because employees are an integral part of the corporate community, promotion practices must be considered by all as being fair and equitable. In Japan, the criteria for promotion are usually a combination of seniority and merit. Also, educational background plays a role in promotion decisions. Japanese companies invest heavily in the training and development of their employees, and the practice of job rotation throughout the employees' working life leads to a broad career path in which the employees are exposed to many different enterprise activities.

Perhaps the most pervasive impact on managerial practices comes from lifetime employment. Japanese companies make every effort to ensure stable employment until retirement age (around 55). At times of economic slowdown, companies usually dismiss part-time or seasonal employees, who are not considered members of the permanent work force. Also, instead of being laid off, permanent employees are often transferred to organizational units that are in need of additional help. But the practice of lifelong employment seems to be on its way out. In an interview, Japanese executives suggested that lifelong employment is very costly to a company, resulting in a top-heavy organization structure, and therefore will have to be slowly modified.

Staffing in the United States

The management of human resources in the United States is quite different from that in Japan. American firms also recruit employees from schools, but they hire employees from other companies too. For example, the high turnover rates among those who recently received their Master of Business Administration degree are quite notorious. Rapid advancement is expected, and if it is not forthcoming, an employee may change companies. Professionals, such as engineers or accountants, often identify more with their profession than with their company, and job-hopping is not unusual.

A common practice in American companies is to appraise the performance of new employees rather soon after they join the company. If the performance does not meet the company's expectations, employment may be terminated. But even for those who have been with a company for many years, performance is evaluated at least once a year, and in many cases their performance is reviewed periodically during the year. In general, the focus of performance appraisal is on short-term results and individual contributions to the company's aims. Moreover, differentials in pay increases are often based on individual performance. These differences in pay may be substantial, especially at upper levels of management. Promotions in U.S. companies are based primarily on individual performance.

Although progressive companies provide for continuous development, training is often undertaken with hesitation because of the cost and the concern that the trained person may switch to another firm. Thus, employees are often trained in specialized functions, and this results in a rather narrow career path within the firm. Finally, in many American companies, employees feel that they may be laid off during economically hard times, which, naturally, contributes to job insecurity.

Staffing in China

The staffing practices in China have aspects similar to those in Japan. As in Japan, employees are hired from school. They are expected to stay with the enterprise for a long time. More recently, however, personnel have also been hired from other organizations; but people are usually assigned to their positions by higher authorities. As in Japan, promotion is slow through the ranks but there are regular salary increases.

Lacking in China are dedication and loyalty to both the company (as in Japan) and the profession (as in the United States). Performance reviews are done in China, usually once a year, which is similar to practices in Japan and in the United States. Promotions are supposed to be based primarily on performance, education, and potential ability. However, family ties and good relations with the superior greatly influence advancement within an organization. In the past, training programs were available in China only to the chosen few. Recently, however, training has been provided for more managers by educational television and professional night schools. Moreover, some managers now have to pass an exam sponsored by the State Economic Commission. The jobs of employees are secure; job security implies lifetime employment (known as "iron-rice bowl") regardless of performance.

INTERNATIONAL FOCUS:
TRAINING AND DEVELOPMENT FOR THE GLOBAL MARKET:
THE GERMAN/EUROPEAN MODEL

Germany is slowly accepting the idea that management is learnable and teachable. Because managerial education provided by universities is insufficient, companies have developed their own programs or made cooperative arrangements with schools. One such cooperative arrangement is the apprenticeship system.

Combination of Internal and External Training: The Apprenticeship System

An apprentice obtains practical experience by working in the company and learns theoretical concepts in a vocational school. University of Chicago Professor Gary Becker suggests that the German approach to vocational training may be useful for reducing the number of high school dropouts in the United States.[2] He suggests that some young people would prefer to be in a training-employment program rather than continue their studies in high school. Owing to their lack of interest in academic subjects, some students simply drop out of school.

Although they are not managerial training programs as such, the in-company apprenticeship programs play a vital role in preparing future managers for their job. These programs, supplemented by additional education, provide the foundation for the development of first-line supervisors in Germany.

Young people who choose the 3-year apprenticeship training work 3 to 4 days a week and spend 1 or 2 days a week in the vocational school. The government sets the standards for over 400 occupations. For example, an apprentice auto mechanic may be required to learn some basic skills, such as how to use a file, lathe, and drill, while working in the company. These activities may be supervised by a trainer (supervising ten to fifteen young people), a manager, and a director. The apprentices' work usually does not contribute to the short-term profit of the firm. Typically, these apprentices engage in projects, such as preparing an iron cube, that are carefully evaluated for accuracy, surface preparation, proper and precise angles, and so on. Advanced auto mechanic training requires working on more complex car components, such as automatic transmissions or engines.

In addition to having apprentices attend vocational training courses, many big firms offer in-house classroom training. Thus apprentices not only learn about the products or services of the firm but also may be taught foreign languages, which are important for technicians or managers sent to other countries. Social activities are not neglected either during the apprenticeship training. For example, apprentices have opportunities to participate in company-sponsored hiking tours, competitive sports such as soccer or track-and-field events, and other recreational activities. In a sense, apprenticeship training is really a continuation of basic schooling with an emphasis on job skills. This is reflected in the fact that at the end of the training, apprentices take an exam administered by the public vocational school. In addition, the apprentices must meet company requirements.

Although the wages for the apprentices are low, the training is quite costly to the company, especially since a trainee may leave the company after completing the program. Hewlett-Packard in former West Germany hires about 80 apprentices each year at a cost of about $5000 per apprentice. Most apprentices stay with their company, and so the long-term investment for the company pays off. Without apprenticeship programs, German firms would not be so successful in marketing their quality products and services around the world.

The German airline Lufthansa has an advertisement showing apprentices inspecting an airplane engine. The message is that investment in the training of technicians results in higher product and service quality. About half a million German firms train 1.8 million teenagers, or 6 percent of the work force, and about 70 percent of Germany's high school students choose vocational education.[3]

The importance of technical training is illustrated in the effort by Daimler-Benz, the maker of Mercedes cars. In 1987, over 5500 people were involved in technical professional training, with about 1600 graduating in that year.[4] During the apprenticeship training, the young people divide their time between working on the job and attending school.[5] In this way, practical experience is supplemented by theoretical knowledge that can be applied on the job. Teaching skilled workers and trained technicians the theoretical foundation of their work creates professionals who will continually make efforts to improve productivity.

The Vocational Academy (VA)

While apprenticeship training emphasizes technical knowledge and skills, it does not usually teach managerial skills. Only recently have the needs for teaching managerial skills and integrating theory with practice been recognized. A new program, the Vocational Academy (Berufsakademie), has been devised to address these needs. Because of its success, a more detailed discussion is in order.

In 1974, the state of Baden-Wuerttemberg, together with firms such as Daimler-Benz and Bosch, started the Vocational Academy (also called the Stuttgarter Model, named after the city of Stuttgart). This managerial training model, which focuses on technology, social sciences, and business, rather than on academic subjects, has been considered an important alternative to university studies. The Academy has the following characteristics:[6]

1. Theoretical and vocational education are closely integrated. The educational process consists of two sets of learning modules, one for theory and the other for practice.
2. Students must have a vocational contract with an enterprise or a social institution to be admitted to the Academy.
3. The Academy and the enterprise have equal authority in determining the educational goals.
4. The first step is achieved after 2 years, when students must take a state-recognized vocation-qualifying exam.
5. The complete educational process spans 3 years, or six semesters. The students must take a second exam, and upon passing it, they receive a degree that is similar to a university degree in engineering.

Ten years after the inception of the VA, surveys indicated that professional opportunities were considerably higher for VA graduates than for those who did not receive this training. Applications for admission to VAs far exceed available study opportunities, with as many as twenty young persons competing for one educational slot. While VA programs originated in the cities of Stuttgart and Mannheim, they are currently established in eight cities, with approximately 3000 enterprises participating, offering twenty-two curricula.[7]

One can conclude that the Stuttgarter Educational Model, integrating theory and practical experience, fills an important business education gap not filled by traditional universities and apprenticeship programs. This relatively new cooperative model, involving the Academy, industry, and government, has shown encouraging results. It may stimulate U.S. companies to search for alternative training methods for developing managers and increasing productivity.

The New European Manager

So far the discussion has centered on training and development for lower- and middle-level managers; now the focus shifts to training for upper-level management. Managers in many European firms have been criticized for an apparent lack of sufficient knowledge and skills necessary for managing globally. Specifically, demands on today's global managers include the ability to think globally, an understanding of the mentalities of managers in other EC and non-EC countries, managerial experience abroad, and proficiency in speaking at least two foreign languages.

The European Community 1992 program underscores the need for developing globally minded managers. A research study of eleven European firms by an international consulting group found that many managers do not meet the Eurodemands of the future, although respondents in the study recognized the need for international managerial experience. Not only do the Euromanagers need to gain experience abroad, but firms also need to realize that non-Europeans will have to be recruited and trained in the European headquarters of multinational corporations. The following examples illustrate the exception rather than the rule under which companies operate. The Deutsche Bank (German Bank) has a development program for foreigners who spend at least 1 year at the Frankfurt headquarters. Bosch, a manufacturer of a variety of products ranging from refrigerators to auto accessories, invites foreigners, Spaniards in particular, to Germany for training. Bosch also requires its German trainees to spend at least 6 months abroad. While these international opportunities are attractive for young managers, there is concern, especially among older managers, that being away from headquarters may inhibit career advancement.

According to the Korn/Ferry consulting group, the following characteristics are *very important* for ideal Euromanagers:

- Having a university or college education
- Having work experience abroad
- Understanding economics
- Being a generalist
- Being proficient in English and French as foreign languages[8]

The research study found that German, French, and Italian managers had little work experience abroad. German and Italian managers lacked general manager experience, while German and British managers had insufficient skills in communicating in the French language. In team-orientation and global thinking, the Germans and Italians ranked low. The Germans also ranked low in communication and motivation abilities. In respect to the question pertaining to "willingness to contribute above average," English and French managers ranked low, while in decision making, Italian managers got a low rating. Although these are generalizations, they indicate that many European managers are not sufficiently prepared for the competitive environment that will be created by the European Single Market in 1992 and beyond.

What Business Schools Should Do

German universities have not been adequately preparing managers for the 1990s. German law does not allow state-supported schools to offer Master of Business Administration degrees; but there are some seventy M.B.A. schools throughout the rest of Europe, including the following:[9]

Rotterdam School of Management (RSM), in The Netherlands

The International Institute for Management Development (IMD), in Lausanne, Switzerland

Graduate School of Business Administration (GSBA), in Zurich, Switzerland

Institute Superieur des Affaires (ISA), in Jouy-en-Josas, France

Manchester Business School, in England

Scuola Di Direzione Aziendale Dell' Universita Luigi Bocconi (SDA Bocconi), in Milan, Italy

Institut Europeen d'Administration des Affaires (INSEAD), in Fontainebleau, France

Nijenrode School—The Netherlands School of Business, in Breukelen

Escuela Superior De Administracion Y Direccion De Empresas (ESADE), in Barcelona, Spain

London Business School, in England

Summary and Conclusion about the German/European Model of Manager Development

The 1990s will be marked by fierce global competition in which only the most productive organizations will survive. This competitive environment necessitates a second look at human resource training and development. Managers should evaluate the suitability of cooperative training by industry and educational institutions as practiced in Germany. The model of the new Euromanager may inspire more effective and relevant approaches for training future executives.

GLOBAL CAR INDUSTRY CASE: MEET THE CARMAKERS' CEOs[10]

Strategies are largely determined by the CEOs of companies. It is therefore important to learn about the career paths of the top executives of selected major car manufacturers. The accompanying table summarizes some characteristics of those executives. Three key leaders—one from Japan, one from the United States, and one from Germany—have been selected for further discussion.

Soichiro Honda, CEO at Honda

Relatively little is known about Soichiro Honda, who was the soft-spoken CEO of Honda Motor Company. He did not write an autobiography and rarely granted an interview. He was not a member of the "in-group" of Japanese carmakers either. Nor was he a friend of Japan's MITI (the Ministry of International Trade and Industry) or government bureaucrats. Instead, he was one who was fascinated with motor vehicles and had an intense interest in the needs of his automotive customers. For example, when the customers wanted motorcycles after World War II, MITI's officials did not cooperate and help Honda exploit the demand. When he wanted to produce cars, MITI officials argued that Japan needed fewer, not more, car manufacturers.

Honda began car production with the very small Civic model. Today, the model range extends from the representative Civic to the Accord and to the fairly luxurious Acura. In 1991, Honda expanded its model line with the introduction of

CHIEF EXECUTIVE OFFICERS OF SELECTED CAR COMPANIES*

Lee Iacocca, Chrysler, United States	Harold Poling, Ford Motor Company, United States	Robert Stempel, General Motors, United States	Carl Hahn, Volkswagen, Germany	Edzard Reuter, Daimler-Benz, Germany
B.S. in industrial engineering, M.S.E. in mechanical engineering	B.A. in economics, business administration	B.S. in mechanical engineering, M.B.A.—business administration	Studied business administration, economics (doctorate) in Germany, France, and Switzerland	Studied mathematics, physics, and law
Career path: technical, engineering	*Career path:* finance and accounting	*Career path:* technical, engineering	*Career path:* OEEC, Continental Rubber, VW export, marketing	*Career path:* finance, corporate planning
Company situation: strong in minivans, jeeps; several models are aging	*Company situation:* need for cost cutting; car sales weakening; high leverage because of Jaguar acquisition	*Company situation:* need for cost cutting; wants to revamp product line	*Company situation:* high cost structure; expansion into former East Germany	*Company situation:* high cost structure; cash-rich; needs new product line

* The information has been drawn from a variety of sources, including "The Corporate Elite" (no author shown), *Business Week*, Special Issue (Oct. 19, 1990); Edzard Reuter, *Vom Geist der Wirtschaft—Europa zwischen Technokraten and Mythokraten* (Stuttgart: Deutsche Verlags-Anstalt GmbH, 1986); personal correspondence; Maynard M. Gordon, *The Iacocca Management Technique* (New York: Dodd, Mead & Company, 1985); Lee Iacocca with William Novak, *Iacocca—An Autobiography* (New York: Bantam Books, 1984).

the Accord EX wagon, which is the family version of its best-selling Accord in America.

Although Mr. Honda retired some time ago (and in 1991, he passed away), his tenure influenced the direction of the company. His leadership style was quite different from that of other carmakers' CEOs. His desire to explore new things was reflected in the company philosophy. When he began producing Honda motorcycles for the U.S. market, few thought that he would succeed. His strategy was based not on extensive market research but rather on intuition. His obsession with quality and the desire to please customers led to the development of the successful car line, including the best-selling Honda Accord. But the U.S. success is not mirrored in the Japanese market, where Honda ranks third, selling less than one-fourth as many cars as Toyota does. Mr. Honda's other passion concerned safety. He insisted that his workers take their tasks seriously and protect their customers from injuries that could result from poor work. Indeed, he created a Japanese foundation for car safety.

Another aspect of Honda's philosophy was his dealings with people. He made no distinction between blue-collar and white-collar workers or between the rich and poor people he came in contact with. His attitude toward people was reflected in the policies of Honda's Ohio plant, where workers, managers, and even the president eat in the same cafeteria. His passion for egalitarianism may have helped him become close to his customers; thus he was able to recognize their motor transportation needs.

Lee Iacocca, CEO at Chrysler

Lee Iacocca, the top corporate manager of Chrysler, differs from Honda's former CEO in many ways. For one, Iacocca is a member of Detroit's elite and likes many of the CEO privileges, including the use of a private jet. His leadership orientation is more toward elitism rather than toward egalitarianism.

Iacocca is probably the most recognized CEO among U.S. car companies. Besides receiving credit for developing the successful Mustang while working at Ford, he became best known for managing Chrysler's bailout by the federal government. In August 1983 he announced that the company repaid the government-guaranteed loan 7 years ahead of schedule. When he took over the helm at Chrysler, he found an unsound organization structure, insufficient financial controls, a lack of attractive new products, and the need for marketing strategy. The turnaround strategy required some drastic measures, including the firing of thirty-three of the thirty-five vice presidents.

In looking into the future, Iacocca said that in order to compete, one has to have quality products. His view is that one has to go back to the basics in the car business and do them well.

Edzard Reuter, CEO at Daimler-Benz

Edzard Reuter, Daimler-Benz's CEO, studied mathematics, physics, and law. Before joining Daimler, he held various managerial positions in a variety of companies, the last one at the Bertelsmann Group, a publishing firm.

When Reuter joined Daimler, he worked at first in finance. Later he was responsible for corporate planning. After serving as a deputy member of the board for a few years, he became a full member in 1976. A year later, he also took charge of the Technical Planning Department. During that time, important decisions were made in reorganizing the product lines and production, especially in the automobile sector. In 1980, he assumed responsibility for the Finance and Business Management section. Since 1987, he has been the chairman of the Daimler-Benz Board of Management.

Besides being the chairman at Daimler-Benz, Reuter is a member of many other institutions. For example, he is the chairman of the Supervisory Board of AEG AG (a company that could be compared with General Electric in the United States) and Berliner Bank AG. He is also a member of the Supervisory Board of Karlsruher Lebensversicherung AG and Alliance AG Holding (both insurance companies). But his interests go beyond business, as shown by his being a member of several boards of foundations that promote the arts.

Under Reuter's leadership, Daimler-Benz has made several strategic moves, including a drastic reorganization. The Daimler-Benz Holding Company oversees and coordinates the three groups: Mercedes-Benz, AEG, and German Aerospace. The keystones of the new strategy are microelectronics and system techniques. The car sector will remain the core business. On the other hand, the defense-related divisions may have to be curtailed because of the end of the cold war between the East and West. Reuter envisions Daimler-Benz as a global company, effectively using new technologies, new materials, and the latest information and systems knowledge.*

1. Which leadership style is most appealing to you? Why?
2. What background (technical/production, marketing, finance, or any other) is most suitable for the CEO of a major car company? May the suitability vary with the demands at a particular time?
3. If you were on the selection committees at Honda, Chrysler, and Daimler-Benz, what characteristics would you look for in choosing the next president of each of the three companies?

* Strategy formulation was discussed in detail in the Part 2 closing, "Global Planning."

REFERENCES

1. Sources of information are given in note 6 in the Part 2 closing References. In addition, see Robert Neff, Stewart Toy, Paul Magnusson, and William J. Holstein, "Can Japan Cope?" *Business Week* (Apr. 23, 1990), pp. 46–49; Yumiko Ono and Marcus W. Brauchli, "Japan Cuts the Middle-Management Fat," *The Wall Street Journal* (Aug. 8, 1989); Todd Barrett, "Mastering Being in America," *Business Week* (Feb. 5, 1990), p. 84; Urban C. Lehner and Alan Murray, "Youth in Japan, U.S. Reinforce Culture Gap between the Nations," *The Wall Street Journal* (June 15, 1990); and James W. Schmotter, "Japanese M.B.A.s—Made in the U.S.A.," *The Wall Street Journal* (July 23, 1990).
2. Gary S. Becker, "Tuning in to the Needs of High School Dropouts," *Business Week* (July 3, 1989).
3. Nancy J. Perry, "The New, Improved Vocational School," *Fortune* (June 19, 1989), pp. 127–138.
4. "Betriebliche Bildungsarbeit 1987," internal publication by Daimler-Benz.
5. Peter F. Drucker, "What We Can Learn from the Germans," *The Wall Street Journal* (Mar. 6, 1986).
6. "Information zu den Berufsakademien des Landes Baden-Wuerttemberg" (undated).
7. "Interesenten Stehen Schlange," IWD (1986).
8. Brigitta Lentz, "Der polyglotte Supermann," *Manager Magazine* (May 1989), pp. 257–270.
9. "MBA-Schulen auf dem Pruefstand. Die Top Ten 1988" (Frankfurt: Cox Communication, 1988), in Albert Staehli, "Helvetische Spitzenausbildung fuer Europas Topmanagers," *The Best of Switzerland* (Zurich, Switzerland: Jean Frey AG, 1989); Andrew Fisher, "Putting Europe's Business Schools under the Microscope," *Financial Times* (Sept. 22, 1989); William H. Cox and Ingrid Cox, *Der MBA in Europa* (Frankfurt: Allgemeine Zeitung, 1987); and brochures by the institutions.
10. The information has been drawn from a variety of sources, including Joel Kotkin, "Mr. Iacocca, Meet Mr. Honda," *Inc.* (November 1986), pp. 37–39; Karen Lowry Miller and James B. Treece, "Honda's Nightmare: Maybe You Can't Go Home Again," *Business Week* (Dec. 24, 1990), p. 36; Keita Asari, "Soichiro Honda on Himself and His Machines," *Economic Eye* (September 1985), pp. 27–32; Richard E. Miller and M. Reza Vaghefi, "The New Chrysler Corporation: Fall and Rise," *Journal of Management Case Studies* (Fall 1987), pp. 252–268.

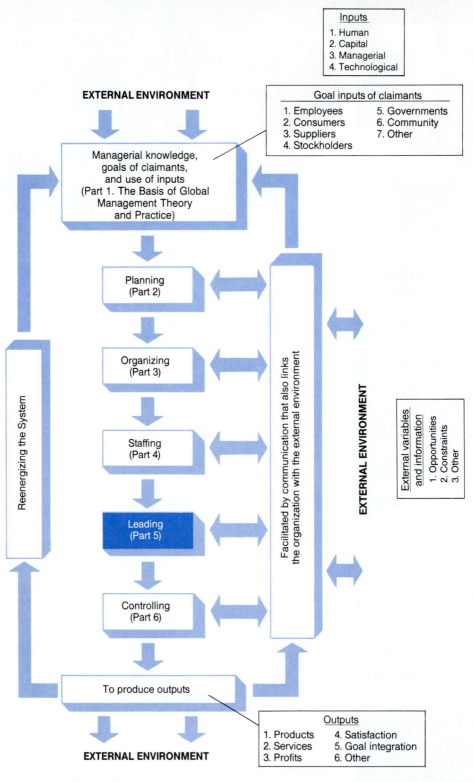

SYSTEMS APPROACH TO MANAGEMENT

Chapter 9

Motivating employees is one of the most consistent challenges any manager faces.[1]

Curtis W. Cook

Human Factors and Motivation

Chapter Objectives

After reading this chapter, you should be able to:

1. Define the nature of leading and leadership.
2. Describe the basic human factors that affect managing.
3. Explain the meaning of motivation, motivators, and satisfaction.
4. Describe McGregor's Theory X and Theory Y.
5. Explain the various leading theories of motivation and their strengths and weaknesses.
6. Analyze special motivational techniques, with particular emphasis on the quality of working life and job enrichment.
7. Present a systems and situational approach to motivation.

Management and leadership are often thought of as the same thing. Although it is true that the most effective manager will almost certainly be an effective leader and that leading is an essential function of managers, there is more to managing than just leading. As indicated in previous chapters, managing involves doing careful planning, setting up an organization structure that will aid people in achieving plans, and staffing the organization structure with people who are as competent as possible. The measurement and correction of people's activities through controlling is also an important function of management, as Part 6 will show. However, all these managerial functions accomplish little if managers do not know how to lead people and to understand the human factors in their operations in such a way as to produce desired results.

The managerial function of **leading** is defined as the process of influencing people so that they will contribute to organization and group goals. As the discussion of this function will show, it is in this area that the behavioral sciences make their major contribution to managing. In its analysis of the pertinent knowledge in leading, Part 5 of this book will focus on the human factors, motivation, leadership, and communication.

In this chapter, discussion centers on a variety of human factors. **Managing** requires the creation and maintenance of an environment in which individuals work together in groups toward the accomplishment of common objectives. This chapter emphasizes the importance of knowing and taking advantage of human and motivating factors, but that does not mean managers should become amateur psychiatrists. The manager's job is not to manipulate people but, rather, to recognize what motivates people.

HUMAN FACTORS IN MANAGING

It is obvious that while enterprise objectives may differ somewhat in various organizations, the individuals involved also have needs and objectives that are especially important to them. Through the function of leading, managers help people see that they can satisfy their own needs and utilize their potential and at the same time contribute to the aims of an enterprise. Managers should thus have an understanding of the roles assumed by people, the individuality of people, and the personalities of people.

Multiplicity of Roles

Individuals are much more than merely a productive factor in management's plans. They are members of social systems of many organizations; they are consumers of goods and services, and thus they vitally influence demand; they are members of families, schools, churches, trade associations, and political parties. In these different roles, they establish laws that govern managers, ethics that guide behavior, and a tradition of human dignity that is a major characteristic of our society. In short, managers and the people they lead are interacting members of a broad social system.

No Average Person

People act in different roles, but they are also different themselves. There is no average person. Yet in organized enterprises, the assumption is often made that there is. Firms develop rules, procedures, work schedules, safety standards, and position descriptions—all with the implicit assumption that people are essentially alike. Of course, this assumption is necessary to a great extent in organized efforts, but it is equally important to acknowledge that individuals are unique—they have different needs, different ambitions, different attitudes, different desires for responsibility, different levels of knowledge and skills, and different potentials.

Unless managers understand the complexity and individuality of people, they may misapply the generalizations about motivation, leadership, and communication. Principles and concepts, although generally true, have to be adjusted to fit specific situations. In an enterprise, not all the needs of individuals can be completely satisfied, but managers do have considerable latitude in making individual arrangements. Although position requirements are usually derived from enterprise and organization plans, this fact does not necessarily exclude the possibility of arranging the job to fit the person in a specific situation.

The Importance of Personal Dignity

Managing involves achieving enterprise objectives. Achieving results is important, but the means must never violate the dignity of people. The concept of individual dignity means that people must be treated with respect, no matter what their position in the organization. The president, vice president, manager, first-line supervisor, and worker all contribute to the aims of the enterprise. Each is unique, with different abilities and aspirations, but all are human beings, and all deserve to be treated as such.[2]

Consideration of the Whole Person

We cannot talk about the nature of people unless we consider the whole person, not just separate and distinct characteristics, such as knowledge, attitudes, skills, or personality traits. A person has them all to different degrees. Moreover, these characteristics interact with one another, and their predominance in specific situations changes quickly and unpredictably. The human being is a total person influenced by external factors. People cannot divest themselves of the impact of these forces when they come to work. Managers must recognize these facts and be prepared to deal with them.

The recent trend of downsizing organizations and the mergers of enterprises have had a traumatic effect on middle managers in many organizations.[3] In the drive to improve efficiency, middle-level manager jobs have been eliminated. The drastic reduction in personnel in many U.S. enterprises has had unexpected consequences. For example, it was assumed that the working life of the remaining managers would be enriched by more meaningful jobs. The reality is that many managers now feel that they are overworked and that their contributions go unappreciated.

The restructuring of organizations has resulted in great job insecurity and low morale. Managers are often reluctant to share information because they want to protect their jobs. Moreover, they hesitate to speak freely in meetings because they do not want to risk crossing their boss. Middle managers feel that they do not get sufficient information from top managers, who often do not provide vision and leadership for the enterprise.

On the other hand, top executives, such as Roger Smith, the chairman of General Motors, complain about the resistance of rank-and-file managers to change. Whatever the situation, the bitterness and alienation of many lower-level managers affect morale and productivity. If U.S. companies want to be competitive, employees must be committed to enterprise goals. To elicit this dedication requires corporate concern for the individual, recognition of his or her dignity as a human being, and reasonable job security with an opportunity for personal growth and development.

MOTIVATION AND MOTIVATORS

Human motives are based on needs, whether consciously or subconsciously felt. Some are primary needs, such as the physiological requirements for water, air, food, sleep, and shelter. Other needs may be regarded as secondary, such as self-esteem, status, affiliation with others, affection, giving, accomplishment, and self-assertion. Naturally, these needs vary in intensity and over time among different individuals.

Motivation

Motivation is a general term applying to the entire class of drives, desires, needs, wishes, and similar forces. To say that managers motivate their subordinates is to say that they do those things which they hope will satisfy these drives and desires and induce the subordinates to act in a desired manner.

Managers are responsible for providing an environment conducive to performance. But individuals themselves are responsible for self-motivation. One approach is through strategic career management (which was discussed in Chapter 14). George Odiorne, a management professor, scholar, and experienced consultant, made specific recommendations.[4] Here are some:

1. Set a goal for yourself, and do not lose sight of it. Lee Iacocca (the president of Chrysler) set the goal of becoming vice president at the Ford Motor Company by age 35, and for 15 years this aim motivated him and guided his behavior.
2. Supplement your long-term objectives with short-term goals and specific actions. It has been said that to get something done is to begin.
3. Learn a challenging new task each year. Learning to become a manager does not stop with a bachelor's or master's degree in business. A degree is the real beginning, not the end, of learning. Learning and applying the new microcomputer technology might be such a challenging task.
4. Make your job a different one. Set improvement objectives for your position. With some imagination, you probably can considerably increase your productivity.
5. Develop an area of expertise. Build on your strengths, or develop one of your weaknesses into a strength. You might want to be known as the best accountant or the best engineer in your specific area of competence.
6. Give yourself feedback and reward yourself. Setting verifiable goals provides you with a standard against which you can measure your performance. Why not have a special dinner to celebrate your accomplishments?

The Need-Want-Satisfaction Chain

It is possible, then, to look at motivation as involving a chain reaction: Felt needs give rise to wants or goals sought, which cause tensions (that is, unfulfilled desires), which give rise to actions toward achieving goals, which finally result in satisfaction. This chain is shown in Figure 16-1.

The chain explanation is complex. In the first place, except for physiological needs, such as food, needs are not independent of a person's environment. Many physiological needs, however, are stimulated by environmental factors: The smell of food may cause hunger, a lower thermometer reading may cause chills, or the sight of a cold drink may cause an overwhelming thirst.

Environment has a major influence on our perception of secondary needs. The promotion of a colleague may kindle one's desire for a higher position. A

FIGURE 16-1

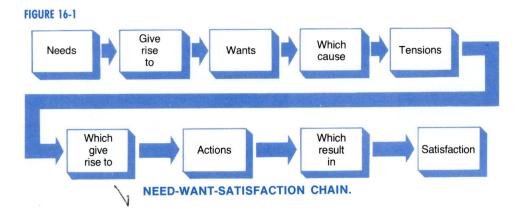

NEED-WANT-SATISFACTION CHAIN.

challenging problem may whet one's desire to accomplish something by solving it. A congenial social group may increase one's need for affiliation; and, of course, being alone more than one wants to be can give a strong motivation for wanting to be with people.

In the second place, the need-want-satisfaction chain does not always operate as simply as portrayed. Needs do cause behavior, but needs also may result from behavior. Satisfying one need may lead to a desire to satisfy more needs. For example, a person's need for accomplishment may be made keener by the satisfaction gained from achieving a desired goal, or it may be dulled by failure. The one-way nature of the chain has also been challenged by the work of some biological scientists who have found that needs are not always the cause of human behavior but may be a result of it. In other words, behavior is often what people do and not why they do it.

Complexity of Motivation

It takes only a moment's thought to realize that at any given time, an individual's motives may be quite complex and often conflicting. A person may be motivated by a desire for economic goods and services (groceries, a better house, a new car, or a trip), and even these desires may be complex and conflicting (should one buy a new house or a new car?). At the same time, an individual may want self-esteem, status, a feeling of accomplishment, or relaxation (who has not felt a conflict between the time demands of a job and the desire to play golf or go to a movie?).

Motivators. **Motivators** are things that induce an individual to perform. While motivations reflect wants, motivators are the identified rewards, or incentives, that sharpen the drive to satisfy these wants. They are also the means by which conflicting needs may be reconciled or one need heightened so that it will be given priority over another.

A manager can do much to sharpen motives by establishing an environment favorable to certain drives. For example, people in a business that has developed a reputation for excellence and high quality tend to be motivated to contribute to this reputation. Similarly, the environment of a business in which managerial performance is effective and efficient tends to breed a desire for high-quality management among most, or all, managers and personnel.

A motivator, then, is something that influences an individual's behavior. It makes a difference in what a person will do. Obviously, in any organized enterprise, managers must be concerned about motivators and also inventive in their use. People can often satisfy their wants in a variety of ways. A person can, for example, satisfy a desire for affiliation by being active in a social club rather than in a business, meet economic needs by performing a job just well enough to get by, or satisfy status needs by spending time working for a political party. What a manager must do, of course, is use those motivators which will lead people to perform effectively for the enterprise that employs them.

Difference between motivation and satisfaction.   **Motivation** refers to the drive and effort to satisfy a want or goal. **Satisfaction** refers to the contentment experienced when a want is satisfied. In other words, motivation implies a drive toward an outcome, and satisfaction is the outcome already experienced, as shown in Figure 16-2.

From a management point of view, then, a person might have high job satisfaction but a low level of motivation for the job, or the reverse might be true. Understandably, the probability exists that highly motivated persons with low job satisfaction will look for other positions. Likewise, people who find their positions rewarding but are being paid considerably less than they desire or think they deserve will probably search for other jobs.

MOTIVATION: THE CARROT AND THE STICK

The various leading theories of motivation and motivators seldom make reference to the carrot and the stick. This metaphor relates, of course, to the use of rewards and penalties in order to induce desired behavior. It comes from the old story that to make a donkey move, one must put a carrot in front of him or jab him with a stick from behind.

Despite all the research on and theories of motivation that have come to the

FIGURE 16-2

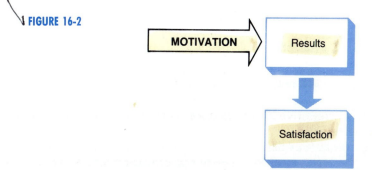

DIFFERENCES BETWEEN MOTIVATION AND SATISFACTION.
Motivation is the drive to satisfy a want (achieve an outcome); satisfaction is experienced when the outcome has been achieved.

fore in recent years, reward and punishment are still considered strong motivators. For centuries, however, they were too often thought of as the only forces that could motivate people. As the succeeding sections will explain, there are many other motivators.

At the same time, in all theories of motivation, the inducements of some kinds of "carrots" are recognized. Often the "carrot" is money in the form of pay or bonuses. Even though money is not the only motivating force, it has been and will continue to be an important one. The trouble with the money "carrot" approach is that too often everyone gets a carrot, regardless of performance, through such practices as salary increases and promotion by seniority, automatic "merit" increases, and executive bonuses not based on individual manager performance.

The "stick," in the form of fear—fear of loss of job, loss of income, reduction of bonus, demotion, or some other penalty—has been and continues to be a strong motivator. Yet it is admittedly not the best kind. It often gives rise to defensive or retaliatory behavior, such as union organization, poor-quality work, executive indifference, failure of a manager to take any risks in decision making, or even dishonesty. But fear of penalty cannot be overlooked. Whether managers are first-level supervisors or chief executives, the power of their position to give or withhold rewards or impose penalties of various kinds gives them an ability to control, to a very great extent, the economic and social well-being of their subordinates. It is hardly a wonder that many subordinates are "yes-sayers," simply agreeing with their superiors rather than using their considered judgment.

AN EARLY BEHAVIORAL MODEL: McGREGOR'S THEORY X AND THEORY Y

One view about the nature of people has been expressed in two sets of assumptions developed by Douglas McGregor and commonly known as "Theory X" and "Theory Y."[5] Managing, McGregor suggested, must start with the basic question of how managers see themselves in relation to others. This viewpoint requires some thought on the perception of human nature. Theory X and Theory Y are two sets of assumptions about the nature of people. McGregor chose these terms because he wanted neutral terminology without any connotation of being "good" or "bad."

Theory X Assumptions

The "traditional" assumptions about the nature of people, according to McGregor, are included in Theory X as follows:

1. Average human beings have an inherent dislike of work and will avoid it if they can.
2. Because of this human characteristic of disliking work, most people must be coerced, controlled, directed, and threatened with punishment to get them to put forth adequate effort toward the achievement of organizational objectives.
3. Average human beings prefer to be directed, wish to avoid responsibility, have relatively little ambition, and want security above all.

Theory Y Assumptions

The assumptions under Theory Y are seen by McGregor as follows:

1. The expenditure of physical effort and mental effort in work is as natural as play or rest.
2. External control and the threat of punishment are not the only means for producing effort toward organizational objectives. People will exercise self-direction and self-control in the service of objectives to which they are committed.
3. The degree of commitment to objectives is in proportion to the size of the rewards associated with their achievement.
4. Average human beings learn, under proper conditions, not only to accept responsibility but also to seek it.
5. The capacity to exercise a relatively high degree of imagination, ingenuity, and creativity in the solution of organizational problems is widely, not narrowly, distributed in the population.
6. Under the conditions of modern industrial life, the intellectual potentialities of the average human being are only partially utilized.

These two sets of assumptions obviously are fundamentally different. Theory X is pessimistic, static, and rigid. Control is primarily external, that is, imposed on the subordinate by the superior. In contrast, Theory Y is optimistic, dynamic, and flexible, with an emphasis on self-direction and the integration of individual needs with organizational demands. There is little doubt that each set of assumptions will affect the way managers carry out their managerial functions and activities.

Clarification of the Theories

McGregor was apparently concerned that Theory X and Theory Y might be misinterpreted.[6] The following points will clarify some of the areas of misunderstanding and keep the assumptions in proper perspective. First, Theory X and Theory Y assumptions are just that: They are assumptions only. They are not prescriptions or suggestions for managerial strategies. Rather, these assumptions must be tested against reality. Furthermore, these assumptions are intuitive deductions and are not based on research. Second, Theories X and Y do not imply "hard" or "soft" management. The "hard" approach may produce resistance and antagonism. The "soft" approach may result in laissez-faire management and is not congruent with Theory Y. The effective manager recognizes the dignity and capabilities, as well as the limitations, of people and adjusts behavior as demanded by the situation. Third, Theories X and Y are not to be viewed as being on a continuous scale, with X and Y on opposite extremes. They are not a matter of degree; rather, they are completely different views of people.

Fourth, the discussion of Theory Y is not a case for consensus management, nor is it an argument against the use of authority. Under Theory Y, authority is seen as only one of the many ways a manager exerts leadership. Fifth, different tasks and situations require a variety of approaches to management. At times, authority and structure may be effective for certain tasks, as found in the research by John J. Morse and Jay W. Lorsch.[7] They suggest that different approaches are effective in different situations. Thus, the productive enterprise is one that fits the task requirements to the people and the particular situation.

THE HIERARCHY OF NEEDS THEORY

One of the most widely mentioned theories of motivation is the hierarchy of needs theory put forth by psychologist Abraham Maslow.[8] Maslow saw human needs in the form of a hierarchy, ascending from the lowest to the highest, and he concluded that when one set of needs is satisfied, this kind of need ceases to be a motivator.

The Needs Hierarchy[9]

The basic human needs placed by Maslow in an ascending order of importance and shown in Figure 16-3 are these:

1. *Physiological needs.* These are the basic needs for sustaining human life itself, such as food, water, warmth, shelter, and sleep. Maslow took the position that until these needs are satisfied to the degree necessary to maintain life, other needs will not motivate people.
2. *Security, or safety, needs.* These are the needs to be free of physical danger and of the fear of losing a job, property, food, or shelter.
3. *Affiliation, or acceptance, needs.* Since people are social beings, they need to belong, to be accepted by others.
4. *Esteem needs.* According to Maslow, once people begin to satisfy their need to belong, they tend to want to be held in esteem both by themselves and by others. This kind of need produces such satisfactions as power, prestige, status, and self-confidence.
5. *Need for self-actualization.* Maslow regards this as the highest need in his hierarchy. It is the desire to become what one is capable of becoming—to maximize one's potential and to accomplish something.

Questioning the Needs Hierarchy

Maslow's concept of a hierarchy of needs has been subjected to considerable research. Edward Lawler and J. Lloyd Suttle collected data on 187 managers in two different organizations over a period of 6 to 12 months.[10] They found little evidence to support Maslow's theory that human needs form a hierarchy. They did note, however, that there were two levels of needs—biological and other needs—and that the other needs would emerge only when biological needs were reasonably satisfied. They found, further, that at the higher level, the strength of needs varied with the individual; in some individuals social needs predominated, while in others self-actualization needs were strongest.

In another study of Maslow's needs hierarchy involving a group of managers over a period of 5 years, Douglas T. Hall and Khalil Nougaim did not find strong evidence of a hierarchy.[11] They found that as managers advance in an organization,

FIGURE 16-3

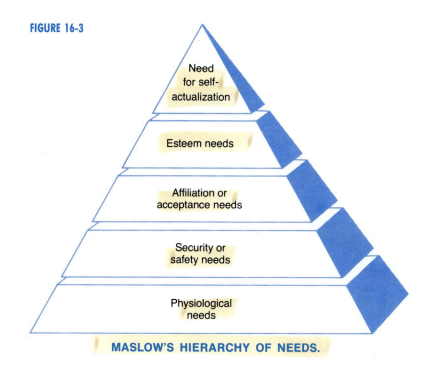

Need for self-actualization

Esteem needs

Affiliation or acceptance needs

Security or safety needs

Physiological needs

MASLOW'S HIERARCHY OF NEEDS.

their physiological and safety needs tend to decrease in importance, and their needs for affiliation, esteem, and self-actualization tend to increase. They insisted, however, that the upward movement of need prominence resulted from upward career changes and not from the satisfaction of lower-order needs.

THE MOTIVATION-HYGIENE APPROACH TO MOTIVATION

Maslow's needs approach has been considerably modified by Frederick Herzberg and his associates.[12] Their research purports to find a **two-factor theory** of motivation. In one group of needs are such things as company policy and administration, supervision, working conditions, interpersonal relations, salary, status, job security, and personal life. These were found by Herzberg and his associates to be only **dissatisfiers** and not motivators. In other words, if they exist in a work environment in high quantity and quality, they yield no dissatisfaction. Their existence does not motivate in the sense of yielding satisfaction; their lack of existence would, however, result in dissatisfaction. Herzberg called them *maintenance, hygiene,* or *job context factors.*

In the second group, Herzberg listed certain **satisfiers**—and therefore motivators—all related to *job content.* They include achievement, recognition, challenging work, advancement, and growth in the job. Their existence will yield feelings of satisfaction or no satisfaction (not dissatisfaction). As Figure 16-4 indicates, the satisfiers and dissatisfiers identified by Herzberg are similar to the factors suggested by Maslow.

FIGURE 16-4

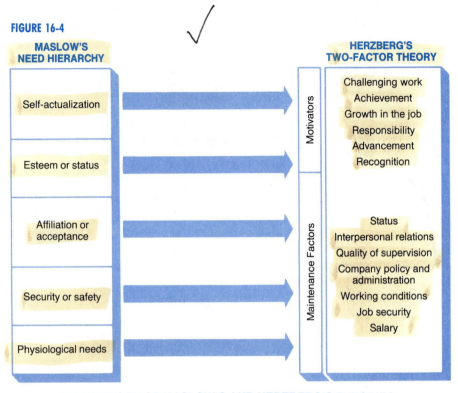

COMPARISON OF MASLOW'S AND HERZBERG'S THEORIES
OF MOTIVATION.

The first group of factors (the dissatisfiers) will not motivate people in an organization; yet they must be present, or dissatisfaction will arise. The second group, or the job content factors, Herzberg found to be the real motivators because they have the potential of yielding a sense of satisfaction. Clearly, if this theory of motivation is sound, managers must give considerable attention to upgrading job content.

The Herzberg research has not gone unchallenged.[13] Some researchers question Herzberg's methods, saying that his investigation methods tended to prejudice his results. For example, the well-known tendency of people to attribute good results to their own efforts and to blame others for poor results is thought to have prejudiced Herzberg's findings. Other researchers, not following his methods, have arrived at conclusions that do not support Herzberg's theory.

THE EXPECTANCY THEORY OF MOTIVATION

Another approach, one that many believe goes far in explaining how people are motivated, is the **expectancy theory.** One of the leaders in advancing and explaining this theory is the psychologist Victor H. Vroom. He holds that people will be motivated to do things to reach a goal if they believe in the worth of that goal and if they can see that what they do will help them in achieving it.[14] In a sense, this is a modern expression of what Martin Luther observed centuries ago when he said, "Everything that is done in the world is done in hope."

In greater detail, Vroom's theory is that people's motivation toward doing anything will be determined by the value they place on the outcome of their effort (whether positive or negative), multiplied by the confidence they have that their efforts will materially aid in achieving a goal. In other words, Vroom makes the point that motivation is a product of the anticipated worth that an individual places on a goal and the chances he or she sees of achieving that goal. In his own terms, Vroom's theory may be stated as

$$\text{Force} = \text{valence} \times \text{expectancy}$$

where **force** is the strength of a person's motivation, **valence** is the strength of an individual's preference for an outcome, and **expectancy** is the probability that a particular action will lead to a desired outcome. When a person is indifferent about achieving a certain goal, a valence of zero occurs; there is a negative valence when the person would rather not achieve the goal. The result of either would be, of course, no motivation. Likewise, a person would have no motivation to achieve a goal if the expectancy were zero or negative. The force exerted to do something will depend on *both* valence and expectancy. Moreover, a motive to accomplish some action might be determined by a desire to accomplish something else. For example, a person might be willing to work hard to get out a product for a valence in the form of pay. Or a manager might be willing to work hard to achieve company goals in marketing or production for a promotion or pay valence.

The Vroom Theory and Practice

One of the great attractions of the Vroom theory is that it recognizes the importance of various individual needs and motivations. It thus avoids some of the simplistic features of the Maslow and Herzberg approaches. It does seem more realistic. It fits the concept of harmony of objectives: Individuals have personal goals different from organization goals, but these can be harmonized. Furthermore, Vroom's theory is completely consistent with the system of managing by objectives.

The strength of Vroom's theory is also its weakness. His assumption that perceptions of value vary among individuals at different times and in various places appears to fit real life more accurately. It is consistent also with the idea that a manager's job is to *design* an environment for performance, necessarily taking into account the differences in various situations. On the other hand, Vroom's theory is difficult to apply in practice. Despite its difficulty in application, the logical accuracy of Vroom's theory indicates that motivation is much more complex than the approaches of Maslow and Herzberg seem to imply.

The Porter and Lawler Model

Lyman W. Porter and Edward E. Lawler III derived a substantially more complete model of motivation, built in large part on expectancy theory. In their study, they applied this model primarily to managers.[15] It is summarized in Figure 16-5.

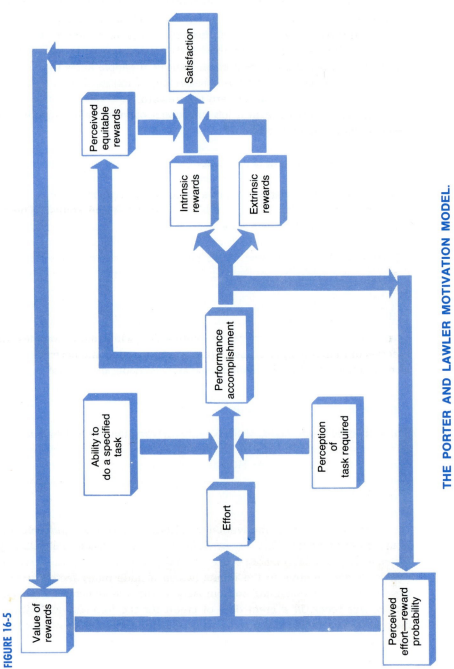

Adapted from L. W. Porter and E. E. Lawler, *Managerial Attitudes and Performance* (Homewood, Ill.: Richard D. Irwin, Inc., 1968), p. 165.

FIGURE 16-5

THE PORTER AND LAWLER MOTIVATION MODEL.

Value of rewards

Perceived effort—reward probability

Ability to do a specified task

Effort

Perception of task required

Performance accomplishment

Intrinsic rewards

Extrinsic rewards

Perceived equitable rewards

Satisfaction

As this model indicates, the amount of effort (the strength of motivation and energy exerted) depends on the value of a reward plus the amount of energy a person believes is required and the probability of receiving the reward. The perceived effort and probability of actually getting a reward are, in turn, influenced by the record of actual performance. Clearly, if people know they can do a job or if they have done it, they have a better appreciation of the effort required and know better the probability of getting a reward.

Actual performance in a job (the doing of tasks or the meeting of goals) is determined principally by effort expended. But it is also greatly influenced by an individual's ability (knowledge and skills) to do the job and by his or her perception of what the required task is (the extent to which the person understands the goals, required activities, and other elements of a task). Performance, in turn, is seen as leading to intrinsic rewards (such as a sense of accomplishment or self-actualization) and extrinsic rewards (such as working conditions and status). These rewards, tempered by what the individual sees as equitable, lead to satisfaction. But performance also influences sensed equitable rewards. Understandably, what the individual sees as a fair reward for effort will necessarily affect the satisfaction derived. Likewise, the actual value of rewards will be influenced by satisfaction.

Implications for Practice

The Porter and Lawler model of motivation, while more complex than other theories of motivation, is almost certainly a more adequate portrayal of the system of motivation. To the practicing manager, this model means that motivation is not a simple cause and effect matter. It means, too, that managers should carefully assess their reward structures and that through careful planning, managing by objectives, and clearly defining duties and responsibilities through a good organization structure, the effort-performance-reward-satisfaction system can be integrated into an entire system of managing.

EQUITY THEORY

An important factor in motivation is whether individuals perceive the reward structure as being fair. One way of addressing this issue is through **equity theory,** which refers to an individual's subjective judgments about the fairness of the reward she or he got, relative to the inputs (which include many factors, such as effort, experience, and education), in comparison with the rewards of others. J. Stacy Adams has received a great deal of credit for the formulation of the equity (or inequity) theory.[16] The essential aspects of the equity theory may be shown as follows:

$$\frac{\text{Outcomes by a person}}{\text{Inputs by a person}} = \frac{\text{outcomes by another person}}{\text{inputs by another person}}$$

There should be a balance of the outcomes/inputs relationship for one person in comparison with that for another person.

FIGURE 16-6

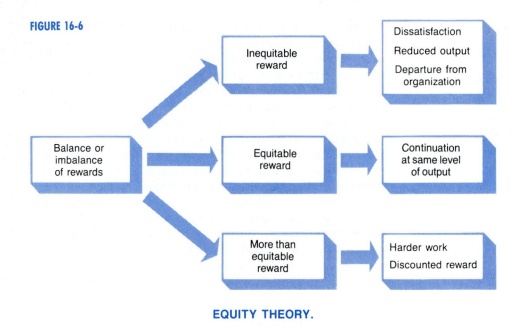

EQUITY THEORY.

If people feel that they are inequitably rewarded, they may be dissatisfied, reduce the quantity or quality of output, or leave the organization. If people perceive the rewards as equitable, they probably will continue at the same level of output. If people think the rewards are greater than what is considered equitable, they may work harder. It is also possible that some may discount the rewards. These three situations are illustrated in Figure 16-6.

One of the problems is that people may overestimate their own contributions and the rewards others receive. Certain inequities may be tolerated for some time by employees.[17] But prolonged feelings of inequity may result in strong reactions to an apparently minor occurrence. For example, an employee being reprimanded for being a few minutes late may get angry and decide to quit the job, not so much because of the reprimand but because of long-standing feelings that the rewards for his or her contributions are inequitable in comparison with others' rewards. Likewise, a person may be very satisfied with a weekly salary of $500 until he or she finds out that another person doing similar work gets $10 more.

REINFORCEMENT THEORY

The psychologist B. F. Skinner of Harvard developed an interesting—but controversial—technique for motivation. This approach, called **positive reinforcement** or **behavior modification,**[18] holds that individuals can be motivated by proper design of their work environment and praise for their performance and that punishment for poor performance produces negative results.

Skinner and his followers do far more than praise good performance. They analyze the work situation to determine what causes workers to act the way they do, and then they initiate changes to eliminate troublesome areas and obstructions to performance. Specific goals are then set with workers' participation and assistance, prompt and regular feedback of results is made available, and performance improvements are rewarded with recognition and praise. Even when performance does not equal goals, ways are found to help people and praise them for the good things they do. It has also been found highly useful and motivating to give people full information on a company's problems, especially those in which they are involved.

This technique sounds almost too simple to work, and many behavioral scientists and managers are skeptical about its effectiveness. However, a number of prominent companies have found the approach beneficial. Emery Air Freight Corporation, for example, observed that this approach saved the company a substantial amount of money by merely inducing employees to take great pains to ensure that containers were properly filled with small packages before shipment.[19]

Perhaps the strength of the Skinner approach is that it is so closely akin to the requirements of good managing. It emphasizes removal of obstructions to performance, careful planning and organizing, control through feedback, and the expansion of communication.

McCLELLAND'S NEEDS THEORY OF MOTIVATION

David C. McClelland has contributed to the understanding of motivation by identifying three types of basic motivating needs.[20] He classified them as the need for power (n/PWR), need for affiliation (n/AFF), and need for achievement (n/ACH). Considerable research has been done on methods of testing people with respect to these three types of needs, and McClelland and his associates have done substantial research, especially on the need for achievement.[21]

All three drives—power, affiliation, and achievement—are of particular relevance to management, since all must be recognized to make an organized enterprise work well.

Need for Power

McClelland and other researchers have found that people with a high need for power have a great concern for exercising influence and control.[22] Such individuals generally are seeking positions of leadership; they are frequently good conversationalists, though often argumentative; they are forceful, outspoken, hardheaded, and demanding; and they enjoy teaching and public speaking.

Need for Affiliation

People with a high need for affiliation usually derive pleasure from being loved and tend to avoid the pain of being rejected by a social group. As individuals, they are likely to be concerned with maintaining pleasant social relationships, to enjoy a sense of intimacy and understanding, to be ready to console and help others in trouble, and to enjoy friendly interaction with others.

Need for Achievement[23]

People with a high need for achievement have an intense desire for success and an equally intense fear of failure. They want to be challenged, and they set moderately difficult (but not impossible) goals for themselves. They take a realistic approach to risk; they are not likely to be gamblers but, rather, prefer to analyze and assess problems, assume personal responsibility for getting a job done, and like specific and prompt feedback on how they are doing. They tend to be restless, like to work long hours, do not worry unduly about failure if it does occur, and tend to like to run their own shows.

How McClelland's Approach Applies to Managers

In research studies by McClelland and others, entrepreneurs—people who start and develop a business or some other enterprise—showed very high need-for-achievement and fairly high need-for-power drives but were quite low in their need for affiliation. Managers generally showed high on achievement and power and low on affiliation, but not as high or low as entrepreneurs.

McClelland found the patterns of achievement motivation clearest in people in small companies, with the president normally having very high achievement motivation. In large companies, what is quite interesting is that he found chief executives to be only average in achievement motivation and often stronger in drives for power and affiliation. Managers in the upper-middle level of management in such companies rated higher than their presidents in achievement motivation. Perhaps, as McClelland indicated, these scores are understandable. The chief executive has "arrived," and those below are striving to advance.

The question is often raised as to whether all managers should rate high on achievement motivation. People who do rate high tend to advance faster than those who do not. But because so much of managing requires other characteristics besides achievement drive, every company should probably have many managers who, while possessing fairly strong achievement motivation, also have a high need for affiliation. This latter need is important for working with people and for coordinating the efforts of individuals working in groups.

SPECIAL MOTIVATIONAL TECHNIQUES

After looking at the theories of motivation, one may well ask what they mean to managers. What motivational techniques can managers use? While motivation is so complex and individualized that there can be no single best answer, some of the major motivational techniques can be identified.

Money

As mentioned earlier, in the discussion of the carrot and the stick, money can never be overlooked as a motivator. Whether in the form of wages, piecework (getting paid for units produced at a certain quality level) or any other incentive pay, bonuses, stock options, company-paid insurance, or any of the other things that may be given to people for performance, money is important. And, as some writers have pointed out, money is often more than monetary value. It can also mean status or power.

Economists and most managers have tended to place money high on the scale of motivators,[24] while behavioral scientists tend to place it low. Probably neither view is right.[25] But if money is to be the kind of motivator that it can and should be, managers must remember several things.

First, money, as money, is likely to be more important to people who are raising a family, for example, than to people who have "arrived" in the sense that their money needs are not so urgent. Money is an urgent means of achieving a minimum standard of living, although this minimum has a way of getting higher as people become more affluent. For example, an individual who was once satisfied with a small house and a low-priced car may now be able to derive the same satisfaction only from a large and comfortable house and a fairly luxurious automobile. And yet it is impossible to generalize in even these terms. For some people money will always be of the utmost importance, while for others it may never be.

The lure of money and power can lead to inappropriate and illegal actions. Ivan F. Boesky was accused of insider trading that resulted in huge personal profits—and a $100 million fine. The scandal, one of the worst on Wall Street since the 1920s, shook public confidence with the fear that stock trading may be rigged.[26] Money is often used for motivating, but it also addresses itself to human greed, which dulls the conscience and may lead to unethical and illegal behavior.

Second, it is probably quite true that in most kinds of businesses and other enterprises, money is used as a means of keeping an organization adequately staffed and not primarily as a motivator. Various enterprises make wages and salaries competitive within their industry and their geographic area to attract and hold people.

Third, money as a motivator tends to be dulled somewhat by the practice of making sure that salaries of various managers in a company are reasonably similar. In other words, organizations often take great care to ensure that people on comparable levels are given the same, or nearly the same, compensation. This is understandable, since people usually evaluate their compensation in light of what their equals are receiving.

Fourth, if money is to be an effective motivator, people in various positions, even though at a similar level, must be given salaries and bonuses that reflect their individual performance. Even if a company is committed to the practice of comparable wages and salaries, a well-managed firm need never be bound to the same practice with respect to bonuses. In fact, it appears that unless bonuses for managers are based to a major extent on individual performance, an enterprise is not buying much motivation with them. The way to ensure that money has meaning, as a reward for accomplishment and as a means of giving people pleasure from accomplishment, is to base compensation as much as possible on performance.

It is almost certainly true that money can motivate only when the prospective payment is large relative to a person's income. The trouble with many wage and salary increases, and even bonus payments, is that they are not large enough to motivate the receiver. They may keep the individual from being dissatisfied and from looking for another job, but unless they are large enough to be felt, they are not likely to be a strong motivator.[27]

Participation

One technique that has been given strong support as a result of motivation theory and research is the increased awareness and use of participation. Only rarely are people not motivated by being consulted on action affecting them—by being "in on the act." In addition, most people in the center of an operation have knowledge both of problems and of solutions to them. As a consequence, the right kind of participation yields both motivation and knowledge valuable for enterprise success.

Participation is also a means of recognition. It appeals to the need for affiliation and acceptance. Above all, it gives people a sense of accomplishment. But encouraging participation should not mean that managers weaken their positions. Although they encourage participation of subordinates on matters with which the latter can help, and although they listen carefully, on matters *requiring their decision* they must decide themselves.

Quality of Working Life (QWL)

One of the most interesting approaches to motivation is the **quality of working life** (QWL) program, which is a systems approach to job design and a promising development in the broad area of job enrichment, combined with a grounding in the sociotechnical systems approach to management (see Table 2-2 in Chapter 2). QWL is not only a very broad approach to job enrichment but also an interdisciplinary field of inquiry and action combining industrial and organization psychology and sociology, industrial engineering, organization theory and development, motivation and leadership theory, and industrial relations. Although QWL rose to prominence only in the 1970s, there are now hundreds of case studies and practical programs and a number of QWL centers, primarily in the United States, Great Britain, and Scandinavia.[28]

QWL has received enthusiastic support from a number of sources. Managers have regarded it as a promising means of dealing with stagnating productivity, especially in the United States and Europe. Workers and union representatives have also seen it as a means of improving working conditions and productivity and as a means of justifying higher pay. Government agencies have been attracted to QWL as a means of increasing productivity and reducing inflation and as a way of obtaining industrial democracy and minimizing labor disputes.

Perspective

QWL in Action

In the development of a QWL program, certain steps are normally undertaken. Usually, a labor-management steering committee is set up, ordinarily with a QWL specialist or staff, which is charged with finding ways of enhancing the dignity, attractiveness, and productivity of jobs through job enrichment and redesign. The participation of workers and their unions (if an operation is unionized) in the effort is thought to be very important, not only because of the exercise of industrial democracy but also because of the great practical advantage it offers: People on a job are the ones who are best able to identify what would enrich the job for them and make it possible for them to be more productive. This typical QWL technique tends to solve the problem encountered in many job enrichment cases in which workers have mistakenly not been asked what would make the job more interesting for them.

Out of the deliberations of this committee, a number of changes may be suggested in the design of jobs and in the entire working environment. The recommendations of the committee may extend to such matters as reorganization of the organization structure, means of improving communication, problems that may never have surfaced before and their solutions, changes in work arrangements through technical modifications such as the redesign of an assembly line, better quality control, and other things that might improve organization health and productivity.

It is no wonder that QWL, with such possible important yields, has been spreading fast, especially in larger companies. Nor is it a surprise that leaders in adopting QWL programs should be such well-managed companies as General Motors, Procter & Gamble, American Aluminum (ALCOA), and AT&T.

JOB ENRICHMENT

Research on and analysis of motivation point to the importance of making jobs challenging and meaningful. This applies to the jobs of managers as well as to those of nonmanagers. Job enrichment is related to Herzberg's theory of motivation, in which factors such as challenge, achievement recognition, and responsibility are seen as the real motivators. Even though his theory has not gone unchallenged, it has led to a widespread interest, both in the United States and overseas, in developing ways to enrich job content, particularly for nonmanagerial employees.

Job enrichment should be distinguished from job enlargement (but some authors do not make this distinction). **Job enlargement** attempts to make a job more varied by removing the dullness associated with performing repetitive operations. It means enlarging the scope of the job by adding similar tasks without enhancing responsibility. For example, a production line worker may install not only the bumper on a car but also the front hood. Critics would say that this is simply adding one dull job to another, since it does not increase the worker's responsibility. In **job enrichment,** the attempt is to build into jobs a higher sense of challenge and achievement. Jobs may be enriched by variety. But they also may be enriched by (1) giving workers more freedom in deciding about such things as work methods, sequence, and pace or the acceptance or rejection of materials; (2) encouraging participation of subordinates and interaction between workers; (3) giving workers a feeling of personal responsibility for their tasks; (4) taking steps to make sure that workers can see how their tasks contribute to a finished product and the welfare of the enterprise; (5) giving people feedback on their job performance, preferably before their supervisors get it; and (6) involving workers in the analysis and change of physical aspects of the work environment, such as the layout of the office or plant, temperature, lighting, and cleanliness.

The Claims of Job Enrichment

A number of companies have introduced programs of job enrichment. The first company to do so on a fairly large scale was Texas Instruments, and other companies, such as AT&T, Procter & Gamble, and General Foods, have had considerable experience with it. In all these companies, claims have been made that productivity was increased, that absenteeism and turnover were reduced, and that morale improved.

Perhaps the most glowing claims for job enrichment are contained in the 1973 report of a study made by the U.S. Department of Health, Education, and Welfare.[29] As the result of an analysis of worker attitudes and the quality of working life, this study concluded that (1) the primary cause of dissatisfaction of workers is the nature of their work—the quality of their working life—and (2) blue-collar workers will work harder if their jobs are enriched and expanded so as to give them greater control over their work and more freedom from their supervisor.

Limitations of Job Enrichment

Even the strongest supports of job enrichment readily admit that there are limitations in its application.[30] One of these is technology. With specialized machinery and assembly line techniques, it may not be possible to make all jobs very meaningful. Another limitation is cost. General Motors tried six-person and three-person teams in the assembly of motor homes but found that this approach was too difficult, slow, and costly. On the other hand, two Swedish auto manufacturers, Saab and Volvo, have used the team approach and have found costs to be only slightly higher, and they believe that this increase was more than offset by reductions in absenteeism and turnover.

There is also some question as to whether workers really want job enrichment, especially of the kind that changes the basic content of their jobs. Various surveys of worker attitudes, even the attitudes of assembly line workers, have shown that a high percentage of workers are not dissatisfied with their jobs and that few want "more interesting" jobs. What these workers seem to want above all is job security and pay. Moreover, workers are concerned that changing the nature of tasks to increase productivity may mean a loss of jobs.

The limitations of job enrichment apply mainly to jobs requiring low skill levels. The jobs of highly skilled workers, professionals, and managers already contain varying degrees of challenge and accomplishment. Perhaps these could be enriched considerably more than they are. But this can probably be done best by modern management techniques such as managing by objectives, utilizing more policy guidance with delegation of authority, introducing more status symbols in the form of titles and office facilities, and tying bonuses and other rewards more closely to performance.

Problems with Job Enrichment

On the surface, job enrichment as a response to motivating factors is an attractive idea, but it apparently has not worked as well as anticipated. There do seem to be a number of problems in the way it has been approached.

One of the major problems appears to be the tendency of top managers and personnel specialists to apply their own scale of values for challenge and accomplishment to other people's personalities. Some people are challenged by jobs that would appear dull to many others. In one company, an employee who had spent his life doing no more than keeping daily records of orders received honestly felt he had one of the most important jobs in the company. In another business, a woman who had had a job-enriched position with a variety of tasks told her supervisor that she was greatly relieved to be freed of such responsibility when she was given a repetitive assembly line job. Similarly, a woman who was found to have considerable leadership ability in her outside activities with the Girl Scouts and Parent-Teacher Association turned down a supervisory position because her present job allowed her to think about the problems and programs she was interested in outside the company.

Another difficulty is that job enrichment is usually imposed on people; they are told about it, rather than being asked whether they would like it and how their jobs could be made more interesting. This appeared to be, at least in part, the problem General Motors encountered in enlarging the jobs of assembly line workers at the Vega plant in Lordstown, where workers interpreted the attempts to make jobs more varied and meaningful as only a scheme of the company to get them to work harder. One should never overlook the importance of consultation, of getting people involved.

Also, there has been little or no support of job enrichment by union leaders. If job enrichment were so important to workers, it would probably be translated into union demands, a move that apparently has seldom occurred.

Making Job Enrichment Effective

Several approaches can be used to make job enrichment appeal to higher-level motivations. First, organizations need a better understanding of what people want. As a number of motivation researchers have pointed out, wants vary with people and situations. Research has shown that workers with few skills want such factors as job security, pay, benefits, less restrictive plant rules, and more sympathetic and understanding supervisors. As people move up the ladder in an enterprise, they find that other factors become increasingly important. But little job enrichment research has been done on high-level professionals and managers.

Second, if productivity increases are the main goal of enrichment, the program must show how workers will benefit. For example, in one company with fleets of unsupervised two-person service trucks, a program of giving these employees 25 percent of the cost savings from increased productivity, while still making it clear that the company would profit from their efforts, resulted in a startling rise in output and a much greater interest in these jobs.

Third, people like to be involved, to be consulted, and to be given an opportunity to offer suggestions. They like to be considered as people. In one aerospace missile plant, increased morale and productivity, as well as greatly reduced turnover and absenteeism, resulted from the simple technique of having all employees' names on placards at their workstations and of having each program group—from parts production and assembly to inspection—work in an area in which machines and equipment were painted a different color.

Fourth, people like to feel that their managers are truly concerned with their welfare. Workers like to know what they are doing and why. They like feedback on their performance. They like to be appreciated and recognized for their work.

A SYSTEMS AND CONTINGENCY APPROACH TO MOTIVATION

The foregoing analysis of theory, research, and application demonstrates that motivation must be considered from a systems and contingency point of view. Given the complexity of motivating people with individual personalities and in different situations, risks of failure exist when any single motivator, or group of motivators, is applied without taking into account these variables. Human behavior is not a simple matter but must be looked upon as a system of variables and interactions of which certain motivating factors are an important element.

Dependence of Motivation on Organizational Climate

Motivating factors definitely do not exist in a vacuum. Even individual desires and drives are conditioned by physiological needs or by needs arising from a person's background. But what people are willing to strive for is also affected by the organizational climate in which they operate. At times a climate may curve motivations; at other times it may arouse them.

Motivation, Leadership, and Managership

The interaction of motivation and organizational climate not only underscores the systems aspects of motivation but also emphasizes how motivation both depends on and influences leadership styles and management practice. Leaders and managers (who, if effective, will almost certainly be leaders) must respond to the motivations of individuals if they are to design an environment in which people will perform willingly.[31] Likewise, they can design a climate that will arouse or reduce motivation. Styles of leadership will be discussed in Chapter 17.

As for the ways and means by which managers design an environment for performance, they are really the subject of this entire book. In short, managers do this when they see that verifiable goals are set, strategies are developed and communicated, and plans to achieve objectives are made. They do it also in designing a system of organizational roles in which people can be effective. (It should be pointed out in this connection that "organization structure" is not used here in the restrictive bureaucratic sense.) Managers do it also when they make sure that the structure is well staffed. Their styles of leadership and their ability to solve communication problems are also central to managing. And managers do much to create an effective environment when they make sure that control tools, information, and approaches furnish people with the feedback knowledge they must have for effective motivation.

SUMMARY

Leading is the process of influencing people so that they will contribute to organization and group goals. People assume different roles, and there is no average person. While working toward goals, a manager must take into account the dignity of the whole person.

Motivation is not a simple concept; instead, motivation pertains to various drives, desires, needs, wishes, and other forces. Managers motivate by providing an environment that induces organization members to contribute. The need-want-satisfaction chain is somewhat oversimplified. Indeed, motives are often conflicting.

There are different views and assumptions about human nature. McGregor called his sets of assumptions about people Theory X and Theory Y. Maslow's theory holds that human needs form a hierarchy ranging from the lowest-order needs (physiological needs) to the highest-order need (the need for self-actualization). According to Herzberg's two-factor theory, there are two sets of motivating factors. In one set are the dissatisfiers, which are related to the job context (circumstances, conditions). The absence of these factors results in dissatisfaction. In the other set are the satisfiers, or motivators, which are related to the content of the job.

Vroom's expectancy theory of motivation suggests that people are motivated to reach a goal if they think that the goal is worthwhile and can see that their activities will help them achieve the goal. The Porter and Lawler model has many variables. Essentially, performance is a function of ability, the perception of the task required, and effort. Effort is influenced by the value of rewards and the perceived effort-reward probability. Performance accomplishment, in turn, is related to rewards and satisfaction.

Equity theory refers to an individual's subjective judgment about the fairness of the reward received for inputs in comparison with the rewards of others. Reinforcement theory was developed by Skinner, who suggested that people are motivated by praise of desirable behavior; people should participate in setting their goals and should receive regular feedback with recognition and praise. McClelland's theory is based on the need for power, the need for affiliation, and the need for achievement.

Special motivational techniques include using money, encouraging participation, and improving the quality of working life (QWL). Job enrichment aims at making jobs challenging and meaningful. Although there have been some successes, certain limitations must not be overlooked.

The complexity of motivation requires a contingency approach that takes into account the environmental factors, including the organizational climate.

KEY IDEAS AND CONCEPTS FOR REVIEW

Leading	Vroom's expectancy theory
Human factors in managing	Porter and Lawler's motivation model
Individual dignity	Equity theory
Motivation	Positive reinforcement
Need-want-satisfaction chain	Behavior modification
Motivators	McClelland's needs theory
McGregor's Theory X and Theory Y assumptions	Quality of working life (QWL)
	Job enrichment
Maslow's needs hierarchy	Organizational climate and motivation
Herzberg's motivation-hygiene approach	

FOR DISCUSSION

1. What is motivation? How does effective managing take advantage of, and contribute to, motivation?
2. Why is the need-want-satisfaction chain too simplified an explanation of motivation?
3. What are Theory X and Theory Y assumptions? State your reasons for agreeing or disagreeing with these assumptions. What are some misunderstandings of Theories X and Y?
4. Why has the Maslow theory of needs been criticized? To what extent, if any, is it valid?
5. Compare and contrast the Maslow and Herzberg theories of motivation. On what grounds has the Herzberg theory been criticized? Why would you suspect that Herzberg's approach has been so popular with practicing managers?
6. Explain Vroom's expectancy theory of motivation. How is it different from the Porter and Lawler approach? Which appeals to you as being more accurate? Which is more useful in practice?
7. Explain McClelland's theory of motivation. How does it fit into a systems approach? What does the impact of organizational climate show?
8. "You cannot motivate managers. They are self-propelled. You just get out of their way if you really want performance." Comment.
9. To what extent, and how, is money an effective motivator?
10. What motivates you in striving toward excellence in your work at school? Are these motivating forces shown in any of the models discussed in this chapter?

EXERCISES/ACTION STEPS

1. The instructor may take a survey in the class and ask the students to respond to two questions: (1) "Can you describe in detail when you felt exceptionally good about your

job?" and (2) "Can you describe in detail when you felt exceptionally bad about your job?" Students should write their answers on a sheet of paper. Then each individual should be encouraged to share his or her good and bad work experiences with the class. The instructor can classify these responses according to Herzberg's two-factor theory and point out the weakness in this research design.
2. Collect information on an organization you know, and identify the reasons why people contribute to the goals of the enterprise.

CASES

CASE 16-1
MANAGING THE HEWLETT-PACKARD WAY[32]

William R. Hewlett and David Packard, two organizational leaders who demonstrated a unique managerial style, began their operation with $538 in 1939, in a one-car garage. Eventually they built a very successful company that now produces more than 10,000 products, such as computers, peripheral equipment, test and measuring instruments, and handheld calculators. Perhaps even better known than its products is the distinct managerial style preached and practiced at Hewlett-Packard (HP). It is known as the HP Way.

The values of the founders—who withdrew from active management in 1978—still permeate the organization. The HP Way emphasizes honesty, a strong belief in the value of people, and customer satisfaction. The managerial style also emphasizes an open-door policy, which promotes team effort. Informality in personal relationships is illustrated by the use of first names. Management by objectives is sup-

plemented by what is known as managing by wandering around. By strolling through the organization, top managers keep in touch with what is really going on in the company.

This informal organizational climate does not mean that the organization structure has not changed. Indeed, the organizational changes in the 1980s in response to environmental changes were quite painful. However, these changes resulted in extraordinary company growth during the 1980s.

1. Is the Hewlett-Packard way of managing creating a climate in which employees are motivated to contribute to the aims of the organization? What is unique about the HP Way?
2. Would the HP managerial style work in any organization? Why, or why not? What are the conditions for such a style to work?

INTERNATIONAL CASE 16-2
THE HUMAN FACTOR AT OLIVETTI IN ITALY[33]

Olivetti had an excellent reputation as a typewriter company. Adjusting to new technology, it has become an office equipment company and a systems networking services firm. It is one of the oldest Italian companies, with a history dating back to the early 1900s.

From the early period until 1960, the company was known for being progressive with good economic

results. On the other hand, the time between 1960 and the latter part of the 1970s was marked by some economic decline. In 1978, Carlo De Benedetti took leadership of the company, and the result was an initial success. But later, the firm encountered problems such as slow growth.

The personal values of the leadership have

played an important role in the operation of the company. Camillo Olivetti, who started his firm in 1908, was quite involved in social activities; in fact, he was a member of the Italian Socialist party. Adriano Olivetti, the son of Camillo Olivetti, saw the firm as a mover of a "new" society and as a center for a new social structure. Under his leadership, the company was characterized by innovative, social ideals. For example, Olivetti was a leader in Italy of efforts to reduce working hours. Also, organizational titles were de-emphasized, if not abolished. Leadership based on social principles was quite uncommon in Italy at that time. Employees identified themselves very closely with the company. When Adriano Olivetti died in 1960, the company was deprived of a strong leader.

In 1978, however, Carlo De Benedetti started another era. Although De Benedetti made many changes, they were congruent with the social ideals of the founders. For example, he introduced flexible working hours, with a great deal of freedom given to the work force. He also promoted the entrepreneurial spirit of the employees.

Olivetti has had very good relations with the unions. In the late 1980s and early 1990s, Olivetti underwent radical organization changes that required a reduction in the work force. The layoffs were arranged with the cooperation of the unions. Indeed, the 1990s will have major challenges for Olivetti.

1. What impact did Olivetti's CEOs have on the human organization?
2. How could Olivetti obtain union cooperation in laying off employees?
3. Would you like to work for a company like Olivetti? Why, or why not?

REFERENCES

1. Curtis W. Cook, "Guidelines for Managing Motivation," in Max D. Richards (ed.), *Readings in Management,* 6th ed. (Cincinnati: South-Western Publishing Company, 1982), p. 373.
2. This is also one of the important messages in the *Second Draft—Pastoral Letter on Catholic Social Teaching and the U.S. Economy* (Oct. 7, 1985). The letter *Economic Justice for All: Catholic Social Teaching and the U.S. Economy* was approved in November 1986.
3. John A. Byrne, Wendy Zellner, and Scott Ticer, "Caught in the Middle—Six Managers Speak Out on Corporate Life," *Business Week* (Sept. 12, 1988), pp. 80–88; Peter Nulty, "How Managers Will Manage," *Fortune* (Feb. 2, 1987), pp. 47–50.
4. Most of the recommendations are based on *The George Odiorne Letter* (Nov. 8, 1985).
5. Douglas McGregor, *The Human Side of Enterprise* (New York: McGraw-Hill Book Company, 1960).
6. Harold M. F. Rush, *Behavioral Science—Concepts and Management Application* (New York: National Industrial Conference Board, 1969), pp. 13–16; Douglas McGregor, *The Professional Manager* (New York: McGraw-Hill Book Company, 1969), chap. 5.
7. John J. Morse and Jay W. Lorsch, "Beyond Theory Y," *Harvard Business Review* (May–June 1970), pp. 61–68.
8. Abraham Maslow, *Motivation and Personality* (New York: Harper & Row, 1954).
9. A variation of Maslow's hierarchy of needs theory of motivation has been suggested by Clayton P. Alderfer, which he refers to as the ERG (existence, relatedness, and growth) theory of needs. See his *Existence, Relatedness, and Growth: Human Needs in Organizational Settings* (New York: The Free Press, 1972).
10. Edward Lawler III and J. Lloyd Suttle, "A Causal Correlation Test of the Need-Hierarchy Concept," *Organizational Behavior and Human Performance* (April 1972), pp. 265–287.
11. Douglas T. Hall and Khalil Nougaim, "An Examination of Maslow's Hierarchy in an Organization Setting," *Organizational Behavior and Human Performance* (February

1968), pp. 12–35. For an additional evaluation of the need-hierarchy theory, see John B. Miner, *Theories of Organizational Behavior* (Hinsdale, Ill.: The Dryden Press, 1980), chap. 2.

12. Frederick Herzberg, Bernard Mausner, Robert A. Peterson, and D. Capwell, *Job Attitudes: Review of Research and Opinion* (Pittsburgh: Psychological Services of Pittsburgh, 1957); Frederick Herzberg, Bernard Mausner, and Barbara B. Snyderman, *The Motivation to Work* (New York: John Wiley & Sons, 1959).

13. See, for example, H. Randolph Bobbitt and O. Behling, "Defense Mechanism as an Alternate Explanation of Herzberg's Motivator—Hygiene Results," *Journal of Applied Psychology* (January 1972), pp. 24–27; D. A. Ondrack, "Defense Mechanism and the Herzberg Theory: An Alternate Test," *Academy of Management Journal* (March 1974), pp. 79–89; Edwin A. Locke and Roman J. Whiting, "Sources of Satisfaction and Dissatisfaction among Solid Waste Management Employees," *Journal of Applied Psychology* (April 1974), pp. 145–156.

14. Victor H. Vroom, *Work and Motivation* (New York: John Wiley & Sons, 1964). See also David A. Nadler and Edward E. Lawler III, "Motivation: A Diagnostic Approach," in J. Richard Hackman, Edward E. Lawler III, and Lyman W. Porter (eds.), *Perspectives on Behavior in Organizations*, 2d ed. (New York: McGraw-Hill Book Company, 1983), pp. 67–87.

15. Lyman W. Porter and Edward E. Lawler III, *Managerial Attitudes and Performance* (Homewood, Ill.: Richard D. Irwin, 1968); also Cynthia M. Pavett, "Evaluation of the Impact of Feedback on Performance and Motivation," *Human Relations* (July 1983), pp. 641–654.

16. J. Stacy Adams, "Toward an Understanding of Inequity," *Journal of Abnormal and Social Psychology*, vol. 67 (1963), pp. 422–436; J. Stacy Adams, "Inequity in Social Exchange," in L. Berkowitz (ed.), *Advances in Experimental Social Psychology* (New York: Academy Press, 1965), pp. 267–299.

17. Richard A. Cosier and Dan R. Dalton, "Equity Theory and Time: A Reformulation," *Academy of Management Review* (April 1983), pp. 311–319. See also Richard C. Huseman, John D. Hatfield, and Edward W. Miles, "A New Perspective on Equity Theory: The Equity Sensitivity Construct," *Academy of Management Review* (April 1987), pp. 222–234.

18. Fred Luthans and Robert Kreitner, *Organizational Behavior Modification and Beyond: An Operant and Social Learning Approach* (Glenview, Ill.: Scott, Foresman and Company, 1984).

19. For an extensive discussion of the benefits of behavior modification, see W. Clay Hamner and Ellen P. Hamner, "Behavior Modification on the Bottom Line," in J. Richard Hackman et al., *Perspectives on Behavior* (1983), pp. 310–324.

20. David C. McClelland, *The Achievement Motive* (New York: Appleton-Century-Crofts, 1953), *Studies in Motivation* (New York: Appleton-Century-Crofts, 1955), and *The Achieving Society* (Princeton, N.J.: Van Nostrand Company, 1961). See also his "Achievement Motivation Can Be Developed," *Harvard Business Review* (January–February 1965), pp. 6–24, 178, and (with David G. Winter) *Motivating Economic Achievement* (New York: The Free Press, 1969).

21. For a thorough evaluation of the theory, see John B. Miner, *Theories of Organizational Behavior* (1980), chap. 3.

22. See, for example, David C. McClelland and David H. Burnham, "Power Is the Great Motivator," *Harvard Business Review* (March–April 1976), pp. 100–110.

23. David C. McClelland, "That Urge to Achieve," in Max D. Richards (ed.), *Readings in Management*, 7th ed. (Cincinnati: South-Western Publishing Company, 1986), pp. 367–375.

24. See Aaron Bernstein and Michael A. Pollock, "Executive Pay: Who Made the Most," *Business Week* (May 5, 1985), pp. 78–103.

25. George S. Odiorne, "When Money Has Lost Its Motivational Power, What Else Can You Use to Motivate Your People?" *The George Odiorne Letter* (Mar. 21, 1986), pp. 1–3.

26. William B. Glaberson, Jeffrey M. Laderman, Christopher Power, and Vicky Cahan, "Who'll Be the Next to Fall?" *Business Week* (Dec. 1, 1986), pp. 28–30; Chris Welles and Gary Weiss, "A Man Who Made a Career of Tempting Fate," *Business Week* (Dec. 1, 1986), pp. 34–35.

27. For a discussion of a compensation plan, see Jay R. Schuster, "Compensation Plan Design," *Management Review* (May 1985), pp. 21–25. Also, more recently, employee ownership has become more common; see J. C. Louis, "Employee Ownership: The Rising Tide," *Management Review* (March 1985), pp. 40–43.

28. For a pioneering work in this field, see Louis E. Davis and Albert B. Cherns, *Quality of Working Life* (New York: The Free Press, 1975). Among the more prominent QWL centers are the Tavistock Institute in Great Britain, under Eric L. Trist; the center at the University of California, Los Angeles, under Louis E. Davis; and the Institute for Social Research in Industry in Trondheim, Norway, under M. Elder.

29. DHEW, *Work in America* (Washington: Government Printing Office, 1973). See also Antone Alber, "Job Enrichment for Profit," *Human Resource Management* (Spring 1979), pp. 15–25.

30. The appropriateness of job enrichment depends on the situation. The need for balancing internal and external factors has been pointed out by Randall B. Dunham, Jon L. Pierce, and John W. Newstrom, "Job Context and Job Content: A Conceptual Perspective," *Journal of Management* (Fall–Winter 1983), pp. 187–202.

31. Abraham Zaleznik makes a distinction between managers and leaders, but the difference is primarily in the way he describes managers (a rather negative way), which certainly is not our view of an effective manager. See Abraham Zaleznik, "Managers and Leaders: Are They Different?" *Harvard Business Review* (May–June 1986), p. 48.

32. Information has been gathered from several sources, including Walter Guzzardi, Jr., "The U.S. Business Hall of Fame, *Fortune* (Mar. 14, 1988), pp. 142–144; *HP Annual Report, 1987*; Jonathan B. Levine, "Mild-Mannered Hewlett-Packard Is Making like Superman," *Business Week* (Mar. 7, 1988), pp. 110–114; Michael A. Verespej, "Where People Come First," *Industry Week* (July 16, 1990), pp. 22–32.

33. Information has been obtained from a variety of sources, including *Olivetti Group, Annual Reports 1988, 1989;* M. Molteni, "Ing. C. Olivetti & Co.," *Economia Aziendale Corso Progredito Universita* (Milano: Luigi Bocconi, 1983).

Chapter 17

Leadership

Chapter Objectives

After reading this chapter, you should be able to:

1. Define leadership and identify its ingredients.
2. Describe the trait approaches to leadership and recognize their limitations.
3. Discuss various leadership styles based on the use of authority.
4. Explain Likert's four systems of management.
5. Identify the two dimensions of Blake and Mouton's managerial grid and the resulting extreme leadership styles.
6. Recognize that leadership can be seen as a continuum.
7. Explain the contingency approach to leadership.
8. Describe the path-goal approach to leadership effectiveness.

Although some people treat the terms "managership" and "leadership" as synonyms, the two should be distinguished. As a matter of fact, there can be leaders of completely unorganized groups, but there can be managers, as conceived here, only where organized structures create roles. Separating leadership from managership has important analytical advantages. It permits leadership to be singled out for study without the encumbrance of qualifications relating to the more general issue of managership.

Leadership is an important aspect of managing.[2] As this chapter will show, the ability to lead effectively is one of the keys to being an effective manager; also, undertaking the other essentials of managing—doing the entire managerial job—has an important bearing on ensuring that a manager will be an effective leader. Managers must exercise all the functions of their role in order to combine human and material resources to achieve objectives. The key to doing this is the existence of a clear role and a degree of discretion or authority to support managers' actions.

The essence of leadership is followership.[3] In other words, it is the willingness of people to follow that makes a person a leader. Moreover, people tend to follow those whom they see as providing a means of achieving their own desires, wants, and needs.

Leadership and motivation are closely interconnected. By understanding motivation, one can appreciate better what people want and why they act as they do. Also, as noted in the previous chapter, leaders may not only respond to subordinates' motivations but also arouse or dampen them by means of the organizational climate they develop. Both these factors are as important to leadership as they are to managership.

DEFINING LEADERSHIP

Leadership has different meanings to various authors.[4] In this book, **leadership** is defined as influence, that is, the art or process of influencing people so that they will strive willingly and enthusiastically toward the achievement of group goals.

Ideally, people should be encouraged to develop not only willingness to work but also willingness to work with zeal and confidence. Zeal is ardor, earnestness, and intensity in the execution of work; confidence reflects experience and technical ability. Leaders act to help a group attain objectives through the maximum application of its capabilities. They do not stand behind a group to push and prod; they place themselves before the group as they facilitate progress and inspire the group to accomplish organizational goals. A good example is an orchestra leader, whose function is to produce coordinated sound and correct tempo through the integrated effort of the musicians.[5] Depending on the quality of the director's leadership, the orchestra will respond.

Perspective

Leadership at Southwest Airlines[6]

Let us consider the leadership style of Herbert Kelleher, the chairman of Southwest Airlines. He attempts to create a family feeling among his employees by remembering their names and personally sending out birthday cards. In an attempt to stay competitive in the deregulated airline industry, he asked for, and received, considerable concessions from employees and their union. His hands-on leadership style won him the respect and followership of his employees. The austerity measures apply equally to management and employees. His office, for example, is in a barracks-style building. Leading by example those who follow him, he seems concerned about both the tasks to be done and the people who work for him. His leadership style is also congruent with the airline's policy of providing friendly service and keeping costs low.

INGREDIENTS OF LEADERSHIP

Leaders envision the future; they inspire organization members and chart the course of the organization. Chrysler's Lee Iacocca and General Electric's Jack Welch have provided a vision for their companies. Leaders must instill values—whether they be concern for quality, honesty, and calculated risk taking or concern for employees and customers.[7]

Every group of people that performs near its total capacity has some person as its head who is skilled in the art of leadership. This skill seems to be a compound of at least four major ingredients: (1) the ability to use power effectively and in a responsible manner, (2) the ability to comprehend that human beings have different motivation forces at different times and in different situations, (3) the ability to inspire, and (4) the ability to act in a manner that will develop a climate conducive to responding to and arousing motivations.

The first ingredient of leadership is power. The nature of power and the differences between power and authority were discussed in Chapter 11.

The second ingredient of leadership is a fundamental understanding of people. As in all other practices, it is one thing to know motivation theory, kinds of motivating forces, and the nature of a system of motivation but another thing to be able to apply this knowledge to people and situations. A manager or any other leader who at least knows the present state of motivation theory and who understands the elements of motivation is more aware of the nature and strength of human needs and is better able to define and design ways of satisfying them and to administer so as to get the desired responses.

The third ingredient of leadership is the rare ability to inspire followers to apply their full capabilities to a project. While the use of motivators seems to center on subordinates and their needs, inspiration also comes from group heads. They may have qualities of charm and appeal that give rise to loyalty, devotion, and a strong desire on the part of followers to promote what leaders want. This is not a matter of need satisfaction; it is, rather, a matter of people giving unselfish support to a chosen champion. The best examples of inspirational leadership come from hopeless and frightening situations: an unprepared nation on the eve of battle, a prison camp with exceptional morale, or a defeated leader undeserted by faithful followers. Some may argue that such devotion is not entirely unselfish, that it is in the interests of those who face catastrophe to follow a person they trust. But few would deny the value of personal appeal in either case.

The fourth ingredient of leadership has to do with the style of the leader and the climate he or she develops. As Chapter 16 has shown, the strength of motivation greatly depends on expectancies, perceived rewards, the amount of effort believed to be required, the task to be done, and other factors that are part of an environment, as well as an organizational climate. Awareness of these factors has led to considerable research on leadership behavior and to the development of various pertinent theories. The views of those who have long approached leadership as a psychological study of interpersonal relationships have tended to converge with the personal viewpoint expressed in this book, that is, that the primary tasks of managers are the design and maintenance of an environment for performance.

Almost every role in an organized enterprise is made more satisfying for participants and more productive for the enterprise by those who can help others fulfill their desire for such things as money, status, power, and pride of accomplishment. The fundamental **principle of leadership** is this: *Since people tend to follow those who, in their view, offer them a means of satisfying their own personal goals, the more managers understand what motivates their subordinates and how these motivations operate, and the more they reflect this understanding in carrying out their managerial actions, the more effective they are likely to be as leaders.*

Perspective

Can Leadership Be Taught?

A frequently raised question is whether leadership can be taught. Professor Noel Tichy of the University of Michigan estimates that 80 percent of leadership growth derives from experience on the job, whereas 20 percent can be acquired through training and study.[8] This, of course, is difficult to prove and depends on the individual, but it points out that on-the-job training and classroom training must go hand in hand. At an early stage in their careers, potential leaders at Johnson & Johnson are given the opportunity to demonstrate their ability to manage one of the company's rather autonomous business units. The idea behind this practice is that a tough assignment can be an opportunity for learning and development.

Because of the importance of leadership in all kinds of group action, there is a considerable volume of theory and research concerning it.[9] It is difficult to summarize such a large body of research in a form relevant to day-to-day management. However, examined below are several major types of leadership theory and research, together with outlines of some basic kinds of leadership styles.

TRAIT APPROACHES TO LEADERSHIP

Prior to 1949, studies of leadership were based largely on an attempt to identify the traits that leaders possess.[10] Starting with the "great man" theory that leaders are born and not made, a belief dating back to the ancient Greeks and Romans, researchers have tried to identify the physical, mental, and personality traits of various leaders. The "great man" theory lost much of its acceptability with the rise of the behaviorist school of psychology.

Many studies of traits have been made.[11] Ralph M. Stogdill found that various researchers have identified specific traits related to leadership ability: five physical traits (such as energy, appearance, and height), four intelligence and ability traits, sixteen personality traits (such as adaptability, aggressiveness, enthusiasm, and self-confidence), six task-related characteristics (such as achievement drive, persistence, and initiative), and nine social characteristics (such as cooperativeness, interpersonal skills, and administrative ability).[12]

The discussion of the importance of traits to leadership goes on; more recently, the following key leadership traits were identified: drive (including achievement, motivation, energy, ambition, initiative, and tenacity), leadership motivation (the aspiration to lead but not to seek power as such), honesty and integrity, self-confidence (including emotional stability), cognitive ability, and an understanding of the business. Less clear is the impact of creativity, flexibility, and charisma on leadership effectiveness.[13]

In general, the study of leaders' traits has not been a very fruitful approach to explaining leadership. Not all leaders possess all the traits, and many nonleaders may possess most or all of them. Also, the trait approach gives no guidance as to *how much* of any trait a person should have. Furthermore, the dozens of studies that have been made do not agree as to which traits are leadership traits or what their relationships are to actual instances of leadership. Most of these so-called traits are really patterns of behavior.

A new era began in 1987 when former Soviet leader Mikhail Gorbachev initiated the policies of *glasnost,* which provided openness and opportunities for critics, and *perestroika,* which promoted a restructuring of the economy. He probably initiated more changes in the latter part of the 1980s than any other person.

In order to understand the person, it is necessary to look at his background and discover how he came to power and what kinds of leadership traits he possessed. Gorbachev came from the southern farming region. Those who know him describe him as incorruptible, with a dislike for Stalinism. In a sense, he was an "outsider" who was very effective in networking, which began at Moscow University and continued throughout his political life. His eager-to-please style helped him to make contacts with powerful people. It has been reported that he read Dale Carnegie's American best-seller *How to Win Friends and Influence People* to improve his style. His dealings with people may have helped him to overcome failures such as his farm policies, which worked in one area but were very unsuccessful in other regions.

Whether the changes in the former Soviet Union were the sole result of Mikhail Gorbachev's leadership style or due to the changing world order is hard to say. It may be simply that he was the right person for this particular time.

LEADERSHIP BEHAVIOR AND STYLES

There are several theories on leadership behavior and styles. This section focuses on (1) leadership based on the use of authority, (2) Likert's four systems of management, (3) the managerial grid, and (4) leadership involving a variety of styles, ranging from a maximum to a minimum use of power and influence.

Styles Based on Use of Authority

Some earlier explanations of leadership styles classified them on the basis of how leaders use their authority. Leaders were seen as applying three basic styles. The **autocratic** leader commands and expects compliance, is dogmatic and positive, and leads by the ability to withhold or give rewards and punishment. The **democratic,** or **participative,** leader consults with subordinates on proposed actions and decisions and encourages participation from them. This type of leader ranges from the person who does not take action without subordinates' concurrence to the one who makes decisions but consults with subordinates before doing so.

The **free-rein** leader uses his or her power very little, if at all, giving subordinates a high degree of independence in their operations. Such leaders depend largely on subordinates to set their own goals and the means of achieving them, and they see their role as one of aiding the operations of followers by furnishing them with information and acting primarily as a contact with the group's external environment. Figure 17-1 illustrates the flow of influence in the three leadership situations.

There are variations within this simple classification of leadership styles. Some autocratic leaders are seen as "benevolent autocrats." Although they listen considerately to their followers' opinions before making a decision, the decision is their own. They may be willing to hear and consider subordinates' ideas and concerns, but when a decision is to be made, they may be more autocratic than benevolent.

A variation of the participative leader is the person who is supportive. Leaders in this category may look upon their task as not only consulting with followers and carefully considering their opinions but also doing all they can to support subordinates in accomplishing their duties.

The use of any style will depend on the situation. A manager may be highly autocratic in an emergency; one can hardly imagine a fire chief holding a long meeting with the crew to consider the best way of fighting a fire. Managers may also be autocratic when they alone have the answers to certain questions.

A leader may gain considerable knowledge and a better commitment on the part of persons involved by consulting with subordinates. As already noted, this is true in developing verifiable objectives under systems of managing by objectives. Furthermore, a manager dealing with a group of research scientists may give them free rein in developing their inquiries and experiments. But the same manager might be quite autocratic in enforcing a rule stipulating that employees wear a protective covering when handling certain potentially dangerous chemicals.

Perspective

Do Women Lead Differently?

Women as managers may use a different leadership style than men. One study found that women see leadership as changing the self-interest of followers into concern for the total enterprise by using interpersonal skills and personal traits to motivate subordinates.[15] This "interactive leadership" style involves sharing information and power, inspiring participation, and letting people know that they are important. Men, in contrast, are more likely to see leadership as a sequence of transactions with their subordinates. Moreover, they more often use control of resources and the authority of their position to motivate their people. This does not mean that all successful women and men use the respective leadership styles. Certainly, some men use "interactive leadership" in guiding their subordinates, and some women use the traditional command structure in directing their followers.

Likert's Four Systems of Management

Professor Rensis Likert and his associates at the University of Michigan have studied the patterns and styles of leaders and managers for three decades.[16] In the

FIGURE 17-1

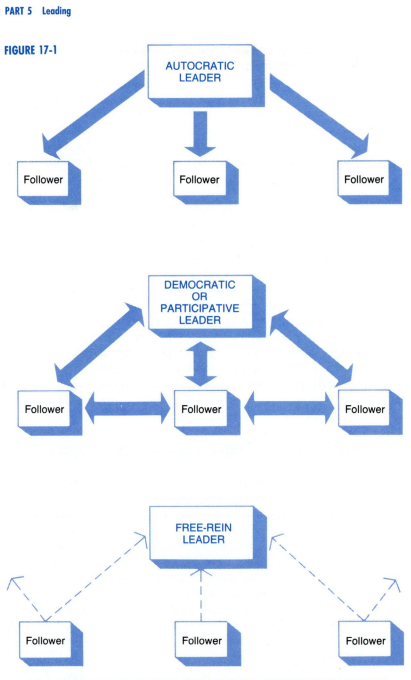

THE FLOW OF INFLUENCE WITH THREE LEADERSHIP STYLES.

course of this research, Likert has developed certain ideas and approaches important to understanding leadership behavior. He sees an effective manager as strongly oriented to subordinates, relying on communication to keep all parties working as a unit. All members of the group, including the manager or leader, adopt a supportive attitude in which they share in one another's common needs, values, aspirations, goals, and expectations. Since it appeals to human motivations, Likert views this approach as the most effective way to lead a group.

As guidelines for research and for the clarification of his concepts, Likert has suggested four systems of management. **System 1** management is described as "exploitive-authoritative"; its managers are highly autocratic, have little trust in subordinates, motivate people through fear and punishment and only occasional rewards, engage in downward communication, and limit decision making to the top. **System 2** management is called "benevolent-authoritative"; its managers have a patronizing confidence and trust in subordinates, motivate with rewards and some fear and punishment, permit some upward communication, solicit some ideas and opinions from subordinates, and allow some delegation of decision making but with close policy control.

System 3 management is referred to as "consultative." Managers in this system have substantial but not complete confidence and trust in subordinates, usually try to make use of subordinates' ideas and opinions, use rewards for motivation with occasional punishment and some participation, engage in communication flow both down and up, make broad policy and general decisions at the top while allowing specific decisions to be made at lower levels, and act consultatively in other ways.

Likert saw **System 4** management as the most participative of all and referred to it as "participative-group." System 4 managers have complete trust and confidence in subordinates in all matters; they always get ideas and opinions from subordinates and constructively use them. They also give economic rewards on the basis of group participation and involvement in such areas as setting goals and appraising progress toward goals. They engage in much communication down and up and with peers, encourage decision making throughout the organization, and operate among themselves and with their subordinates as a group.

In general, Likert found that those managers who applied the System 4 approach to their operations had the greatest success as leaders. Moreover, he noted that departments and companies managed by the System 4 approach were most effective in setting goals and achieving them and were generally more productive. He ascribed this success mainly to the degree of participation and the extent to which the practice of supporting subordinates was maintained.

Figure 17-2 shows the profile of a new manager in a General Motors assembly plant. The organization operated previously in System 3 but moved toward System 4. This manager, aided by the survey feedback improvement approach, used the data of the profile to focus on those areas that needed improvement.

Although there is considerable support for System 4 theory, the approach is not without its critics.[17] The research focus of this theory is on small groups, yet the discussion is frequently extrapolated and applied to the total organization.

FIGURE 17-2

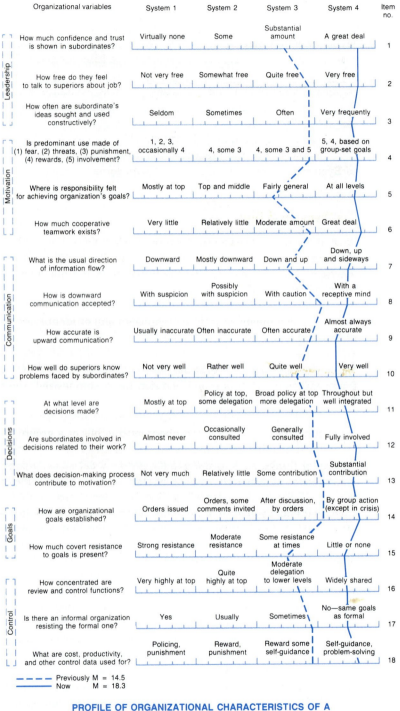

PROFILE OF ORGANIZATIONAL CHARACTERISTICS OF A
NEW PLANT MANAGER AT A GENERAL MOTORS PLANT.

R. Likert and J. G. Likert, *New Ways of Managing Conflict* (New York: McGraw-Hill Book Company, 1976), p. 75. Used with permission.

Furthermore, the research has primarily been conducted at lower organizational levels and may not be supported when data from top-level managers are separated.[18] Likert and his associates realize the need for clarity in role definitions, but at the same time they suggest, for example, matrix departmentation, which usually increases role conflict and uncertainty. Since System 4 is often introduced when companies are profitable, the results attributed to the survey feedback method may actually be due to the general prosperity of the firm. It appears, then, that those evaluating System 4 theory should take careful account of the surrounding circumstances. For the practicing manager this means that the benefits attributed to System 4 theory must be viewed with some caution.

The Managerial Grid

A well-known approach to defining leadership styles is the **managerial grid,** developed some years ago by Robert Blake and Jane Mouton.[19] Building on previous research that showed the importance of a manager's having concern both for production and for people, Blake and Mouton devised a clever device to dramatize this concern. This grid, shown in Figure 17-3, has been used throughout the world as a means of training managers and of identifying various combinations of leadership styles.

The grid dimensions.   The grid has two dimensions: concern for people and concern for production. As Blake and Mouton have emphasized, their use of the phrase "concern for" is meant to convey "how" managers are concerned about production or "how" they are concerned about people, and not such things as "how much" production they are concerned about getting out of a group.

"Concern for production" includes the attitudes of a supervisor toward a wide variety of things, such as the quality of policy decisions, procedures and processes, creativeness of research, quality of staff services, work efficiency, and volume of output. "Concern for people" is likewise interpreted in a broad way. It includes such elements as degree of personal commitment toward goal achievement, maintenance of the self-esteem of workers, placement of responsibility on the basis of trust rather than obedience, provision of good working conditions, and maintenance of satisfying interpersonal relations.

The four extreme styles.   Blake and Mouton recognize four extremes of style. Under the **1.1** style (referred to as "impoverished management"), managers concern themselves very little with either people or production and have minimum involvement in their jobs; to all intents and purposes, they have abandoned their jobs and only mark time or act as messengers communicating information from superiors to subordinates. At the other extreme are the **9.9** managers, who display in their actions the highest possible dedication both to people and to production. They are the real "team managers" who are able to mesh the production needs of the enterprise with the needs of individuals.

FIGURE 17-3

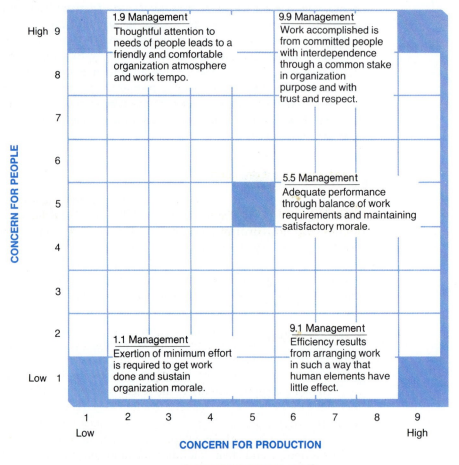

CONCERN FOR PEOPLE

High 9 — 1.9 Management
Thoughtful attention to needs of people leads to a friendly and comfortable organization atmosphere and work tempo.

9.9 Management
Work accomplished is from committed people with interdependence through a common stake in organization purpose and with trust and respect.

5.5 Management
Adequate performance through balance of work requirements and maintaining satisfactory morale.

1.1 Management
Exertion of minimum effort is required to get work done and sustain organization morale.

9.1 Management
Efficiency results from arranging work in such a way that human elements have little effect.

Low 1

1   2   3   4   5   6   7   8   9
Low   High

CONCERN FOR PRODUCTION

THE MANAGERIAL GRID.

Adapted from R. R. Blake and J. S. Mouton, *The Managerial Grid* (Houston, Tex.: Gulf Publishing Company, 1964), p. 10.

Another style is **1.9** management (called "country club management" by some), in which managers have little or no concern for production but are concerned only for people. They promote an environment in which everyone is relaxed, friendly, and happy and no one is concerned about putting forth coordinated effort to accomplish enterprise goals. At another extreme are the **9.1** managers (sometimes referred to as "autocratic task managers"), who are concerned only with developing an efficient operation, who have little or no concern for people, and who are quite autocratic in their style of leadership.

By using these four extremes as points of reference, every managerial technique, approach, or style can be placed somewhere on the grid. Clearly, **5.5** managers have medium concern for production and for people. They obtain adequate, but not outstanding, morale and production. They do not set goals too high, and they are likely to have a rather benevolently autocratic attitude toward people.

The managerial grid is a useful device for identifying and classifying managerial styles, but it does not tell us *why* a manager falls into one part or another of the grid. To determine the reason, one has to look at underlying causes, such as the personality characteristics of the leader or the followers, the ability and training of managers, the enterprise environment, and other situational factors that influence how leaders and followers act.

Leadership as a Continuum

The adaptation of leadership styles to different contingencies has been well characterized by Robert Tannenbaum and Warren H. Schmidt, developers of the **leadership continuum** concept.[20] As Figure 17-4 shows, they see leadership as involving a variety of styles, ranging from one that is highly boss-centered to one that is highly subordinate-centered. The styles vary with the degree of freedom a leader or manager grants to subordinates. Thus, instead of suggesting a choice between the two styles of leadership—authoritarian or democratic—this approach offers a range of styles, with no suggestion that one is always right and another is always wrong.

The continuum theory recognizes that which style of leadership is appropriate depends on the *leader,* the *followers,* and the *situation.* To Tannenbaum and Schmidt, the most important elements that may influence a manager's style can be seen along a continuum as (1) the forces operating in the manager's personality, including his or her value system, confidence in subordinates, inclination toward leadership styles, and feelings of security in uncertain situations; (2) the forces in subordinates (such as their willingness to assume responsibility, their knowledge and experience, and their tolerance for ambiguity) that will affect the manager's behavior; and (3) the forces in the situation, such as organization values and traditions, the effectiveness of subordinates working as a unit, the nature of a problem and the feasibility of safely delegating the authority to handle it, and the pressure of time.

In reviewing their continuum model in 1973 (it was first formulated in 1958), Tannenbaum and Schmidt placed circles around the model, as shown in Figure 17-4, to represent the influences on style imposed by both the organizational environment and the societal environment.[21] This was done to emphasize the open-system nature of leadership styles and the various impacts of the organizational environment and of the social environment outside an enterprise. In their 1973 commentary, they put increased stress on the interdependency of leadership style and environmental forces—such as labor unions, greater pressures for social responsibility, the civil rights movement, and the ecology and consumer movements—that challenge the rights of managers to make decisions or handle their subordinates without considering interests outside the organization.

FIGURE 17-4

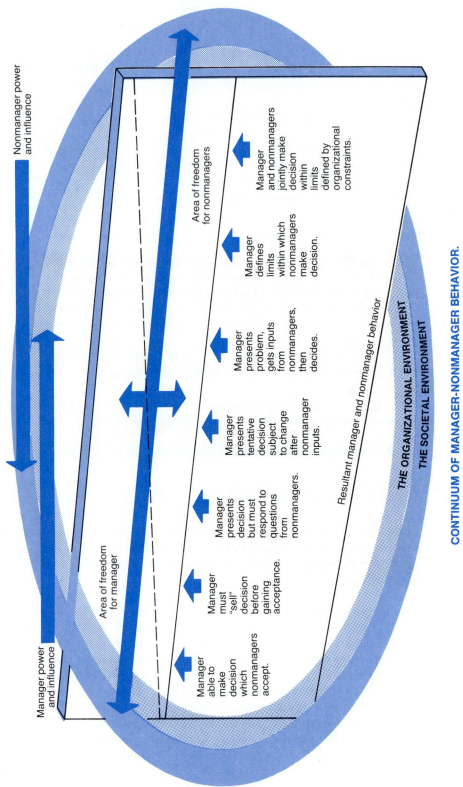

CONTINUUM OF MANAGER-NONMANAGER BEHAVIOR.

Used with permission from R. Tannenbaum and W. H. Schmidt, "Retrospective Commentary" on "How to Choose a Leadership Pattern," *Harvard Business Review*, vol. 51, no. 3 (May–June 1973), p. 167.

International Perspective

Leadership at Italian ITALTEL

In 1981, when Marisa Bellisario became director and CEO of ITALTEL, a state-owned telecommunication equipment manufacturer in Italy, the company was in trouble: high losses, large debts, insufficient research and development, and an overstaffed, unionized organization.[22] Ms. Bellisario took some major steps to turn the company around and to improve productivity. Here are some examples of the new direction:

- Restructuring the organization into business units
- Reducing the number of employees by more than one-third between 1980 and 1985, which was accomplished through open communication and cooperation with the union
- Leading the company into electronics, which required retraining of employees
- Developing a program to upgrade low-skilled women in the work force
- Pushing for intra-European cooperation with companies in France, England, and what was then West Germany
- Improving efficiency through innovation in products and manufacturing processes

Leadership such as this has to be analyzed in terms of the characteristics of the leader (technical, human, conceptual, and design skills); good relations with the followers, especially the unionized work force; and the situation, which in the early 1980s demanded a strong leader to deal with the crisis.

SITUATIONAL, OR CONTINGENCY, APPROACHES TO LEADERSHIP

As disillusionment with the "great man" and trait approaches to understanding leadership increased, attention turned to the study of situations and the belief that leaders are the product of given situations. A large number of studies have been made on the premise that leadership is strongly affected by the situation from which the leader emerges and in which he or she operates. That this is a persuasive approach is indicated by the rise of Hitler in Germany in the 1930s, the earlier rise of Mussolini in Italy, the emergence of Franklin Delano Roosevelt in the Great Depression of the 1930s in the United States, and the rise of Mao Tse-tung in China in the period after World War II. This approach to leadership recognizes that there exists an interaction between the group and the leader. It supports the follower theory that people tend to follow those whom they perceive (accurately or inaccurately) as offering them a means of accomplishing their own personal desires. The leader, then, is the person who recognizes these desires and does those things, or undertakes those programs, designed to meet them.

Situational, or contingency, approaches obviously have much meaning for managerial theory and practice. They also tie into the system of motivation discussed in Chapter 16, and they are important for practicing managers, who must consider the situation when they design an environment for performance.

Fiedler's Contingency Approach to Leadership

Although their approach to leadership theory is primarily one of analyzing leadership style, Fred E. Fiedler and his associates at the University of Illinois have suggested a **contingency theory of leadership.**[23] The theory holds that people become leaders not only because of the attributes of their personalities but also because of various situational factors and the interactions between leaders and group members.

Critical dimensions of the leadership situation.

On the basis of his studies, Fiedler described *three critical dimensions* of the leadership situation that help determine what style of leadership will be most effective:

1. *Position power.* This is the degree to which the power of a position, as distinguished from other sources of power, such as personality or expertise, enables a leader to get group members to comply with directions; in the case of managers, this is the power arising from organizational authority. As Fiedler points out, a leader with clear and considerable position power can obtain good followership more easily than one without such power.
2. *Task structure.* With this dimension, Fiedler had in mind the extent to which tasks can be clearly spelled out and people held responsible for them. If tasks are clear (rather than vague and unstructured), the quality of performance can be more easily controlled and group members can be held more definitely responsible for performance.
3. *Leader-member relations.* Fiedler regarded this dimension as the most important from a leader's point of view, since position power and task structure may be largely under the control of an enterprise. It has to do with the extent to which group members like, trust, and are willing to follow a leader.

Leadership styles.

To approach his study, Fiedler set forth two major styles of leadership. One of these is primarily task-oriented; that is, the leader gains satisfaction from seeing tasks performed. The other is oriented primarily toward achieving good interpersonal relations and attaining a position of personal prominence.

Favorableness of situation was defined by Fiedler as the degree to which a given situation enables a leader to exert influence over a group. To measure leadership styles and determine whether a leader is chiefly task-oriented, Fiedler used an unusual testing technique. He based his findings on two sources: (1) scores on the *least preferred coworker* (LPC) scale—these are ratings made by people in a group as to those with whom they would least like to work; and (2) scores on the *assumed similarity between opposites* (ASO) scale—ratings based on the degree to which leaders see group members as being like themselves, on the assumption that people will like best, and work best with, those who are seen as most like themselves. Today the LPC scale is most commonly used in research. In developing this scale, Fiedler asked respondents to identify the traits of a person with whom they could work least well.[24] Respondents described the person by rating sixteen items on a scale of attributes, such as the following:

Pleasant : _____ : _____ : _____ : _____ | _____ : _____ : _____ : _____ : Unpleasant

Rejecting : _____ : _____ : _____ : _____ | _____ : _____ : _____ : _____ : Accepting

On the basis of his studies with this method, as well as studies done by others, Fiedler found that people who rated their coworkers high (that is, in favorable terms) were those who derived major satisfaction from successful interpersonal relationships. People who rated their "least preferred coworker" low (that is, in unfavorable terms) were seen as deriving their major satisfaction from task performance.

From his research, Fiedler came to some interesting conclusions. Recognizing that personal perceptions may be unclear and even quite inaccurate, Fiedler nonetheless found the following to be true:

> Leadership performance depends as much on the organization as it depends on the leader's own attributes. Except perhaps for the unusual case, it is simply not meaningful to speak of an effective leader or an ineffective leader; we can only speak of a leader who tends to be effective in one situation and ineffective in another. If we wish to increase organizational and group effectiveness we must learn not only how to train leaders more effectively but also how to build an organizational environment in which the leader can perform well.[25]

Fiedler's contingency model of leadership is presented as a graph in Figure 17-5. This figure is really a summary of Fiedler's research, in which he found that in "unfavorable" or "favorable" situations the task-oriented leader would be the most effective. In other words, when leader position power is weak, the task structure is unclear, and leader-member relations are moderately poor, the situation is unfavorable for the leader and the most effective leader will be one who is task-oriented. (Each dot in the graph represents findings from a research study; see the lower right-hand corner for the task-oriented leader.) At the other extreme, in which position power is strong, the task structure is clear, and leader-member relations are good—a favorable situation for the leader—Fiedler found that the task-oriented leader will also be most effective. However, if the situation is only moderately unfavorable or favorable (the middle of the scale in the figure), the human relations–oriented leader will be most effective.

In a highly structured situation, such as in the military during a war, where the leader has strong position power and good relations with members, there is a favorable situation in which task orientation is most appropriate. The other extreme, an unfavorable situation with moderately poor relations, an unstructured task, and weak position power, also suggests task orientation by the leader, who may reduce anxiety or ambiguity that could be created by the loosely structured situation. Between the two extremes (the middle of the scale in Figure 17-5), the suggested approach emphasizes cooperation and good relations with people.

FIGURE 17-5

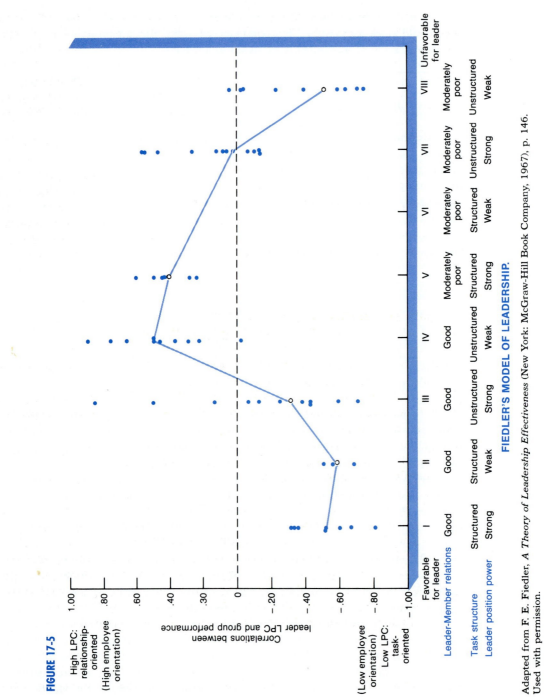

FIEDLER'S MODEL OF LEADERSHIP.

Adapted from **F. E. Fiedler,** *A Theory of Leadership Effectiveness* (New York: McGraw-Hill Book Company, 1967), p. 146. Used with permission.

Fiedler's research and management.   In reviewing Fiedler's research, one finds that there is nothing automatic or "good" in either the task-oriented or the people-satisfaction-oriented style. Leadership effectiveness depends on the various elements in the group environment. This might be expected. Cast in the desired role of leaders, managers who apply knowledge to the realities of the group reporting to them will do well to recognize that they are practicing an art. But in doing so, they will necessarily take into account the motivations to which people will respond and their ability to satisfy them in the interest of attaining enterprise goals.

Several scholars have put Fiedler's theory to the test in various situations. Some have questioned the meaning of the LPC score, and others suggest that the model does not explain the causal effect of the LPC score on performance. Some of the findings are not statistically significant, and situational measures may not be completely independent of the LPC score.

Despite such criticism, it is important to recognize that effective leadership style depends on the situation. Although this idea may not be new, Fiedler and his colleagues drew attention to this fact and stimulated a great deal of research.

The Path-Goal Approach to Leadership Effectiveness

The **path-goal theory** suggests that the main function of the leader is to clarify and set goals with subordinates, help them find the best path for achieving the goals, and remove obstacles. Proponents of this approach have studied leadership in a variety of situations.[26] As stated by Robert House, the theory builds on various motivational and leadership theories of others.[27]

In addition to the expectancy theory variables, other factors contributing to effective leadership should be considered. These situational factors include (1) characteristics of subordinates, such as their needs, self-confidence, and abilities; and (2) the work environment, including such components as the task, the reward system, and the relationship with coworkers (see Figure 17-6).

Leader behavior is categorized into four groups:

1. *Supportive leadership* behavior gives consideration to the needs of subordinates, shows a concern for their well-being, and creates a pleasant organizational climate. It has the greatest impact on subordinates' performance when they are frustrated and dissatisfied.
2. *Participative leadership* allows subordinates to influence the decisions of their superiors and can result in increased motivation.
3. *Instrumental leadership* gives subordinates rather specific guidance and clarifies what is expected of them; this includes aspects of planning, organizing, coordinating, and controlling by the leader.
4. *Achievement-oriented leadership* involves setting challenging goals, seeking improvement of performance, and having confidence that subordinates will achieve high goals.

Rather than suggesting that there is one best way to lead, this theory suggests that the appropriate style depends on the situation. Ambiguous and uncertain

FIGURE 17-6

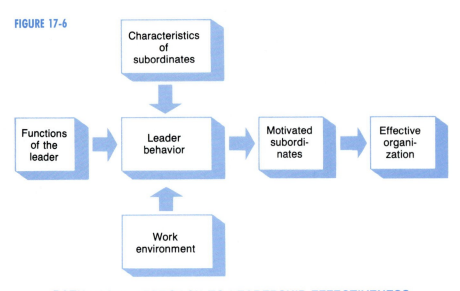

PATH–GOAL APPROACH TO LEADERSHIP EFFECTIVENESS.

situations can be frustrating for subordinates, and a more task-oriented style may be called for. In other words, when subordinates are confused, then the leader may tell them what to do and show them a clear path to goals. On the other hand, for routine tasks, such as those found on the assembly line, additional structure (usually provided by a task-oriented leader) may be considered redundant; subordinates may see such efforts as overcontrolling, which, in turn, may be dissatisfying. To put it differently, employees want the leader to stay out of their way because the path is already clear enough.

The theory proposes that the behavior of the leader is acceptable and satisfies subordinates to the extent that they see it as a source for their satisfaction. Another proposition of the theory is that the behavior of the leader increases the effort of subordinates, that is, it is motivating, insofar as (1) this behavior makes satisfaction of the needs of subordinates dependent on effective performance and (2) the behavior enhances the subordinates' environment through coaching, directing, supporting, and rewarding.

The key to the theory is that the leader influences the paths between behavior and goals. The leader can do this by defining positions and task roles, by removing obstacles to performance, by enlisting the assistance of group members in setting goals, by promoting group cohesiveness and team effort, by increasing opportunities for personal satisfaction in work performance, by reducing stresses and external controls, by making expectations clear, and by doing other things that meet people's expectations.

The path-goal theory makes a great deal of sense to the practicing manager. At the same time, one must realize that the model needs further testing before the approach can be used as a definite guide for managerial action.

SUMMARY

Leadership is the art or process of influencing people so that they contribute willingly and enthusiastically toward group goals. Leadership requires followership. There are various approaches to the study of leadership, ranging from the trait to the contingency approach. One such approach focuses on three styles: the autocratic; the democratic, or participative; and the free-rein. Likert identified four systems of management, ranging from System 1 (exploitive-authoritative) through System 4 (participative-group), which he considers the most effective system.

The managerial grid identifies two dimensions: concern for production and concern for people. On the basis of these dimensions, four extreme styles and a "middle-of-the-road" style are identified. Leadership can also be viewed as a continuum. At one extreme of the continuum, the manager has a great deal of freedom, while subordinates have very little. At the other extreme, the manager has very little freedom, whereas subordinates have a great deal.

Still another approach to leadership, built on the assumption that leaders are the product of given situations, focuses on the study of situations. Fiedler's contingency approach takes into account the position power of the leader, the structure of the task, and the relations between the leader and group members. The conclusion is that there is no one best leadership style and that managers can be successful if placed in appropriate situations. The path-goal approach to leadership suggests that the most effective leaders help subordinates achieve enterprise and personal goals.

KEY IDEAS AND CONCEPTS FOR REVIEW

Leadership
Ingredients of leadership
Leadership traits
Leadership styles based on the use of
    authority
Likert's four systems of management

Managerial grid
Leadership as a continuum
Situational approach to leadership
Fiedler's contingency theory
Path-goal approach to leadership

FOR DISCUSSION

1. What do you see as the essence of leadership?
2. How are leadership theory and styles related to motivation?
3. Why has the trait approach as a means of explaining leadership been so open to question?
4. Can you see why the managerial grid has been so popular as a training device?
5. Select a business or political leader you admire, and identify his or her style of leading by applying the managerial grid or the continuum-of-behavior model of Tannenbaum and Schmidt.

6. What is Fiedler's theory of leadership? Applying it to cases of leaders you have known, do you perceive it as being accurate?
7. What are the advantages and limitations of the path-goal approach to leadership?
8. If you were selected to be the group leader for a class project (e.g., to make a case study of a particular company), which leadership style or what behavior would you use? Why?

EXERCISES/ACTION STEPS

1. Analyze a situation in which you were the leader. Which leadership approach discussed in this chapter helps explain why you were a leader?
2. Analyze a case in this book by using the group approach. Specifically, the class should be divided into groups of about five students. Each group should select a spokesperson, who will present the analysis of the case to the class. For each group, one observer (this person should not be a participant in the case discussion) should describe the interactions in the group. Was there a leader in the group? If the answer is "yes," why was he or she considered a leader? Was it owing to his or her personality, the other group members (followers), or the nature of the task (situation)? Explain the group processes in light of any leadership theory or concepts discussed in this chapter.

CASES

CASE 17-1
WHO ARE THE EFFECTIVE LEADERS?[28]

In a search for effective leaders, 206 CEO respondents from *Fortune* 500 and Service 500 companies identified as the three top leaders Don Petersen (No. 1) at Ford, Lee Iacocca at Chrysler, and Jack Welch at General Electric. The overwhelming majority of those questioned felt that there is no leadership crisis in the United States. On the other hand, those holding another view pointed to the ineffectiveness of managers in competing in the global market; the excessive focus on short-term results, often at the expense of long-term company health; and the lack of investment in plants.

About two-thirds of the respondents thought that leadership can be taught, especially through job rotation, in-company training, and delegation of authority. But there was also the realization that latent leadership qualities have to be the foundation for leadership.

Although not on the basis of the survey, *Fortune* identified the following factors for successful business leadership:

- Trust in subordinates is the foundation for delegating authority. A manager gets things done through people.
- Leaders must provide a vision for the enterprise and inspire others to commit themselves to this vision.
- Leaders must take command in times of crisis. Even those who subscribe to participative management realize that at critical times they have to take charge.
- Taking risks is a part of business—not careless risks, but calculated ones. Probably those who have never

failed (who played it safe) may not have managed well.

- Leaders need to be very competent in their fields and command the respect of employees.
- A top executive surrounded by "yes-sayers" will get an incorrect view of what is really going on within and outside the organization. Thus, executives should invite dissenting views.
- Effective leaders see and understand the big picture. They simplify complex situations and problems so that they can be understood.

1. Who were the leaders identified in the survey? Why do you think they have been effective?
2. What were the leadership characteristics identified by *Fortune?* Do you agree with the seven statements about the characteristics? Should other factors be taken into account?
3. Do you think that leadership can be taught? Explain.
4. How do the leadership characteristics relate to the managerial functions?

INTERNATIONAL CASE 17-2
LEADERSHIP AT LUFTHANSA[29]

Leadership depends on the leader, the followers, and the situation. Heinz Ruhnau, the CEO at Lufthansa, has had an interesting career, one that has equipped him for dealing with internal and external forces.

As a young man, he was an apprentice in electrical tool and die making. He studied business administration, and after graduation, he became a union official. Later he served in the senate in Hamburg. The federal government called on him to serve as state secretary in the Department of Transportation. In this role, he also was a member of the board of directors of Lufthansa before taking over as the chief executive officer of the airline.

External factors do have a bearing on Ruhnau's effectiveness, for the German government owns about 77 percent of Lufthansa. This means that the leader has to be familiar with the workings of the government.

An understanding of the internal environment is also essential for leadership. A need for change is usually recognized by the work force when a company is in severe difficulties. But how does a leader change an enterprise when it is relatively successful and employees do not see an urgent need for change? Lufthansa was quite successful despite an elaborate and inefficient bureaucracy. How does a leader cope with such a situation? According to Ruhnau, "You can't cure a bureaucracy. You have to kill it."

Ruhnau shook up the company through reorganization, which, in turn, set off a storm. Specifically, through organizational rearrangements, management was given more decision power, with fewer requirements for consulting with workers. In Germany, in general, employees have considerable influence on company policy through worker representation. The actions by Ruhnau, a former labor leader, shocked some employees and surprised others, winning him few friends. Yet Ruhnau felt that the increasing competition in the airline industry demanded a lean organization and fast responses to the changing environment.

While the reorganization resulted in less consultation with workers, Ruhnau wants to stay close to them. This is illustrated by his behavior. When he flies, for example, he talks to all flight attendants and even serves coffee to the crew.

1. Why do you think Ruhnau is successful as a CEO despite his controversial reorganization?
2. What other ways can be used to revitalize a company besides reorganization? What would you do?
3. Would it be possible in the United States for a union boss to become the CEO of a company?
4. Is a close relationship between a company and government desirable? Why, or why not?

REFERENCES

1. Jeremy Main, "Wanted: Leaders Who Can Make a Difference," *Fortune* (Sept. 28, 1987), p. 102.
2. Kotter makes the distinction that management pertains to dealing with complexities, while leadership relates to coping with change. See John P. Kotter, "What Leaders Really Do," *Harvard Business Review* (May–June 1990), pp. 103–111.
3. For a review of research on followership, see Trudy Heller and Jon Van Til, "Leadership and Followership: Some Summary Propositions," *Journal of Applied Behavioral Science*, vol. 18, no. 3 (1982), pp. 405–414. For other discussions, see William Litzinger and Thomas Schaefer, "Leadership through Followership," *Business Horizons* (September–October 1982), pp. 78–81; Clayton P. Alderfer, "Teaching Personality and Leadership: A Course of Followership," *The Organizational Behavior Teaching Review*, vol. XII, no. 4 (1987–1988), pp. 12–33.
4. See Bernard M. Bass, *Stogdill's Handbook of Leadership: A Survey of Theory and Research*, rev. ed. (New York: The Free Press, 1981).
5. See also Peter F. Drucker, "The Coming of the New Organization," *Harvard Business Review* (January–February 1988), pp. 45–53.
6. "Why Herb Kelleher Gets So Much Respect from Labor," *Business Week* (Sept. 24, 1984), pp. 112–114; "The Corporate Elite," *Business Week* (Oct. 19, 1990), p. 229.
7. Jeremy Main, "Wanted: Leaders Who Can Make a Difference," *Fortune* (Sept. 28, 1987), pp. 92–102.
8. Main, "Wanted: Leaders" (1987).
9. For an evaluation of the extensive research, see John B. Miner, "The Validity and Usefulness of Theories in an Emerging Organizational Science," *Academy of Management Review* (April 1984), pp. 296–306.
10. For a discussion of leadership traits, see Gary A. Yukl, *Leadership in Organizations* (Englewood Cliffs, N.J.: Prentice-Hall, 1981), chap. 4.
11. David A. Kenny and Stephen J. Zaccaro, "An Estimate of Variance Due to Traits in Leadership," *Journal of Applied Psychology* (November 1983), pp. 678–685.
12. Ralph M. Stogdill, *Handbook of Leadership: A Survey of Theory and Research* (New York: The Free Press, 1974). See also his earlier study, "Personal Factors Associated with Leadership: A Survey of the Literature," *Journal of Psychology*, vol. 25 (1948), pp. 35–71.
13. Shelley A. Kirkpatrick and Edwin A. Locke, "Leadership: Do Traits Matter?" *Academy of Management Executive* (May 1991), pp. 48–60.
14. Peter Galuszka, "How Gorby Got to the Top," *Business Week* (June 18, 1990), p. 15; James B. Hayes, "Wanna Make a Deal in Moscow?" *Fortune* (Oct. 22, 1990), pp. 113–115; Mikhail Gorbachev, *Perestroika: New Thinking for Our Country and the World* (New York: Harper & Row, 1987).
15. Judy B. Rosener, "Ways Women Lead," *Harvard Business Review* (November–December 1990), pp. 119–125.
16. See especially his *New Patterns of Management* (New York: McGraw-Hill Book Company, 1961) and *The Human Organization* (New York: McGraw-Hill Book Company, 1967), from which material in this section has been drawn. Also see Rensis Likert and Jane G. Likert, *New Ways of Managing Conflict* (New York: McGraw-Hill Book Company, 1976).
17. John B. Miner, *Theories of Organizational Structure and Process* (Hinsdale, Ill.: The Dryden Press, 1982), chap. 2.

18. David G. Bowers, "Hierarchy, Function and the Generalizability of Leadership Practices," in James G. Hunt and Lars L. Larson (eds.), *Leadership Frontiers* (Kent, Ohio: Kent State University Press, 1975), pp. 167–180.

19. Robert R. Blake and Jane Mouton, *The Managerial Grid* (Houston, Tex.: Gulf Publishing Company, 1964) and *Building a Dynamic Corporation through Grid Organization Development* (Reading, Mass.: Addison-Wesley Publishing Company, 1969). The grid concept has been further refined in Robert R. Blake and Jane S. Mouton, *The Versatile Manager: A Grid Profile* (Homewood, Ill.: Richard D. Irwin, 1981) and *The Managerial Grid III* (Houston, Tex.: Gulf Publishing Company, 1985).

20. Robert Tannenbaum and Warren H. Schmidt, "How to Choose a Leadership Pattern," *Harvard Business Review* (March–April 1958), pp. 95–101. See also Heinz Weihrich, "How to Change a Leadership Pattern," *Management Review* (April 1979), pp. 26–28, 37–40.

21. Tannenbaum and Schmidt, "How to Choose a Leadership Pattern," reprinted with a commentary by the authors in *Harvard Business Review* (May–June 1973), pp. 162–180.

22. The perspective is based on a variety of sources, including Lawrence Ingrassia, "A Revitalized ITALTEL Wants to Test Wings in the Global Market," *The Wall Street Journal* (June 17, 1985); Parker Hodges, "The Continental Challenge," *Datamation* (Nov. 1, 1985); "ITALTEL's New Chief Gets What She Wants," *Business Week* (Apr. 30, 1984); "European Companies Link Up for Strategic Growth," *International Management* (June 1985); and personal correspondence.

23. Fred E. Fiedler, *A Theory of Leadership Effectiveness* (New York: McGraw-Hill Book Company, 1967). See also Fred E. Fiedler and Martin M. Chemers, *Leadership and Effective Management* (Glenview, Ill.: Scott, Foresman and Company, 1974); Fred E. Fiedler and Martin M. Chemers, with Linda Mahar, *Improving Leadership Effectiveness* (New York: John Wiley & Sons, 1977).

24. Fiedler, *A Theory of Leadership Effectiveness* (1967), p. 41.

25. Fiedler, p. 261.

26. For a meta-analysis of the research on the path-goal theory, see Julie Indvik, "Path-Goal Theory of Leadership: A Meta-Analysis," in John A. Pearce II and Richard B. Robinson, Jr. (eds.), *Academy of Management Best Papers—Proceedings, 1986,* Forty-Sixth Annual Meeting of the Academy of Management, Chicago (Aug. 13–16, 1986), pp. 189–192.

27. Robert J. House, "A Path-Goal Theory of Leadership Effectiveness," *Administrative Science Quarterly* (September 1972), pp. 321–338; Robert J. House and Terence R. Mitchell, "Path-Goal Theory of Leadership," in Harold Koontz, Cyril O'Donnell, and Heinz Weihrich (eds.), *Management: A Book of Readings*, 5th ed. (New York: McGraw-Hill Book Company, 1980), pp. 533–540; Alan C. Filley, Robert J. House, and Steven Kerr, *Managerial Process and Organizational Behavior* (Glenview, Ill.: Scott, Foresman and Company, 1976), chap. 12.

28. Kate Ballen, "The No. 1 Leader Is Petersen of Ford," *Fortune* (Oct. 24, 1988), pp. 69–70, and Kenneth Labich, "The Seven Keys to Business Leadership," *Fortune* (Oct. 24, 1988), pp. 58–66.

29. The information has been drawn from a variety of sources, including a speech by Heinz Ruhnau, published in the *Lufthansa Jahrbuch '85* (Cologne, West Germany: Deutsche Lufthansa Aktiengesellschaft, 1985/86); Susan Carey, "Lufthansa Jettisons Bureaucratic Baggage," *The Wall Street Journal* (Sept. 30, 1986).

Committees do have legitimate functions and, properly used, they constitute an invaluable management tool.[1]

Cyril O'Donnell

Committees and Group Decision Making*

Chapter Objectives

After reading this chapter, you should be able to:

1. Explain the nature of various types of committees.
2. Outline the reasons why committees and groups are used, with special attention to their use in decision making.
3. Present the disadvantages of committees, especially in decision making.
4. Explain the nature of plural executives and the board of directors.
5. Outline the ways committees tend to be misused.
6. Discuss the requirements for using committees effectively.
7. Describe the advantages and disadvantages of small groups other than committees in managing.

* Note that decision making is also discussed in Chapter 8.

One of the most ubiquitous and controversial devices of organization is the committee. Whether it is referred to as a "board," "commission," "task force," or "team," its essential nature is the same. **A committee** is *a group of persons to whom, as a group, some matter is committed.* It is this characteristic of group action that sets the committee apart from other organization devices, though, as will be seen, not all committees involve group decision making.

Committees are a fact of organizational life. Although committees are widely criticized, properly conducted committee meetings used for the right purpose can result in a greater motivation, improved problem solving, and increased output.[2] In a study of subscribers to the *Harvard Business Review*, only 8 percent of the respondents indicated that they would eliminate committees if it were within their power.[3] The problem, then, is not the existence of committees but rather the way they are conducted and where they are used.

THE NATURE OF COMMITTEES

Because of variation in the authority assigned to committees, much confusion has resulted as to their nature.

Group Processes in Committees

Some say that groups go through four stages: (1) forming (the members of a group get to know each other), (2) storming (the members determine the objective of the meeting; conflicts arise), (3) norming (the group agrees on norms and some behavior rules), and (4) performing (the group gets down to the task). While these characteristics may be found in most groups, they may not necessarily follow the sequential steps.[4]

People play certain roles in committees. Some seek information; others give information. Some try to encourage others to contribute; others are followers. Finally, some try to coordinate the group's effort or to achieve a compromise when disagreements occur, while others take a more aggressive role.

To be effective in a group, one must not only listen to what is said but also observe the nonverbal behavior. Furthermore, noting the seating of members may give some clues as to the social bonds among the committee participants. Those who know each other often sit next to each other. The seating arrangement may have an impact on group interaction. Often the chairperson sits at the head of a rectangular table. At Daimler-Benz, the maker of Mercedes-Benz cars, the board of directors sits at a round table to de-emphasize the position of the chairperson.

Functions and Formality of Committees

Some committees undertake managerial functions, and others do not. Some make decisions, while others merely deliberate on problems without authority to decide. Some have authority to make recommendations to a manager, who may or may not accept them, while others are formed to receive information, without making recommendations or decisions.

A committee may be either line or staff, depending on its authority. If its authority involves decision making affecting subordinates responsible to it, it is a plural executive—a *line committee* that also carries out managerial functions; if its authority relationship to a superior is advisory, then it is a *staff committee*.

Committees may also be formal or informal. If established as part of the organization structure, with specifically delegated duties and authority, they are *formal*. Most committees with any permanence fall into this class. Committees that are *informal* are organized without specific delegation of authority, usually by some person desiring group thinking or a group decision on a particular problem. For example, a manager may have a problem on which he or she needs advice or agreement from other managers or specialists outside his or her department. The manager may, therefore, call a special meeting for the purpose of solving the problem.

Committees may be relatively *permanent*, or they may be *temporary*. One would expect formal committees to be more permanent than the informal ones, although this is not necessarily so. A formal committee might be established by order of a company president, with appropriate provision in the organization structure, for the sole purpose of studying the advisability of building a new factory and be disbanded immediately upon the completion of its task. And an informal committee set up by the factory manager to advise on the improvement of product quality or to help coordinate delivery dates with sales commitments might continue indefinitely.

However, the executive who merely calls assistants into the office or confers with department heads is not creating a committee. It is sometimes difficult to draw a sharp distinction between committees and other small groups. The essential characteristic of the committee is that it is a group charged with dealing with a specific problem or problem areas.

The Use of Committees in Different Organizations

Committees are in wide use in all types of organizations. In government, one finds a large number of standing and special committees in every legislative body. In education, university faculties, concerned about academic freedom and distrustful of administrative power, traditionally circumscribe the authority of presidents and deans with a myriad of committees. In one large university more than 300 standing committees share in administration or advise on policy.

Committees are also prevalent in business. A board of directors is a committee, as are its various constituent groups, such as the executive committee, the finance committee, the audit committee, and the bonus committee. Occasionally, one finds a business managed by a management committee instead of a president. And almost invariably under the president there will be a variety of management or policy committees, planning committees, wage and salary review committees, grievance committees, task forces for particular projects, and numerous other standing and special committees. Moreover, at each level of the organization structure, one or more committees are likely to be found. A perhaps extreme example of the use of committees in a large bank is shown in Figure 18-1.

REASONS FOR USING COMMITTEES

One need not look far for reasons for the widespread use of committees. Although the committee is sometimes regarded as having democratic origins and as being characteristic of democratic society, the reasons for its existence go beyond mere desire for group participation. Committees are widely used even in authoritarian organizations, such as the People's Republic of China.

Group Deliberation and Judgment

Perhaps the most important reason for the use of committees is the advantage of gaining group deliberation and judgment—a variation of the adage that "two heads are better than one." Very few important business problems fall entirely into an enterprise function such as production, engineering, finance, or sales. Most problems require more knowledge, experience, and judgment than any individual possesses.

It should not be inferred that group judgment can be obtained only through the use of committees. The staff specialist who confers individually with many persons in a given phase of a problem can obtain group judgment without the formation of committees. Similarly, an executive may ask key subordinates or other specialists for their analysis and recommendations. At times group judgment can thus be obtained more efficiently, in terms of time, than by using the deliberations of a committee.

However, one of the advantages of group deliberation and judgment, not to be obtained without an actual meeting, is the discussion of ideas and the cross-examination of the participants. Committees may help the clarification of problems and development of new ideas. Such group interactions have been found to be especially enlightening in policy matters. Indeed, at times, group deliberation may be superior to individual judgment.

FIGURE 18-1

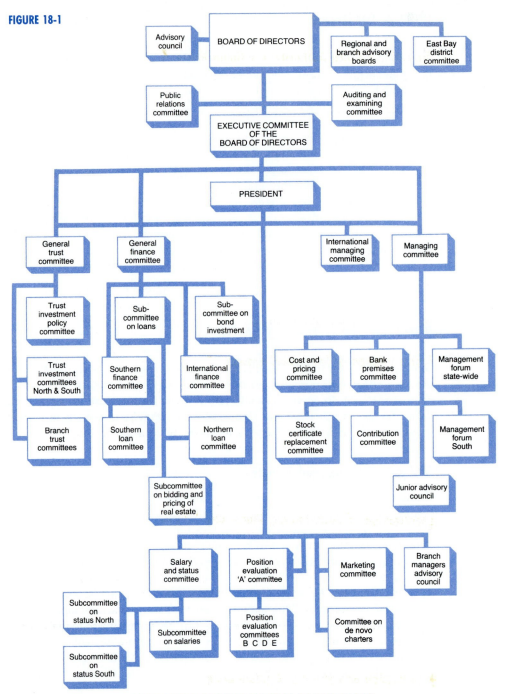

COMMITTEE ORGANIZATION IN A LARGE BANK.

This bank has supplemented its management organization structure with a large number of committees and subcommittees. All these groups exert influence on management policy and decision, and certain committees, such as the position evaluation committee, actually make decisions. Others, such as the advisory council of the board of directors and the regional and branch advisory boards, operate only in an advisory capacity. Likewise, the general trust committees make actual decisions. Most of the committees have as their members senior or other key managers from all the important departments and divisions of the company. The junior advisory council, however, consists of lower-level managers or those about to be placed in a managerial capacity. While it carries on important analyses and projects and advises senior management groups, its primary purpose is training junior managers for future increased responsibilities in the bank.

Fear of Too Much Authority in a Single Person

Another reason for the widespread use of committees is the fear of delegating too much authority to a single person. This fear, especially pronounced in government, dictated to the framers of the American Constitution not only the establishment of a two-house legislature and a multimember Supreme Court but also the division of the powers of government among the Congress, the Supreme Court, and the President. Despite this fear of centralized authority, the founders of the American republic placed the *administration* of laws in the hands of a single top executive. Yet, as former President Nixon discovered, the legislature has the power to remove or force the resignation of the chief executive.

A committee may be established to make recommendations on a problem largely because the CEO or department head does not wish to take full responsibility for making a decision. Bonus committees, which may decide on the amount and the distribution of bonuses for outstanding managers, are an example. Major financial and capital investment policies are also often developed by committees, partly because of unwillingness to give a single individual complete authority to make such important decisions.

Representation of Interested Groups

Representation plays a part in the establishment and staffing of committees in business. Boards of directors are often selected on the basis of groups interested in the company and, perhaps more often, on the basis of groups in which the company has an interest. When executives have a particularly difficult internal problem involving managers and specialists in various departments and activities, they may choose committee members in such a way as to give these interested parties representation.

Coordination of Departments, Plans, and Policies

There is general agreement that committees are very useful for coordinating activities among various organizational units. They are also useful for coordinating plans and policies as well as their implementation. The dynamics of modern enterprises place a heavy burden on the managers to integrate plans and activities.

A committee permits individuals not only to obtain firsthand knowledge of the plans and of their own rule in the execution of them but also to make suggestions for the improvement of plans.

Transmission and Sharing of Information

Committees are useful for transmitting and sharing information. All group members affected by a mutual problem or project can learn about it simultaneously, and decisions and instructions can be received uniformly with opportunities for clarification. This may save time. The spoken word may clarify a point better than even carefully written memorandums.

Consolidation of Authority

A manager in a department, branch, or section often has only a portion of the authority necessary to accomplish a program. As noted in Chapter 11, this is known as splintered authority. One way to handle a problem in this situation is to refer it upward in the organizational hierarchy until it reaches a point at which the requisite authority exists. But this place is often in the office of the president, and the problem may not be of sufficient importance to be decided at that level.

For example, a customer of a machine-tool manufacturer may wish a slight but unusual change in the design of a piece of equipment. The customer approaches the sales department, which (if there is no established procedure for handling this change) cannot act without the authority of the engineering department, the production department, and the cost estimating department. In such a case, the sales manager might establish a special purpose committee to study the problem, to agree on the nature and cost of the change, and to use the combined authority of its members to approve the request.

The informal use of committees gives much flexibility to an organization. However, consolidating splintered authority through a committee should be watched carefully. It should be determined whether the organizational structure itself should be changed in order to concentrate in one position the appropriate authority to make *recurring* decisions.

Motivation through Participation

Committees permit wide participation in decision making. Persons who take part in planning a program or making a decision usually feel more enthusiastic about accepting and executing it. Even limited participation can be helpful.

The use of committees to motivate subordinates to support a program or decision requires skillful handling. It is by no means certain that deliberations of this kind will kindle enthusiastic support, for they can also result in the deepening of existing divisions among participants. On the other hand, there are people who seem to be against every move unless they have been previously consulted. Thus, it requires a skillful chairperson to direct conflicting interests toward common objectives.

Avoidance of Action

It cannot be denied that committees are sometimes appointed by managers when they want to avoid action. One of the surest ways to delay the handling of a problem, and even to postpone a decision indefinitely, is to appoint a committee (and sometimes several subcommittees) to study the matter. At times, committee members are chosen in a way aimed at delaying action.

DISADVANTAGES OF COMMITTEES

Although there are good reasons for using committees, there are also disadvantages of doing so. Committees are costly; they may result in compromises at the least common denominator; they may lead to indecision; they can be self-destructive; they also can split responsibility; finally, they can lead to a situation in which a few persons impose their will on the majority.

Disparaging attitudes toward committees are reflected in such sayings as the following:

"A camel is a horse invented by a committee."

"A committee is made up of the unfit selected by the unwilling to do the unnecessary."

"A committee is a place where the loneliness of thought is replaced by the togetherness of nothingness."

High Cost in Time and Money

Committee action can be very costly in terms of time. A committee may require members to travel some distance to reach a meeting. During the meeting, all members have the right to be heard, to have their viewpoints discussed, to challenge and cross-examine the presentations of others, and to analyze the reasons for a considered group conclusion. The spoken word, though valuable for emphasis and clarification, is seldom concise, and the "thinking out loud" is sometimes a waste of time for those who must listen. If the committee is supposed to reach a unanimous or nearly unanimous decision, the discussion is likely to be lengthy. And if a decision can be reached quickly, the meeting may have been unnecessary in the first place.

The monetary cost of committee discussion can also be very high. One must consider not only the cost of executive time but even more the cost to the company of the loss of the executive time that would otherwise have been devoted to other important duties. On the other hand, it is quite possible that the cost of executive time in a group meeting might be less than when a superior meets individually with subordinates.

This cost in time and money becomes all the more disadvantageous when a committee is assigned a problem that could just as well, or better, be solved by an individual or by an individual with the help of a smaller and lesser-paid staff. Therefore, a cost benefit analysis of the advisability of establishing a committee may have to be made.

Compromise at the Least Common Denominator

When committees are required to come to some conclusion or to reach some decision, there is the danger that their action will not result in an optimum solution. If the matter under consideration is so simple that differences of opinion do not exist, the use of committee time is probably wasteful. If differences of opinion exist, the point at which all or a majority of the committee members can agree tends to be at the least common denominator. Most often this is not as strong and positive a course of action as that undertaken by an individual, who has only to consider the facts as he or she sees them and then reach a conclusion.

There is the danger of compromising at the level of the least common denominator of agreement. Small groups of people frequently seek—from feelings of politeness, mutual respect, and humility—to reach conclusions on which all can agree. Since committee members are often selected from organization equals, reluctance to force a conclusion on a recalcitrant member presenting a minority view is understandable. This may, however, increase the probability of making weak decisions.

Indecision

Another disadvantage of committees is that the discussion of peripheral or tangential subjects takes up valuable time and often results in adjournment without action. Moreover, committee meetings are often characterized by both an official and a hidden agenda. The *hidden agenda* pertains to the disguised individual motives of members. It is not unusual for these motives to prevent the committee from reaching agreement on the official topic of discussion.

Tendency to Be Self-Destructive

Indecisiveness may give the chairperson or a strong member an opportunity to force the committee into a decision the way he or she wants it to go. Almost invariably, one person in a group emerges as the leader. But when an individual becomes dominant, the nature of the committee as a decision-making group of equals changes. What emerges is an executive with a group of followers or advisers. Executives often delude themselves into believing that a committee operates on group management principles as a group of equals when, as a matter of fact, the "team" is composed of subordinate advisers or even yes-sayers following a leader.

Splitting of Responsibility

When authority to study a problem, make recommendations, or arrive at a decision is delegated to a group, the fact is that the authority is dispersed throughout the group. Thus, individual members hardly feel the same degree of responsibility that they would if they personally were charged with the same task. This splitting of responsibility is one of the chief disadvantages of a committee. Since no one feels personally accountable for the actions of the group, no individual feels personally responsible for any action taken by it.

Tyranny by a Few Persons

As has been pointed out, committees tend to seek unanimous or nearly unanimous conclusions or decisions. A few members who may represent a minority view are thus in a strong position to impose their will on the majority of members. By their insistence on acceptance of their position, or of a compromise position, they may exercise an unwarranted tyranny over the majority. An individual jury member in the American legal system has such power. We recall an important committee of nine members in which a tradition for unanimous agreement developed. One member actually controlled the committee, not through force of leadership but through the power to withhold his vote.

THE PLURAL EXECUTIVE AND THE BOARD OF DIRECTORS[5]

Most committees are nonmanagerial in nature. However, some groups are given the power to make decisions and to undertake one or all of the managerial functions of planning, organizing, staffing, leading, and controlling. It is this latter type of committee that is referred to as the **plural executive.**[6] An example of the plural executive is the board of directors.

Authority of the Board of Directors

The extent of authority to manage and to make decisions held by a plural executive is not always easy to ascertain. Some committees, such as the board of directors, clearly have this power, although they may not exercise it.

Usually the president is the dominant figure on the board, with the other members often being little more than advisers. In other words, the plural executive is not always what it seems, and a single executive often makes the decisions.

Role of the Plural Executive in Policy-Making

The plural executive is often found in the field of strategy or policy-making.[7] Many companies have an executive or management committee to develop major plans and adopt basic strategies. Such committees go by various names: General Motors has its executive and finance committees, United States Rubber Company its operating policy committee, the Sun Chemical Company its management committee, Lockheed Aircraft Corporation its corporate policy committee, and the Koppers Company its policy committee.

The extent of authority of these committees varies considerably, although their influence on decision making is perhaps greater in strategic planning than in any other area. These committees also engage in control, for their concern with strategic plans must be followed up to make sure that events conform to decisions.

Furthermore, these committees are often useful in settling differences of opinion or in settling questions of organizational jurisdiction. The plural executive is an ideal arbitrator of disputes, since a determination by a group will usually be accepted by contesting parties as being more impartial than that of a single arbiter.

Where committees are successful in strategy formulation, they are dependent on accurate and adequate staff work. A committee can hardly develop a proposal, forecast probable profits and costs from alternative courses of action, or investigate the numerous tangible and intangible factors influencing a basic decision. These are matters for study, and the committee is a notoriously poor study or research device. Therefore, if group deliberation is to be productive, facts and analyses must be developed and presented so that the members have readily available the data on which to base a decision.

As the European Community moves toward unification of the twelve member countries, the appropriate model for industrial democracy or worker participation in managerial decisions has to be selected. This issue will become especially critical for cross-border mergers. Companies may choose from three models of worker participation. The first model is based on the German codetermination law (*Mitbestimmung*). This approach requires that firms with over 1000 employees elect half of the supervisory board. The second model is based on the works council used especially in the Benelux countries. Employee representatives get financial reports; they are also consulted before board meetings. The third is the traditional collective bargaining model. But this model may be modified by the inclusion of certain aspects of the first and second models.

Role of the Plural Executive in Policy Execution

Companies may distinguish between policy-making and policy execution. The former may be concerned primarily with the establishment of broad principles by which the administration is guided, while the latter is concerned with the daily conduct of the company's affairs. The plural executive is used for formulating policies. Policy implementation is carried out primarily by managers who set standards and procedures to guide and govern the execution of policies, establish controls to ensure adherence to standards, improve interdivisional coordination, and meet various emergencies as they arise.

In the 1960s and 1970s, more outsiders than insiders were selected for boards of directors; in fact, in the 1970s, outsiders constituted a majority of many boards of major companies. But in the latter part of the 1980s, many who were called declined the invitation, and now, more insiders are again favored on many boards.

There are many reasons why people from the outside do not want to serve on a board of directors. For one, members are increasingly required to study the issues brought before them more carefully, and this demands a great deal of their time. Moreover, board members are concerned about the possibility of being held liable for their decisions. It is true that companies may provide liability insurance, but several insurance companies have reduced their coverage, increased the premium, and even withdrawn coverage.[10]

To attract capable directors and to make boards more effective, some ideas for reform have been circulated. Some want directors to own stocks in the companies they serve. It is suggested that this would result in more careful deliberation of the issues. Others say that board members should be nominated by a committee composed of outside members. Still others recommend that members have an independent staff to study the various issues. There is also the idea that the boards should reflect the various claimants. For example, in the early 1980s Douglas A. Frazer of the United Automobile Workers sat on the board of Chrysler. He, in a sense, was required to wear two "hats": He had to represent labor, and at the same time he had to consider the overall health of the company and its various claimants. This practice, by the way, is quite common in Germany and other European countries, where, by law, labor must be represented on the boards of major companies.

Whatever the changes are going to be, and some seem to be necessary, the role of the board of directors is likely to change in the future.

✓ MISUSE OF COMMITTEES

The committee form has often fallen into disrepute through misuse. The five following abuses should be avoided when committees are set up and operated.

As Replacement for a Manager

The weakness of the committee as a managing device has already been noted. If decision making is to be sharp, clear, prompt, and subject to unquestioned responsibility, it is better exercised by an individual. One can hardly say that a committee has no place in management, but the advantages of group thinking and participation in policy questions can be gained in most cases through advisory committees. Most business committees function this way, leaving the real decision making and managing to the line executives to whom they report. As Ralph Cordiner, former president of the General Electric Company, has said, "We have no committees to make decisions that individuals should make."

For Research or Study

A group of people meeting together can hardly engage in research or study, even though it may well weigh and criticize the results of each of these activities. When the solution to a problem requires data not available to a committee, no discussion or consideration can turn up the missing information. Gathering information is essentially an individual function, even though individuals may be coordinated into a team with individual research assignments. Most committees, therefore, need a research staff to provide at least analyses of alternative courses of action, historical summaries, or well-considered forecasts.

For Unimportant Decisions

Even where a committee is clothed with advisory authority only, the disadvantages of this device should dictate that its use be limited to important matters. Moreover, no intelligent specialist or manager can help feeling uncomfortable when time is wasted by a group deliberating at length on trivial subjects.

For Decisions beyond Participants' Authority

At times, executives with the requisite authority cannot attend a committee meeting. Instead, they send subordinates who have not had the superiors' authority delegated to them or who hesitate to bind the superiors. The result is that the committee cannot function as intended. Delays result because the substituting participants refer questions to their superiors. Thus, much of the advantage of group decision making and deliberation is lost.

To Consolidate Divided Authority

A disadvantage of departmentation is that authority is so delegated that in some cases, no one except the chief executive officer has adequate authority to do what must be done. Even within departments or sections, authority may be so splintered that group meetings are necessary to consolidate authority for making decisions. If the problem of divided authority can be eliminated by changing the organization structure or by delegating authority, the use of a committee is inappropriate.

SUCCESSFUL OPERATION OF COMMITTEES

Managers spend a great deal of time in committees. The use of committees is due not only to the democratic tradition in American social life but also to a growing emphasis on group management and group participation in organizations. In attempting to overcome some of the disadvantages of committees, managers may find the following guidelines useful.

Authority

A committee's authority should be spelled out so that the members know whether their responsibility is to make decisions, make recommendations, or merely deliberate and give the chairperson some insights into the issue under discussion.

Size

The size of a committee is very important. As shown in Figure 18-2, the complexity of interrelationships greatly increases with the size of the group. If the group is too large, there may not be enough opportunities for adequate communication among its members. On the other hand, if the group consists of only three persons, there is the possibility that two may form a coalition against the third member. No precise conclusions can be drawn here about the appropriate size. As a general rule, a committee should be large enough to promote deliberation and include the breadth of expertise required for the job but not so large as to waste time or foster indecision. The optimum committee size is thought by some to be at least five or six members but not more than fifteen or sixteen. An analysis of small-group research indicates that the ideal committee size may be five when the five members possess adequate skills and knowledge to deal with problems facing the committee.[11] It is obvious that the larger the group, the greater the difficulty in obtaining a "meeting of the minds" and the more time necessary to allow everyone to contribute.

Membership[12]

The members of a committee must be selected carefully. If a committee is to be successful, the members must be representative of the interests they are expected to serve. They must also possess the required authority and be able to perform well in a group. Finally, the members should have the capacity for communicating well and reaching group decisions by integrated group thinking rather than by inappropriate compromise.

Subject Matter

The subject must be carefully selected. Committee work should be limited to subject matter that can be handled in group discussion. Certain kinds of subjects lend themselves to committee action, while others do not. Jurisdictional disputes and strategy formulation, for example, may be suitable for group deliberation, while certain isolated, technical problems may be better solved by an expert in the specialized field. Committees will be more effective if an agenda and relevant information are circulated well in advance so that the members can study the subject matter before the meeting.

FIGURE 18-2

**INCREASED COMPLEXITY OF RELATIONSHIPS
THROUGH INCREASE IN GROUP SIZE.**

Chairperson

The selection of the chairperson is crucial for an effective committee meeting. Such a person can avoid the wastes and drawbacks of committees by planning the meeting, preparing the agenda, seeing that the results of research are available to the members ahead of time, formulating definite proposals for discussion or action, and conducting the meeting effectively. The chairperson sets the tone of the meeting, integrates the ideas, and keeps the discussion from wandering.

Minutes

Effective communication in committees usually requires circulating minutes and checking conclusions. At times, individuals leave a meeting with varying interpretations as to what agreements were reached. This can be avoided by taking careful minutes of the meeting and circulating them in draft form for correction or modification before the final copy is approved by the committee.

Cost Effectiveness

A committee must be worth its cost. It may be difficult to count the benefits, especially such intangible factors as morale, enhanced status of committee members, and the committee's value as a training device to enhance teamwork. But the committee can be justified only if the costs are offset by tangible and intangible benefits.

OTHER GROUPS IN MANAGING

Although the committee is of special importance as an organization device, it is really only one of many types of groups that are found in organizations. In addition to committees, there are teams, conferences, task forces, and negotiation sessions, all involving group activities.

A **group** may be defined as two or more people acting interdependently in a unified manner toward the achievement of common goals. A group is more than a collection of individuals; rather, through their interactions, new forces and new properties are created that need to be identified and studied in themselves. The goals may pertain to specific tasks, but they may also mean that the people share some common concerns or values or an ideology. Thus, group members are attracted to each other by some social bonds.

Characteristics of Groups

Groups—and the focus is on groups in an organization—have a number of characteristics. First, group members share one or more common goals, such as the goals of a product group to develop, manufacture, and market a new product. A second characteristic of groups is that they normally require interaction and communication among members. It is impossible to coordinate the efforts of group members without communication. Third, members within a group assume roles. In a product group, for example, individuals are responsible for designing, producing, selling, or distributing a product. Naturally, the roles are in some kind of relationship to each other in order to achieve the group task. Fourth, groups usually are a part of a larger group. The product group may belong to a product division that produces many products of a similar nature. Large groups may also consist of subgroups. Thus, within the product group may be a subgroup specializing exclusively in the selling of the product. Also, groups interface with other groups. Thus, product group A may cooperate with product group B in the distribution of their products. It is evident, then, that the systems point of view, which focuses on the interrelatedness of parts, is essential in understanding the functioning of groups.

There are a number of other sociological characteristics of groups that must be recognized. Groups develop **norms,** which refer to the expected behavior of the group members. If individuals deviate from the norms, pressure is exerted to make them comply. This can be functional when, for example, a person who frequently shows up late for work is admonished by other group members. But there are also situations in which groups may be dysfunctional. For example, ambitious, highly motivated employees may be pressed to produce in congruence with generally accepted norms rather than according to their abilities.

Perspective

Pressure toward Conformity— How Would You Respond?

In a widely publicized experiment, S. E. Asch showed the impact of pressure of the group toward conformity.[13] Members of a small group were asked to match a standard line (8 inches long) with three comparison lines (6¼, 8, and 6¾ inches long—see Figure 18-3). One member of the group (the naive subject) was not aware that all the other students in the group (confederates of the experimenter) were instructed to occasionally give wrong answers, such as saying that the 6¾-inch line was as long as the 8-inch standard line. The setting was arranged so that the naive subject was one of the last ones to make a judgment. It was found that an "innocent" member made wrong choices when the confederates did so unanimously. In later interviews, subjects reported that they wanted to agree with the majority. This illustrates that even in a rather uncomplicated task, people may decide against their better judgment owing to group pressure. These findings explain to some extent the influence of group pressure toward conformity and how it may result in managerial decisions that are less than optimal.

A Special Kind of Group: The Focus Group

Focus groups have been used for some time in market research. For example, actual or potential customers are asked in a group setting to comment on a product

FIGURE 18-3

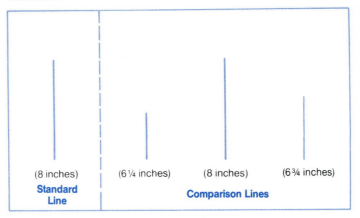

(8 inches)   (6 ¼ inches)   (8 inches)   (6 ¾ inches)

**Standard
Line**   **Comparison Lines**

**WHICH COMPARISON LINE IS
THE SAME LENGTH AS THE STANDARD LINE?**

or service before large-scale research is undertaken. The comments may be taped
or notes may be taken. The responses are then analyzed to determine the customers' attitudes toward, perceptions of, or satisfaction with the product or service.

Elements of focus groups have also been used in Europe.[14] Germany's public
participated in value forums to determine long-term energy policies. The experience indicated that (1) the public can contribute to value forums, (2) the participants
were satisfied with this kind of procedure, and (3) the participants were eager to
help resolve inconsistencies.

Focus groups may also be used for evaluating managerial aspects within an
organization. The Public Service Company of New Mexico established six focus
groups to elicit responses about its performance appraisal, compensation, and
benefits systems.[15] On the basis of the findings, the company implemented a more
flexible benefits program, a program for job redesign, and a new decision-making
process. Rather than imposing organizational changes, the company allowed the
employees to become actively involved in the change process.

Functions and Advantages of Groups

Groups have many functions. They are powerful in changing behavior, attitudes,
and values and in disciplining members. As noted, deviant members may be
pressured to adhere to group norms. In addition, groups are used for decision
making, negotiating, and bargaining. Thus, group members with diverse backgrounds may bring different perspectives to the decision-making process. This does
not mean, however, that group decisions are always better than individual decisions.

Group concepts are very important for the topics covered in other chapters
in this book. Specifically, different group structures influence *communication* patterns. Thus, communication will differ when it is channeled through one key
member or when it flows freely among all the group members. One can hardly

consider a number of people a team when each member communicates only with the boss; teamwork requires open communication among all members. Effective group interactions may also affect *motivation*. For example, group members participating in setting objectives may become committed to the achievement of group goals. Finally, *leadership* must be seen in the context of group processes. A grasp of group concepts helps in understanding the interactions between leaders and followers as well as the interactions among all the group members. In short, an understanding of groups is important for carrying out all managerial functions, particularly the function of leading. Groups are a fact of organized and unorganized life. It is important to know how they work and to use them in an effective and efficient manner in situations that favor group actions.

Groups also have advantages for individuals. Groups do provide social satisfaction for their members, a feeling of belonging, and support for the needs of individuals. Another benefit of groups is that they promote communication. It may be the give-and-take in a formal meeting, or it can take the form of the grapevine, which is the informal communication through which group members become aware of "what is really going on in the firm." Groups also provide security. Labor unions are sometimes formed precisely for this reason—to give job security to their members. Finally, groups provide opportunities for promoting self-esteem through recognition from and acceptance by peers.

Disadvantages of Groups

Group activities also may present problems. Certainly, the disadvantages of committees mentioned above are relevant here. As pointed out in the discussion of committees, when a compromise can be reached only at the least common denominator or when decisions must be postponed, the use of groups may be costly in time and money. A chairperson or a strong member may use the group for selfish purposes rather than for the well-being of the enterprise. Responsibility may be divided so that no one feels accountable for a decision. Finally, a few members may tyrannize the group and inhibit its proper functioning. In other words, all the problems and dangers found in committees are potentially present with groups.

SUMMARY

A committee is a group of persons to whom, as a group, some matter is committed. Committees may be line or staff, formal or informal, permanent or temporary. Committees are used for obtaining group deliberation and judgment, for preventing one person from accumulating too much authority, and for presenting the views of different groups. Committees are also used for coordinating departments, plans, and policies, as well as for sharing information. At times, a manager may not have all the authority needed for making a decision. Thus, authority is consolidated through committees. Moreover, committees often increase motivation by letting people participate in the decision-making process. But sometimes committees are used to postpone a decision and to avoid action.

Committees also have disadvantages: They can be costly; their actions may result in compromises at the least common denominator; their discussions may lead to indecision; and they have the tendency to be self-destructive when one person dominates the meetings. Another drawback is that responsibility is split, with no one person feeling responsible for a decision. Moreover, a small group of committee members may insist on the acceptance of their unwarranted view against the will of the majority.

A plural executive, such as a board of directors, is a committee with the power to make managerial decisions. The authority of the board of directors varies widely. While the board often gets involved in strategy formulation and policy-making, implementation of the policies is usually done by managers.

Effective operation of a committee requires determining its authority, choosing an appropriate size, selecting members carefully, using it only for the proper subject matter, appointing an effective chairperson, taking and circulating minutes, and using it only when its benefits exceed its costs.

A committee is one kind of group; another kind is, for example, a team. The experiment by Asch showed the impact of group pressure toward conformity. Thus, people may give wrong answers against their better judgment when other group members take an opposing position. The focus group is a special kind of group that elicits responses from customers, the public, or employees. Before an organization uses group actions, it must consider the advantages and disadvantages of groups.

KEY IDEAS AND CONCEPTS FOR REVIEW

Committee

Four stages in group processes

Line and staff committees

Formal and informal committees

Permanent and temporary committees

Eight reasons for using committees

Disadvantages of committees

Plural executive

Misuses of committees

Seven recommendations for making
    committees successful

Characteristics of groups

Experiment by Asch

Focus group

Advantages and disadvantages of groups

FOR DISCUSSION

1. A prominent novelist-critic of the management scene has said: "I don't think we can go on very much longer with the luxurious practice of hiring ten men to make one man's decision. With all its advantages, professional management tends to encourage bureaucratic corpulence." Comment.
2. Distinguish between a "committee," a "team," and a "group."
3. Where in an organization, if anyplace, would you suggest that committees be used? Why?
4. What are the reasons for using committees? If there are good reasons, why are committees criticized so much?
5. What is meant by the term "plural executive"?

6. What is the relative effectiveness of individual and committee action in functional activities? Identify the activities that can be undertaken most effectively by a committee.
7. Describe and discuss the nature of misapplications of committees.
8. What would you recommend for making committees effective?
9. What are the major characteristics of groups in organizations?

EXERCISES/ACTION STEPS

1. Discuss one of the cases in this chapter in a group of students. Divide the class into groups of various sizes (e.g., groups of 3, 6, 9, and 12 students). Each group is to analyze a case and make recommendations. A spokesperson should be selected in each group to present the group's view on the case. On what basis was the spokesperson selected? What are the similarities and differences between a spokesperson and a chairperson? Discuss the advantages and problems encountered in the groups of various sizes. What do you think is the "ideal" group size?
2. Interview two managers, and ask about their experiences in committees. Do they have a positive or a negative view of committees? What have they found to be most important for making committees effective and efficient? What do they think the "ideal" size for a committee is?

CASES

CASE 18-1
THE HUMBOLD RETAIL CHAIN

At a time when most retailers had a decline in earnings, the Humbold Retail Chain showed great increases. The executives at Humbold attribute the profit performance largely to the relatively new managerial style, which emphasizes group decision making and personnel policies similar to those used by the Japanese, with an emphasis on job security and harmonic relationships with both employees and customers.

The current chairman of the board (who, however, is soon to retire) practices consensus management, giving managers ample opportunities to participate in most major decisions. This, in turn, helps managers to understand what is going on at the various levels in the organization. At the same time, the team approach facilitates the development of managers. For example, one committee deals with policy areas such as strategic issues. Through group partici-

pation, younger managers become familiar with the critical issues facing the firm.

While most managers at Humbold feel that the group management approach is working well, Richard Newstrom, a young manager with a master's degree from a highly respected business school, is not quite as optimistic about this approach. He thinks that managers waste their time in committee meetings and that group decisions are compromises and may not be optimal. In order to emphasize his point, he quotes a number of clichés about the weaknesses of committees.

His colleagues, however, point out that the team approach breaks down some of the departmental barriers and facilitates coordination among divisions. They admit that developing plans in a group may be time-consuming, but their implementation is swift. Moreover, they argue that the team approach encourages managers to explore many more alternatives than with individual decision making, and people in different age groups and with different perspectives have an input.

Newstrom does not agree with his colleagues. He suggests that the team approach at Humbold works only because of the managerial style of its chairman and that as soon as he retires, collaboration among managers will come to an end.

1. What are the advantages and disadvantages of the group decision approach?
2. What accounts for the negative attitudes toward committees?
3. How can committees, or teams, be made more effective?

CASE 18-2
COMMITTEE MANAGEMENT AT THE UNIVERSITY OF CALIFORNIA

Many universities, notably the larger ones, operate extensively through committee management, especially in the appointment and promotion of persons to tenured associate and full professorships. One example of a university where committees are extensively used in this area is the University of California (its various campuses).

For appointment or promotion to the position of associate professor or full professor (each carries tenure), the University of California uses the following steps:

• A candidate is reviewed thoroughly by the staffing committee of his or her department or school.
• If the candidate passes there, the action is sent to the chairperson or dean for review and then to the office of the executive vice-chancellor of the campus, where it is referred to the campus budget and promotion committee.
• The budget and promotion committee immediately refers the case to a specially appointed ad hoc committee of five faculty members, of whom only one or two may be from the candidate's department or school.

• The ad hoc committee reviews the case and makes a recommendation to the budget and promotion committee.
• The budget and promotion committee reviews the case and makes recommendations to the executive vice-chancellor and chancellor of the campus.
• The executive vice-chancellor and chancellor review the case, and after this review, the case is sent to the academic vice president of the university with recommendations.
• The university's academic vice president and president review the case and, if their decision is favorable, send it with recommendations to the regents of the university for final action.

1. How would you like to be reviewed for appointment or promotion by this hierarchy of committees?
2. What strengths or weaknesses do you see in this procedure?
3. Assuming that you see certain weaknesses and perhaps dangers in this kind of committee management, what do you suggest be done?

REFERENCES

1. Cyril O'Donnell, "Ground Rules for Using Committees," *Management Review* (October 1961), pp. 63–67.
2. J. Presley and S. Keen, "Better Meetings Lead to Higher Productivity: A Case Study," *Management Review* (April 1975), pp. 16–22.

3. R. Tillman, Jr., "Committees on Trial," *Harvard Business Review* (May–June 1960), pp. 6–12, 162–173. For a discussion of characteristics of committees and their functions, see John J. Gabarro and Anne Harlan, "Process Observation," in Leonard A. Schlesinger, Robert G. Eccles, and John J. Gabarro (eds.), *Managing Behavior in Organizations* (New York: McGraw-Hill Book Company, 1983), pp. 93–100.

4. Walter Kiechel III, "How to Take Part in a Meeting," *Fortune* (May 26, 1986), pp. 177–180.

5. For an excellent and very thorough discussion of the board of directors, see Stanley C. Vance, *Corporate Leadership—Boards, Directors, and Strategy* (New York: McGraw-Hill Book Company, 1983); see also Idalene F. Kesner and Roy B. Johnson, "Boardroom Crisis: Fiction or Fact," *Academy of Management Executive* (February 1990), pp. 23–35.

6. For an early discussion of the plural executive, see William H. Mylander, "Management by the Executive Committee," *Harvard Business Review* (May–June 1955), pp. 51–58.

7. See Barry Baysinger and Robert E. Hoskisson, "The Composition of Boards of Directors and Strategic Control: Effects on Corporate Strategy," *Academy of Management Review* (January 1990), pp. 72–87.

8. Simcha Ronen, *Comparative and Multinational Management* (New York: John Wiley & Sons, 1986), chap. 9; Eric G. Friberg, "Moves Europeans Are Making," *Harvard Business Review* (May–June 1989), p. 85.

9. Laurie Baum, "The Job Nobody Wants," *Business Week* (Sept. 8, 1986), pp. 56–61; William B. Glaberson and William J. Powell, Jr., "A Landmark Ruling That Puts Board Members in Peril," *Business Week* (Mar. 18, 1985), pp. 56–57; "Inside Look at Life in the Corporate Board Room," *U.S. News & World Report* (Jan. 28, 1985), pp. 71–72; Jay Lorsch interviewed by Jack Young, "Pawns or Potentates: The Reality of America's Corporate Boards," *Academy of Management Executive* (November 1990), pp. 85–87; William A. Sahlman, "Why Sane People Shouldn't Serve on Public Boards," *Harvard Business Review* (May–June 1990), pp. 28–36; Elmer W. Johnson, "An Insider's Call for Outside Direction," *Harvard Business Review* (March–April 1990), pp. 46–55; Rosswell B. Perkins, "Avoiding Director Liability," *Harvard Business Review* (May–June 1986), pp. 8–14.

10. A rather new Delaware law gives some protection to directors from negligence suits. But angry stockholders can still sue them. See Leo Herzel, Richard W. Shepro, and Leo Katz, "Next-to-Last Word on Endangered Directors," *Harvard Business Review* (January–February 1987), pp. 38–43.

11. See Alan C. Filley, "Committee Management: Guidelines from Social Science Research," *California Management Review* (Fall 1970), pp. 13–21.

12. For an early discussion of membership selection, see Cyril O'Donnell, "Ground Rules for Using Committees," *Management Review* (October 1961), pp. 63 ff.

13. See David Krech, Richard S. Crutchfield, and Egerton L. Ballachey, *Individual in Society* (New York: McGraw-Hill Book Company, 1962), pp. 507–508.

14. Ralph L. Keeney, Detlof von Winterfeldt, and Thomas Eppel, "Eliciting Public Values for Complex Policy Decisions," *Management Science* (September 1990), pp. 1011–1030.

15. Orlando Esquibel, Jack Ning, and John Sugg, "New Salary System Supports Changing Culture," *HRM Magazine* (October 1990), pp. 43–48.

The new technologies of communications have the power to change the competitive game for almost all companies of all sizes.[1]

Eric K. Clemons and
F. Warren McFarlan

Communication

Chapter Objectives

After reading this chapter, you should be able to:

1. Describe the communication function in an organization.
2. Diagram a model of the basic communication process.
3. Explain the flow of communication in an organization.
4. Describe the characteristics of written, oral, and nonverbal communication.
5. Identify barriers and breakdowns in communication and suggest approaches to improve it.
6. Describe the role of the electronic media in communication.

Although communication applies to all phases of managing, it is particularly important in the function of leading. **Communication** is the transfer of information from a sender to a receiver, with the information being understood by the receiver. This definition, then, becomes the basis for the communication process model discussed in this chapter. The model focuses on the sender of the communication, the transmission of the message, and the receiver of the message. The model also draws attention to noise, which interferes with good communication, and feedback, which facilitates communication. This chapter also examines the impact of the electronic media on communication.

THE COMMUNICATION FUNCTION IN ORGANIZATIONS

It is no exaggeration to say that the communication function is the means by which organized activity is unified. It may be looked upon as the means of which social inputs are fed into social systems. It is also the means by which behavior is modified, change is effected, information is made productive, and goals are achieved. Whether it is within church, a family, a scout troop, or a business enterprise, the transfer of information from one individual to another is absolutely essential.

The Importance of Communication

Over the years, the importance of communication in organized effort has been recognized by many authors. Chester I. Barnard, for example, viewed communication as the means by which people are linked together in an organization to achieve a common purpose.[2] This is still the fundamental function of communication. Indeed, group activity is impossible without communication, because coordination and change cannot be effected.

Psychologists have also been interested in communication. They emphasize human problems that occur in the communication process of initiating, transmitting, and receiving information. They have focused on the identification of barriers to good communication, especially those that involve the interpersonal relationships of people. Sociologists and information theorists, as well as psychologists, have concentrated on the study of communication networks.

Leadership demands information about what is really going on in the organization. Managers who never leave the office and who rely on formal communication channels may receive only the information that places subordinates in a favorable light. To overcome their isolation, managers need to supplement the formal communication channels with informal ones.

In their search for excellent companies, Thomas Peters and Robert Waterman noted that managers at United Airlines practice what has been labeled "management by walking around."[3] A similar practice is called "management by wandering around" at Hewlett-Packard. The belief is that managers will improve informal communication channels by walking through the plant.

However, a survey of CEOs in *Fortune* 500 enterprises indicated that executives spend little time with lower-level employees.[4] Professor Henry Mintzberg, who previously studied the activities of executives, interpreted the findings as showing that "management by walking around" is not very prevalent in these large companies. Managers spend a lot of time with those who are at similar organizational levels. Yet by wandering around, managers could obtain a great deal of information not available through formal communication channels.

The Purpose of Communication

In its broadest sense, the purpose of communication in an enterprise is to effect change—to influence action toward the welfare of the enterprise. Communication is essential for the *internal* functioning of enterprises, because it integrates the managerial functions. Communication is especially needed to (1) establish and disseminate the goals of an enterprise, (2) develop plans for their achievement, (3) organize human and other resources in the most effective and efficient way, (4) select, develop, and appraise members of the organization, (5) lead, direct, motivate, and create a climate in which people want to contribute, and (6) control performance.

Figure 19-1 graphically shows not only that communication facilitates the managerial functions but also that communication relates an enterprise to its *external* environment. It is through information exchange that managers become aware of the needs of customers, the availability of suppliers, the claims of stockholders, the regulations of governments, and the concerns of a community. It is through communication that any organization becomes an open system interacting with its environment, a fact whose importance is emphasized throughout this book.

FIGURE 19-1   **THE MANAGEMENT PROCESS**

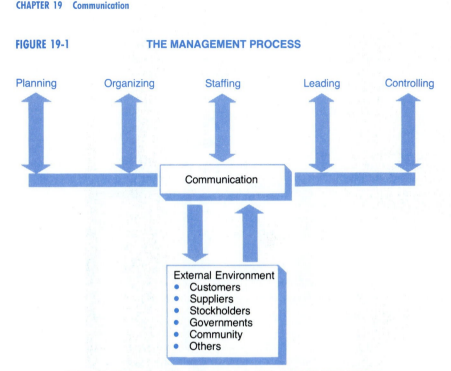

THE PURPOSE AND FUNCTION OF COMMUNICATION.

THE COMMUNICATION PROCESS

Simply stated, the **communication process,** diagrammed in Figure 19-2, involves the sender, the transmission of a message through a selected channel, and the receiver. Let us examine closely the specific steps in the process.

The Sender of the Message

Communication begins with the sender, who has a *thought* or an idea which is then encoded in a way that can be understood by both the sender and the receiver. While it is unusual to think of *encoding* a message into the English language, there are many other ways of encoding, such as translating the thought into computer language.

Use of a Channel to Transmit the Message

The information is transmitted over a *channel* that links the sender with the receiver. The message may be oral or written, and it may be transmitted through a memorandum, a computer, the telephone, a telegram, or television. Television, of course, also facilitates the transmission of gestures and other visual clues. At times, two or more channels are used. In a telephone conversation, for instance, two people may reach a basic agreement that they later confirm by a letter. Since

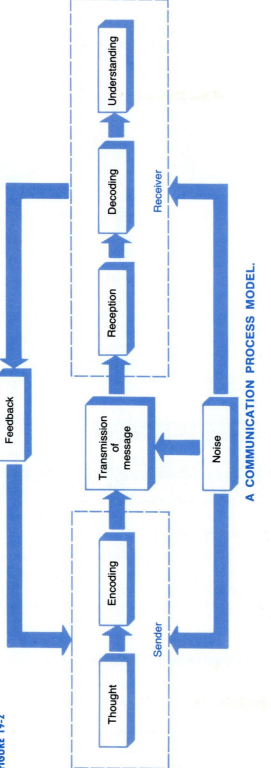

FIGURE 19-2

A COMMUNICATION PROCESS MODEL.

many choices are available, each with advantages and disadvantages, the proper selection of the channel is vital for effective communication.[5]

The Receiver of the Message

The receiver has to be *ready* for the message so that it can be decoded into thought. A person thinking about an exciting football game may pay insufficient attention to what is being said about an inventory report, for example, thus increasing the probability of a communication breakdown. The next step in the process is *decoding,* in which the receiver converts the message into thoughts. Accurate communication can occur only when both the sender and the receiver attach the same or at least similar meanings to the symbols that compose the message. Thus, it is obvious that a message encoded into French requires a receiver who understands French. Less obvious, and frequently overlooked, is the fact that a message in technical or professional jargon requires a recipient who understands such language. So communication is not complete unless it is understood. *Understanding* is in the mind of both the sender and the receiver. Persons with closed minds will normally not completely understand messages, especially if the information is contrary to their value system.

International Perspective

Cross-Cultural Barriers

Misunderstandings increase when communicating is done in different languages. The German language, for example, is rather distinct in its formality and the way people are addressed. The formal *Sie* is seldom replaced by *Du*. Only after people know each other for a long time and only after they know each other very well is the informal *Du* used. Similarly, adults usually address each other with *Herr* ("Mr.") or *Frau* ("Mrs."). The use of the first name is common only among relatives, very close friends, or children and teenagers. A non-German who is addressed with the formal *Sie* or the formal *Frau* or *Herr* may interpret such usage as meaning that the person does not like him or her or wants to maintain a social distance. This may not be true at all; the usage is simply dictated by cultural norms. On the other hand, if a casual acquaintance is being addressed in German by his or her first name, that person may be offended. While such distinctions in a language may appear unimportant to a non-German, they not only create communication barriers but also may result in damaged relationships and possibly in a loss of business.

Noise Hindering Communication

Unfortunately, communication is affected by "noise," which is anything—whether in the sender, the transmission, or the receiver—that hinders communication. For example:

- A noise or a confined environment may hinder the development of a clear thought.
- Encoding may be faulty because of the use of ambiguous symbols.
- Transmission may be interrupted by static in the channel, such as may be experienced in a poor telephone connection.
- Inaccurate reception may be caused by inattention.
- Decoding may be faulty because the wrong meaning may be attached to words and other symbols.
- Understanding can be obstructed by prejudices.
- Desired change may not occur because of the fear of possible consequences of the change.
- Since language is an especially important factor in cross-cultural communication, not only verbal expression but also gestures and posture can result in "noise," hindering communication.

Feedback in Communication

To check the effectiveness of communication, a person must have *feedback*. One can never be sure whether or not a message has been effectively encoded, transmitted, decoded, and understood until it is confirmed by feedback. Similarly, feedback indicates whether individual or organizational change has taken place as a result of communication.

Situational and Organizational Factors in Communication

Many situational and organizational factors affect the communication process. Such factors in the external environment may be educational, sociological, legal-political, and economic. For example, a repressive political environment will inhibit the free flow of communication. Another situational factor is geographic distance. A direct face-to-face communication is different from a telephone conversation with a person on the other side of the globe and different from an exchange of cables or letters. Time must also be considered in communication. The busy executive may not have sufficient time to receive and send information accurately. Other situational factors that affect communication within an enterprise include the organization structure, managerial and nonmanagerial processes, and technology. An example of the latter is the pervasive impact of computer technology on handling very large amounts of data.

In summary, the communication model provides an overview of the communication process, identifies the critical variables, and shows their relationships. This, in turn, helps managers pinpoint communication problems and take steps to solve them or, even better, prevent the difficulties from occurring in the first place.

✓ COMMUNICATION IN THE ORGANIZATION

In today's enterprises, information must flow faster than ever before. Even a short stoppage on a fast-moving production line can be very costly in terms of lost output.

It is, therefore, essential that production problems be communicated quickly for corrective action. Another important element is the amount of information, which has greatly increased over the years, frequently causing an information overload. What is often needed is not more information but relevant information. It is necessary to determine what kind of information a manager needs to have for effective decision making. Obtaining this information frequently requires getting information from managers' superiors and subordinates and also from departments and people elsewhere in the organization.

The Manager's Need to Know

To be effective, a manager needs information necessary for carrying out managerial functions and activities. Yet even a casual glance at communication systems shows that managers often lack vital information for decision making, or they may get too much information, resulting in overload. It is evident that managers must be discriminating in selecting information. A simple way for a manager to start is to ask, "What do I really need to know for my job?" Or, "What would happen if I did not get this information on a regular basis?" It is not maximum information that a manager needs but pertinent information. Clearly, there is no universally applicable communication system; rather, a communication system must be tailored to the manager's needs.

The Communication Flow in the Organization

In an effective organization, communication flows in various directions: downward, upward, and crosswise. Traditionally, *downward* communication was emphasized, but there is ample evidence that if communication flows only downward, problems will develop. In fact, one could argue that effective communication has to start with the subordinate, and this means primarily *upward* communication. Communication also flows *horizontally*, that is, between people on the same or similar organizational levels, and *diagonally*, involving persons from different levels who are not in direct reporting relationships with one another. The different kinds of information flows are diagrammed in Figure 19-3.

Downward communication.   Downward communication flows from people at higher levels to those at lower levels in the organizational hierarchy. This kind of communication exists especially in organizations with an authoritarian atmosphere. The kinds of media used for *oral* downward communication include instructions, speeches, meetings, the telephone, loudspeakers, and even the grapevine. Examples of *written* downward communication are memorandums, letters, handbooks, pamphlets, policy statements, procedures, and electronic news displays.[6]

Unfortunately, information is often lost or distorted as it comes down the chain of command. Top management's issuance of policies and procedures does not ensure communication. In fact, many directives are not understood or even read. Consequently, a feedback system is essential for finding out whether information was perceived as intended by the sender.

Downward flow of information through the different levels of the organization

FIGURE 19-3

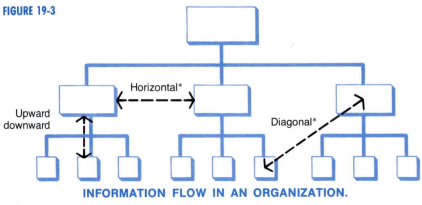

INFORMATION FLOW IN AN ORGANIZATION.

* Since horizontal and diagonal communication flows have some common characteristics, we call them crosswise communication and discuss them together later in this chapter.

is time-consuming. Indeed, delays may be so frustrating that some top managers insist that information be sent directly to the person or group requiring it.

Upward communication.   Upward communication travels from subordinates to superiors and continues up the organizational hierarchy. Unfortunately, this flow is often hindered by managers in the communication chain who filter the messages and do not transmit all the information—especially unfavorable news—to their bosses. Yet objective transmission of information is essential for control purposes. Upper management needs to know specifically production performance facts, marketing information, financial data, what lower-level employees are thinking, and so on.

Upward communication is primarily nondirective and is usually found in participative and democratic organizational environments. Typical means for upward communication—besides the chain of command—are suggestion systems, appeal and grievance procedures, complaint systems, counseling sessions, joint setting of objectives, the grapevine, group meetings, the practice of an open-door policy, morale questionnaires, exit interviews, and the ombudsperson.

The concept of the **ombudsperson** was used relatively little in the United States until recently. It originated in Sweden, where a civil servant could be approached by a citizen to investigate complaints about the federal bureaucracy. Now some U.S. companies have established a position for a person who investigates employees' concerns. Anheuser-Busch, Control Data, General Electric, McDonnell Douglas, and AT&T are just a few of the companies using the ombudsperson for promoting upward communication. There is now even a Corporate Ombudsman Association. At General Dynamics, over 3000 calls were made to the ombudsperson in 1986, suggesting that workers trust the person in such a position.[7] Companies have found that the position of the ombudsperson can provide a valuable upward communication link and avert front-page scandals and legal costs by bringing improprieties to the attention of the appropriate person before they become major problems.

Effective upward communication requires an environment in which subordinates feel free to communicate. Since the organizational climate is greatly influenced by upper management, the responsibility for creating a free flow of upward communication rests to a great extent—although not exclusively—with superiors.

Perspective

Lack of Upward Communication Can Be Disastrous

The lack of upward communication can be disastrous. In the 1986 space shuttle disaster, vital information apparently did not reach the top management at NASA.[8] Other examples of a breakdown of upward communication are these: Bank of America's top officials were surprised about the poor quality of their mortgage portfolio, which resulted in substantial losses for the bank. E. F. Hutton's executives were apparently unaware of the incorrect check-writing scheme of their lower-level managers.

In some organizations, upward communication is hindered by an organization culture and climate that "punishes" managers who communicate bad news or information with which top management does not agree. Indeed, the tendency to report only good news upward is quite common. Yet correct information is absolutely necessary for managing an enterprise.[9]

So what can managers do to facilitate the free flow of information? First, managers must create an informal climate that encourages upward communication. An open-door policy is only useful when it is practiced. Second, the formal structure of information flow must be clear. Third, managers can learn a great deal by just wandering through the corridors. Hewlett-Packard is often mentioned as an example of open communication because of the practice of "management by wandering around."

Crosswise communication.   Crosswise communication includes the *horizontal* flow of information, among people on the same or similar organizational levels, and the *diagonal* flow, among persons at different levels who have no direct reporting relationships with one another. This kind of communication is used to speed information flow, to improve understanding, and to coordinate efforts for the achievement of organizational objectives. A great deal of communication does not follow the organizational hierarchy but cuts across the chain of command.

The enterprise environment provides many occasions for *oral* communication. They range from informal meetings of the company bowling team and lunch hours employees spend together to more formal conferences and committee and board meetings. This kind of communication also occurs when individual members of different departments are grouped into task teams or project organizations. Finally, communication cuts across organizational boundaries when, for example, staff members with functional or advisory authority interact with line managers in different departments.

In addition, *written* forms of communication keep people informed about the enterprise. These written forms include the company newspaper or magazine and bulletin board notices. Modern enterprises use many kinds of oral and written crosswise communication patterns to supplement the vertical flow of information.

Because information may not follow the chain of command, proper safeguards need to be taken to prevent potential problems. Specifically, *crosswise* communication should rest on the understanding that (1) crosswise relationships will be encouraged wherever they are appropriate, (2) subordinates will refrain from making commitments beyond their authority, and (3) subordinates will keep superiors informed of important interdepartmental activities. In short, crosswise communication may create difficulties, but it is a necessity in many enterprises in order to respond to the needs of the complex and dynamic organizational environment.

Written, Oral, and Nonverbal Communication

Written and oral communication media have favorable and unfavorable characteristics; consequently, they are often used together so that the favorable qualities of each can complement the other. In addition, visual aids may be used to supplement both oral and written communications. For example, a lecture in a management training session may be made more effective when written handouts, transparencies, videotapes, and films are used. Evidence has shown that when a message is repeated through several media, the people receiving it will more accurately comprehend and recall it.

In selecting media, one must consider the communicator, the audience, and the situation. An executive who feels uncomfortable in front of a large audience may choose written communication rather than a speech. On the other hand, certain audiences who may not read a memo may be reached and become motivated by direct oral communication. Situations may also demand a specific medium. For example, former President Reagan, an effective communicator, used press conferences in trying to clarify the arms shipments to Iran. Face-to-face interaction was demanded by the news media to deal with the many aspects of the transactions.

Written communication.   French managers are almost obsessed with the use of written communication, not only for formal messages but also for informal notes. A French manager of the Citroen carmaker stated that unless something is written down, it has no reality.[10]

Written communication has the *advantage* of providing records, references, and legal defenses. A message can be carefully prepared and then directed to a large audience through mass mailings. Written communication can also promote uniformity in policy and procedure and can reduce costs, in some cases.

The *disadvantages* are that written messages may create mountains of paper, may be poorly expressed by ineffective writers, and may provide no immediate feedback. Consequently, it may take a long time to know whether a message has been received and properly understood.

Oral communication.   A great deal of information is communicated orally. Oral communication can occur in a face-to-face meeting of two people or in a manager's presentation to a large audience; it can be formal or informal, and it can be planned or accidental.

The principal *advantage* of oral communication is that it makes possible speedy interchange with immediate feedback. People can ask questions and clarify points. In a face-to-face interaction, the effect can be noted. Furthermore, a meeting with the superior may give the subordinate a feeling of importance. Clearly, informal or planned meetings can greatly contribute to the understanding of the issues.

However, oral communication also has *disadvantages*. It does not always save time, as any manager knows who has attended meetings in which no results or agreements were achieved. These meetings can be costly in terms of time and money.

Nonverbal communication.   People communicate in many different ways. What a person says can be reinforced (or contradicted) by nonverbal communication, such as facial expressions and body gestures. Nonverbal communication is expected to support the verbal, but it does not always do so. For example, an autocratic manager may pound a fist on the table while announcing that from now on participative management will be practiced; such contradictory communications will certainly create a credibility gap. Similarly, managers may state that they have an open-door policy, but then they may have a secretary carefully screen people who want to see them; this creates an incongruence between what they say and what they do. This is an illustration of "noise" in the communication process model (Figure 19-2). Clearly, nonverbal communication may support or contradict verbal communication, giving rise to the saying that actions often speak louder than words.

✓ BARRIERS AND BREAKDOWNS IN COMMUNICATION

It is probably no surprise that managers frequently cite communication breakdowns as one of their most important problems. However, communication problems are often symptoms of more deeply rooted problems. For example, poor planning may be the cause of uncertainty about the direction of the firm. Similarly, a poorly designed organization structure may not clearly communicate organizational relationships. Vague performance standards may leave managers uncertain about what is expected of them. Thus, the perceptive manager will look for the causes of communication problems instead of just dealing with the symptoms. Barriers can exist in the sender, in the transmission of the message, in the receiver, or in the feedback. Specific communication barriers are discussed below.

Lack of Planning

Good communication seldom happens by chance. Too often people start talking and writing without first thinking, planning, and stating the purpose of the message. Yet giving the reasons for a directive, selecting the most appropriate channel, and choosing proper timing can greatly improve understanding and reduce resistance to change.

Unclarified Assumptions

Often overlooked, yet very important, are the uncommunicated assumptions that underlie messages. A customer may send a note stating that she will visit a vendor's plant. Then she may assume that the vendor will meet her at the airport, reserve a hotel room, arrange for transportation, and set up a full-scale review of the program at the plant. But the vendor may assume that the customer is coming to town mainly to attend a wedding and will make a routine call at the plant. These unclarified assumptions in both instances may result in confusion and the loss of goodwill.

Semantic Distortion

Another barrier to effective communication is semantic distortion, which can be deliberate or accidental. An advertisement that states "We sell for less" is deliberately ambiguous; it raises this question: Less than what? Words may evoke different responses. To some people, the word "government" may mean interference or deficit spending; to others, the same word may mean help, equalization, and justice.

Poorly Expressed Messages

No matter how clear the idea in the mind of the sender of communication, the message may still be marked by poorly chosen words, omissions, lack of coherence, poor organization, awkward sentence structure, platitudes, unnecessary jargon, and a failure to clarify its implications. This lack of clarity and precision, which can be costly, can be avoided through greater care in encoding the message.

Communication Barriers in the International Environment[11]

Communication in the international environment becomes even more difficult because of different languages, cultures, and etiquette.[12] Translating advertising slogans is very risky. The slogan "Put a Tiger in Your Tank" by Exxon was very effective in the United States, yet it is an insult to the people in Thailand. Colors have different meanings in various cultures. Black is often associated with death in many Western countries, while in the Far East white is the color of mourning. In business dealings it is quite common in the United States to communicate on a first-name basis, yet in most other cultures, especially those with a pronounced hierarchical structure, persons generally address one another by their last names.[13]

In the Chinese culture, words may not convey what people really mean because they may want to appear humble.[14] For example, when a promotion is offered, the person may say that he or she is not qualified enough to assume great responsibility. But the expectation is that the superior will urge the subordinate to accept the promotion and mention all the virtues and strengths of the candidate, as well as his or her suitability for the new position.

Communication patterns differ in various countries with respect to the degree to which they are explicit or implicit. In countries such as Germany and the United States, one expects that persons mean what they say. The need for precision is illustrated in the popularity of management by objectives, where goals are stated precisely in quantitative, measurable terms whenever possible. In contrast, Japanese communication is implicit; the meaning has to be inferred. For example, Japanese dislike saying "no" in communication; instead, they couch a negative answer in ambivalent terms. This has been demonstrated many times in trade agreements between Japan and the United States, as well as between Japan and Europe.

The degree of explicitness or implicitness in communication varies among nations. An emphasis on explicit communication is found among the Swiss-Germans, while implicit communication patterns prevail among the Japanese. Thus the range from explicit communication to implicit communication is as follows: Swiss-Germans, Germans, North Americans, French, English, Italians, Latin Americans, Arabs, and Japanese.[15] While this may be, to some extent, an overgeneralization, managers who are aware of the different communication patterns can benefit from this knowledge.

To overcome communication barriers in the international environment, large corporations have taken a variety of steps. Volkswagen, for example, provides extensive language training. Furthermore, the company maintains a large staff of translators. Frequently, local nationals, who know the host-country's language and culture, are hired for top positions. In the United States, foreign firms find it advantageous to hire students from their own country who are attending U.S. universities.

Loss by Transmission and Poor Retention

In a series of transmissions from one person to the next, the message becomes less and less accurate. Poor retention of information is another serious problem. Thus, the necessity of repeating the message and using several channels is rather obvious. Consequently, companies often use more than one channel to communicate the same message.

Poor Listening and Premature Evaluation

There are many talkers but few listeners. Everyone probably has observed people entering a discussion with comments that have no relation to the topic. One reason may be that these persons are pondering their own problems—such as preserving their own egos or making a good impression on other group members—instead of listening to the conversation. Listening demands full attention and self-discipline. It also requires that the listener avoid premature evaluation of what another person has to say. A common tendency is to judge, to approve or disapprove what is being said, rather than trying to understand the speaker's frame of reference. Yet listening without making hasty judgments can make the whole enterprise more effective and more efficient. For example, sympathetic listening can result in better labor-management relations and greater understanding among managers. Specifically, sales personnel may better understand the problems of production people, and the credit manager may realize that an overly restrictive credit policy may lead to a disproportionate loss in sales. In short, listening with empathy can reduce some of the daily frustrations in organized life and result in better communication.

Impersonal Communication

Effective communication is more than simply transmitting information to employees. It requires face-to-face contact in an environment of openness and trust. The Perspective illustrates how this simple but effective communication technique may be overlooked.

Perspective

The Closed-Circuit Television Failure[16]

A company was about to install a sophisticated $300,000 closed-circuit television system to improve the transmission of information to employees. When a management consultant recommended instead that the president join his people during the coffee break, rather than sipping his coffee in a closed group of top executives, the president was skeptical. The suggestion seemed radical, but he agreed to try it. The experiment was a failure because the president found that his employees would not talk to him. After some soul-searching, the president again tried meeting with his employees face-to-face during the coffee break, but this time he talked about *their* concern (the opening of a European plant that could result in the elimination of jobs). To the president's surprise, employees talked openly about what was on their minds. In fact, the communication went so well that the president requested that his executive group mingle with their people "kaffeeklatsches."

As the events in the Perspective indicate, real improvement of communication often requires not expensive and sophisticated (and impersonal) communication media but the willingness of superiors to engage in face-to-face communication. Such informal gatherings, without status trappings or a formal authority base, may be threatening to a top executive, but the risks involved are outweighed by the benefits that better communication can bring.

Distrust, Threat, and Fear

Distrust, threat, and fear undermine communication. In a climate containing these forces, any message will be viewed with skepticism. Distrust can be the result of inconsistent behavior by the superior, or it can be due to past experiences in which the subordinate was punished for honestly reporting unfavorable, but true, information to the boss. Similarly, in light of threats—whether real or imagined—people tend to tighten up, become defensive, and distort information. What is needed is a climate of trust, which facilitates open and honest communication.

Insufficient Period for Adjustment to Change

The purpose of communication is to effect change that may seriously concern employees: shifts in the time, place, type, and order of work or shifts in group arrangements or skills to be used. Some communications point to the need for further training, career adjustment, or status arrangements. Changes affect people in different ways, and it may take time to think through the full meaning of a message. Consequently, for maximum efficiency, it is important not to force change before people can adjust to its implications.

Information Overload[17]

One might think that more and unrestricted information flow would help people overcome communication problems.[18] But unrestricted flow may result in too much information. People respond to information overload in various ways.[19] First, they may *disregard* certain information. A person getting too much mail may ignore letters that should be answered. Second, if they are overwhelmed with too much information, people *make errors* in processing it. For example, they may leave out the word "not" in a message, which reverses the intended meaning. Third, people may *delay* processing information either permanently or with the intention of catching up in the future. Fourth, people may *filter* information. Filtering may be helpful when the most pressing and most important information is processed first and the less important messages receive lower priority. However, chances are that attention will be given first to matters that are easy to handle, while more difficult but perhaps critical messages are ignored. Finally, people respond to information overload by simply *escaping* from the task of communication. In other words, they ignore information or do not communicate information because of an overload.

Some responses to information overload may be adaptive tactics that can, at times, be functional. For example, delaying the processing of information until the amount is reduced can be effective. On the other hand, withdrawing from the task of communicating is usually not a helpful response. Another way to approach the overload problem is to reduce the demands for information. Within an enterprise, this may be accomplished by insisting that only essential data be processed, such as information showing critical deviations from plans. Reducing external demands for information is usually more difficult because these demands are less controllable by managers. An example may be the government's demand for detailed documentation on governmental contracts. Companies that do business with the government simply have to comply with these requests.

Other Communication Barriers

Besides the mentioned barriers to effective communication, there are many others. In *selective perception* people tend to perceive what they expect to perceive. In communication this means that they hear what they want to hear and ignore other relevant information.

Closely related to perception is the influence of *attitude,* which is the predisposition to act or not to act in a certain way; it is a mental position regarding a fact or state. Clearly, if people have made up their minds, they cannot objectively listen to what is said.

Still other barriers to communication are differences in *status* and *power* between the sender and the receiver of information. Also, when information has to pass through several *levels* in the organization hierarchy, it tends to be distorted.

TOWARD EFFECTIVE COMMUNICATION

The communication process model introduced at the beginning of this chapter (Figure 19-2) helps identify the critical elements in the communication process. At each stage, breakdowns can occur—in the encoding of the message by the sender,

FIGURE 19-4

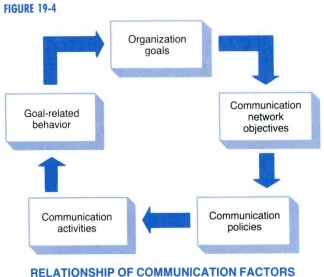

**RELATIONSHIP OF COMMUNICATION FACTORS
TO ORGANIZATION GOALS.**

From H. H. Greenbaum, "The Audit of Organizational Communication,"
Academy of Management Journal, vol. 17, no. 4 (December 1974),
p. 743. Used by permission.

in the transmission of the message, and in the decoding and understanding of the message by the receiver. Certainly, noise can interfere with effective communication at each stage of the process.

There are several approaches that can be used to improve communication. One is to make a communication audit. The findings then become the basis for organization and system changes. Another approach is to apply communication techniques, with the focus on interpersonal relations and listening.

The Communication Audit

One way to improve communication in an organization is to conduct a communication audit.[20] Such an audit is a tool for examining communication policies, networks, and activities. Organizational communication is viewed as a group of communication factors related to organizational goals, as shown in Figure 19-4.

What is interesting in this model is that communication is considered not for its own sake but rather as a means to achieve organizational goals, a fact sometimes forgotten by those concerned only with interpersonal relations. This model is consistent with the systems model of the operational approach to managing (see Figure 1-5). In the systems model, as you will recall, the communication system integrates the managerial functions of planning, organizing, staffing, leading, and controlling. In addition, it is important to remember that the communication system has another function, namely to link the enterprise with its environment.

The four major communication networks that need to be audited are as follows:

1. The regulative or task-related network pertaining to policies, procedures, rules, and superior-subordinate relationships
2. The innovative network, which includes problem solving, meetings, and suggestions for change
3. The integrative network, which consists of praise, rewards, promotions, and those items that link enterprise goals with personal needs
4. The informative-instructive network, which includes company publications, bulletin boards, and the grapevine[21]

The communication audit, then, is a tool for analyzing communication related to many key managerial activities. It is used not only to deal with problems when they occur but also to prevent them from occurring in the first place. The format of the audit can take many shapes and may include observations, questionnaires, interviews, and analyses of written documents. Although the initial audit of the communication system is highly desirable, it needs to be followed by periodic reports.

Guidelines for Improving Communication

Effective communication is the responsibility of all persons in the organization, managers as well as nonmanagers, who work toward a common aim. Whether communication is effective can be evaluated by the intended results. The following guidelines can help overcome the barriers to communication:

1. Senders of messages must clarify in their minds what they want to communicate. This means that one of the first steps in communicating is clarifying the purpose of the message and making a plan to achieve the intended end.
2. Effective communication requires that encoding and decoding be done with symbols that are familiar to the sender and the receiver of the message. Thus the manager (and especially the staff specialist) should avoid unnecessary technical jargon, which is intelligible only to the experts in their particular field.
3. The planning of the communication should not be done in a vacuum. Instead, other people should be consulted and encouraged to participate: to collect the facts, analyze the message, and select the appropriate media. For example, a manager may ask a colleague to read an important memo before it is distributed throughout the organization. The content of the message should fit the recipients' level of knowledge and the organizational climate.
4. It is important to consider the needs of the receivers of the information. Whenever appropriate, one should communicate something that is of value to them, in the short run as well as in the more distant future. At times, unpopular actions that affect employees in the short run may be more easily accepted if they are beneficial to them in the long run. For instance, shortening the workweek may be more acceptable if it is made clear that this action will strengthen the competitive position of the company in the long run and avoid layoffs.
5. There is a saying that the tone makes the music. Similarly, in communication the tone of voice, the choice of language, and the congruency between what is said and how it is said influence the reactions of the receiver of the message. An autocratic manager ordering subordinate supervisors to practice participative management will create a credibility gap that will be difficult to overcome.
6. Too often information is transmitted without communicating, since communication is complete only when the message is understood by the receiver. And one never knows whether communication is understood unless the sender gets feedback. This is accomplished by asking questions, requesting a reply to a letter, and encouraging receivers to give their reactions to the message.
7. The function of communication is more than transmitting information. It also deals with emotions that are very important in interpersonal relationships between superiors, subordinates, and colleagues in an organization. Furthermore, communication is vital for creating an environment in which people are motivated to work toward the goals of the enterprise while they achieve their personal aims. Another function of communication is control. As explained in the discussion of management by objectives (MBO), control does not necessarily mean top-down control. Instead, the MBO philosophy emphasizes self-control, which demands clear communication with an understanding of the criteria against which performance is measured.

8. Effective communicating is the responsibility not only of the sender but also of the receiver of the information. Thus, listening is an aspect that needs additional comment.

Listening: A Key to Understanding

The rushed, never-listening manager will seldom get an objective view of the functioning of the organization. Time, empathy, and concentration on the communicator's messages are prerequisites for understanding. People want to be heard, want to be taken seriously, want to be understood. Thus, the manager must avoid interrupting subordinates and putting them on the defensive. It is also wise both to give and to ask for feedback, for without it one can never be sure whether the message is understood. To elicit honest feedback, a manager should develop an atmosphere of trust and confidence and a supportive leadership style, with a de-emphasis on status (such as barricading oneself behind an extrawide executive desk).

Listening is a skill that can be developed. Keith Davis and John W. Newstrom proposed ten guides to improve listening: (1) Stop talking, (2) put the talker at ease, (3) show the talker that you want to listen, (4) remove distractions, (5) emphathize with the talker, (6) be patient, (7) hold your temper, (8) go easy on arguments and criticism, (9) ask questions, and (10) stop talking! The first and the last guides are the most important; people have to stop talking before they can listen.[22]

Carl R. Rogers and F. J. Roethlisberger suggest a simple experiment.[23] It goes like this. The next time you have an argument, try to use the following simple rule: A person may speak only after the ideas and feelings of the previous speaker are repeated accurately to the speaker's satisfaction. This rule sounds simple yet is difficult to practice. It requires listening, understanding, and empathy. But managers who have used this technique have reported a considerable number of cases in which they were not communicating accurately.

Some Tips for Improving Written Communication

Effective writing may be the exception rather than the rule; indeed, education and intelligence do not guarantee good writing. Many people fall into the habit of using technical jargon that can be understood only by experts in the same field. Common problems in written communications are that writers omit the conclusion or bury it in the report, are too wordy, and use poor grammar, ineffective sentence structure, and incorrect spelling. Yet a few guidelines may do much to improve written communication:[24]

Use simple words and phrases.

Use short and familiar words.

Use personal pronouns (such as "you") whenever appropriate.

Give illustrations and examples; use charts.

Use short sentences and paragraphs.

Use active verbs, as in "The manager *plans* . . . ."

Avoid unnecessary words.

John Fielden suggests that the writing style should fit the situation and the effect the writer wants to achieve.[25] Specifically, he recommends a *forceful* style when the writer has power; the tone should be polite but firm. The *passive* style is appropriate when the writer is in a position lower than that of the recipient of the message. The *personal* style is recommended for communicating good news and making persuasive requests for action. The *impersonal* style is generally right for conveying negative information. The *lively* or *colorful* style is suitable for good-news items, advertisements, and sales letters. On the other hand, a *less colorful* style, combining the impersonal with the passive, may be appropriate for common business writing.

Some Tips for Improving Oral Communication

For some people, including executives, the thought of having to give a speech may cause nightmares. Yet giving speeches and having fun doing it can be learned. A classic example of how one can learn oral communication is the Greek statesman Demosthenes, who, after feeling very discouraged following the poor delivery of his first public speech, became one of the greatest orators through practice, practice, and more practice.

Managers need to inspire, to lead, to communicate a vision. A clear idea of the organizational purpose is essential but insufficient for leading. This vision must be articulated. This means not only stating the facts but also delivering them in a way that inspires the employees of the organization by catering to their values, their pride, and their personal objectives.

Most of the tips for improving written communication also apply to the improvement of oral communication. But there is more. Rational reasoning needs to be supplemented by emotional appeal, and the message must be delivered in an understandable manner to the employees. Jay A. Conger suggests the following guidelines for oral communication and, especially, for articulating the organization's mission:[26]

1. State the mission in a way that is congruent with positive values and beliefs.
2. Incorporate organizational and societal values in the statement of enterprise goals. Use stories and give examples illustrating these goals.
3. Show the importance of the mission, the reason for establishing it, and the underlying assumption as to why the company will be successful in achieving it.
4. Deliver the message in an easy-to-understand language, using metaphors, analogies, and stories.
5. Practice oral communication, and elicit feedback on your speech.
6. Show your enthusiasm and emotions in articulating your vision for the company.

ELECTRONIC MEDIA IN COMMUNICATION

Managers have studied and are gradually adopting various electronic devices that improve communication. Electronic equipment includes mainframe computers, minicomputers, personal computers, electronic mail systems, and electronic typewriters, as well as cellular telephones for making telephone calls from cars and beepers for keeping in contact with the office. The impact of computers on all phases of the management process will be discussed in Chapter 21 in connection with management information systems and will therefore be mentioned only briefly here. Let us first look at telecommunication in general and at the increasing use of teleconferencing in particular.

Telecommunication

Although telecommunication is just emerging, a number of companies have already effectively utilized the new technology in a variety of ways, as shown by the following examples:[27]

- A large bank supplies hardware and software to its customers so that they can easily transfer funds to their suppliers.
- Several banks now make bank-by-phone services available even to individuals.
- Facsimile (fax) service transmits information within minutes to countries on the opposite side of the globe.
- Car companies stay in close contact with their suppliers, informing them about their needs and thus reducing inventory costs.
- Telecommunication provides an important link for just-in-time inventory systems.
- The computerized airline reservation system facilitates making travel arrangements.
- One large medical supply company gained a competitive edge by providing hospital purchasing agents with the opportunity to enter supply orders directly at a computer terminal.
- Many firms now have detailed personnel information—including performance appraisals and career development plans—in a data bank.

As you can see, there are many applications of telecommunication. But to make telecommunication systems effective, the technical experts must make every effort to identify the real needs of managers and customers and to design systems that are useful.[28] Let us now turn to a specific application of the new technology: teleconferencing.

Teleconferencing

For some time now companies such as IBM, Bank of America, and Hughes have used teleconferencing.[29] However, owing to the wide variety of systems, including audio systems, audio systems with snapshots displayed on a video monitor, and live video systems, the term "teleconferencing" is difficult to define. In general, most people think of a **teleconference** as a group of people interacting with each other by means of audio and video media with moving or still pictures.

Full-motion video is frequently used to hold meetings among managers. Not only do they hear each other, but they can also see each other's expressions or discuss some visual display. This kind of communication is, of course, rather expensive, and audio in combination with still video may be used instead. This method of communication may be useful for showing charts or illustrations during a technical discussion.

Advantages.   Some of the potential advantages of teleconferencing include savings in travel expenses and travel time. Also, conferences can be held whenever necessary, since there is no need to make travel plans long in advance. Because meetings can be held more frequently, communication is improved between, for example, headquarters and geographically scattered divisions.

Disadvantages.   There are also drawbacks to teleconferencing. Because of the ease in arranging meetings in this manner, they may be held more often than necessary. Moreover, since this approach uses rather new technology, the equipment is subject to breakdowns. Most important, perhaps, teleconferencing is still a poor substitute for meeting with other persons face-to-face. Despite these limitations, increased use of teleconferencing is likely in the future.

The Use of Computers for Information Handling

Electronic data processing now makes it possible to handle large amounts of data and to make information available to a large number of people. Thus, one can obtain, analyze, and organize timely data quite inexpensively. But it must never be forgotten that data are not necessarily information; information must inform someone. The new computer graphics can inform visually, displaying important company information. At PepsiCo Inc., managers used to dig through reams of computer printouts for information; now they can quickly display a colored map showing their competitive picture.[30] There will be more about the impact of the computer on the process of managing in Chapter 21.

SUMMARY

Communication is the transfer of information from a sender to a receiver, with the information being understood by the receiver. The communication process begins with the sender, who encodes an idea that is sent in oral, written, visual, or some other form to the receiver. The receiver decodes the message and gains an understanding of what the sender wants to communicate. This, in turn, may result in some change or action. But the communication process may be interrupted by "noise," that is, by anything that hinders communication. In an organization, managers should have the information necessary for doing a good job. The information may flow not only downward or upward in the organization structure but also horizontally or diagonally. Communication can be in written form, but more information is communicated orally. In addition, people communicate through gestures and facial expressions.

Communication is hindered by barriers and breakdowns in the communication process. Understanding these barriers, making a communication audit, and applying the guidelines for effective communicating and listening facilitate not only understanding but also managing. Electronic media can improve communication, as illustrated by teleconferencing and the application of computers, two of many approaches to handling the increasing amount of information in organizations.

KEY IDEAS AND CONCEPTS FOR REVIEW

Communication	Nonverbal communication
Communication process model	Barriers and breakdowns in
"Noise" in communication	communication
Downward communication	Responses to information overload
Ombudsperson	Communication audit
Crosswise communication	Guidelines for improving communication
Written and oral communication—	Listening as a key to understanding
advantages and disadvantages of each	Teleconferencing

FOR DISCUSSION

1. Briefly describe the communication process model. Select a communication problem, and determine the cause (or causes) by applying the model in your analysis.
2. List different channels for transmitting a message. Discuss the advantages and disadvantages of the various channels.
3. What are some kinds of downward communication? Discuss those used most frequently in an enterprise you are familiar with. How effective are the various types?
4. What are some problems in upward communication? What would you suggest for overcoming the difficulties?
5. What are the advantages and disadvantages of written and oral communication? Which do you prefer? Under what circumstances?
6. What is information overload? Do you ever experience it? How do you deal with it?
7. How well do you listen? How could you improve your listening skills?
8. Discuss the role of electronic media in communication.

EXERCISES/ACTION STEPS

1. Recall a situation that occurred at home or at work, and identify the communication problems you observed or experienced. Discuss how the communication model in this chapter can help you locate the problems.
2. Go to the library and do research on a public figure who communicates well. Discuss this person's characteristics as they relate to communication.

CASES

CASE 19-1
HAYNES FASHION STORES, INCORPORATED

After graduating from college, Joyce Haynes went to work for her father, Dudley Haynes, who was president of Haynes Fashion Stores, Incorporated, a chain of women's apparel stores. The company had been founded by Ms. Haynes's grandfather over 50 years ago. With her grandfather's and, for the past 20 years, her father's drive and knowledge of women's fashions and of how to buy and sell them, the company had developed from a single store in Hartford, Connecticut, to a fairly large and highly profitable chain of thirty stores in the New England area. Dudley Haynes was much like his father before him. He knew what he was doing and how to do it, and he prided himself on being able to keep his hands on details in buying, advertising, and store management. Every one of his store managers, as well as his top vice presidents and headquarters staff people, met with him every 2 weeks in Hartford. Between these meetings, Mr. Haynes spent 2 or 3 days each week visiting the stores and working with store managers.

His major worries were communication and motivation. Although he felt that all his managers and staff people listened carefully at the conferences he held, their subsequent actions made him wonder whether they had heard him at all. He observed that many of his policies were not being strictly followed in the stores; he often had to rewrite advertising copy; and in some of the stores the employees had joined the clerks union. He increasingly heard things he did not like, such as reports that many employees and even some managers felt they did not know the company's goals and believed they could do better if they had a chance to communicate with the executives at headquarters. He also had a strong feeling that many

of his managers and most of the store clerks were merely doing their jobs without showing any real imagination or drive. An additional concern was the fact that some of his best people had quit and taken positions with a competitor.

When his daughter walked into his office to begin work as his special assistant, he said: "Joyce, I'm worried about how things are going. Apparently, my two problems are communication and motivation. Now, I know that you took some courses in management in school. I've heard you talk of the problems, barriers, and techniques of communication, and you've mentioned some fellows—Maslow, Herzberg, Vroom, McClelland, and others—who knew a great deal about motivation. While I doubt that these psychology types knew much about business and I feel that I know what motivates people—primarily money, good bosses, and a good place to work—I wonder if you've learned anything that will help me communicate better. What do you suggest?"

1. If you were Ms. Haynes, what would you say to your father?
2. How would you go about analyzing the communication problem, and what difficulties do you see already from the case?
3. Suggest ways that the motivation and communication theories you have studied might be applied to Haynes Fashion Stores. Is there anything else you would want to know?
4. How would you apply the Rogers and Roethlisberger experiment discussed in this chapter to the case?

CASE 19-2
COULD THE CHALLENGER ACCIDENT HAVE BEEN AVOIDED?[31]

The Challenger Space Shuttle accident on January 28, 1986, gripped the nation more than any other event in the last dozen years or so. It was a tragic accident in which seven people died. There is now some evidence that the astronauts may have survived the initial explosion and may have died on impact when the space shuttle hit the water. The purpose of recounting the Challenger accident is to briefly explain what happened, why it may have happened, how it may have been prevented, and what one can learn from it.

The Challenger mission consisted of two complex systems: the technical system and the managerial system. The technical problem was the troublesome O-rings, which under pressure and low temperatures became ineffective and did not provide the required seal. Engineers and managers were aware of the problem. So why was the go-ahead given for launching the spacecraft? Can it be explained by the way the managerial system worked?

The engineers at Morton Thiokol, the contractor for the booster rocket, argued against the launch, citing previous problems at low temperatures. Management, on the other hand, may have felt pressure from NASA to go ahead with the launch. Roger Boisjoly, one of the engineers who argued strongly against the launch, stated that he received looks from management that seemed to say: "Go away and don't bother us with the facts." He said that he felt helpless. Another engineer was told to take off his engineering hat and put on his management hat.

Eventually, the go-ahead was given by managers. Engineers were excluded from the final decision. What, then, were some possible reasons for the disaster? Some argued that there was a lack of communication between engineers and managers. They have different goals: safety versus on-time launching. Others suggested that people with responsibilities did not want to hear the bad news. Thus, no listening. Still others suggested that there was insufficient provision for upward communication outside the chain of command. There was also a suggestion that status differences between engineers and managers and between upper- and lower-level managers may have played a role in inhibiting upward communication. Perhaps there was also false confidence in the mission because of past luck. Managers and engineers knew the problem, but nobody was killed before. Moreover, no one in the organizational unit wanted to be the "bad guy" to halt the launch. Morton Thiokol may also have been concerned about a pending contract.

The result of the series of events was the death of seven Americans: Jarvis, McAuliffe, McNair, Onizuka, Resnik, Scobee, and Smith. The question on our minds is: Could this accident have been prevented?

1. What can you learn from this disaster that may be relevant to your organization or an organization you know?
2. What do you think was the cause, or were the causes, of the Challenger disaster?

REFERENCES

1. Eric K. Clemons and F. Warren McFarlan, "Telecom: Hook Up or Lose Out," *Harvard Business Review* (July–August 1986), p. 91.
2. Chester I. Barnard, *The Functions of the Executive* (Cambridge, Mass.: Harvard University Press, 1938).
3. Thomas J. Peters and Robert H. Waterman, Jr., *In Search of Excellence* (New York: Harper & Row, 1982), chap. 5.
4. Maggie McComas, "Atop of the Fortune 500: A Survey of the C.E.O.s," *Fortune* (Apr. 28, 1986), pp. 26–31.

5. See also Carol Saunders and Jack William Jones, "Temporal Sequences in Information Acquisition for Decision Making: A Focus on Source and Medium," *Academy of Management Review* (January 1990), pp. 29–46.

6. Walter Kiechel III, "No Word from on High," *Fortune* (Jan. 6, 1986), pp. 125–126.

7. Michael Brody, "Listen to Your Whistleblower," *Fortune* (Nov. 24, 1986), pp. 77–78.

8. Michael Brody, "NASA's Challenge: Ending Isolation at the Top," *Fortune* (Mar. 12, 1986), pp. 26–32.

9. Charles E. Beck and Elizabeth A. Beck, "The Manager's Open Door and the Communication Climate," *Business Horizons* (January–February 1986), pp. 15–19.

10. Jean-Louis Barsoux and Peter Lawrence, "The Making of a French Manager," *Harvard Business Review* (July–August 1991), pp. 58–67.

11. See also Nancy J. Adler, *International Dimensions of Organizational Behavior,* 2d ed. (Boston: PWS-Kent Publishing Company, 1991).

12. See John D. Daniels, Ernest W. Ogram, Jr., and Lee H. Radebaugh, *International Business,* 3d ed. (Reading, Mass.: Addison-Wesley Publishing Company, 1982), chaps. 4 and 19; Simcha Ronen, *Comparative and Multinational Management* (New York: John Wiley & Sons, 1986), chap. 4.

13. V. H. Kirpalani, *International Marketing* (New York: Random House, 1985), chap. 4.

14. Chin-Ning Chu, *The Chinese Mind Games* (Beaverton, Oreg.: AMC Publishing, 1988).

15. Martin Rosch, "Communications: Focal Point of Culture," *Management International Review,* vol. 27, no. 4 (1987).

16. Roger D'Aprix, "The Oldest (and Best) Way to Communicate with Employees," *Harvard Business Review* (September–October 1982), pp. 30–32.

17. See also Rodger W. Griffeth, Kerry D. Carson, and Daniel B. Marin, "Information Overload: A Test of an Inverted U Hypothesis with Hourly and Salaried Employees," *Academy of Management Best Papers—Proceedings 1988,* Forty-Eighth Annual Meeting of the Academy of Management, Anaheim, Calif. (Aug. 7–10, 1988), pp. 232–235.

18. See also Eric M. Eisenberg and Marsha G. Witten, "Reconsidering Openness in Organizational Communication," *Academy of Management Review* (July 1987), pp. 418–426.

19. For a detailed discussion of this topic, see J. C. Miller's analysis of information overload in Daniel Katz and Robert L. Kahn, *The Social Psychology of Organizations* (New York: John Wiley & Sons, 1978), pp. 451–455.

20. Howard H. Greenbaum, "The Audit of Organizational Communication," *Academy of Management Journal* (December 1974), pp. 739–754.

21. Howard H. Greenbaum and N. D. White, "Biofeedback at the Organizational Level: The Communication Audit," *The Journal of Business Communication* (Summer 1976), pp. 3–15.

22. Keith Davis and John W. Newstrom, *Human Behavior at Work: Organizational Behavior,* 7th ed. (New York: McGraw-Hill Book Company, 1985), p. 436.

23. Carl R. Rogers and F. J. Roethlisberger, "Barriers and Gateways to Communication," *Business Classics: Fifteen Key Concepts for Managerial Success* (Boston: Resident and Fellows of Harvard College, 1975), pp. 44–50.

24. Davis and Newstrom, *Human Behavior at Work* (1985), p. 438.

25. John S. Fielden, "What Do You Mean You Don't Like My Style?" *Harvard Business Review* (May–June 1982), pp. 128–138.

26. Adapted from Jay A. Conger, "Inspiring Others: The Language of Leadership," *Academy of Management Executive* (February 1991), pp. 31–45.

27. Eric K. Clemons and F. Warren McFarlan, "Telecom: Hook Up or Lose Out," *Harvard Business Review* (July–August 1986), pp. 91–97; Anne R. Field and Catherine L. Harris, "The Information Business," *Business Week* (Aug. 25, 1986), pp. 82–90.

28. For a series of articles on telecommunications, see *The Wall Street Journal—A Special Report: Telecommunications* (Feb. 24, 1986).

29. Robert Johansen and Christine Bullen, "What to Expect from Teleconferencing," *Harvard Business Review* (March–April 1984), pp. 164–174.

30. "Management Warms Up to Computer Graphics," *Business Week* (Aug. 13, 1984), pp. 96–101.

31. Information for this case was drawn from a variety of sources, including Congressional hearings and a presentation by Roger Boisjoly.

Summary of Major Principles, or Guides, for Leading

For the managerial function of leading, several principles, or guides, can be summarized. They are the following:

Principle of harmony of objectives.   The more managers can harmonize the personal goals of individuals with the goals of the enterprise, the more effective and efficient the enterprise will be.

Principle of motivation.   Since motivation is not a simple cause and effect matter, the more managers carefully assess a reward structure, look upon it from a situation and contingency point of view, and integrate it into the entire system of managing, the more effective a motivational program will be.

Principle of leadership.   Since people tend to follow those who, in their view, offer them a means of satisfying their personal goals, the more managers understand what motivates their subordinates and how these motivators operate, and the more they reflect this understanding in carrying out their managerial actions, the more effective they are likely to be as leaders.

Principle of communication clarity.   Communication tends to be clear when it is expressed in a language and transmitted in a way that can be understood by the receiver.

The responsibility of the sender is to formulate the message so that it is understandable to the receiver. This responsibility pertains primarily to written and oral communication and points to the necessity for planning the message, stating the underlying assumptions, and applying the generally accepted rules for effective writing and speaking.

Principle of communication integrity.   The greater the integrity and consistency of written, oral, and nonverbal messages, as well as of the moral behavior of the sender, the greater the acceptance of the message by the receiver.

Principle of supplemental use of informal organization.   Communication tends to be more effective when managers utilize the informal organization to supplement the communication channels of the formal organization.

Informal organization is a phenomenon managers must accept. Information, true or not, flows quickly through the informal organization. Consequently, managers should take advantage of this device to correct misinformation and to provide information that cannot be effectively sent or appropriately received through the formal communication system.

Global Leading

This part closing is on global leading. First, leading is practiced differently in various countries. The comparisons here are among Japan, the United States, and the People's Republic of China. Next, the international focus is on selected global aspects of leading—specifically, the influence of different cultures. Finally, a global car industry case involving two U.S. carmakers is presented to illustrate managerial leading in the international context.

LEADING PRACTICES IN JAPAN, THE UNITED STATES, AND THE PEOPLE'S REPUBLIC OF CHINA[1]

Leading is the process of influencing people so that they will contribute to organizational aims; it is concerned with motivation, leadership, and communication. The managerial practices in leading are summarized in the accompanying table for Japan, the United States, and China.

Leading in Japan

Japanese managers are seen as social integrators who are a part of the work group. Using a paternalistic leadership approach, managers show great concern for the welfare of their subordinates. Common values and team spirit facilitate cooperation. The role of managers is to create an environment of esprit de corps, and they are willing to help out in doing the same work their subordinates do. In an attempt to maintain harmony at almost any cost, managers avoid face-to-face confrontation. This means that things may be purposely left ambiguous. Leadership requires followership, and managers are aided by the fact that individuals are expected to

COMPARISONS OF JAPANESE, U.S., AND CHINESE LEADING*		
Japanese management	**U.S. management**	**Chinese management**
1. Leader acting as a social facilitator and group member	1. Leader acting as the decision maker and head of the group	1. Leader acting as the head of the group (committee)
2. Paternalistic style	2. Directive style (strong, firm, determined)	2. Directive style (Parent-Child relations, in transactional analysis terms)
3. Common values facilitating cooperation	3. Often divergent values; individualism sometimes hindering cooperation	3. Common values; emphasis on harmony
4. Avoidance of confrontation, sometimes leading to ambiguities; emphasis on harmony	4. Face-to-face confrontation common; emphasis on clarity	4. Avoidance of confrontation
5. Critical communication top-down and bottom-up; noncritical communication often bottom-up	5. Communication primarily top-down	5. Communication top-down

* Sources of information are given in note 6 in the Part 2 closing References.

subordinate their self-interest to that of the group and the organization. While managers may not be very directive, influence is exerted through peer pressure. In fact, close personal relationships are nurtured not only because employees work together on common tasks but also because they meet and associate outside the work environment. The result is a confluence of organizational and private life.

Communication patterns parallel those for decision making. Critical communication is top-down and bottom-up, while noncritical communication is often bottom-up. This communication pattern is promoted by Japanese managers who take a great deal of time communicating with their subordinates, emphasizing face-to-face contact rather than memos.

Leading in the United States

The managerial function of leading is carried out quite differently in U.S. companies. Leaders are seen as decision makers heading the group; they are expected to be directive, strong, firm, and determined. Their task is to integrate diverse values, but the emphasis on individualism in the society in general and in organizations in particular may hinder cooperation. It is expected that managers will take decisive actions and clarify the direction of the group or the enterprise, even if this requires face-to-face confrontation with those who may disagree. Although managers work hard, they value their private life and separate it from their working life. Within the organization, the communication pattern is to a great extent from the top down through the hierarchy, with considerable emphasis given to written communication.

Leading in China

The managerial function of leading in China has characteristics of Japanese and U.S. practices. The leader is the head of the group (in committees, for example), and the leadership style is generally quite directive. One interviewee described the relationship between the leaders and followers as Parent-Child, in transactional analysis terms. In other words, it is expected that the leaders' commands will be obeyed. Leaders, in turn, are responsible to higher authorities for performance and goals but not for meeting customer needs and demands (this, however, is slowly changing). Similar to leading in Japan, leading in China is aided by common values and an emphasis on harmony rather than confrontation. On the other hand, communication is primarily top-down, as in many U.S. corporations.

INTERNATIONAL FOCUS: LEADING IN DIFFERENT CULTURES[2]

The managerial function of leading focuses on interactions among people. Managers operating in the global environment need to understand at least some cultural aspects of the country in which they plan to work. The influence of the nation's culture on the organization culture may not be immediately recognized, yet it is reflected in organizational behavior and managerial practices.

Culture and Managerial Behavior

Culture is not easy to define. As pointed out previously, one way to describe culture is as a pattern of behavior related to values and beliefs that were developed over a period of time. Symbols, for example, may indicate what members of a society or an organization value. Indeed, one may distinguish between the culture of a nation and that of an organization. The external environment influences the way people interact within an organization. It must also be recognized that within a country the culture may differ widely, not only in countries as large and diverse as the United States but also in geographically small and relatively homogeneous countries such as Germany. Northern Germans behave differently than the people in southern Germany. It is with this precaution that culture and its impact on organizations must be viewed.

Today's managers need to develop a global perspective; a parochial view is inappropriate. In the past, many U.S. corporations (except the multinational ones) saw little reason to develop a global view. The immense U.S. market was often sufficient for small and medium-sized firms. These companies did not see the need to expand beyond the national boundaries and venture to foreign countries, with different cultures, different languages, and increased risks. But now hardly any company can ignore the global environment, even if the firm has no plans to operate abroad. Increasingly, foreign firms are entering the U.S. market. Moreover, many U.S. firms employ people from different nations with different cultures.

Cultural differences affect managerial behavior and practices such as planning (for example, short- versus long-term orientation), organizing (for example, the kind of organizational structure or the attitude toward delegation), staffing (for example, selection based on family relationships rather than professional qualifications), leading (for example, the use of the participative, rather than directive, leadership style), and controlling (for example, the use of tight and close control versus broad controls).

Culture also affects interpersonal relations, such as those found in negotiations. In Russia, for example, people in business may not seek long-term relations with their negotiating partners. Also, one should not be surprised to see very few Russians smiling in public. In the Russians' business dealings, toasts are very common, so Westerners would be well advised not to try to keep up with the way Russians drink alcoholic beverages.

Americans may find doing business with the English relatively easy. Not only do Americans and the English share many cultural aspects, but they also communicate in the same native language, which facilitates interpersonal relations. However, the British do not like to discuss business at the dinner table.

In France, conflict is a common part of daily life. The French attempt to seek the truth in universal laws. They also base their personal trust on the character of the individual rather than on professional achievement. Moreover, competitive drive is not as pronounced in France as it is in the United States. The social class structure and the status related to this structure are very important for social interactions within and outside the organization.

Since business relationships with Japanese firms are becoming more frequent, and since Westerners are often unaware or uncertain of Japanese cultural aspects in social interactions, some guidelines will be provided.

The Importance of Understanding the Culture While Doing Business in Japan

People from Western countries may feel uncomfortable doing business in Japan. While it may be extremely difficult to understand the subtleties of the Japanese culture, thorough preparation may be vitally important for harmonious business relationships.

Establishing business relationships. It is virtually impossible to meet new Japanese business partners without establishing contacts long before the trip to Japan. Appointments need to be preceded by connections and letters planning the meetings. While it may be difficult to learn the Japanese language, one should at least learn greetings and some common phrases. In a male-dominated society such as Japan, Western women may feel uncomfortable at first. However, they are aided by the fact that the Japanese are very polite to foreigners in general. Moreover, even Japanese women have made some career advancements in recent years in Japanese firms.

For the Japanese, face-to-face communication is very important. They want to know their foreign partners very well before doing business with them. Moreover, it must be remembered that Japanese managers try to reach a consensus among themselves before responding to questions or making statements. One of the authors had the opportunity to visit a major Japanese carmaker. Questions directed at the Japanese host were first discussed by the managers (in Japanese) before one of the managers provided answers.

Recognizing what the Japanese may think about Westerners.
The Japanese may admire the innovativeness of Westerners as well as their energy in getting things done. On the other hand, foreigners are often viewed as being impatient, making quick acquaintances but friendships of little depth. Moreover, the Japanese often feel that deprivation, such as that experienced after World War II, made them hard workers. Some Japanese political and business leaders feel that Japan should now be assuming economic leadership in the world. These same leaders realize that the economic prosperity of their more than 120 million people depends on exports and the operation of Japan's multinational corporations abroad. Furthermore, Japan has only limited natural resources and must import all its oil from abroad.

Understanding the art of gift giving.
One can distinguish between two kinds of gifts: personal and corporate. Personal gifts may include picture books or items for which the home country or state is known. Other items may include golf balls, caps, tie clips, or Native American jewelry. If the Japanese partner has children, then T-shirts, children's books, or pens or pencils may be appropriate gifts. Corporate gifts may include pens, T-shirts, bookmarks, or other items with the company logo. These items should be made in the home country, not in Japan.

The way gifts are presented is also important. Presents should be wrapped in colors appropriate for the occasion, such as blue, brown, gray, or green. Showy colors, such as pink or red, and flowered paper are not appropriate. Moreover, black and white, known as funeral colors, should also be avoided. Giving and receiving gifts is done with both hands. Gift packages are generally not opened in front of the giver, in case it may embarrass him or her. If a gift consists of several similar items, avoid giving four items of a kind, as this may imply "death," or nine items, since the word "nine" means "choking."

Meeting with the Japanese.
Business meetings in Japan are generally more formal than in the United States. The preliminary aspects take a great deal of time, yet they are essential for a successful meeting. Unless introduced, one introduces himself or herself first to the senior Japanese businessperson. At this time, business cards are exchanged. If the ranking, or senior, person is not known, it usually becomes evident from the behavior of subordinates, who show great respect toward this person. Moreover, it is usually the senior person who enters the room first. At the meeting, the ranking person usually sits at the middle position at the table or in the middle among his advisers. (Note that there are hardly any women in top-management positions, although women have made some career advancements in recent years.)

The presentation of the business card is an essential ritual. Never leave your home without your business cards when going to Japan. Ideally, the cards should be in English and Japanese. Younger persons, or those of lower ranking, present their card first to the Japanese business partner. On the other hand, lower-level foreign managers only give their card when the Japanese CEO has offered his.

The card should be presented with both hands unless the cards are exchanged with a handshake. Also, the printed side (the English side if the other side is in Japanese) should be held faceup and in such a way that the Japanese businessperson can read it without having to turn the card. While the Japanese have a custom of bowing, a friendly nod by the foreign person will suffice.

Meetings serve not only for "making deals" but also for establishing relationships. The Japanese would like to know whether they feel comfortable enough to deal with the counterpart. This means that they want to know whether a person is trustworthy, has a thorough knowledge of the product or service offered, and is listening and being receptive to their needs. Americans are often perceived as being too talkative or too pushy in obtaining a decision.

Modern managers need to develop a perspective with a global geographic and multicultural orientation. Being aware of cultural differences is a prerequisite for personal and organizational success.

GLOBAL CAR INDUSTRY CASE:
CAN FORD AND GENERAL MOTORS REGAIN THEIR LEADERSHIP?[3]

Ford and General Motors face tough global competition, for Japanese carmakers have been gaining market share in the United States. Ford Motor Company responded with the rather successful Taurus model, using extensively teamwork concepts. General Motors, on the other hand, built a completely new manufacturing and assembly plant in Tennessee. The departures from traditional managing were spearheaded by Ford's Donald Petersen and GM's Roger Smith.

Management by Teamwork at Ford

In the early 1980s Ford Motor Company was in trouble. It was even said that "FORD" stood for "fix or repair daily." Indeed, the Ford story shows how a company can be turned around. The Ford Taurus and Mercury Sable were the turning points for the company; they illustrate that models produced by U.S. carmakers can compete with the very successful Japanese imports.

Problems can become opportunities, and during the 1980 recession there were many difficulties to overcome. It became clear that Ford had to compete not only against other U.S. carmakers but also against auto manufacturers throughout the world. Drastic steps were necessary: Ford invested $3 billion in its new models, made quality its number-one concern, and learned from other carmakers, especially the Japanese.

One of the first undertakings was to replace the old bureaucratic structure with the team approach, or program management. Previously, it took 5 years to produce a new model. The old "sequential" approach was as follows: The product planners developed the general concept of the new model, which was then given to the designers. After the design stage, engineers got involved, developing specifications for manufacturing and for the various suppliers. This process was sequential, with little communication among the various groups. When manufactur-

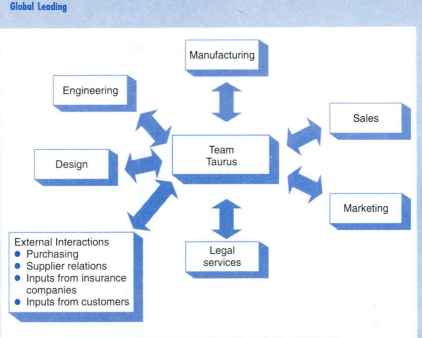

TEAM APPROACH TO PRODUCT DEVELOPMENT.

ing, for example, got the specifications, little flexibility was possible, even if changing the design would facilitate assembly. If a problem was discovered at the manufacturing stage, designers and engineers had to be involved again, this time to correct the problem. However, if parts were already purchased or dies already made, changes were costly; some were simply not made because of the delay that would be involved. In this approach, the overall responsibility was not clearly defined.

Ford recognized the need for dramatic changes, which were incorporated in the project "Team Taurus." Rather than having each unit do the various tasks sequentially, the company established a team consisting of planners, designers, engineers, manufacturing people, and even suppliers (see the accompanying figure). Thus, representatives from all units were involved in the project right from the beginning. This way, difficulties could be resolved before they became major problems. Ford also involved assembly line workers in the development of the model. They were asked to comment on difficulties they had with assembling the parts and to make recommendations for improvements.

Rather than adopting the attitude of "we know best," Ford people carefully studied cars made by other manufacturers and learned about their best features. For example, Ford noted the accuracy of the Toyota fuel gauge and the good tire storage of the BMW, as well as the design of Audi's accelerator pedal. Ford also tested different seats on young and old, male and female, drivers. Through extensive market studies, Ford learned about other customer preferences.

The chairman, Donald Petersen, gives credit for Ford's turnaround to his team. But *he* took the $3 billion risk in developing the new line of cars. He delegated authority down the organizational hierarchy to the ranks of the workers.

Decision making is no longer the prerogative of top management; it is done by the team that takes action. Petersen practiced "management by wandering around" (MBWA), visiting the factories and listening to workers.

GM's Gamble with the Saturn

Eight years in the making, GM's Saturn was conceived as the car to beat the Japanese. Chairman Roger Smith departed from tradition to set up an unconventional, independent subsidiary to meet the Japanese challenge. Between 1985 and 1990, Japanese carmakers' market share increased 7 percent, while GM's declined 11 points.

GM is confident of Saturn's quality, its excellent handling, and its low vibration. But the company's aim was more than to come out with a new product. What GM achieved are Saturn's new organization culture, its new management-labor relations, its participative management style, and its new manufacturing approach. Employees undergo intensive training. Barriers between labor and management are eliminated. For example, the president and the employees eat together in the same cafeteria. All employees are salaried. Workers begin at 80 percent of the pay on the pay scale of GM's United Automobile Workers (UAW) union. However, productivity is rewarded with extra pay. Workers participate in decision making. New employees receive 5 days of training, and training continues after the initial period, with 5 percent of the working time devoted to further development.

The layout of GM's new manufacturing and assembly plant in Spring Hill, Tennessee, near Nashville, differs from the traditional one. For example, the plant has no central loading dock. Instead, parts arrive in several places, where workers immediately check for defects. The assembly line is designed with the workers in mind. The guiding idea is to achieve higher productivity with less stress. Workers, for example, ride with the car on the assembly line while doing their work. Then they simply walk back to the next car.

But the Saturn project underwent changes after its initial conception. The original idea of a subcompact car was changed to one of a compact size. The price tag nearly doubled. The wheelbase got longer. The planned 6000-member work force was cut in half, and the planned investment of $5 billion was reduced to $3 or $3.5 billion. Saturn's rather conventional styling received mixed reviews. There were also critics within GM who barked at the heavy investment in the project.

For GM, the Saturn represents a major gamble. Analysts think that the production output will need to be increased to make the project profitable. The new organization culture, emphasizing participative management, teamwork, and new production layouts, needs to stand the test of time. While the venture appears to be risky, it might have been even riskier to continue in the old way.

1. Compare Ford's traditional sequential procedure with the team approach used for developing new models.
2. Discuss Ford's new production design and its impact on the managerial system. What are the implications for leadership?
3. Why did GM's Roger Smith initiate the Saturn project?

4. Do you think that the new organization culture and the new leadership style will be successful? Why is this a new approach?

5. Would you buy a Saturn, or would you prefer one of its competitors, such as the Honda Civic or the Toyota Corolla? What factors are important in your buying decision?

REFERENCES

1. Sources of information are given in note 6 in the Part 2 closing References. In addition see Lee Smith, "Japan's Autocratic Managers," *Fortune* (Jan. 7, 1985), pp. 56–65; Hirotake Takeuchi, "Productivity: Learning from the Japanese," *California Management Review* (Summer 1981), pp. 5–20. For a discussion of Japan's young leaders, see Frederick Hiroshi Katayama, "Six Who Will Make a Difference," *Fortune* (Mar. 30, 1987), pp. 50–53; Adi Ignatius, "Beleaguered Bosses—For China's Managers, Keeping Plants Going Is a Daily Struggle," *The Wall Street Journal* (Apr. 13, 1990).

2. For further reading see Nancy J. Adler, *International Dimensions of Organizational Behavior*, 2d ed. (Boston: PWS-Kent Publishing Company, 1991); Simcha Ronen, *Comparative and Multinational Management* (New York: John Wiley & Sons, 1986); Philip R. Harris and Robert T. Moran, *Managing Cultural Differences*, 2d ed. (Houston: Gulf Publishing Company, 1987); Christalyn Brannen, *Going to Japan on Business* (Berkeley, Calif.: Stone Bridge Press and BLC Intercultural, 1991); John C. Condon, *With Respect to the Japanese* (Yarmouth, Maine: Intercultural Press, 1984); David J. Lu, *Inside Corporate Japan: The Art of Fumble-Free Management* (Tokyo: Charles E. Tuttle, 1987); Robert Neff, Ted Holden, Karen Lowry Miller, and Joyce Barnathan, "Hidden Japan—The Scandals Start to Reveal How the System Really Works," *Business Week* (Aug. 26, 1991), pp. 34–38; Robert Neff, "Japan's Small Smoke-Filled Room," *Business Week* (Aug. 26, 1991), pp. 42–44; Robert Whiting, *You Gotta Have Wa* (New York: Vintage Books, 1990); Mark Zimmerman, *How to Do Business with the Japanese* (New York: Random House, 1985).

3. The Ford and General Motors cases are based on a variety of sources, including Brian Dumaine, "A Humble Hero Drives Ford to the Top," *Fortune* (Jan. 4, 1988), pp. 23–24; Alex Taylor III, "Who's Ahead in the World Auto War," *Fortune* (Nov. 9, 1987), pp. 74–88; James B. Treece, Mark Maremont, and Larry Armstrong, "Will the Auto Glut Choke Detroit?" *Business Week* (Mar. 7, 1987), pp. 54–62; David Woodruff and Stephen Phillips, "Ford Has a Better Idea: Let Someone Else Have the Idea," *Business Week* (Apr. 30, 1990), pp. 116–117; James B. Treece, "Here Comes GM's Saturn," *Business Week* (Apr. 9, 1990), pp. 56–62. For further information see Alex Taylor III, "Can GM Remodel Itself?" *Fortune* (Jan. 13, 1992), pp. 26–34; James B. Treece, "The Board Revolt—Business As Usual Won't Cut It Anymore at a Humbled GM," *Business Week* (Apr. 29, 1992), pp. 30–36.

PART 6

Controlling

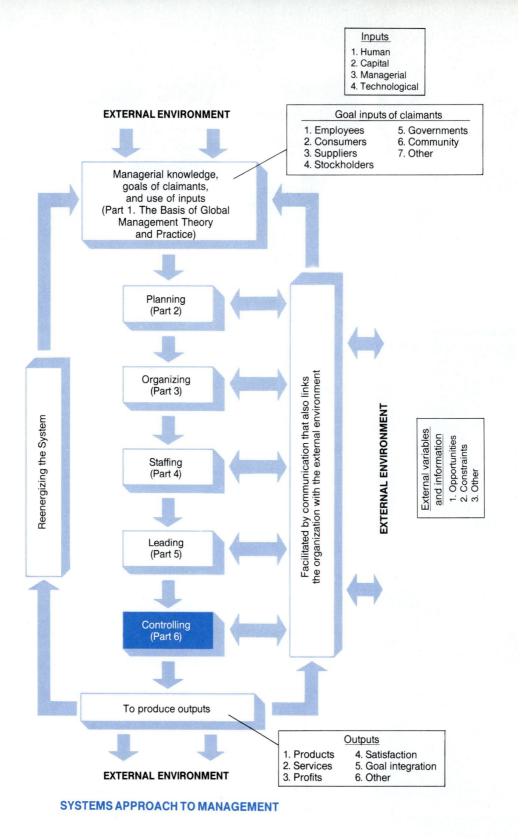

SYSTEMS APPROACH TO MANAGEMENT

To understand why the organization
wants activities controlled, one must
look to the organization's goals.[1]
Stephen G. Green
and M. Ann Welsh

The System and
Process of Controlling

Chapter Objectives

After reading this chapter, you should be able to:

1. Describe the steps in the basic control process.
2. Enumerate and explain the critical control points and standards.
3. Illustrate applications of the feedback system.
4. Demonstrate that because of the time lags in feedback control, real-time information will not solve all the problems of management control.
5. Show that feedforward control systems can make management control more effective.
6. List and explain the requirements for effective controls.

The managerial function of **controlling** is the measurement and correction of performance in order to make sure that enterprise objectives and the plans devised to attain them are being accomplished. Planning and controlling are closely related. In fact, some writers on management think that these functions cannot be separated. It is wise to separate them conceptually, however, which is why they are discussed individually in Parts 2 and 6 of this book. Still, planning and controlling may be viewed as the blades of a pair of scissors; the scissors cannot work unless there are two blades. Without objectives and plans, control is not possible, because performance has to be measured against some established criteria.

Controlling is the function of every manager from president to supervisor. Some managers, particularly at lower levels, forget that the primary responsibility for the exercise of control rests in every manager charged with the execution of plans. Although the scope of control varies among managers, those at all levels have responsibility for the execution of plans, and control is therefore an essential managerial function at every level.

Although control is often treated superficially in management literature, Giovanni B. Giglioni and Arthur G. Bedeian found a valuable body of knowledge in the following areas: control concepts, the process of control, characteristics of control systems, the problems encountered in control and the lessons learned from them, the variety of control models and techniques, and some principles for effective and efficient control.[2] Part 6 will cover all these topics, as well as others such as management information systems and tools for production and operations management.

THE BASIC CONTROL PROCESS

Control techniques and systems are essentially the same for cash, office procedures, morale, product quality, and anything else. The **basic control process,** wherever it is found and whatever is being controlled, involves three steps: (1) establishing standards, (2) measuring performance against these standards, and (3) correcting variations from standards and plans.

Establishment of Standards

Because plans are the yardsticks against which managers devise controls, the first step in the control process logically would be to establish plans. However, since plans vary in detail and complexity, and since managers cannot usually watch everything, special standards are established. **Standards** are, by definition, simply criteria of performance. They are the selected points in an entire planning program at which measures of performance are made so that managers can receive signals about how things are going and thus do not have to watch every step in the execution of plans.

There are many kinds of standards. Among the best are verifiable goals or objectives, as suggested in the discussion of managing by objectives (see Chapter 6). You will learn more about standards, especially those that point out deviations at critical points, in the next section.

Measurement of Performance

Although such measurement is not always practicable, the measurement of performance against standards should ideally be done on a forward-looking basis so that deviations may be detected in advance of their occurrence and avoided by appropriate actions. The alert, forward-looking manager can sometimes predict probable departures from standards. In the absence of such ability, however, deviations should be disclosed as early as possible.[3]

If standards are appropriately drawn and if means are available for determining exactly what subordinates are doing, appraisal of actual or expected performance is fairly easy. But there are many activities for which it is difficult to develop accurate standards, and there are many activities that are hard to measure. It may be quite simple to establish labor-hour standards for the production of a mass-produced item, and it may be equally simple to measure performance against these standards, but if the item is custom-made, the appraisal of performance may be a formidable task because standards are difficult to set.

Moreover, in the less technical kinds of work, not only may standards be hard to develop but also appraisal will be difficult. For example, controlling the work of the finance vice president or the industrial relations director is not easy because definite standards are not easily developed. The superior of these managers often relies on vague standards, such as the financial health of the business, the attitude of labor unions, the absence of strikes, the enthusiasm and loyalty of subordinates, the expressed admiration of business associates, and the overall success of the department (often measured in a negative way by lack of evidence of failure). The superior's measurements are often equally vague. At the same time, if the department seems to be making the contribution expected of it at a reasonable cost and without too many serious errors, and if the measurable accomplishments give evidence of sound management, a general appraisal may be adequate. The point is that as jobs move away from the assembly line, the shop, or the accounting machine, controlling them becomes more complex and often even more important.

Correction of Deviations

Standards should reflect the various positions in an organization structure. If performance is measured accordingly, it is easier to correct deviations. Managers know exactly where, in the assignment of individual or group duties, the corrective measures must be applied.

Correction of deviations is the point at which control can be seen as a part of the whole system of management and can be related to the other managerial functions. Managers may correct deviations by redrawing their plans or by modifying their goals. (This is an exercise of the principle of navigational change.) Or they may correct deviations by exercising their organizing function through reassignment or clarification of duties. They may correct, also, by additional staffing, by better selection and training of subordinates, or by that ultimate restaffing measure—firing. Or, again, they may correct through better leading—fuller explanation of the job or more effective leadership techniques.

Special Considerations in Controlling International Companies

Controlling domestic companies is often difficult. More difficult is exercising control of enterprises operating in different countries. The geographic distances make certain controls, such as observation, very difficult, despite modern jet service.

Control standards have to be adjusted to the local environment. Subsidiaries in low-labor-cost countries may have lower cost budgets than companies in countries with a high-cost labor force. And productivity in countries with low labor costs may lag behind that of other countries.

Transfer pricing between the headquarters and the subsidiaries or between subsidiaries may distort the profitability and return-on-investment pictures. A similar distortion can occur through currency fluctuations among the various countries. Moreover, erratic or chronic inflation makes the setting of standards and measurement against those standards difficult.

Other factors should also be considered in controlling. As pointed out in the discussion of organizing, the organization structure should facilitate control. Multinational corporations require a different departmentation from that of domestic firms. Another way to exercise control is to prevent deviations from occurring by selecting competent managers in the first place.[4] In the past, multinational corporations sent experienced managers to head their subsidiaries in other countries. More recently, however, companies have been selecting and training managers of the nationality of the country in which they operate. Furthermore, managers with special skills for cultural adaptation may come from a country other than where the headquarters or the subsidiary is located. For example, at one time, the CEO of Volkswagen of America was neither a German nor an American but a Canadian.

The way control is exercised differs in various countries. In the United States, for example, attempts are made to pinpoint responsibility for deviations from standards. In many Asian countries, superiors try to let the person who does not meet the standards "save face." Moreover, standards may not even be set in measurable terms in the first place. How, then, can control be exercised? In countries such as Japan where group work is common, peer pressure may be a very effective means for exercising control.

In short, controlling—that is, setting standards, measuring performance, and taking corrective actions—must be flexible enough to take into account the organizational and country-specific environment.

CRITICAL CONTROL POINTS AND STANDARDS

Standards are yardsticks against which actual or expected performance is measured. In a simple operation a manager might control through careful personal observation of the work being done. However, in most operations this is not possible because of the complexity of the operations and the fact that a manager has far more to do than personally observe performance for a whole day. A manager must choose points for special attention and then watch them to be sure that the whole operation is proceeding as planned.

The points selected for control should be *critical,* in the sense either of being limiting factors in the operation or of showing better than other factors whether plans are working out. With such standards, managers can handle a larger group of subordinates and thereby increase their span of management, with resulting cost savings and improvement of communication. The **principle of critical-point control,** one of the more important control principles, states: *Effective control requires attention to those factors critical to evaluating performance against plans.*

Questions for Selecting Critical Points of Control

The ability to select critical points of control is one of the arts of management, since sound control depends on them. In this connection, managers must ask themselves such questions as these: What will best reflect the goals of my department? What will best show me when these goals are not being met? What will best measure critical deviations? What will tell me who is responsible for any failure? What standards will cost the least? For what standards is information economically available?

Types of Critical-Point Standards

Every objective, every goal of the many planning programs, every activity of these programs, every policy, every procedure, and every budget become standards against which actual or expected performance might be measured. In practice, however, standards tend to be of the following types: (1) physical standards, (2) cost standards, (3) capital standards, (4) revenue standards, (5) program standards, (6) intangible standards, (7) goals as standards, and (8) strategic plans as control points for strategic control.

Physical standards.   Physical standards are nonmonetary measurements and are common at the operating level, where materials are used, labor is employed, services are rendered, and goods are produced. They may reflect quantities such as labor-hours per unit of output, pounds of fuel per horsepower produced, ton-miles of freight traffic carried, units of production per machine-hour, or feet of wire per ton of copper. Physical standards may also reflect quality, such as hardness of bearings, closeness of tolerances, rate of climb of an airplane, durability of a fabric, or fastness of a color.

Cost standards.[5]   Cost standards are monetary measurements and, like physical standards, are common at the operating level. They attach monetary values to specific aspects of operations. Illustrative of cost standards are such widely used measures as direct and indirect costs per unit produced, labor cost per unit or per hour, material cost per unit, machine-hour costs, costs per plane reservation, selling costs per dollar or unit of sales, and costs per foot of oil well drilled.

Capital standards.   There are a variety of capital standards, all arising from the application of monetary measurements to physical items. They have to do with the capital invested in the firm rather than with operating costs and are therefore primarily related to the balance sheet rather than to the income statement. Perhaps the most widely used standards for new investment, as well as for overall control, is return on investment. The typical balance sheet will disclose other capital standards, such as the ratios of current assets to current liabilities, debt to net worth, fixed investment to total investment, cash and receivables to payables, and notes or bonds to stock, as well as the size and turnover of inventories.

Revenue standards.   Revenue standards arise from attaching monetary values to sales. They may include such standards as revenue per bus passenger–mile, average sale per customer, and sales per capita in a given market area.

Program standards.   A manager may be assigned to install a variable budget program, a program for formally following the development of new products, or a program for improving the quality of a sales force. Although some subjective judgment may have to be applied in appraising program performance, timing and other factors can be used as objective standards.

Intangible standards.   More difficult to set are standards not expressed in either physical or monetary measurements. What standards can a manager use for determining the competence of the divisional purchasing agent or personnel director? What can one use for determining whether the advertising program meets both short- and long-term objectives? Or whether the public relations program is successful? Are supervisors loyal to the company's objectives? Is the office staff alert? Such questions show the difficulty of establishing standards or goals for clear quantitative or qualitative measurement.

Many intangible standards exist in business, partially because adequate research into what constitutes desired performance has not been done above the level of the shop, the district sales office, the shipping room, or the accounting department. Perhaps a more important reason is that where human relationships count in performance, as they do above the basic operating levels, it is very hard to measure what is "good," "effective," or "efficient." Tests, surveys, and sampling techniques developed by psychologists and sociometrists have made it possible to probe human attitudes and drives, but many managerial controls over interpersonal relationships must continue to be based on intangible standards, considered judgment, trial and error, and even, on occasion, sheer hunch.

Goals as standards.   With the present tendency for better-managed enterprises to establish an entire network of verifiable qualitative or quantitative goals at every level of management, the use of intangible standards, while still important, is diminishing. In complex program operations, as well as in the performance of managers themselves, modern managers are finding that through research and thinking it is possible to define goals that can be used as performance standards. While the quantitative goals are likely to take the form of the standards outlined above, the definition of qualitative goals represents an important development in the area of standards. For example, if the program of a district sales office is spelled out to include such elements as training salespeople in accordance with a plan with specific characteristics, the plan and its characteristics themselves furnish standards that tend to become objective and, therefore, "tangible."

Strategic plans as control points for strategic control.   A great deal has been written about strategic planning, but relatively little is known about strategic control. According to a book on the topic, **strategic control** comprises systematic monitoring at strategic control points as well as modifying the organization's strategy on the basis of this evaluation.[6] The book's authors agree with the viewpoint expressed in this text, namely that planning and controlling are closely related. Therefore, strategic plans require strategic control. Moreover, since controls facilitate comparisons of intended goals with actual performance, they also provide opportunities for learning, which, in turn, is the basis for organization change. Finally, through the use of strategic control one gains insights not only about organizational performance but also about the ever-changing environment by monitoring it.

CONTROL AS A FEEDBACK SYSTEM

Managerial control is essentially the same basic control process as that found in physical, biological, and social systems. Many systems control themselves through information feedback, which shows deviations from standards and initiates changes. In other words, systems use some of their energy to feed back information that compares performance with a standard and initiates corrective action. A simple feedback system was shown in Chapter 5 (see Figure 5-2).

Perspective

Examples of Feedback Systems

The house thermostate is a system of feedback and information control. When the house temperature falls below the preset level, an electric message is sent to the heating system, which is then activated. When the temperature increases and reaches the set level, another message shuts off the heater. This continual measurement and turning on and off of the heater keeps the house at the desired temperature. A similar process activates the air-conditioning system. As soon as the temperature exceeds the preset level, the air-conditioning system cools the house to the desired temperature. Likewise, in the human body, a number of feedback systems control temperature, blood pressure, motor reactions, and other conditions. Another example of feedback is the grade a student receives on a midterm test. This is intended, of course, to give the student information about how he or she is doing and, if performance is less than desirable, to send a signal suggesting improvement.

Management control is usually perceived as a feedback system similar to that which operates in the common household thermostat.[7] This can be seen clearly by looking at the feedback process in management control shown in Figure 20-1. This system places control in a more complex and realistic light than would regarding it merely as a matter of establishing standards, measuring performance, and correcting for deviations. Managers do measure actual performance, compare this measurement against standards, and identify and analyze deviations. But then, to make the necessary corrections, they must develop a program for corrective action and implement this program in order to arrive at the performance desired.

REAL-TIME INFORMATION AND CONTROL

One of the interesting advances arising from the use of the computer and from electronic gathering, transmission, and storage of data is the development of systems of **real-time information.**[8] This is information about what is happening while it is happening. It is technically possible through various means to obtain real-time data on many operations. For years, airlines have obtained information about vacant seats simply by entering a flight number, a trip segment (for example, Los Angeles to New York), and date into a memory system, which immediately responds with information on seat availability. Supermarkets and department stores have electronic cash registers in operation that immediately transmit data on every sale to a central data storage facility, where inventory, sales, gross, profit, and other data can be obtained as they occur. A factory manager can have a system that reports at any time the status of a production program in terms of such things as the production point reached, labor-hours accumulated, and even whether the project is late or on time in the manufacturing process.

FIGURE 20-1

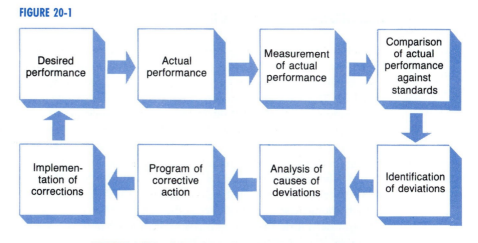

FEEDBACK LOOP OF MANAGEMENT CONTROL.

Some people see real-time information as a means of getting real-time control in areas of importance to managers—in other words, control effected at the very time information shows a deviation from plans. But reference to the management control feedback loop in Figure 20-1 shows that real-time information does not, except possibly in the simplest and most unusual cases, make possible real-time control. It is possible in many areas to collect real-time data that measure performance. It may also be possible in many of these cases to compare these data with standards and even to identify deviations. But the analysis of causes of deviations, the development of programs of correction, and the implementation of these programs are likely to be time-consuming tasks.

In the case of quality control, for example, it may take considerable time to discover what is causing factory rejects and more time to put corrective measures into effect. In the more complex case of inventory control, particularly in a manufacturing company, which has many items—raw materials, component parts, goods in process, and finished goods—the correction time may be very long. Once it is learned that an inventory is too high, the steps involved in getting it back to the desired level may take a number of months. And so it goes with most other instances of management control problems: Time lags are unavoidable.

This does not mean that prompt measurement of performance is unimportant. The sooner managers know that activities for which they are responsible are not proceeding in accordance with plans, the faster they can take action to make corrections. Even so, there is always the question of whether the cost of gathering real-time data is worth the few days saved. Often it is, as in the case of the airline business, in which ready information on seat availability is likely to be crucial to serving customers and filling airplanes. But in a major defense company producing one of the highest-priority defense equipment items, there was little real-time information in an otherwise highly sophisticated information control system. Even for this program, it was thought that the benefit of gathering real-time data was not worth the expense because the correction process took so long.

FEEDFORWARD CONTROL[9]

The time lag in the management control process shows that control must be directed toward the future if it is to be effective. It illustrates the problem of only using feedback from the output of a system and measuring this output as a means of control. It shows the deficiency of historical data such as those received from acounting reports. One of the difficulties with such historical data is that they tell business managers in November that they lost money in October (or even September) because of something that was done in July. At this late time, such information is only a distressingly interesting historical fact.

What managers need for effective control is a system that will tell them, in time to take corrective action, that problems will occur if they do not do something about them now. Feedback from the output of a system is not good enough for control. It is little more than a postmortem, and no one has found a way to change the past.

Future-directed control is largely disregarded in practice, mainly because managers have been so dependent for purposes of control on accounting and statistical data.[10] To be sure, in the absence of any means of looking forward, reference to history—on the questionable assumption that what is past is prologue—is admittedly better than no reference at all.

Techniques of Future-Directed Control

Neglect of future-directed control does not mean that nothing has been done. One common way many managers have practiced it is through careful and repeated use of forecasts based on the latest available information: By comparing what is desired with the forecasts, managers can introduce program changes that will make the forecasts more promising. For example, if a company makes a sales forecast indicating that sales will be at a lower level than desirable, managers may develop new plans for advertising, sales promotion, or the introduction of new products in order to improve the sales forecast.

Likewise, most businesses and other enterprises engage in future-directed control when managers carefully plan the availability of cash to meet requirements. Businesses, for example, would hardly find it wise to wait for a report at the middle or end of May to determine whether they had enough cash in the banks to cover checks issued in April.

One of the better techniques of future-directed control in use today is network planning, exemplified by PERT (Program Evaluation and Review Technique) networks (a topic to be discussed in Chapter 21). This technique of planning and control enables managers to see that they will have problems in such areas as costs or on-time delivery unless they take action now.

Feedforward in Human Systems

There are many examples of feedforward control in human systems. A motorist, for example, who wishes to maintain a constant speed in going up a hill would not usually wait for the speedometer to signal a drop in speed before depressing the

FIGURE 20-2

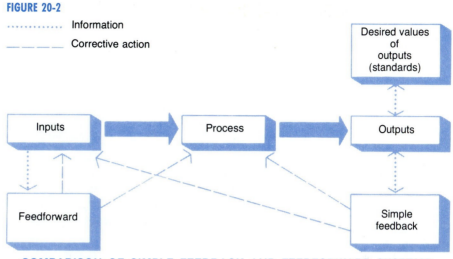

············ Information

— — — — Corrective action

COMPARISON OF SIMPLE FEEDBACK AND FEEDFORWARD SYSTEMS.

accelerator. Instead, knowing that the hill represents a disturbing variable in the system, the driver would probably correct for this by pressing the accelerator before speed falls. Likewise, a hunter will always aim ahead of a duck's flight to correct for the time lag between a shot and a hoped-for hit.

Feedforward versus Feedback Systems[11]

Simple feedback systems measure outputs of a process and feed into the system or the inputs of the system corrective actions to obtain desired outputs. For most management problems, because of time lags in the correction process, this is not good enough. Feedforward systems monitor *inputs* into a process to ascertain whether the inputs are as planned; if they are not, the inputs, or perhaps the process, are changed in order to obtain desired results.

A comparison of feedforward and feedback systems is depicted in Figure 20-2. In a sense, a feedforward control system is really a kind of feedback system. However, the information feedback is at the *input* side of the system so that corrections can be made before the system output is affected. Also, even with a feedforward system, a manager would still want to measure the final system output, since nothing can be expected to work perfectly enough to ensure that the final output will always be exactly as desired.

Feedforward in Management*

An idea of what feedforward means in management control can be conveyed through the examples of cash and inventory planning systems. Figures 20-3 and 20-4 illustrate what is involved.

---

* Sometimes called "preliminary control" or "steering control."

FIGURE 20-3

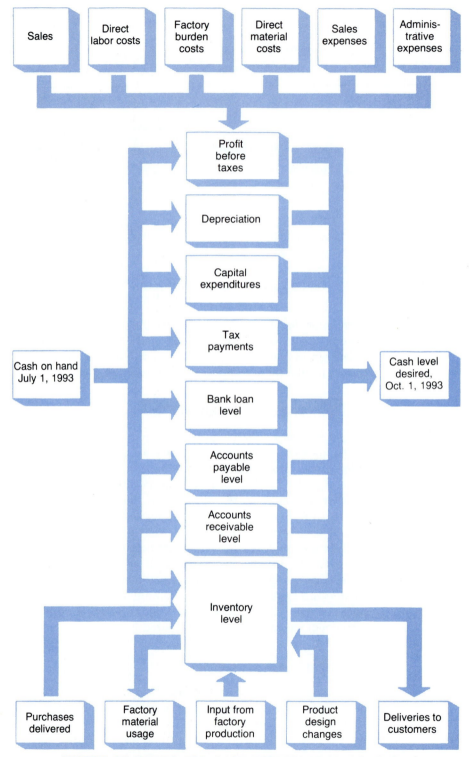

SYSTEM OF INPUTS FOR CASH FEEDFORWARD CONTROL.

FIGURE 20-4

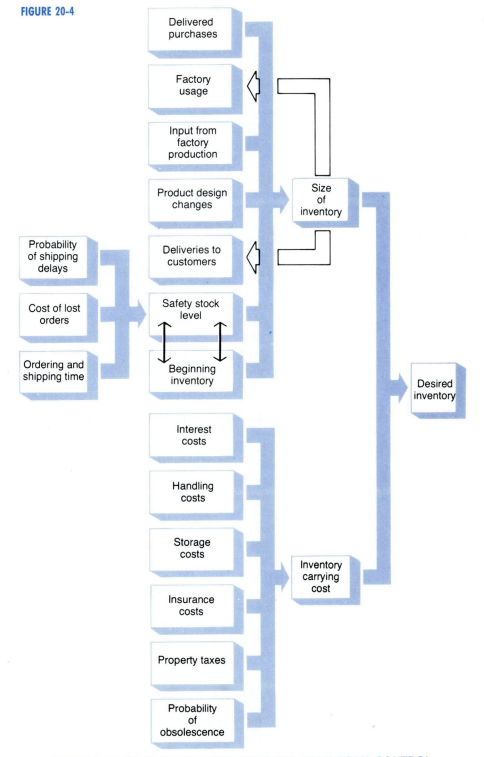

SYSTEM OF INPUTS FOR FEEDFORWARD INVENTORY CONTROL.

The somewhat simplified schematic figures of input variables shown in the charts for cash and for inventory planning and control indicate that if managers are to exercise effective control over either cash or inventories, they must identify each as an interacting system. As can be seen in each instance, some of the variables interact, and some have either a negative or a positive effect on either cash or inventory.

Also, if the system of variables and their impact on a process are accurately portrayed—and each enterprise should design its own system, appropriate to the realities of its situation—a deviation from any planned input can result in an unplanned output unless something is done about it in time. For example, in the case of the inventory model, if delivered purchases are greater than planned or if factory usage turns out to be less than planned, the result will be a higher-than-planned inventory unless corrective action is taken. Of course, to make feedforward work in practice, inputs must be carefully monitored.

In the best kind of feedforward control program, the model of input variables should include inputs in the system model that materially influence the key inputs. For example, delivered purchases tend to increase inventories; but these deliveries are, of course, dependent on orders placed, and the placing of orders is in turn dependent on other factors.

The system of feedforward may appear to be rather complex. But for major problem areas, at least, it should not be difficult to identify system input variables, to see them as an interacting system, and to computerize the model. From that point it should be an easy matter to gather information on the inputs and to determine on a regular basis their effect on the desired end result. Certainly, in view of its importance to meaningful management control, this would not appear to be too much trouble to take.

One of the problems in all feedforward control systems is the necessity of watching for what engineers call "disturbances." These are factors which have not been taken into account in the input model but which may have an impact on the system and the desired end result. Obviously, it would be impracticable to take into account in a model all inputs that might possibly affect the operation of a program. For example, for a company with a long history of an adequate flow of bank loans for financing needs, the possibility that the company's bank may suddenly have to restrict credit might not have been a variable put into the input system. Or the bankruptcy of a large customer or supplier might be an unanticipated, and unprogrammed, input variable. Since unprogrammed events do sometimes occur and may upset a desired output, monitoring regular inputs must be supplemented by watching for, and taking into account, unusual and unexpected "disturbances."

Requirements for Feedforward Control

The requirements for a workable feedforward control system may be summarized as follows:

1. Make a thorough and careful analysis of the planning and control system,

2. Develop a model of the system.
3. Take care to keep the model up to date; in other words, the model should be reviewed regularly to see whether the input variables identified and their interrelationships continue to represent realities.
4. Collect data on input variables regularly, and put them into the system.
5. Regularly assess the variations of actual input data from planned-for inputs, and evaluate the impact on the expected end result.
6. Take action. Like any other technique of planning and control, all that the system can do is indicate problems; people must obviously take action to solve them.

REQUIREMENTS FOR EFFECTIVE CONTROLS

All alert managers want to have an adequate and effective system of controls to assist them in making sure that events conform to plans.[12] It is sometimes not realized that the controls used by managers must be designed for the specific task and person they are intended to serve. While the basic process and the fundamentals of control are universal, the actual system requires special design.

Indeed, if controls are to work, they must be specially tailored. In short, they must be tailored to plans and positions, to the individual managers and their personalities, and to the needs for efficiency and effectiveness.

Tailoring Controls to Plans and Positions

All control techniques and systems should reflect the plans they are designed to follow. Every plan and every kind and phase of an operation has unique characteristics. What managers need is the information that will tell them how the plans for which they are responsible are progressing. Certainly, the information needed for following the progress of a marketing program will be quite different from that needed for checking on a production plan.

In the same way, controls should be tailored to positions. What will be appropriate for a vice president in charge of manufacturing will certainly not be suitable for a shop supervisor. Controls for the sales department will differ from those for the finance department, and both will differ from controls for the purchasing department. A small business will need some controls that differ from those in a large business. The very nature of control emphasizes the fact that the more controls are designed to deal with and reflect the specific nature and structure of plans, the more effectively they will serve managerial needs.

Certain techniques, such as those involving budgets, standard hours and costs, and various financial ratios, have general application in various situations. However, none of these widely used techniques is completely applicable in any given situation. Managers must always be aware of the critical factors in their plans and operations requiring control, and they must use techniques and information suited to them.

Controls should also reflect the organization structure. Being the principal means of clarifying the roles of people in an enterprise, organization structure shows who is responsible for the execution of plans and for any deviation from them. Thus the more carefully controls are designed to reflect the place in the organization where responsibility for action lies, the more they will enable managers to correct deviations from plans.

Tailoring Controls to Individual Managers

Controls must also be tailored to individual managers. Control systems and information are, of course, intended to help individual managers carry out their function of control. If they are not of a type that a manager can or will understand, they will not be useful. It really does not matter whether people cannot understand a control technique or control information or whether they are just unwilling to understand it. In either case, it is not understood. What individuals cannot understand they will not trust. And what they do not trust they will not use.

Some people—for instance, certain statisticians and accountants—like their information in the form of complex tables of data or voluminous computer printouts; in such cases, they should have it that way. Other people like their information in chart form; if so, it should be furnished that way. And a few people—for instance, scientists and mathematicians—may even like their information in mathematical model form; in this event, it should be given to them that way. It is sometimes said that if people will not understand the information they need in any other way, one should consider giving it to them in comic-book form. The important thing is that people should get the information they need in a form they will understand and use.

What is said about tailoring information for understanding is true also of control techniques. Even quite intelligent people may be "turned off" by some of the sophisticated techniques of the expert. Sophisticated techniques of planning and control, like variable budgeting or network planning, can fail in practice solely because the systems either were not comprehensible to the people who had to use them or appeared to be too complex for them. Experts in these matters must not try to show others how expert they are; rather, they should design a system at the level of ready comprehension so that people will use it. Obtaining 80 percent of the possible benefit from a fairly crude system is far better than obtaining no benefit from a more perfect, but unworkable, system.

Making Sure That Controls Point Up Exceptions at Critical Points

One of the most important ways of tailoring controls to the needs for efficiency and effectiveness is to make sure that they are designed to *point up exceptions*. In other words, controls that concentrate on exceptions from planned performance allow managers to benefit from the time-honored exception principle and detect those areas that require their attention.

But it is not enough merely to look at exceptions. Some deviations from standards have little meaning, and others have a great deal. Small deviations in certain areas may have greater significance than larger exceptions in other areas.

A manager, for example, might be concerned if the cost of office labor deviated from the budget by 5 percent but might be unworried if the cost of postage stamps deviated from the budget by 20 percent.

Consequently, the exception principle should be accompanied in practice by the *principle of critical-point control*. It is not enough just to look for exceptions; one must look for them at critical points. Certainly, the more that managers concentrate their control efforts on exceptions, the more efficient their control will be. But this principle had best be considered in light of the fact that effective control requires that managers pay primary attention to those things which are most important.

Seeking Objectivity of Controls

Management necessarily has many subjective elements, but whether a subordinate is doing a good job should ideally not be a matter for subjective determination. If controls are subjective, a manager's or a subordinate's personality may influence judgments of performance and make them less accurate; but people have difficulty in explaining away control of their performance, particularly if the standards and measurements are kept up to date through periodic review. This requirement may be summarized by saying that effective control requires objective, accurate, and suitable standards.

Ensuring Flexibility of Controls

Controls should remain workable in the face of changed plans, unforeseen circumstances, or outright failures. If controls are to remain effective despite failure or unexpected changes of plans, they must be flexible.

The need for flexible control can readily be illustrated. A budget system may project a certain level of expenses and grant authority to managers to hire labor and purchase materials and services at this level. If, as is usually the case, this budget is based on a forecast of a certain level of sales, it may become meaningless as a system of control if the actual sales volume is considerably above or below the forecast. Budget systems have been brought into ill repute among some companies because of inflexibility in such circumstances. What is needed, of course, is a system that will reflect sales variations as well as other deviations from plans. This requirement is provided by the flexible, or variable, budget, as Chapter 21 will show.

Fitting the Control System to the Organizational Culture

To be most effective, any control system or technique must fit the organizational culture. For example, in an organization where people have been given considerable freedom and participation, a tight control system may go so strongly against the grain that it will be doomed to failure. On the other hand, if subordinates have been managed by a superior who allows little participation in decision making, a generalized and permissive control system will hardly succeed. People who have little desire to participate or who have not been accustomed to participating are likely to want clear standards and measurements and specific directions.

Achieving Economy of Controls

Controls must be worth their cost. Although this requirement is simple, it is often difficult to accomplish in practice. A manager may have difficulty in ascertaining what a particular control system is worth or what it costs. Economy is relative, since the benefits vary with the importance of the activity, the size of the operation, the expense that might be incurred in the absence of control, and the contribution the system can make.

A limiting factor of control systems is their cost; this, in turn, will depend a great deal on managers' selecting for control only critical factors in areas important to them. If tailored to the job and to the size of the enterprise, control will probably be economical. One of the economies of large-scale enterprise is being able to afford expensive and elaborate control systems. Often, however, the magnitude of the problems, the wider area of planning, the difficulty of coordinating plans, and poor management communication in a large organization require such expensive controls that their overall efficiency suffers in comparison with lesser controls in a small business. Control techniques and approaches are efficient when they bring to light actual or potential deviations from plans with the minimum of costs.

Establishing Controls That Lead to Corrective Action

An adequate system will disclose where failures are occurring and who is responsible for them, and it will ensure that some corrective action is taken. Control is justified only if deviations from plans are corrected through appropriate planning, organizing, staffing, and leading.

SUMMARY

The managerial function of controlling is the measurement and correction of performance in order to ensure that enterprise objectives and the plans devised to attain them are being accomplished. It is a function of every manager from president to supervisor.

Control techniques and systems are basically the same regardless of what is being controlled. Wherever it is found and whatever is being controlled, the basic control process involves three steps: (1) establishing standards, (2) measuring performance against these standards, and (3) correcting variations from standards and plans. There are different kinds of standards, and they should point out deviations at critical points.

Managerial control is usually perceived as a simple feedback system similar to the common household thermostat. However, no matter how quickly information is available on what is occurring (even real-time information, which is information on what is happening as it happens), there are unavoidable delays in analyzing deviations, developing plans for taking corrective action, and implementing these programs. In order to overcome these time lags in control, it is suggested that managers utilize a feedforward control approach and not rely on simple feedback alone. Feedforward control requires designing a model of a process or system and monitoring inputs with a view to detecting future deviations of results from standards and plans, thereby giving managers time to take corrective action.

If controls are to work, they must be specially tailored (1) to plans and positions, (2) to individual managers, and (3) to the needs for efficiency and effectiveness. To be effective, controls also should be designed to point up exceptions at critical points, to be objective, to be flexible, to fit the organizational culture, to be economical, and to lead to corrective action.

KEY IDEAS AND CONCEPTS FOR REVIEW

Controlling
Steps in controlling
Critical-point control
Types of critical-point standards
Feedback systems
Real-time information system

Techniques of future-directed control
Feedforward control in management
Requirements for feedforward control
Requirements for effective controls
Exception principle

FOR DISCUSSION

1. Planning and control are often thought of as a system; control is also often referred to as a system. What is meant by these observations? Can both statements be true?
2. Why is real-time information not good enough for effective control?
3. What is feedforward control? Why is it important to managers? Besides the examples of cash and inventory control mentioned in this chapter, can you think of any other areas in which feedforward would be used? Select one of these and explain how you would proceed.
4. If you were asked to institute a sytem of "tailored" controls in a company, how would you go about it? What would you need to know?
5. Develop a set of standards for any area of interest to you over which you might wish to exercise effective control.

EXERCISES/ACTION STEPS

1. Design a control system for measuring the progress you make in your course work. Apply the feedback and feedforward concepts discussed in this chapter.
2. Interview two managers about the controls used in their companies. Can you identify standards against which performance can be accurately measured? How is performance measured against the standards, and how timely is the reporting of deviations? If deviations are detected, how long does it take before corrections are made in specific situations?

CASE 20-1
THE KAPPA CORPORATION

As George House, vice president for finance, and Helen Robbins, controller, walked into the office of Adrian Barnes, chairperson and chief executive officer of Kappa Corporation, they were met with the following outburst from the company's top officer:

"Why doesn't someone tell me things? Why can't I know what is going on around here? Why am I kept in the dark? No one informs me about how the company is doing, and I never seem to hear of our problems until they become crises. Now, I want you both to work out a system for keeping me informed, and I want to know by next Monday how you will do it. I am tired of being isolated from the things I must know if I am to take responsibility for this company."

After George House had left Mr. Barnes's office, he turned to the controller and muttered, "Everything he wants to know or could possibly want to know is in that stack of reports on the table in back of his desk."

1. Who was right—Adrian Barnes or George House? Was Barnes getting information?
2. What would you do to make sure that the chairperson does get the information he needs for control purposes?

INTERNATIONAL CASE 20-2
CONTROLLING DECENTRALIZED UNILEVER[13]

Unilever is a large multinational corporation, operating more than 500 companies in about 80 countries. *Fortune* magazine ranked Unilever twentieth among the multinationals. Most of the corporation's business is in consumer goods, such as food, personal products, and detergents. The Anglo-Dutch parent companies are in London and Rotterdam.

In order to control and coordinate the corporation, top management sets the major goals. The decentralized divisions are responsible for developing their own strategic plans. To maintain control in this decentralized structure, only the most proficient and experienced managers are given profit and loss responsibility; these managers also have a great deal of flexibility in decision making.

However, decentralization has not always worked. One of Unilever's U.S. subsidiaries, Lever Brothers, once responsible for all household, personal, and food products, had a great deal of freedom to make decisions. The hands-off approach by headquarters, less-than-sufficient investments, and a too careful approach to marketing may have contributed to a relatively poor performance in the United States. In the late 1980s, however, things began to change. For one, Lever now handles only laundry and soap products, marketed under names such as Wisk, Surf, Snuggle, Dove, and Lifebuoy. Snuggle, for example, had over 20 percent of the U.S. market in 1989.

The U.S. operations include Lever Brothers, Chesebrough-Pond's, Elizabeth Arden, Calvin Klein Cosmetics, Thomas J. Lipton (teas, dried foods, and other foods), Van Den Bergh Foods, and Ragu Foods. To control and integrate the U.S. operations and the other operations around the world demands coordination.

Committees play an important part in the coordination of the enterprise. To become a member of the top-management team, one has to prove himself or herself by performing well in special committee assignments, which serve as a kind of apprenticeship program for future managers. Committees, in general, are notorious for delaying decisions. Not so at Unilever. These committees are driven by a sense of urgency for action.

1. How does Unilever control the worldwide operation?

2. Committees are notoriously ineffective. Why do you think they have been effective at Unilever?

3. What kinds of standards would you recommend for controlling?

REFERENCES

1. Stephen G. Green and M. Ann Welsh, "Cybernetics and Dependence: Reframing the Control Concept," *Academy of Management Review* (April 1988), pp. 287–301.

2. For an excellent summary of pioneering writers on control, see Giovanni B. Giglioni and Arthur G. Bedeian, "A Conspectus of Management Control Theory: 1900–1972," *Academy of Management Journal* (June 1974), pp. 292–305.

3. Richard L. Daft and Norman B. Macintosh, "The Nature and Use of Formal Control Systems for Management Control and Strategy Implementation," *Journal of Management* (Fall 1984), pp. 43–66.

4. Preventive control is further discussed in Chapter 23.

5. See also Charles B. Ames and James D. Hlavacek, "Vital Truths about Managing Your Costs," *Harvard Business Review* (January–February 1990), pp. 140–147.

6. Peter Lorange, Michael F. Scott Morton, and Sumantra Ghoshal, *Strategic Control* (St. Paul, Minn.: West Publishing Company, 1986), p. xvii. See also Daft and Macintosh, "The Nature and Use of Formal Control Systems" (1984).

7. There are also limitations and problems in relying on feedback. See Geert Hofstede, "The Poverty of Management Control Philosophy," in Max D. Richards (ed.), *Readings in Management,* 2d ed. (Cincinnati, Ohio: South-Western Publishing Company, 1986), pp. 302–315. Some of the limitations of traditional controls will be discussed in Chapter 23.

8. See, for example, Kenneth C. Laudon and Jane Price Laudon, *Management Information Systems* (New York: Macmillan Publishing Company, 1991).

9. For a discussion of feedforward control techniques, see Harold Koontz and Robert W. Bradspies, "Managing through Feedforward Control," in Harold Koontz, Cyril O'Donnell, and Heinz Weihrich (eds.), *Management: A Book of Readings,* 5th ed. (New York: McGraw-Hill Book Company, 1980), pp. 576–585. Much of the material in this section is drawn from that paper.

10. The idea of future-directed control was emphasized by one of the authors many years ago. See Harold Koontz, "A Preliminary Statement of Principles of Planning and Control," *Academy of Management Journal* (April 1958), pp. 45–61. Now many authors discuss this concept, but they give it different names. For example, the term "steering controls" has been used by James A. F. Stoner and Charles Wankel, *Management,* 3d ed. (Englewood Cliffs, N.J.: Prentice-Hall, 1986), p. 579, and John R. Schermerhorn, Jr., *Management for Productivity,* 2d ed. (New York: John Wiley & Sons, 1986), p. 402.

11. See also Harold Sirkin and George Stalk, Jr., "Fix the Process, Not the Problem," *Harvard Business Review* (July–August 1990), pp. 26–33.

12. See also Robert N. Anthony, John Dearden, and Norton M. Bedford, *Management Control Systems,* 5th ed. (Homewood, Ill.: Richard D. Irwin, 1984).

13. The material for this case was collected from a variety of sources, including Andrew Brown, "Unilever Fights Back in the U.S.," *Fortune* (May 26, 1986), p. 35; "Unilever: Back to Minding the Store in Europe with the Lines It Knows Best," *Business Week* (Mar. 14, 1983), p. 138; "The World's Biggest Industrial Corporations," *Fortune* (July 31, 1989); Walecia Konrad, "The New, Improved Unilever Aims to Clean Up in the U.S.," *Business Week* (Nov. 27, 1989), pp. 102–106.

Chapter 21

Control Techniques and Information Technology

Over the past 40 years, the technique of decision making his been greatly advanced by the development of a wide range of tools—in particular, the tools of operations research and management science, and the technology of expert systems.[1]

Herbert A. Simon

Chapter Objectives

After reading this chapter, you should be able to:

1. Explain the nature of budgeting and types of budgets.
2. Discuss modern techniques of budgeting, including variable budgeting and zero-base budgeting.
3. Describe nonbudgetary control devices
4. Explain time-event network analysis as a major technique of planning and control.
5. Explain the nature and problems of program budgeting.
6. Discuss the special need for effective procedures planning and control.
7. Describe the nature and applications of information technology.
8. Recognize the importance of computers in handling information.
9. Explain the challenges created by the new information technology

Although the basic nature and purpose of management control do not change, a variety of tools and techniques have been used over the years to help managers control. As this chapter will show, all these techniques are in the first instance tools for planning. They illustrate the fundamental truth that the task of controls is to make plans succeed; naturally, in doing so, controls must reflect plans, and planning must precede control.

Some of these tools may be classed as traditional in the sense that they have long been used by managers, although variable budgeting and zero-base budgeting, for example, are refinements of traditional budgeting. Others, like Program Evaluation and Review Technique (PERT) and program budgeting, represent a newer generation of planning and control tools. While there are many more of these than discussed here, the new tools generally reflect the systems techniques long used in the physical sciences. Operations research (discussed in Chapter 22) is such a technique. Since information is vital for managing effectively, this chapter also examines the newer information technology and its challenges, as well as the use of computers.

In spite of all the newer techniques of planning and control, the traditional tools are still extremely important.

CONTROL TECHNIQUES: THE BUDGET[2]

A widely used device for managerial control is the budget. Indeed, it has sometimes been assumed that budgeting is *the* device for accomplishing control. However, many nonbudgetary devices are also essential.

The Concept of Budgeting

Budgeting is the formulation of plans for a given future period in numerical terms. As such, budgets are statements of anticipated results, either in financial terms—as in revenue and expense and capital budgets—or in nonfinancial terms—as in budgets of direct-labor-hours, materials, physical sales volume, or units of production. It has sometimes been said, for example, that financial budgets represent the "dollarizing" of plans.

The Purpose of Budgeting

By stating plans in terms of numbers and breaking them into parts that parallel the parts of an organization, budgets correlate planning and allow authority to be delegated without loss of control. In other words, reducing plans to numbers forces a kind of orderliness that permits the manager to see clearly what capital will be spent by whom and where, and what expense, revenue, or units of physical input or output the plans will involve. Having ascertained this, the manager can more freely delegate authority to effect the plans within the limits of the budget. Moreover, a budget, to be useful to a manager at any level, must reflect the organizational pattern. Only when plans are complete, coordinated, and developed enough to be fitted into departmental operations can a useful departmental budget be prepared as an instrument of control.

Types of Budgets

Budgets may be classified into several basic types, with a budget summary (discussed in Chapter 23) portraying the total planning picture of all the budgets: (1) revenue and expense budgets, (2) time, space, material, and product budgets, (3) capital expenditure budgets, and (4) cash budgets.

Revenue and expense budgets.   By far the most common budgets spell out plans for revenues and operating expenses in dollar terms. The most basic of these is the sales budget (for a simple example, see Table 21-1), which is a formal and detailed expression of the sales forecast. Just as the sales forecast is the cornerstone of planning, so is the sales budget the foundation of budgetary control. Although a company may budget other revenues, such as expected income from rentals, royalties, or miscellaneous sources, the revenue from sales of products or services furnishes the principal income to pay operating expenses and yield profits.

Operating expense budgets of the typical enterprise can be as numerous as the expense classifications in its chart of accounts and the units of organization in its structure. These budgets may deal with individual items of expense, such as travel, data processing, entertainment, advertising, telephone, and insurance. Sometimes a department head will budget only major items and lump together other items in one control summary. For example, if the manager of a small department is expected to take one business trip a year at a cost of $720, budgeting this cost each month at $60 would mean little for monthly planning or control.

Time, space, material, and product budgets.   Many budgets are better expressed in quantities rather than in monetary terms. Although such budgets are usually translated into monetary terms, they are much more significant at a certain stage in planning and control if they are expressed in terms of quantities. Among the more common of these are the budgets for direct-labor-hours, machine-hours, units

TABLE 21-1 A TYPICAL SALES BUDGET (For the year ending December 31, 1994)			
Product and area	Unit sales volume	Unit selling price	Total sales
Product A:			
Area 1	26,000	$10	$260,000
Area 2	15,000	10	150,000
Area 3	20,000	10	200,000
Total			$610,000
Product B:			
Area 1	30,000	$15	$450,000
Area 2	20,000	15	300,000
Area 3	22,000	15	330,000
Total			$1,080,000
Total revenue from sales			$1,690,000

of materials, square feet allocated, and units produced. Most firms budget product output, and most production departments budget their share of the output of components of the final product. In addition, it is common to budget labor, in either labor-hours or labor-days or by types of labor required. Obviously, such budgets cannot be well expressed in monetary terms, since the dollar cost would not accurately measure the resources used or the results intended.

Capital expenditure budgets.   Capital expenditure budgets outline specifically capital expenditures for plant, machinery, equipment, inventories, and other items. Whether for a short term or a long one, these budgets require care because they give definite form to plans for spending the funds of an enterprise. Since a business takes a long time to recover its investment in plant and equipment, capital expenditure budgets should usually be tied in with fairly long-range planning.

Cash budgets.   The cash budget is simply a forecast of cash receipts and disbursements against which actual cash "experience" is measured. Whether called a budget or not, this is one of the most important controls in an enterprise. The availability of cash to meet obligations as they fall due is the first requirement of existence, and handsome business profits do little good when tied up in inventory, machinery, or other noncash assets. Cash budgeting also shows the availability of excess cash, thereby making it possible to plan for profit-making investment of surpluses.

Dangers in Budgeting

Budgets are used for planning and control. Unfortunately, some budgetary control programs are so complete and detailed that they become cumbersome, meaningless, and unduly expensive.

Overbudgeting. There is a danger in overbudgeting through spelling out minor expenses in detail and depriving managers of needed freedom in managing their departments. For example, a department head in a poorly budgeted company was hindered in an important sales promotion because expenditures for office supplies exceeded budgeted estimates; new expenditures had to be limited, even though his total departmental expenses were well within the budget and he had funds to pay personnel for writing sales promotion letters. In another department, expenses were budgeted in such useless detail that the actual budgeting cost of many items exceeded the expenses controlled.

Overriding enterprise goals. Another danger lies in allowing budgetary goals to become more important than enterprise goals. In their zest to keep within budget limits, managers may forget that they owe primary loyalty to enterprise objectives. In one company with a budgetary control program, the sales department could not obtain needed information from the engineering department on the grounds that the latter's budget would not stand such expense! This conflict between partial and overall control objectives, the excessive departmental independence generated, and the lack of coordination are symptoms of inadequate management, since plans should constitute a supporting and interlocking network and every plan should be reflected in a budget in a way that will aid in achieving enterprise goals.

Perspective

"It's Not in My Budget"

How often have you heard managers say: "This is a good idea, but it's not in my budget"? Budgets often control the wrong things. They measure inputs but ignore outputs such as the quality of the product or customer satisfaction. These items are difficult to measure, yet they may be the key to success or failure of the business. Managers may make unwise decisions to meet the budget, especially if incentive pay is involved for staying within the budget. They may not invest in research and development, or make capital investments for productivity, or invest in activities that will result eventually in greater market share because these investments do not show immediate results. Some of these items should be included in the long-range plan rather than in the 1-year budget. Real savings may come from more efficient machines, new products, or other creative ideas, not from adhering to the budget. The 3M Company includes in its strategic forecasts "nonincremental growth opportunities" for laboratories that come up with a new product for which neither costs nor revenues can be predicted with great certainty.[3]

Hiding inefficiencies. Another danger in budgeting is that it may be used to hide inefficiencies. Budgets have a way of growing from precedent; the fact that a certain expenditure was made in the past can become evidence of its reasonableness in the present. Thus, if a department once spent a given amount for supplies, this cost becomes a minimum for future budgets. Also, managers sometimes learn that budget requests are likely to be pared down in the course of final approval, and therefore they ask for much more than they need. Unless budget making is accomplished by constant reexamination of standards and conversion factors by which planned action is translated into numerical terms, the budget may become an umbrella under which slovenly and inefficient management can hide.

Causing inflexibility. Perhaps inflexibility is the greatest danger in budgets. Even if budgeting is not used to replace managing, the reduction of plans to numerical terms gives them a kind of misleading definiteness. It is entirely possible that events will prove that a larger amount should be spent for this kind of labor or that kind of material and a smaller amount for another or that sales will exceed or fall below the amount forecast. Such differences may make a budget obsolete almost as soon as it is formulated; if managers must stay within the straitjacket of their budgets in the face of events like these, the usefulness of budgets is reduced or nullified. This is especially true when budgets are made for long periods in advance.

Variable Budgets

Because dangers arise from inflexibility in budgets and because maximum flexibility consistent with efficiency underlies good planning, attention has been increasingly given to **variable,** or **flexible,** budgets. These are designed to vary usually as the volume of sales or some other measure of output varies and so are limited largely to expense budgets. The variable budget is based on an analysis of expense items to determine how individual costs *should* vary with volume of output. Some costs do not vary with volume, particularly in so short a period as 1 month, 6 months, or a year. Among these are depreciation, property taxes and insurance, maintenance of plant and equipment, and costs of keeping a minimum staff of supervisory and other key personnel. Some of these standby, or period, costs—such as those of maintaining a minimum number of key or trained personnel for advertising or sales promotion and for research—depend on managerial policy.

Costs that vary with volume of output range from those that are completely variable to those that are only slightly variable. The task of variable budgeting involves selecting some unit of measure that reflects volume; inspecting the various categories of costs (usually by reference to the chart of accounts); and, by statistical studies, methods of engineering analyses, and other means, determining how these costs should vary with volume of output. At this stage, each category of costs is related to volume, sometimes with recognition of "steps" as volume increases. Each department is given these variable cost items, along with definite dollar amounts for its fixed, or standby, costs. Periodically—usually each month—department heads are then given the volume forecast for the immediate future, from which is calculated the dollar amounts of variable costs that make up the budget. In this way, a basic budget can be established for 6 or 12 months in advance, but it can be made variable with shorter-term changes in sales and output.

The variable budget chart in Figure 21-1 is based on the assumption that period costs will remain the same for a volume output of 0 to 6000 units. In most cases, a variable budget will represent a range of output in which plant, managerial, organizational, and other elements of period cost will be the same. But, in practice, this may be over a range of 3000 to 10,000 units. If it were less than 3000 units, a different variable budget would be required with the level of period costs more suitable for the smaller volume; if it were more than 10,000 units, another variable budget would be necessary to reflect the level of period costs necessitated by a larger operation.

Perspective

Example of a Variable Budget

A typical variable budget resulting from the analysis in the text is shown in Table 21-2. This expense budget, for an entire company, is based on a range of expected monthly sales volume of $575,000 to $875,000. The assumption is that if sales were thought to be below $575,000, the company would probably have to reorganize its operations to sustain this smaller volume profitably. On the other hand, if monthly sales rose above $875,000, an expansion of company plant and organization would require a completely new variable budget.

When using the various kinds of variable budgets, department managers must still make future plans. It may be easy to tell a certain supervisor that during the month of May he can have twelve trained electronic assemblers; then, several weeks later, that he may have fifteen in June; and a month later, that his budget for July will permit him to have only ten. But the problems of hiring and training

TABLE 21-2   A TYPICAL VARIABLE BUDGET FOR AN ENTIRE COMPANY
(In thousands of dollars)

Item of expense	Monthly sales volume						
	$575	$625	$675	$725	$775	$825	$875
Material	$184	$200	$216	$232	$248	$264	$280
Direct labor	70	76	82	88	94	100	106
Overhead costs	150	155	161	168	170	171	174
Cost of production	$404	$431	$459	$488	$512	$535	$560
Engineering	$ 35	$ 36	$ 38	$ 38	$ 38	$ 38	$ 40
Research and development	10	10	10	10	12	12	12
Sales and advertising	64	66	69	72	73	74	75
Administrative costs	60	62	63	63	64	65	66
Total costs	$573	$605	$639	$671	$699	$724	$753
Profit from operations	$2	$20	$36	$54	$76	$101	$122
Percentage of profit to sales	0.3%	3.2%	5.4%	7.5%	9.8%	12.3%	14%

FIGURE 21-1

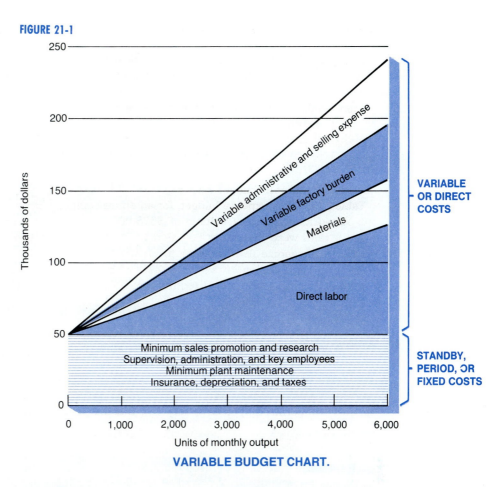

VARIABLE BUDGET CHART.

competent personnel make the process of accomplishing these variations more costly than the savings they are intended to produce. In other words, efficiency may demand that department managers not vary certain of their expenses with short-term variations in volume. In the search for flexibility in budgets, as with other tools of management, an intelligent manager will not lose sight of basic objectives and efficiencies by blindly following any system.

Variable budgets work best when sales or other measures of volume can be reasonably well forecast and when longer-range plans are made, so that the level of expense will not have to be changed so often and on such short notice as to make the job of supervisors intolerable. Under these circumstances, one might well ask: What are the advantages of variable budgeting? Although a fixed budget will work as well with good plans and sales forecasts, a variable budget *forces* study of, and preoccupation with, factors that translate workload into labor or expense needs. Conversion factors—carefully worked out and applied in advance—are necessary for any good budgeting. This, rather than flexibility itself, appears to be the principal advantage of variable budgeting.

Alternative and Supplementary Budgets

Another method of obtaining variable budgeting is to establish **alternative budgets.** Sometimes a company will establish budgets for a high level of operation, a medium level, and a low level, and the three budgets will be approved for the company as a whole and for each organizational segment for 6 or 12 months in advance. Then, at stated times, managers will be informed as to which budget to use in their planning and control. Alternative budgets are a modification of variable budgets, the latter being virtually infinitely variable instead of being limited to a few alternatives.

Budget flexibility is also obtained with a plan referred to as the **supplemental monthly budget.** Under this plan, a 6-month or 1-year budget is prepared for the primary purpose of outlining the framework of the company's plans, coordinating them among departments, and establishing department objectives. This is a basic or minimum budget. Then a supplementary budget is prepared each month on the basis of the volume of business forecast for that month. This budget gives each manager authority for scheduling output and spending funds above the basic budget if, and to the extent that, the shorter-term plans so justify. It avoids some of the detailed calculations necessary under the typical variable budget. But these budget approaches do not usually have the advantage of forcing a complete analysis of all costs and relating them to volume.

Zero-Base Budgeting

Another type of budgeting, the purpose of which has much in common with the purpose of a well-operated system of variable budgeting, is **zero-base budgeting.** The idea behind this technique is to divide enterprise programs into "packages" composed of goals, activities, and needed resources and then to calculate costs for each package from the ground up. By starting the budget of each package from base zero, budgeters calculate costs afresh for each budget period; thus they avoid the common tendency in budgeting of looking only at changes from a previous period.

This technique has generally been applied to so-called support areas, rather than to actual production areas, on the assumption that there is some room for discretion in expenditures for most programs in such areas as marketing, research and development, personnel, planning, and finance. The various programs thought to be desirable are costed and reviewed in terms of their benefits to the enterprise and are then ranked in accordance with those benefits and selected on the basis of which package will yield the benefit desired.

The principal advantage of this technique is, of course, the fact that it forces managers to plan each program package afresh. As managers do so, they review established programs and their costs in their entirety, along with newer programs and their costs.

Effective Budgetary Control

If budgetary controls are to work well, managers must remember that budgets are designed only as tools and not as replacements for managing, that they have limitations, and that they must be tailored to each job. Moreover, they are the tools of all managers and not only of the budget director or the controller. The only persons who can administer budgets, since they are plans, are the managers responsible for budgeted programs. No successful budget program can be truly "directed" or "administered" by a budget director. This staff officer can assist in the preparation and use of budgets by the responsible managers, but unless the entire company management is to be turned over to the budget officer, this person should not be given the job of making budget-commitment or expenditure decisions.

Top-management support. To be most effective, budget making and administration must receive the wholehearted support of top management. Establishing an office of budget director by decree and then forgetting about it leads to haphazard budget making and to saddling subordinate managers with another procedure or set of papers to prepare. On the other hand, if top management actively supports budget making and grounds a budget firmly on plans, requires divisions and departments to make and defend their budgets, and participates in this review, then budgets encourage alert management throughout the organization.

Participation. Related to the participation of top management, another means of making budgets work is to make sure that all managers expected to operate and live under budgets have a part in their preparation. Real participation in budget making is necessary to ensure success. Most budget directors and controllers recognize this fact, but too often in practice participation amounts to managers' being simply pressured to "accept" budgets.

Although budgets do furnish a means of delegating authority without loss of control, there is a danger, as noted earlier, that they will be so detailed and inflexible that little real authority is, in fact, delegated. Some executives even believe that the best budget to give managers is one that lumps all their allowable expenditures for a period of time into a single amount and then gives them complete freedom regarding how these funds are to be spent in pursuance of the company's goals. This kind of decentralization has much to recommend it, although better planning and control might be achieved by allowing the department manager to participate actively in budget making. It may be a good idea, however, to give department managers a reasonable degree of latitude in changing their budgets and in shifting funds, as long as they meet their *total* budgets.

Standards. One of the keys to successful budgeting is to develop and make available standards by which programs and work can be translated into needs for labor, operating expenses, capital expenditures, space, and other resources. Many budgets fail for lack of such standards, and some upper-level managers hesitate to allow subordinates to submit budget plans for fear that they may have no logical basis for reviewing budget requests. With conversion factors available, superior managers can review such requests and justify their approval or disapproval of them. Moreover, by concentrating on the resources required to do a planned job, managers can base their request on what they need to have for meeting output goals and improving performance. They no longer must cope with arbitrary across-the-board budget cuts—a very frustrating technique. In fact, across-the-board cuts are the surest evidence of poor planning and loss of control.

Information. Finally, if budgetary control is to work, managers need ready information about actual and forecast performance under budgets by their departments. This information must be designed to show them how well they are doing. Unfortunately, such information is usually not available until it is too late for the manager to avoid budget deviations.

TRADITIONAL NONBUDGETARY CONTROL DEVICES

There are, of course, many traditional control devices not connected with budgets, although some may be related to, and used with, budgetary controls. Among the more important of them are (1) statistical data, (2) special reports and analyses, (3) the operational audit, and (4) personal observation.

Statistical Data

Statistical analyses of the innumerable aspects of an operation and the clear presentation of statistical data, whether of a historical or a forecast nature, are important to control. It is probably safe to say that most managers understand statistical data best when the data are presented in chart or graphic form, since trends and relationships are then easier to see. Moreover, if data are to be meaningful, even when presented on charts, they should be formulated in such a way that comparisons with some standard can be made. What is the significance of a 3 or a 10 percent rise or fall in sales or costs? Who is responsible? Clear presentation of statistical data in graphic, tabular, or chart form is an art that requires imagination.

Moreover, since no manager can do anything about history, it is essential that statistical reports show trends so that the viewer can extrapolate where things are going. This means that most data, when presented on charts, should be made available as averages to rule out variations due to accounting periods, seasonal factors, accounting adjustments, and other periodic differences. In the 12-month moving average, for example, the total for 12 consecutive months, divided by 12, is used. The difference in clarity can be seen in the comparative data presented graphically in Figure 21-2.

Special Reports and Analyses

For control purposes, special reports and analyses help in particular problem areas. Although routine accounting and statistical reports furnish a good share of necessary information, there are often areas in which they are inadequate. One successful manager of a complicated operation hired a small staff of trained analysts and gave them no assignment other than that of investigating and analyzing activities under his control. This group developed a surprising sense for situations in which things did not seem just right. Almost invariably, their investigation disclosed opportunities for cost improvement or better utilization of capital that no statistical chart would have revealed.

It may be that some of the funds being spent for elaborate information

FIGURE 21-2

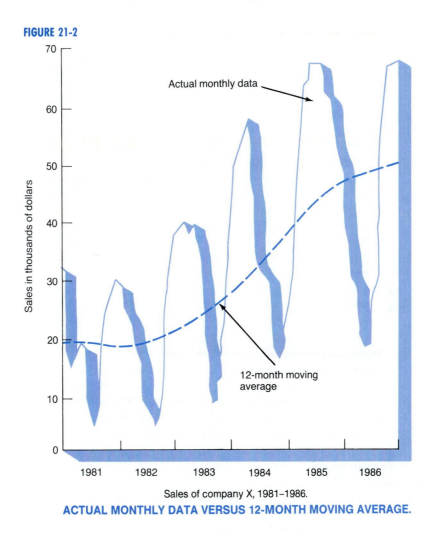

Sales of company X, 1981–1986.
ACTUAL MONTHLY DATA VERSUS 12-MONTH MOVING AVERAGE.

programs could be more profitably spent for special analyses. Their nonroutine nature can highlight the unusual and, in so doing, reveal places for significant improvement in efficiency. In routinely searching for pennies and accounting for them, managers may be overlooking opportunities for saving dollars.

Operational Audit

Another effective tool of managerial control is the internal audit, or, as it is now coming to be called, the operational audit. **Operational auditing,** in its broadest sense, is the regular and independent appraisal, by a staff of internal auditors, of the accounting, financial, and other operations of an enterprise. Although often limited to the auditing of accounts, in its most useful form operational auditing includes appraisal of operations in general, weighing actual results against planned results. Thus, operational auditors, in addition to assuring themselves that accounts properly reflect the facts, appraise policies, procedures, use of authority, quality of management, effectiveness of methods, special problems, and other phases of operations.

Personal Observation

One should never overlook the importance of control through personal observation. Budgets, charts, reports, ratios, auditors' recommendations, and other devices are essential to control. But the manager who relies wholly on these devices and sits, so to speak, in a soundproof control room reading dials and manipulating levers can hardly expect to do a thorough job of control. Managers, after all, have the task of seeing that enterprise objectives are accomplished by *people*, and although many scientific devices aid in ensuring that people are doing that which has been planned, the problem of control is still one of measuring activities of human beings. It is amazing how much information an experienced manager can get from personal observation, even from an occasional walk through a plant or an office. In some companies this is called "management by walking around." (See the discussion of "management by walking around" in Chapter 19.)

TIME-EVENT NETWORK ANALYSES

Another planning and control technique is a time-event network analysis called the Program Evaluation and Review Technique (PERT). Before the development of PERT, there were other techniques designed to assess how the parts of a program fit together during the passage of time and events.

Gantt Charts

The first of these techniques was the chart system (see Figure 21-3) which was developed by Henry L. Gantt early in the twentieth century and which culminated in the bar chart bearing his name. Although simple in concept, this chart, showing time relationships between "events" of a production program, has been regarded as revolutionary in management. What Gantt recognized was that total program goals should be regarded as a series of interrelated supporting plans (or events) that people can comprehend and follow. The most important developments of control reflect this simple principle as well as basic principles of control, such as picking out the more critical elements of a plan to watch carefully.

Milestone Budgeting

As a result of the development of further techniques from the principles of the Gantt chart, and with better appreciation of the network nature of programs, "milepost" or "milestone" budgeting and PERT were devised, contributing much to better planning and control of many projects and operations. Used by an increasing number of companies in recent years in controlling engineering and development, milepost or milestone budgeting breaks a project down into controllable

FIGURE 21-3

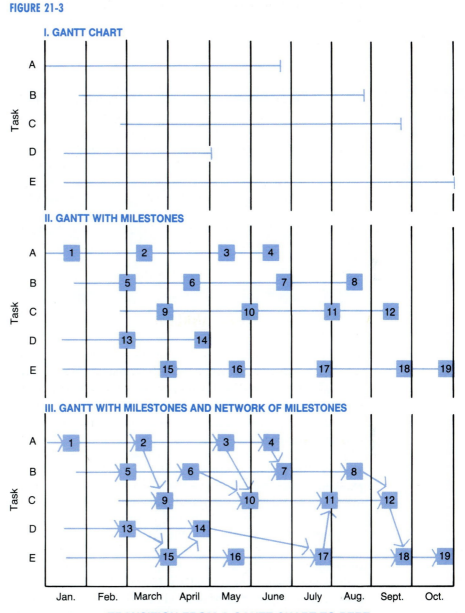

I. GANTT CHART

II. GANTT WITH MILESTONES

III. GANTT WITH MILESTONES AND NETWORK OF MILESTONES

Jan.   Feb.   March   April   May   June   July   Aug.   Sept.   Oct.

TRANSITION FROM A GANTT CHART TO PERT.

The Gantt chart in I above shows the scheduled time of accomplishing a task, such as procurement (Task A), and the related schedules of doing other tasks, such as manufacture of parts (Task B). When each of these tasks is broken down into milestones, such as the preparation of purchase specifications (Task A-1), and when network relationships among the milestones of each task to those of other tasks are worked out, the result provides the basic elements of a PERT chart.

pieces and then carefully follows them. As noted in the discussion of planning, even relatively simple projects contain a network of supporting plans or projects. In this approach to control, "milestones" are defined as identifiable segments. When accomplishment of a given segment occurs, cost or other results can be determined.

The best way to plan and control an engineering project is to break it down into a number of events—for example, completion of preliminary drawings, an experimental model, a package design, a packaged prototype, and a production design. Or a project might be broken down vertically into subprojects—for example, the design of a circuit, a motor, a driving mechanism, a sensing device, a signal feedback device, and similar components—that can be completed individually, in a time sequence, so that components are ready when needed. Milestone budgeting allows a manager to see a complex program as a series of simpler parts and thus to maintain some control through knowing whether a program is succeeding or failing.

Program Evaluation and Review Technique (PERT)

Developed by the Special Projects Office of the U.S. Navy,[4] the Program Evaluation and Review Technique (PERT) was first formally applied to the planning and control of the Polaris Weapon System in 1958 and worked well in expediting the successful completion of that program. For a number of years, it was so enthusiastically received by the armed services that it became virtually a required tool for major contractors and subcontractors in the armament and space industry. Although PERT is no longer much heard of in defense and space contracts for reasons that will be noted presently, its fundamentals are still essential tools of planning and control. Moreover, in a host of nongovernmental applications, including construction, engineering and tooling projects, and even such simple things as the scheduling of activities to get out monthly financial reports, PERT or its companion network technique, the Critical Path Method (CPM), may be used.

Major features.   **PERT** is a time-event network analysis system in which the various events in a program or project are identified, with a planned time established for each. These events are placed in a network showing the relationships of each event to the other events. In a sense, PERT is a variation of milestone budgeting (see Figure 21-3).

Figure 21-4 shows a PERT flowchart for the major assembly of an airplane. This example illustrates the basic nature of PERT. Each *circle* represents an event—a supporting plan whose completion can be measured at a given time. The circles are numbered in the order in which the events occur. Each *arrow* represents an activity—the time-consuming element of a program, the effort that must be made between events. *Activity time*, represented by the numbers beside the arrows, is the elapsed time required to accomplish an event.

FIGURE 21-4

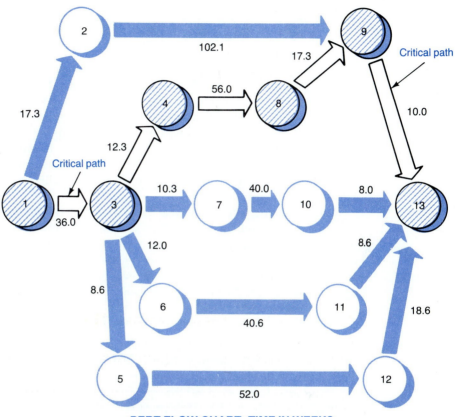

PERT FLOW CHART: TIME IN WEEKS.

Major assembly of an airplane. Events (major milestone of progress) are: (1) order program go-ahead; (2) initiate engine procurement; (3) complete plans and specifications; (4) complete fuselage drawings; (5) submit GFAE* requirements; (6) award tail assembly subcontract; (7) award wings subcontract; (8) complete manufacture of fuselage; (9) complete assembly of fuselage engine; (10) receive wings from subcontractors; (11) receive tail assembly from subcontractors; (12) receive GFAE; (13) complete aircraft.

*Note: GFAE stands for government-furnished airplane equipment.

In this example only a single time is shown for each activity, but in the original PERT program there were *three time estimates*: "optimistic" time, an estimate of the time required if everything goes exceptionally well; "most likely" time, an estimate based on the time the project engineer really believes is necessary for the job; and "pessimistic" time, a time estimate based on the assumption that some logically conceivable bad luck—other than a major disaster—will be encountered. These estimates are often included in PERT because it is very difficult, in many engineering and development projects, to estimate time accurately. When several estimates are made, they are usually averaged, with special weight given to the most likely estimate; a single estimate is then used for calculations.

The next step is to compute the *critical path*, that is, the sequence of events which takes the longest time and which has zero (or the least) slack time. In Figure 21-4, the critical path comprises events 1–3–4–8–9–13. Over this path, the activity time for this sequence of events is 131.6 weeks; if promised delivery is in 135 weeks, even this critical path will have been completed 3.4 weeks ahead of time. Some of the other paths are almost as long as the critical path. For example, the path 1–2–9–13 is 129.4 weeks. This is not unusual in PERT charts, and it is customary to identify several crucial paths in order of importance. Although the critical path has a way of changing as key events are delayed in other parts of the program, identifying it at the start makes possible close monitoring of this particular sequence of events to ensure that the total program is on schedule.

Typical PERT analyses involve hundreds or thousands of events. Even though smaller PERT analyses can be done manually, estimates indicate that when more than 200 to 300 events are involved, it is virtually impossible to handle the calculations without a computer.

It is customary to summarize very large and complex time-event networks by subnetworks and to prepare the summarized network for top-management consideration. Thus, the top-management network might include some forty or fifty major events, each a summary of a number of subsidiary events. In fact, it is possible to group, or to break down, events so that there is a PERT network appropriate to every level of management.

Strengths and weaknesses.   There are five important *advantages* of PERT. First, it forces managers to plan, because it is impossible to make a time-event analysis without planning and seeing how the pieces fit together. Second, it forces planning all the way down the line, because each subordinate manager must plan the event for which he or she is responsible. Third, it concentrates attention on critical elements that may need correction. Fourth, it makes possible a kind of forward-looking control; a delay will affect succeeding events and possibly the whole project unless the manager can make up the time by shortening the time allocated to some action in the future. Fifth, the network system with its subsystems enables managers to aim reports and pressure for action at the right spot and level in the organization structure at the right time.

PERT also has certain *limitations*. Because of the importance of activity time to its operation, the technique is not useful when a program is nebulous and no reasonable "guesstimates" of schedule can be made; even in this case, however, insurance can be "bought" by such practices as putting two or more groups of people to work on an event when costs permit. A major disadvantage of PERT has been its emphasis on time only, not on costs. While this focus is suitable for programs in which time is of the essence or in which, as so often is the case, time and costs have a close, direct relationship, the tool is more useful when considerations other than time are introduced into the analysis. (There is, however, another program called PERT/COST that does consider costs.)

PERT is not a cure-all. It will not do the planning, although it forces planning. It will not make control automatic, although it establishes an environment where sound control principles can be appreciated and used. And it apparently involves rather less expense than one might expect. Setting up the network, its analysis, and its interpretation and reporting from it probably require little, if any, more expense than most other planning and control techniques, unless, of course, these are made unduly complicated.

PROGRAM BUDGETING

One of the widely publicized tools of planning and control, used primarily in government operations but applicable to any kind of enterprise, is *program planning and budgeting (PPB),* or, more simply, *program budgeting.* Although really not more, at least in its fundamentals, than what budgeting should always be, its emphasis and approach deserve analysis.

What Program Budgeting Is

Program budgeting is basically a systematic method for allocating the resources of an enterprise in ways that will most effectively help the enterprise to meet its goals. By emphasizing goals and programs to meet them, it overcomes the ordinary weakness of all kinds of budgets, even in business, of being too closely tied to the time frames of accounting periods of months, quarters, or years. By concentrating on goals and programs in light of available resources, it stresses the desirability of assessing costs against benefits when selecting the best course toward accomplishing a program goal.

Problems in Applying Program Budgeting in Government

For most government agencies, program budgeting has not been the great tool in practice that its logic would imply. There are a number of reasons why it has not.

In the first place, many federal, state, and local government executives, particularly at the middle and lower levels of management, do not understand the philosophy and theory of the technique; they have been given directives and forms but have not really known what the system entails. A second major hurdle has been the lack of clearly defined goals; obviously, no one can plan and budget for an unknown or fuzzy goal. Another difficulty is the lack of attention to planning premises; even with clear program goals, the program budgeter is in the dark without knowledge of critical planning premises. Another problem arises from the long tradition in government of line budgeting; most legislators, accustomed to line budgets, often will not tolerate other budgets unless they are recast in a line-item form. Also, many government budgetary divisions or staffs have been reluctant to make the change from their practice and procedures of annual budgets to longer-range program budgets. Other roadblocks include the fact that accounting data are seldom consistent with program budgeting, the lack of information in many areas to make meaningful cost effectiveness analyses, and the political problems of reorganizing government departments to improve concentration of program responsibility.

PROCEDURES PLANNING AND CONTROL

Procedures present a rewarding area of planning and control to which a systems approach can be applied. They are desirable tools for efficiently getting things done in a given way or for control. But procedures can also make for departmental rigidity that thwarts innovation and response to change. Although they *should* be designed to implement plans and to respond to change, they too often are not.

Effective planning and control of procedures depend on recognizing that they are inherently systems. Procedures normally extend into various departments, and it is a rare procedure that does not concern itself with more than two. This increases the importance of their control. Accounting departments, for example, tend to regard their procedures as concerned purely with their function, and yet a simple payroll or expense account procedure reaches into every nook and cranny of the company and affects many nonaccounting activities. Personnel, purchasing, and other functional departmental procedures do likewise.

How Procedures Get Out of Control

Procedures often get out of control because of the specialized approach of each organization function in setting them up for its particular operation. Accounting procedures may conflict with, or overlap, purchasing procedures, differ slightly from personnel procedures, and somewhat duplicate sales department procedures. Duplication, overlapping, and conflict are usually elusive and partial; there is rarely either complete duplication or clear disagreement. Different forms and records commonly are called for, though they use the same subject matter. This, of course, can be expensive.

Procedures also get out of control when managers try to use them to solve problems instead of solving the problems through better policies, clearer delegations, or improved direction. Then again, many procedures are instituted to correct a mistake that might never be made again. In one case, a division head ordered the development of a complete system of procedures to prevent the duplication of one serious customer complaint. This complaint had happened only once. A clear policy statement, simple routing of complaints, and the assignment of complaint handling to the service manager would have taken care of the situation and avoided any recurrence.

Procedures also evade control by becoming obsolete, either because they are not kept up to date or because failure to police them permits deviations in practice. Moreover, procedures have a way of becoming customs, ingrained in departments and in individuals who have a stubborn resistance to change. And managers find it expedient to impose new procedures on the old, a haphazard practice.

Finally, a major reason why procedures get out of control is that managers are often not clear as to what procedures should do, how much they cost, when they are duplicated, how to overhaul them, and how to control them. And to top all this, managers often fail to obtain the interest and support of top managers in the tedious and unromantic planning and control procedures. There are, however, guidelines that make the planning and control of procedures more effective.

Guidelines for Effective Procedures

Minimize procedures.   Limit procedures to those situations in which they are clearly called for. The costs of procedures in paper handling, stifled thinking, delay, and lack of responsiveness to change are such as to make a concerned manager think twice before initiating them. Managers must weigh the potential gain in money or necessary control against the disadvantages and costs.

Make sure procedures are plans.   Since procedures are plans, they must be designed to reflect and help accomplish enterprise (not just departmental) objectives and policies. Have they been planned? If they are necessary, are they designed effectively and efficiently to accomplish plans? For example, a procedure to handle orders for spare parts or repair defective parts should expedite a job so as to meet customer service standards without undue delay.

Analyze procedures.   Procedures should be carefully analyzed to ensure a minimum of duplication, overlapping, and conflict. For proper analysis, the procedures must be visualized. This, in turn, necessitates mapping them, with their various steps identified and interrelated. That this is not always easy is exemplified by a defense material procedure which, when charted, took a piece of paper 27 feet long and involved over 250 related required actions!

Recognize procedures as systems.   Any given procedure, whether it specifies the handling of payroll, procurement, inventory planning and control, or some other activity, is in itself a system of interrelated activities normally in a network rather than a pure linear form. Therefore, groups of procedures are usually interrelated systems.

Estimate the cost of procedures.   The analysis of a procedure should include an estimate of what its operation will cost. While some costs cannot be ascertained, such as the cost of possible frustration to those involved, an estimate may bring into sharper focus the answer to this question: Is this procedure worthwhile?

Police the operation of procedures.   To be sure that procedures are needed and are doing the job intended, it is necessary to police them. This requires three steps: (1) Knowledge of procedures must be made available in manual or some other form to those who must follow them. (2) Employees must be taught how to operate under them and, ideally, why the procedures are necessary and what purpose they are designed to serve. (3) There must be machinery to ensure that people do understand and are employing up-to-date procedures and that they are doing the job intended. This requires constructive auditing.

Procedures Analysis and Electronic Data Processing

An encouraging consequence of present systems and procedures planning and the analysis of procedures as systems is that procedures are often programmed on electronic data processing (EDP) equipment. However, there remains the danger that the systems and procedures expert will become so enamored of programming as to forget that electronic automation of procedures can reflect the system of procedures only as it exists.

Despite this danger, EDP has stimulated broad analysis and improvement of procedures. A strong effort needs to be made to ensure that a procedure is workable and clear before it is automated. Nevertheless, the systems approach of the programmer forces an orderly approach to procedures analysis. Since, at the very least, a procedure cannot be put on a machine without having been mapped, the very process of mapping often reveals the existence of overlapping and the need for simplification, as well as the means of achieving it.

The need is great for experts who understand the nature of procedures as management tools and their importance in accomplishing enterprise objectives. Systems and procedures analysis—like information technology, discussed next—is high-level, difficult, and challenging work.

INFORMATION TECHNOLOGY[5]

The systems model of management shows that communication is needed for carrying out the managerial functions and for linking the organization with its external environment. The management information system (MIS) provides the communication link that makes managing possible.

The term **management information system** has been used differently by various authors. It is defined here as *a formal system of gathering, integrating, comparing, analyzing, and dispersing information internal and external to the enterprise in a timely, effective, and efficient manner.*

The management information system has to be tailored to specific needs and may include *routine* information, such as monthly reports; information that points out *exceptions,* especially at critical points; and information necessary to *predict* the future. The guidelines for designing a management information system are similar to those for designing systems and procedures and other control systems. Since they have been discussed elsewhere, they need not be elaborated here.

Electronic equipment permits fast and economical processing of huge amounts of data. The computer can, with proper programming, process data toward logical conclusions, classify them, and make them readily available for a manager's use. In fact, data do not become information until they are processed into a usable form that informs.

Expansion of Basic Data

The focus of attention on management information, coupled with its improved processing, has led to the reduction of long-known limitations. Managers have recognized for years that traditional accounting information, aimed at the calculation of profits, has been of limited value for control. Yet in many companies this has been virtually the only regularly collected and analyzed type of data. Managers need all kinds of nonaccounting information about the external environment, such as social, economic, political, and technical developments. In addition, managers need nonaccounting information on internal operations. The information should be qualitative as well as quantitative.

While not nearly enough progress has been made in meeting these requirements, the computer, plus operations research, has led to an enormous expansion of available managerial information. One sees this especially in relation to data on marketing, competition, production and distribution, product cost, technological change and development, labor productivity, and goal accomplishment.

Information Indigestion

Managers who have experienced the impact of better and faster data processing are justly concerned with the danger of "information indigestion." With their appetite for figures whetted, the data originators and processors are turning out material at an almost frightening rate. Managers are complaining that they are being buried under printouts, reports, projections, and forecasts which they do not have time to read or cannot understand or which do not fill their particular needs.

International Perspective

Telecommunications Battles in Europe[6]

Recently, information technology has become combined with the evolving knowledge of telecommunications. Videotex, videoconferencing, cellular conferencing, and PABX (private automated branch exchange) are just a few examples of the application of the new technology. Still-picture phones are already in operation in Japan and may soon be introduced in other parts of the world.

In the past, Europe's telecommunications industry was protected by national governments. However, the EC 1992 program is bringing many changes. National orientation of the governments may have to give way to cross-border proliferation of the new technology. The 1987 "Green Paper" of the European Community recommends dramatic changes for eliminating national prerogatives. Similarly, the European Telecommunications Standards Institute (ETSI) attempts to set EC standards. Countries such as France, Greece, Italy, and Spain have been resisting changes, as they would require those countries to open their protected markets. In response to the changing environment, European companies are developing strategies of cooperation among themselves in order to meet the international challenges from U.S. and Japanese firms.

The telecommunications revolution. With computer voice and visual technology, there are almost limitless combinations. Videoconferencing, video telephones, and faxes are just a few of the potential applications.

Any of the twelve EC-member states accounts for only a small portion of the total European market. Consequently, U.S. and Japanese firms have great opportunities in the standardized market of the future. *Networks* such as integrated services digital networks (ISDNs), PABXs, and LANs (local area networks) are expected to grow through the adoption of common standards.

Another area of opportunities is in *terminal equipment*. Data and video terminals as well as car phones will become quite common during the 1990s. And so will the applications of telex and voice phone services. The new information technologies are suitable for meeting the specific needs of customers, both commercial and private. The videotex in France is one example of applying the new technologies. Another is the access of customers to databases for making, for example, airline and hotel reservations. Electronic mail and financial services such as electronic banking are still other applications of the information technologies.

Forging new alliances.   Developing the new technologies is costly. To share the costs, companies form strategic alliances such as illustrated by Alcatel (telecommunications manufacturer) and GEC.

In a number of strategic moves, the German giant Siemens has gained a stronghold in the United Kingdom and former East Germany. U.S. companies have not been idle. AT&T enhanced its strength through a cooperative arrangement with ITALTEL of Italy. Similarly, the "Baby Bells" are considering entering the European market. Motorola, known for its digital mobile telephones, is well positioned in the European market. To improve European competitiveness, European industries launched ESPRIT (European Strategic Program for Research and Development in Information Technologies) and RACE (Research and Development for Advanced Communication Technologies for Europe) in 1987.[7]

The European market is highly fragmented. But some countries, mainly the United Kingdom, the Netherlands, and Germany, began coordinating their activities, especially in the early and middle 1980s. Realizing the competitive disadvantages, the EC developed a policy of integrating its services. At the same time, EC countries opened their markets and allowed competition from foreign firms.

Intelligence Services

One attempt at solving the problem of information overload is the establishment of intelligence service and the development of a new profession of intelligence experts.[8] The service is provided by specialists who know (or find out) what information managers need and who know how to digest and interpret such information for managerial use. Some companies have established organizational units under such names as "administrative services" or "management analyses and services" for making information understandable and useful.[9]

THE USE OF COMPUTERS IN HANDLING INFORMATION

The computer can store, retrieve, and process information. Often a distinction is made between kinds of computers. The *mainframe* is a full-scale computer, often costing millions of dollars, that is capable of handling huge amounts of data. Some of these "supercomputers" are used for engineering, simulation, and the manipulation of large databases. The *minicomputer* has less memory and is smaller than the mainframe. This kind of computer is often connected with peripheral equipment. The *microcomputer* is even smaller and may be a desk computer, home computer, personal computer, portable computer, or small computer for a business system. Increasingly, however, minicomputers are used by large organizations either as stand-alone computers or as parts of a network.

But the distinction between the various classes of computers is disappearing. With the introduction of the new microcomputers based on the 80386 microprocessor, these computers have become very powerful. However, the full utilization of the hardware (the computers) depends to a considerable degree on the lagging development of the software programs.

Among the many business applications of the computer are material requirements planning, manufacturing resource planning, computer-aided control of manufacturing machinery, project costing, inventory control, and purchasing. The computer also aids design and engineering, an application that made the U.S. space program possible. Then there are the many uses in processing financial information such as accounts receivable and accounts payable, payroll, capital budgeting, and financial planning. Computer-aided communication impacts not only on decision making but also on organizational design.[10]

The Impact of Computers on Managers at Different Organizational Levels

Information needs differ at various organizational levels. Therefore, the impact of computers will also be different.

At the *supervisory level*, activities are usually highly programmable and repetitive. Consequently, the use of computers is widespread at this level. Scheduling, daily planning, and controlling of the operation are just a few examples.

Middle-level managers, such as department heads or plant managers, are usually responsible for administration and coordination. But much of the information important to them is now also available to top management if the company has a comprehensive information system. For this reason, some people think that the need for middle-level managers will be reduced by the computer. Others predict that their roles may be expanded and changed.

Top-level managers are responsible for the strategy and overall policy of the organization.[11] In addition to determining the general direction of the company, they are responsible for the appropriate interaction between the enterprise and its environment. Clearly, the tasks of CEOs are not easily programmable. Yet top managers can use the computer to retrieve information from a database that facilitates the application of decision models.[12] This enables the company to make timely responses to changes in the external environment. Still, the use of the computer will probably affect the jobs of top managers less severely than it will affect the jobs of those at lower levels.

The Application and Impacts of Microcomputers

The personal computer (PC) is becoming increasingly appealing to managers because it is flexible and relatively inexpensive and can be used more quickly than the mainframe computer. Its applications include the following:

Budget preparation	Simulation models
Graphic presentations	Forecasting
Electronic spreadsheets	Electronic mail
Financial analyses	Tapping into databases
Word processing	Time-sharing

The implications of the increasing use of the microcomputer are manifold. There is a need for specialized staff support, education for managers and nonmanagers, and a redefinition of jobs. For example, the distinction between line and staff is becoming less clear. The information that was formerly gathered by staff can now be obtained with ease by other managers when they access a common database. On the other hand, information that was the prerogative of upper-level managers can also be made available to personnel at lower levels, possibly resulting in the shift of power to lower levels in the organization. But not all information should be accessible to all people in the company. Thus, one of the problems currently faced by many firms is maintaining the security of information.

Perspective

Apple's Move into the Corporate Office[13]

The first attempt by Apple Computer to invade the industrial market was not very successful. A second attempt seems to be more promising. One reason is the increasing popularity of desktop publishing, an area where Apple has certain advantages over the IBM Personal Computer. In the past, Apple developed a strong market position in education. However, this market is quite price-sensitive and is growing rather slowly, making it imperative to move into the office market.

Cooperation between Apple and Aldus (which prepares the software) opened the door to many corporate offices that had a need for desktop publishing. Brochures or reports that in the past had to be sent to the printshops can now be produced faster and with less expense in-house. Moreover, some newer Macintosh computers by Apple are now "open" to the addition of microprocessing boards supplied by other vendors. So, with the ease of use and the graphic capabilities of its computers, Apple aims to invade and conquer the important office market. But it will not be easy to compete against powerful IBM and firms selling IBM-compatible clones.

✓ CHALLENGES CREATED BY INFORMATION TECHNOLOGY

Eliminating the unauthorized use of information is just one of many challenges. Others include reducing resistance to the use of computers, adapting to speech recognition devices and telecommuting, and implementing computer networks.

Resistance to Computer Application

While high school students may feel comfortable using the computer, some managers fear it. One study revealed that the typical executive affected by this phobia is male, is about 50 years old, and has worked most of his life for the same company. This fear might explain why certain managers are reluctant to use the computer. They are afraid of looking unskilled if they are not able to understand the new technology or do not have the typing skills often necessary for entering data into the computer. In the past, typing was considered the task of the secretary, not the manager.[14]

A survey of CEOs in *Fortune* 500 companies showed that over 50 percent of the respondents never used the computer and over 70 percent of them did not have a computer in their office.[15] On the other hand, a majority of the top executives thought that computers assist managers in doing their jobs, which suggests that computers are considered useful below the level of the CEO. Those not favorably inclined to the use of computers made various comments, such as that their time is too valuable to be spent learning computer skills.

The application of graphics can help overcome the resistance to computers. Instead of being buried in reams of computer printouts, information is displayed as easy-to-understand graphics. PepsiCo, for example, invested $250,000 in decision support graphics over 3 years, generating 80,000 charts and slides.[16] At any rate, as more sophisticated technology makes the use of the computer easier, its acceptance is likely to increase.

Speech Recognition Devices

Another way to encourage the use of computers is through speech recognition devices.[17] The aim is to input data into the computer by speaking in a normal manner, rather than by using the keyboard. Several companies are working on such devices, but it may still take several years before they can be widely applied, although simple speech recognition has been in limited use for some time. Merely expanding the vocabulary through a larger memory is not enough. Imagine the program sophistication needed to distinguish between similar sounds such as "then" and "than," "to" and "too" and "two." Despite the complex problems, some people think that the efforts made in this area will result in products that may revolutionize office operation.

Telecommuting

The widespread use of computers and the ease of linking them through telephone lines to a company's mainframe computer have led to **telecommuting.** This means that a person can work at a computer terminal at home instead of commuting to work.[18] Some of the advantages claimed include greater flexibility in scheduling work, the avoidance of traffic congestion, and a reduced need for office space.

The futurist Alvin Toffler envisioned an "electronic cottage" with computer terminals installed at home. But John Naisbitt, in his book *Megatrends*, is skeptical of the idea and suggests that after telecommuting for some time, workers will miss the office gossip and the human interactions with workers.[19] Some companies that have contracted work to telecommuters have been criticized for not providing the benefits usually given to office workers. At Pacific Bell, however, participants in the voluntary program are considered full-time employees.[20] Moreover, some employees go to the office at least once a week to check their mail and to mingle with coworkers.

With the increasing traffic congestion, especially in metropolitan areas, one may see a somewhat greater use of telecommuting. But it is doubtful that it will replace the office as we know it today.[21]

Computer Networks

The widespread use of stand-alone computers often results in duplication of efforts. The database in the mainframe or the minicomputer, for example, may not be accessible from the desktop computer. Therefore, computer networks have been developed that link workstations with each other, with larger computers, and with peripheral equipment.

Persons at several workstations can communicate with each other as well as access other computers.[22] Moreover, workstations can be connected to costly hardware that may be underutilized by a single user. For example, several users can share laser printers or tape backup units that ensure saving of the data files. There are many other applications of computer networks, such as electronic mail and the gathering and disseminating of industry data and future trends. Although computer networking is still in its infancy, new technological developments are rapidly changing the system of information handling.

SUMMARY

A variety of tools and techniques have been used to help managers control. These techniques are generally, in the first instance, tools for planning, and they illustrate the fact that controls must reflect plans. Some of these tools have long been used by managers; others, such as variable budgeting and zero-base budgeting, are more recent refinements of traditional budgeting. The Program Evaluation and Review Technique (PERT) represents a newer generation of planning and control tools.

One of the older control devices is the budget. Budgeting is the formulation of plans for a given future period in numerical terms. There are several types of budgets: (1) revenue and expense budgets, (2) time, space, material, and product budgets, (3) capital expenditure budgets, and (4) cash budgets. There are a number of dangers in budgeting, but the major danger, inflexibility, can be largely avoided by using variable budgets. These are budgets designed to vary with the volume of output, with expenses divided among those items that vary usually as the volume of sales or some other measure of output varies. Flexibility may also be obtained by providing alternative or supplementary budgets. Budgeting is made much more precise by zero-base budgeting, in which programs are divided into "packages." The costs for each package are calculated from a base of zero. In order to make budgetary control effective in practice, managers must always realize that budgets are tools and are not intended to replace managing.

Among the traditional nonbudgetary control devices are statistical data and their analyses, special reports and analyses, the operational audit, and personal observation.

One of the newer techniques of planning and control is the time-event network analysis. The Program Evaluation and Review Technique (PERT) is a refinement of the original Gantt charts, which were designed to show, in bar-chart form, the various things that must be done, and when, in order to accomplish a program. PERT is also a refinement of "milestone" budgeting, in which the things that have to be done are broken down into identifiable and controllable pieces called milestones. When milestones are connected to form a network and the time required to complete each milestone is identified, the result is a PERT time-event network. Using the sequences of events and the times required for them, one can determine the critical path, which is the sequence that takes the longest time and has zero (or the least) slack time.

Program budgeting is a systematic method for allocating resources. It is used primarily in government operations. Procedures should be designed to implement plans. Procedures can be made effective through proper planning and controlling and by using the guidelines suggested in this chapter.

The management information system (MIS) is a formal system of gathering, integrating, comparing, analyzing, and dispersing information internal and external to the enterprise in a timely, effective, and efficient manner.

Computers (mainframes, minicomputers, and microcomputers) are now extensively used. Their impact on managers at various organizational levels differs. Information technology provides many challenges. Some managers still resist using computers, but speech recognition devices encourage computer use. Computers have also contributed to telecommuting, which means that persons may work at home at a computer terminal that is linked to a company's mainframe computer. Increasingly, computer networks link workstations with each other, with larger computers, and with peripheral equipment.

KEY IDEAS AND CONCEPTS FOR REVIEW

Budgeting	Zero-base budgeting
Types of budgets	Nonbudgetary control devices
Budgeting problems	Operational audit
Variable budgets	Gantt charts
Alternative and supplementary budgets	Milestone budgeting

Critical path in PERT
Program planning and budgeting (PPB)
Guidelines for effective procedures
Management information system (MIS)
Mainframe computer
Program Evaluation and Review
  Technique (PERT)

Minicomputer
Microcomputer
Impact of computers on managers
Application of microcomputers
Speech recognition devices
Telecommuting
Computer networks

FOR DISCUSSION

1. The techniques of control appear to be as much techniques of planning as they are of control. In what ways is this true? Why would you expect it to be so?
2. "Variable budgets are flexible budgets." Discuss.
3. It is often claimed that an operating expense budget must be set at a level lower than expected in order to ensure the attainment of cost and profit goals. Do you agree?
4. To what extent, and how, can budgeting be approached on a grass roots basis, that is, from the bottom of the organization upward?
5. If you were going to institute a program of special control reports and analyses for a top manager, how would you go about it?
6. PERT is a management invention that takes basic principles and knowledge and, through design to get a desired result, comes up with a useful technique of planning and control. Analyze PERT with this in mind.
7. Give examples of how information technology has affected you.
8. Why do you think computers have a different impact on managers at various organization levels?

EXERCISES/ACTION STEPS

1. Use PERT to plan your college study program. What are the advantages in using this technique? What are some problems?
2. Select an organization you know and show how it uses computers.

CASES

CASE 21-1
THE WHOLESALE DRUG COMPANY

The Wholesale Drug Company grew rapidly to become one of the largest firms of its kind. The success was due primarily to the leadership of the president, Ms. Johnson. Since many similar, but smaller, enterprises used computers for recordkeeping and data processing, Ms. Johnson was under great pressure to install a computerized control system to keep track of twenty distribution centers scattered throughout the nation.

Up to that time, expenses and income were

recorded by means of a relatively simple ledger sheet and a journal showing the data for the twenty centers. This kind of recordkeeping, which was done by hand, allowed for easy comparison of the centers. Payrolls were done in a similar manner, and checks were usually processed within 24 hours. At that time five people and two supervisors were employed in the accounting department.

Several computer companies looked at the system, but their analysis showed that cost savings were hardly possible. However, one firm made a rather convincing case for a new data processing system. The consulting firm predicted the following benefits: (1) faster processing of information, (2) more detailed information on the operation, and (3) a reduction in costs.

After 2 years of using the new system, Ms. Johnson, who had reluctantly agreed to the computerization, related the following story: "Before the use of the computer, we had seven people in the account-

ing department. Now we have nine plus seven people in the data processing center. It is true that it takes only a few minutes to get the output from the computer, but we cannot run the program until the last distribution center provides the data. Unfortunately, this means delays, because we depend on the slowest operational unit for their input. It is true that we can get more detailed information, but I do not know if anybody ever looks at it. It is just too time-consuming to find the relevant information in the stacks of computer printouts and to interpret the data. I just wish we could go back to the old ledger system. But we invested so much money, and have reached a point of no return."

1. Why did the computerized system not live up to its expectations?
2. What should Ms. Johnson do now?
3. How would you design a computerized system? What factors would you consider?

CASE 21-2
INFORMATION TECHNOLOGY AT AMERICAN AIRLINES[23]

The information system at American Airlines has become an integral part of the overall strategy to gain a competitive edge in the industry. The extensive use of computers began in the 1950s in payroll and inventory control and extended to customer service. In the early 1960s, American developed the widely known SABRE system ("SABRE" stands for Semi-Automated Business Research Environment). It is one of the most sophisticated passenger reservation systems used by travel agents and customers. Through the PRODIGY computer access system, customers now have access to the Personal Reservation System called "EAASY SABRE."

Shortly after implementing SABRE, American also used the system for other tasks, such as controlling freight shipments, as well as dispatching and tracking flights. When the government deregulated the airline industry in 1978, the information system became an even more important tool for competing against the low-cost airlines such as the former People Express, Jet America, America West, and other carriers, whose labor costs were as much as 40 to 50 percent lower.

American Airlines' strategy was to use the information technology to compete in a variety of ways. One application was to have as many aircraft seats as possible filled without having many passengers "bumped" through overbooking. Another application was to obtain the proper balance between discount and regular fares. It was estimated that revenues could be increased by $65 million a year by shifting 1 percent of discount fares to the full fare—clearly a competitive advantage in a market where price changes occur daily and on occasion even hourly.

Another application of the information system was to find the most efficient way to fly in order to reduce fuel cost, which is the second largest expense. Some airplanes have sensors on board to monitor essential equipment; the operational information is sent to the ground station. Maintenance can then be planned effectively and performed more efficiently when the aircraft lands. Still another application of the computer was to determine the most profitable routes.

The complexity of scheduling over 13,000 pilots and flight attendants on 1300 daily flights is horrendous. The high cost of overtime can put an airline at a competitive disadvantage.

Robert L. Crandall, chairman and president of American Airlines, thinks that information systems are the key for success. He stated: "We have taken what was once a basic reservation system and built it into an integrated information system that drives our corporate strategy as much as it is driven by that strategy." In 1990, more than 85,500 SABRE terminals were used by travel agencies in 47 countries.

While American has been the industry leader in the use of information technology, competition is on the horizon. The 1992 program of the European Community (EC) is designed to eliminate trade and many political barriers. The European airline industry will also be deregulated by the end of 1992. Rather than engaging in mergers, airlines probably will be integrated into a network linking selected carriers together. An illustration of the new cooperation among airlines involves the two computer reservation systems Galileo and Amadeus. Thus, American Airlines—with a strategy of expanding in the European market, the largest market in the industrialized world with over 340 million people—will have ample competition.

1. Discuss the evolving use of information technology at American Airlines.
2. Should American expand its position in Europe? What are the arguments for and against this expansion?

REFERENCES

1. Herbert A. Simon, "Making Management Decisions: The Role of Intuition and Emotion," *Academy of Management Executive* (February 1987), p. 57.
2. Primarily because of the negative implications of budgeting in the past, the more positive phrase "profit planning" is sometimes used, and the budget is then known as the "profit plan."
3. Thomas A. Stewart, "Why Budgets Are Bad for Business," *Fortune* (June 4, 1990), pp. 179–190.
4. The technique was also separately developed as the Critical Path Method by engineers at the Du Pont Company at virtually the same time. Only PERT is discussed here because the Critical Path Method, although different in some respects, utilizes the same principles.
5. See also Richard E. Walton, *Up and Running—Integrating Information Technology and the Organization* (Boston: Harvard Business School Press, 1989); E. Wainright Martin, Daniel W. DeHayes, Jeffrey A. Hoffer, and William C. Perkins, *Managing Information Technology—What Managers Need to Know* (New York: Macmillan Publishing Company, 1991); George Gilder, "Into the Telecosm," *Harvard Business Review* (March–April 1991), pp. 150–161; Blake Ives and Richard O. Mason, "Can Information Technology Revitalize Your Customer Service?" *Academy of Management Executive* (November 1990), pp. 52–69.
6. William Lee and Patricia Robin, "Opportunities in the Changing European Telecommunications Scene," *The Journal of European Business* (November–December 1989), pp. 26–34; Brenton R. Schlender, "Who's Ahead in the Computer Wars," *Fortune* (Feb. 12, 1990), pp. 58–66; Andrew Kupfer, "The Go-Anywhere Phone Is at Hand," *Fortune* (Nov. 5, 1990), pp. 143–148; Edgar Carl Law, "1992—The Pivotal Year for European Telecommunications," *Business Communications Review* (July–August 1988), pp. 70–72; Timothy Aeppel, "Siemens Confronts History in Takeover," *The Wall Street Journal* (Aug. 12, 1991).

7. For alliances and combines in Japan, see Charles H. Ferguson, "Computers and the Coming of the U.S. Keiretsu," *Harvard Business Review* (July–August 1990), pp. 55–70.

8. See also Michael Hammer, "Reengineering Work: Don't Automate, Obliterate," *Harvard Business Review* (July–August 1990), pp. 104–112.

9. For organizational issues in establishing an MIS (management information system) unit, see Mark Klein, "Information Politics," *Datamation* (Aug. 1, 1985), pp. 87–92.

10. George P. Huber, "A Theory of the Effects of Advanced Information Technologies on Organizational Design, Intelligence, and Decision Making," *The Academy of Management Review* (January 1990), pp. 47–71.

11. Clark Holloway thinks that in the 1990s supercomputers may share many functions of top executives. See his article "Strategic Management and Artificial Intelligence," *Long Range Planning* (October 1983), pp. 89–93. The use of information technology for formulating a strategy is discussed by Sid L. Huff, "Information Technology and Corporate Strategy," *Business Quarterly* (Summer 1985), pp. 18 ff.

12. While some argue that senior managers can keep better control of the operation as well as of subordinates, others consider the impact on top management minimal. For discussions of this topic, see John Dearden, "SMR Forum: Will the Computer Change the Job of Top Management?" *Sloan Management Review* (Fall 1983), pp. 195–204; John C. Camillus and Albert L. Lederer, "Corporate Strategy and the Design of Computerized Information Systems," *Sloan Management Review* (Spring 1985), pp. 35 ff.

13. Brian O'Reilly, "Apple Finally Invades the Office," *Fortune* (Nov. 9, 1987), pp. 52–64.

14. See also Alice LaPlante, "Baby-Sitting the Boss," *InfoWorld* (Aug. 8, 1988), pp. 1 and 89.

15. Lisa L. Spiegelman, "Top-Level Managers Not Using PCs, Survey Finds," *InfoWorld* (May 26, 1988), p. 24.

16. "Management Warms Up to Computer Graphics," *Business Week* (Aug. 13, 1984), pp. 96–101.

17. Paul Duke, Jr., "Can We Talk?" *The Wall Street Journal, A Special Report: Technology in the Work Place* (Nov. 10, 1986).

18. Geoff Lewis, Jeffrey Rothfeder, Resa W. King, Mark Maremont, and Thane Peterson, "The Portable Executive," *Business Week* (Oct. 10, 1988), pp. 102–112.

19. John Naisbitt, *Megatrends* (New York: Warner Books, 1982), chap. 1.

20. David Needle, "Telecommuting: Off to a Slow Start," *InfoWorld* (May 19, 1986), pp. 43–46.

21. Margrethe H. Olson, "Do You Telecommute?" *Datamation* (Oct. 15, 1985), pp. 129–132.

22. For a discussion of local area networks, see Laurie Flynn, "LANs," *InfoWorld* (Oct. 27, 1986), pp. 45–46.

23. Remarks by Robert L. Crandall, chairman and president of American Airlines, at the Cooperative Users of Recognition Equipment 1985 Conference, Dallas (June 18, 1985); Jeffrey M. Lenorovitz, "Airlines Will Cooperate, Not Merge, after Deregulation of Europe in 1992," *Aviation Week & Space Technology* (Sept. 5, 1988), pp. 133 and 135; Kevin Kelly, Todd Mason, Christopher Power, and James E. Ellis, "American Aims for the Sky," *Business Week* (Feb. 20, 1989), pp. 54–58; Kenneth Labich, "The Computer Network That Keeps American Flying," *Fortune* (Sept. 24, 1990), p. 46; Max D. Hopper, "Rattling SABRE—New Ways to Compete on Information," *Harvard Business Review* (May–June 1990), pp. 118–125.

Chapter 22

Many service jobs exist because of hard-goods producing industries.[1]
Wickham Skinner

Productivity and Operations Management*

Chapter Objectives

After reading this chapter, you should be able to:

1. Identify the nature of productivity issues and suggest ways to improve effectiveness and efficiency.
2. Describe the nature of production and operations management as an applied case of managerial planning and control.
3. Discuss the managerial techniques found to be especially useful for operations planning and control as well as other areas of enterprise operations.
4. Describe techniques for improving productivity.
5. Suggest some probable future developments in operations planning and control.

* Additional topics in production and operations management are discussed in other parts of the book. See, for example, Chapter 8 for various aspects of decision making, including the topic of decision support systems; Chapter 13 for job design; and Chapter 21 for procedures planning and control, management information systems, and different kinds of control techniques.

In a real sense, the whole book is about the improvement of productivity. But this important topic will receive special attention in this chapter, with an emphasis on the micro level of production and operations management.[2]

PRODUCTIVITY PROBLEMS AND MEASUREMENT

Undoubtedly, productivity will be one of the major concerns of managers in the 1990s and probably beyond. This concern extends beyond the boundaries of the United States into many other parts of the world. Even Japan, which is admired for productivity improvements, is now concerned about remaining competitive in the world market.[3]

Productivity Problems

Productivity implies measurement, which, in turn, is an essential step in the control process. Although there is general agreement about the need for improving productivity, there is little consensus about the fundamental causes of the problem and what to do about them.[4] The blame has been assigned to various factors. Some people place it on the greater proportion of less skilled workers with respect to the total labor force, but others disagree. There are those who see the cutback in research and the emphasis on immediate results as the main culprit. Another reason given for the productivity dilemma is the growing affluence of people, which makes them less ambitious. Still others cite the breakdown in family structure, the workers' attitudes, and government policies and regulations. Increasingly, attention shifts to management as the cause of the problem—as well as the solution, which is the focus of this book.

Measurement of Productivity of Knowledge Workers

As defined in Chapter 1, **productivity** is *the input-output ratio within a time period with due consideration for quality*. This definition can be applied to the productivity of organizations, managers, staff personnel, and workers. Measurement of skills work is relatively easy, but it becomes more difficult for knowledge work. The difference between the two kinds of work is the relative use of knowledge and skills. Thus, a person on the production line would be considered a skills worker, while the assistant to the manager with planning as his or her main function would be a knowledge worker. Managers, engineers, and programmers are knowledge workers because the relative amount of their work does not consist of utilizing skills, as would be the case for bricklayers, mechanics, and butchers. But the job title cannot be the sole guide for making distinctions. The owner of a gas station may schedule the day's tasks, determine priorities, and direct subordinates, but the owner may also change brakes, adjust the carburetor, or realign the front wheels on a car.

It is clear that, in general, the productivity of the knowledge worker is more difficult to measure than that of the skills worker. (Note also that worker productivity measurement is somewhat artificial because it often ignores the cost of capital.) One difficulty in measuring the productivity of knowledge workers is that some outputs are really activities that help achieve end results. Thus, the engineer contributes indirectly to the final product. Another difficulty is that knowledge workers often assist other organizational units. The advertising manager's efforts should improve sales, but it is hard to say for sure what the exact contribution is. Still another difficulty is that the quality of the knowledge workers' outputs is often difficult to measure. The effects of a strategic decision, for example, may not be evident for several years, and even then the success or failure of the new strategic direction may depend on many external forces beyond the control of the manager.

Perspective

Approaches to Productivity Improvement

There is no one best approach to productivity improvement, but there are many.[5] Here are some examples:

- Kaiser Aluminum and Chemical Corporation emphasized the formulation of improvement objectives, the measurement of performance against these objectives, an effective reporting system, and frequent reinforcement of good performance.
- Hughes Aircraft Company, in which a very large percentage of the employees are knowledge workers, provided principles and guidelines for productivity improvement covering areas such as recognition of good performance, use of work modules, design of meaningful work, emphasis on goals, and development of the ability to work with people.

It is evident, then, that productivity improvement is achieved by the good management practices advocated throughout this book.[6] But the discussion will now turn to the specific area of production and operations management, where measurement is relatively easy and consequently has been the focus of productivity improvement programs in the past.

PRODUCTION AND OPERATIONS MANAGEMENT[7]

One of the major areas in any kind of enterprise, whether business, government, or others, is production and operations management. It is also the area where managing as a scientifically based art got its start. The contributions of such management pioneers as Frederick Taylor, Henry Gantt, and Frank Gilbreth, to mention only a few, indicate that their interest was largely in improving productivity and manufacturing products most efficiently while still recognizing, as they did, the importance of the human factor as an indispensable input.

In the past, **production management** was the term used to refer to those activities necessary to manufacture products. However, in recent years, the area has been generally expanded to include such activities as purchasing, warehousing, transportation, and other operations from the procurement of raw materials through various activities until a product is available to the buyer. The term **operations management** refers to activities necessary to produce and deliver a service as well as a physical product.

There are, of course, other essential activities undertaken by a typical enterprise. In addition to production, these enterprise functions often include research and development, engineering, marketing and sales, accounting, and financing. This chapter deals only with what has come to be called "operations management" or "production management," and often "production and operations management" (POM). It should be pointed out that this is not, of course, the same thing as "operational"-management theory. As explained earlier, operational-management theory is the study of the practice (managing) which that theory or science is designed to underpin.

OPERATIONS MANAGEMENT SYSTEMS

Operations management has to be seen as a system. Figure 22-1 gives an overview of the operations function. In the operations management model the *inputs* include needs of customers, information, technology, management and labor, fixed assets, and variable assets that are relevant to the transformation process. Managers and workers use the information and physical factors to produce outputs. Some physical elements, such as land, plant site, buildings, machines, and warehouses, are relatively permanent. Other physical elements, such as materials and supplies, are consumed in the process of producing outputs. The *transformation process* incorporates planning, operating, and controlling the system. There are many tools and techniques available to facilitate the transformation process. The model also reflects a constant concern for improving the system. *Outputs* consist of products and services and may even be information, such as that provided by a consulting organization.

FIGURE 22-1

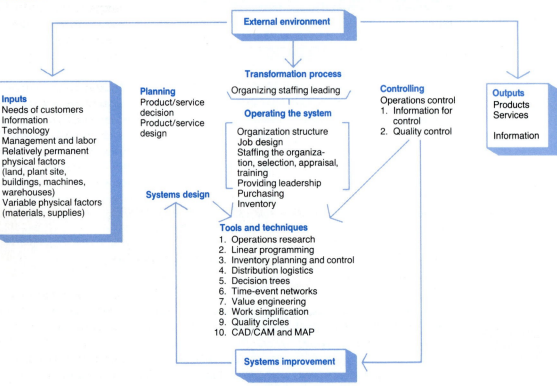

OPERATIONS MANAGEMENT SYSTEM.

The last part of the model shows that operations are influenced by *external factors,* such as safety regulations or fair labor practices. Since the external environment is discussed elsewhere in this book (especially in Chapter 3 and in Part 2, "Planning"), it will not be expanded on here; the important point is that operations management must be an open system interacting with its surroundings.

The operations management model (Figure 22-1) serves as a framework for the discussions that follow. There is a close relationship between this model and the one introduced in Chapter 1 (Figure 1-5), since this operations model may be regarded as a subsystem of a total management system. Examples of operations systems[8] with inputs, transformation (sometimes also called "process"), and outputs are presented in Table 22-1.

Planning Operations

Objectives, premises, and strategies of an enterprise (discussed in Part 2 of this book) determine the search for and the selection of the product or service. In this discussion, the production of physical products is emphasized, but the concepts can

TABLE 22-1 EXAMPLES OF OPERATIONS SYSTEMS		
Inputs	**Transformation**	**Outputs**
1. Plant, factory machines, people, materials	Assembling bicycles	Completed bicycles
2. Students with limited knowledge, skills, and attitudes	Lectures, cases, experiential exercises, term papers	Students with enhanced knowledge, skills, and attitudes
3. Client problem	Consulting: data-collection analysis, evaluation of alternatives, selection of alternative, recommendation	Consulting report recommending course of action

also be applied to the provision of services. After an end product has been selected, the specifications are determined and the technological feasibility of producing it is considered. The design of an operations system requires decisions concerning the location of facilities, the process to be used, the quantity to be produced, and the quality of the product.

International Perspective

Maquiladora: Alternative Plant Locations[9]

In planning their operations, companies increasingly take a global perspective. U.S. companies have a special relationship with neighboring Mexico that resulted in the Maquiladora program. Although it began in 1966, the program expanded in the early 1980s after the economic crisis in Mexico. It began near the Mexican-U.S. border but has been extended throughout Mexico. The basic idea is to establish a Maquiladora company to produce or assemble products that cannot be sold in the Mexican market and, in return, obtain exemption from duties. These plants are partly or wholly owned by foreigners, initially U.S. firms but now also companies from Japan, South Korea, and Taiwan. They include familiar names such as Casio, Hitachi, Matsushita, Sanyo, Samsung, and Lucky Goldstar. The "Big Three" U.S. carmakers have manufacturing facilities in northern Mexico. Altogether, there are over 1400 Maquiladora plants in Mexico, employing about 400,000 people.

One primary reason for setting up shop is the low labor rate in Mexico. Trico, a windshield manufacturer in Buffalo, New York, participated in the Maquiladora project, which may have contributed to the company's survival. The benefits often cited are that Maquiladora provides jobs and hard currency and also promotes economic development.

However, critics charge that workers are exploited and that U.S. employers pay the Mexican workers much less than Mexican companies do. U.S. employers are accused of exploiting the most vulnerable workers: girls and young women, who constitute two-thirds of the work force. Other criticisms are that the Maquiladora does not sufficiently contribute to technology transfer. Nor does it help to develop a skilled work force, because workers receive little training. In the United States, criticism of the program comes primarily from labor unions, which are concerned about the loss of jobs.

Special interests in a product decision.   One of the basic decisions an enterprise makes is selecting a product or products it intends to produce and market. This requires gathering product ideas that will satisfy the needs of customers and contribute to the goals of the enterprise while being consistent with the strategy of the firm.[10] In a product decision, the various interests of functional managers must be considered. For example, a production manager may want a product that can be produced without difficulty, at a reasonable cost, and with long production runs. Engineers may share many of these aims, but they are often looking for engineering sophistication rather than ways of producing the product at a reasonable cost.

The sales or marketing manager's interest is likely to be the needs of customers, and his or her aim is to increase the sales of products through ready availability and competitive prices. Moreover, sales managers may want to offer a broad product line without considering the engineering, production, transportation, and warehousing costs and the problems involved. The finance manager's concerns are likely to be costs and profits, high return on investment, and low financial risks. The divergent interests of these functionally oriented managers and professionals influence what products will be produced and marketed, but it is the general manager who has to integrate the various interests and balance revenues with costs, profits with risks, and long-term with short-term growth.

Product and production design.   The design of a product and its production require a number of activities. The following steps have often been suggested:

1. Create product ideas by searching for consumer needs and screening the various alternatives.
2. Select the product on the basis of various considerations, including data from market and economic analyses, and make a general feasibility study.
3. Prepare a preliminary design by evaluating various alternatives, taking into consideration reliability, quality, and maintenance requirements.
4. Reach a final decision by developing, testing, and simulating the processes to see if they work.
5. Decide whether the enterprise's current facilities are adequate or if new or modified facilities are required.
6. Select the process for producing the product; consider the technology and the methods available.
7. After the product is designed, prepare the layout of the facilities to be used, plan the system of production, and schedule the various things that must be done.

Systems design.   In producing a product, companies can consider several basic kinds of production layouts.[11] One alternative is to arrange the layout in the order in which the product is *produced* or *assembled*. For example, a truck assembly line may be arranged so that the preassembled front and rear axles are attached to the frame, followed by the installation of the steering, the engine, and the transmission. Then the brake lines and electrical cables are connected, and other parts are assembled and painted. Finally, the truck is road-tested.

A second alternative is to lay out the production system according to the *process* employed. In a hospital, for example, specific steps are likely to be followed: the admission of the patient, the treatment of the patient (which usually involves specific subprocesses), billing for service, and dismissal. This may be followed up by posthospitalization treatment.

In a third kind of layout (sometimes called *fixed-position* layout) the product stays in one place for assembly. This layout is used for the assembly of extremely large and bulky items such as printing presses, large strip-mining machines, and ships.

The fourth kind of layout is arranged according to the nature of the *project*. Building a bridge or tunnel is normally a one-time project designed to fit specific geographic requirements.

In the fifth kind of layout the production process is arranged to facilitate the *sale* of products. In a supermarket basic food items, such as dairy products, are normally located away from the checkout counters. This causes customers to walk through the long aisles and, it is hoped, select other items on the way to the dairy section.

A sixth basic approach to production layout is to design the process so that it facilitates *storage or movement* of products. Storage space is costly, and an effective and efficient design can keep the storage costs low. Also, in order to reach an item, it should not be necessary to move many other items.

Operating the System[12]

After a product has been selected and the system for producing it has been designed and built, the next major step is to operate the system. This requires setting up an organization structure, staffing the positions, and training people. Managers are needed who can provide the supervision and leadership to carry out activities necessary to produce desired products or provide services. Other activities, such as purchasing and maintaining the inventory, are also required in operating the system. The aim is to obtain the best productivity ratio within a time period with due consideration for quality.

Controlling Operations with Emphasis on Information Systems

Controlling operations, as in any other case of managerial control, requires setting performance criteria, measuring performance against them, and taking actions to correct undesirable deviations. Thus, one can control production, product quality and reliability levels, inventory levels, and work-force performance. A number of tools and techniques have been developed to do this. Because their application extends beyond operations or production, they have been discussed previously. Some, however, are important to operations; examined here is the role of information systems in operations control.

One type of planning and control system, one which has been available for several years, integrates information on virtually an instantaneous basis, thereby reducing considerably the delays that usually impede effective control. With the development of computer hardware and software, it is now possible for virtually any measurable data to be reported as events occur. Systems are available for quickly and systematically collecting data bearing on total operation, for keeping these data readily available, and for reporting without delay the status of any of a large number of projects at any instant. They are thus primarily information systems designed to provide effective planning and control.[13]

Perspective

How an Information System Facilitates Operations

Applied widely now to purchasing, storing, manufacturing, and shipping, information systems may operate through dispatch stations and input centers located throughout a plant. At the dispatch centers, events are recorded as they occur, and the information is dispatched immediately to a computer. For example, when a worker finishes an assigned task on the assembly of a product, the work-order time card is put into a transactor, which electrically transmits to a computer the information that item x has passed through a certain process, has accumulated y hours of labor, may or may not be on schedule, and other pertinent data. The input centers are equipped to originate information needed for a production plan automatically from programmed instructions, purchase orders, shop orders, and other authorizations. These data are fed into a computer and compared against plans, which are used as standards against which actual operations can be compared.

In addition to providing fast entry, comparison, and retrieval of information, such an integrated operations control system furnishes needed information for planning programs in such areas as purchasing, production, and inventory control. Moreover, it permits almost instantaneous comparison of results with plans, pinpointing where they differ and providing a regular (daily or more often, if needed) system of reports on deviations from plans, such as items that are behind schedule or costs that are running above budget.

Other planning, control, and information systems have been developed to reflect quickly the interaction between production and distribution operations and such key financial measures as costs, profit, and cash flow. Companies with real-time computer models can give operating managers virtually instant analysis of such "what-if" questions as the effects of reducing or increasing output, the impact of a reduction in demand, and the sensitivity of the system to labor cost increases, price changes, and new equipment additions. To be sure, system models, simulating actual operations and their impact on financial factors, are primarily planning tools. But so are most control techniques. However, by making possible exceptionally quick responses to the many "what-if" questions of operating managers, system models can greatly reduce the time elapsed in correcting for deviations from plans and can materially improve control.

These and other systems that use the technology of fast computation clearly promise to hasten the day when planning all the areas of production can be more precise and controlling more effective. The drawback is not cost; rather, it is the failure of managers to spend time and mental effort conceptualizing the system and its relationships or to see that someone else in the organization does so. Nevertheless, as pointed out in Chapter 20, fast information availability can never provide true real-time controls of the time delays in any feedback system. Only a feedforward approach can overcome these delays.

OPERATIONS RESEARCH FOR PLANNING, CONTROLLING, AND IMPROVING PRODUCTIVITY

A number of techniques employed in many kinds of planning and controlling are especially useful in managing operations. This is understandable, since most of the special techniques that have been developed are based on mathematical models and the use of quantitative data. Conceptual models and fairly exact quantitative data are available in many areas for production and operations management.

It was advantageous to discuss some of these techniques in the chapters on decision making and control techniques. Of special interest here to managers of production and operations are the tools of operations research. Later in this chapter other techniques will also be discussed.

The Concept of Operations Research

Operations research is a product of World War II, although its forerunners in scientific methods, higher mathematics, and such tools as probability theory go back far beyond that period. The accelerated growth of operations research in recent years has followed the trend of applying the methods of physical scientists and engineers to economic and political problems. It has also been made possible by the development of rapid computing machines, particularly those using electronics, since much of the advantage of operations research depends on the ability to apply, at low cost, involved mathematical formulas and to use data with complex relationships. There are almost as many definitions of operations research as there are writers on the subject. For the purposes of this discussion, the most acceptable definition is that **operations research** is the application of scientific methods to the study of alternatives in a problem situation, with a view to obtaining a quantitative basis for arriving at the best solution. Thus, the emphasis is on scientific methods, on the use of quantitative data, on goals, and on the determination of the best means of reaching the goals. In other words, operations research might be called "quantitative common sense."

The Essentials of Operations Research

Managers have long attempted to solve management problems scientifically, but operations researchers have supplied an element of novelty in the orderliness and completeness of their approach. They have emphasized defining the problem and goals, carefully collecting and evaluating data, developing and testing hypotheses, determining relationships among data, developing and checking predictions based on hypotheses, and devising measures to evaluate the effectiveness of a course of action.

Thus, the essential characteristics of operations research as applied to decision making can be summarized as follows:

1. It emphasizes *models*—the logical physical representation of a reality or problem. Models can, of course, be simple or complex. For example, the accounting formula "Assets minus liabilities equals proprietorship" is a model, since it represents an idea and, within the limits of the terms used, symbolizes the relationship among the variables involved.
2. It emphasizes *goals* in a problem area and the development of measures of effectiveness in determining whether a given solution shows promise of achieving these goals. For example, if the goal is profit, the measure of effectiveness may be the rate of return on investment, and every proposed solution will arrange the variables so that the end result can be weighed against this measure.
3. It incorporates in a model the *variables* in a problem, or at least those that appear to be important to its solution. Managers can control some variables; others may be uncontrollable factors in the problem.
4. It puts the model and its variables, constraints, and goals in *mathematical terms* so that they may be clearly identified, subjected to mathematical simplification, and readily utilized for calculation by substitution of quantities for symbols.
5. It *quantifies* the variables in a problem to the extent possible, since only quantifiable data can be inserted into a model to yield a measurable result.
6. It supplements much unavailable data with such usable mathematical and statistical devices as the *probabilities* in a situation, thus often making the mathematical and computing problem workable within a small margin of error despite gaps in accurate quantifiable data.

Of all these characteristics, perhaps the basic tool—and the major contribution—of operations research is the conceptual model. There are many types of models that can be constructed and used. Some assert logical relationships among variables. These may be referred to as "simulative" or "descriptive" if they are designed only to describe the relationship of elements in a situation. The models useful for planning are referred to as "decision" or "optimizing" models, designed to lead to the selection of a best course of action among available alternatives.

Operations Research Procedure

Applying operations research generally involves the following six steps:

1. Formulate the problem. As in any other planning problem, the operations researcher must analyze the goals and the system in which the solution must operate. That complex of interrelated components in a problem area, referred to by operations researchers as a "system," is the environment of a decision, and it represents planning premises. It may take in an entire business operation or be limited to planning production for presses and lathes. It is still, however, an interconnected complex of related human or material components. Obviously, unless managers can greatly simplify the problem by applying the principle of the limiting factor (that is, unless they eliminate alternatives that don't resolve the immediate problem), the more comprehensive the system, the more complex the problem.

2. Construct a mathematical model. The next step is to restate the problem as a system of relationships in a mathematical model. For a single goal, with at least some variables subject to control, the general form of the operations research model is

$$E = f(x_i, y_j)$$

where E = measure of effectiveness of system
x_i = controllable variables
y_j = variables beyond control

This model may be classified as either a decision model or a simulation model. When it is being used as a decision model, values inserted for the uncontrollable variables (y_j) and the controllable variables (x_i) are manipulated to yield the greatest measure of effectiveness (E). For example, suppose that marketing managers wished to find out what actions on their part would yield the most total sales dollars. The model might include such uncontrollable variables as competitors' prices, gross national product, and price-level changes and such controllable variables as number of salespeople, commissions allowed, product prices, and advertising expenditures.

Although all models are intended to represent reality, with simulation models the users put in the model a set of factual values for the controllable variables and assume a set of values for the uncontrollable variables. By using one or more sets of values for the uncontrollable variables (because often they cannot be known), one can compute various E's until the E believed to be satisfactory is found. In this event, of course, there is no way of knowing whether an optimal solution has been found. There is something to be gained by restating a problem in concrete (visible) terms. Often a decision model cannot be used because a lack of input data prevents the accurate simulation of reality (at least the important elements of reality) and because it may be very complex and difficult to build.

3. Derive a solution from the model.
There are two basic procedures for arriving at a solution from a model. In the *analytical* procedure, mathematical deduction is used in order to reach, as nearly as possible, a mathematical solution before quantities are inserted to get a numerical solution. This can be an important contribution to complex decision making. Variables can be reduced or restated in terms of common variables. Certain variables (for example, sales) can appear in a number of places in a model, and the user can factor some out or reduce them. In other cases, the user can consolidate and simplify a series of mathematical equations. The result of this analytical procedure is that the user has placed a complex series of relationships into as simple a mathematical form as possible. In addition, this analysis may disclose, mathematically, that certain variables are unimportant to a reasonable solution and may be dropped from consideration.

The second procedure is referred to as *numerical*. In this, the analyst simply tries different values for the controllable variables to see what the results will be and then develops a set of values that seems to give the best solution. The numerical procedure varies from pure trial and error to complex iteration. In iteration, the analyst undertakes successive trial runs to approach an optimal solution. In some complex cases, such as the iterative procedures used in linear programming, rules have been developed to help analysts more quickly undertake trials and identify the optimum solution when it is reached.

4. Test the model.
Because a model, by its very nature, is only a representation of reality and because it is seldom possible to include all the variables, models should usually be tested. This can be done by using the model to solve a problem and comparing the results with what actually happens. The tests can be carried out by using past data or by trying the model out in practice to see how it measures up to reality.

5. Provide controls for the model and the solution.
Because a once-accurate model may cease to represent reality, because the variables that are beyond the user's control may change, or because the relationships of variables may shift, provision must be made for control of the model and the solution. This is done in the same way any other control is undertaken, by providing means for feedback so that significant deviations can be detected and changes made. In many complex models, such as those used for production or distribution planning, the effect of the deviations must be weighed against the cost of feeding in the correction or against the usually greater cost of revising the entire program. As a result, the decision may sometimes be made not to correct the model or the inputs.

6. Put the solution into effect.
The final step is to put the model and the inputs into operation. In anything but the simplest programs, this will involve revising and clarifying procedures so that the inputs (including control feedback information) become available in an orderly fashion, and this, in turn, often requires reorgani-

zation of an enterprise's available information. What many users of operations research have found to be a major stumbling block is that no one is willing to undertake the hard work of developing better information to use with the models. Accounting and other data normally available in a company are often not adequate for the requirements of successful operations research. Many managers, intrigued with the possibilities of operations research, wish that some of the research effort of experts, now so widely employed in constructing elegant models, could be channeled toward reorganizing information.

Other problems in making operations research useful for managers involve getting people to understand, appreciate, and use the techniques of operations research and deciding such questions as what computing facilities to use, how to use them, and how the information outputs are to be made useful and understandable to those responsible for decisions. In this connection, operations researchers would do managers a real favor by frankly admitting the nature of and margin of uncertainty in their solution.

All this is to say that operations researchers are not nearly done with their task when their model is reduced to paper and tested. Mathematical gymnastics may be interesting to the pure philosopher, but managers must make responsible decisions, and the operations researcher who would be useful to managers must be more than a mathematical gymnast.

Linear Programming

A technique for determining the optimum combination of limited resources to obtain a desired goal, **linear programming** is one of the most successful applications of operations research. It is based on the assumption that a linear, or straight-line, relationship exists between variables and that the limits of variations can be determined. For example, in a production shop, the variables may be units of output per machine in a given time, direct-labor costs or material costs per unit of output, the number of operations per unit, and so on. Most or all of these may have linear relationships, within certain limits; by solving linear equations, one can establish the optimum in terms of cost, time, machine utilization, and other objectives. Thus, this technique is especially useful in cases where input data can be quantified and objectives are subject to definite measurement.

As one might expect, the technique has had its most promising use in such problem areas as determining shipping rates and routes, and the utilization of production and warehouse facilities to achieve the lowest overall costs, including transportation costs. Because the technique depends on linear relationships and many decisions do not involve these or cannot be simulated accurately enough, newer and more complex systems of nonlinear programming have come into use.

Inventory Planning and Control

Perhaps in the history of operations research more attention has been directed to inventory control than to any other practical area of operations. The essential systems relationships can be seen as a little "black box," as depicted in Figure 22-2.

FIGURE 22-2

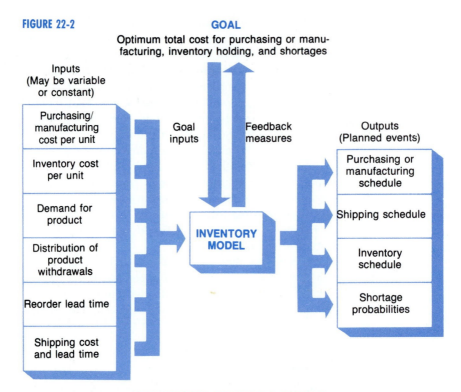

INVENTORY CONTROL MODEL.

In mathematical form, these conceptual relationships are expressed by the following equation:

$$Q_e = \sqrt{\frac{2DS}{H}}$$

where Q_e = economic order quantity (EOQ)
   D = demand per year
   S = setup costs
   H = inventory holding (carrying) cost per item, per year

The model in Figure 22-2 illustrates several things. It forces consideration of the goals desired and of the need for placing values on outputs and inputs. It also furnishes a manager with the basis for plans and with standards by which to measure performance.[14] However, with all its advantages, this is a subsystem and does not incorporate other subsystems, such as production planning, distribution planning, and sales planning.

The **economic order quantity** (EOQ) approach to determining inventory levels has been used by firms for many years. It works reasonably well for finding order quantities when demand is predictable and fairly constant throughout the year (that is, there are no seasonable patterns). However, for determining inventory levels of parts and materials used for some production processes, the EOQ approach does not work well. For example, poor quality of parts may increase the demand for these production inputs. Thus, demand is likely to be intermittent, resulting in inventory shortages at some times and excesses at other times. Firms determining inventory levels in these manufacturing settings have found that inventory control approaches such as material requirements planning (MRP) and Kanban (just-in-time) systems perform better than EOQ.[15]

Just-in-Time Inventory System

One reason for Japan's high manufacturing productivity is the cost reductions it achieves through its **just-in-time** (JIT) inventory method.[16] In this system, the supplier delivers the components and parts to the production line "just in time" to be assembled. Other names for this or very similar methods are **zero inventory** and **stockless production.**[17]

The just-in-time method was successfully used after World War II by the Toyota automobile company. In the United States General Motors, Ford, Chrysler, and American Motors use more advanced versions of JIT. But other companies also have used JIT with favorable results. Consider Black & Decker, which produces, among other things, small appliances such as coffee makers and irons: When its plant in North Carolina switched to JIT, inventory was reduced by 40 percent and 30 percent fewer forklift trucks were required. Moreover, quality losses were reduced 60 percent and labor productivity increased by 15 percent.[18]

For the JIT method to work, a number of requirements must be fulfilled: (1) The quality of the parts must be very high; a defective part could hold up the assembly line. (2) There must be dependable relationships and smooth cooperation with suppliers.[19] (3) Ideally, the suppliers should be located near the company, with dependable transportation available.[20]

Perspective
To Make or Buy, That Is the Question for GM[21]

General Motors (GM) is facing great challenges. During the 1986–1987 period GM saw its market share and its sales slip. Some of its plants are not competitive, with some of its parts costing 15 percent more than if they were purchased from suppliers. This is an important factor because GM produces 70 percent of the parts used in its cars. In contrast, Ford produces approximately 50 percent and Chrysler 30 percent of its parts. However, the United Automobile Workers union is opposed to outsourcing (purchasing parts from outside sources) and wants to protect workers' security.

Distribution Logistics[22]

An exciting and profit-promising way of using systems logistics in planning and control is the expansion of inventory control to include other factors; this system is referred to here as **distribution logistics.** In its advanced form, it treats the entire logistics of a business—ranging from sales forecasting through purchasing and processing material and inventorying to shipping the finished goods—as a single system. The goal is usually to optimize the total costs of the system in operation while furnishing a desired level of customer service and meeting certain constraints, such as financially limited inventory levels. A large mass of relationships and information is gathered into one system in order to optimize the whole. It is entirely possible that transportation, manufacturing, or any other single area of cost will not be optimized but that the total cost of material management will be.

Schematically, a distribution logistics system might appear as shown in Figure 22-3. This model would be expressed mathematically as an operating system. The figure shows the relationships between the goal desired, the input variables and

FIGURE 22-3

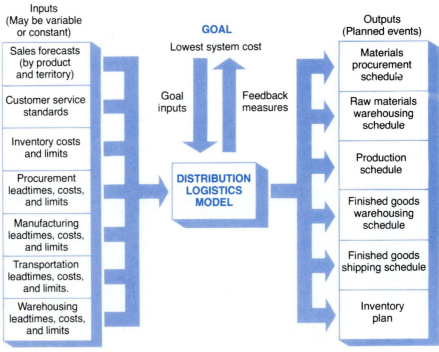

DISTRIBUTION LOGISTICS MODEL.

limits, and the expected outputs. By optimizing *total* costs in a broad area of operation, the system might show that it would be cheaper to use more expensive transportation on occasion rather than to carry high inventories. Or it might show that production at less-than-economic order quantities would be justified in order to get better transportation or warehousing utilization or to meet customer service standards with limited inventories.

Limitations of Operations Research

So far, operations research has been used to solve only a fairly limited number of managerial problems. Its limitations should not be overlooked.

In the first place, there is the sheer magnitude of the mathematical and computing aspects. The number of variables and interrelationships in many managerial problems, plus the complexities of human relationships and reactions, calls for a higher order of mathematics than nuclear physics does. The late mathematical genius John von Neumann found, in his development of the theory of games, that his mathematical abilities soon reached their limit in a relatively simple strategic problem. Managers are, however, a long way from fully using the mathematics now available.

In the second place, although probabilities and approximations are being substituted for unknown quantities and although scientific methods can assign values to factors that could never be measured before, a major portion of important managerial decisions still involves qualitative factors. Until these can be measured, operations research will have limited usefulness in these areas, and decisions will continue to be based on nonquantitative judgments.

Related to the fact that many management decisions involve unmeasurable factors is the lack of information needed to make operations research useful in practice. In conceptualizing a problem area and constructing a mathematical model to represent it, people discover variables about which they need information that is not now available. To improve this situation, persons interested in the practical applications of operations research should place far more emphasis on developing this required information.

Still another limitation is the gap between practicing managers and trained operations researchers. Managers in general lack a knowledge and appreciation of mathematics, just as mathematicians lack an understanding of managerial problems. This gap is being dealt with, to an increasing extent, by the business schools and, more often, by business firms that team up managers with operations researchers. But it is still the major reason why firms are slow to use operations research.

A final drawback of operations research—at least in its application to complex problems—is that analyses and programming are expensive, and many problems are not important enough to justify this cost. However, in practice this has not really been a major limitation.

OTHER TOOLS AND TECHNIQUES FOR IMPROVING PRODUCTIVITY

Besides operations research there are other techniques. Discussed below is the application of time-event networks, value engineering, work simplification, quality circles, total quality management, computer-aided design, computer-aided manufacturing, and the manufacturing automation protocol.

Time-Event Networks

As discussed in Chapter 21, time-event network analysis is a logical extension of the famous Gantt chart. Often referred to as the Program Evaluation and Review Technique (PERT) and in its essentials as the Critical Path Method (CPM), this technique of planning and control has wide potential use in many applications. But PERT and its various refinements, like PERT/COST, have considerable potential for use in many aspects of planning and controlling operations.

Value Engineering

A product can be improved and its cost lowered through **value engineering,** which consists of analyzing the operations of the product or service, estimating the value of each operation, and attempting to improve that operation by trying to keep costs low at each step or part. The following specific steps are suggested:

1. Divide the product into parts and operations.
2. Identify the costs for each part and operation.
3. Identify each part's relative contribution value to the final unit or product.
4. Find a new approach for those items which appear to have a high cost and low value.

Work Simplification

Work methods can also be improved through **work simplification,** which is the process of obtaining the participation of workers in simplifying their work. Training sessions are conducted to teach concepts and principles of techniques such as time and motion studies, work-flow analyses, and the layout of the work situation.

Quality Circles

A quality control circle, or simply **quality circle** (QC), is a group of people from the same organizational area who meet regularly to solve problems they experience at work.[23] Members are trained in solving problems, in applying statistical quality control, and in working in groups. Usually a facilitator works with each group, which normally consists of six to twelve members. The QCs may meet 4 hours a month. Although QC members may receive recognition, they usually do not receive monetary rewards.

For some time now, Japanese companies have been successful in marketing products. To a great extent this has been due to the quality of their products, but this has not always been the case. In fact, in the 1950s and 1960s many products made in Japan had the image of poor quality.

In order to compete in the world market, Japanese firms had to improve the quality of their products.[24] The campaign to improve the quality of Japanese products was initiated by regulatory action taken by the Japanese government. Shortly after World War II ended, the Japanese, realizing that their economic situation depended on increasing exports, encouraged their government to set up a system of regulations mandating that all exporters submit to a government agency a sample of each product to be exported and that they meet demanding requirements for quality before receiving a permit to export.

The legislative drive for quality was supported by various management techniques encouraging or requiring product quality. One of the interesting techniques is the quality control circle, now in widespread use in Japan. At first, employees were trained in the analysis of quality problems. But now other problems are also dealt with, such as cost reduction, workshop facilities improvement, safety problems, employee morale, pollution control, and the education of employees.

Quality circles evolved from suggestion programs. In both approaches, workers participate in solving work-related problems. Although in suggestion programs the problems are usually quite specific, those dealt with by quality control circles are often more complex and require the involvement of several team members. The team consists primarily of rank-and-file workers and sometimes also includes supervisors. So-called efficiency experts are usually excluded from the team.

It is interesting to note that while the concept of quality control originated in the United States, the Japanese appear to have perfected it.[25] More recently, American firms have "rediscovered" the importance of quality, as stressed, for example, in the advertisements for Chrysler and Ford automobiles. At any rate, there is no reason to doubt that quality circles can be used by American companies, which are now faced with a competitive situation in a world market that demands quality products.

While specific approaches to quality improvement depend on the situation, certain guidelines can be helpful:[26]

1. Quality improvement must not be a fad; it must be a long-term, continuous effort. There are always oportunities for improvement.
2. While top-management commitment is of vital importance, everybody in an organization, from top to bottom, must be committed to quality.
3. Most quality problems require the cooperation and coordination of many

functional departments: production design, testing, engineering, manufacturing, marketing, and so on. These problems must also be the concern of labor and management.

4. Ideas and suggestions for quality improvements can come from many, often unexpected, sources. Tap ideas from the most important resource: people.

5. Quality control should be done at crucial steps in the operations process. Set quality criteria for each important step. It is not enough to test the product at the end of an assembly line, for example. If a problem develops, find the underlying cause; ask why something went wrong.

6. A quality improvement plan is not enough. Provisions must be made for its implementation. So, above all: act.

Total Quality Management (TQM)[27]

After World War II, Japanese products were often known for their poor quality. Now, products from Japan ranging from cars to electronics are recognized for their high quality. One reason is the way quality is managed.

Recently, **total quality programs** have been implemented by several companies. The term "total quality management" (TQM) has various meanings. In general, **TQM** involves the organization's long-term commitment to the continuous improvement of quality—throughout the organization, and with the active participation of all members at all levels—to meet and exceed customers' expectations. This top-management-driven philosophy is considered a way of organizational life.[28] In a sense, TQM is simply effective management.

Although the specific programs may vary, they usually require a careful analysis of the customers' needs, an assessment of the degree to which these needs are currently met, and a plan to fill the possible gap between the current and the desired situation. The success of this quality improvement approach often needs the cooperation of suppliers. Furthermore, to make the TQM program effective, top managers must be involved. They must provide a vision, reinforce values emphasizing quality, set quality goals, and deploy resources for the quality program. It is obvious that TQM demands a free flow of information—vertically, horizontally, and diagonally.

Training and development are very important for developing skills and for learning how to use tools and techniques, such as statistical quality control. This continual effort for improving quality requires an environment that can be called a "learning organization." Any quality improvement effort needs not only the support but also the involvement of management, from the top to the bottom, as well as nonmanagerial employees. Persons need to be empowered to initiate and implement the necessary changes. In the modern, interlocking organization, teamwork often becomes a prerequisite for an effective and efficient operation.

The quality improvement efforts need to be continuously monitored through ongoing data collection, evaluation, feedback, and improvement programs. TQM is not a one-time effort; instead, it is a continual, long-term endeavor that needs to be recognized, reinforced, and rewarded.

When done effectively, TQM should result in greater customer satisfaction, fewer defects and less waste, increased total productivity, reduced costs and improved profitability, and an environment in which quality has high priority.

A concern for quality should not be restricted to businesses. Deming's principles for quality improvement also apply to government. The mayor of Madison, Wisconsin, demonstrated how they can be implemented in city government.[29] The first test came in the motor equipment division. After the initial success, a formal quality program was started citywide. What is surprising is that resistance to the program came not from unions or from the city council but from middle-level bureaucrats who saw their power being eroded by the reduction in departmental barriers and by greater teamwork.

In Japan the concern for quality starts with the CEO, whereas in the United States, quality has been the primary concern of lower-level managers and quality control engineers. But this pattern is beginning to change. Former President Reagan designated October 1988 as "National Quality Month." To reinforce the commitment to quality, some of the largest companies—such as Coca-Cola, Ford, GM, and IBM—participated in the National Quality Forum.

While there is still skepticism regarding whether most CEOs are really serious about quality, the chairman of one large, multinational corporation provides a good role model. Colby H. Chandler, Kodak's CEO, started his career as a quality control engineer. His philosophy is "Quality pays for itself many times over." Quality is closely linked to productivity and engineering, which have been greatly improved by computers and the new software programs. Kodak's strategy is driven by research and development as well as concern for productivity and quality. If top-management involvement in these issues is a trend in the United States, then companies may again achieve product leadership.

CAD/CAM and MAP

Product design and manufacturing have been changing greatly in recent years, largely because of the application of computer technology. Computer-aided design (CAD), computer-aided manufacturing (CAM), and the manufacturing automation protocol (MAP) are some of the cornerstones of the factory of the future.

CAD/CAMs help engineers design products much more quickly than they could with the traditional paper-and-pencil approach. This will become increasingly important, since product life cycles are getting shorter. Capturing the market quickly is crucial in the very competitive environment. Moreover, firms can respond more rapidly to the requests of customers with specific requirements. The ultimate aim of many companies is "computer-integrated manufacturing."[31]

Automobile companies, as well as firms such as Deere, Boeing, and Eastman Kodak, developed what is called **manufacturing automation protocol** (MAP), which is a network of machines and various office devices. MAP is a sophisticated extension of local area networks (LANs). One of the most committed supporters of MAP was Roger Smith, former chairman of General Motors, who saw it as a key to the factory of the future. At General Motors, for example, MAP is used to link robots with numerically controlled machine tools. The company has achieved considerable savings by using the new method to change the production line when introducing a different kind of front axle for an automobile. What previously took 3 days now takes only 10 minutes. With the new technology, General Motors and other U.S. manufacturers hope to overtake Japanese firms, which now are quite advanced in automation.[32]

Perspective

IBM's PC Convertible and Laser Printer[33]

The IBM laptop PC Convertible was the first computer built in the United States completely by robots. It is manufactured on an automated assembly line with modular workstations that put together, check, and package the computers without people turning even a screw. What is special about this assembly line is that it not only can produce the Convertible but also can assemble other personal computers, printers, and even household appliances. This production line is probably the first of its kind in the world, and it may help IBM stay competitive with its Asian rivals.

IBM also simplified the design of its laser printer. It has fewer parts than the competing Hewlett-Packard printer. In the development of the printer, IBM assembled design and manufacturing engineers to form a team for speeding up the process of bringing the product to the market. Because of the simplicity of the printer design, it was less expensive to use labor rather than robots.

THE FUTURE OF OPERATIONS MANAGEMENT[34]

What factors show signs of influencing future developments in this field? Several major trends can be expected in operations management.[35]

1. The increased complexity of technology will be reflected in the products themselves as well as in the processes used to produce them.[36] Fifteen years ago few people would have expected that sophisticated home computers could be produced at a price affordable by the average consumer.
2. Automation is becoming increasingly more important in the production process.[37] General Motors, which pioneered the application of robots, is importing a new generation of robots from Japan. New machine tools, microproces-

sors, sensory technology, and computer controls now make it possible to reduce machine setup time and costs.[38] This means a greater variety of products at lower cost. In the past, lower cost tended to be achieved through high-volume production of a particular model. Now, through high technology, setup times are reduced dramatically. This means a better use of machines with lower direct-labor costs. Moreover, work-in-process inventories can thereby be reduced. Finally, maintenance costs are reduced by simplifying processes, controls, and machines. These simplification technologies were pioneered by Toyota when it doubled its automobile model range without incurring the high costs traditionally associated with a variety of models.

3. The service industry in the United States is providing an increasingly important portion of the gross national product. This means that the concepts and principles of "production" have been advantageously adapted to such nonmanufacturing activities as banking, health care, and tourism.

4. The production function will become increasingly a global challenge.[39] Car engines produced in Japan and Germany are now installed in American cars. Moreover, major car manufacturers in the United States have made arrangements to produce cars in Japan and market them under their own names in the United States and elsewhere.

In short, then, productivity, and the concern for measuring it, will continue to be a challenge for managers operating in an increasingly competitive global market. Operations management systems are expected to become more productive through the application of operations research, a variety of other tools, and information technology.

SUMMARY

Productivity is a major concern of managers. It implies measurement, an essential step in the control process. The productivity measurement of skills workers is generally easier than that of knowledge workers such as managers. Yet managerial productivity is very important, especially for organizations operating in a competitive environment.

Production management refers to those activities necessary to manufacture products; it may also include purchasing, warehousing, transportation, and other operations. Operations management has a similar meaning, referring to activities necessary to produce and deliver a service as well as a physical product.

The operations management systems model (Figure 22-1) shows inputs, the transformation process, outputs, and the feedback system. A variety of tools and techniques make operations more productive. Seven steps are often involved in planning and designing a product and its production. Companies can choose from six different kinds of production layouts. In order to operate the system, the managerial functions of organizing, staffing, and leading must be carried out effectively. Controlling requires an information system often supported by computers.

Among the various tools for planning and controlling operations is operations research, which is the application of scientific methods to the study of alternatives in a problem situation to obtain a quantitative basis for arriving at the best solution. The operations research procedure consists of six steps. Examples of tools are linear programming, inventory planning and control, the just-in-time inventory system, and distribution logistics. Other tools and techniques are time-event networks, value engineering, work simplification, quality circles, total quality management, and a variety of computer-aided approaches.

KEY IDEAS AND CONCEPTS FOR REVIEW

Productivity
Production management
Operations management
Operations management system
Steps in product and production design
Production layouts
Operations research
Essential characteristics of operations
   research
Six steps of operations research procedure
Linear programming
Inventory planning and control

Just-in-time (JIT) inventory system
Distribution logistics
Time-event networks
Value engineering
Work simplification
Quality circles
Total quality management (TQM)
Computer-aided design (CAD), computer-
   aided manufacturing (CAM), and
   manufacturing automation protocol
   (MAP)
Trends in operations research

FOR DISCUSSION

1. How would you measure the productivity of managers and other knowledge workers? Explain in detail.
2. Why is the field of production and operations management such a good one to use as a case example of planning and control techniques? Why do you believe that this area was favored for analysis and productivity improvement by the pioneers in the field of management?
3. Distinguish between the planning and control techniques that are usually found only in production and operations management and those that are found useful in all areas of management. Why is this so?
4. Explain the nature of and reasons for each step usually found in the development of a production and operations management program.
5. There are many typical layouts used in the design of a production program. Which one is ordinarily used for the manufacture of automobiles? Why? Which one do you believe was used for construction of the trans-Alaska pipeline. Why?
6. Real-time information can be widely used in the area of production, but this does not solve the problem of control. Why?
7. What tools generally found in operations research have been widely used in production and operations management? Do they have anything in common? If so, what is it?
8. What makes distribution logistics a more useful and complex tool for planning and control than an inventory model?
9. Why do you believe that quality control circles have been used so much in Japan?

EXERCISES/ACTION STEPS

1. After the class has been divided into groups of four or five students, consider Case 22-1 and try to answer the six questions raised by Lampert's business colleague. For the second question, each group should display a drawing of its lamp, including the main specifications (e.g., voltage) and several uses. One member of each group should try to "sell" the lamp to the class. If the class size is large enough, one group should act as an independent panel, evaluating each lamp proposal in terms of creativity, aesthetics, feasibility, and other criteria developed by the group.
2. Draw the layout of your apartment or your house, and indicate the pathways you walk while doing your typical daily chores. Show any rearrangements you could make that would increase your effectiveness and personal productivity.

CASES

CASE 22-1
LAMPERT & SONS COMPANY

John Lampert, president of Lampert & Sons Company, a small manufacturing firm producing electrical appliances, was an entrepreneur with a technical background. He recently moved into a new house, and his wife asked him to install some spotlights to accent various areas in the house, such as bookshelves, a sculpture, and certain items in a wall unit.

At the local lighting stores, the lamps that might fit the purpose cost far more than Mr. Lampert was willing to pay. He felt that there was a real need for a low-cost, attractive spotlight or clamp-on lamp. He discussed his idea with a business colleague, who raised a number of questions such as these:

- Is there really a need for such a product?
- What should such a lamp look like?
- How or where should it be produced (e.g., in his plant in the Midwest or abroad, such as in Korea, Hong Kong, or Taiwan)?

- What arrangements would have to be made if the lamp were to be produced by Lampert & Sons?
- What kind of distribution channel (or channels) should be used to sell the product?
- How would he maintain the quality if the price of the lamp was to be kept low?

After this discussion, Mr. Lampert realized that he really had not thought through his idea and could not satisfactorily answer several of the questions.

1. If you were a small-business consultant, how would you answer the questions Mr. Lampert's colleague raised?
2. What other actions would you recommend for making the decisions to design the product, to set up a production system, and to control the operation, especially the quality?
3. What decision-making tools and techniques could assist you in making these decisions?

INTERNATIONAL CASE 22-2
GENERAL ELECTRIC IS "ENLIGHTENING" HUNGARY[40]

Can Western management approaches turn a state-owned Hungarian company into a profit-oriented enterprise? That was the question GE's executive

George Varga answered with a "yes." When GE joined forces with the Hungarian Tungsram company to produce light bulbs, it became a management experiment that required the teaching of basic managerial concepts such as inventory control, accounts receivable, and the importance of profits.

GE selected the Hungarian-born, 54-year-old George Varga to head this operation. He was not a newcomer but had 28 years of experience with GE in a variety of positions, the last one being in the Netherlands. Varga surrounded himself with seasoned managers who were sensitive to the different cultural environments and managerial practices. Staffing decisions, for example, had to be changed from those practiced in the West, where an overstaffed bureaucracy would be streamlined through layoffs. Not so in Hungary. Cost savings had to be accomplished in ways other than by laying off people. Instead, methods such as better inventory control had to be introduced.

If this management experiment succeeds in the long run, GE may become competitive. Labor costs are low in Hungary. At Tungsram the average pay is $3000 a year, compared with about $30,000 in the United States and Western Europe. With this venture, GE may gain a foothold in the European market, where the company has been relatively weak.

1. What are some of the considerations in operating a manufacturing plant in a foreign country? How does it differ from setting up a plant in the United States?
2. What characteristics (technical, human, and management skills) should a manager have to operate a plant in a foreign country?
3. How would you "manage" the local work force?

REFERENCES

1. Wickham Skinner, "What Matters to Manufacturing," *Harvard Business Review* (January–February 1988), p. 11.
2. Certain sections of the discussion of productivity in this chapter are based on Heinz Weihrich, *Management Excellence* (New York: McGraw-Hill Book Company, 1985).
3. See also Kuniyasu Sakai, "The Feudal World of Japanese Manufacturing," *Harvard Business Review* (November–December 1990), pp. 38–49.
4. See, for example, Vernon M. Buehler and Y. Krishna Shetty (eds.), *Productivity Improvement* (New York: AMACOM, 1981), reporting on the experiences of companies in improving their productivity. See also Bernard J. Reilly and Joseph P. Fuhr, Jr., "Productivity: An Economic and Management Analysis with a Direction towards a New Synthesis," *Academy of Management Review* (January 1983), pp. 108–117.
5. Buehler and Shetty, *Productivity Improvement* (1981).
6. See also Joseph A. Maciariello, Jeffrey W. Burke, and Donald Tilley, "Improving American Competitiveness: A Management Systems Perspective," *Academy of Management Executive* (November 1989), pp. 294–303.
7. In the preparation of this chapter, the authors received considerable assistance from Richard B. Chase and Nicholas J. Aquilano, *Production and Operations Management* (Homewood, Ill.: Richard D. Irwin, 1981). See also Alfred D. Chandler, "The Enduring Logic of Industrial Success," *Harvard Business Review* (March–April 1990), pp. 130–140; Peter F. Drucker, "The Emerging Theory of Manufacturing," *Harvard Business Review* (May–June 1990), pp. 94–102; John E. Ettlie, "What Makes a Manufacturing Firm Innovative?" *Academy of Management Executive* (November 1990), pp. 7–20.
8. The input-transformation-output model is widely used in the discussion of operations management. See, for example, Chase and Aquilano, *Production* (1981); Harold Fearon, William A. Ruch, Patrick G. Decker, Ross R. Reck, Vincent G. Reuter, and C. David Wieters, *Fundamentals of Production/Operations Management* (St. Paul, Minn.: West Publishing Company, 1979); Elwood S. Buffa and James S. Dyer, *Management Science/Operations Research* (New York: John Wiley & Sons, 1981).

9. Don Hellriegel, "Maquiladoras: A Managerial Perspective," invited address at Managing in a Global Economy III, Eastern Academy of Management, Hong Kong (June 11–15, 1989); M. P. McEnrue and K. Kwong, "Managing in a Global Economy: Emerging Human Resources and Production Management Issues as Offshore Manufacturing Moves to Mexico," *Managing in a Global Economy III, Proceedings of the Third International Conference* (Hong Kong: Eastern Academy of Management, 1989), pp. 82–86; Stephen Baker, Todd Vogel, and Adrienne Bard, "Will the New Maquiladoras Build a Better Mañana? *Business Week* (Nov. 14, 1988), pp. 102, 106; Stephen Baker, Adrienne Bard, and Elizabeth Weiner, "The Magnet of Growth in Mexico's North," *Business Week* (June 6, 1988), pp. 48–50.

10. For a discussion of the relationship between strategy and operations management, see Wickham Skinner, *Manufacturing in the Corporate Strategy* (New York: John Wiley & Sons, 1978); Stephen C. Wheelwright, "Operations as Strategy Lessons from Japan," *Stanford GSB* (Fall 1981–1982), pp. 3–7.

11. See Chase and Aquilano, *Production* (1981), sec. 2; see also Arthur C. Laufer, *Operations Management* (Cincinnati, Ohio: South-Western Publishing Company, 1979), chap. 16.

12. See also Kuniyasu Sakai, "The Feudal World of Japanese Manufacturing," *Harvard Business Review* (November–December 1990), pp. 38–49.

13. For a detailed discussion of information and control, see Edward E. Lawler III and John G. Rhode, *Information and Control in Organizations* (Santa Monica, Calif.: Goodyear Publishing Company, 1976).

14. For the application of analytical techniques and the use of graphics, see David J. Armstrong, "Sharpening Inventory Management," *Harvard Business Review* (November–December 1985), pp. 42–58. For a variety of graphics software for the microcomputer, see David Needle, "Presentation Graphics Software," *InfoWorld* (Sept. 22, 1986).

15. Robert N. Mefford, "The Productivity Nexus of New Inventory and Quality Control Techniques," *Engineering Costs and Production Economics* (The Netherlands), vol. 17 (1989), pp. 21–28. See also Richard B. Chase and Nicholas J. Aquilano, *Production and Operations Management,* 4th ed. (Homewood, Ill.: Richard D. Irwin, 1985), chap. 18.

16. See also Lance Heiko, "Some Relationships between Japanese Culture and Just-in-Time," *Academy of Management Executive* (November 1989), pp. 319–321; for a critical analysis, see Ernest H. Hall, Jr., "Just-in-Time Management: A Critical Assessment," *Academy of Management Executive* (November 1989), pp. 315–318.

17. Alan L. Saipe and Richard J. Schonberger, "Don't Ignore Just-in-Time Production," *Business Quarterly* (Spring 1984), pp. 60–66.

18. Saipe and Schonberger, "Don't Ignore Just-in-Time Production" (1984).

19. Richard C. Walleigh, "What's Your Excuse for Not Using JIT?" *Harvard Business Review* (March–April 1986), pp. 38–54.

20. For an evaluation of just-in-time techniques, see Chiradet Ousawat and Kenneth D. Ramsing, "An Evaluation of the Just-in-Time Techniques in a Multi-Stage, Multi-Product Production System," in Frank Hoy (ed.), *Academy of Management Best Papers—Proceedings 1987,* Forty-Seventh Annual Meeting of the Academy of Management, New Orleans, La. (Aug. 9–12, 1987), pp. 296–300. See also Marshall Schminke and Stephen Chapman, "Organization Theory and Implementing JIT: Understanding *Why* as Well as What and How," in Frank Hoy (ed.), *Academy of Management Best Papers—Proceedings 1988,* Forty-Eighth Annual Meeting of the Academy of Management, Anaheim, Calif. (Aug. 7–10, 1988), pp. 303–307.

21. James B. Treece, "It's Time for a Tune-Up at GM," *Business Week* (Sept. 7, 1987), pp. 22–23.

22. Donald J. Bowersox, "The Strategic Benefits of Logistics Alliances," *Harvard Business Review* (July–August 1990), pp. 36–45.

23. Edward E. Lawler III and Susan A. Mohrman, "Quality Circles after the Fad," *Harvard Business Review* (January–February 1985), pp. 65–71. See also S. G. Goldstein, "Organizational Dualism and Quality Circles," *Academy of Management Review* (July 1985), pp. 504–517.

24. For a discussion of quality circles in Japan and in the United States, see Tai K. Oh, "The Fate of QC Circles in the U.S.: A Case Study Testing the Cultural, Convergence, and Tradition-Modernity Theories," in Ryine T. Hsieh and Steven A. Scherling (eds.), *Proceedings of the Academy of International Business, Southeast Regional Conference, Taipei,* vol. 1 (June 26–28, 1986), pp. 749–759. See also Peter B. Petersen, "The Contribution of W. Edwards Deming to Japanese Management Theory and Practice," in Hoy (ed.), *Academy of Management Best Papers* (1987), pp. 133–137.

25. Hamid Noori, "The Taguchi Methods: Achieving Design and Output Quality," *Academy of Management Executive* (November 1989), pp. 322–326.

26. Joel Dreyfuss, "Victories in the Quality Crusade," *Fortune* (Oct. 10, 1988), pp. 80–88.

27. Quality has been discussed in a variety of articles, such as Frederick F. Reichheld and W. Earl Sasser, Jr., "Zero Defections: Quality Comes to Services," *Harvard Business Review* (September–October 1990), pp. 105–111; Genichi Taguchi and Don Clausing, "Robust Quality," *Harvard Business Review* (January–February 1990), pp. 65–75. For the relationships between quality and productivity see Robert N. Mefford, "Quality and Productivity: The Linkage," *International Journal of Production Economics,* vol. 24 (1991), pp. 137–145.

28. For major contributions to TQM, see Philip B. Crosby, *Quality Is Free—The Art of Making Quality Certain* (New York: McGraw-Hill Book Company, 1979); W. Edwards Deming, *Out of the Crisis* (Cambridge, Mass.: Massachusetts Institute of Technology, Center for Advanced Engineering Study, 1986); Armand V. Feigenbaum, *Total Quality Control* (New York: McGraw-Hill Book Company, 1983); Masaaki Imai, *Kaizen* (New York: Random House, 1986); J. M. Juran, *Managerial Breakthrough* (New York: McGraw-Hill Book Company, 1964).

29. Joseph Sensenbrenner, "Quality Comes to City Hall," *Harvard Business Review* (March–April 1991), pp. 64–75.

30. George Melloan, "Computers Elevate Quality Standards," *The Wall Street Journal* (Oct. 11, 1988); *Eastman Kodak Company Annual Report,* 1985.

31. Gene Bylinsky, "GM's Road Map to Automated Plants," *Fortune* (Oct. 28, 1985), pp. 89–102. For another discussion of computer-integrated manufacturing (CIM), see Robert S. Kaplan, "Must CIM Be Justified by Faith Alone?" *Harvard Business Review* (March–April 1986), pp. 87–95.

32. Bylinsky, "GM's Road Map" (1985). For difficulties with the new technology, especially at General Motors' Hamtramck plant in Michigan, which was supposed to be the showcase of high technology, see Amal Nag, "Auto Makers Discover 'Factory of the Future' Is Headache Just Now," *The Wall Street Journal* (May 13, 1986).

33. Bill Saporito, "IBM's No-Hands Assembly Line," *Fortune* (Sept. 15, 1986), pp. 105–109; Jeremy Main, "Manufacturing the Right Way," *Fortune* (May 21, 1990), pp. 54–64.

34. See also J. T. Black, *The Design of the Factory with a Future* (New York: McGraw-Hill, 1991).

35. Fearon et al., *Fundamentals* (1979). See also Joseph Finkelstein and David Newman, "The Third Industrial Revolution: A Special Challenge to Managers," *Organizational Dynamics* (Summer 1984), pp. 53–65.

36. For a discussion of flexible automation, see Ramchandran Jaikumar, "Postindustrial Manufacturing," *Harvard Business Review* (November–December 1986), pp. 69–76. A holistic approach to developing new products has been suggested by Hirotaka Takeuchi and Ikujiro Nonaka, "The New Product Development Game," *Harvard Business Review* (January–February 1986), pp. 137–146.

37. For a discussion of how robotics is changing organizations and manufacturing tasks, see Daniel E. Whitney, "Real Robots Do Need Jigs," *Harvard Business Review* (May–June 1986), pp. 110–116.

38. "The Big Revolution on the Factory Floor," *The Wall Street Journal* (July 12, 1982).

39. For futuristic ideas about floating factories, see Alonzo L. McDonald, "Of Floating Factories and Mating Dinosaurs," *Harvard Business Review* (November–December 1986), pp. 82–86.

40. This discussion is based on a variety of sources, including Shawn Tully, "GE in Hungary: Let There Be Light," *Fortune* (Oct. 22, 1990), pp. 127–142; Jonathan B. Levine, Gail E. Schares, and Zachary Schiller, "GE Carves Out a Road East," *Business Week* (July 30, 1990), pp. 32–33.

> While no one can prevent all disasters, organizations can adopt a systematic and comprehensive perspective for managing them more effectively.[1]
>
> Ian I. Mitroff, Paul Shrivastava, and Firdaus E. Udwadia

Overall Control and toward the Future through Preventive Control

Chapter Objectives

After reading this chapter, you should be able to:

1. Discuss the concept of overall control.
2. Describe the most widely used techniques of overall control of an enterprise.
3. Present the principle of preventive control and distinguish its nature and application from those of the many direct controls.
4. Explain the nature and potential of the management audit and the enterprise self-audit.
5. Summarize the major challenges facing management and explain what needs to be done to develop excellent managers.

Most controls are designed for specific things: policies, wages and salaries, employee selection and training, research and development, product quality, costs, pricing, capital expenditures, cash, and other areas where we wish performance to conform to plans. Such controls are partial in the sense that they apply to a part of an enterprise and do not measure total accomplishments against total goals. There clearly is a need for some overall measures, and it is not surprising that many are expressed in financial terms.

Many of the controls are based on feedback by measuring deviations from plans. Also, the traditional approach is to find out who is responsible for the undesirable deviation and to get that person to correct it. This is direct control. But, as discussed later in this chapter, this kind of control is based on some questionable assumptions. Would it not be better to prevent undesirable deviations from occurring in the first place? Most people would answer, "Of course." It is therefore recommended that "preventive control" be applied; with this approach, a highly qualified manager will make fewer mistakes, thus reducing (but certainly not eliminating) the need for direct control. But let us first discuss the more traditional—and important—overall controls of budget summaries and other financial analyses.

CONTROL OF OVERALL PERFORMANCE

Planning and control are increasingly being treated as an interrelated system. Along with techniques for partial control, control devices have been developed for measuring the overall performance of an enterprise—or an integrated* division or project within it—against total goals.

* "Integrated" is used here as meaning that an operation includes the functions necessary to gain an overall objective. Thus, a product division of a company would normally include engineering, manufacturing, and marketing, and these functions represent enough of a total operation for the division manager—even though subject to some direction and control from headquarters—to be held basically responsible for a profit. To a lesser degree, an engineering design operation might be regarded as integrated: If its head supervises all the engineering functions and specialties necessary for complete product design, he or she can then be held responsible for the efficient accomplishment of the project.

There are many reasons for control of overall performance. In the first place, just as overall planning must apply to enterprise or major division goals, so must overall controls be applied. In the second place, decentralization of authority—especially in product or territorial divisions—creates semi-independent units, and these must be subjected to overall controls to avoid the chaos of complete independence. In the third place, overall controls permit measuring an integrated area manager's *total* effort, rather than parts of it.

Many overall controls in business are, as one might expect, financial. Business owes its continued existence to profit making; its capital resources are a scarce, life-giving element. Since finance is the binding force of business, financial controls are certainly an important objective gauge of the success of plans.[2]

Financial measurements also summarize, as a common denominator, the operation of a number of plans. Further, they accurately indicate total expenditures of resources in reaching goals. This is true in all forms of enterprises. Although the purpose of an educational or government enterprise is not to make monetary profits, any responsible manager must have some way of knowing what goal achievement has cost in terms of resources. Proper accounting is important not only for business but for government as well. Professor Robert N. Anthony at Harvard points out that in government, accounting often hides important facts. Otherwise, how could it have happened that several cities, including New York, were nearly bankrupt before their financial conditions became clear?[3]

Financial controls, like any other control, have to be tailored to the specific needs of the enterprise or the position. Doctors, lawyers, and managers at different organizational levels do have different needs for controlling their area of operation.[4] Financial analyses also furnish an excellent "window" through which accomplishment in nonfinancial areas can be seen. A deviation from planned costs, for example, may lead a manager to find the causes in poor planning, inadequate training of employees, or other nonfinancial factors.

✓ BUDGET SUMMARIES AND REPORTS

A widely used control of overall performance takes the form of a summary of budgets. A **budget summary,** being a résumé of all the individual budgets, reflects company plans so that sales volume, costs, profits, utilization of capital, and return on investment may be seen in their proper relationship. In these terms it shows top mangement how well the company as a whole is succeeding in meeting its objectives.

For the best control through a budget summary, a manager must first be satisfied that total budgets are an accurate and reasonably complete portrayal of the company's plans. The manager should study the budget reports and any material accompanying them to determine whether the comparison of budget and actual costs shows the real nature of any deviations. For example, a company head criticized his factory manager for being considerably over his labor budget in a month when the labor force had been materially reduced and the temporary increase in expenses was due to severance pay.

Minor discrepancies should receive appropriately little attention. The purpose of a control system is to draw attention to important variations, and both the budget reports and the attention paid to them should reflect this. Above all, a manager should never forget that a budget summary is no substitute for profitable operation. Budgeting is never more perfect than the planning behind it, and plans—especially long-range plans—are subject to the imperfections caused by change and uncertainty. There may even be times when a manager must forget the budget and take special action to meet unexpected events. Budgets are meant to be tools, and not masters, of managers.

On the other hand, managers should not underestimate the value of budget summaries in providing an effective means for overall control in situations of decentralized authority. Budget summaries furnish a means whereby enterprise objectives can be clearly and specifically defined and departmental plans can be made to contribute toward such objectives. Should the budget summary and the reports of actual events indicate that the enterprise as a whole is not tending toward its objectives, top managers have a convenient and positive means of finding out where the deviations are occurring. The summaries thus furnish a useful guide for corrective action.

✓PROFIT AND LOSS CONTROL

The income statement for an enterprise as a whole serves important control purposes, mainly because it is useful for determining the immediate revenue or cost factors that have accounted for success or failure. Obviously, if it is first put in the form of a forecast, the income statement is an even better control device in that it gives managers a chance, before things happen, to influence revenues, expenses, and, consequently, profits.

The Nature and Purpose of Profit and Loss Controls

Since the survival of a business usually depends on profits, and since profits are a definite standard against which to measure success, many companies use the income statement for divisional or departmental control. Because it is a statement of all revenues and expenses for a given time, it is a true summary of the results of business operations. Profit and loss control, when applied to divisions or departments, is based on the premise that if it is the purpose of the entire business to make a profit, each part of the enterprise should contribute to this purpose.[5] Thus, the ability of a part to make an expected profit becomes a standard for measuring its performance.

In profit and loss control, each major department or division details its revenues and expenses—normally including a proportionate share of company overhead—and calculates periodically its profit or loss. Some units have their own accounting group; in others, the statement is prepared by the central accounting department. In either case, the organizational unit, because it is expected to turn in a separate record of profitable operation, is considered by headquarters in much the same way that subsidiary companies are considered by a holding company.

For a long time Eastman Kodak Company, with headquarters in Rochester, New York, was considered an excellent company. In the mid-1980s, however, the company encountered difficulties, partly because of the strong U.S. dollar and the tough competition from Japan's Fuji Films, Kodak's main rival. In 1986 the profit picture changed for the better, with an increase of about 14 percent in earnings.

What, then, accounted for the turnaround? Among the various reasons for the change are the following:

1. The decline of the value of the U.S. dollar had a positive effect on profits. It also made Kodak more competitive with Fuji.
2. Cost was reduced by a reduction in the work force of almost 25,000.
3. In 1986 Kodak introduced 100 new products, including new films (for example, the VR-G films with vibrant colors) and a new 35-mm camera.
4. Kodak is also selling minilabs for developing films; these labs use great amounts of chemicals and paper made by Kodak.
5. The company diversified into areas such as optical-disk data storage, long-life batteries, and electronic publishing.
6. The reorganization resulted in seventeen fairly autonomous business units, a setup that enables the company to respond more quickly to changes in the market.

Kodak is also preparing for the more distant future, realizing that it has to expand its domain beyond photography. Thus, the company is venturing into health care, drugs (for example, to fight cancer), electronic imaging, and data storage (it acquired the floppy-disk maker Verbatim in 1985). In 1988 Sterling Drug, Inc., was acquired for over $5 billion, which made Kodak a major player in the pharmaceutical industry.

The 1990s pose new challenges for Kodak, a leader in photography. New technology threatens the company's future. Sony and Canon offer cameras that can show their still pictures on TV, using compact-disk (CD) technology. But the quality of these pictures is not as good as that of traditional pictures. Kodak's dilemma is deciding whether to adopt the CD technology and, at the same time, risk hurting its traditional photographic business.

Kodak's interim solution is Photo CD, which combines electronic imaging with traditional photography. This new system still uses film that needs to be developed in the laboratory, but the customer receives, as a new option, pictures stored on CDs. These pictures can then be edited by the customer and re-submitted to the laboratory, which prepares edited prints. This new Photo CD system uses computer-age technology without killing Kodak's core business in traditional photography.

Profit and loss control usually is practicable only for major segments of a company, since the paperwork involved in building up profit and loss statements for smaller departments tends to be too heavy. Also, profit and loss control usually implies that managers of a division or department have fairly wide authority to run their part of the business as they see fit, with profit the primary standard of success. However, many companies that do not so decentralize authority have nonetheless found profit and loss control valuable. The focus on profit and the sensitivity of the organizational unit to it are worthwhile even when managers have limited independence in seeking profit as they wish.

The more integrated and complete the organization unit, the more accurate a measuring stick profit and loss control can be. For this reason, it works best in product or territorial divisions, where both sales and production functions for a product or service are under one general manager. For example, it is much easier to use the standard of profit for measuring the operations of the general manager of the Buick division of General Motors than it would be to use it for the supervisor of the motor-block-boring section of the manufacturing department of this division.

At the same time, companies organized on a functional basis do occasionally employ profit and loss control. The heat-treating department may produce and "sell" its service to the machining department, which in turn "sells" its product to the assembly department, which in turn "sells" a complete product to the sales department. This can be done, although the paperwork required is often not worth the effort, and the problem of determining the right transfer price may occasion much negotiation or many difficult executive decisions. If the transfer is made at cost, clearly only the sales department will show a profit or a loss. If it is made at a figure above cost, the question of what price to charge arises.

In most instances, profit and loss control is not applied to central staff and service departments. Although these departments could "sell" their services, the most satisfactory practice is to place them under some other form of control, such as the variable expense budget.

Limitations of Profit and Loss Control

Profit and loss control suffers its greatest limitation from the cost of the accounting and paper transactions involving intracompany transfer of costs and revenues. Duplication of accounting records, efforts involved in allocating the many overhead costs, and the time and effort required to calculate intracompany sales can make this control too costly if it is carried too far.

Profit and loss control also may be inadequate for overall performance. Top managers may not wish to give too much authority to their division managers, and they may desire the additional assurances of good budgetary control. In addition, profit and loss control in and of itself does not provide a standard of desirable profits or policy controls in the area of product-line development or in other matters of long-term overall company concern.

Another limitation of profit and loss control, especially if it is carried very far in the organization, is that departments may come to compete with an aggressive detachment not helpful to enterprise coordination. On the other hand, in many companies there is not enough feeling of departmental responsibility for company profit, and departments may develop the smugness of a monopolist with an assured market. The parts fabrication department that knows its products must be "bought" by the assembly department, the manufacturing or the service department that can force its output on the sales department, and the engineering group that has a monopolistic hold on both production and sales are dangerous monopolists indeed. Profit and loss control can break down these islands of monopoly. So, in spite of limitations—and especially if accompanied by an intracompany pricing policy which requires that departments meet competitive prices of suppliers outside the enterprise, rather than a policy which is based on cost—profit and loss control can give top managers an extraordinary measure of overall control.

CONTROL THROUGH RETURN ON INVESTMENT (ROI)

One of the most successfully used control techniques is that of measuring both the absolute and the relative success of a company or a company unit by the ratio of earnings to investment of capital. The return-on-investment approach, often referred to simply as ROI, has been the core of the control system of the Du Pont Company since 1919. A large number of companies have adopted it as their key measure of overall performance. This yardstick is the rate of return that a company or a division can earn on the capital allocated to it. This tool, therefore, regards profit not as an absolute but as a return on capital employed in the business. The goal of a business is seen, accordingly, not necessarily as optimizing profits but as optimizing returns from capital devoted to business purposes. This standard recognizes the fundamental fact that capital is a critical factor in almost any enterprise and, through its scarcity, limits progress. It also emphasizes the fact that the job of managers is to make the best possible use of assets entrusted to them.

The Return-on-Investment System in Action

As the system has been used by the Du Pont Company, return on investment involves consideration of several factors. Return is computed on the basis of capital turnover (that is, total sales divided by capital, or total investment) multiplied by earnings as a percentage of sales. This formula recognizes that a division with a high capital turnover and low percentage of earnings to sales may be more profitable in terms of return on investment than another with a high percentage of profits to sales but with low capital turnover. As can be seen, the system measures effectiveness in the use of capital. Investment includes not only the permanent plant facilities but also the working capital of the unit. In the Du Pont system, investment and working capital represent amounts invested without reduction for liabilities or reserves, on the grounds that such a reduction would result in a fluctuation in operating investments as reserves or liabilities change, which would distort the rate of return and render it less meaningful. Earnings are, however, calculated after normal depreciation charges, on the basis that true profits are not earned until allowance is made for the write-off of depreciable assets.

Return-on-investment control is perhaps best summarized in chart form, as in Figure 23-1. Here, analysis of variations in rate of return leads into every financial aspect of the business. Rate of return is the common denominator used in comparing divisions, and differences can easily be traced to their causes.

However, other companies have taken the position that the return on investment should be calculated on fixed assets less depreciation. Such companies hold that the depreciation reserve represents a write-off of the initial investment and that funds made available through such charges are reinvested in other fixed assets or used as working capital. Such a treatment appears more realistic to operating people, partly because it places a heavier rate-of-return burden on new fixed assets than on worn or obsolete ones.

In any control through return on investment, the number of ratios and comparisons behind the yardstick figure cannot be overlooked. Although improvement in rate of return can come from a higher percentage of profit to sales, improvement may also come from increasing the rate of turnover by lowering price and reducing return on sales. Moreover, the ratio of return on investment might be improved by getting more products (and sales) out of a given plant investment or by reducing the cost of sales for a given product.

Application of ROI to Product Lines

Functional-line organizations without integrated product divisions have applied return-on-investment control to their various product lines. By grouping its many products into a number of major classifications, a typical company follows through with the allocation of sales, costs, and investment in fixed assets and working capital to arrive at the same kind of rate-of-return analysis used by multidivision companies. A simplified example of these results is shown in Table 23-1.

To use the rate-of-return yardstick (as return on assets employed) for product lines, the company has allocated certain expenses and assets, but these allocations apparently have not caused much difficulty. Most production costs are maintained by product, and common costs, such as sales branch expenses, are allocated by volume of sales. More difficulty is incurred in determining asset usage by product lines, but cash, accounts receivable, and administrative and sales facilities are allocated in accordance with sales, while inventories and factory and plant equipment are prorated to the various products on the basis of special analyses.

In addition to comparing rates of return on assets of products, as indicated in Table 23-1, this company compared actual experience with trends for the various products (identified for purposes of simplicity as the "base year" in the table). An advantage of these comparisons is that the company is able to keep a sharp eye on its product lines, with a view to determining where capital is being most efficiently employed and as a guide toward obtaining a balanced use of capital for greatest overall profit. Thus, the company has been able to identify products that are either strong and established, new and improved, or past their peak growth and profitability.

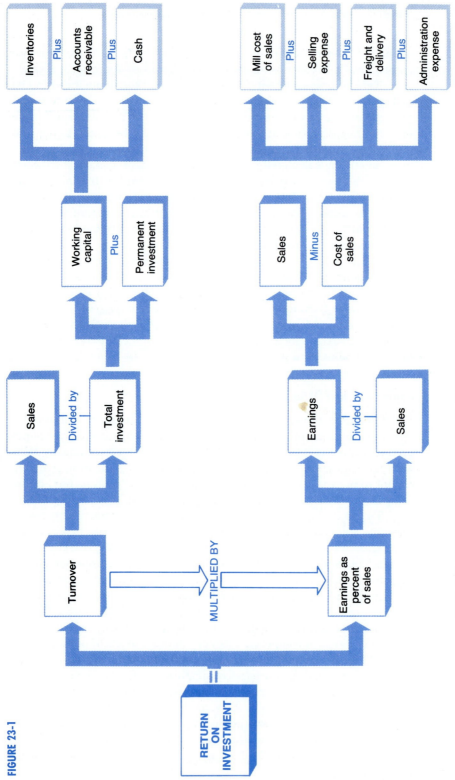

FIGURE 23-1

THE RELATIONSHIP OF FACTORS AFFECTING RETURN ON INVESTMENT.

TABLE 23-1   COMPARATIVE RATES OF RETURN ON ASSETS EMPLOYED: MULTIPRODUCT COMPANY
(In thousands of dollars)

	Total sales		Assets employed		Operating income*		
	Amount	Percent of total	Amount	Per dollar of sales	Amount	Percent return on sales	Percent return on assets
Base year:							
Product A	$ 39,300	40	$ 20,700	52.9%	$ 4,800	12.2	23.1
Product B	29,500	30	16,900	57.3	2,800	9.4	16.4
Product C	19,600	20	8,900	45.1	2,100	10.8	23.9
Product D	9,800	10	2,700	27.5	500	5.1	18.5
Total	$ 98,200	100	$ 49,200	50.1%	$10,200	10.4	20.8
Current year:							
Product A	$ 48,100	25	$ 28,400	59.0%	$ 5,600	11.6	19.7
Product B	96,200	50	75,300	78.3	8,500	8.8	11.2
Product C	38,500	20	19,500	50.7	3,900	10.2	20.1
Product D	9,600	5	2,900	29.9	500	5.2	17.2
Total	$192,400	100	$126,100	65.5%	$18,500	9.6	14.6

* Before interest on borrowed money and federal income taxes.

Advantages of ROI

One of the principal advantages of using return on investment to control overall performance is that it, like profit and loss control, focuses managerial attention on the central objective of the business—making the best profit possible on the capital available. It measures the efficiency of the company as a whole and of its major divisions or departments, its products, and its planning. It takes attention away from mere increase in sales volume or asset size or even from the level of costs, and it draws attention to the combination of factors that promotes successful operation.

Another advantage of control by return on investment is that it is effective where authority is decentralized. It not only is an absolute guide to capital efficiency but also offers the possibility of comparing efficiency in the use of capital within the company and in relation to efficiency in such use by other enterprises. By holding departmental managers responsible for performance in terms of the dollars invested in their parts of the business, it forces them to look at their operations from the point of view of top management. Managers often insist on heavy capital investments for new equipment or drive for lower prices to increase sales without taking into account the possible effect of their requests on the company as a whole. They also often feel isolated, particularly in large businesses, with respect to their performance. If managers are furnished with a guide to efficiency that applies to a business as a whole, they develop a keener sense of responsibility for their department or division, and top managers can more easily hold subordinate managers responsible.

A further advantage of return-on-investment control, if it is complete and shows all the factors bearing on the return, is that it enables managers to locate weaknesses. If inventories are rising, the rate of return will be affected; or if other factors camouflage inventory variations and leave the rate looking good, tracing back influences will disclose any weaknesses of the inventory situation and open the way for consideration of a remedy.

Limitations of ROI

With all its advantages and its widespread use by well-managed and successful companies, this method of control is not foolproof. Difficulties involve availability of information on sales, costs, and assets and proper allocation of investment and return for commonly sold or produced items. Does the present accounting system give the needed information? If not, how much will it cost to get it, through either changes in the system or special analyses? If assets are jointly used or costs are common, what method of allocation among divisions or departments should be used? Should a manager be charged with assets at their original costs, their replacement costs, or their depreciated values? Setting up a return-on-investment control system is no simple task.

Another question is: What constitutes a reasonable return? Comparisons of rates of return are hardly enough, because they do not tell the top manager what the rate of return should be. Perhaps as good a standard as any is one that meets or surpasses the level of competing firms, since, in a practical sense, the best tends to be measured not by an absolute level but by the level of the competition for capital.

One of the dangers of overemphasis on the rate of return is that it may lead to undesirable inflexibility in investing capital for new ventures. Many companies using this important measuring tool have set minimum rates that a division, new product program, or investment must meet before the allocation of additional capital is approved. It is said that even Du Pont, for many years, would not approve a new product program that did not promise a minimum return on investment of 20 percent. According to one executive of the company, this rigid minimum caused Du Pont to pass up such great product opportunities as xerography and the Land (Polaroid) camera. More recently, the company has used a more flexible minimum rate of return, requiring a higher rate when risks are greater and a lower rate when results are very promising or more certain or when an investment supplements an established business.

Perhaps the greatest danger in return-on-investment control, as with any other system of control based on financial data, is that it can lead to excessive preoccupation with financial factors within a firm or an industry. Undue attention to ratios and financial data can cause a firm to overlook environmental factors such as social and technical developments. It might also lead a company to overlook the fact that capital is not the only scarce resource with which a business can grow, prosper, and endure. Every bit as scarce are competent managers, good employee morale, and good customer and public relations. A well-managed company would never regard any financially based control as the sole gauge of overall performance.

For several decades, Renault was operated as if profits were not important. The company was one of the biggest in Europe until it dropped to sixth place in 1984, accompanied by great losses. But the company turned around dramatically. Since Renault is a state-owned enterprise, France's government had the power to fire the chairman, which it did in 1985 and replaced him with Georges Besse. His order was to make money.

Mr. Besse reduced the work force by 25 percent, reduced many bonuses, and virtually froze the wages. Mr. Besse's short reign was ended when he was murdered. His successor, Raymond Levy, continued the cost-cutting approach, along with an emphasis on quality improvement. In fact, he wants to make Renault the most profitable car company in Europe. Rather than having operations in many overseas countries, Renault wants to concentrate on the European market. For this reason, it sold its 46 percent ownership in American Motors to the Chrysler Corporation.

The cost-cutting measures have raised productivity to 13.5 cars per employee per year. This is similar to the productivity of U.S. car companies, but it is far below that of Japanese firms. Critics have also charged that cost reductions are not enough—management must also have a vision and a strategy, which seem to be lacking. While the company has come a long way in a short time, performance must be measured not only against its past but also against the performance of international competitors.

✓ DIRECT CONTROL VERSUS PREVENTIVE CONTROL

The preceding analysis of controls stresses the variety of approaches that managers follow to make results conform to plans. At the basis of control is the fact that the outcome of plans is dependent on the people who carry them out. For instance, a poor educational system cannot be controlled by criticizing its product, the unfortunate graduate; a factory turning out inferior products cannot be controlled by consigning products to the scrap heap; a firm plagued with customer complaints cannot be controlled by ignoring the complainers. Responsibility for controllable deviations lies with whoever has made unfortunate decisions. Any hope of abolishing unsatisfactory results lies in changing the future actions of the responsible person through additional training, modification of procedures, or new policy. This is the crux of controlling the quality of management.

There are two ways of seeing to it that the responsible people modify future action. The normal procedure is to trace the cause of an unsatisfactory result back to the persons responsible for it and get them to correct their practices. This may be called **direct control.** The alternative in the area of management is to develop better managers who will skillfully apply concepts, techniques, and principles and who will look at managing and managerial problems from a systems point of view, thus eliminating undesirable results caused by poor management. This will be referred to as **preventive control.***

✓ DIRECT CONTROL

In every enterprise, hundreds, and even thousands, of standards are developed to compare the actual output of goods or services—in terms of quantity, quality, time, and cost—with plans. A negative deviation indicates—in terms of goal achievement, cost, price, personnel, labor-hours, or machine-hours—that performance is less than good or normal or standard and that results are not conforming to plans.

Causes of Negative Deviations from Standards

The causes of negative deviations will often determine whether control measures are possible. Although an incorrect standard may cause deviations, if the standard is correct, plans may fail because of (1) uncertainty and (2) lack of knowledge, experience, or judgment on the part of those who make the decisions or take actions.

Uncertainty.   Elements affecting a given plan may be grouped into facts, risks, and uncertainty. Facts, such as number of employees, costs, or machine capacity, are known. Considerably less is known about the element of risk. Insurable risks are readily converted to factual status through the payment of a known premium, and the costs of certain noninsurable risks may be included in a business decision on the basis of probability. But most risks arise from uncertainty. The total of facts and risks is small compared with the element of uncertainty, which includes everything about which nothing is certain. For instance, the success of a plan to manufacture aluminum pistons will depend not only on known facts and risks but also on such uncertainties as future world conditions, competition of known and yet unknown metals, and power technology that may eliminate all piston prime movers. Not even probability can be estimated for all the uncertain factors, and yet they can wreck a plan.

Managerial errors caused by unforeseeable events cannot be avoided. The fixing of personal responsibility by direct control techniques is of little avail in such situations.

Lack of knowledge, experience, or judgment.   Plans may misfire and negative deviations occur when people appointed to managerial posts lack the necessary background. The higher in the organizational structure managers are placed, the broader the knowledge and experience they need. Long years as an engineer, a sales manager, a production executive, or a controller may be inadequate qualifications for a top manager.

If the cause of error is poor judgment, whether due to inadequate training,

---

*In previous editions of this text a different terminology was used. On the basis of colleagues' recommendations, the terms "preventive" control and "direct" control are used in this edition.

to lack of experience, or to failure to use appropriate information in decision making, corrections can be made. Managers can improve their education, be transferred to acquire broader experience, or be cautioned to take better stock of the situation before making decisions.

Questionable Assumptions Underlying Direct Control

In addition to its cost, the shortcomings of direct control may also be the results of questionable assumptions which hold that (1) performance can be measured,[8] (2) personal responsibility exists, (3) the time expenditure is warranted, (4) mistakes can be discovered in time, and (5) the person responsible will take corrective steps.

Assumption that performance can be measured. At first glance, almost any enterprise appears to be a maze of controls. Input, output, cost, price, time, complaints, and quality are subject to numerous standards, and the standards may be expressed in terms of goal achievement, time, weight, tolerances, averages, ratios, dollars, and indexes. In terms of usefulness, the standards may be correct, acceptable, or merely better than nothing. Close analysis will often reveal shortcomings of two types. The first type concerns measurement. The ability of a manager to develop potential managers, the effectiveness of research, and the amount of creativity, foresight, and judgment in decision making can seldom be measured accurately.

The second type of shortcoming concerns the location of the control. Managers know that critical stages exist in acquiring input factors, manipulating them to produce a finished product, and selling and delivering the product. In a factory operation, for example, critical stages would include receiving inspection, inspection for each assembly process, shipping, and billing. These are critical because effective control here will minimize costs. No amounts of control at other points can make up for lack of control at these stages.

Assumption that personal responsibility exists. Sometimes no manager is responsible for poor results. An increase in interest rates or inflation may cause the costs of many activities to rise precipitously; scarcity of a particular fuel may necessitate use of less economical sources of power; and markets may shrink for reasons unconnected with the firm.

Assumption that the time expenditure is warranted. Whether managers undertake the inquiry themselves or assign it to others, executive time must be spent in ferreting out causes of poor results. Large scrap losses, for example, may call for meetings attended by persons representing quality control, production planning, engineering, purchasing, and manufacturing. Because time has passed, recalling facts may be quite difficult. These drawbacks may convince managers that the cost of investigation exceeds any benefit they may derive. This often precludes investigation of clear violations of standards.

Assumption that mistakes can be discovered in time. Discovery of deviations from plans often comes too late for effective action. Although true control can be applied only to future action, most controls depend on historical data—all that most managers have available. Managers should, of course, interpret such data in terms of their implications for the future.

The cost of errors in major areas—such as cash or inventories—has led to the use of feedforward techniques as the basis for control. Since these are often difficult to use, the natural tendency to rely on historical reports seriously blocks adequate controls. Feedforward control techniques offer hope, but as yet they have not been widely developed or utilized. No manager really has control unless he or she can correct mistakes. And the best way to correct mistakes is to avoid them.

Assumption that the person responsible will take corrective steps.   Fixing the responsibility may not lead to correction. High production costs, for example, might be traced back to a marketing manager who insists that "slight" product modification will make selling easier and that this involves "really" no change in a production run. If the marketing manager is a member of top management, a subordinate investigator may be intimidated. Although great effort may be made to correct subordinate managers, it is sometimes very difficult to correct an executive to whom one reports.

THE PRINCIPLE OF PREVENTIVE CONTROL

The principle of preventive control embraces the idea that most of the responsibility for negative deviations from standards can be fixed by applying fundamentals of management. It draws a sharp distinction between analyzing performance reports, essential in any case, and determining whether managers act in accordance with established principles in carrying out their functions. The **principle of preventive control,** then, can be stated as follows: *The higher the quality of managers and their subordinates, the less will be the need for direct controls.*

The extensive adoption of preventive control must await a wider understanding of managerial principles, functions, and techniques as well as management philosophy. While such an understanding is not achieved easily, it can be gained through university training, on-the-job experience, coaching by a knowledgeable superior, and constant self-education. Moreover, as progress is made in appraising managers as managers, preventive control can be expected to have more practical meaning and effectiveness.

Assumptions of the Principle of Preventive Control

The desirability of preventive control rests on three assumptions. These hold that (1) qualified managers make a minimum of errors, (2) managerial performance can be measured, and management concepts, principles, and techniques are useful diagnostic standards in measuring managerial performance, and (3) the application of management fundamentals can be evaluated.

Assumption that qualified managers make a minimum of errors.   J. P. Morgan has often been quoted as saying that the decisions of good managers are right two-thirds of the time. However, an accurate analysis of the quality of decision making should not rely on the quantity of errors but should be concerned with the nature of the errors. J. Paul Getty once said that his concern in his worldwide empire was not the percentage of decisions in which an executive was right or wrong—the executive could be wrong on only 2 percent of them and seriously endanger a company if the errors were critical. Managers can logically be held strictly accountable for the performance of their functions because these functions should be undertaken in conformance with the fundamentals of management.[9] However, accountability cannot be exacted for errors attributable to factors beyond managers' authority or their ability to forecast the future with a reasonable degree of accuracy.

Assumption that management fundamentals can be used to measure performance.   The chief purpose of this book has been to draw together concepts, principles, theory, and basic techniques or approaches of management and relate them to a system of managerial functions. As stated in previous chapters, the completeness and certitude of these vary considerably, depending largely on the state of knowledge concerning managing. There is, for instance, greater general acceptance of some of the principles of organizing than there is of the principles relating to other functions. Nevertheless, it can be said that the fundamentals set forth here are useful in measuring managerial performance, even though this statement will undoubtedly be refined and better verified by future specialists.

Assumption that the application of management fundamentals can be evaluated.   Evaluation can provide for periodic measurement of the skill with which managers apply management fundamentals. This can be done not only by judging performance against these fundamentals but also by casting them into a series of fairly objective questions. An approach to the proper evaluation of managers as managers was set forth in Chapter 14. The ability to set and achieve verifiable objectives is one measure of a manager's performance, but much depends on being able to evaluate the performance of a manager as a manager. As crude as these standards of measurement may be at the present state of the art of managing, they can still highlight the extent to which an individual has the knowledge and ability required to fill the managerial role.

Advantages of Preventive Control

Controlling the quality of managers and thus minimizing errors has several advantages. First, greater accuracy is achieved in assigning personal responsibility. The ongoing evaluation of managers is practically certain to uncover deficiencies and should provide a basis for specific training to eliminate them.

Second, preventive control should hasten corrective action and make it more effective. It encourages control by self-control. Knowing that errors will be uncovered in an evaluation, managers will themselves try to determine their responsibility and make voluntary corrections. For example, a report of excessive scrap will probably cause the department supervisor to determine quickly whether the excess was due to poor direction of subordinates or to other factors. The same report will cause the chief inspector to look into whether inspections employees acted properly, the purchasing agent to check the material purchased against engineering specifications, and the engineers to determine whether appropriate material was specified. All these actions can be immediate and voluntary. Managers who conclude privately that they were in error are likely to do their best to prevent recurrence, for they realize their responsibility.

Third, preventive control may lighten the managerial burden now caused by direct controls. Preventing problems from occurring often requires less effort than correcting them after deviations have been detected.

Fourth, the psychological advantage of preventive control is impressive. Many subordinates feel that superiors do not rate fairly, that they rely on hunch and personality, and that they use improper measuring standards, but performance appraisal of the kind suggested in Chapter 14 can go far in removing this feeling. Subordinate managers know what is expected of them, understand the nature of managing, and feel a close relationship between performance and measurement.

THE MANAGEMENT AUDIT AND THE ENTERPRISE SELF-AUDIT

A question might be raised as to how a management audit may be distinguished from an enterprise self-audit. The latter emphasizes where a company is and where it is probably going in the face of present and future economic, political, and social developments. The **enterprise self-audit,** then, is really an audit of an organization's operations and only indirectly an audit of its managerial system.

The **management audit,** on the other hand, is not nearly as broad as the enterprise self-audit in that it aims only at evaluating the quality of management and the quality of managing as a system. It will be discussed first.

The Management Audit

Application of the principle of preventive control has led to action in several directions. One of the most promising and effective has been the improvement of programs in recent years to appraise individual managers. Primarily, this has taken the form of appraising performance against the standard of setting and achieving verifiable goals. However, much must still be done to make even this widely accepted approach effective. A second essential aspect of this process, still done only on a limited and experimental basis, is the appraisal of managers in their role as *managers*. Both these approaches were discussed in Chapter 14.

Another direction in which the principle of preventive control has led is toward a developing interest in management audits. Compared with other forms of management evaluations, these aim not at evaluating managers as individuals but rather at looking at the entire system of managing an enterprise. While little progress has been made in such management audits, some pioneering programs have been undertaken.

Management audits and accounting firms.   Although many management consulting firms have undertaken various kinds of appraisals of management systems, usually as a part of an organization study, the greatest interest in pursuing management audits has been demonstrated by accounting audit firms. One of the significant developments of recent years has been their entry into the field of management services of a broad consultancy nature. While this has been an attractive field of expansion for these auditing companies, since they are already inside an organization and financial information furnishes a ready window on problems of managing, it does open some question of conflict of interest. In other words, the question is often raised whether the same firm can be in the position of a management consultant furnishing both advice and services and still be completely objective as an accounting auditor. To be sure, accounting firms have attempted to avoid this problem by organizationally separating these two activities.

Regardless of whether auditing firms should be in management services, the fact is that they are. Since many are experienced in both auditing and management services, it is only a short step to management auditing. If it is possible for these firms to set up a completely detached and objective management auditing operation, and if this can be staffed by individuals with truly professional knowledge and ability in management, then the result may be an acceleration in the practice of management auditing. As long as the various professional and academic associations with a specific interest in management seem to be doing little in this field, perhaps accounting firms will show the way.

The certified management audit.   Another possibility for the future is the development of a **certified management audit,** an independent appraisal of a company's management by an outside firm. For years investors and others have relied on an independent certified accounting audit designed to make certain that the company's records and reports reflect sound accounting principles. From the standpoint of investors and even from that of managers and those desiring to work for a company, an independent audit of management quality would be extremely important. It is probably not an overstatement to say that an investor would get more value from a certified management audit than from a certified accounting audit, since the future of a company is likely to depend more on the quality of its managers than on any other single factor.

To ensure objectivity, the certified management audit should be the responsibility of a recognized outside firm, staffed with individuals who are qualified to appraise a company's managerial system and the quality of its managers and who have a reporting responsibility, like that of most accounting auditors, to the board of directors or another responsible top-management group. Although the management audit would require considerable study from the inside and a set of reasonably objective standards, it probably would take little more time than a thorough accounting audit. Moreover, except for the audit of top-level managers and the preparation of a final analysis of the company's management as a total system, much work on the management audit could be done, as in the case of accounting audits, with the help of suitable inside managerial and staff personnel. Furthermore, as with the accounting audit, once a group of special auditors becomes familiar with a company, subsequent audits take less time than the first.

It is quite obvious that any management audit report must go far beyond the typical accounting auditor's statements. It must do more than say that a management group has followed "generally accepted standards of management." In a meaningful report the quality of managers and the system within which they manage must be assessed objectively in fairly specific terms. This requirement, as one can see, gives rise to problems. How many accounting or management consulting firms can really be expected to be objective where, as so often occurs, managerial deficiencies exist at the top and when the firms are retained by, and report to, these same top managers? This is not an easy hurdle to overcome; the problems will persist until almost completely objective standards can be agreed on by true professionals and applied impartially. One cannot help but wonder whether this might not necessitate a specially licensed group that is independent of present accounting and management consulting firms and that reports, as a professional organization, to some agency independent of the firm being audited.

The Enterprise Self-Audit

J. O. McKinsey, who achieved an outstanding position in the realm of management several decades ago, came to the conclusion that a business enterprise should periodically make a "management audit," an appraisal of the enterprise in all its aspects in light of its present and probable future environment. Although McKinsey called this appraisal a management audit, it is actually an audit of the entire enterprise.

The **enterprise self-audit** appraises the company's position to determine where it is, where it is heading under present programs, what its objectives should be, and whether revised plans are needed to meet those objectives. In most enterprises, objectives and policies become obsolete. If an enterprise does not change course to suit the changing social, technical, and political environment, it loses markets, personnel, and other requirements for continued existence. The enterprise self-audit is designed to force managers to meet this situation.

Procedure.   The self-audit may be made annually or every 3 or 5 years. The first step is to study the outlook of the firm's industry. What are recent trends and prospects? What is the outlook for the product? Where are the markets? What technical developments are affecting the industry? How may demand be changed? What political or social factors may affect the industry? Note that similar questions may be raised in the formulation of the firm's strategy (see Chapter 7).

The second step in the self-audit is to appraise the position of the firm in the industry, both current and prospective. Has the company maintained its position? Has it expanded its influence and markets? Or has competition reduced its position? What is the competitive outlook? To answer such questions, the company may undertake studies on competitor standing, development of competition, customer reactions, and other factors bearing on its position within the industry.

On the basis of such studies, the next logical step for the company is to reexamine its basic objectives and major policies to decide where it wishes to be in, say, 3, 5, or 10 years. After this reexamination, the company may audit its organization, policies, procedures, programs, facilities, financial position, personnel, and management. This examination should identify any deviations from objectives and facilitate the revision of many major and minor plans.

Contribution of the self-audit.   Most top managers do not think in terms of an enterprise's future or evaluate overall performance in relation to long-range objectives. The enterprise self-audit has the distinct advantage of forcing them to appraise overall performance in terms not only of current goals but also of future ones. Top managers who expend mental effort for this kind of audit will almost certainly be well repaid and will be surprised at how many day-to-day decisions will be simplified by a clear picture of where the business is attempting to go.

A similar audit is often done when a company evaluates a firm it wishes to acquire. Without in any way detracting from the major importance of financial performance, it is realized that a firm's value depends on its future rather than its past. For this evaluation to be made, an examination of financial factors needs to be supplemented by a consideration of such factors as product lines and basic competition, marketing strengths, research and development record, personnel and public relations, and the quality of management. If these are of importance to a buyer of a company, one cannot help but wonder why they should not be significant on a regular and continuing basis to a firm.

DEVELOPING EXCELLENT MANAGERS

Although the introductory analyses of the tasks of a manager are presented in this book as a start toward understanding the science underlying managerial practice, more is required. There are many considerations in ensuring the development of excellent managers; some of the more important ones are discussed below. Surely, effective future managerial practice will depend, at least, on these.

Instilling a Willingness to Learn

If managers are to avoid the stultifying effect of basing too much of their learning on experience, they must be aware of the dangers of experience.[10] As indicated earlier in this book, undistilled experience can lead an individual toward assuming that events or programs of the past will or will not work in a different future. But managers need more than this. They need to be willing to learn and to take advantage of new knowledge and new techniques. This necessitates a humble approach to their successes and limitations. It demands a recognition that there is no finishing school or terminal degree for management.

Accelerating Management Development

The preceding discussion underlines the urgent importance of accelerated programs of management development. This implies not only more pertinent management seminars and conferences but also other means of transmitting to practicing managers in as simple and useful a way as possible the new knowledge and tools in the field of management.

One of the major challenges in this connection is that of compressing and transmitting the available knowledge. Every field of art based on a burgeoning science has the same problem. No field has completely solved it, although certain areas, such as specialized aspects of medicine and dentistry, have made considerable progress.

There is no adequate answer for this problem. It does appear that those on the management faculties of our universities have an obligation to practicing managers to do much of the task of compressing and transmitting new knowledge as easily and quickly as possible. There is still inadequate evidence that many university professors see the social importance of this role. Also, one might expect a greater contribution from various management associations, as well as from management consultants, who can certainly greatly improve their value to clients by transmitting new knowledge. Perhaps more can be done through intelligent digesting of articles and books. Also, a series of special management clinics could be established on a regular basis. By spending a day every few weeks at such a clinic, managers at all levels in alert companies could be brought up to date on a specific area of new knowledge and techniques.

Planning for Innovation

As competition becomes sharper, as problem solving grows in complexity, and as knowledge expands, one expects that the managers of the future will have to place greater importance on planning for innovation. Even now it is widely recognized that a business enterprise, at least, must "innovate or die," that new products do not just happen, and that new marketing ideas do not often occur by luck. The manager of the future must place more emphasis than ever before on developing an environment for effective planning. This will involve, even more than it does at present, planning goals that call for stretch; creating policy guidelines to channel thinking toward them without stifling imagination; designing roles in which people can be creative and yet constructive; keeping abreast of the entire external environment (discussed in greater detail in Chapters 3 and 4), which affects every kind of organization; and recognizing the urgency of channeling research toward desired ends.

Measuring and Rewarding Management

One of the significant concerns of the managers of the future will be the importance both of objectively measuring managerial performance and of rewarding good performance, imposing sanctions on a poor operation, and providing corrective action where it is indicated. Managers must be willing to work toward establishing objective measures of performance through both an analysis of verifiable results and a measurement of the abilities of individuals as managers.

Tailoring Information

Another important consideration for the manager of the future will be obtaining the right information in the right form and at the right time. Tailoring information, as outlined in this book, requires a high order of intelligence and design. Until more managers realize that very little of their operation can be planned and controlled through "handbook" approaches, and until more managers recognize that they themselves must become involved in tailoring the information they require, progress will continue to be slow in this area. As long as information design is confused with the clerical work of information gathering and summarizing, managers will understandably continue to fret about the inadequacy of the data on which they are forced to act.

Expanding Research and Development in Tools and Techniques

All the issues mentioned above should command greater managerial attention. In addition, a great need exists for more real research and development in management tools and techniques themselves. The level of research effort and support in the field of management is woefully low. It is also not particularly great in the disciplines underlying management or, for that matter, in the entire area of social science. Nevertheless, it is probable that research in the underlying disciplines far outpaces that in the central area of management.

There are many reasons for this. General management research is difficult, exceedingly complex, and dynamic. It is an area in which facts and proved relationships are hard to come by and in which the controlled experiment of the laboratory is difficult to use without dangerous oversimplification. Likewise, management research is expensive, and the funds that have gone into it are abysmally inadequate.

Still another reason for the low state of management research is that there are few clinical analyses, despite a considerable volume of clinical experience. Consulting efforts of both professional consultants and individual academics, extensive management case collections, and studies and analyses made internally in business, government, and other enterprises almost certainly encompass a huge mass of undigested, largely unsummarized, and relatively useless information. If this clinical experience could be given the analytical and summarizing work so common in the health sciences, there might now be considerable evidence of what is workable in practice and where deficiencies exist.

Undertaking this research requires patience and understanding. Perfection of analysis to include all kinds of variables is a laudable goal for a researcher. But, particularly in the field of management, a little light can be a massive beam in a hitherto dark area. We must often settle for small advances so that cumulatively, and over time, we may gain larger ones.

Developing More Managerial Inventions

Research without development is insufficient. One of the major challenges for the manager of the future is the need for developing more managerial inventions. It is interesting that so much creative talent has been channeled into the invention of physical designs and chemical compositions while so little has gone into social inventions. The Gantt chart has sometimes been regarded as the most important social invention of the first half of the twentieth century. Other management inventions include the variable budget, rate-of-return-on-investment analysis, and PERT. Mere reference to these inventions underscores the fact that they are creative tools developed from a base of principles on the one hand and needs on the other. Reference to them indicates also that they are useful devices in improving the art of managing.

Inventions tend to reflect the cultural level of an art. There are few of them in management. Surely, even the present inadequate cultural level can be coupled with urgent needs to give rise to many more management innovations, particularly if the people concerned are willing to spend some time and money to direct their energies toward these inventions. It is very easy to see that one significant management invention, such as any of those mentioned in the previous paragraph, can make important contributions to management effectiveness and economy of operations. Applied research and development in this field surely justify a considerable expenditure of time and money.

Creating Strong Intellectual Leadership

That intellectual leadership in management is urgently needed can hardly be denied. Managing can no longer be only a practical art requiring merely native intelligence and experience. The rapid growth of underlying knowledge and the obvious need for even more, particularly knowledge that is organized and useful for improvement of practice, are requirements of tremendous significance.

For people in every type of enterprise, at any part of the globe, the challenge of creating a highly productive society is great. History teaches us that when needs exist and are recognized, leadership usually rises to inspired solutions. The challenging needs are here, waiting the application of knowledge discussed in this book, which is aimed at making you more effective as a person and as a manager so that you can lead a productive organization.

TOWARD A UNIFIED, GLOBAL THEORY OF MANAGEMENT

Today, the framework of planning, organizing, staffing, leading, and controlling (with some slight variations at times) has become the most popular way of structuring managerial knowledge.[11] Management textbooks based on this framework are widely used around the world. Still, there are challenging tasks ahead for integrating the body of managerial knowledge into a unified theory.

Chapter 2 of this book dealt with the many schools of, or approaches to, management. There is evidence that the management theory jungle not only continues to flourish but gets denser, with nearly twice as many schools or approaches as were found more than 30 years ago.

At the same time, there are signs that the various schools of thought are converging. Realizing that these are only signs along the road to a more unified and operational theory of management and that there is more of this road to travel, let us briefly examine some of these tendencies toward convergence.

The Empirical Approach: Distilling Basics

In reviewing the many programs that use cases as a means of educating managers, one finds that there appears to be much greater emphasis on distilling fundamentals than there was two or three decades ago. Likewise, in the field of business policy, by which term these case approaches have tended to be known, there has been increased emphasis on teaching and research that goes beyond recounting what happened in a given situation to analyzing the underlying causes.[12] One major result of all this has been a new emphasis on strategic management. Furthermore, many textbooks on policy and strategy now have many international cases and considerable text material of distilled knowledge.[13]

Systems Thinking—Not a Separate Approach

Practicing managers as well as the operational theorists increasingly use the basics of systems theory in analyzing managerial jobs. On the macro level, managers, especially those in multinational corporations, are viewing their operations as a global interdependent system. Japanese managers, for example, are in charge of their manufacturing plants in the United States, and U.S. managers direct their firms in Europe and other countries.

Situational and Contingency Approaches—Not New or Separate

It is now clear that the concepts of situational, or contingency, management are merely a way of distinguishing between science and art, knowledge and practice. As pointed out at the beginning of this book, science and art are two different but complementary things. Those writers and scholars who have emphasized situational, or contingency, approaches have done the field of management theory and practice a great service by stressing that what the intelligent manager actually does depends on the realities of a situation, whether it is in the United States or abroad.

The Confluence of Motivation and Leadership Theories

Another interesting sign of the move toward a unified operational theory of management is the way that research and analysis have tended to merge motivation and leadership theories.[14] As explained in Chapters 16 and 17, leadership research and theory have found that people tend to follow those who offer them a means of satisfying their own desires. Thus, explanations of leadership have been increasingly related to motivation.

Implied by most recent research and theory is the clear message that effective leaders design a system that takes into account the expectations of subordinates, the variability of motives among individuals, the factors specific to a situation, the need for clarity of role definition, interpersonal relations, and types of rewards.

The New, Managerially Oriented "Organization Development"

Both "organization development" and the field ordinarily referred to as "organization behavior" have grown out of the interpersonal and group behavior approaches to management. Many specialists in these areas are now beginning to see that basic management theory and techniques fit well into their programs of behavioral intervention.

Fortunately, a review of the latest organization behavior books indicates that many authors in this field are beginning to understand that the study of behavioral elements in group operations must be more closely integrated with the study of organization structure design, staffing, planning, and control. This is a hopeful sign. It is a recognition that analysis of individual and group behavior, at least in managed situations, easily and logically falls into place in the scheme of operational-management theory.

The Impact of Technology: Researching an Old Problem

That technology has an important impact on organizational structure, behavior patterns, and other aspects of managing has been recognized by practitioners for many years. Fortunately, academic researchers in recent years have directed their attention to the impact of technology on managerial effectiveness.

Perspective

The Organization of the Future

The concept of the modern organization as it exists today in the United States originated with Pierre S. Du Pont and Alfred P. Sloan. It was Sloan who structured General Motors with an emphasis on centralized staff and decentralized operation. Policy-making and operations were distinguished. Control was maintained through a number of control techniques and budgets. This kind of organization worked remarkably well and is still the predominant way large enterprises are organized today. However, new technology, new demands in the environment, and a new work force call for a new kind of organization based on information.

Peter F. Drucker, one of the most perceptive writers on management, predicted that in 20 years large organizations will have only a third of the managers they have today, and the organizational levels will be reduced by more than half.[15] He suggests that future organizations will be information- and knowledge-based. They will consist of specialists and may be more like the universities, hospitals, or symphony orchestras of today.

The Merger of Theory and Practice

For some time now, scholars and practitioners have been looking at the total job of managing. As pointed out in Chapter 2, the 7-S framework for management analysis proposed by McKinsey & Company, a respected management consulting firm, is indeed close to the operational, or management process, model.

Research Supporting the Operational, or Management Process, Approach

Some recent research studies have focused on the total managerial job. An example of this research was presented by Fred Luthans in his presidential speech at the

Academy of Management in August 1986.[16] His findings are, in general, congruent with the operational approach to managing as used in this book. In his 4-year study of more than 300 managers at different levels and in various kinds of organizations, he found that "real" managers carry out the following activities: (1) routine communication (see Part 5 in this book), (2) traditional managerial activities such as planning, decision making, and controlling (Parts 2 and 6 in this book), (3) human resource management activities (Parts 4 and 5), and (4) networking, by which is meant socializing, politicking, and interacting with outsiders (some of these concepts relate to the discussion of informal organization, coordination, and power presented in Part 3). Luthans found a significant relationship between networking activities and managerial success (measured by a promotional index). The next level of analysis focused on managers' effectiveness (consisting of perceived work unit performance in terms of quantity and quality, as well as subordinates' commitment and satisfaction). The findings showed the strongest relationships between effectiveness and routine communication, followed by human resource management and traditional management. Although the research does not address all the key managerial activities (such as structuring the organization or clarifying authority-responsibility relationships), it takes a comprehensive look at what successful and effective managers really do.

Clarification of Semantics: Some Hopeful Signs

One of the greatest obstacles to disentangling the jungle has been the problem of semantics. People writing and lecturing on management and related fields have tended to use the same terms in different ways (or to use different terms for the same concept). This is exemplified by the variety of meanings given to such terms as "organization," "line and staff," "authority," "responsibility," and "policies," to mention a few. While this semantics swamp still exists and the general acceptance of standardized meanings of key terms and concepts is still a long way off, there are some hopeful signs on the horizon.

It has become rather common now for leading management texts to include a glossary of key terms and concepts, and an increasing number of textbooks are beginning to use terms in a similar way. Furthermore, the Fellows of the International Academy of Management, a select group comprising management scholars and managerial leaders from more than thirty countries, have responded to the demands of members and undertaken the development of a glossary of management concepts and terms in a number of languages. It is necessary to agree not only on the translation of terms (although some terms such as "operations research" or "management" are used without translations in different languages) but also on the precise meaning, understandable to all.

The Internationalization of Management[17]

The term "global village" may appropriately describe the world we live in today. Advances in technology in aerospace, communications, fiber optics, and computers link people from around the globe.

While Japan sends its young people to the United States to study management techniques (and Japanese managers are eager readers of U.S. best-sellers on management), managers in the United States often look to Japan for ways of implementing some of these techniques and theories more effectively. Recently, Korean managers have come with their style—which in many ways is similar to that of the Japanese—to lead their subsidiaries in the United States.[18] Samsung, Lucky Goldstar, Daewoo, and Hyundai are just a few of the Korean companies establishing themselves (quite successfully) in the United States. One Japanese manager admits that the Koreans, lacking the homogeneous culture of the Japanese, may be more flexible in adapting to the U.S. environment.

The point here is not that one approach is better than another but, rather, that many countries can contribute to managerial theory and practice.[19] A special commission presented a sobering report on industrial competitiveness to the President of the United States.[20] In an environment of global competition, only the best companies will succeed, and management, it can be suggested, will be an important factor for this success.[21]

A perceptive observer will note that the role of managers is expanding. New approaches are required to avoid managerial obsolescence and improve managerial productivity. There is a need for more effective planning, flexible approaches to organizing, better managing of human resources, an environment favorable for motivation, and methods for effective and efficient control that use the new information technology. Above all, the field of management requires intellectual and inspirational leadership in the United States and around the world to make organizations more productive for the benefit of humanity.

SUMMARY

Many overall controls are financial. One widely used control of overall performance is the budget summary, which is a summary of all operating revenue and expense budgets. Another kind of control is profit and loss control. Still another overall control technique is the exercise of control through calculating and comparing return on investment. This approach is based on the idea that profit should be considered not as an absolute measure but as a return on the capital employed in a segment of a business. An example is the well-known Du Pont return-on-investment (ROI) model.

In carrying out the controlling function, managers have two basic approaches. The most usual one, direct control, consists of developing standards for desired performance and then comparing actual performance against these standards. The normal procedure is to trace the cause of an unsatisfactory result back to the persons responsible for it and get them to correct their practices.

The other approach is preventive control, in which an attempt is made to prevent negative deviations from standards by ensuring that managers at all levels apply effectively the fundamentals of management. The principle of preventive control is stated as follows: The higher the quality of managers and their subordinates, the less will be the need for direct controls. The assumptions that underlie the principle of preventive control are that (1) qualified managers make a minimum of errors, (2) management fundamentals can be used to measure performance, and (3) the application of management fundamentals can be evaluated.

There are two kinds of audits. The management audit aims at evaluating the quality of management and the quality of managing as a system. The enterprise self-audit evaluates the organization's operations and only indirectly the managerial system.

Without question, the role of managers is expanding and changing. With new knowledge being developed and social forces requiring managers to take advantage of it, the danger that managers will become obsolete for their tasks is growing more serious. Many factors can help avoid this possibility: managers who are willing to learn, acceleration of programs of management development, more effective planning for innovation, better methods for evaluating and rewarding managerial performance, more tailored information, and greater emphasis on managerial research, development, and inventions. The best intellectual leadership in management is urgently required to meet these challenges.

Chapter 2 highlighted the various approaches to management, which constitute a kind of jungle. The operational, or management process, approach, as used in this book, is an attempt to unify these different orientations. There are indeed signs that business is moving toward a unified, global theory of management.

KEY IDEAS AND CONCEPTS FOR REVIEW

Budget summary

Profit and loss control

Limitations of profit and loss control

Return on investment (ROI)

Advantages and limitations of ROI control

Direct control

Questionable assumptions underlying direct control

Principle of preventive control

Advantages of preventive control

Management audit

Certified management audit

Enterprise self-audit

Essentials for developing excellent managers

Trends toward a unified, global theory of management

FOR DISCUSSION

1. Why do most controls of overall performance tend to be financial? Should they be? What else would you suggest?
2. "Profit and loss control is defective in that it does not emphasize return on investment; the latter is defective in that it places too great an emphasis on present results, possibly endangering future results." Discuss.
3. In applying the rate of return on investment as a control tool, would you favor using an undepreciated or a depreciated asset base?
4. If preventive control were completely effective, would a company need any direct controls?
5. Select any major area of management theory and principles, and discuss how it can be applied to reality.

6. In reference to specific management problem areas, such as new product development, organization structure, or budgets, what are the ways that managers can introduce flexibility, and what are the inflexibilities usually encountered in each?

7. How do you anticipate that the computer will affect the manager's role at the top-management level and at the middle-management level? How will it affect first-level supervision?

8. What can be done about the problem of top-level executive malnutrition?

9. What are some of the hopeful signs that indicate business is moving toward a unified, global theory of management?

EXERCISES/ACTION STEPS

1. Interview two managers in business firms, and ask them about the kinds of controls used to measure overall performance. What are the similarities and differences of the responses of the two managers?

2. Choose any federal, state, or local government agency you wish, and check whether or not it has some kind of overall control. If it does not, could you develop a system or program for evaluating overall performance?

CASES

CASE 23-1
BANKAMERICA CORPORATION[22]

BankAmerica, once the largest bank in the United States, ranked 299th among the 300 most admired companies identified by *Fortune* magazine.[23] In this group BankAmerica was among the least admired companies in terms of quality of management, innovativeness, and other characteristics.

In the early 1980s, the bank was one of the most profitable banks in the nation. At that time, it had over 87,000 employees and more than 2000 offices in about 100 countries. But over a period of 5 years, loans worth more than $4 billion were written off, many of them to home builders, shipping firms, farmers, and foreign customers. In 1986 Samuel Armacost stated that the situation was under control,[24] yet the stock price dropped sharply in that year. The headquarters building in San Francisco was sold, followed by the sale of Charles Schwab & Co., BankAmerica's brokerage subsidiary, in 1987.

The bank had expanded its mortgage business in 1979 and 1980 with the expectation that the interest rates would fall. Instead, they skyrocketed in the early 1980s. Being stuck with low mortgages but paying high interest rates on deposits put a great burden on the institution. Deregulation resulted in an easing of interest-rate ceilings and created a dynamic environment for which most financial institutions were not prepared. Savings and loan associations became more like banks in their operations. Increased competition resulted in lower margins, which, in turn, led some inefficient organizations to fail or to be acquired by other institutions.

Competition came not only from other banks but also from many other institutions. General Motors, for example, became one of the top consumer lenders. Other firms going into the finance business were Sears, Ford Motor Company, National Steel, General Electric, and American Express, just to mention a few.

BankAmerica, like many other banks, also made loans to less developed countries. One of the reasons was to spread the risks for savers and investors. But some of the loans were not collectible.

In 1986 Armacost was replaced by A. W. Clausen, who was also his predecessor.

1. Did BankAmerica get out of control? If your answer is "yes," how did it happen?

2. What safeguards would you recommend so that it does not happen again? What, for example, would you recommend so that loan officers do not make risky loans?

INTERNATIONAL CASE 23-2
PLANNING AND CONTROL AT VOLKSWAGEN[25]

Siegfried Hoehn, director of strategy and investment at Volkswagen A.G. (VW), writing from the perspective of a practitioner, points out that the information system affects the whole system of managing, but especially planning and controlling. Figure 23-2 provides an overview of the planning and control model used by the VW Group.

Although the planning and control system at

FIGURE 23-2

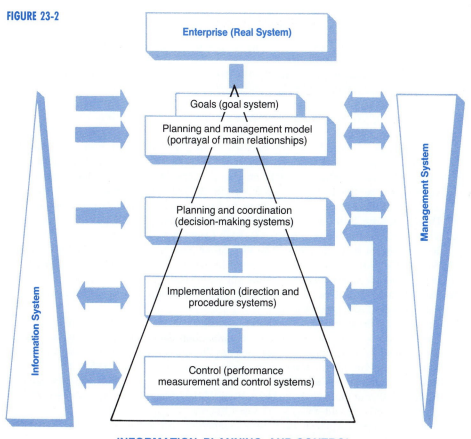

**INFORMATION, PLANNING, AND CONTROL
IN THE MANAGEMENT SYSTEM OF THE VOLKSWAGEN GROUP.**

From Siegfried Hoehn, "How Information Technology Is Transforming Corporate Planning," *Long Range Planning* (August 1986), p. 19. Used with permission.

VW is quite comprehensive, Hoehn suggests that new developments in information technology will change planning and control in the future. Some of the trends include the use of integrative systems, multifunction terminals, telecommunication networks, and computer systems. Moreover, greater decentralization allows the system to be tailored to the specific functions of the users. The application of computers facilitates the automation of workplaces, with computers doing more of the routine work.

1. Describe the relationship between planning and controlling.
2. In what ways will new technology influence planning and controlling?
3. Why does the model show the information flowing upward?

REFERENCES

1. Ian I. Mitroff, Paul Shrivastava, and Firdaus E. Udwadia, "Effective Crisis Management," *Academy of Management Executive* (November 1987), p. 283.
2. For a discussion of different kinds of measurement, see Joseph W. Wilkinson, "The Meanings of Measurement," in Max D. Richards (ed.), *Readings in Management*, 7th ed. (Cincinnati: South-Western Publishing Company, 1986), pp. 318–324.
3. Robert N. Anthony, "Games Government Accountants Play," *Harvard Business Review* (September–October 1985), pp. 161–170.
4. Michael J. Sandretto, "What Kind of Cost System Do You Need?" *Harvard Business Review* (January–February 1986), pp. 110–118.
5. Frances Gaither Tucker and Seymour M. Zivan, "A Xerox Cost Center Imitates a Profit Center," *Harvard Business Review* (May–June 1985), pp. 168–174.
6. Leslie Helm, "Why Kodak Is Starting to Click Again," *Business Week* (Feb. 23, 1987), pp. 134–138; Leslie Helm and Barbara Buell, "Kodak Fights Fuji with 'Me-Too' Tactics," *Business Week* (Feb. 23, 1987), p. 138; Alex Taylor III, "Kodak Scrambles to Refocus," *Fortune* (Mar. 3, 1986), pp. 34–39; Clare Ansberry, "Kodak Plans to Cut Work Force by about 4,500, and to Sell Units," *The Wall Street Journal* (Aug. 24, 1989); Joan E. Rigdon, "Kodak Tries to Prepare for Filmless Era without Inviting Demise of Core Business," *The Wall Street Journal* (Apr. 18, 1991).
7. Thomas Kamm and Philip Revzin, "Difficult Drive: Renault Works to Lift Auto Quality, Profits, Regain Its Lost Luster," *The Wall Street Journal* (Oct. 12, 1987).
8. See also Geert Hofstede, "The Poverty of Management Control Philosophy," in Richards (ed.), *Readings in Management* (1986), pp. 302–315.
9. See also Derek F. du Toit, "Confessions of a So-So Controller," *Harvard Business Review* (July–August 1985), pp. 50–56.
10. On the other hand, the contributions of managers in their forties and fifties are often underestimated. They are often the ones who keep the organization going and should be involved in important decisions. See Jay W. Lorsch and Haruo Takagi, "Keeping Managers Off the Shelf," *Harvard Business Review* (July–August 1986), pp. 60–65.
11. See also Stephen J. Carroll and Dennis J. Gillen, "Are the Classical Management Functions Useful in Describing Managerial Work?" *Academy of Management Review* (January 1987), pp. 38–51.
12. See, for example, Michael E. Porter, *Competitive Advantage* (New York: The Free Press, 1985).
13. One example of a book with extensive text material, readings, and cases is George A. Steiner, John B. Miner, and Edmund R. Gray, *Management Policy and Strategy*, 3d

ed. (New York: The Macmillan Company, 1986); another book with extensive text material is Fred R. David, *Fundamentals of Strategic Management* (Columbus, Ohio: Merrill Publishing Company, 1986). An example of a book with many international cases is Thomas J. McNichols, *Policymaking and Executive Action*, 6th ed. (New York: McGraw-Hill Book Company, 1983).

14. A high degree of motivation can also be obtained through self-leadership. See, for example, Charles C. Manz, "Self-Leadership: Toward an Expanded Theory of Self-Influence Processes in Organizations," *Academy of Management Review* (July 1986), pp. 585–600.

15. See Peter F. Drucker, "The Coming of the New Organization," *Harvard Business Review* (January–February 1988), pp. 45–53.

16. See also Fred Luthans, Richard M. Hodgetts, and Stuart A. Rosenkrantz, *Real Managers* (Cambridge, Mass.: Ballinger Publishing Company, 1988). The book has also been reviewed by Craig C. Pinder in *Academy of Management Review* (October 1988), pp. 661–663.

17. See also Tom Peters, "Prometheus Barely Unbound," *Academy of Management Executive* (November 1990), pp. 70–84; Rosabeth Moss Kanter, "Transcending Business Boundaries: 12,000 World Managers View Change," *Harvard Business Review* (May–June 1991), pp. 151–164.

18. Laurie Baum, "Korea's Newest Import: Management Style," *Business Week* (Jan. 19, 1987), p. 66.

19. F. T. Murray and Alice Haller Murray, "SMR Forum: Global Managers for Global Businesses," *Sloan Management Review* (Winter 1986), pp. 75 ff.; Andrew Kupfer, "How to Be a Global Manager," *Fortune* (Mar. 14, 1988), pp. 52–58.

20. *Global Competition—The New Reality,* The Report of the President's Commission on Industrial Competitiveness, vol. 1 (Washington: GPO, January 1985).

21. Louis Kraar, "The New Powers of Asia," *Fortune* (Mar. 28, 1988), pp. 126–132.

22. This case is based on a variety of sources, including Harvey Rosenblum and Diane Siegel, *Competition in Financial Services: The Impact of Nonbank Entry,* Federal Reserve Bank of Chicago, Staff Study #83-1, p. 17; Teresa Carson, "Who Needs BankAmerica? Not Joe Pinola," *Business Week* (Feb. 23, 1987), p. 46; Jonathan B. Levine, "1985 Won't Be Any Better for BofA," *Business Week* (June 24, 1985), p. 46; "Banks Give Farmers Loans and Pray for Bailout," *The Wall Street Journal* (June 6, 1985); Harlan S. Byrne and Jonathan R. Laing, "Asset or Liability? Tom Clausen Returns to B of A," *Barrans* (October 1986); Nina Easton, "Some Branch Tightening Ahead of Bank of America," *American Banker* (Feb. 23, 1987).

23. Edward C. Baig, "America's Most Admired Corporations," *Fortune* (Jan. 19, 1987), pp. 18–31.

24. Gary Hector, "The Most Beleaguered Banker," *Fortune* (Jan. 5, 1987), p. 86.

25. Siegfried Hoehn, "How Information Technology Is Transforming Corporate Planning," *Long Range Planning* (August 1986), pp. 18–30; see also John C. Papageorgiou, "Decision Making in the Year 2000," *Interfaces* (April 1983), pp. 77–86.

Summary of Major Principles, or Guides, for Controlling

From the discussions in the previous chapters on management control, there have emerged certain essentials, or basic truths. These, which are referred to as "principles," are designed to highlight aspects of control that are regarded as especially important. In view of the fact that control, even though representing a system itself, is a subsystem of the larger area of management, certain of these principles are understandably similar to those identified in discussions of the other managerial functions. Principles of control can be grouped into three categories, reflecting their purpose and nature, structure, and process.

The Purpose and Nature of Control

The purpose and nature of control may be summarized by the principles listed below.

Principle of the purpose of control. The task of control is to ensure that plans succeed by detecting deviations from plans and furnishing a basis for taking action to correct potential or actual undesired deviations.

Principle of future-directed controls. Because of time lags in the total system of control, the more a control system is based on feedforward rather than simple feedback of information, the more managers have the opportunity to perceive undesirable deviations from plans before they occur and to take action in time to prevent them.

These two principles emphasize that the purpose of control in any system of managerial action is ensuring that objectives are achieved through detecting deviations and taking action designed to prevent or correct them. Moreover, control, like planning, should ideally be forward-looking. This principle is often disregarded in practice, largely because the present state of the art in managing has not regularly provided for systems of feedforward control. Managers have generally been dependent on historical data, which may be adequate for collecting taxes and determining stockholders' earnings but are not good enough for the most effective control. If means of looking forward are lacking, reference to history, on the questionable assumption that "what is past is prologue," is better than not looking at all. But time lags in the system of management control make it imperative that greater efforts be undertaken to make future-directed control a reality.

Principle of control responsibility. The primary responsibility for the exercise of control rests in the manager charged with the performance of the particular plans involved.

Since delegation of authority, assignment of tasks, and responsibility for certain objectives rest in individual managers, it follows that control over this work should be exercised by each of these managers. An individual manager's responsibility cannot be waived or rescinded without changes in the organization structure.

Principle of efficiency of controls. Control techniques and approaches are efficient if they detect and illuminate the nature and causes of deviations from plans with a minimum of costs or other unsought consequences.

Control techniques have a way of becoming costly, complex, and burdensome. Managers may become so engrossed in control that they spend more than it is worth to detect a deviation. Detailed budget controls that hamstring a subordinate, complex mathematical controls that thwart innovation, and purchasing controls that delay deliveries and cost more than the item purchased are examples of inefficient controls.

Principle of preventive control. The higher the quality of managers in a managerial system, the less will be the need for direct controls.

Most controls are based in large part on the fact that human beings make mistakes and often do not react to problems by undertaking their correction adequately and promptly. The more qualified managers are, the more they will perceive deviations from plans and take timely action to prevent them.

The Structure of Control

The principles that follow are aimed at pointing out how control systems and techniques can be designed to improve the quality of managerial control.

Principle of reflection of plans. The more that plans are clear, complete, and integrated, and the more that controls are designed to reflect such plans, the more effectively controls will serve the needs of managers.

It is not possible for a system of controls to be devised without plans, since the task of control is to ensure that plans work out as intended. There can be no doubt that the more clear, complete, and integrated these plans are, and the more that control techniques are designed to follow the progress of these plans, the more effective the controls will be.

Principle of organizational suitability. The more that an organizational structure is clear, complete, and integrated, and the more that controls are designed to reflect the place in the organization structure where responsibility for action lies, the more the controls will facilitate correction of deviations from plans.

Plans are implemented by people. Deviations from plans must be the responsibility primarily of managers who are entrusted with the task of executing planning programs. Since it is the function of an organization structure to define a system of roles, it follows that controls must be designed to affect the role in which responsibility for performance of a plan lies.

Principle of individuality of controls.   The more that control techniques and information are understandable to individual managers who must utilize them, the more they will actually be used and the more they will result in effective control.

Although some control techniques and information can be utilized in the same form by various kinds of enterprises and managers, as a general rule controls should be tailored to meet the individual needs of managers. Some of this individuality is related to position in the organization structure, as noted in the previous principle. Another aspect of individuality is the tailoring of controls to the kind and level of managers' understanding. Company presidents as well as supervisors have thrown up their hands in dismay (often for quite different reasons) at the unintelligible nature and inappropriate form of control information. Control information that a manager cannot or will not use has little practical value.

The Process of Control

Control, often being so much a matter of technique, rests heavily on the art of managing, on know-how in given instances. However, there are certain principles that experience has shown have wide applicability.

Principle of standards.   Effective control requires objective, accurate, and suitable standards.

There should be a simple, specific, and verifiable way to measure whether a planning program is being accomplished. Control is accomplished through people. Even the best manager cannot help being influenced by personal factors, and actual performance is sometimes camouflaged by a dull or a sparkling personality or by a subordinate's ability to "sell" a deficient performance. Good standards of performance, objectively applied, will more likely be accepted by subordinates as fair and reasonable.

Principle of critical-point control.   Effective control requires special attention to those factors critical to evaluating performance against plans.

It would ordinarily be wasteful and unnecessary for managers to follow every detail of plan execution. What they must know is that plans are being implemented. Therefore, they concentrate attention on salient factors of performance that will indicate any important deviations from plans. Perhaps all managers can ask themselves what things in their operations will best show them whether the plans for which they are responsible are being accomplished.

The exception principle.   The more that managers concentrate control efforts on significant exceptions, the more efficient will be the results of their control.

This principle holds that managers should concern themselves with significant deviations—the especially good or the especially bad situations. It is often confused with the principle of critical-point control, and the two do have some kinship.

However, critical-point control has to do with recognizing the points to be watched, while the exception principle has to do with watching the size of deviations at these points.

Principle of flexibility of controls. If controls are to remain effective despite failure or unforeseen changes of plans, flexibility is required in their design.

According to this principle, controls must not be so inflexibly tied in with a plan as to be useless if the entire plan fails or is suddenly changed. Note that this principle applies to failures of plans, not failures of people operating under plans.

Principle of action. Control is justified only if indicated or experienced deviations from plans are corrected through appropriate planning, organizing, staffing, and leading.

There are instances in practice in which this simple truth is forgotten. Control is a wasteful use of managerial and staff time unless it is followed by action. If deviations are found in experienced or projected performance, action is indicated, in the form of either redrawing plans or making additional plans to get back on course. The situation may call for reorganization. It may require replacing subordinates or training them to do the task desired. Or it may indicate that the fault is a lack of direction and leadership in getting a subordinate to understand the plans or in motivating him or her to accomplish them. In any case, action is implied.

Global Controlling and Global Challenges

Like the closing sections in Parts 1 to 5, this part closing is about the global environment. In this part closing, the focus is on controlling. First, controlling practices in Japan, the United States, and the People's Republic of China are discussed. Second, the international focus is on the implications of the European Community's program—EC 1992—for managing in the New Europe. Finally, two global car industry cases are presented, one dealing with the importance of quality and the other one highlighting global competitive challenges for carmakers.

CONTROLLING PRACTICES IN JAPAN, THE UNITED STATES, AND THE PEOPLE'S REPUBLIC OF CHINA[1]

In the view of Western managers, controlling involves setting standards, measuring performance, and correcting undesirable deviations. But to the Japanese, this process is less direct, as shown in the accompanying table.

Controlling in Japan

As noted in the discussion of decision making, the group—its dynamics and its pressures—has a profound impact on the managerial process. In an office without dividing walls, peers are well aware of the performance of their colleagues. Moreover, managers are a part of the work group rather than being separated from employees by an office door. The measurement of individual performance is not against specific verifiable objectives; instead, emphasis is placed on group performance. Also, the Japanese approach of letting subordinates "save face" would be

COMPARISONS OF JAPANESE, U.S., AND CHINESE CONTROLLING*		
Japanese management	**U.S. management**	**Chinese management**
1. Control by peers	1. Control by superior	1. Control by group leader (superior)
2. Control focus on group performance	2. Control focus on individual performance	2. Primary control focus on groups—but also focus on individuals
3. Saving face	3. Fixing blame	3. Trying to save face
4. Extensive use of quality control circles	4. Limited use of quality control circles	4. Limited use of quality control circles

* Sources of information are given in note 6 in the Part 2 closing References.

incongruent with fixing the blame for deviations from plans on individuals. Control emphasizes process, not numbers. The Japanese are well known for their concern for quality. Yet this has not always been the case. In the 1950s and 1960s, Japanese products had an image of shoddy quality. This image has changed; good quality is one of the characteristics now associated with Japanese products. This is due, in part, to the success of quality control, which requires grass roots involvement with very active participation in quality control circles.

Controlling in the United States

Control in the United States often means measuring performance against pre-established precise standards. Management by objectives, widely practiced in this country, requires the setting of verifiable objectives against which individual performance is measured. Thus the superior can trace deviations to specific individuals, and this often results in fixing blame. In an attempt to maximize individual results, group performance may suffer. We all can think of examples in which self-interest of individuals was placed before group or organizational interest.

The use of quality control programs is not new. Hughes Aircraft Company, for example, had such programs for a long time under the names Zero Defects and Value Engineering. Many of these programs were developed in this country and later used by the Japanese for improvement of product quality and productivity.

Controlling in China

In China, control is exercised primarily by group leaders. The control focus is primarily on the group but also on the individual. Factory managers, for example, are expected to meet their yearly quota. Thus, Chinese control practices are a mixture of U.S. and Japanese managerial practices. In identifying deviations from standards, there is a tendency to let the persons responsible for subperformance save face (this is similar to the Japanese practice). There is some use of quality circles, but it is not a common practice.

Conclusions about Managerial Practices in Different Countries

The comparisons of planning, organizing, staffing, leading, and controlling practices in Japan, the United States, and China make it clear that the *application* of the principles and managerial concepts differs in these countries. It is also clear that managers with a global orientation will learn about management as it is practiced not only in their own country but also in other places in the world. Chinese managers look at both Japanese and U.S. managerial practices and compare them with their past experiences, as shown in the discussions of the managerial functions. Some practices from the United States and Japan may be transferable, but others are not.[2] The environment, especially sociocultural factors, does influence practice.[3] But its impact may have been overstated.

INTERNATIONAL FOCUS:
IMPLICATIONS OF EC 1992 FOR MANAGERS IN THE NEW EUROPE

The European Community of 1992 will affect most U.S. companies, whether they are operating within national boundaries or abroad. Strong European firms will become tough competitors in the United States. To be successful in the global market, enterprises need to use their capabilities to cope with the demands in the external environment.

The External Environment[4]

In developing an *enterprise profile* for their companies, executives must wrestle with fundamental questions about the firm's geographic domain, its competitive situation, and its top-management orientation.

The *geographic domain* determination requires raising questions such as "Where are our customers, and where are those who should be our customers but are not at the present?" If the intention is to operate in the European market, a clear understanding of the new dynamics created by EC 1992 is required.

The *competitive situation* will be greatly altered by the European Community. Market share is only one indicator of the firm's potential. Others are price, quality, service, product innovation, distribution systems, facilities, and locations. Factors that were keys to success in the past may become altered in a global market. The competitive analysis becomes especially intricate for companies operating in international markets.

The direction of the firm is shaped by people, especially top executives. Some managers may have to alter their *orientation* from a national viewpoint to a global perspective. The new demands on managers, reinforced by EC 1992, are thinking in global terms, understanding the mentalities of managers in EC and non-EC countries, gaining managerial experience abroad, and developing proficiency in speaking at least two foreign languages.

In the analysis of the external environment, many diverse factors need to be considered. As indicated in the above discussion, *economic* power will shift through the 1992 program. This shift will be accompanied by many *social* and *political* changes. We will see, for example, a greater uniformity in laws and regulations that can be both threats and opportunities.

Products need to be adjusted not only to the local demands but also to the state of the fast-changing technology. *Technology* transfer is rapid. Companies need to build organization structures that can take advantage of technological breakthroughs such as superconductivity or nuclear fusion.

Demographic shifts need to be taken into account. The opening of borders is likely to result in the movement of people from one country to another. For example, workers from other countries who worked in former West Germany are entitled to a number of benefits, which, in turn, increase the debt burden on Germans. Moreover, the age composition will be different for the various EC countries. This means that despite the creation of a common market, marketing will still have to be tailored to the needs of the people in each country.

Markets and competition will undergo dramatic changes. The number and kinds of competitors will change. Thus companies have to ask: "Who are our competitors, and how do we compare with the competition?" "What are the strengths and weaknesses of the competitors, and what are their strategies?" And finally, each company has to determine how it can best compete in the European environment.

There are, of course, other factors that are critical to a specific organization and that need to be taken into consideration, such as the availability of raw materials and suppliers or the adequacy of the transportation system.

The Internal Environment of Companies[5]

The demands of the external environment must be matched with the weaknesses and strengths in management, the organization structure, operations, finance, and other internal factors.

Managers not only must be proficient in carrying out the managerial functions of planning, organizing, staffing, leading, and controlling but also must widen their horizon beyond national boundaries. Furthermore, they need to understand the difference between countries in labor relations, personnel policies, selection, training, and development.

Organization structures must reflect the demands of the new Europe. In some cases exportation of goods or licensing agreements may have to be replaced by joint ventures, subsidiaries, mergers, and acquisitions. Strategic alliances can take many forms, ranging from joint ventures to marketing agreements. In the eighties, U.S. firms engaged in over 2000 alliances with European companies.[6] Many competing companies have joined forces. General Electric has links with firms in Europe, Japan, and South Korea. Ford works with Japanese Nissan on a minivan, and it also has ties with Mazda. In addition, the company has joint operations with Volkswagen in Argentina and Brazil. AT&T works with the Dutch Philips. Clearly, national boundaries are becoming less important as the move toward a global market continues.

Operations must be carefully analyzed in terms of research and development capabilities, marketing, distribution channels, and brand-name protection. For example, high-technology companies may have to respond to the demands of Europeans of conducting research in their countries. Other competitive factors may be productivity, labor cost, pricing, appropriate customer identification, service, and the company image.

The *financial* markets will be greatly affected by the 1992 program. The easier availability of capital in Europe may cause scarcity of capital in the United States. Companies need to assess their weaknesses and strengths in terms of profitability, financial planning, the accounting system, and the impact of the tax structure. In Germany, for example, the tax law will eliminate the tax breaks on capital gain. This will affect small and medium-size companies—for example, by making them candidates for acquisition.

Choice of Strategy

There are a variety of strategies available for U.S. enterprise.[7] One is the *exportation* of goods and services to the European Community. In general, U.S. firms have had only limited success in exporting. Another strategy is the *joint venture,* which has had mixed results, as exemplified by the cooperative arrangement between Olivetti and AT&T. Still, as pointed out above, several firms now do consider the joint venture option. The most successful approaches have been setting up wholly owned *subsidiaries* or *branches,* as shown by well-established companies such as Opel (a subsidiary of General Motors), Ford Motor Company, and IBM.

In evaluating the alternatives, firms must consider opportunities in light of the *risks* involved. The new European environment, with its 340-plus million rather affluent people, provides many profit opportunities for new products and services. Yet some companies may not be able to afford the risks. On the other hand, when taking a long-term view, a firm may not be able to afford not taking the risk of entering the market.

In January and February 1989 alone, U.S. firms bought into twenty-three European firms for $973 million. These were the highest cross-border purchases (the next highest were by the United Kingdom and Italy).[8] Some observers see a flood of U.S. investments in Europe in the future. United Parcel Service (UPS) has already bought eight delivery companies in the United Kingdom, Belgium, Denmark, and France. Outside the twelve-member EC, UPS made similar purchases in Switzerland and Finland.

While some U.S. companies are consolidating their positions in Europe—for example, Sara Lee bought a coffee and tea firm in the Netherlands and a ladies' stockings firm in France—other U.S. firms are new in the European market. Whirlpool, one of the largest U.S. manufacturers of appliances, found a way to enter the EC market by engaging in a joint venture with the Dutch firm N.V. Philips to make major appliances for marketing under the Philips name. Whether new on the European scene or already established, many firms from outside the EC are trying to establish or consolidate their base as a result of EC 1992.

There is concern that free competition and full deregulation may precipitate bankruptcies and restructuring and cost some 500,000 jobs during the first two years.[9] One report forecasts that at the beginning 500,000 jobs may be lost and that no jobs may be gained until 1994. The long-term outlook, however, is that 1.8 million jobs will be created through the EC.[10]

Strategic choices must be made in light of competitors. Not only will one encounter highly competitive European firms, but Japanese companies will also become formidable rivals. For example, Japanese chemical companies have already been active by participating in joint ventures, engaging in licensing, or making direct investments.[11] While Sweden's Volvo saw a drop in its car shipments to the United States, the company compensated for it with its plans to shift some of its operations to EC countries.[12] Since Sweden is not a member of the EC, Volvo's strategy, in keeping with its concern about "Fortress Europe," is to attempt to gain a market position in the Community.

Many large multinational firms have taken steps to prepare for possible protectionist measures as a result of EC 1992. These strategic choices often are acquisitions, mergers, strategic alliances (joint ventures or agreements for cooperation), and rationalization. The Deutsche Bank (German bank), for example, *acquired* Bank of America's branches in Italy. Brown & Boveri, a Swiss electrical company, merged with Sweden's ASEA.[13] The American Telephone and Telegraph Company engaged in a *joint venture* with ITALTEL, a state-owned telecommunication equipment manufacturer in Italy. Many firms have adopted a strategy of cost reduction through *rationalization*. Ford's goal is to become Europe's low-cost automobile manufacturer. The Swedish Electrolux Company closed several factories and consolidated its manufacturing facilities in several European countries in order to become more competitive. Rationalization is especially important for European firms because their social costs (for example, unemployment support, disability benefits, and health care) are generally higher than for firms in the United States, Canada, and Asian countries.

While many large concerns have made strategic decisions in anticipation of a Single Market, smaller firms—especially older, traditional ones—are generally ill-equipped for the changes. One strategy may be to get established in a small European market, watch carefully the developments, and adjust to the new evolving regulations.[14] Small American firms may consider alliances with the not-so-powerful (economically) countries such as Ireland, Greece, Portugal, and Spain.[15] Yet there is no assurance that those firms which were already in Europe by 1992 will have opportunities equal to those of European firms. For example, the new rules may be based on European manufacturing processes or standards, and complying with them may be costly to U.S. firms.

Dr. Wisse Dekker, the chairman of the Supervisory Board of N.V. Philips in Holland and a leading advocate of the European market, has some advice for American firms. While it is common for U.S. managers to be driven by a short-term orientation and quarterly profit results, it may be more appropriate for the European situation to balance profit performance with continuity. In other words, after deciding on a strategy, managers should be persistent in pursuing it, keeping in mind the long-term goal.[16]

Future Challenges in the New Europe

Because of the EC 1992 program, U.S. companies will have to make difficult strategic decisions about their European operations. The elimination of trade barriers and the move toward a unified market will make Europe an economic powerhouse.

Many established multinational corporations are well positioned to take advantage of the opportunities provided by the free flow of goods and services. Other firms are rushing to establish a European base either through acquisitions and mergers or through partial ownership, as in joint ventures. Although the 1992 program aims for a free market, outsiders such as the United States, Japan, and non-EC nations fear trade restrictions.

Carefully monitoring the developments and preparing contingency plans may yield the best prospects for taking advantage of the huge European market. For companies, the stakes are high in the largest single market of the industrialized world—and so are the opportunities in the New Europe.

GLOBAL CAR INDUSTRY CASE A: QUALITY AND CONTINUOUS IMPROVEMENT— THE COMPETITIVE EDGE?[17]

As U.S. carmakers are improving the quality of their cars, the Japanese are redefining the quality concept. Traditionally, quality meant reliability and an automobile free from product defects. However, the evolving quality concept is more than that. It holds that a car should be engineered to "feel good" and to "feel right." It also means that the product should feel comfortable and be engineered to satisfy customer wants. Thus, a car needs to be engineered so that it has its own personality. For Toyota, quality means "building the very best and giving the customer what he (she) wants."

A New Quality Concept

Japanese carmakers view this new quality concept as an art. Their approach focuses on customer needs. Nissan, for example, employed anthropologists to find out why people buy cars. On the basis of customer information, Nissan developed an "active" suspension system that improves the car's riding quality. To find out what customers like, Japanese carmakers carefully examined the features in popular competing luxury cars such as Mercedes and BMW. For example, Toyota bought Mercedes, BMW, and Jaguar cars before designing the LS 400 luxury car. After putting their competitors' cars through very demanding tests, they took them apart and tried to improve them. This resulted in both a reduction in the drag coefficient and lower weight (characteristics that improve mileage), a reduction of inside noise, and the development of fuel-efficient engines. To keep the costs of luxury cars at a reasonable level, the Japanese invested heavily in efficient manufacturing equipment, which allows them to build cars that are less expensive than their European counterparts.

New Product Development and Continuous Improvement

In contrast to U.S. manufacturers, the Japanese give considerable freedom to their design engineers, who are not necessarily Japanese nationals. The idea for the successful Mazda Miata came from a Californian product planner. Another Californian designed the original styling. The Accord wagon was designed by Americans in Torrance, California. It is produced by American workers in Marysville, Ohio. Honda estimates that the car came 2 months earlier to the market than if it had been designed in Japan, over 6000 miles away.

U.S. and Japanese car companies differ in the degree of authority given to their engineers. At Toyota, the chief engineer has broad responsibilities, including developing the concept for the car, deciding how to produce it, and selecting suppliers. The chief engineer even participates in developing the marketing strategy and scanning the environment for trends such as safety, exhaust, and fuel efficiency regulations. In U.S. companies, in contrast, the responsibilities are much more narrowly defined.

Quality and productivity can be obtained in various ways. Toyota, for example, emphasizes the *kaizen* concept, which requires continuous improvement. The thinking behind this concept is that continuously taking small steps in improvements will be the key to long-term success. So far, this strategy has worked well for Toyota, which is considered by some to be the best carmaker in the world. But success could lead to complacency. Therefore, Toyota creates an environment of continuous dissatisfaction with the present state, which, in turn, stimulates the drive for continuous improvement and reorganization. In 1990, for example, Toyota reorganized by removing two levels of middle managers. The number of staff personnel and executives was drastically reduced. Shoichiro Toyoda, Toyota's CEO, who has a Ph.D. in engineering, took charge of product development. Toyota, which was once considered a conservative company, is now becoming more open to new ideas and to the development of stylish models, as exemplified by the minivan Previa, designed in California. Another factor that reduces complacency is that executives in Japan are housed not in luxurious quarters but in a simple building with a vinyl-floor lobby. It has been described as being less impressive than a typical U.S. high school. Toyota also saves money by having its headquarters located in Toyota City, some 300 miles away from the expensive Tokyo location.

Not all Japanese carmakers use the same approach to designing cars with the new quality concept. Honda, for example, asked its product designers to come up with the ideal family car "personality." In fact, Honda people visited U.S. families in their homes to talk about their personal hobbies and what features they liked in cars. For sharing their opinions, families received $50. Probably this was a very wise investment. Lexus employees are also close to their customers; they call them to find out what they like about their newly purchased cars. Mazda is known for its *kansei* engineering, which pays attention to the rational and emotional aspects of the customers. For example, engineers measure the driver's heart rate to discern human reactions under various driving conditions. In short, Mazda tries to develop model "personalities" for different types of consumers.

The short product development cycles allow Japanese carmakers to include the latest technological innovations in their new models. On the average, the Japanese develop new models every 4.5 years. The Honda product development cycle is only 4 years. In contrast, U.S. firms need much longer cycles, and at the German carmaker Daimler-Benz it takes 7 years or longer to develop new models.

Improvement of Operating Efficiency and Effectiveness

Effective and efficient operation is a key to success in the global, competitive environment. At Toyota, *kanban*—the just-in-time system—contributes to the company's successful operation. In use for over 20 years, the system has been continuously improved. It is used not only for inventory control but also for other operations. Customers, for example, can order cars according to their specifications and take delivery in 7 to 10 days. Since the dealers order the cars directly from the factory, their inventory costs are very low.

Other factors that make Toyota's operation effective are achieved through the heavy investment in research and development and new manufacturing technologies. It is estimated that it takes 13 labor-hours to build a car at Toyota, while it takes 19 hours at Honda and 22 hours at Nissan. With these cost savings, Toyota is in a very favorable financial position, with $22 billion in reserves. But this money has been accumulated not only from producing cars but also from making shrewd investments. It has been said that the company makes more money from its investments than from its cars.

Toyota's Global Strategy

The strategy of using *kaizen* and *kanban* has been quite successful. But Toyota's executives do not rest on their success; they have their eyes set on the future. While the company is operated out of Japan, it expands globally. It has a test track in Arizona, plans to build a third plant in the United States, and is enlarging its design center in America. Toyota is also expanding in Southeast Asia, Latin America, and Europe. Expanding in the European Community will be more difficult than in the United States. Europeans, especially the French and Italians, are attempting to protect their own market from the Japanese. Britain, on the other hand, has invited Japanese carmakers to build their plants in that country. The European Community's EC 1992 program will remove some of the restrictions for the Japanese. Toyota's aim is to become a truly global company, designing, manufacturing, and marketing cars around the world.

Can U.S. Carmakers Compete in the Global Environment?

The question, then, is: Can U.S. car companies compete in this global environment? Crisis can lead to opportunities. When the Buick plant in Flint, Michigan, was scheduled to close, partly because of its low quality relative to the quality at other

GM plants, salaried and hourly workers got together to address the basics of quality management. Weekly meetings were held with suppliers, and these resulted in better-quality components. Quality responsibility was assigned to assembly line workers. Engineers worked on the assembly line to gain firsthand knowledge of some of the problems encountered by the production people. In time, this plant became one of the most efficient in the GM group.

American carmakers are catching up with Japanese quality. But, as noted at the beginning of this case, as they are catching up, the Japanese are redefining quality, which goes beyond reliability and includes many needs of the customers. In the global car market, quality counts. Can U.S. firms keep up with, and perhaps even overtake, their foreign competitors?

1. If you were the CEO of General Motors or Ford, what would you do to help your firm stay competitive? Would you argue for import quotas? Why, or why not?
2. If you were the CEO of Mercedes-Benz, what strategy would you develop to make your company's cars price-competitive with Japanese luxury cars?
3. What features in a car influence your buying decision? Explain.

GLOBAL CAR INDUSTRY CASE B: COMPETITIVE CHALLENGES FOR CARMAKERS[18]

The interdependencies of countries can best be illustrated by the global automobile war. About 175 companies produce over 45 million cars, buses, and trucks, which are sold around the world. The competition is so fierce that no country has a clear competitive advantage in all areas. In executive leadership, the American Lee Iacocca of Chrysler is often mentioned. In referring to prestige, the European firm Mercedes-Benz is frequently cited. The Japanese are considered tough competitors, known for high productivity and adaptability. More recently, inexpensive Korean cars have invaded the U.S. market. The beneficiaries of this competition are the car buyers, who can choose from a great variety of features such as the reliability of Japanese cars, the handling of European cars, the low cost of Korean cars, and the comfort of the traditional American family car.

Challenges and Opportunities

The car companies face many other problems besides competition: overcapacity in the United States and Europe; traffic congestion in metropolitan areas, which may limit the demand for cars; increasing concern about protectionism in Europe as well as in Japan; and environmental concerns. European, Japanese, and U.S. companies are working on cars that are environmentally friendly. For example, Toyota is working on a solar car, Volkswagen on a multifuel car, and General Motors on a hybrid electric minivan. Even so, there are opportunities such as the demand for large and sporty cars in the United States and the potential markets around the world. Although it has not yet materialized, there is an enormous expected demand for automobiles in former Eastern-bloc nations and less developed countries. The unification of Germany and the opening of the borders in Eastern-bloc countries will open the doors to a huge market for European, Japanese, and U.S. carmakers. Carl H. Hahn, Volkswagen's CEO, is so optimistic that he wants to spend $34 to $35 billion over a 5-year period to expand capacity—a risky decision in an already glutted market. He has a vision of a "federated," decentralized company running the VW, Audi, SEAT (Spain), and Skoda (Czechoslovakia) operations almost around the world.

How, then, do the world's carmakers respond to or prepare for such challenges? Each company tries to use its own strength to compete in the world market. Fiat, an Italian car company, seems to have worked out its labor problems and can now focus on beating Volkswagen, the European leader. The strength of VW is its automated assembly line. Moreover, VW has cooperative ventures with more than ten carmakers, including the German Daimler-Benz and Porsche, Japanese Nissan, Swedish Volvo, and Spanish SEAT. Volkswagen is also considering a $2 billion venture with Ford to produce small trucks in Europe.

Strategies and Tactics of Carmakers

Germany has become the second-largest market for Japanese cars (the largest is the United States). The strategies of the Japanese carmakers in Germany is similar to that in the United States: Get into the market; learn from mistakes and correct them quickly; listen to the customers; and have a flexible production line to adapt to customers' tastes. Carl Hahn, the chairman of VW, admitted that the Japanese cannot be beaten on productivity. The motto underlying a joint project with the Japanese seems to be: "If you can't beat them, join them." Thus, Volkswagen and Toyota will produce pickup trucks designed by the Japanese.

Listening to the customers was one of the keys to the success of Japanese car companies in Germany. They changed the styling of their cars to accommodate European preferences, and they equipped their cars with better suspension and steering to make them suitable for the German freeways, which have no speed limit. Similarly, they identified the need for minivans and four-wheel-drive vehicles and offered models to fill those needs.

One reason why many Japanese carmakers can respond quickly to changes in the market is the fact that they deal with many suppliers. It has been estimated that Toyota, for example, buys about 80 percent of its parts from suppliers. The company also strengthened its market position in the United States through a joint venture with General Motors, producing cars in Fremont, California. Indeed, many Japanese carmakers have cooperative arrangements with foreign companies. The exception is Honda, which is quite independent. With its Japanese facilities used to their limits, Honda was one of the first foreign manufacturers (besides Volkswagen, which has closed its U.S. plant) to establish a plant in the United States. The company's success led to the introduction of a new luxury car marketed under the name Acura.

In the past, General Motors' full model line and its enormous size were considered strengths. But it is now realized that these characteristics can also be weaknesses, hindering adaptation to changes in the environment. GM's vertical integration, in which the company produces some 70 percent of its own parts, may contribute to its inflexibility. Although GM operates worldwide, there has been little cooperation between the U.S. company and its foreign subsidiaries in the past. In contrast, Ford Motor Company has become truly international, with close coordination among its design centers in the United States, England, and Germany. Chrysler has enlarged its capacity through the purchase of American Motors. The company tries to stay competitive by adapting to changes in consumer demands through the use of flexible manufacturing techniques.

The Japanese Car Market

Japan is a fast-growing market for imported cars. Most of the car companies are European. The Volkswagen-Audi Group holds the No. 1 position in 1989 import registrations. In the past, its cars were sold through independent dealers, but since 1990 they have been distributed through exclusive dealerships. The next spot for imported vehicles in Japan is held by BMW, which established its own dealerships. Mercedes-Benz ranks third. The recent cooperation between this company and Mitsubishi may strengthen Mercedes's position in Japan. Among the U.S. carmakers, General Motors ranks sixth, Ford Motor Company eighth, and Chrysler fifteenth. It is interesting to note that Honda cars produced in America and imported into Japan rank ninth. Honda planned to send some 50,000 cars built in Ohio to Japan, but it shipped only about 12,000 in 1990. Among the sixteen major car companies, five are from Germany, four are from the United States, two are from Britain and two more from Sweden, and one each is from France, Italy, and South Korea.

It is quite clear now that executives of major car companies have to take a global view of their business. While opportunities have increased through internationalization, threats are always present. A shift in direction of the interdependent economies or a dramatic change in oil prices can make or break the automobile market. The challenges for the carmakers' executives are great indeed.

1. Why have Japanese car companies been so successful in the United States and in Germany?
2. What kind of organization structure is best for competing in the international car war? Why?
3. What kinds of problems do you expect when carmakers from different countries join forces?

REFERENCES

1. Sources of information are given in note 6 in the Part 2 closing References. In addition see W. Edwards Deming, *Out of the Crisis* (Cambridge, Mass.: MIT Center for Advanced Engineering Study, 1986); Howard W. Gitlow and Shelly J. Gitlow, *Deming Guide to Achieving Quality and Competitive Position* (Englewood Cliffs, N.J.: Prentice-

Hall, 1986); Nancy Mann, *The Keys to Excellence: The Story of the Deming Philosophy* (Santa Monica, Calif.: Preswick Books, 1986); William W. Scherkenbach, *The Deming Route to Quality and Productivity: Roadmaps and Roadblocks* (Milwaukee, Wis.: American Society for Quality Control, 1986); Mary Walton, *The Deming Management Method* (New York: Dodd, Mead, and Company, 1986).

2. See, for example, Thomas E. Maher, "Condemning Japan while Imitating Her Management Techniques: No Solution for America's Problems," *SAM Advanced Management Journal* (Winter 1985), pp. 31–35.

3. China Handbook Editorial Committee, *Culture* (Beijing: Foreign Languages Press, 1982); China Handbook Editorial Committee, *Education and Science* (Beijing: Foreign Languages Press, 1983).

4. The external factors are discussed in most textbooks on strategic management, such as James Brian Quinn, Henry Mintzberg, and Robert M. James, *The Strategy Process* (Englewood Cliffs, N.J.: Prentice-Hall, 1988), pt. 1. One of the early contributions was by George A. Steiner, *Top Management Planning* (New York: The Macmillan Company, 1969).

5. For a discussion of internal factors for formulating a strategy, see the many textbooks on business policy or Heinz Weihrich, "The TOWS Matrix—A Tool for Situational Analysis," *Long Range Planning* (April 1982), pp. 52–64.

6. Louis Kraar, "Your Rivals Can Be Your Allies," *Fortune* (Mar. 27, 1989), pp. 66–76.

7. See, for example, Harold Koontz and Heinz Weihrich, *Management*, 9th ed. (New York: McGraw-Hill Book Company, 1988), chap. 25.

8. John Lichfield, "Trans-Atlantic Company Acquisitions Gain Momentum," *Europe* (April 1989), pp. 24–25.

9. J. B. Phillips, "1992: Gearing Up for the New Europe," *Institutional Investor* (July 1988), pp. 124–130.

10. Leigh Bruce, "1992: The Bad News," *International Management* (September 1988), pp. 22–26.

11. Richard I. Kirkland, Jr., "Outsider's Guide to Europe in 1992," *Fortune* (Oct. 24, 1988), pp. 121–127.

12. Blanca Riemer, Jonathan Kapstein, John Templeman, and Richard A. Melcher, "The Europeans' Big Problem: What to Do with All That Cash," *Business Week* (Apr. 24, 1989), pp. 42–43.

13. John E. Magee, "1992: Moves Americans Must Make," *Harvard Business Review* (May–June 1989), pp. 78–84.

14. George V. Priovolos, "Small Businesses Can Benefit from European Economic Changes if They Take Precautions," *Marketing News* (Sept. 26, 1988), p. 6.

15. Kate Bertrand, "Scrambling for 1992," *International Marketing* (February 1989), pp. 49–59.

16. Nan Stone, "The Globalization of Europe: An Interview with Wisse Dekker," *Harvard Business Review* (May–June 1989), pp. 90–95.

17. Material for this case was drawn from a variety of sources, including David Woodruff, Karen Lowry Miller, Larry Armstrong, and Thane Peterson, "A New Era for Auto Quality," *Business Week* (Oct. 22, 1990), pp. 84–96; Wendy Zellner, "Buick City: The Factory That's Getting Things Right," *Business Week* (Oct. 22, 1990), p. 87; Alex Taylor III, "Why Toyota Keeps Getting Better and Better and Better," *Fortune* (Nov. 19, 1990), pp. 66–79; Alex Taylor III, "Japan's New U.S. Car Strategy," *Fortune* (Sept. 10, 1990), pp. 65–80.

18. The information for this case was drawn from a variety of sources, including Alex Taylor III, "Who's Ahead in the World Auto War," *Fortune* (Nov. 9, 1987), pp. 74–88; Thomas

F. O'Boyle, "German Pride in Cars Doesn't Stop Japan," *The Wall Street Journal* (Oct. 21, 1987); James B. Treece, "Detroit Is Bracing for a One-Two Punch," *Business Week* (Nov. 16, 1987), pp. 136–144; John Templeman, "What Ended VW's American Dream," *Business Week* (Dec. 7, 1987), p. 63; James B. Treece, Mark Maremont, and Larry Armstrong, "Will the Auto Glut Choke Detroit?" *Business Week* (Mar. 7, 1988), pp. 54–62; Rahul Jacob, "Foreign Car Sales Go Vroom in Japan," *Fortune* (Apr. 9, 1990), p. 10; Laxmi Nakarmi and Larry Armstrong, "Honk if You'd Buy a Hyundai," *Business Week* (Sept. 10, 1990), p. 52; Karen Lowry Miller and James B. Treece, "Honda's Nightmare: Maybe You Can't Go Home Again," *Business Week* (Dec. 24, 1990), p. 36; John Templeman and James B. Treece, "Carl Hahn's High-Octane Growth Plan for VW," *Business Week* (Mar. 18, 1991), pp. 46–47; for the many changes taking place in Eastern Europe, see Gail E. Schares, Ken Olsen, Lynne Reaves, and Elizabeth Weiner, "Reawakening—A Market Economy Takes Root in Eastern Europe," *Business Week* (Apr. 15, 1991), pp. 46–50; David Woodruff, Thane Peterson, and Karen Lowry Miller, "The Greening of Detroit," *Business Week* (Apr 8, 1991), pp. 54–60; Bernard Avishai, "A European Platform for Global Competition: An Interview with VW's Carl Hahn," *Harvard Business Review* (July–August 1991), pp. 103–113.

Glossary

Absoluteness of responsibility. See *Responsibility, absoluteness of.*

Administrators. See *Managers.*

Apprenticeship system in Germany. An apprentice obtains practical experience by working in the company and learns theoretical concepts in vocational schools.

Approach to management, contingency or situational. An analysis of management that emphasizes the fact that what managers do in practice depends on a given set of circumstances or the "situation" and that there is no single "best way" to manage. (Fig. 2-2)

Approach to management, cooperative social system. An analysis of management concerned with both interpersonal and group behavioral aspects leading to a system of cooperation. (Fig. 2-2)

Approach to management, decision theory. An analysis of management that focuses on the making of decisions, persons or groups making decisions, and the decision-making process. Some theorists use decision making as a springboard to study all enterprise activities. The boundaries of study are no longer clearly defined. (Fig. 2-2)

Approach to management, empirical or case. An analysis of management that studies experience through cases, identifying successes and failures. (Fig. 2-2)

Approach to management, group behavior. An analysis of management that studies the behavior of people in groups. The approach is based on sociology and social psychology. The focus is on group behavior patterns. The study of large groups is often called "organization behavior." (Fig. 2-2)

Approach to management, interpersonal behavior. An analysis of management that focuses on interpersonal behavior, human relations, leadership, and motivation. It is based primarily on individual psychology. (Fig. 2-2)

Approach to management, managerial roles. A means of analyzing management by observing what managers actually do and from such observations coming to conclusions as to what managerial activities (or roles) are.

Approach to management, mathematical or "management science." An analysis of management primarily seen as mathematical processes, concepts, symbols, and models. This approach views management as a purely logical process, expressed in mathematical symbols and relationships. (Fig. 2-2)

Approach to management, McKinsey's 7-S framework. An analysis of management that organizes managerial knowledge around the following categories: strategy, structure, systems, style, staff, shared values, and skills.

Approach to management, operational or process. An analysis of management that draws together concepts, principles, techniques, and knowledge from other fields and managerial approaches. The attempt is to develop science and theory with practical application. The approach distinguishes between managerial and nonmanagerial knowledge. It develops a classification system built around the managerial functions of planning, organizing, staffing, leading, and controlling.

Approach to management, systems approach. An analysis that emphasizes systems concepts with broad applicability. Systems have boundaries, but they also interact with the external environment; i.e., organizations are open systems. (Fig. 2-2)

Approaches to management, sociotechnical systems. An analysis of management viewing managerial situations as involving a combination of interacting social and technical systems. (Fig. 2-2)

Art. Practice; skill acquired by experience.

Assessment center. A technique to aid in the selection and evaluation of potential managers whereby candidates are subjected to various tests and exercises and their performance is observed and evaluated by assessors.

Authority, organizational.   See *Organizational authority.*

Authority, parity with responsibility.   The principle that responsibility for action should not be greater than authority delegated, nor should it be less. Authority is the discretionary power to carry out assignments, and responsibility is the obligation owed a delegator to accomplish these activities.

Board of directors.   A plural executive, that is, a committee, with power to exercise authority and make decisions, which normally stands at the top of a corporation and is charged by law with the responsibility of "managing" the corporation.

Bounded rationality.   Rational action limited because of lack of information, time, or ability to analyze alternatives in light of a goal sought; unclear goals; or the human tendency not to take risks in making a decision, to "play it safe." See also *Satisficing.*

Brainstorming.   An approach to improve problem discovery and solving by encouraging unfettered suggestions and ideas, usually from a group of individuals.

Break-even point analysis.   Charting and analyzing relationships, usually between sales and expenses, to determine at what size or volume point an operation breaks even between a loss and a profit; it can be used in any problem area where marginal effects can be pinpointed.

Budget.   A statement of plans and expected results expressed in numerical terms: a "numberized" program.

Budget, program.   See *Program budgeting.*

Budget summary.   A master summary of operating and capital budgets, usually with a forecast income statement and balance sheet.

Budgets, variable or flexible.   See *Variable budgets.*

Budgets, zero-base.   See *Zero-base budgeting.*

Business units.   See *Strategic business unit.*

Centralization of authority.   The tendency to restrict delegation of decision making in an organization structure, usually by holding authority at or near the top of the organization structure.

Commitment principle.   The idea that logical planning should cover a period of time in the future necessary to foresee, through a series of actions, the fulfillment of commitments involved in a current decision.

Committee.   A group of persons to whom, as a group, some matter is committed for purposes of information, advice, interchange of ideas, or decision.

Communication.   The transfer of information from one person to another, with the information being understood by the receiver.

Comparative management.   The study and analysis of management in different environments and in various countries.

Computer-aided design (CAD).   The application of computer technology to design products much more quickly than with the traditional paper-and-pencil approach.

Computer-aided manufacturing (CAM).   The application of computer technology to the manufacturing process. The ultimate goal for some companies is "computer-integrated manufacturing," which computerizes the total manufacturing process.

Concepts.   Mental images of anything formed by generalization from particulars; for example, a word or term.

Contingency approach to leadership.   A theory that leadership depends on the group task situation and the degree to which the leader's style, personality, and approach fit the group.

Contingency management.   Managing that recognizes differences or contingencies in people, at various times and in actual situations; also referred to as "situational management"; an approach that emphasizes that there can be no "one best way" in all situations.

Contingency model of leadership effectiveness.   A leadership model developed by Fred Fiedler that postulates that a leader's effectiveness depends on three variables: (1) how well a leader is accepted by subordinates, (2) the degree to which subordinates' positions are routine and clearly spelled out in contrast to being vague and undefined, and (3) the formal authority in the position occupied by a leader.

Contingency planning.   Planning for possible future environments which are not expected to occur but which may occur; if this possible future is widely different from that premised, alternative premises and plans are required.

Contingency strategies.   Strategies developed to be used when unforeseen events or circumstances may make a selected strategy obsolete or unsuitable.

Control of overall performance. Control designed to measure the total performance of an enterprise, an integrated division of it, or a major program or project.

Control process. The basic managing process that involves (1) establishing standards, (2) measuring performance against standards, and (3) correcting for undesirable deviations.

Controlling. The managerial function of measuring and correcting individual and organizational performance to ensure that events conform to plans. It involves measuring performance against goals and plans, showing where deviations from standards exist and helping to correct them.

Cooperative system. A system, as perceived by Chester Barnard, whose purpose is cooperation and which comprises physical, biological, social, and psychological elements.

Coordination. Achieving harmony of individual and group efforts toward the accomplishment of group purposes and objectives.

Corporate social responsibility. There is no complete agreement about the definition of this term. In a broad context it means that corporations consider seriously the impact of the enterprise's actions on society.

Cost effectiveness analysis. A search for the best ratio of benefits and costs. This means, for example, finding the least costly way of reaching an objective, or getting the greatest value for given expenditures.

Creativity. The ability to develop new concepts, ideas, and problem solutions.

Decentralization of authority. The tendency to disperse decision-making authority in an organization structure.

Decentralization of performance. The geographic dispersal of operations in an enterprise.

Decision making. The selection of a course of action from among alternatives; a rational selection of a course of action.

Decision support system (DSS). The application of computers to facilitate the decision-making process of semistructured tasks.

Decision trees. An approach toward seeing risks and probabilities in a problem situation involving uncertainty, or chance events, by sketching in the form of a "tree" decision points, chance events,

and the probabilities involved in various courses that might be undertaken.

Delegation of authority. The vesting of a decision-making discretion in a subordinate.

Delegation of authority, process of. The determination of results expected from a subordinate, the assignment of tasks, the delegation of authority for accomplishing these tasks, and the holding of people responsible for the accomplishment of such tasks.

Delphi technique. A technique normally used for forecasting such future events and conditions as technological developments by obtaining estimates of experts in a field and feeding back summaries of these estimates for additional estimates by those experts, until a reasonable degree of convergence in estimates is obtained.

Department. A distinct area, division, or branch of an enterprise over which a manager has authority for the performance of specified activities and results.

Departmentation by customer. The grouping of activities around customers.

Departmentation by function. The grouping of activities in departments in accordance with the characteristic functions an enterprise undertakes; for example, in a manufacturing company—marketing, production, engineering, and finance.

Departmentation by process or equipment. The grouping of activities around a process or type of equipment used, such as electronic data processing or painting departments.

Departmentation by product. The grouping of activities around a product or product line.

Departmentation by territory or geography. The grouping of activities by territorial segments; geographic departmentation.

Direct control. Control techniques designed to identify and correct for deviations in plans.

Distribution logistics. An operations research optimizing model that treats the entire logistics of an enterprise—from sales forecasting through purchasing and processing of materials and inventorying them to shipping of finished goods to sales warehouses—as a single system.

Effectiveness. The achievement of objectives; the achievement of desired effects.

Efficiency. Achievement of the ends with the least amount of resources; accomplishment of objectives at the least cost or other unsought consequences.

Enterprise self-audit. The making by an enterprise of

an audit, or appraisal, or its position, where it is heading under present programs, what its objectives should be, and whether revised plans are needed to meet these objectives.

Entrepreneurs.   People with the ability to see an opportunity; the ability to obtain the necessary capital, labor, and other inputs; and the know-how to put together an operation successfully. They also have the willingness to take the personal risk of success or failure.

Environment, economic.   That environment of managers which has to do with such elements as labor availability, quality, and price; capital, materials, price levels, productivity, availability of high-quality entrepreneurs and managers, government fiscal and tax policy, customers, and demands for goods and services.

Environment, ethical.   That environment of managers which has to do with generally accepted sets of standards of personal conduct. See also *Ethics*.

Environment, political.   That environment of managers which has to do with the complex of laws, regulations, and government agencies and their actions.

Environment, social.   That environment of managers which has to do with the attitudes, desires, expectations, degrees of intelligence, beliefs, and customs of people in any given group or society; social forces.

Environment, technological.   That environment of managers which has to do with such elements as knowledge of ways of doing things; inventions; and techniques in the areas of processes, machines, and tools.

Environmental forecasting.   Forecasting the future environment—economic, technological, social, ethical, and political—as it may affect the enterprise.

Equity theory.   Refers to individuals' subjective judgments about the equity or fairness of the reward they receive in relation to their inputs (which include factors such as effort, experience, and education) in comparison with others' rewards.

Ethics.   A system of moral principles or values dealing with moral judgment, duty, and obligation; the discipline concerned with what is good or bad, right or wrong. See also *Environment, ethical*.

European Community 1992 (EC 1992) program objective.   The objective of Europe 1992 is to create a single market through the removal of trade barriers, and a free movement of goods, people, services, and capital.

Executives.   See *Managers*.

Expectancy theory of motivation.   The theory that people will be motivated by their expectancy that a particular action on their part will lead to a desired outcome.

Feedback.   An informational input in a system transmitting messages of system operation to indicate whether the system is operating as planned; information concerning any type of planned operation relayed to the responsible person for evaluation.

Feedforward control.   A control system that attempts to identify future deviations from plans, early enough to take action before the deviations occur, by developing a model of system or process inputs, monitoring these inputs, and taking action in time to prevent undesired or unplanned system outputs.

Flexibility (in planning) principle.   The more that flexibility (the ability to change direction without undue cost, embarrassment, or friction) can be built into plans, the less the danger of losses incurred by unexpected events. The cost of flexibility should be weighed against its advantages.

Functional authority.   The right delegated to an individual or a department to control specified processes, practices, policies, or other matters relating to activities undertaken by persons in other departments.

Functions of managers.   See *Managers, functions of*.

Gantt chart.   A technique for planning and control developed by Henry L. Gantt showing by bars on a chart the time requirements for the various tasks, or "events," of a production or other program.

Global or transnational corporation.   An organization in which managers view the whole world as one market.

Goal of managers.   See *Managers, goal of*.

Goals.   See *Objectives, or goals*.

Grapevine.   A kind of informal organization network over which information tends to flow, usually regularly, between persons who know and trust each other.

Hierarchy of needs.   Psychologist Abraham Maslow's theory that basic human needs exist in an ascending order of importance (physiological, security or safety, affiliation or acceptance, esteem, and self-actualization) and that once a lower-level need is satisfied, actions appealing to it cease to motivate.

Hygiene factors in motivation. Psychologist Herzberg's theory that certain human needs motivate and others merely cause dissatisfaction if they are not met; in other words, the meeting of this latter class of needs is a "maintenance" or "hygiene" factor; these are such factors in a work situation as salary, company policy and administration, quality of supervision, working conditions, interpersonal relations, status, and job security.

Informal organization. Generally, patterns of human behavior and relationships coexisting with, or lying outside, the formal organization structure. According to Professor Keith Davis it is "a network of personal and social relations not established or required by the formal organization but arising spontaneously as people associate with one another."

Job design. The structuring of a job in terms of content, function, and relationships. It may focus on individual positions or on work groups.

Job enrichment. Programs of building into jobs a high sense of meaning, challenge, and potential for accomplishment.

Just-in-time (JIT) inventory system. A supplier's delivery of components and parts to the production line "just in time" to be assembled. Other names for this or similar methods are "zero inventory" and "stockless production."

Kaizen. A Japanese term which points at the importance of continuous improvements. The idea is that continuously taking small steps in improvements will be the key to long-term success.

Kansei engineering. The Japanese practice of paying attention to the rational and emotional aspects of customers and developing model "personalities" for different types of customers.

Leadership continuum. The concept advanced by Tannenbaum and Schmidt in which leadership is seen as involving a variety of styles ranging from highly boss-centered to highly subordinate-centered, depending on situations and personalities.

Leadership, definition of. Influence, or the art or process of influencing people so that they strive willingly and enthusiastically toward the accomplishment of group goals.

Leading. The function of managers involving influencing people so that they will contribute to organization and group goals; it has to do predominantly with the interpersonal aspect of managing.

Limiting factor, principle of. In choosing from among alternatives, the more individuals can recognize and solve for those factors which are limiting or critical to the attainment of the desired goal, the more clearly, accurately, and easily they can select the most favorable alternative.

Line. An authority relationship in organizational positions where one person (a manager) has responsibility for the activities of another person (the subordinate). It is commonly, but erroneously, thought of as a department or a person, and not a relationship; it is also commonly, but inaccurately, thought of as the major departments of an enterprise believed to be most closely contributing to the achievement of enterprise objectives, such as marketing and production in a manufacturing company.

Linear programming. A technique for determining the optimum combination of limited resources to obtain a desired goal; it is based on the assumption that a linear relationship exists between variables and that the limits of variables can be determined.

Mainframe computer. A full-scale computer that is capable of handling huge amounts of data. Some of these "supercomputers" are used for engineering, simulation, and the manipulation of large databases.

Management. The process of designing and maintaining an environment in which individuals work together in groups to accomplish efficiently selected aims.

Management as an art. The use of underlying knowledge (science) and application of it to realities in a situation, usually with blend or compromise, to obtain practical results; managing is an art, but "management" is more properly used to refer to the body of knowledge—science—underlying this art.

Management as a science. Organized knowledge—concepts, theory, principles, and techniques—underlying the practice of managing; science systematically explains phenomena in managing, as it does in any other field.

Management auditing. Auditing the quality of managers through appraising them as individual managers and appraising the quality of the total system of managing in an enterprise.

Management by objectives (MBO).   An approach sometimes used for performance appraisal against verifiable objectives. There is no complete agreement on MBO. In this book, management by objectives is a comprehensive managerial system, integrating many key activities, consciously directed toward effective and efficient achievement of organizational and individual objectives.

Management information system.   A formal system to gather, integrate, compare, analyze, and disperse information internal and external to the enterprise in a timely, effective, and efficient manner.

Management inventory.   A technique, usually by use of a chart, whereby managers in an enterprise are designated as promotable now, promotable in one year, having potential for future promotion, satisfactory but not promotable, or having to be terminated. Another term for "inventory chart" is "management replacement chart."

Management theory jungle.   The term applied by Harold Koontz in 1961 to identify the existence of a variety of schools of, or approaches to, management theory and knowledge. He found just six such schools or approaches in 1961 but in 1979 identified eleven. He found that the schools or approaches tended to vary in their semantics and their view of management and approached the theory of management from different specialists' points of view.

Management training.   The provision of opportunities through various approaches and programs to improve a person's knowledge of, and proficiency in, the managerial task.

Manager development.   The progress a person makes in learning how to manage effectively.

Managerial appraisal.   Evaluating the performance of managers in their positions, ideally evaluating performance in setting and achieving verifiable objectives and performance as a manager.

Managerial environment.   See *Environment, economic; Environment, ethical; Environment, political; Environment, social; Environment, technological.*

Managerial grid.   A way of analyzing leadership styles, developed by Blake and Mouton, whereby leaders are classified on a grid with the two dimensions of concern for people and concern for production.

Managerial know-how.   Managerial knowledge applied effectively in practice; it includes both knowledge of the science underlying managing and the artful ability to apply it to realities.

Managers.   Those who undertake the task and functions of managing, at any level in any kind of enterprise.

Managers, functions of.   Planning, organizing, staffing, leading, and controlling.

Managers, goal of.   To so establish and maintain an environment for performance that individuals will contribute to group objectives with least cost—in money, time, effort, materials, discomfort, or dissatisfaction—to create a surplus value, or "profit."

Manufacturing automation protocol (MAP).   A network of machines and various office devices hooked together. General Motors, for example, has been known for linking robots with numerically controlled machine tools.

Matrix organization.   A form of organization in which two or more basic types of departmentation are combined. In engineering and marketing this is likely to be a combination of project or product and functional departments, with one overlaying the other. Often referred to as "grid" organization structures, or "project" or "product" management.

Microcomputer.   Smaller than the minicomputer; may be a desk computer, home computer, personal computer, portable computer, or computer for a small-business system.

Milestone budgeting.   Budgeting by breaking down a program or project into identifiable and controllable pieces, or "milestones."

Minicomputer.   Smaller than the mainframe computer but more powerful than the microcomputer, and often connected with peripheral equipment.

Mission, or purpose.   The basic function or task of an enterprise or agency or any department of it.

Motivators.   Forces that induce individuals to act or perform; forces that influence human behavior.

Multinational corporations.   Corporations headquartered usually in one country, but having operations in other countries.

Navigational change, principle of.   The more planning decisions commit for the future, the more important it is that managers periodically check on events and expectations and redraw plans as necessary to maintain a course of action toward a desired goal; this implies a willingness to change plans.

Objectives, or goals.   The ends toward which activity is aimed—the end points of planning.

Objectives, verifiable. An objective is verifiable if, at some target date in the future, a person can look back with certainty and determine whether or not it has been accomplished; goals or objectives may be verifiable if expressed either quantitatively (i.e., in numbers) or qualitatively (a program with certain specific characteristics to be put into effect by a certain date).

Operational-management theory and science. See *Approach to management, operational or process.*

Operations management. Activities necessary to produce and deliver a product or service. See also *Production management.*

Operations research. The use of mathematical models to reflect the variables and constraints in a situation and their effect on a selected goal, ordinarily thought of as using optimizing models; the application of scientific method in a problem situation with a view to providing a quantitative basis for arriving at an optimum solution in terms of goals sought.

Organization. A concept used in a variety of ways such as (1) a system or pattern of any set of relationships in any kind of undertaking, (2) an enterprise itself, (3) cooperation of two or more persons, (4) all behavior of all participants in a group, and (5) the intentional structure of roles in a formally organized enterprise.

Organization culture. The general pattern of behavior, shared beliefs, and values that members of an organization have in common.

Organization development (OD). A systematic, integrated, and planned approach to improving the effectiveness of groups of people and of the whole organization; OD uses various techniques for identifying and solving problems.

Organizational authority. The degree of discretion in organizational positions conferring on persons occupying these positions the right to use their judgment in decision making.

Organizational role. An organizational position designed for individuals to fill; to be meaningful to people, it should incorporate (1) verifiable objectives, (2) a clear concept of the major duties or activities involved, (3) an understood area of discretion, or authority, (4) the availability of information and resources necessary to accomplish a task.

Organizing. Establishing an intentional structure of roles for people to fill in an organization.

Parity of authority and responsibility. See *Authority, parity with responsibility.*

Partial controls. Controls designed to measure performance in a specific activity, such as quality, cash, production, or sales.

Path-goal approach to leadership effectiveness. An approach that sees as the main function of the leader clarifying and setting goals with subordinates, helping them to find the best path for achieving the goals, and removing obstacles.

PERT (Program Evaluation and Review Technique). A time-event network analysis system in which the various events in a program or project are identified, with the planned time for each, and are placed in a network showing the relationships of each event to other events: from the sequence of interrelated events, the path of those events in which there is zero (or the least) slack time in terms of planned completion is the "critical path"; PERT/TIME systems deal only with time; PERT/COST systems introduce costs of each event and are usually combined with elapsed time of each event or series of events.

Peter Principle. Principle enunciated by Laurence J. Peter and Raymond Hall that managers tend to be promoted until they reach the level of their incompetence.

Planning. Selecting missions and objectives—and the strategies, policies, programs, and procedures for achieving them; decision making; the selection of a course of action from among alternatives.

Planning premises. The planning assumptions—the expected environment in which plans will operate; they may be forecasts of the planning environment or basic policies and existing plans that will influence any given plan.

Plans, types of. Purpose or mission, objectives, strategies, policies, procedures, rules, programs, and budgets.

Plural executive. A committee, or group, that has the authority to execute, as a group, managerial functions.

Pluralistic society. A society in which many organized groups present various interests. Each group has an impact on other groups, but no one group has an inordinate amount of power.

Policies. General statements or understandings that guide thinking in decision making; the essence of policies is the existence of discretion, within certain limits, in guiding decision making.

Positive reinforcement.   Psychologist Skinner's theory that people are best motivated by properly designing their work environment, giving them prompt feedback on performance, and finding ways to help them and praise them for the good things they do.

Power.   The ability of individuals or groups to induce or influence the beliefs or actions of other persons or groups. Several kinds of power may be identified, such as legitimate power, expertness, referent power, reward power, and coercive power.

Preference, or utility, theory.   The theory that individual attitudes toward risk will vary from statistical probabilities, with some individuals being willing only to take lower risks than indicated by probabilities ("risk averters") and others taking greater risks ("gamblers").

Principles.   Fundamental truths, or what are believed to be truths at a given time, explaining relationships between two or more sets of variables, usually an independent variable and a dependent variable; may be descriptive, explaining what will happen, or prescriptive (or normative), indicating what a person should do: in the latter case, principles reflect some scale of values, such as efficiency, and therefore imply value judgments.

Procedures.   Plans that establish a required method of handling future activities. They are chronological sequences of required actions. They are guides to action rather than to thinking, and they detail the exact manner in which certain activities must be accomplished.

Production management.   Those activities necessary to manufacture products or create services. It includes activities such as purchasing, warehousing, transportation, and other operations to procure raw materials until the product or service is bought by the customer.

Productivity.   The output-input ratio within a time period with due consideration for quality.

Profit.   The surplus of sales dollars over expense dollars.

Profit and loss control.   A control technique designed to measure a division or some other part of a business enterprise by calculating the total profit (or loss) performance of that entity.

Program.   A complex of goals, policies, procedures, rules, task assignments, steps to be taken, resources to be employed, and other elements necessary to carry out a given course of action and normally supported by capital and operating budgets.

Program budgeting.   A budgeting approach, used primarily by government agencies, emphasizing goals, the programs to achieve them, and budgetary allocations designed to support such programs.

Promotion.   A change within the organization to a higher position that has greater responsibilities and usually requires more advanced skills and knowledge than the previous position. Promotion normally brings greater status and an increase in pay.

Promotion based on open competition.   The policy of filling positions or making promotions from the most qualified people available, whether from inside or outside a given enterprise.

Promotion from within.   The practice of making all promotions in an enterprise from people within it if it is possible to do so.

Purpose.   See *Mission, or purpose.*

Quality control circles (or quality circles).   Participation of workers in solving work-related problems. Often several people, usually rank-and-file workers, are involved in solving the problems.

Quality of working life (QWL).   Programs representing a systems approach to job design and job enrichment that will make jobs more interesting and challenging. QWL programs are closely associated with the sociotechnical systems approach.

Rationality.   Analysis requiring a clear goal, a clear understanding of alternatives by which a goal can be reached, an analysis and evaluation of alternatives in terms of the goal sought, needed information, and a desire to optimize.

Real-time information.   Information on events as they occur.

Recentralization of authority.   The recall of some or sometimes all authority previously delegated.

Recruitment of managers.   Attracting candidates for managerial positions in order to meet the objectives of the enterprise.

Responsibility.   The obligation owed by subordinates to their superiors for exercising authority delegated to them in a way to accomplish results expected.

Responsibility, absoluteness of.   The idea that responsibility cannot be delegated. The responsibility of subordinates to their superiors for performance is absolute, and superiors cannot escape responsibility for the organization activities of their subordinates.

Return-on-investment control.   A control technique designed to measure a division or some other part of a business enterprise by looking on the profit made as a percentage of the investment in assets in that entity.

Risk analysis. An approach to problem analysis that weighs risk in a situation by introducing probabilities to give a more accurate assessment of risks involved.

Rules. Required action or nonaction, allowing no discretion; e.g., "positively no smoking."

Sales forecast. A prediction of expected sales, by product or service and price, for a period of time in the future; sales forecasts are derived from plans and are also major planning premises.

Satisficing. A term used by Herbert A. Simon to denote the tendencies of managers, normally in instances of bounded rationality, in making decisions to pick a course of action that is deemed "good enough" under the circumstances. See *Bounded rationality*.

Scalar relationships. Authority relationships are said to be scalar when subordinates report to their immediate superiors and when their superiors report directly, as subordinates, to their superiors (i.e., in "scales"). In other words, the chain of command that runs from the top of an organization to its lowest ranks.

Science. Organized knowledge of pertinence to an area, usually an area of practice.

Scientific management. A term originally used as denoting the work and approach of F. W. Taylor and his associates in analyzing management. It implies that the methods of scientific inquiry, analysis, and summary can be applied to the activities of managers. It later implied time study and similar methods used by Taylor and his followers to analyze activities of people in organizations. Basically, it sought to develop (1) ways of increasing productivity by making work easier to perform and (2) methods for motivating people to take advantage of labor-saving techniques it developed. It may be summarized as (1) replacing rules of thumb with rules of science, (2) obtaining harmony rather than discord, (3) achieving cooperation rather than chaotic individualism, (4) working for maximum rather than restricted output, (5) developing workers to the fullest extent possible.

Sensitivity training. A form of training based on behavior of persons in groups and, through undirected group interchange, designed to make these persons more aware of their feelings and the feelings of others toward them.

Situational approach to leadership. The approach that studies leadership on the premise that it is strongly influenced by the situation from which the leader emerges and in which he or she operates.

Situational management. See *Contingency management*.

Social audit. A commitment to systematic assessment of and reporting on some meaningful, definable domain of the company's activities that has a social impact.

Social responsibility of managers. The responsibility of managers, in carrying out their socially approved missions, to be responsive to, to be congruent with, and to interact and live with the forces and elements of their social environment.

Social responsiveness. The ability of an enterprise to relate policies and operations to the environment that are beneficial to both the organization and the society.

Sociotechnical system. A system viewed as an interconnection of physical (technical) and social elements in an organization. (Fig. 2-2)

Span of control. See *Span of management*.

Span of management. The phenomenon that there is a limit to the number of persons a manager can supervise, even though this limit varies depending on situations and the competence of a manager.

Splintered authority. The situation where the total authority to accomplish a given result rests in more than one position and must be pooled, or combined, to make the required decision.

Staff. A relationship in an organizational position where an incumbent's task is to give some other person advice or counsel.

Staffing. Filling, and keeping filled, the positions in the organization structure with competent people. This is done through (1) identifying work-force requirements, (2) inventorying the people available, (3) recruiting, (4) selecting candidates for positions, (5) placing candidates, and (6) promoting, (7) appraising, (8) planning the career of, (9) compensating, and (10) training or otherwise developing people.

Strategic business unit (SBU). A distinct little business set up as a unit in a larger company to ensure that a certain product or product line is promoted and handled as though it were an independent business.

Strategies, contingency. See *Contingency strategies*.

Strategy.   The determination of the purpose (or mission) and the basic long-term objectives of an enterprise, and the adoption of courses of action and allocation of resources necessary to achieve these aims.

Supervisors.   Same as managers, but ordinarily used to apply to managers at the lowest level, or first line, of managing.

System, definition of.   A set or assemblage of things connected, or interdependent and interacting, so as to form a complex unity; a whole composed of parts in orderly arrangement according to some scheme or plan. For any system there must be boundaries that separate it from its environment.

System, open.   A system having interaction with its environment and exchanging information, energy, or material with that environment.

Tactics.   Action plans by which strategies are implemented.

Technology.   The sum total of knowledge of ways of doing things; it includes inventions, techniques, and the vast store of organized knowledge of how to do things.

Telecommuting.   A situation where a person can work at home at a computer terminal instead of commuting to work by car, public transportation, or some other means.

Teleconference.   A group of people interacting with each other by means of audio and video media with moving or still pictures.

Theory.   The systematic grouping of interdependent concepts and principles that give a framework to, or tie together, significant knowledge.

Theory X and Theory Y.   Assumptions about the nature of people as suggested by Douglas McGregor. For example, Theory X suggests that people dislike work and will avoid it if they can. On the other hand, Theory Y suggests, for instance, that the expenditure of physical and mental effort in work is as natural as play or rest.

Theory Z.   Theories using the letter "Z," proposed by several authors. In general, Theory Z refers to selected Japanese managerial practices adapted to the environment of the United States as suggested by William Ouchi. For example, one of the characteristics of Type Z organizations is the emphasis on interpersonal skills needed for group decision making.

Trait appraisals.   Evaluation of people, whether managers or nonmanagers, on the basis of personality traits and work-oriented characteristics.

Unity of command.   Having each subordinate report to only one superior. The principle of unity of command implies only that the more an individual reports to a single superior, the less the problem of conflict in instructions and the greater the feeling of personal responsibility for results.

Value engineering.   Analyzing the operation of a product or service, estimating the value of each operation, and attempting to improve the operation by trying to keep costs low at each step or part.

Variable budgets.   Budgets constructed by distinguishing between period costs (costs that vary only with time or remain fixed over time) and variable costs (costs that vary to some extent with the volume of enterprise output) and showing budgeted expenses of an organizational unit as they vary with volume.

Verifiable objectives.   See *Objectives, verifiable*.

Zero-base budgeting.   Budgeting in which enterprise programs are divided into "packages" comprising goals, activities, and needed resources, and costs are calculated for each package from the ground up.

Name Index

Product and Organization Index

Subject Index